THE REIGN OF
HENRY III

THE REIGN OF

HENRY III

D.A. CARPENTER

THE HAMBLEDON PRESS

LONDON   AND   RIO   GRANDE

Published by The Hambledon Press, 1996
The Tower Building, 11 York Road, London SE1 7NX, Great Britain
80 Maiden Lane, Suite 704, New York, NY 10038, USA

www.continuumbooks.com

ISBN: 1852851376

Printed on acid-free paper in
Great Britain and bound by
Biddles Ltd, King's Lynn, Norfolk

Contents

Acknowledgements   vii

Preface   ix

1   The Dating and Making of Magna Carta   1

2   Justice and Jurisdiction under King John and King Henry III   17

3   The Fall of Hubert de Burgh   45

4   Chancellor Ralph de Neville and Plans of Political Reform, 1215–1258   61

5   King, Magnates and Society: The Personal Rule of King Henry III, 1234–1258   75

6   The Gold Treasure of King Henry III   107

7   Matthew Paris and Henry III's Speech at the Exchequer in October 1256   137

8   The Decline of the Curial Sheriff in England, 1194–1258   151

9   What Happened in 1258?   183

10   King Henry III and the Tower of London   199

11   Simon de Montfort: The First Leader of a Political Movement in English History   219

12   The Lord Edward's Oath to Aid and Counsel Simon de Montfort, 15 October 1259   241

13   An Unknown Obituary of King Henry III from the Year 1263   253

14   King Henry III's 'Statute' against Aliens: July 1263   261

15   Simon de Montfort and the Mise of Lewes   281

16   St Thomas Cantilupe: His Political Career   293

17   English Peasants in Politics, 1258–1267   309

18   Was There a Crisis of the Knightly Class in the Thirteenth Century? The Oxfordshire Evidence   349

19   The Beginnings of Parliament   381

20   King Henry III and the Cosmati Work at Westminster Abbey   409

21   The Burial of King Henry III, the *Regalia* and Royal Ideology   427

Index   463

The author and the publisher are most grateful to the Isobel Thornley Bequest for a generous grant towards the publication of this book.

Acknowledgements

These essays appeared first in the following places. The author and the publisher gratefully acknowledge the kind consent of the original publishers to reprint them.

1 This essay appears here for the first time.
2 This essay appears here for the first time.
3 *Journal of British Studies*, 19 (1980), pp. 1–17.
4 *Thirteenth Century England II. Proceedings of the Newcastle upon Tyne Conference 1987*, ed. P.R. Coss and S.D. Lloyd (Boydell and Brewer, Woodbridge, 1988), pp. 69–80.
5 *Speculum*, 60 (1985), pp. 39–70.
6 *Thirteenth Century England I: Proceedings of the Newcastle upon Tyne Conference 1985*, ed. P.R. Coss and S.D. Lloyd (Boydell and Brewer, Woodbridge, 1986), pp. 61–88.
7 This essay appears here for the first time.
8 *English Historical Review*, 101 (1976), pp. 1–32.
9 *War and Government in the Middle Ages: Essays in Honour of J.O. Prestwich*, ed. J. Gillingham and J.C. Holt (Boydell and Brewer, Woodbridge, 1984), pp. 106–119.
10 *The London Journal*, 19 (1995), pp. 96–107.
11 *History*, 76 (1991), pp. 3–23.
12 *Bulletin of the Institute of Historical Research*, 58 (1985), pp. 226–37.
13 *England in the Thirteenth Century: Proceedings of the 1984 Harlaxton Symposium*, ed. W.M. Ormrod, 1985, Harlaxton College, pp. 45–51.
14 *English Historical Review*, 107 (1992), pp. 925–44.
15 *Bulletin of the Institute of Historical Research*, 58 (1985), pp. 1–11.
16 *St Thomas Cantilupe Bishop of Hereford: Essays in his Honour*, ed. M. Jancey (Hereford Cathedral, 1982), pp. 57–72.
17 *Past and Present*, 136 (1992), pp. 3–42.
18 *English Historical Review*, 95 (1980), pp. 721–52.
19 This essay will also appear in *The House of Commons: 700 Years of British Tradition*, ed. J.S. Moore and R. Smith (Manorial Society of Great Britain, London 1996).
20 *The Cloister and the World: Essays in Medieval History in Honour of Barbara Harvey*, ed. J. Blair and B. Golding (Oxford University Press, Oxford, 1996), pp. 178–95.
21 This essays appears here for the first time.

Brand's books – *The Origins of the English Legal Profession* (Oxford, 1992) and *The Making of the Common Law* (London, 1992) – are essential reading both for legal developments in the thirteenth century and much else besides. Simon Lloyd has made Henry III's crusading and Sicilian ambitions (the background to my essay on the king's gold treasure) much more understandable. Paul Binski's new book has a bravura treatment of Henry III's relations with Westminster Abbey.[6] Two valuable general works which help put these specialist studies in perspective are Michael Prestwich's *English Politics in the Thirteenth Century* (London, 1990), with a judicious analysis of recent historiography, and Alan Harding's *England in the Thirteenth Century* (Cambridge, 1993).

Numerous friends have helped with these essays by reading drafts and answering sometimes interminable questions, often asked without warning and at awkward times. I thank them all in the footnotes. Much earlier debts were to two inspiring teachers of history (in very different ways) at Westminster school, namely Roy Haines and Charles Keeley. I was lucky to spend a year in the Westminster Abbey Library and Muniment Room under the civilised, meticulous and humorous tutelage of Lawrence Tanner. At Christ Church Oxford I was taken through Stubbs's *Select Charters* by John Mason, and his lectures, I often think, have remained the foundation of my knowledge of English medieval history. My thesis on sheriffs of Oxfordshire in the thirteenth century was supervised by John Prestwich and I have benefited from his insight and criticism ever since, as the footnotes to two of the most recent essays published here, those on Henry III's 'statute' against Aliens and the dating and making of Magna Carta, bear witness. I thank Barbara Harvey for constant encouragement and support.

I have often profited from the questions and ideas of the undergraduates who have studied medieval history with me at Christ Church and St Hilda's College, Oxford; Aberdeen University, Queen Mary College, London; and now at King's College, London. A more particular debt is owed to my doctoral students at King's, from all of whom I have learnt much. Like many others, I am grateful to Peter Coss and Simon Lloyd for establishing the biennial conferences, held first at Newcastle upon Tyne and now at Durham, which have brought together historians of thirteenth-century England and their work. Within London I would like particularly to record my thanks for the help and inspiration of Paul Brand, Michael Clanchy, David Crook, John Gillingham, Jinty Nelson and Nigel Saul. I am lucky to have lived for many years within easy reach of the Institute of Historical Research and the Public Record Office in Chancery Lane and I thank the staff of both for much tolerant help. This book will appear in the same year as the closure of the PRO in Chancery Lane, and it is dedicated, in a way, to the Round Room, Long Room, and several of the rooms upstairs, where much of the research for these essays was carried out.

---

[6] S. Lloyd, *English Society and the Crusade* (Oxford, 1988), Chapter 6; P. Binski, *Westminster Abbey and the Plantagenets: Kingship and the Representation of Power, 1200–1400* (Yale, 1995).

To My Parents

1

The Dating and Making of Magna Carta

The four original engrossments of Magna Carta conclude with the famous statement, 'Given by our hand [the hand of King John] in the meadow which is called Runnymede between Windsor and Staines on the fifteenth day of June in the seventeenth year of our reign [15 June 1215]': *Data per manum nostram in prato quod vocatur Ronimed inter Windlesoram et Stanes, quinto decimo Junii, anno regni nostri decimo septimo.*[1] Despite this explicit assertion, generations of historians have concluded that 15 June 1215 was not the true date of Magna Carta. Instead, they have suggested that it was only several days later that the Charter reached final form, and was engrossed and sealed. The first modern scholar to develop this view was W.S. McKechnie. McKechnie argued that on Monday 15 June King John accepted and sealed not Magna Carta, but the Articles of the Barons on which Magna Carta was founded. The next days were spent in the negotiations which produced Magna Carta itself, copies of the final document being sealed and presented to the barons on 19 June, the day on which peace was proclaimed.[2] In an article of 1957 and in his book, *Magna Carta*, published in 1965, J.C. Holt modified and extended McKecknie's hypothesis.[3] He argued that the Articles of the Barons were accepted and sealed by the king not on 15 June but five days earlier on the 10th.[4] On the 15th, they were generally agreed as a basis for a settlement. Four days were then spent in negotiations and the terms of the Charter were settled by 19 June, the day of the peace.[5] Even then the Charter may have existed only in draft form; quite probably the first copies to be engrossed and sealed were those referred to on 24 June.[6] C.R. Cheney, writing independently of Holt, thought, like McKechnie, that the Ar-

---

[1] The text of Magna Carta with a parallel translation forms appendix IV of the first edition of J.C. Holt's *Magna Carta* and appendix 6 of the second edition for which see notes 3 and 16 below. I am most grateful to John Gillingham and John Prestwich for commenting on a draft of this essay.

[2] W.S. McKechnie, *Magna Carta. A Commentary on the Great Charter of King John*, (2nd edn., Glasgow, 1914), pp. 36–42.

[3] J.C. Holt, 'The Making of Magna Carta', *Eng. Hist. Rev.*, 62(1957),pp. 401–22, reprinted in *Magna Carta and Medieval Government* (London, 1985), ch. 9, between pp. 217–38; J.C. Holt, *Magna Carta* (Cambridge, 1965), ch. 6 within which the substance of the 1957 article is repeated. Where I have cited the article it has been from *Magna Carta and Medieval Government*.

[4] Holt, *Magna Carta*, pp. 154–9.

[5] Ibid., pp. 159,161, 164–5.

[6] Ibid., pp. 165–6; idem., 'The Making of Magna Carta', p. 236.

ticles were sealed on 15 June but argued that it was not till 23 June that a final draft of the Charter was ready to be engrossed and sealed.[7] The 15 June date actually attached to the Charter was nothing more or less than 'fictitious'.[8]

The view that 15 June was not the real date of the Charter has won widespread acceptance. W.L. Warren, in his biography of King John, published in 1961, followed Holt in having the Articles of the Barons sealed on 10 June. The 15 June in the Charter was 'simply a nominal date'. More time was needed for the Charter's precise terms to be worked out, and it was only distributed after the peace on 19 June.[9] In 1965 Helen Cam, likewise, did not dissent from Holt's basic chronology, and had 'no doubt that the document [Magna Carta] as we have it was not completed until 19 June'.[10] The position was much the same in 1994 in R.V. Turner's new biography of King John. Turner stated that John sealed the Articles of the Barons on 10 June. Final agreement on the terms of Magna Carta was reached by the 19th, and copies were engrossed and sealed sometime between then and the 24th. The date of the 15th does not feature in his account at all.[11] It reflects the power of Holt's arguments in particular that 10 June, a date for which there is no documentary evidence, has become firmly established as the date for the sealing of the Articles of the Barons, while 15 June, as the date for the Charter, although vouched for by the Charter itself, has virtually disappeared from the historical map.[12]

In all of this there has been but one dissentient voice, that of V.H. Galbraith. In an article published in 1968,[13] Galbraith supported the 10 June date which Holt had suggested for the Articles of the Barons. He also accepted that the Charter itself was only engrossed and sealed on or after 19 June.[14] However, Galbraith had discovered in the Huntington Library in California a fourteenth-century copy of the Charter which differed from the known originals in various ways. It concluded with the statement that it had been 'Given by our own hand at Windsor on the fifteenth day of June in the seventeenth year of our reign', whereas the originals, as we have seen, placed John not at Windsor on the 15th but at Runnymede. Galbraith argued that the Huntington version was a copy of the penultimate draft of the Charter, which was modified during ne-

[7] C.R. Cheney, 'The Eve of Magna Carta', *Bulletin of the John Rylands Library*, 38(1955–6), pp. 310–41, especially pp. 330,332–3, reprinted with the same pagination as ch. 13 in C.R. Cheney, *The Papacy and England, 12th-14th Centuries* (London, 1982).

[8] C.R. Cheney, 'The Twenty-Five Barons of Magna Carta', *Bulletin of the John Rylands Library*, 50(1967–8), pp. 280–307, at p. 280, reprinted with the same pagination as ch. 14 in Cheney, *The Papacy and England, 12th-14th Centuries.*

[9] W.L. Warren, *King John* (London, 1961), p. 236.

[10] H.M. Cam, *Magna Carta : Event or Document?* (Selden Soc. Lecture, London 1965), p. 9.

[11] R.V. Turner, *King John* (London, 1994) pp. 236–8.

[12] However, G.R.C. Davis, *Magna Carta* (The British Library, 1963), reprinted with revisions on numerous occasions, followed Cheney rather that Holt and thus thought the Articles were sealed on 15 June. See pp. 15, 39 (of the 1989 reprint).

[13] V.H. Galbraith, 'A Draft of Magna Carta (1215)', *Proceedings of the British Academy*, 53 (1967), pp. 345–60, reprinted with the same pagination as ch. 5 of his *Kings and Chronicles* (London, 1982).

[14] Ibid., pp. 353, 354, 358.

gotiations on the 15th to form the final draft agreed later that day at Runnymede, a draft which was the warrant for the subsequent chancery engrossments of the Charter.[15] Galbraith's view that a final draft of the Charter was thus agreed on 15 June has, however, had limited impact. In an appendix to the second edition of his *Magna Carta*, published in 1992,[16] Holt accepted that the Huntington version could well have been a draft presented at Runnymede and, after discussion and amendment, have become the warrant for the final version. This would explain why 15 June was the date in all the engrossments.[17] Holt's comment, however, left open the question of when the final version was agreed,[18] and in the main text of his book he felt no need to revise what he had written in 1965.[19] Thus he still considered it 'extremely unlikely' that the Charter was agreed on 15 June, and suggested instead that 'the drafting of final terms took at least four days'.[20] Turner essentially followed Holt's line and indeed made no reference to Galbraith's arguments at all.[21]

The debate over the making and dating of Magna Carta has been conducted with courtesy and restraint.[22] All sides have recognised that, given the state of the evidence, they are advancing hypotheses which may be wrong and criticising views which may be right.[23] The discovery of some new draft of the Charter may throw out the most confident reconstructions. It is very much in this spirit that the following essay has been written. It argues that a final draft of the Great Charter was agreed on 15 June. It thus reaches the same conclusion as Galbraith though largely through different routes. It also suggests that

---

[15] Ibid., pp. 347, 352.

[16] J.C. Holt, *Magna Carta* (2nd edn., Cambridge, 1992). Henceforth all quotations, unless indicated, are from the second edition.

[17] Ibid., pp. 445–6.

[18] Having acknowledged that Galbraith's hypothesis could indeed be right, Holt added (*Magna Carta*, p. 446): 'If there is a difficulty it is in the date and the warranty'. He then went on to raise the possibility that there was more than one draft, referring to the version of the charter with the date 16 June (referred to on p. 15 below).

[19] Holt, *Magna Carta*, p. 250 (compare p. 161 of the first edition). To a sentence in the first edition (p. 161) in which he mentioned other views about the events of 15 June, Holt added in the second edition (p. 249) that 'another again [has argued] that a surviving 'draft' of the Charter was completed then and became the warrant for the final version'. A footnote then gave a reference to Galbraith's article and the discussion in the appendix (pp. 445–6). Later in the chapter Holt made a major addition to the text (between pp. 256–7; see below note 78).

[20] Ibid., p. 250. Holt cited evidence which implied that John was already confident on 18 June that peace would be proclaimed the next day: ibid., pp. 250, 253 n. 67; 'The Making of Magna Carta', p. 230.

[21] Turner, *King John*, pp. 236–8. Galbraith's article is cited in a different context on p. 237 n. 17.

[22] See Holt's critique of Cheney: 'The Making of Magna Carta', pp. 236–8. Galbraith noted where his findings supported Holt's arguments but not where they were at variance from them: 'A Draft of Magna Carta', p. 353. For Holt's tribute to Galbraith, see the Preface to *Magna Carta and Medieval Government*.

[23] Holt, 'The Making of Magna Carta', pp. 218, 227, 237; idem, *Magna Carta*, p. 249; Cheney, 'The Eve of Magna Carta', pp. 329, 333. See below notes 33, 37, 42.

the Charter, having been finalised on the 15th, was immediately engrossed and sealed. Here it returns to a view which has been almost totally out of fashion since the days of Sir James Ramsay, Kate Norgate and Bishop Stubbs.[24] These points are only partly pedantic. They cast new light on the Charter's puzzling clauses and John's political skills; they clarify how the Charter emerged and why its peace collapsed.

Any inquiry into the date of Magna Carta must begin with the statement, quoted above, with which it concludes: 'Given by our hand[the hand of King John] in the meadow which is called Runnymede between Windsor and Staines on the fifteenth day of June in the seventeenth year of our reign [15 June 1215]:' *Data per manum nostram in prato quod vocatur Ronimed inter Windlesoram et Stanes, quinto decimo Junii, anno regni nostri decimo septimo.* It is remarkable how lightly this testimony has been set aside. The *data per manum* clause first appears in Angevin royal charters in the reign of Richard I, being modelled on the forms of the papal chancery. Had the datary under John been always the same person, the chancellor for example, or the king himself, we might well wonder whether the clause was anything more than formulaic.[25] In fact, however, throughout the reign there were frequent changes of datary. It was sometimes the chancellor but more usually a chancery clerk, who indeed often continued to act when the chancellor was present at court.[26] John himself nearly always gave the charters when the beneficiary was the chancellor or the normal datary; occasionally he gave them on other occasions as well.[27] Between September and December 1199, for example, charters were given by the chancellor (Hubert Walter), by King John himself (a charter to the priory of Bodmin), by Simon archdeacon of Wells and John de Grey acting together, and by both of them acting apart.[28] In the regnal year 1213–14 the enrolled charters were given by Richard Marsh, Peter des Roches bishop of Winchester and, on John's ex-

---

[24] Sir J.H. Ramsay, *The Angevin Empire* (Oxford, 1903), pp. 474, 478; K. Norgate, *John Lackland* (London, 1902), pp. 233–4; W. Stubbs, *The Constitutional History of England*, i, (5th edn., Oxford, 1891), p. 569.

[25] There is a full study of the clause in Jean Borthwick Edwards, 'The English Royal Chamber and Chancery in the Reign of King John' (unpublished Cambridge University D.Phil. thesis, 1974), pp. 118–32. This was a thesis supervised by C.R. Cheney, who brought it to my attention. For the clause see also R.L. Poole, *Lectures on the History of the Papal Chancery* (Cambridge, 1915), pp. 38–9, 48, 55–6, 138–42; *The Memoranda Roll for the Michaelmas Term 1 John*, ed. H.G. Richardson (Pipe Roll Soc., new ser., 21, 1943), pp. lx–lxi; V.H. Galbraith, *Studies in the Public Records* (London, 1948), pp. 127–30; C.R. Cheney, *English Bishops' Chanceries* (Manchester, 1950), pp. 81–90; P. Chaplais, *English Royal Documents* (Oxford, 1971), pp. 14–15.

[26] For example *Rotuli Chartarum in Turri Londinensi Asservati*, ed. T. Duffus Hardy (Record Commission, 1837), pp. 137,147,153b.

[27] For example, *Rotuli Chartarum*, pp. 63b, 83, 86, 88, 127b, 157, 167b, 169b, 171; *Foedera, Conventiones, Litterae . . .* , ed. T. Rymer, new edn., I, part i, ed. A. Clarke and F. Holbrooke (Record Commission, 1816), p. 93. See Galbraith, *Studies in the Public Records*, pp. 127–30. For an example of the chancellor giving a charter when the beneficiary was a frequent datary: *Rotuli Chartarum*, p. 154b.

[28] *Rotuli Chartarum*, pp. 62–63b.

pedition to France, Ralph de Neville.[29] None of them were given by the nominal chancellor, Walter de Grey archbishop of York, or by the king. In 1215–16 all the enrolled charters were given by Richard Marsh, who was by this time chancellor, which lends all the more significance to Magna Carta being given by the king himself.[30]

All this implies that the *data per manum* clause did have some meaning. But what was it? Chancery practice might be variable and haphazard. We have no 'Dialogue of the Chancery' to guide us through it. On the *data per manum* front, however, there are some pointers. The first, most obviously, is that the clause was saying something about the individual charter to which it was attached: it was the charter which was 'given by the hand'. The second is that the clause appeared not merely on the engrossments but on the drafts from which they were copied.[31] Taken together, these pointers suggest one likely explanation of the clause, namely that it indicated the person who had authorised the engrossment of the charter from the final draft, and when and where he had done so.[32] The first engrossment of Magna Carta, therefore, was probably copied from a final draft which concluded with the statement that it was given by King John at Runnymede on 15 June. The natural interpretation of this clause is that it was indeed then and there that King John 'gave the Charter by the hand', that is authorised its engrossment.[33]

If this is right, it is hard, on the face of it, to see how an agreement on 15 June that the Articles of the Barons should form the basis of the settlement,

[29] Ibid., pp. 192b-196b.

[30] Ibid., pp. 209b-221b.

[31] Edwards, 'The English Royal Chamber and Chancery in the Reign of John', p. 122, and see pp. 81–9, 95. When original charters can be compared with the enrolments on the charter rolls, differences sometimes appear between them. This suggests that the enrolments in question were made from drafts but not the final ones. Since the *data per manum* clause is almost always present on the enrolments, it must have been on the drafts. It certainly appears on what Galbraith took to be the penultimate draft of Magna Carta. It should be noted, however, that enrolments were sometimes made from the engrossments rather than from the drafts: see Edwards, 'The English Royal Chamber and Chancery in the Reign of John', p. 82 and, in particular, *Rotuli Chartarum*, p. 150. See also Richardson's discussion in *Memoranda Roll 1 John*, pp. xliii-iv, xlix-li, and Sir H.C. Maxwell-Lyte, *Historical Notes on the Use of the Great Seal of England* (London, 1926), p. 359.

[32] This was also Edwards's conclusion: 'I think the most likely explanation is that the dating clause bore witness to the fact that approval had been granted for that charter to be engrossed and issued': 'The English Royal Chamber and Chancery in the Reign of John', p. 124. Cheney, in the course of his study of the *data per manum* clause in English bishops' chanceries stated that 'the person named in some sense authorized the issue of the document', and that the appearance of *data per manum nostram* 'may be taken to indicate that the bishop's usual datary was not at hand and that the bishop authorized the document': C.R. Cheney, *English Bishops' Chanceries, 1100–1250*, pp. 85 n.7, 89. Holt seems to accept that the dating clause in some way indicated the authority for the drawing up of Magna Carta: see below note 34.

[33] Cheney ('The Eve of Magna Carta', p. 329) saw the force of this conclusion, observing of the view that the Charter was indeed completed by 15 June, 'I do not see how this hypothesis can be disproved. It has the advantage of requiring no elaborate explanation of the date set upon the charter. That date is taken at its face-value.'

could have been taken as authorising the Charter, and have thus determined its date, as both Holt and Cheney have suggested.[34] Magna Carta was founded on the Articles but differed significantly from them. The Articles lacked the Charter's long preamble stating on whose advice the king had acted; they lacked the Charter's chapter on the liberties of the church (cap. 1); its fixing of the size of relief (cap. 2); its explanation of how the king should obtain the 'common counsel' of the kingdom (cap. 14); its stipulation that earls and barons should be amerced by their peers (cap. 21); its promise that evil customs in the localities should be abolished *within forty days* (cap. 48); its promise at some vaguer time in the future to give full justice on the afforestations of Henry II and Richard I (cap. 53); and its requirement, in the security clause, that breaches of the Charter be redressed again *within forty days*. The Charter also omitted sections in the Articles, notably the promise to do justice without delay on the disseisins committed by Henry II and Richard I,[35] and the promise, at the end, not to invalidate the Charter by appealing to the pope. The Articles run to just over six printed pages in Stubbs's *Select Charters*; Magna Carta runs to nearly eleven.[36] The changes between the two documents were not simply ones of definition and drafting; many were highly controversial. It seems unlikely, therefore, that an agreement to the Articles could have been seen as authorising the Charter. Once a final draft of the Charter was ready John must have authorised it afresh; if that authorisation took place later than 15 June, why does the *data per manum* clause not say so?[37]

Now, it might be possible to advance an answer to this question, namely by suggesting that the *data per manum* clause was carried over from one draft of the Charter to the next, perhaps indeed from some ceremonial agreement to the Articles on 15 June, and was never updated. But the evidence tells against this assumption. Rather, as one would expect, successive versions of the Charter were given fresh *data per manum* clauses as they went along.[38] Galbraith, as

---

[34] Holt, *Magna Carta*, pp. 248–9: 'That something did happen [on 15 June] is established by the dating clause of the Charter and it can only have been something which could be accepted as authorizing the Charter as a final settlement. The most likely explanation is that all parties present agreed to accept the Articles as a basis for a settlement'. This would 'provide a point of authorization for the final terms of the Charter, for the Articles were the foundation on which the Charter was built'. Cheney observed of his hypothesis that 'Like the orthodox view, it assumes that the day on which the Articles were sealed (which we suppose to be 15 June) provided the chancery with a date to set upon the Charter.', 'The Eve of Magna Carta', p. 333.

[35] Articles cap. 25; Magna Carta, cap. 52; Holt, *Magna Carta*, pp. 435, 464–7.

[36] *Select Charters and other Illustrations of English Constitutional History*, ed. W. Stubbs, ninth edn., revised throughout by H.W.C. Davis (Oxford, 1913), pp. 285–291–302.

[37] Cheney saw the force of this point without, to my mind, carrying it to its logical conclusion: 'Yet the Articles were not a warrant [for the Charter], in the ordinary sense, and there must have been a later day when the draft charter was at last prepared, and approved, by the king, which would have served equally well for dating the document', 'The Eve of Magna Carta', p. 333. Galbraith also observed that 'the Articles were not the warrant for the 1215 charter', 'A Draft of Magna Carta', p. 353.

[38] This may have happened with ordinary royal charters too since, where there are differences

we have seen, has suggested that the Huntington version of the Charter was the penultimate draft. It was 'given by the king's hand' on 15 June at Windsor. Later in the day, negotiations moved to Runnymede and the final draft of Magna Carta emerged. It was given a new and up to date *data per manum* clause. Instead of giving the Charter on 15 June at Windsor, John now gave it on 15 June at Runnymede.[39]

The evidence so far surveyed strongly suggests that a final draft of the Charter was authorised by King John on 15 June. What, then, has persuaded historians to reject the 15 June date? For McKecknie a central point was his belief that it was only on 15 June at Runnymede that the Articles of the Barons were presented to King John. Given the differences between the Articles and the Charter, it followed that several days of negotiation were then necessary to move from the one to the other.[40] This argument was largely laid to rest by Holt. He advanced evidence, circumstantial but persuasive, to suggest that the Articles were agreed between John and the baronial envoys as early as 10 June.[41] Holt himself pointed out that this threw open the whole date of Magna Carta and made it quite possible that it was ready by the 15th.[42] But he believed that other considerations rendered this extremely unlikely.[43] Since the date in the Charter implied that something had happened on the 15th, he suggested that there was then a solemn and general agreement to accept the Articles as a basis for the Charter. If that was true, it followed once again that several days more of negotiation were necessary to produce the final document.[44]

Holt's other considerations centred on the single most important piece of

---

continued
between enrolments and engrossments, the latter sometimes have later dating clauses. See Edwards, 'The English Royal Chamber and Chancery in the Reign of John', pp. 122,87. One puzzle are the enrolments which have dates later than the engrossments. In all of this allowance has to be made for mistakes and carelessness.

[39] Galbraith, 'A Draft of Magna Carta', pp. 351–2. Likewise (on one interpretation) when a baronial faction tried to reopen negotiations on 16 June they drafted a charter with a new dating clause. See below p. 15. In the negotiations for Magna Carta dating clauses were added to the drafts in the hope or expectation of authorisation, not after it had taken place. Edwards, on the other hand, suggested that the dating clause was added to the draft once it had been approved; 'The English Royal Chamber and Chancery in the Reign of John', p. 125. Practice probably varied.

[40] McKechnie, *Magna Carta*, pp. 36–42.

[41] Holt, 'The Making of Magna Carta', pp. 220–7. The substance of the argument is repeated in Holt, *Magna Carta*, pp. 242–8, 429–31.

[42] Holt, 'The Making of Magna Carta', p. 227: 'If the *Articuli* were accepted on 10 June, then the whole problem of the date of Magna Carta is thrown open . . . ; the baronial envoys and the king, therefore, could have continued discussions after the 10th and had the Charter ready by the 15th . . . it is still possible that the Charter was drafted by or on that day.'

[43] Holt's conviction on this point seems to have strengthened between the article in 1957 and the first edition of *Magna Carta* in 1965. Contrast 'The Making of Magna Carta', pp. 227–8 and *Magna Carta* (1st edn.,), p. 161 repeated on p. 250 of the 2nd edn.

[44] Holt, *Magna Carta*, pp. 248–9. See 'The Making of Magna Carta', p. 230: 'If the authorization of the Charter is to be found in a general acceptance of the *Articuli* on 15 June, then the Charter cannot have been drafted until some time later.'

evidence which has served to discredit the date of 15 June for the Charter; the fact that it was not till Friday 19 June that peace was made and the king took the homages of the rebellious barons. 19 June, as the day of the final peace, is indeed the one immovable rock in the whole debate since it is referred to specifically in a royal letter: 'You are to know that a firm peace has been made by the grace of God between us and our barons on the Friday next after the feast of St Trinity at Runnymede near Staines; so that we have taken their homages there on the same day'.[45] Two things were thought to follow from this. First, it seemed unlikely that the Charter was finalised as early as 15 June, for that would have left an inexplicable 'vacuum' (the word is Cheney's) until the peace on the 19th.[46] Secondly, and here Holt, Cheney and Galbraith stood virtually together, it was inconceivable that John would have granted liberties to those who were still in rebellion against him. This made it highly improbable that the Charter was engrossed, sealed and distributed until after the peace on 19 June.[47]

To the problem of the vacuum, we will return in due course. Here we will deal with the impossibility of granting the Charter to those in rebellion. From one point of view, John would have regarded this objection as irrelevant to his purpose, for he was, in part, issuing Magna Carta over the heads of the baronial rebels. As we will see later, by 15 June he had secured the best deal he could expect. If he must grant the Charter, he would make it look as spontaneous as possible.[48] He hoped that the Charter would lead to peace, but, if it did not, it might at least divide his enemies and win him wide support.[49] Yet it is equally true that John would have fiercely denied that the liberties in the Charter could be enjoyed by rebels. Here Holt, Cheney and Galbraith were completely right. But that did not stop John engrossing, sealing and distributing the Charter before the peace. The nearest parallel is with November 1216, when

---

[45] *Rotuli Litterarum Patentium in Turri Londinensi Asservati*, ed. T. Duffus Hardy (Record Commission, 1835), p. 143b. The peace was also referred to in two other royal letters witnessed on 19 June: *Rot. Litt. Pat.*, p. 180b; *Rotuli Litterarum Clausarum in Turri Londinensi Asservati*, ed. T. Duffus Hardy, 2 vols. (Record Commission, 1833–4), i, 215 (Holt, *Magna Carta*, pp. 493–5).

[46] Cheney, 'The Eve of Magna Carta', p. 330. See Holt, *Magna Carta*, p. 250, and 'The Making of Magna Carta', p. 228.

[47] Holt, *Magna Carta*, pp. 253, 261: 'The King would not grant, nor would the barons accept, a concession of privileges while still at war, for it would offend the majesty of the one and deny legal title to the other.'; 'The king would not have executed a solemn grant in perpetuity in favour of men who were not yet in his peace'. Likewise Galbraith, 'A Draft of Magna Carta', pp. 353–4: 'The charter, though drafted, was not yet operative. It had still to be engrossed in multiple exemplars, and probably remained unsealed until the baronial *diffidatio* had been erased by the renewal of their homage on the 19th.' Cheney even thought that the Charter could not have been finally drafted till after the peace; 'The Eve of Magna Carta', p. 330: 'Moreover, it may be questioned whether a solemn charter of this sort would be finally drafted before the king took the homage of the barons who had defied him.'

[48] For the appearance of the Charter as a 'freely given grant', see Holt, *Magna Carta*, p. 261.

[49] I owe the above line of argument to John Prestwich, He adds that in public pronouncements John was always very reluctant to acknowledge the fact of the rebellion. See Holt, *Magna Carta*, p. 241.

Henry III issued a new version of Magna Carta although half the kingdom was in rebellion against him. The fact of the rebellion limited not the king's actions but the circle of those who benefited from them. It is true that in 1215, as in 1216, the liberties in the Charter were granted 'to all the freemen of our realm', but it went without saying that such freemen were within the king's allegiance. The fact that the 1215 Charter, again like that of 1216, was addressed to 'all [the king's] *faithful* men' made that clear.[50] The liberties in the Charter were thus the exclusive concern of the king's *fideles*. Rebels, of course, could look enviously upon those liberties, but they would only enjoy them once they too had become faithful men. Indeed, that was part of the point. We can see this happening in the case of Earl David of Huntingdon. On 21 June, John ordered Fortheringhay Castle to be returned to him (under the terms of the Charter) 'as soon as he has done homage to us'.[51] In other words, as soon as David became one of the king's *fideles*, he profited from the Charter. The same was true of everyone else. There was no question, therefore, of John allowing rebels to enjoy the liberties in the Charter but that principle remained inviolate whether it was issued before or after 19 June.[52]

We turn now to some further considerations which both confirm that the Charter was finalised in draft at early as 15 June and suggest that it was immediately engrossed, sealed and, in a limited way, distributed. These considerations lie partly within the text of the Charter and partly in the immediate political circumstances which produced it.

Curious features of the Charter are its preamble and witness list. In the preamble John announced that he had acted on the advice of two archbishops, seven bishops, Pandulf the papal envoy, the master of the Templers, four earls and twelve other magnates and ministers. At the end of the Charter, quite unusually, there was no witness list; merely the statement that the witnesses were as above; in other words they were the same as the advisers in the preamble.[53] Now none of these advisers were drawn from the ranks of the rebels. Since they were specifically the king's *fideles*, before 19 June that had to be the case. After the peace on 19 June, on the other hand, former rebels who had renewed their homage could have acted as advisers and/or witnesses. Indeed on 20 June at Runnymede a royal charter was attested by the earl of Clare, William de Mowbray, Eustace de Vesci, Roger de Montbegon, Robert Grelle and Gilbert de Gant, all former rebels.[54] These facts strongly suggest that the beginning and end of the charter were finalised before the final peace on 19 June.

---

[50] Holt, *Magna Carta*, pp. 448–51; Stubbs, *Select Charters*, pp. 336–7.

[51] *Rot. Litt. Pat.*, p. 144. See Holt, *Magna Carta*, p. 253.

[52] The force of the argument advanced here would have been weakened had the Charter been couched throughout in terms of a bargain between the king and the barons which would only become operative after the peace. But this is not at all the case. There is an element of bargain at the end when oaths are taken on behalf of both sides to observe the Charter; but the general form of the Charter is of a freely given grant, as Holt points out: Holt, *Magna Carta*, p. 261.

[53] Ibid., pp. 448–9, 472–3 (cap. 63).

[54] *Rot. Chartarum*, p. 210b.

They do not prove that the finalisation took place on 15 June, but they sit happily with that hypothesis and with the further suggestion that the document was immediately closed by engrossment and sealing. The later one puts the final draft, and the longer one thinks it remained unengrossed, unsealed and thus capable of alteration, the more surprising it becomes that it did not include former rebels amongst its witnesses; something which would certainly have given the document more weight and solemnity.[55]

Closely related to the puzzle of the witnesses is the question of the twenty-five barons of the security clause. On the face of it, one of the most remarkable features of the Charter is its failure to name the twenty-five and this for a reason equally remarkable: as chapter 61 says, the barons had still to chose them.[56] Without the twenty-five, the Charter was worthless. It was to any four of their number that breaches were to be reported; if the breaches were not redressed the four were to report to the twenty-five who were empowered to implement the Charter by force. Everyone in the land was to take an oath to obey the orders of the twenty-five.[57] But how could this work if no one knew who the twenty-five were? The answer is that it was left to the twenty-five to proclaim themselves to the counties.[58] They were not very successful, if we may judge from the silence of contemporary chroniclers as to their identity.[59] The task of the twenty-five and the chances of enforcing the Charter would have been immeasurably improved had they been named within it. The reason why they were not was twofold, or so we may suggest. First, and to this point we will return, the Charter was negotiated on the baronial side by a small group of envoys who doubted their authority to chose the twenty-five. Second, when the negotiations concluded on 15 June, the Charter was immediately closed by engrossment and sealing. Had it remained open until after the peace, by which time the twenty-five had almost certainly been chosen, then it could and quite probably would have named them.

Other singular features of the Charter are its two references to the settlement of peace, the *reformacio pacis*. In the conclusion to the Charter, John forgave all transgressions committed because of the discord from Easter 1215 'until

[55] The Charter of 1216 followed the format of the 1215 Charter, inevitably since it too was issued in the middle of a rebellion. The Charter of 1217, although issued after the peace, had neither a long list of those on whose advice the king had acted, nor a witness list. This may have been because of the protracted way in which it was produced and proclaimed in 1217–18. A witness list at last reappeared with the Charter of 1225. See Stubbs, *Select Charters*, pp. 336, 339, 341, 344 (see also pp. 345, 348), 351.

[56] Holt, *Magna Carta*, pp. 468–9.

[57] Ibid., pp. 468–73.

[58] Thus the sheriffs were ordered on 19 June to make everyone swear the oath to the twenty-five 'at their mandate' and 'in their [the twenty-five's] presence': *Rot. Litt. Pat.*, p. 180b (Holt *Magna Carta*, pp. 493–4).

[59] The names of the twenty-five are known from only three sources; the works of Matthew Paris; a Reading Abbey MS; and a marginal annotation in a late thirteenth-century legal collection: Holt, *Magna Carta*, pp. 478–80.

the conclusion of peace', *usque ad pacem reformatam*.[60] Again, it is slightly curious, if the Charter was not completed in draft until 18 or 19 June, when the intended date of the peace was known, and if it was not closed by engrossment and sealing until after the peace, that the date of that peace was not given in the document. It was after all an extremely important point over which there was a good deal of confusion.[61] John sought to clarify the issue in royal letters. He would have found it much easier had the date been in the Charter.

The second reference to the peace in the Charter is even more instructive. It comes in chapter 51.

> And immediately after concluding peace (*statim post pacis reformacionem*) we will remove from the kingdom all alien knights, crossbowmen, serjeants, [and] mercenary soldiers who have come with horses and arms to the harm of the kingdom.[62]

The reference to the peace here is in no way accidental. On the contrary, it was inserted at a late stage in the negotiations for it is not in the Articles of the Barons. There the clause (cap. 41) simply reads:

> And that the king will remove alien knights, mercenary soldiers, crossbowmen and routiers and serjeants who have come with horses and arms to the harm of the kingdom.[63]

No other clause had an insertion of this kind. Elsewhere, the Charter insisted that John do something *statim*, 'immediately', for example in chapters 47, 48, 49, 52, 53 and 56. In three chapters (those on the reversal of John's afforestations, the inquiry into evil customs in the localities, and the return of hostages) the *statim* was inserted between the Articles and the Charter, just as it was in the chapter on the mercenaries.[64] But only in the chapter on the mercenaries was the *statim* linked with the *post pacis reformacionem*. Why was this? Now it might be possible to argue that the *post pacis reformacionem* was added at baronial insistence to give *statim* more force, to give it, in effect, some sort of 'time-limit', in which case it could have been inserted right up to the moment of the peace, whatever its date.[65] But it seems highly unlikely that the barons would have singled out the mercenaries in this way, thereby in effect weakening the force of the *statim* in the other clauses, over several of which no less immediate action was certainly required.[66] There is, therefore, another and,

---

[60] Holt, *Magna Carta*, pp. 472–3 (cap. 62).

[61] Hence the very different dates given by chroniclers for the peace: Holt, 'The Making of Magna Carta', p. 237.

[62] Holt, *Magna Carta*, pp. 464–5.

[63] Ibid., p. 438.

[64] Articles, caps. 47, 39, 38; Charter, caps. 47, 48, 49; Holt, *Magna Carta*, pp. 437–8, 464–5.

[65] For Holt mentioning in passing that the *post pacis reformacionem* provided a 'time-limit', see *Magna Carta*, pp. 356–7.

[66] As just mentioned, between the Articles and the Charter, the barons inserted *statim* in the chapters on the reversal of John's afforestations, the launching of the local inquiry, the return of

to my mind, more plausible explanation, namely that the *post pacis reformacionem* was introduced, not by the barons in order to strengthen the *statim*, but
by the king in order to qualify it. He did so because he knew there might be a
considerable delay between the issuing of the Charter on 15 June and the actual conclusion of peace, if indeed there was peace at all. It thus became essential for him to make clear that, until there was peace, he would not disarm by
dismissing his mercenary soldiers. That was both a safeguard to his own position and an incentive to the barons to accept the settlement.

The political circumstances gave John every reason to anticipate delay, and
it was those circumstances which both explain why the Charter was immediately sworn, engrossed and sealed, and why it was four days before it led to
peace. We need to approach the political situation by looking briefly at how
the Charter emerged. The Articles of the Barons, as Holt has argued, were
probably accepted as a basis for negotiation on 10 June. There then followed
several days of highly detailed bargaining and drafting before the final
version of the Charter emerged on the 15th. That bargaining and drafting
was most likely carried out by fairly small delegations from either side,
something also suggested, as we have seen, by the failure of the baronial
envoys to chose the twenty-five barons of the security clause. When the
negotiations were over, the baronial envoys swore to the terms on behalf of
the barons and the royal representatives swore on behalf of the king. This is
not the usual view of the oath described at the end of the Charter. Holt
believed that it took place after the renewal of homage on 19 June, being
sworn by the king and the general body of the barons. Cheney likewise
thought in terms of a general oath.[67] But this is not at all what Magna Carta
says. The text runs as follows:

continued
the hostages and the dismissal of the mercenaries. On both the hostages and the local inquiry,
John was forced to take action on 19 June immediately after the peace: *Rot. Litt. Pat.*, pp. 143b,
180b (Holt, *Magna Carta*, pp. 493–5). There were probably equally strong feelings about John's
promise, here both in the Articles (cap. 25) and Magna Carta (cap. 52), to restore *statim* those
whom he had disseised without lawful judgement of their peers, and here too there was action
immediately after the peace: *Rot. Litt. Claus.*, i, 215; Holt, *Magna Carta*, pp. 435, 464–5, 165, 359–62.
The first sign that John was dismissing his mercenaries does not come till 23 June: *Rot. Litt. Pat.*, p.
144; Holt, *Magna Carta*, pp. 356, 496. The dismissal of the mercenaries *statim post pacis reformacionem* stood in immediate contrast to the previous chapter's promise (both in the Articles and the
Charter) to dismiss certain alien sheriffs and castellans (the relations of Gerard d'Athée) merely
penitus: Holt, *Magna Carta*, pp. 356–7, 438, 464–5 (Articles, 40; Magna Carta, 50). Either John put
up a stiffer resistance on this issue, refusing to agree to immediate dismissal, or baronial feelings
ran less high.
    [67] Holt, *Magna Carta*, p. 253: 'The terms were secured by a further oath, described in the Char-
ter itself, in which all parties present, the barons as well as the king, swore to observe the terms it
embodied in good faith and without evil intent.' Cheney, 'The Eve of Magna Carta', p. 335: 'The
nearest approach to the terms of a treaty is in the final record that both king and barons have
sworn to observe all the foregoing faithfully.' For Holt's suggestion that the oath was sworn after
the renewal of homage on 19 June, see *Magna Carta*, p. 254.

Moreover an oath has been sworn both on our behalf and on behalf of the barons that all these things aforesaid shall be observed in good faith and without evil intent.

Juratum est autem tam ex parte nostra quam ex parte baronum, quod hec omnia supradicta bona fide et sine malo ingenio observabuntur.[68]

The Charter, therefore, does not say that either John or the barons swore to observe its terms. Rather the oath was sworn on their behalf. *Ex parte nostra. Ex parte baronum.* The phrases are immensely significant because they are precisely those used in 1215 of the arbitrators and negotiators acting on behalf of either side. On 9 May John announced that 'we are placing ourselves on four barons of England whom we will chose *ex parte nostra* and the barons opposed to us are placing themselves on four others whom they will chose *ex parte sua.*'[69] This attempt to reach a settlement was abortive but, a month later, it was envoys coming *ex parte baronum*, who negotiated the terms of Magna Carta. On 8 June John gave safe conducts to 'all those who come *ex parte baronum* to Staines on Tuesday in Penetecost week [9 June] . . . to make and agree peace between us and our barons'. The safe conduct was to last until the close of the following Thursday (11 June). Later, the truce was extended from 11 June until the morning of 15 June itself.[70] These envoys, therefore, first agreed the Articles of the Barons as the basis for negotiation and then proceeded to hammer out the actual Charter. Having reached agreement at Runnymede on 15 June, they swore to its terms *ex parte baronum*. The king's negotiators swore on his behalf, *ex parte nostra.*[71] The Charter does not prove that this oath took place on 15 June, but, given its implication that it was sworn by the negotiators, that date is far more likely than one some time after the negotiations were finished. Both sides had, in fact, good grounds for proceeding at once to swearing, engrossment and sealing.

As Galbraith showed by comparing the penultimate draft of the Charter with the final version, John on the last day of the negotiations had gained two important concessions. He had raised the relief for a barony from 100 marks to a £100, thus making it the equal to the relief for an earldom; and he had watered down the guarantee not to seek anything from the pope which would nullify the Charter to the much vaguer promise not to seek anything 'from

---

[68] Holt, *Magna Carta*, pp. 472–3 (cap. 63). Holt prefers to translate: 'Moreover an oath has been sworn, both on our part and on the part of the barons . . . '.

[69] *Rot. Chartarum*, p. 209b; *Rot. Litt. Pat.*, p. 141 (Holt, *Magna Carta*, pp. 492–3). See Holt, *Magna Carta*, pp. 232–5.

[70] *Rot. Litt. Pat.*, pp. 142b–143.

[71] There appears to be no list of those who swore the oath on behalf of the king but Matthew Paris preserved a list of those who swore to observe the orders of the twenty-five barons of the security clause: *Matthaei Parisiensis . . . Chronica Majora*, ed. H.R. Luard, 7 vols. (Rolls Ser., 1872–83), ii, 605–6.

anyone'.[72] John, therefore, wanted to close down the negotiations and make sure of these victories. By so doing he also kept the names of the twenty-five barons out of the Charter. The only way to close down, to show everyone that that was that, was to proceed immediately to the swearing, engrossment and sealing of the Charter. John thus kicked the ball back firmly into the barons' half. He challenged them to accept the settlement and threatened, implicitly or explicitly, to make it public if they failed to do so.

The baronial envoys looked at matters differently, but came to the same conclusions. On the one hand, they had strong reasons for keeping the Charter open until it could include the names of the twenty-five, as we have seen. On the other hand, there were terrible dangers in doing this. The baronial radicals might destroy the whole business by making impossible demands. John seemed eager to settle, but he might change his mind and demand fresh concessions. Alternatively, he might, as we have suggested, go public with the Charter, thus utterly wrong-footing the barons.[73] It was better to settle. Once that decision was made, there were imperative reasons for proceeding at once not merely to the oaths, but to engrossment and sealing. Legally there may have been no need for this.[74] Politically, there was every need. The baronial envoys had doubtless received some authority for their negotiations *ex parte baronum* but that did not mean what they brought back would be accepted.[75] They had already shied away from choosing the twenty-five barons. They now had the difficult task of selling the Charter to their fellows at Runnymede and further afield, and bringing them in to a ceremony of peace. It was vital, against this background, to show that John really had agreed to the Charter, which was why, no doubt, he 'gave' it with his own hand.[76] It was even more vital to actually display the Charter engrossed and sealed. Holt himself has made a similar point with respect to the Articles of the Barons. The reason why they were sealed by the king, he has suggested, was so that the baronial envoys could demonstrate to the rest of their party that they had indeed reached an agreement.[77] How much more was that the case with the Charter itself. Given the distrust of King John, one can imagine the shouts of scepticism and derision which would have greeted

---

[72] Galbraith, 'A Draft of Magna Carta', pp. 348, 350–1.

[73] Holt sees the need to ward off baronial radicals as a reason for the sealing of the Articles of the Barons: *Magna Carta*, p. 247.

[74] For the argument that it was the oaths, rather than the engrossment and sealing of the Charter, which made John's concessions law: see Holt, *Magna Carta*, pp. 253–4.

[75] See also Holt, *Magna Carta*, pp. 247–8. Presumably, as was envisaged on 9 May, the barons had chosen and 'placed' themselves on their representatives: *Rot. Chartarum*, p. 209b; *Rot. Litt. Pat.*, p. 141 (Holt, *Magna Carta*, pp. 492–3).

[76] Galbraith (*Studies in the Public Records*, p. 129) likewise suggests that John gave the Charter himself at baronial insistence: 'the personal assumption of responsibility by the King was . . . full of meaning'.

[77] Holt, *Magna Carta*, pp. 246–7, 431. Much of what Holt says between pp. 246–8, about the negotiations for the Articles of the Barons, I would apply to the negotiations for the Charter itself.

some attempt to read a mere draft of the agreement, without sight or sign of an authentic Charter with the King's great seal attached to it.[78]

The fact was that sections of the baronage were deeply hostile to the settlement. The concession John had wrung at the last moment over baronial reliefs was bitterly resented and there may have been attempts to revive the issue. Hence a draft of the Charter survives (in a later copy), with the relief for a barony back at 100 marks, given by the king's hand at Runnymede on *16 June*, the day *after* the final engrossed version. One explanation for this apparent anomaly is that this was a draft prepared by a baronial faction attempting to reopen the Charter.[79] Another issue which was time consuming and contentious was the security clause. The barons had somehow to chose the twenty-five, probably no easy business. There were also, almost certainly, disputes over the form of the clause itself, which, as it stood, reflected all too clearly how the barons had settled with the king without depriving him of physical power; a mistake not repeated in 1258. John might have to dismiss his mercenaries and accept baronial control of London, but he still retained the rest of his army and all his castles. Here too there may well have been an attempt to reopen the issue, for Roger of Wendover preserves an alternative draft of the security clause in which castellans, loyal to the twenty-five barons and sworn to obey their orders, were to be appointed to the castles of Northampton, Kenilworth, Nottingham and Scarborough.[80]

Yet another contentious issue was that of the forest. In the baronial demands earlier in 1215, embodied in the so called 'Unknown' Charter, the afforestations of Henry II were to be immediately reversed.[81] This promised the elimination of the royal forest altogether from many parts of England. Not surprisingly, John resisted tooth and nail, and succeeded in removing all mention of Henry II's afforestations from the Articles of the Barons. When the baronial envoys revealed this to their party they were sharply rebuffed, for the question resurfaced in the Charter: John promised to do justice in the matter of Henry II's afforestations when he returned from or abandoned his crusade; not much, but something. More immediately relevant was the stipulation, introduced between the Articles and the Charter, that the evil customs of the forests, revealed by the local inquiry, were to be abolished 'within forty days'.[82] This time it was John's turn to protest and, in effect, to reopen or second guess the Charter, for he extracted a proclamation from Langton and the bishops to the ef-

---

[78] For Holt's suggestion that the terms were read out (in an Anglo-Norman translation), before the barons renewed their homage, see the important new section in *Magna Carta* between pp. 256–7.

[79] Holt, *Magna Carta*, p. 446. On the other hand it is possible that 16 June was no more than the error of a copyist.

[80] *Chronica Majora*, ii, 603; Holt, *Magna Carta*, pp. 345, 445. Holt suggests that this was a draft rejected before the agreement to the Articles of the Barons but adds that one cannot rule out the possibility that it remained in circulation.

[81] Holt, *Magna Carta*, p. 428 (cap. 9).

[82] Ibid., pp. 466–7, 464–5 (caps. 53,48).

fect that both sides, during the negotiations, had understood that all customs necessary to the working of the forests should remain.[83] None the less John had won a great victory over the Forest. It was left to the Charter of the Forest in 1217 to try once more to tackle the problem.

Against this background it is scarcely surprising that it took several days to persuade the barons to accept the peace. Indeed some never were persuaded, for the Barnwell annalist says that certain of the Northerners (for whom the forest was a particular grievance) left the gathering at Runnymede and, on the pretext that they had not been there, began hostilities.[84]

To conclude. The baronial envoys probably agreed the Articles of the Barons with the king as a basis for negotiation on 10 June. Hard and detailed bargaining in the following days produced a final draft of the Charter at Runnymede on 15 June. On that day, the baronial envoys swore to its terms *ex parte baronum* and the king's negotiators swore on behalf of the king *ex parta nostra.* John then 'gave' the draft with his hand, and it was immediately engrossed and sealed. John had no long term commitment to the Charter but he hoped that it might, in various combinations, end the war, divide his opponents and gain him support. The baronial envoys, for their part, believed that they had squeezed from John all that they could. In the next few days, at what were probably a series of acrimonious meetings, they displayed the Charter and tried to persuade their colleagues to accept it. Some of the Northerners refused to do so and departed. Other barons circulated new drafts of the Charter and strove to reopen the negotiations. In the end, however, the twenty-five barons of the security clause were elected and a substantial number of rebels agreed to accept the settlement. On 19 June they renewed their homages to King John and peace was proclaimed. In the next few days further engrossments of the Charter were made and distributed to the counties. The period between the granting of the Charter on 15 June and the proclamation of peace on the 19th was thus full of doubt, recrimination and activity. As Holt has remarked, the Charter 'created work'.[85] For several days at the start of its life, its acceptance hung in the balance. It could not survive for long.[86]

[83] *Foedera*, I, i, 134 (Holt, *Magna Carta*, pp. 498–9). To the stipulation that the evil customs revealed by the inquiry were to be abolished 'within forty days', John tacked on the saving clause that either he or his justiciar must be informed first: Articles, cap. 39; Magna Carta, cap. 48 (Holt, *Magna Carta*, pp. 437, 464–5). In two of the original engrossments, this reservation was added in at the bottom of the Charter, thus quite possibly reflecting the way drafts were altered in the course of the negotiations: Holt, *Magna Carta*, p. 464 note 1 and p. 441.

[84] *Memoriale Fratris Walteri de Coventria*, ed. W. Stubbs, 2 vols. (Rolls Ser., 1872–3), ii, 222.

[85] Holt, *Magna Carta*, p. 252.

[86] I have not considered the accounts given by the chroniclers of the events at Runnymede because they are too vague to be of value. The Barnwell chronicler implies that the Charter preceded the peace. The Dunstable annalist indicates the reverse. See *Memoriale Fratris Walteri de Coventria*, ii, 221; *Annales Monastici*, ed. H.R. Luard, 5 vols. (Rolls Ser., 1864–9), iii, 43; Holt, *Magna Carta*, p. 259.

2

Justice and Jurisdiction under King John and King Henry III

J.C. Holt's *The Northerners* has long been recognised as a great work of medieval history.[1] Published in 1961, it illuminated, in an altogether new way, the ties of neighbourhood, tenure, kin and faction which permeated local society. It likewise showed in altogether new detail how the pressures exerted by royal government on that society produced the rebellion of 1215. Holt's second book *Magna Carta*, published in 1965, lacked perhaps the characters of *The Northerners* – the Thomas of Moultons and Simon of Kymes – but was entirely new in the depth and surety with which it placed the Charter within the society, government and politics of Angevin England.[2] Essentially *The Northerners* and *Magna Carta* are companion works. Together they provide a unique and profound insight into the nature of the English medieval polity.

Although he has rarely written in detail about the period after 1215, Holt's work has had an important influence on those who have sought, since the 1970's, to reinterpret the reigns of the Plantagenet kings. The last chapter of *Magna Carta* 'The Re-Issues and the Myth', provides by far the best introduction to the constitutional conflicts under Henry III while *The Northerners* and *Magna Carta* together suggest the essential questions to be asked about the nature of Henry's rule.[3] Above all, perhaps, Holt's methodology, the way he embraces both central government and local society, and traces the complex interactions between the two, has pointed the way forward for students of later medieval England.[4]

For medieval historians, therefore, the second edition of *Magna Carta*, published in 1992, was a major event.[5] For some years beforehand, Holt had given indications as to what it might contain. There was, for example, to be both a clause by clause commentary on the Charter and a major new chapter on jus-

---

[1] J.C. Holt, *The Northerners: A Study in the Reign of King John* (Oxford, 1961).

[2] Idem, *Magna Carta* (Cambridge, 1965).

[3] Holt has written perceptively about the origins of parliament in the thirteenth century: J.C. Holt, 'The Prehistory of Parliament' in *The English Parliament in the Middle Ages: A Tribute to J.S. Roskell*, ed. R.G. Davies and J.H. Denton (Manchester, 1981), pp. 1–28. J.C. Holt, *Robin Hood* (London, 1982) is also essentially a study of the period after 1215.

[4] Holt has also been particularly encouraging to younger scholars, as I know from his comments as referee on the first piece I submitted to *English Historical Review*.

[5] J.C. Holt, *Magna Carta*, 2nd edn. (Cambridge, 1992). All subsequent quotations are from this edition.

tice and jurisdiction.[6] In the event, the commentary, as Holt explains in the preface to the second edition, has been omitted, partly for reasons of space, but the chapter on justice and jurisdiction does indeed appear.[7] It is substantial, some sixty-five pages long, and demonstrates the familiar virtues of Holt's work. It advances, in forthright fashion, a hypothesis both highly original and highly important. It demonstrates a remarkable grasp of both legal procedures and large numbers of law cases. It is extremely accurate;[8] and, in the key passages, it is written in Holt's familiar emphatic style: 'This is the clue to the judicial provisions of the Charter. By and large it approved of what the undertenant had enjoyed and condemned what the tenant-in-chief had suffered. Hence it sought to give the magnate a legal security like that enjoyed by the freeman. During the minority of Henry III this was largely achieved. The protection of the law moved up, not down, the social scale'.[9] These short, punchy sentences are typical Holt.

After an introduction like this, readers will expect me to say that the new chapter is totally misconceived, and that is exactly what I am going to say. Or perhaps not entirely and not without qualification. Some parts of Holt's hypothesis seem completely convincing, while others depend on how one 'reads' a series of complex and sometimes fragmentary law cases, about which it is quite possible to hold different opinions. In the following pages I will firstly set out Holt's hypothesis; secondly suggest its difficulties; and thirdly advance some ideas of my own about how the administration of justice changed after 1215. In doing this, my aim is to open up the subject for debate rather than close it down with answers.

Put briefly, Holt's hypothesis is as follows.[10] Before 1215 it was only undertenants who were able to enjoy the benefits of the common law. They could begin their litigation over matters of right, disseisin and inheritance through freely and automatically available write *de cursu* ('of course'). The cases thus started proceeded with speed and regularity, before royal judges but with limited royal interference, towards either verdict and sentence or agreement via final concord. Tenants-in-chief, on the other hand, litigating against each other over land held in chief from the king, were rarely so lucky. The common law procedures open to the undertenant were closed to them. Instead, they were subject directly to the king's feudal jurisdiction and suffered the highly arbitrary and

---

[6] Idem, *Magna Carta and Medieval Government* (London, 1985), preface.

[7] Idem, *Magna Carta*, pp.xiii-xiv, 123–87.

[8] Anyone who has worked through a Holt chapter will testify to the accuracy of both the citations and the more general use of evidence. In the preface to the second edition (p.xiv) Holt thanks me for pointing out some errors in the first edition. But these were less than a handful. Sir James's immediate response to my letter was a card in which he pointed out that I had got the date of John's death wrong in *The Minority of Henry III* (p.12).

[9] Holt, *Magna Carta*, p.123. For further comment on Holt's epigrammatic style, see *Law and Government in Medieval England: Essays in Honour of Sir James Holt*, ed. G. Garnett and J. Hudson (Cambridge, 1994), p.ix.

[10] Holt, *Magna Carta*, pp.123–87.

expensive justice which John provided. After 1215 all this changed. The procedures of the common law became available to tenants-in-chief, in particular through the appearance of a new writ, directly suited to their needs, *praecipe in capite*. The tenants-in-chief thus escaped from the direct feudal jurisdiction of the king. Their cases too proceeded with comparative regularity and despatch. They too came to enjoy the benefits of the common law. This was the great victory of 1215.

It may be helpful to look at this in a little more detail. Holt begins by considering the difficulties faced by tenants-in-chief before 1215. For a variety of reasons they could make little use of the ordinary writs *de cursu*, of which the most important were those of right, *novel disseisin* and *mort d'ancestor*.[11] The writ of right, for example, ordered a lord to do right to A over land he was seeking from B. But, in a case between barons litigating over land held in chief, the lord in question would be the king and the king could not send a writ to himself.[12] Thus the writ of right was unavailable. The only writ which tenants-in-chief could regularly use was the writ *praecipe*, which simply ordered A to return to B the land B was seeking from him, or come before the king or his judges to show why he had not done so. This Holt suggests may well have been the writ through which barons initiated actions of right before 1215. But it was a 'blunderbuss of a writ' and not one *de cursu*. It might be expensive to obtain. It initiated actions which were often slow, formless and fragmented by royal intervention.[13] Thus Holt surveys a large number of cases before 1215 which display these characteristics,[14] as well as revealing just how much money barons had to offer for 'justice' under John.[15] By 1215, therefore, 'the tenant-in-chief might well cast an envious eye towards his litigious undertenants happily pursuing their ends along the tramlines of *mort d'ancestor, novel disseisin*, writs of right and final concords. The plain truth was that in 1215 the undertenant had access to a system of justice which was far more predictable than that available to the great man opposed to his equal in the king's court. With the common law the litigant knew where he stood and how to proceed. The magnate in the king's court was altogether less certain and secure.'[16]

[11] Ibid., pp.127–39.

[12] Ibid., p.128.

[13] Ibid, pp.141–3, with the quotation on p.143, and p.174.

[14] Ibid.,

[15] Ibid., pp. 150–3. The large proffers for justice under John also appear in the cases surveyed in R.V. Turner, *The King and his Courts: The Role of John and Henry III in the Administration of Justice, 1199–1240* (New York, 1968), pp.157–65. For two studies of Turner which show how 'in cases involving magnates the legal issues cannot be separated from political ones', see his 'Exercise of the King's Will in Inheritance of Baronies: the Example of King John and William Briwerre', *Albion*, 22 (1990), pp. 383–401 and his 'The Mandeville Inheritance, 1189–1236: Its Legal, Political and Social Context', *Haskins Society Journal*, 1 (1989), pp. 148–72, both reprinted in Turner's *Judges, Administrators and the Common Law in Angevin England* (London, 1994) from where the quotation comes on p.xxii.

[16] Holt, *Magna Carta*, pp. 163–4. See also p.150: 'There was no easy routine passage from *mort d'ancestor* or an action of right to a final concord as there was with the undertenantry.'

This was soon to change. Immediately after Magna Carta in 1215, John was forced to correct past injustices and make some fifty acts of restoration. Holt suggests that the twenty-five barons of the Charter's security clause played a key part in these restorations. In so doing 'they staked out a claim which marked one of the great unnoticed victories of 1215, more important immediately than the broad assertions about judgement of peers and the law of the land. They established and extended routine process governing seisin and right in cases involving tenants-in-chief'.[17] This victory was clinched during the minority of Henry III by the end of which John's system was dead beyond recall. A whole series of cases involving tenants-in-chief now went through with comparative ease. 'In many cases justice was quick . . . And justice was no longer sold.'[18] A few years later a great baron could argue that even a case involving the succession to an earldom was a 'common plea' and thus, under the terms of Magna Carta, should not be heard before the king at all. 'The tenant-in-chief was escaping from the immediate jurisdiction of the king.'[19]

The mechanism at the heart of these changes was a new writ, *praecipe in capite*. Unlike the old writ of *praecipe*, this was designed specifically to meet the needs of tenants-in-chief for it ordered A to return to B the land B was seeking from him, and 'which he claims to hold of the king in chief', or come before the king or his judges to show why he had not done so. *Praecipe in capite* was also now a writ *de cursu*. It thus enabled tenants-in-chief to litigate against each other with a regularity of procedure previously enjoyed only by undertenants.[20] The appearance of this writ in the eyre which began in 1218 thus 'set the seal on the victory of 1215'.[21] 'The *praecipe in capite* . . . was a great unrecorded baronial victory which gave backbone to cap. 40 of the Charter' (which forbad the denial and sale of justice).[22] To bring home this point, Holt compares cases from 1204 and 1234.[23] At the end of the latter the defeated parties, Hugh Wake and William de Mustac, were told that they could pursue their cause by *mort d'ancestor*, or by writ of right, that is by *praecipe in capite*, 'according to the law of the land' (*secundum legem terrae*). 'The common law', Holt comments, 'had permeated the inner sanctum in which the king held jurisdiction over his immediate vassals. Magna Carta itself did not ensure that; it was nowhere in black and white; but that is what it had brought about.'[24]

Holt's hypothesis is thus about both jurisdictional theory and actual practice. Indeed the two went hand in hand. The withering of the king's feudal

---

[17] Ibid., p167.

[18] Ibid., p.171.

[19] Ibid., p.172.

[20] Ibid., pp.173–4 'In this [an ordinary writ of *praecipe* issued *de cursu*], as in other matters, the undertenant enjoyed a regular procedure which his lord only achieved [via *praecipe in capite*] after 1215' (p.174).

[21] Ibid., p.173.

[22] Ibid., p.174.

[23] Ibid., pp. 174–7.

[24] Ibid., pp. 177–8.

jurisdiction and the growth of the common law made the practice of litigation for great men altogether more straightforward and satisfactory. The hypothesis, as we have seen, is eloquently expressed and powerfully argued. Yet it is only partially convincing. Holt is surely right to stress the difficulties of litigation under John and the disappearance of the great financial proffers for justice thereafter. In that respect litigation after 1215 was less expensive and dangerous than it had been before.[25] We will return to this point again in due course. It is also true that, as the common law grew, the litigation of great men became increasingly caught up in its actions and procedures. But where Holt is wrong is in supposing that this development made such litigation routine and free from royal interference. In this respect he overstates the contrast between before and after 1215. The litigation of great men in the minority of Henry III and thereafter was still contaminated by politics and fragmented by government intervention. Its processes were often tortuous, lengthy and uncertain. It rarely shuttled through on the neat tramlines enjoyed by insignificant men litigating against each other. The lord never achieved the 'regular procedure' enjoyed by the undertenant.[26]

We may begin by looking at the writ *praecipe in capite*, for Holt, as we have seen, the vital mechanism which placed the barons on the tramlines of the common law. This is to exaggerate its importance. *Praecipe in capite* was neither unavailable before 1215 nor, more significantly, any sort of magic elixir thereafter. The evidence for its existence before 1215 appears in a register of writs for Ireland which Paul Brand has dated to 1210, a dating which Holt is inclined to accept.[27] Here we find the following heading: 'Concerning land or concerning a fee which is held of the lord king in chief (*in capite*), let the writ issue which is called *precipe* before the chief justices at a fixed day; for the quantity mentioned above [half a knight's fee or less], without payment'. The writ then follows:

'The King to the sheriff, greeting. Command B. that, justly and without delay, he render to A. half a knight's fee ... in N. which he claims to hold of the lord king for so much service ... and whereof he complains that this B. has deforced him; and if he does not do this ... then summon, by good summoners, the tenant that he be

[25] On the other hand, undercover or disguised payments for justice continued. In order to overturn a judgement in 1254 St Albans abbey secretly gave Richard of Cornwall (regent in England) £100. The abbot also made a voluntary contribution of £50 towards the king's costs in Gascony: *Gesta Abbatum Monasterii Sancti Albani*, ed. H.T. Riley, 3 vols. (Rolls Ser., 1867–9), i, 346; *Matthaei Parisiensis ... Chronica Majora*, ed. H.R. Luard, 7 vols. (Rolls Ser., 1872–83), vi, 293; Public Record Office, London, C 60/51, m.6. All manuscript references are henceforth to documents in the Public Record Office London.

[26] Holt, *Magna Carta*, p.174. See above note 20. Turner, however, *The King and his Courts*, pp.57,64,157,165 (though see also pp.88–90) argues that Henry tampered with the course of justice less than this father.

[27] *Early Registers of Writs*, ed. E. de Haas and G.D.G. Hall (Selden Soc., 87,1970), pp. 1–17; P. Brand, 'Ireland and the Literature of the early Common Law', *Irish Jurist*, new ser., 14 (1979), 95–113, reprinted in *The Making of the Common Law* (London, 1992), pp. 445–72, especially between pp. 450–6; Holt, *Magna Carta*, p.174 n.218.

before our justices on that day to show why he had not done this, and have there the summoners and this writ. Witness etc.'[28]

This is unquestionably the writ *praecipe in capite*. It is also, for property of half a fee or less, a writ *de cursu*, hence the stipulation that it was to be conceded free. Now, the purpose of the Register of 1210 was to introduce English forms to Ireland. As the introductory letter patent put it: 'Since we desire justice according to the custom of our realm of England to be shown to all in our realm of Ireland . . . we have caused the form of writs *de cursu*, by which this is accustomed to be done, to be inserted in the present writing'.[29] The implication, therefore, is that *praecipe in capite* already ran in England as a writ *de cursu*. Holt himself cites what is in effect a *praecipe in capite* issued for property in Northumberland as early as 1200,[30] and the writ may have been used more commonly, given that we often do not know the writs which began baronial litigation under John. Admittedly, in the Irish Register of 1210 *praecipe in capite* was only a writ *de cursu* for half a knight's fee or less, but such restrictions were attached to other writs in Ireland. Whether they also applied to *praecipe in capite* in England seems impossible to say.

The existence of *praecipe in capite* before 1215 is a comparatively minor point. It does not alter Holt's basic picture of litigation under John. And whatever *praecipe in capite*'s theoretical status as a writ *de cursu*, it could be argued that before 1215 it was in practice often hard and expensive to obtain, whereas afterwards it was freely and automatically available. The essential trouble with Holt's hypothesis, however, even thus modified, remains the same, namely that there is limited evidence that *praecipe in capite* after 1215 opened up easy, routine litigation for barons. Indeed, there are some grounds for thinking that the barons never expected it to do so. That, after all, is the message of Magna Carta itself. Holt's statement, that 'the *praecipe in capite* . . . was a great unrecorded baronial victory which gave backbone to cap. 40 of the Charter',[31] is so ringing and emphatic that it almost diverts attention from the point that, yes indeed, Magna Carta has nothing at all to say about it. Yet if the barons and their legal advisers had felt it essential, in order to secure free and speedy justice, to make *praecipe in capite* a writ *de cursu*, or, to take Holt's position, to invent it altogether, why did they not say so in the Charter? After all, it was not as though the Charter was silent about individual writs. Indeed chapter 36 precisely made the writ of inquisition of life and limb a writ 'of course' by stipulat-

---

[28] *Early Registers of Writs*, p.2.

[29] Ibid., p. 1; for the date of the letter see Brand, 'Ireland and the Literature of the Early Common Law', in *The Making of the Common Law*, p.453.

[30] Holt, *Magna Carta*, pp.140–1. Holt himself notes that there may have been some softening before 1215 in the line that the writ *praecipe* itself was a writ *de gracia* for tenants-in-chief: ibid., p.174 and n.218.

[31] Ibid., p.174.

ing that henceforth it should be conceded free and not denied.[32] Yet, as far as their own litigation was concerned, the barons in 1215 preferred to assert general principles of justice rather than initiate specific writs. They were right to do so, for the essential problem with litigation was not just getting the writ; it was what happened thereafter.

If the baronial attitude to *praecipe in capite* in 1215 was comparatively lukewarm, it did not change thereafter. True, the great law book *Bracton*, written in the 1220s and 1230s, assumed that *praecipe in capite* was the normal writ for litigation over baronies.[33] Yet, in some important cases, it was quite clearly not the preferred path. Take the case Holt himself cites to 'bring home the point' that *praecipe in capite* was 'a great unrecorded baronial victory', namely the case in 1234 in which Eustace de Stuteville recovered the manor of Cottingham in Yorkshire from Hugh Wake and William de Mustac.[34] Here Eustace, as Holt observes, began his action not by *praecipe in capite* but by plaint. To be sure, after their defeat, Wake and Mustac were told that they could, if they wished, pursue their action by *mort d'ancestor* or by writ of right (that is by *praecipe in capite*) 'according to the law of the land', hence Holt's comment, as we have seen, that 'the common law had permeated the inner sanctum in which the king held jurisdiction over his immediate vassals'.[35] But did Wake and Mustac appreciate their great unrecorded victory and hurry to the chancery to secure their *praecipe in capite*? Not a bit of it; as far as the evidence goes, they did nothing at all.

In the failure to use *praecipe in capite* around this time Stuteville, Wake and Mustac were scarcely isolated.[36] When, in 1233, Peter de Maulay sought the manor of Upavon from Gilbert Basset he proceeded not by *preaecipe in capite* but by an action of *quo warranto* in which Basset was summoned *coram rege* to show 'by what warrant' he held the manor.[37] Similar *quo warranto* actions were used *coram rege* in 1234–5 by plaintiffs attempting to recover manors which the king had taken from them and given to others between 1232 and 1234, the current holders being summoned to show the warrant for their tenure.[38] On

---

[32] Chapter 34 also forbad the issuing of the writ *praecipe* in such a way as to deprive a freeman of his court.

[33] *Bracton De Legibus et Consuetudinibus Angliae*, ed. G.E. Woodbine, translated and revised by S.E. Thorne, 4 vols. (Cambridge, Mass., 1968–77), ii, 301. For the authorship see below note 119. The indexes to the *Curia Regis Rolls*, 17 vols. (London, 1922–61), which cover the years 1219 to 1243, do not contain many references to *praecipe in capite* but, as before 1215, it is dangerous to draw conclusions from this because it is not always clear what writ has been used to begin litigation.

[34] Holt, *Magna Carta*, p.174; *Curia Regis Rolls*, xv, no.1026.

[35] Holt, *Magna Carta*, p.177.

[36] See also below notes 63, 66 for litigation by writs other than *praecipe in capite*.

[37] *Curia Regis Rolls*, xv, no.131. Basset was summoned to answer the king rather than Maulay himself. Probably the same *quo warranto* procedure was employed by Payn de Chaworth in 1232 in order to wrest the Hertfordshire manors of Lilley and Willian from Richard de Argentan: *Curia Regis Rolls*, xv, no.1426; C 60/32, m.9. For the whole of this quarrel see below note 41.

[38] *Hubert de Burgh* v. *Robert Passelewe* concerning Aspley Guise (Beds.): *Curia Regis Rolls*, xv, no.1058;

occasion, the defeated parties in these cases were told, like Wake and Mustac, that they could take the matter further by seeking another writ or raising the question of right, probably in both cases invitations to proceed via *praecipe in capite*. The offer was accepted by Richard de Argentan, who was trying to recover Lilley and Willian in Hertfordshire from Payn de Chaworth. He did not get very far. In the Easter term of 1236 the king ordered the justices of the bench to adjourn the plea until Trinity, and that, for the moment, was the end of the matter.[39] When Richard's son, Giles de Argentan, resumed hostilities in 1241 it was once again via an action of *quo warranto*, in which he appeared as the king's attorney.[40] This time Lilley and Willian were indeed recovered, only for King Henry to grant them to his steward Paulinus Peyvre. It was left to Giles, a leading Montfortian, to seize the manors in the 1263–5 civil war.[41]

The writ *praecipe in capite* was by this time very much a writ *de cursu*. The action of *quo warranto* was very much one of grace.[42] Yet the latter in these cases was the preferred route. This makes a wider point. For a magnate to succeed in major litigation against another magnate he needed above all the king's support. A *quo warranto* action, an action of grace, showed that he had it. An unblessed action via a writ *de cursu* gave no such signal. In Holt's view what the barons wanted were writs *de cursu* and routine procedures. That might have been true had the playing field been even. But often, of course, it was badly sloped. A writ *de cursu* enabled you to start an action but not to finish it. You might have to deal with a king who would intervene to postpone or forbid judgements and with judges who were too scared or biased to give them; those, at any rate, were common accusations in the reign of Henry III.[43] Indeed, for a

continued

Hubert de Burgh v. Nicholas de Lettres concerning Wheatley (Notts.): no. 1076; *Thomas de la Hay* v. *Mathias de Plessis* concerning Exning (Suff.): nos.1207,1308; *Richard de Argentan* v. *Payn de Chaworth* concerning Lilley and Willian (Herts.): no. 1426; *John Lestrange* v. *Ralph Russell* concerning Road (Som.): no. 1427; *Hubert de Burgh* v. *Anketil Mallore* concerning Arley (Staffs.): no.1475 and *Bracton's Note Book*, ed. F.W. Maitland, 3 vols. (London, 1887), iii, no.1136; *Hubert de Burgh* v. *Mathias Bezille* concerning Westhall (Suff.): *Curia Regis Rolls*, xv, no.1475 and *Bracton's Note Book*, iii, no.1141; *Hubert de Burgh* v. *John de Grey* concerning Purleigh and v. *Alan de Urri* concerning Canewdon and Wickford (all Essex): *Curia Regis Rolls*, xv, no.1895. In *Hubert de Burgh* v. *Nicholas de Lettres*, Lettres was summoned to answer the king; in the other cases the defendant was summoned to answer the plaintiff.

[39] *Curia Regis Rolls*, xv, nos.1426, 1540; *Close Rolls, 1234–7*, p.251.

[40] *Curia Regis Rolls*, xvi, no.1758. By this time the manors were no longer held by Payn de Chaworth, see *Close Rolls, 1234–7*, pp. 465, 483. The pleadings did not cover the Argentan claim.

[41] *Cal. Charter Rolls, 1226–57*, p. 276; *Cal. Inquisitions Miscellaneous*, i, nos.707,711; *Feudal Aids*, i, 429,430. For the background to the conflict over Lilley and Willian, which dated back, as so often, to an ambiguous grant made by King John: see, in addition to the references given above, *Rot. Litt. Clause*, i, 283b,593; *Exc. Rot. Fin.*, i, 147; *Rot. Litt. Claus.*, ii, 139b, 141b, 162; *Cal. Charter Rolls, 1226–57*, pp. 57,85,140; *Close Rolls, 1231–4*, pp. 173, 179, 190–1; *Book of Fees*, pp.14, 124. The Argentans coveted the properties because they adjoined their ancestral seat at Wymondley.

[42] For the distinction, see *Brevia Placitata*, ed. G.J. Turner and T.F.T. Plucknett (Selden Soc., 66, 1947), pp. xlviii-lix.

[43] See below p. 36.

magnate contemplating major litigation against another magnate, was there really such a thing, in practice, as a writ *de cursu?* *Minores* litigating against *minores* doubtless obtained their writs with no questions asked. But the commencement of major litigation required a whole series of political soundings. If, in the end, such litigation was not sanctioned in some way by the king, even writs *de cursu* might turn out to be unavailable.[44] The importance of royal favour was seen all too clearly in Hubert de Burgh's litigation after his rehabilitation in 1234. He brought a series of successful actions to recover the properties which he had lost on his fall. All sorts of reasons were thought up to give judgements in his favour, some of them clean contrary to the facts.[45] Then, with renewed disgrace in 1236, Hubert abandoned his actions and his enemies gathered round to make good their losses.[46] The most successful was the rising minister, Robert Passelewe, who recovered Henlow in Bedfordshire through a judgement just as suspicious as any from which Hubert had profited: it depended on the revelation that the writ which had put Hubert in seisin had been addressed in error to the sheriff of Northamptonshire, instead of the sheriff of Bedfordshire, and that the sheriff of Northamptonshire had in any case never received it, this despite the fact that the writ in question was found on the rolls of the chancery. All this was brought to light by the testimony of the then sheriff of Northamptonshire, Henry of Bath, who was now none other than one of the judges in the case. Henry, it is worth noting, was later dismissed from the bench for malpractice.[47]

The truth is that actions involving great men could never escape from the attentions of the king and considerations of politics and patronage. They could never proceed with the regularity enjoyed by the cases of lesser mortals. As Holt has remarked, the king 'could not achieve consistency. To provide it would impede his political initiative'.[48] This was as true under Henry III as it was under John. Such a conclusion is reinforced if we look briefly at some of the litigation from the minority. The brave new world Holt sees then beginning was foreshadowed, he suggests, by the restorations made by King John immediately after Magna Carta. It was these which first introduced, for tenants-in-chief, regularity of procedure and routine processes into the operations of the

---

[44] For the allegation that Henry III prevented wirts *de cursu* being issued against favoured magnates and ministers: *Documents of the Baronial Movement of Reform and Rebellion*, ed. R.F. Treharne and I.J. Sanders (Oxford, 1973), pp. 270–3; see also *Chronica Majora*, v, 594,689.

[45] For these cases see above note 38. In *Hubert de Burgh v. Anketil Mallore (Bracton's Note Book*, iii, nos.1136, 1141) Hubert's recovery of Arley (Staffs.) depended on the king declaring that he had given Arley to Anketil believing that he could do so lawfully since Hubert had been outlawed, whereas he now realised that the outlawry was null. Yet in fact Anketil (as he himself indicated) had received Arley *before* Hubert's outlawry, Hubert having lost it under the terms of the settlement in November 1232. See *Cal. Patent Rolls, 1232–47*, pp. 28–30; *Cal. Charter Rolls, 1226–57*, pp. 25, 182; *Close Rolls, 1231–4*, pp. 166–7, 217,232; *Curia Regis Rolls*, xvi, no. 145.

[46] *Curia Regis Rolls*, xvi, nos. 5, 145, 1001.

[47] *Curia Regis Rolls*, xvi, no.1001; see *Close Rolls, 1231–4*, pp. 332, 359, 443; *Cal. Charter Rolls, 1226–57*, p. 60; *Book of Fees*, p. 888; *Chronica Majora*, v, 213–5, 223–4, 240.

[48] Holt, *Magna Carta*, p. 157.

king's court.[49] It is hard to see how this was the case. The restorations certainly reflected a principle, that the king should disseise no one unjustly and without judgement. But they hardly established a routine. Some of the restorations may have followed judgements by the twenty-five barons, though the evidence for this is limited. Others depended on local investigations by the sheriffs who were to discover whether or not the complainant had indeed been disseised unjustly. All this was the reverse of routine. It was desperately *ad hoc.*[50]

There was likewise nothing very smooth about the cases in the minority. It is true that these can be read in different ways. Holt himself, in an important qualification, notes that cases arising from conflicting grants of King John, were resolved 'sometimes with considerable political friction and prolonged difficulty in enforcing judgement'. But he believes these were untypical.[51] My own view is the other way around. A typical case in the minority was constantly subject to delay and political intervention. This may seem merely a difference of emphasis, but it is one central to the arguments here discussed.

The case which Holt cites as a model of the changes which had taken place between 1215 and 1217 is the action of *novel disseisin* which Gilbert de Gant brought in 1219 against the count of Aumale to recover his manor of Edenham in Lincolnshire.[52] Here political intervention of the old kind was certainly defeated by the protests of the Lincolnshire county court. But what was important here, it may be suggested, was less the new availability of legal procedures, seen in Gant's ability to proceed via *novel disseisin,* than the new atmosphere, or what Holt himself calls 'the new tone',[53] revealed in the way the county court appealed to Magna Carta and the principle that possession should not be lost 'without judgement'.[54] Equally important, moreover, were simply the immediate politics of the minority. Aumale's backer was King John's former justiciar and the young king's tutor, the Touraigneau Peter des Roches, bishop of Winchester. Bishop Peter promptly supported Aumale's efforts to reopen the case and, presiding over the government, allowed it to continue despite Aumale's excommunication, thus blatantly overturning the custom of the realm.[55] What finally persuaded Aumale to accept defeat in the Michaelmas term of 1220 was Bishop Peter's political eclipse.[56]

[49] Ibid., pp. 165, 167.
[50] In essence, this emerges from Holt's own discussion. ibid., pp. 165–7. *Rot. Litt. Claus,* i, 215–7 and *Rot. Litt. Pat.,* pp. 143b-145b contain the orders for the restorations.
[51] Holt, *Magna Carta,* pp. 170–1.
[52] Ibid., pp. 168–9.
[53] Ibid., p. 168. For the absence of baronial litigation via *novel disseisin* over tenancies-in-chief under John see p. 132, though observe the word of caution in note 41.
[54] *Royal and other Historical Letters illustrative of the Reign of Henry III,* ed. W.W. Shirley, 2 vols. (Rolls Ser., 1862, 1866), i, no. xvi. For Gant's action see *Rolls of the Justices in Eyre for Lincolnshire, 1218–19 . . . ,* ed. D.M. Stenton (Selden Soc., 53, 1934), no.151.
[55] C 60/11, m. 3; *Pipe Roll 3 Henry III,* p.129; *Curia Regis Rolls,* viii, 158; ix, 52–3. See Turner, *The King and his Courts,* pp. 113–14.
[56] *Curia Regis Rolls,* ix, 258. See D.A. Carpenter, *The Minority of Henry III* (London 1990), pp. 182–3 and pp. 102–3, 165–6.

The Edenham case was indeed quickly settled, but this was far from the universal pattern. One action Holt notes as being settled by final concord in 1218 was that between William de Percy and Richard de Percy over the Percy inheritance.[57] A concord was indeed reached in May 1218. Yet it was soon challenged and litigation between the Percies continued intermittently for sixteen years until another settlement in 1234.[58] Another case, which Holt cites specifically as illustrating the speed of justice in the minority, was that between Robert de Vieuxpont and the countess of Eu for the honour of Tickhill, a dispute settled, in Holt's view, in under two years between Michaelmas 1220 and February 1222.[59] But in actual fact this case had been pending since July 1218 when Vieuxpont was allowed to retain the shrieval revenues of Cumberland until he received justice over his claims to Tickhill.[60] In the Hilary term of 1220 the case was adjourned till Easter 'by petition of the lord king and his council'. When Easter approached, the papal legate, Pandulf, accepted the advice of the justiciar, Hubert de Burgh, and agreed that the plea should be adjourned again for 'the times are evil and the malice of men and the times grows daily'. The delay infuriated Vieuxpont, yet he had to wait another eighteen months till February 1222 before the political situation permitted a settlement,[61] this despite the fact that the government had every incentive to reach one; until it did Vieuxpont retained all the revenues of Cumberland without accounting at the exchequer.[62] Another important case less rapid than it seems was that in which the earl of Hereford sought to recover Trowbridge from the countess of Salisbury. This was an attempt to reverse one of John's most notorious disseisins *per voluntatem regis*, that which had ejected Henry de Bohun, earl of Hereford, from Trowbridge and replaced him with William Longespee, earl of Salisbury. To say this plea was begun in 1226 and was concorded in 1230 tells only half the story.[63] The other half is that the plea did not begin at all until William Longespee's death in 1226. Longespee had been a great ally of the

---

[57] Holt, *Magna Carta*, p. 170 and note 196.

[58] *Feet of Fines for the County of York, 1218–1231*, ed. J. Parker (Yorkshire Archaeological Soc., Record ser., 62, 1921), pp. 1–2, 108–111; *Curia Regis Rolls*, ix, 308; xi, nos. 46, 948, 1685, 2432 (substantive pleadings); xii, nos.656, 1444, 1959, 2311; xiii, nos. 570, 586, 856, 1161, 1224 (substantive pleadings), 1546; xv, nos.471, 1046, 1125 (the final settlement); *Close Rolls, 1231–4*, p. 468. For the dispute see Turner, 'Exercise of the King's Will in Inheritance of Baronies: The Example of King John and William Briwerre', *Judges, Administrators and the Common Law*, pp. 280–2, 287.

[59] Holt, *Magna Carta*, pp. 171 and 170 note 194.

[60] E 368/4, m.3d (T. Madox, *The History and Antiquities of the Exchequer*, 2 vols. London, 1769, ii, 68 note t); for the date of this agreement see p.xxvii of Dr Crook's introduction to *Pipe Roll 5 Henry III* (Pipe Roll Soc., new ser., 48, 1984–6).

[61] *Curia Regis Rolls*, viii, 224–5; *Royal Letters*, i, nos. xcii, xcix; *Curia Regis Rolls*, ix, 1–2, 152–3, 212–3; *Feet of Fines for the County of York*, pp.42–3.

[62] Carpenter, *Minority of Henry III*, pp.275–6 and pp. 89, 187–8, 191, 275–6 for the case as a whole.

[63] Holt, *Magna Carta*, p. 170 and note 195. The earl of Hereford seems to have proceeded by a writ of entry *sur disseisin*, a writ which had been *de cursu* since 1204: *Curia Regis Rolls*, xii, no. 2646; Holt, *Magna Carta*, p. 139.

justiciar and pillar of the regime. Until his death left his countess alone and unprotected successive earls of Hereford realised it was pointless to proceed.[64]

Other baronial litigants in the minority would have been surprised to learn that great benefits flowed from new access to the common law. Take the case of Maurice de Gant whom the earl of Chester at Easter 1218 had deprived of the manors of Leeds and Bingley under the terms of a ransom agreement. At a great council in May 1218 Gant sought recovery of the manors. He was unsuccessful: the council decided that Chester should remain in seisin but added that Gant could sue against the earl if he wished. Gant took the council at its word and, in best Holtian fashion, sought remedy through the common law. He obtained a writ of *novel disseisin* and the case came before the justices in eyre in Yorkshire in 1219. It was, however, too hot for them to handle. Since a great council had already passed a judgement in the matter, they simply referred the case back to another great council which met at Oxford in April 1219. This assembly refused to review, let alone overturn, the previous judgement, but added that Gant, if he wished, could implead Chester 'touching right'. If, as seems likely, this was an invitation to have another go via *praecipe in capite*, it was an invitation which Gant declined. He had been round the track once already and had little reason to think that a second circuit would bring better results. He simply gave up and Leeds and Bingley remained with the earl of Chester. This result had everything to do with the political situation. Gant had a strong case, for the ransom agreement should arguably have been rendered invalid under the terms of the peace treaty which closed the civil war, but Chester was immensely powerful and his loyalty immensely important to the regime. In May 1218 he was about to leave England on a crusade. He had already agreed to surrender part of the honour of Richmond. This was no time to risk his disaffection.[65]

A baron who fared even worse than Maurice de Gant was Reginald de Braose. In 1217 he was deprived of the Three Castles after defaulting in a legal action brought by Hubert de Burgh. In form Hubert was seeking to remedy the act of injustice by which King John had deprived him of the Three Castles in the first place.[66] In reality Braose's deprivation smacked of John's own worst sharp practice. Hubert spent the next ten years in a series of convoluted legal manoeuvres designed to buttress his title, seeking first to hold the Three Castles from Reginald, then in chief from the king, and finally from Reginald's nephew John.[67]

[64] Carpenter, *Minority of Henry III*, p.195.
[65] *Rolls of the Justices in Eyre for Yorkshire, 1218–19*, ed. D.M. Stenton (Selden Soc., 56, 1937), nos. 315, 1133; *Cal. Patent Rolls, 1232–47*, p.3; Carpenter, *Minority of Henry III*, pp. 82, 129; Holt, *Magna Carta*, p. 169 note 192.
[66] Hubert proceeded by a writ of entry *sur disseisin: Bracton's Note Book*, iii, no. 1330; *Rot. Litt. Claus.*, i, 404, 386b; *Rot. Chartarum*, p. 160b.
[67] *Curia Regis Rolls*, xi, nos. 1894, 2418, 2788; xii, nos. 59, 307; CP 25(1)/80/5, no. 59; *Cal. Charter Rolls 1226–57*, pp. 74, 83; *Curia Regis Rolls*, xiii, no. 592; CP 25 (1)/ 80/ 5, no. 119. In *The Minority of Henry III*, p. 247 note 16, I was wrong to say that the final agreement to hold the Three Castles from John de Braose was made after Reginald's death. He died a month or so later: *Exc.*

There was nothing routine about that. Meanwhile, between 1217 and 1221, Reginald was involved in litigation designed to wrest Barnstaple and Totnes from respectively Henry de Tracy and Henry fitz Count. Here law and politics were inextricably mixed. Totnes and Barnstaple had been taken by King John from Reginald's father, William de Braose, at the time of his fall. Reginald's case rested on the royal council's promise which had tempted him back into the allegiance of the young king during the war; namely that he could recover his father's lands 'as on the day he best held them'.[68] How lawfully or how easily this promise could be fulfilled depended in part upon the terms on which John had subsequently granted the properties to Tracy and fitz Count. Tracy claimed that he held Barnstaple by hereditary right, a claim Reginald did not challenge.[69] Fitz Count, on the other hand, so Reginald argued, probably correctly, only held during the king's pleasure, and thus could lawfully be deprived.[70] Nonetheless, Reginald abandoned both cases during the Trinity term of 1220.[71] The government simply lacked the will to fulfil its promises.[72] Still there was a silver lining. Next year Reginald did indeed recover Totnes. The reason was entirely political. The situation had been transformed by the sudden fall of Henry fitz Count. And Reginald had earned the government's favour by agreeing to a settlement of the dispute with his nephew, John, and by accepting Hubert de Burgh's tenure of the Three Castles.[73]

These cases from the minority do not suggest that baronial litigation was exactly routine or that it was escaping from the interference of the king and his ministers. Forms and actions of the common law may have been utilised more frequently, but their very complexity made them open to manipulation. Nor is it clear that the barons benefited particularly from the changes in jurisdictional theory with which Holt also deals. Indeed, Holt himself, in discussing the erosion of feudal jurisdiction, makes an important qualification, observing that on its 'ruins' the king's men began to build 'a doctrine of royal prerogative'. As a result the crown did not lose from the dissolution of feudal control over its immediate vassals. Contemporaries, Holt observes, saw no surrender. *Bracton's* list of pleas reserved for the king was much the same as *Glanvil's*.[74] The earls of Chester and Pembroke might have argued in the 1230s that their cases were common pleas which should not follow the king, but their argu-

---

continued

Rot. Fin., i, 172. Hubert's tergiversations were related in part to the *casus regis*, John de Braose being the son of Reginald's elder brother.

[68] *Patent Rolls, 1216–25*, pp. 72–3; *Curia Regis Rolls*, viii, 365.

[69] *Curia Regis Rolls*, viii, 365; see *Rot. Litt. Claus.*, i, 137; *Rot. Litt. Pat.*, p.101.

[70] *Curia Regis Rolls*, viii, 226. See *Rot. Litt. Pat.*, p.89.

[71] *Curia Regis Rolls*, ix, 111–12, 143.

[72] For the initial stages of the cases and the government's efforts to give Braose possession, see *Patent Rolls, 1216–25*, pp. 72, 74–75, 103; *Rot. Litt. Claus.*, i, 376b, 382b, 405b.

[73] *Patent Rolls, 1216–25*, pp. 296–7; Carpenter, *Minority of Henry III*, pp.216, 141–2, 168, 246. The settlement with John de Braose, however, soon collapsed.

[74] Holt, *Magna Carta*, pp. 178–9; and see pp. 172–3.

ments were rejected. The earl of Pembroke was told that his was 'a private plea which specially touches the lord king and a plea which touches the king ought to be determined before him', a claim which already, as Holt suggests, pointed towards a doctrine of jurisdiction based on the royal prerogative.[75] Indeed the two doctrines, feudal and prerogative, at least in the 1230s, were closely interwoven. *Bracton*, in listing the pleas which must be heard *coram rege*, began with 'pleas of baronies, where the demandant claims to hold immediately of the lord king in chief'. This was to hint at a feudal theory, the king's right to hear the case stemming from considerations of tenure. But *Bracton* then added that 'the reason' why the case must come *coram rege* 'is because the matter touches the king himself, in whole or part'.[76] In a way that was to state the obvious. Litigation over land held from the king *ipso facto* was litigation over a matter which touched the king. Feudal jurisdiction and prerogative jurisdiction were here virtually identical. In any case, whatever the change in the theory, the practice was much the same. Great cases involving great men, whether under feudal jurisdiction, prerogative jurisdiction or the common law, remained subject to the highly political supervision of the king.[77]

This situation did not change later in the reign, as the litigation involving Hubert de Burgh itself suggests. True a note of caution needs to be sounded here. The plea rolls of the 1240s and 1250s, many of them unprinted, have yet to be properly analysed. My own impression is that litigation involving magnates over land held in chief was less frequent than it had been under John.[78] That was partly because many of *causes célébres* of the early thirteenth-century had worked themselves out and partly because new ones were less frequently created by actions *per voluntatem regis*, a point to which we will return. But the absence of such cases was also because political pressures continued to distort the judicial process, thus discouraging would be litigants. Certainly those who did go to law in this period experienced slow and bumpy rides.

One example is the dispute over the manor of Redenhall in Norfolk. In 1252 Roger Bigod, earl of Norfolk, claimed this from the knight, Nicholas of Lenham, and three years later, in a final concord, secured the recognition of his right. In return, he granted the manor back to Nicholas for the service of two knights and a rent of £5 a year, and took Nicholas's homage in a ceremony before the justices of the bench.[79] Redenhall was not at this time held in chief;

---

[75] *Curia Regis Rolls*, xvi, no.8; Holt, *Magna Carta*, pp. 178–9, 172–3.

[76] *Bracton*, ii, 301.

[77] Prerogative jurisdiction was not, of course, necessarily separate from common law jurisdiction. The prerogative reserved certain types of pleas for hearing in the king's court (if he so wished) but, once there, they might proceed according to the forms and actions of the common law.

[78] I have been through the printed and unprinted rolls of the 1240s and 1250s looking for interesting and important cases but that does not mean I have always found them.

[79] KB 26/147B, m.13; KB 26/154, m.15; CP 25(1)/158/84, no.1269. For Lenham's properties in Kent and Sussex see *Cal. Charter Rolls, 1226–57*, p.463; *Cal. Inq. Misc.*, i, nos. 739, 759, 1024 (p.314). In 1248 the king had launched a claim for Redenhall 'as an escheat of the lands of the Normans', the Lenhams having acquired the property from a family which had chosen the French

it was part of the honour of Richmond, an honour frequently in the king's hands in the early thirteenth century but now held by the queen's uncle, Peter of Savoy.[80] Still, this remained important litigation which touched the king and his magnates. On the face of it, it had gone through smoothly and without interference. The case was heard before the justices of the bench, not *coram rege*; Nicholas put himself on the grand assize; the case was settled in three years by final concord. The reality was very different. Bigod's claim to Redenhall was highly speculative, being based on the tenure of his great-grandfather before 1177.[81] Yet the action almost certainly had the king's support for, unless it succeeded, Bigod might have some claim to Peter of Savoy's manor of Wissett (Suffolk): this thanks to a promise of King John, ultimately unfulfilled, which had given the Bigods Wisset in place of Redenhall.[82] Lenham had lost, therefore, because he lacked political influence. It was a lesson he soon learnt as he set about spoiling Bigod's victory. In 1257 he leased Redenhall for sixteen years to the queen. Bigod considered this threatened his annual rent, for 'what is given to the queen is given to the king' and the king could not be subject to distraint. He thus disseised the queen's attorneys, was sentenced to pay damages and immediately protested to the king – the assize of *novel disseisin* brought against him had proceeded 'less than rightly'. Henry III characteristically respited the damages and promised to review everything *coram rege*.[83] Next year another settlement was attempted. Nicholas was to grant the manor, with Bigod's consent, to Peter of Savoy himself, who was to hold in chief from the king but pay Bigod his £5 a year. Henry, meanwhile, at Bigod's insistence, waived his rights as overlord to the wardship of the manor and granted them to Bigod and his heirs instead. It may be no accident that this concession, embodied in a charter, was made on 8 May 1258, eight days after Bigod had led the march into the king's hall and confronted the quailing monarch with the demand for

---

continued
allegiance after 1204. Lenham bought off the claim by promising the king 400 marks, a sum subsequently pardoned when he led four knights out with Simon de Montfort to Gascony. See C 60/45, m.3; *Cal. Charter Rolls, 1226–57*, p.333; *Cal. Pat. Rolls, 1247–58*, pp. 26,31; *Close Rolls, 1247–51*, p. 119. For material bearing on the Lenham acquisition of Redenhall see *Pipe Roll 1 John*, p.289; *Feet of Fines for the County of Norfolk, 1198–1202*, ed. B. Dodwell (Pipe Roll Soc., new ser., 27 1959), no.218; *Curia Regis Rolls*, v, 179; vi, 74; *Feet of Fines for the County of Norfolk 1202–15* . . . , ed. B. Dodwell (Pipe Roll Soc., new ser., 32, 1958), no.262; *Cal. Inq. Misc.*, i, no.521; *Rot Litt. Claus.*, ii, 117; *Exc. Rot. Fin.*, i, 99, 143; *Book of Fees*, p. 386; Just 1/578, mm. 28, 99; CP/40/64, m. 114d. The account in F. Blomefield, *An Essay towards a Topographical History of the County of Norfolk*, v (London, 1806), pp. 367–8, is helpful but not entirely accurate. See also *Early Yorkshire Charters*, v, ed. C.T. Clay (Yorkshire Archaeological Soc., record ser., extra ser 2, 1936), pp.3, 315–16.

[80] *Exc. Rot. Fin.*, i, 143; *Rot Litt. Claus.*, ii, 117; *Cal. Charter Rolls, 1226–57*, p.259. It may have been on Peter's behalf that the king laid claim to the manor in 1248.

[81] KB 26/147B, m.13.

[82] *Rot. Chartarum*, p. 151b; *Close Rolls, 1227–31*, pp. 59–60; *Book of Fees*, p. 619; *Cal. Charter Rolls, 1226–57*, p. 259.

[83] Just 1/567, mm. 13,1; *Close Rolls, 1256–9*, p.145. The assize was brought by Nicholas of Lenham because Bigod had deprived him of his 'profit' (*commodum*) from the manor.

the exile of the Poitevins and the general reform of the realm.[84] This second agreement, however, also collapsed and almost immediately. At the beginning of July, in an action *coram rege* at Winchester, Lenham was accused of not rendering due 'suits and services' to Bigod as lord of Earsham hundred, in which Redenhall was situated. When it was stated that Lenham had given all his lands in Norfolk to Peter of Savoy, the rejoinder probably revealed Bigod's thoughts about the whole business: Lenham had done this 'maliciously' in order to obstruct any action against him. Doubtless Lenham would have said he had merely taken revenge for Bigod's speculative litigation the first place.[85] A week after this exchange the agreement between Lenham and Peter of Savoy was recorded in a final concord. Peter was to hold the manor from the king in hereditary right 'performing all services which belong to the land'. No reference at all was made to services to Bigod. On the back of the fine there was a testy note: 'Roger le Bigod, earl of Norfolk and marshal of England, places his claim'.[86] After nearly six years of litigation Bigod was back to square one.[87]

Bigod was, of course, one of the greatest men in the realm and Lenham needed all the help of the queen's Savoyard faction to frustrate him. A less influential magnate, like Thomas de Ferrers, younger son of the earl of Derby, might find things even more difficult. Thomas maintained that his mother, just before her death, had given him her castle and manor of Chartley (Staffs.), together with other properties. This gift his elder brother, William de Ferrers, earl of Derby, refused to respect, despite the king ordering him to do so. Accordingly, in 1249, Thomas began a legal action against William in the court *coram rege*. That Michaelmas term William failed to turn up, having already defaulted on several previous occasions. The sheriff was ordered to distrain him to appear the following Easter. But the case made little progress.[88] The fact was that, in July 1249 just as

---

[84] *Cal. Charter Rolls, 1257–1300*, p. 10. According to the account in the Tewkesbury annals (*Annales Monastici*, ed. H.R. Luard, 5 vols. Rolls ser., 1864–9, i, 164), Bigod also demanded the departure of 'all aliens'. Did this mean Peter of Savoy? Perhaps not since Bigod and Savoy were numbered amongst the seven magnates who confederated together on 12 April: C. Bémont, *Simon de Montfort* (Paris, 1884), pp. 327–8, illustrated on p. 153 of J.R. Maddicott's *Simon de Montfort* (Cambridge, 1994). Conceivably the attempt to reach an agreement in the Redenhall dispute was a consequence of this alliance.

[85] KB 26/158, m. 14d.

[86] CP 25(1)/283/15, no. 351. It may be significant that Peter of Savoy did not witness the king's charter to Bigod of 8 May.

[87] In 1262 Peter of Savoy granted the honour of Richmond, including Redenhall, to the Lord Edward (*Cal. Charter Rolls, 1257–1300*, pp. 42,44) who subsequently enfeoffed Nicholas of Yattendon. The £5 rent owed the Bigods was mentioned in the survey of the manor on Yattendon's death in 1274: *Cal. Inq. Post Mortem*, ii, no.57.

[88] *Cal. Pat. Rolls, 1247–58*, p. 1; *Close Rolls, 1247–51*, pp. 219,224; KB 26/229, m.2d (Curia Regis Rolls, xix, in typescript at PRO, nos. 2413, 2414). See P.E. Golob, 'The Ferrers Earls of Derby: A Study of the Honour of Tutbury (1066–1279)' (unpublished University of Cambridge, Ph.D thesis, 1985), pp. 281–2. In October 1249 the king, having first ordered the barons of the exchequer to suspend a parallel case between Thomas and William over their mother's will, now ordered them to resume it and terminate it 'according to justice'. *Close Rolls, 1247–51*, p.234. A third brother, Hugh, was bringing an action against William for the manor of Salford (Lancs.).

the action got under way, William had cemented his place in royal favour by marrying his son and heir to Alice, one of the king's Lusignan nieces. He then cunningly made some of the disputed property part of their marriage portion. In 1253 Thomas found his case held up because the charter creating the marriage portion had been taken overseas by Alice's brother, William de Valence.[89] Later that year, Thomas tackled the king just before the royal expedition sailed for Gascony, and secured a writ to the regents which reflected all too clearly Henry's own failure to settle the case, his relief at passing the buck to someone else, and the pervasive influence of the earl of Derby.

For Thomas de Ferrers [to the earl of Cornwall and the queen]:

> 'Since for a long time past there have been contentions between our beloved and faithful Thomas de Ferrers and Hugh his brother on the one part and William de Ferrers earl of Derby on the other about certain lands in our kingdom, as you have heard on many occasions, we order you in our place to give full and speedy justice to both parties concerning the foresaid contentions according to the law and custom of our kingdom. And do not omit to do this on account of the favour of the aforesaid earl or anyone else'.[90]

It seems doubtful, however, whether the case made much further progress before the earl's death in 1254, whereupon the custody of his properties was granted to Edward the king's eldest son, who sold them on in 1257 to the queen and Peter of Savoy.[91] This effectively shut the door on further action until Robert de Ferrers, the next earl of Derby, came of age in 1260. Thomas then struck a bargain with Robert and (in 1262) began another legal action to recover Chartley, this time from the widow of the late earl who was holding it in dower.[92] His success and subsequent death without heirs meant that Robert himself eventually inherited Chartley; hence the survival of the Ferrers there, having lost everything else in the great crash of the civil war.[93]

Thomas de Ferrers had at least commenced legal actions but others, in the conditions of the 1240s and 1250s, judged it pointless to do so. This seems to have been the view of Robert fitz Walter, the lord of Daventry.[94] After the death of the countess of Warwick in 1254, Robert's title to the Buckinghamshire manor of Bradenham was indefeasible, yet, as far as can be seen, he made no effort to

[89] *Exc. Rot. Fin.*, ii, 174. This refers to an action before the justices in eyre in Northamptonshire. The eyre roll is badly damaged and I can find no reference to the case: Just 1/615.

[90] *Close Rolls, 1251-3*, p. 499.

[91] *Cal. Pat. Rolls, 1247-58*, pp. 367, 554. For Thomas appointing attorneys in the Michaelmas term of 1253 see KB 26/150, m. 6d.

[92] *Close Rolls, 1261-4*, pp.109-110; Just 1/954, m. 40d ('Pleas Roll temp. Henry III', *Collections for a History of Staffordshire* (William Salt Arch. Soc., 4 1883), p. 152, and see also p.153).

[93] KB 27/18, m. 24d ('Extracts from the Plea Rolls, 1272-94', *Collections for a History of Staffordshire*, William Salt Arch. Soc., part i, vol. 6, 1885), pp. 69-70).

[94] Robert, the son of Walter fitz Simon, was a minor tenant-in-chief and also held Tingry in Buckinghamshire: see *Book of Fees*, pp. 890,935; *Close Rolls, 1251-3*, p. 262; *Close Rolls, 1259-61*. p. 158.

dislodge the countess's husband, John de Plessis, earl of Warwick *iure uxoris*. This was scarcely surprising since the king had made John's career and now supported his continued tenure.[95] In the end, it was only John's death in 1263, the return of Simon de Montfort, the collapse of the king's power and Robert fitz Walter's own Montfortianism which restored Robert to the manor. Even so John de Plessis' son, Hugh de Plessis, seized it again during the civil war.[96]

In another better known case obstruction of the judicial process was specifically alleged. During the Gascon expedition of 1254 two Kentish knights and neighbours came to an agreement. Walter fitz John, short of money, leased his manor of Nashenden (in Rochester) to Roger of Leybourne in return for a £12 annual rent. Since the manor was held in chief the king confirmed the agreement. Back in England in 1255, however, Walter accused Roger of unjustly disseising him of the manor. Roger rejoined that he had entered it under the agreement made in Gascony, whereupon Walter abandoned his action and accepted Roger's right to hold the manor in return for the £12 annual rent. Superficially this looks like litigation, over land held in chief, which had escaped from the king and was going through on the tram lines of the common law. Walter had proceeded by an assize of *novel disseisin* before the justices in eyre in Kent. The action had ended in a concord. Yet again the reality was different. The truth was revealed when the justiciar, Hugh Bigod, visited Kent in 1259. Then Walter complained that he had never received the £12 rent from Roger or been able to distrain him for it. Doubtless this was why he had brought the action of *novel disseisin*. But he had then been equally unable 'to have justice against Roger in the royal court on account of the favour which Roger had at that time since he stood with William de Valence, the brother of the king'. This favour was presumably the reason why Walter had abandoned his *novel disseisin* action.[97]

---

[95] *Cal. Pat. Rolls, 1247–58*, p. 190; *Exc. Rot. Fin.*, ii, 163; *Cal. Inq. Misc.*, i, no.179. Bradenham was held from the earl of Hereford but by socage, or so it was said in 1242: *Book of Fees*, p.879. For the basis of fitz Walter's title see *Bracton's Note Book*, ii, no.855, especially the conclusion, and *Cal. Inq. Post Mortem*, i, no. 558. It is sometimes said (for example in G.E. Cokayne, *The Complete Peerage . . .*, revised by V. Gibbs and others, 12 vols. in 13 (London, 1912–59), x, 548 note c) that John de Plessis also diverted Hook Norton and Kidlington (Oxon.) away from the right heirs. This would have been the case had the family relationships as stated in *Cal. Inq. Post Mortem*, i, no.558 been correct. That they are false is shown by *Bracton's Note Book*, ii, no.855. For the agreements by which John held onto the earldom of Warwick after his wife's death (necessary because they were childless), see *The Beauchamp Cartulary Charters, 1100–1268*, ed. E. Mason (Pipe Roll soc., new ser., 43, 1971–3), nos.249–50; and see E. Mason, 'The Resources of the Earldom of Warwick in the Thirteenth Century', *Midland History*, 3 (1975), 67–75, especially pp. 70–1. John's origins were in Normandy (*Chron. Maj.*, v, 462) but his progress and proceedings created none of the resentment attendant on the rise of the Lusignans. In 1258 he was elected by the baronial twelve to help chose the council of fifteen on which he himself sat. For him sensibly accepting defeat in a law case brought by the men of his manor of Chalgrove, see Curia Regis Rolls, xix (in typescript at Public Record Office), nos. 182, 399, 1649.

[96] *Close Rolls, 1261–4*, pp. 264, 310–11; *Cal. Inq. Post Mortem*, i, no. 558; *Cal. Inq. Misc.*, i, no.630.

[97] Walter alleged that Roger's failure to pay the rent ultimately forced him into another agreement in which he was to hold the manor from Roger in return for paying him five marks a year:

Many of the cases just surveyed had political consequences. Roger Bigod, as we have seen, led the march on the king's hall on 30 April 1258. Nicholas of Lenham, Thomas de Ferrers and Robert fitz Walter of Daventry all joined the rebels in the subsequent civil war.[98] Yet these consequences paled into insignificance before those attendant on the greatest of all failures of the judicial system in the 1240s and 1250s: the failure to settle the great matter of the Montforts. Simon and Eleanor de Montfort claimed that Eleanor had never received her full dower from the lands of her first husband William Marshal, earl of Pembroke. As a result she was losing the extraordinary sum of £933 a year.[99] The Montforts had a strong case. They may have exaggerated their losses but Dr Maddicott's researches have shown that these were nonetheless substantial, probably over £500 a year.[100] The king's reaction to this problem was to say that the Montforts should bring a legal action against the Marshal heirs in order to recover Eleanor's dower from them, and in 1247 the Montforts indeed did so. A day early in 1248 was ultimately given to hear judgement, which the earl, the countess and the heirs all agreed, in the king's presence, to receive 'without essoin and without any delay . . . according to the testimony of the earl and countess and the reply of the heirs, without objection which the parties might be able to make to that judgement'. Yet, despite these elaborate precautions, no judgement was ever passed.[101] Instead, the Montforts abandoned their case. They evidently doubted the king's inclination and ability to force through a settlement, however just their cause; not surprisingly for the Marshal heirs included the most powerful magnates in the land.[102] The king had the greatest difficulty in acting against them on his own account and frequently failed to extract the £400 a year which they owed him. Thus the Montforts nursed their grievance for another decade and ultimately sought a settlement not through litigation but through blackmail. In 1259 they attempted to hold up the ratification of the treaty of Paris until Eleanor's claims were met. Few issues did more to sour relations between Montfort and the king.

Against this background it is not surprising that the revolution of 1258 should have been sparked off by the king's denial of justice to a great magnate, John fitz Geoffrey.[103] Nor is it surprising that the schedules of complaint presented to Louis IX in 1263–4 claimed that King Henry had blatantly transgressed chap-

---

continued

Cal. Pat. Rolls, 1247–58, p.265: Just 1/361, m.13; Just 1/873, m.18d (A.H. Hershey, 'An Introduction to and Edition of the Hugh Bigod Eyre Rolls, June 1258 – February 1259: PRO Just 1 1187 and Just 1/1188' (unpublished University of London Ph.D., 1991), no. B316); *Cal. Inq. Post Mortem*, i, no.467.

   [98] Walter de St John died in 1260: *Cal. Inq. Post Mortem*, i, no. 467; *Exc. Rot. Fin.*, ii, 334,336.

   [99] *Treaty Rolls, 1234–1325*, ed. P. Chaplais (London, 1955), no. 120.

   [100] Maddicott, *Simon de Montfort*, pp. 52–3,183.

   [101] Bémont, *Simon de Montfort* p. 335; KB 26/159, mm. 2d,3,3d; Maddicott, *Simon de Montfort*, p. 131.

   [102] See Maddicott, *Simon de Montfort*, pp. 52–3, 131, 183.

   [103] D.A. Carpenter, 'What Happened in 1258?', below, pp. 183–197. See also H. Ridgeway, 'The Lord Edward and the Provisions of Oxford (1258): A Study in Faction', *Thirteenth Century England*

ter 40 of the Great Charter, where he promised he would never deny or delay justice. Instead, he had intervened to prevent cases going to judgement, permitted judges to be intimidated and retained, and prevented the issue even of writs *de cursu* against favoured magnates and ministers. By contrast those same magnates and ministers, in their own litigation, had been able to obtain whatever writs they wished.[104] Holt, in a footnote to his comment that by 1227 a boundary had been crossed, that King John's system had gone, and things would never be the same again, observes that: 'This did not mean that kings and *curiales* were henceforth unable to override or suborn judicial process. It did mean, however, that when this occurred, as it did very markedly on occasion once Henry III had achieved his majority, the terms of the argument were changed. Cap. 3 of the baronial *gravamina* of January 1264 [referred to above], which uses cap. 40 of Magna Carta to pillory the king's supporters, provides a telling illustration'.[105] This is a significant but puzzling comment, for surely part of Holt's argument is that practice was radically different, not just that the terms of the argument had changed. Just how they had changed is not entirely clear. The conduct of John and his Angevin predecessors had inspired chapter 40 of the Charter which forbad the denial of justice. In 1264 Henry III was accused of breaking that chapter. The terms of the argument were exactly the same.

The judicial process, therefore, was fragmented by politics under Henry III just as it was under King John. But this is far from saying that nothing had changed. In the first place the political pressures exerted on law cases were of very different kinds. John could appear arbitrary, powerful and decisive. The minority government was cautious, weak and havering. In guiding the judicial process, its leading figure, the justiciar Hubert de Burgh, had to balance a whole series of considerations. There was his duty, as justiciar, to dispense justice, a duty all the heavier since the demands of chapter 40 of the Charter. There was his need to appease powerful magnates, reconcile competing factions and thus maintain the peace. There was his desire for private gain. These conflicting demands explain why law cases were often delayed – the adjournment of Robert de Vieuxpont's action because the days were evil was characteristic. But they also explain why, as Holt has rightly noticed, so many cases were in the end settled by compromise. These basic conditions in the minority were, to some degree, repeated during the years of Henry's personal rule. There was the same difficulty in litigating against favoured members of the regime and the same lack of confidence about securing decisive results. The difference was that the system was manipulated with far less skill, thanks to both the king's 'simplicity'

continued
I: Proceedings of the Newcastle upon Tyne Conference 1985, ed. P.R. Coss and S.D. Lloyd (Woodbridge, 1986), pp. 89–99.

[104] *Documents of the Baronial Movement,* pp. 270–5. For further discussion of justice under Henry III, see D.A. Carpenter, 'King, Magnates and Society: the Personal Rule of King Henry III 1234–1258', see below, pp. 75–106.

[105] Holt, *Magna Carta,* p. 168 note 188.

and the destabilising interventions of the Lusignans and the Savoyards: hence the rising tide of complaints about lack of justice.

Likewise it was the contrast between the regimes before and after 1215 which explains, at least in part, another change Holt has rightly stressed, namely the disappearance of the great proffers for justice. This testified both to the moral force of the Charter's chapter 40 and to the government's lack of decisive power. A great proffer for justice implied confidence in the king's ability to provide victory. John inspired such confidence. The minority government, and Henry III thereafter, most certainly did not, as Roger Bigod discovered to his cost. Morality and politics thus marched hand in hand. Not surprisingly, one of the few substantial proffers for justice under Henry III, that of Eustace de Stuteville in the Cottingham case, originated during the regime of Peter des Roches, bishop of Winchester, the period in the reign when the principles of the Charter were most openly flouted and royal government most approached the *vis et voluntas* of King John.[106]

There is, however, another contrast to be drawn between before and after 1215, and that the most important of all, namely the fettering of the king's ability to take arbitrary action against individuals, the fettering that is of actions 'by the will of the king' (*per voluntatem regis*). The perception that John and his Angevin predecessors had deprived men of property and in other ways had acted against them unlawfully and without judgement, *per voluntatem regis*, lay behind two chapters in Magna Carta. Chapter 39 asserted the general principle that no free man was to be imprisoned, disseised, outlawed, exiled or in any way destroyed and moved against 'save by lawful judgement of his peers or by the law of the land'. Chapter 52 went on to give this teeth by either restoring immediately those disseised by John 'without lawful judgement of peers' or, if there was dispute, by referring the cases to the twenty-five barons of the security clause.[107] After 1215 chapter 39 was probably the Charter's most cherished clause. The county court of Lincoln referred to it in the Edenham case when it clamoured for 'the common liberty of the kingdom conceded and sworn' and demanded that Gilbert de Gant's seisin be not overturned 'without judgement'.[108] By and large the king's government down to 1232 heeded such warnings and tried to rule within, or at least give the appearance of ruling within, the terms of chapter 39. However dubious the process, Hubert de Burgh covered his seisin of The Three Castles with a judgement of the king's court in which Archbishop Langton

---

[106] In 1233 Nicholas offered either £1000 not to be disseised of Cottingham without judgement or £333 for the king to take the manor into his hands and hold it until justice had been done to the claimants in his court. After the fall of the bishop's regime he offered £1000 for judgement of the affair in the king's court and this was accepted. See *Curia Regis Rolls*, xv, no. 1026; *Exc. Rot. Fin.*, i, 259; *Close Rolls, 1231–4*, pp. 340, 351, 383, 467, 468–9. The pipe rolls show that Nicholas did pay his fine.

[107] In chapter 52 John also promised, when he returned from or abandoned his crusade, to give full and immediate justice to those who had been disseised without lawful judgement of their peers by Henry II and Richard I.

[108] *Royal Letters of the Reign of Henry III*, i, no. 16.

himself was present.[109] In 1223–4 Hubert and Langton remained within the law when they punished potential rebels, depriving them not of their hereditary lands but of those they held merely at the king's pleasure.[110] The same applied in 1228 to Hubert's removal of Peter de Maulay from Upavon manor in Wiltshire, however much threats of imprisonment were necessary to secure his resignation.[111] Down to 1232 the king's government delayed and denied justice; but it did not, save in a few isolated cases, act *per voluntatem regis*.

All this changed in 1232 when Bishop Peter des Roches at last supplanted Hubert de Burgh. In an extraordinary period between November 1232 and February 1233 no less than seven individuals suffered disseisin *per voluntatem regis* as the rights enshrined in thirteen royal charters and one letter patent were ignored or overthrown.[112] Most blatant and most consequential was the way Henry disseised Gilbert Basset of Upavon manor in Wiltshire, and returned it to Peter de Maulay, despite having granted it to Basset in hereditary right by a royal charter.[113] More arbitrary disseisins followed, including that

---

[109] *Rot. Litt. Claus.*, i, 404, 386b.

[110] Carpenter, *Minority of Henry III*, pp. 346–8.

[111] Maulay was unable to show any royal charter granting him Upavon in hereditary right: *Rot. Litt. Claus.*, i, 11b, 595b; *Close Rolls, 1227–31*, p. 37; *Book of Fees*, p.381; *Curia Regis Rolls*, xv, no.131.

[112] Much new light will be thrown on these disseisins and the period as a whole by Dr Nicholas Vincent's forthcoming biography of Bishop Peter, which he has been kind enough to let me see in draft.

[113] The victims were as follows:

Walerand Tuetonicus: a charter for Clatford (Hants.): *Close Rolls, 1242–7*, p. 304; *Book of Fees*, p. 259; *Cal. Charter Rolls, 1226–57*, p. 130; *Close Rolls, 1227–31*, pp. 509,523; *Close Rolls, 1231–4*, pp. 170–1. Vincent's work brought this disseisin to my attention. He points out that Richard Marshal, earl of Pembroke, was responsible for it, not Bishop Peter, a somewhat ironic fact in view of later events. Walerand was given some compensation.

Richard de Argentan: three charters for Lilley and Willian (Herts): *Cal. Charter Rolls, 1226–57*, pp. 57,85,140; C 60/ 32, m. 9; *Close Rolls, 1231–4*, pp. 173,179,190,191; *Curia Regis Rolls*, xv, no.1426. And see above note 41.

Henry de Heliun: two charters, one for Easingwold (Yorks.) and one for [Great] Fawley (Berks.), *Cal. Charter Rolls, 1226–57*, pp. 122,134; C 60/32, m. 9; *Close Rolls, 1231–4*, pp. 178,489; *Curia Regis Rolls*, xv, no. 1457; *Close Rolls, 1234–7*, p. 277. Richard Marshal had a hand in this disseisin also.

Walter Mauclerc, bishop of Carlisle: four charters; for the county and castle of Carlisle; the treasurership of the exchequer; Melbourne (Derby); and Horncastle (Lincs.) *Cal. Charter Rolls, 1226–57*, pp. 165,52,175,114; *Cal. Pat. Rolls, 1232–47*, pp. 7–8; C 60/32, mm. 8,7; *Close Rolls, 1231–4*, pp. 193, 249, 401, 417, 471. The bishop came to terms and recovered Horncastle but he soon lost it again.

John le Francis: a charter for the *costera* of the wood of Warnel (Cumb.) C60/32, m 7; *Close Rolls, 1231–4*, pp. 9, 193–4, 494. This disseisin was quickly reversed although John's property was considerably damaged.

John Lestrange: a charter for Road (Som.) *Close Rolls, 1231–4*, pp. 183, 453; *Close Rolls, 1227–31*, p. 273; *Cal. Charter Rolls, 1226–57*, p. 124; *Curia Regis Rolls*, xv, no. 1427.

William of Huntercombe: a letter patent for Chalgrove (Oxon.) *Close Rolls 1231–4*, pp. 195, 35; *Patent Rolls, 1225–32*, p. 313; *Close Rolls, 1227–31*, p. 540; *Cal. Charter Rolls, 1226–57*, pp. 108,139; *Curia Regis Rolls*, xv, no. 1047.

Gilbert Basset: a charter for Upavon (Wilts.) *Cal. Charter Rolls, 1226–57*, p. 86 and see above note 111.

which began the dispute over Cottingham.[114] Conceivably the justiciar, Stephen of Seagrave, tried to blur the issue and reassure the king by pointing to the complexity of some of these cases. Many originated in imprecise or conflicting grants made by Henry and his father. Did not Gilbert Basset's loss of Upavon, despite his royal charter, merely right the earlier injustice done to Peter de Maulay? Did not William of Huntercombe's loss of Chalgrove, in defiance of his letter patent, merely uphold an earlier royal charter given to John de Plessis? Still, such conflicting claims were best settled not by arbitrary action but by litigation according to the law and custom of the land. And, in any case, Bishop Peter himself did not hide behind such justifications. He relished the return to the days of John, ridiculed the concept of judgement by peers, and justified actions *per voluntatem* on the grounds that the king possed *plenitudo potestatis*.[115]

The reaction to this revival of arbitrary rule was explosive. Richard Marshal, earl of Pembroke, patron of Gilbert Basset, rebelled; the bishops called for Bishop Peter's dismissal; and in 1234 a humbled King Henry at last complied. The events of 1232 to 1234 showed that the principles of chapter 39 of the Charter were too deeply entrenched to be blatantly set at nought. This was the true moment when a boundary was crossed. That crossing the great lay and ecclesiastical magnates were absolutely determined to mark. In the aftermath of the bishop's fall Henry was given a clear and at times humiliating lesson in kingship;[116] a lesson that he was subject to the law and could not rule *per voluntatem*. To pronounce the lesson the king was given a new teacher. On or soon after 21 May 1234 the senior justice of the bench, William Ralegh, was 'summoned to ride hard westward', to quote the one piece of graphic writing in the whole of Meekings' *oeuvre*.[117] Ralegh's destination was Gloucester, where a great council was meeting. His task was to preside over the sessions of the council and pronounce the judgements which would reverse Henry's acts of injustice.[118] Subsequently he would continue as the presiding judge of a new court *coram rege*.

Ralegh's appointment owed something to his seniority amongst the justices, but much more to his passionately held views on law and kingship. These views are almost certainly reflected in the great book on the laws and customs of England which was put together in the 1220s and 1230s in Ralegh's circle and which now masquerades under the name of his clerk, Henry de Bracton.[119]

---

[114] See the references in note 106 above. For other examples see *Close Rolls, 1231–4*, pp. 235, 470; *Curia Regis Rolls*, xv, no. 1284 (see Turner, *The King and his Courts*, p. 51); and see note 135 for the Gisland case.

[115] *Chronica Majora*, iii, 252; *Treaty Rolls, 1234–1325*, ed. P. Chaplais (London,), no. 15.

[116] Note the perceptive title of Powicke's chapter, 'Henry III's Lesson in Kingship': F.M. Powicke, *Henry III and The Lord Edward*, 2 vols. (Oxford, 1947), ch. 4.

[117] *Curia Regis Rolls*, xv, p. xxvii.

[118] For the reversals see Turner, *The King and his Courts*, pp. 248–51.

[119] The view that *Bracton* was the work of Ralegh and his circle and dates from the 1220s and 1230s has been argued, to my mind convincingly, by S.E. Thorne in his introduction to *Bracton*, iii.

One of the most striking features of *Bracton* is its constitutionalism. It stressed that the king could make law and indeed devise new writs *de cursu* only in concert with great councils.[120] It insisted, even more, that the king was subject to the law and must not rule *per voluntatem*.[121] The tyrannical regime of Bishop Peter must have shocked Ralegh profoundly. It seems highly likely that the passage in *Bracton* which explains that, in cases of treason, 'the peers ought there to be associated with the justices, lest the king in person, or through justices without peers [the justices being his deputies] be both plaintiff and judge', was a direct riposte to Bishop Peter's claim that there were no peers in England and the king could judge and condemn anyone through judges whom he had appointed.[122]

Ralegh's views on law and kingship thus chimed harmoniously with the times. The first session of the great council over which he presided took place at Gloucester on 27 May 1234. The king himself appeared and publicly confessed that he had, in effect, refused the requests of the earl of Pembroke and Gilbert Basset that they be allowed to stand to the judgement of their peers.[123] Ralegh himself pronounced the judgement which nullified the outlawries suffered by Basset, Hubert de Burgh and others.[124] The same session rehearsed the history of the Upavon case and how Henry had eventually disseised Gilbert Basset *de voluntate sua*. Three days later 'by judgement of the court', the manor was returned to Gilbert Basset 'of which', the king again acknowledged 'we disseised him *per voluntatem nostram*'.[125]

This judgement in the Upavon case occasioned one of the best known passages in the whole of *Bracton*, that which canvassed the possibility of resistance to a tyrannical king. As a whole *Bracton's* attitude to resistance was self-confessedly ambivalent; on the one hand, it acknowledged the theory that an errant king should be left to the punishment of God; on the other hand, that the baronage might restrain him.[126] The most famous of these second pas-

---

continued

However for a dissentient view see J.L. Barton, 'The Mystery of Bracton', *Journal of Legal History*, 14, (1993), 1–142. I am grateful to Paul Brand for discussing this question with me. Many references to Ralegh will be found in R.V. Turner, *The English Judiciary in the Age of Glanvill and Bracton, c. 1176–1239* (Cambridge, 1985).

[120] *Bracton*, ii, 19, 21, 305; iv, 285, 289.

[121] Ibid., ii, 33, 110, 166, 169, 305–6; iii, 43; iv, 79, 138–9, 289.

[122] *Chronica Majora*, iii, 251–2; *Bracton*, ii,337. See L. Ehrlich, 'Proceedings against the Crown 1216–1377', in *Oxford Studies in Social and Legal History*, 6, ed. Sir P. Vinogradoff (Oxford, 1921), p. 49 note 1.

[123] *Bracton's Note Book*, ii, no. 857, p. 666.

[124] Ibid., p. 667; *Chronica Majora*, vi, 73. The outlawries were reversed on largely technical grounds and indeed law was made in so doing. See Sir F. Pollock and F.W. Maitland, *The History of English Law*, 2 vols. second edn. with introduction by S.F.C. Milsom (Cambridge, 1968), ii, 581. The refusal of judgement by peers was not the reason for the reversal, nor was there any demand that it should be, but the council was clearly keen to bring this in as part of the story.

[125] *Bracton's Note Book*, ii, no. 857, p. 667; *Close Rolls, 1231–4*, p. 437.

[126] *Bracton*, iii, 43; and see iv, 158–9.

sages ran as follows: 'The king has a superior, namely God. Also the law by which he is made king. Also his curia, namely the earls and barons, because if he is without bridle, that is without law, they ought to put the bridle on him.'[127] The old view that this passage was a much later addition to the original text has been refuted by S.E. Thorne.[128] As a result, it becomes all the more apparent that it was prompted by the May 1234 judgement in the Upavon case, a judgement which William Ralegh almost certainly pronounced.[129] *Bracton's* passage comes in the middle of a section where the author explains that the king's judges cannot pass judgement on royal charters; these must be left to the interpretation and will (*voluntas*) of the king 'since it is for him who establishes to explain his deed'.[130] The author then continues with the observation that while one cannot nullify the king's acts, one can challenge him with having committed and *iniuria* and charge him to amend it lest he fall into the judgement of God. Then follows the famous passage quoted above: 'The king has a superior, namely God. Also the law by which he is made king. Also his curia, namely the earls and barons, because if he is without bridle, that is without law, they ought to put the bridle on him.' The sequence of thought here parallels closely the sequence of events in the Upavon case. In February 1233 Gilbert Basset had proffered the royal charter granting him the manor and had demanded judgement. The judges, quite rightly, had refused to pass judgement on a royal charter and had referred the matter to the king. Henry's obligation was to act justly, which meant (so the opinion was in 1234) that he should have upheld the charter which he himself had granted to Basset. Instead he had disseised him, thereby committing an *iniuria*. Thus it was that in May 1234 'all the magnates in his court, namely the archbishop of Canterbury, the bishops and earls and others' reviewed the case and corrected the injustice.[131] They put a bridle on the king. *Bracton's* discussion of how judges must refer royal charters to the king, therefore, prompted recollection of the *iniuria* Henry committed when this happened in the Upavon case, and how ultimately the *curia* of earls and barons had bridled him.[132] The passage was not merely prompted by the recollection of events, however. It was also there for a purpose: to show that while the king's

---

[127] Ibid., ii, 110.

[128] Ibid., iii, p. xlvi note 9.

[129] Other commentators have related the doctrine in the passage to the reversal of the outlawries: see, for example, H.G. Richardson, 'Azo, Drogheda and Bracton', *Eng. Hist. Rev*, 59 (1944), p. 33, cited by Turner, *The King and his Courts*, pp. 249–50. It certainly fits that episode too but was not prompted by it.

[130] *Bracton*, ii, 109–110.

[131] *Curia Regis Rolls*, xv, no. 131; *Bracton's Note Book*, ii, no. 857, p. 665; *Close Rolls, 1231–4*, p. 437.

[132] As usual, one finds that Maitland got there first: 'It is in connection with this doctrine [expressed in the review of the Upavon case that royal charters must be referred to the king] that the printed text of Bracton has the famous "constitutional" passage' (*Bracton's Note Book*, ii, p. 664 note 7).

voluntas must be awaited in matters of royal charters, that *voluntas* must be exercised in conformity with the law.

In the two years after the Upavon judgement no less than thirteen cases came into the court *coram rege* all turning on the accusation that the king had committed unjust disseisins *per voluntatem*.[133] On 25 June 1234, in the Cottingham case, the king made another public confession of guilt. 'And on this came the king, in whose presence all these things were said . . . and he freely admits that he disseised Eustace [de Stuteville] *per voluntatem suam* without summons and without judgement.' 'And since', the judgement ran, 'he recognises that he disseised Eustace without summons and without judgement *per voluntatem suam* it is considered that this should be emended first. And so Eustace shall recover his seisin . . . '[134] Little more than a week later, Henry was at it again, this time admitting that he had disseised Hubert de Burgh of the manor of Aspley Guise (Beds.) *per preceptum suum*. Hubert too recovered seisin.[135] Next year, when the bishop of Bath complained that Henry 'saving his grace' had seized Cheddar wood *per voluntatem suam injuste* in contravention of the bishop's charters, Henry admitted that he had committed an *iniuria* and pronounced 'with his own mouth' (*ore proprio*) the judgement restoring the wood to the bishop.[136] With that declaration the *vis et voluntas* of Angevin kingship were at an end.

When the great crisis came in 1258 it was totally different from those of 1215 and 1234. In 1215 the Great Charter forced John to reverse his arbitrary disseisins immediately. In 1234 Henry III's disseisins *per voluntatem regis* were overturned by the court *coram rege*. In 1258 nothing was done at all. The issue was dead.[137] The chapter of Magna Carta which Henry III was accused of breaking was chapter 40 which forbad the denial of justice, not 39 which forbad unlawful disseisins. The justiciar set up by the Provisions of Oxford in 1258 was concerned above all with the malpractices of royal and seigneurial officials in the localities; a measure of how far politics had widened out since 1215. He also redressed some of the cases of denial of justice. But he heard only one suit where a magnate alleged disseisin *per voluntatem regis*. This was the exception which proved the rule. For Henry, faced with the accusation that he had dis-

---

[133] *Curia Regis Rolls*, xv, nos. 1026, 1047, 1058, 1076, 1207, 1426, 1246, 1427, 1305, 1475; *Bracton's Note Book*, iii, nos. 1136, 1141; *Curia Regis Rolls*, xv, no. 1895; see also no. 1061. For these cases see above notes 38, 113.

[134] *Curia Regis Rolls*, xv, no. 1026.

[135] *Curia Regis Rolls*, xv, no. 1058. On 14 July Henry issued an embarrassing proclamation explaining the circumstances in which he had disseised the bishop of Carlisle of the lands (at Gisland and elsewhere) which he held from Robert de Vaux: *Cal. Charter Rolls, 1226–57*, pp.60, 76, 189; see *Close Rolls, 1231–4*, pp. 231,241,401; Holt, *The Northerners*, p. 249.

[136] *Curia Regis Rolls*, xv, no. 1305.

[137] Magna Carta and the changed atmosphere after 1215 also restricted the king's ability to impose large reliefs and extract extortionate fines from widows for the right not to marry. The change in the position of widows is splendidly brought out in S.L. Waugh, *The Lordship of England. Royal Wardships and Marriages in English Society and Politics, 1217–1327* (Princeton, 1988), pp. 158–61. However Waugh's book also shows how effectively the kings after 1215 husbanded and exploited their remaining feudal rights and resources.

seised Roger Mortimer of Lechlade manor in Gloucestershire *per voluntatem suam*, did not appear, as in 1234, and make sorrowful admissions of guilt. Instead he set out a perfectly reasonable justification, namely that he had taken the manor into his hands as an escheat 'of the Normans' after the death of Isabella Mortimer, who only held for life. The case was passed between Hugh Bigod, the council and parliament. Various inquiries were ordered. There was clearly a good deal of scepticism about Mortimer's claim and no conclusion was reached before the collapse of the reforming regime in 1261.[138] In the end, at a critical moment in 1263, Henry bought Mortimer out, money well spent given the central role he was to play in the fall of Simon de Montfort.[139]

The principles of chapter 39 of Magna Carta, the expectation of lawful conduct inculcated by the common law, the shock of a civil war which had nearly destroyed the dynasty, the nature of the minority government, and the personality of King Henry III all conspired to reduce the number of actions *per voluntatem regis*. The king was more circumscribed, the magnate safer. All this had repercussions on the course of major litigation. It was less likely to end with some sudden naked act of royal will like that of John which disseised the earl of Hereford of Trowbridge, or that of Henry III which took Upavon from Gilbert Basset. By the same token, fewer grievances were created which gave rise to litigation. But royal intervention still rendered litigation between magnates the reverse of regular and routine. While actions *per voluntatem regis*, like those between 1232 and 1234, could be portrayed in vivid colours as contraventions of the Charter, justice distorted and delayed by the king moved in greyer areas much less easy to depict. Henry III's mistake was in the end to be all too blatant about it. If the common law provided an increasingly structured framework for magnate litigation, the structure was like a maze. Without royal support you were lost. With it you could find a way through or, alternatively, divert your opponent down dead ends and into circular passages. For later medieval kings the arts of management were as important in manipulating the system of justice as they were in controlling the House of Commons. The *vis et voluntas* of Angevin kingship were dead. Justice soiled by politics and patronage had before it a long life.

---

[138] Just 1/1188, mm. 1–2; *Placitorum in Domo Capitulari Westmonasteriensi; Asservatorum Abbreviati* (Record Commission, 1811), pp. 145–6. See *Close Rolls, 1251–3*, pp. 82–3, 95–6, 220. Isabella's hereditary tenure was referred to in a royal letter in 1235 (*Close Rolls, 1234–7*, p. 102 and see *Book of Fees*, p. 50) but was challenged successfully in an action *coram rege* in 1253–4: KB 26/152, m. 1; KB 26/151, m. 30d; *Close Rolls, 1253–4*, p. 67. For the background to the case, see *Rot. de Oblatis et Finibus*, p. 209; *Pipe Roll 6 John*, p. 148; *Rot. Litt. Claus.*, i, 30b; *Magni Rotuli Scaccarii Normanniae*, ed. T. Stapleton, 2 vols. (London, 1840), ii, pp. cxxii–v. One should note, however, that a factor hindering the Mortimer claim was that Lechlade had been given to the earl of Cornwall, who indeed presided over the court *coram rege*, in the king's absence, in 1253–4.

[139] *Cal. Pat. Rolls, 1258–66*, pp.302–3.

3

The Fall of Hubert de Burgh

Few incidents in the reign of Henry III excited more interest and amazement than the fall of Hubert de Burgh. Between 1215 and 1232, Hubert held the office of chief justiciar. After 1219 he progressively dominated the government of England. 'He lacked nothing of royal power', commented the Waverley annalist, 'save the dignity of a royal diadem'[1] Then suddenly in 1232 'the great judge' was swept from court and stripped of all his lands and offices. He became a hunted fugitive. He was dragged from a chapel in which he had taken sanctuary, and incarcerated in chains in Devizes castle. Historians have been attracted by the drama of these events, but they have never provided a coherent explanation of Hubert's dismissal. The accounts of Roger of Wendover and Matthew Paris are confused.[2] Those of Sir Maurice Powicke, though illuminating, are discursive and inaccurate.[3]

The purpose of this paper is to reexamine the fall of England's last great justiciar. It is hoped to show that Powicke exaggerated the extent to which the justiciar's demise was consciously planned by the king, and that he underestimated the force of Hubert's struggle to stay in office. Powicke also failed to stress the connection between the justiciar's fall and events in the early years of the minority. Although Henry III came fully of age in 1227, the politics of the period 1217–34 must be viewed as a whole. Conflicts that burgeoned between 1217 and 1224, and were in some respects the legacy of the reign of John, cast a malign shadow over the next decade. Only when Hubert de Burgh and his arch rival, Peter des Roches, bishop of Winchester, left the political stage in 1234 did the personal rule of Henry III begin.

Hubert de Burgh belonged to a Norfolk 'gentry' family. He came to the fore as a servant of King John, and was made justiciar at Runnymede in 1215. During the civil war, Hubert defended Dover castle against Louis of France, and

[1] H.R. Luard (ed.), *Annales Monastici* (London, 1865), ii, 311. The author would like to thank Miss B.F. Harvey, Dr. J.F.A. Mason, and J.O. Prestwich for commenting upon drafts of this article.

[2] Matthew Paris, *Chronica Majora*, H.R. Luard (ed.), (London, 1876), iii, 217–21. This is the account of Roger of Wendover with additions by Matthew Paris.

[3] F.M. Powicke, *Henry III and The Lord Edward* (hereafter *Henry and Lord Edward* (Oxford, 1947), i, 68–83, *The Thirteenth Century* (Oxford, 1953), pp. 42–51. C. Ellis, *Hubert de Burgh, A Study in Constancy* (London, 1952), the only biography, gives a useful survey of Hubert's career but does not analyze in detail the reasons for his fall.

helped defeat Eustace, the monk, in the sea fight off Sandwich.[4] He was, therefore, one of those to whom Henry III owed his kingdom. He continued as justiciar under the young king, and with the death of the regent William Marshal
(1219) emerged as the chief figure in the government of the country. An explanation of Hubert's eventual eclipse and of the subsequent regime of the
bishop of Winchester must begin with the politics that culminated in the crisis
of 1223–24.[5] In 1223, Hubert de Burgh and Stephen Langton, archbishop of
Canterbury, under the sanction of papal letters, declared the king partially of
age, and they used his new authority to redistribute custody of the castles and
sheriffdoms. Many of the sheriffs and castellans thus dispossessed were old servants and allies of King John and had held office since the civil war. They included Ranulf, earl of Chester (who lost the castles and sheriffdoms of Lancashire
and Shropshire-Staffordshire), and several foreign *curiales*, of whom the most
powerful and prominent was the Norman, Falkes de Bréauté. These men had
resented de Burgh's gathering power even before the attempt to remove them
from their custodies.[6] In 1223, they resisted the changes to the point of civil
war, and strove to oust the justiciar from office. The next year, Falkes de Bréauté
stumbled into an isolated and ill-fated rebellion.[7]

The results of these events were to leave Hubert de Burgh with many enemies and to confirm the antagonism between him and Peter des Roches, bishop
of Winchester. It was des Roches who was to spearhead the attack on Hubert in
1232. A Poitevin by birth, Peter had been made bishop of Winchester by King
John, and was de Burgh's predecessor as justiciar.[8] The friction between the
two men probably originated in a contest to control the young king and his
government. The bishop was Henry's tutor and guardian, but this was a temporary trust. Once the king got beyond the age of pupilage and was removed
from the bishop's custody (probably in 1221) he adhered, so it was complained, entirely to the counsels of the justiciar.[9] In 1221, accusations of treason, allegedly engineered by Hubert de Burgh, were made against Peter des
Roches and several others. Peter was friendly with Falkes de Bréauté; it was
about this time that they planned to go on crusade together.[10] In the crisis of
1223–24, the bishop lost the castles and sheriffdom of Hampshire, offices that
he recovered in 1232. His nephew, Peter des Rivaux, was removed from the

[4] For Hubert's early career, see Ellis, *Hubert de Burgh*.
[5] For the politics of the minority, see K. Norgate, *The Minority of Henry III* (London, 1912).
[6] W. Stubbs (ed.), *The Historical Collections of Walter of Coventry* (London, 1873), ii, 251.
[7] The redistribution began in November 1223 and continued into March, 1224. The opposition effectively surrendered on December 29, 1223; Norgate, *Minority of Henry III*, pp. 203–14,
290–92. Falkes resigned the sheriffdoms and castles of Oxfordshire, Northants, Beds-Bucks, Cambr-
Hunts.
[8] Powicke, *Henry and Lord Edward*, i, 74–76; Norgate, *Minority of Henry III*, pp. 117–19.
[9] Norgate, *Minority of Henry III*, pp. 7, 119–20; 180–81; Stubbs, *Walter of Coventry*, ii 259–60.
[10] H.R. Luard (ed.), *Annales Monastici* (London, 1866), iii, 75. For the accusations see note 14.

king's wardrobe, where he was the senior clerk.[11] Naturally the bishop sided with the dissidents. At a crucial moment during the crisis, Hubert de Burgh accused him of being a traitor and the author of all the evils from which the kingdom had suffered in the reigns of John and his son. Bishop Peter responded with the prophetic oath – 'if it cost him all he had, he would cause the justiciar to be removed from power'.[12]

In any attempt to fulfill this pledge, and having done so fight off opposition, the bishop could look for support to the men embittered by dispossession in 1223–24. Some of these remained out of office and absent from court throughout the eight succeeding years. Others, though restored eventually to favour, were never completely reconciled to Hubert's regime. Falkes de Bréauté died impoverished in France in 1226; but the Earl of Chester, who welcomed Falkes's chief servant, Ralph de Bray, into his service, remained a major force.[13] Then there was the bishop's fellow Poitevin, Peter de Mauley. According to the complaint of Falkes de Bréauté to the pope, the accusations manufactured by the justiciar against de Mauley and the bishop of Winchester in 1221 and de Mauley's consequent ejection from the castellanship of Corfe, were the prelude to the changes of 1223.[14] Other potential partisans were Engelard de Cigogné (from the Touraine), who was accused with des Roches and de Mauley in 1221, and who in 1223 lost the castles of Windsor and Odiham; Brian de Lisle, who was removed as chief justice of the royal forests; and the clerk, Robert Passeleue, the agent of the 1223 opposition at Rome and the probable author of Falkes's *querimonia* to the pope. Although Brian de Lisle, Passeleue (and, of course, the earl of Chester) were English, there was some truth in the view of chroniclers that the bishop and his associates were a group of aliens.[15]

Hubert de Burgh emerged victorious in 1223–24 because he was backed by a powerful coalition of lay and ecclesiastical magnates. Eight years later he could not hope to gain such backing. In 1223–24, the counties and castles were resigned peacefully, largely because the forces gathered by de Burgh at Northampton outnumbered those of the opposition at Leicester.[16] Throughout the later stages of the crisis, the justiciar worked in alliance with Stephen Langton, archbishop of Canterbury. Langton and his suffragans excommunicated disturbers

[11] Norgate, *Minority of Henry III*, pp. 291–92; T.F. Tout, *Chapters in the Administrative History of Medieval England* (Manchester, 1937), i, 191.

[12] Luard, *Annales Monastici*, iii, 84; Norgate, *Minority of Henry III*, pp. 206–07.

[13] *Memoranda Roll 14 Henry III*, p. 32; see *Close Rolls 1227–31*, p. 142; *PRO Lists and Indexes*, ix, 1, 12, 92, 107; PRO Fine Roll 8 Henry III, C. 60/12, m.2.

[14] Stubbs, *Walter of Coventry*, ii, 259–60. De Mauley and the bishop were accused of coming to an agreement with the king of France and arranging to hand over to him Arthur's sister, Eleanor.

[15] Luard *Annales, Monastici*, iii, 68; Norgate, *Minority of Henry III*, p. 291; *Patent Rolls 1216–25*, pp. 285, 423; *Rot. Litt. Claus.*, i, 590. After 1224, Engelard was employed on military expeditions and retained his annual fee. But he held no office and attests no charters enrolled between 1227 and 1232. Brian was restored as joint chief justice of the forest in 1229; *Patent Rolls 1225–32*, p. 278. For Passeleue, Stubbs, *Walter of Coventry*, ii, 262–63; Matthew Paris, *Chronica Majora*, iii, 293. For other foreigners associated with the bishop's regime, see below p. 57.

[16] Matthew Paris, *Chronica Majora*, iii, 83.

of the realm, and many of the castles were surrendered to bishops.[17] Hubert was opposed by William de Forz, earl of Aumale, by Gilbert, earl of Gloucester, and most seriously by Ranulf, earl of Chester. But most of the earls eventually rallied behind the government.[18] In 1232, Hubert's position was much less favourable. For one thing, the issues were different. In 1223, the rights of the king were at stake; in 1232, merely the position of the justiciar – or at least so it appeared at the time. But there were also more personal reasons for de Burgh's isolation. The two bishops who were most prominent at court in 1223–24 were Richard le Poure, bishop of Salisbury, and Joscelin of Wells, bishop of Bath.[19] By 1232, Richard was largely confined to the north as bishop of Durham. Joscelin, though found at court, was no longer influential. Meanwhile de Burgh had quarrelled with Langton's successor as archbishop, Richard Grant, who died in 1231. Throughout the next year the see of Canterbury was vacant.[20] The bishops were generally considered as supporters of the justiciar,[21] but there was no possibility in 1232 of an archbishop and his colleagues intervening in politics as they had in 1223–24, or were to do again in 1234.

Hubert's relations with the great barons had also worsened. They naturally resented the power and perquisites of one who came from a comparatively humble background. In 1232, the earl of Chester was still hostile,[22] and relations were also uneasy with the king's brother, Richard, earl of Cornwall, who had been too young to take a part in the events of 1223–24. In 1227, a dispute over the possession of a manor claimed by Richard led to a military demonstration against the king and the justiciar in which Richard was backed by the earls of Chester, Gloucester, Surrey, Hereford, Derby, Warwick, and Pembroke.[23] In 1223–24, William Marshal II, earl of Pembroke, with his numerous allies had supported the government. This was partly because the earl hated Falkes de Bréauté, with whom he had several long-standing quarrels; and partly because in 1223 de Burgh backed Marshal in his conflict with Llywelyn, and placed him (with his bosom friend, the earl of Salisbury) in command of the royal army in Wales. But relations gradually had declined from this high point, and in 1231 Hubert incurred the displeasure and distrust of the new earl of Pembroke, Richard Marshal, by creating difficulties over his succession to his inheritance.[24]

---

[17] Norgate, *Minority of Henry III*, pp. 210, 290–92.

[18] Norgate, *Minority of Henry III*, pp. 204, 206; Sir James Ramsay, *The Dawn of the Constitution* (Oxford, 1908), p.34.

[19] Stubbs, *Walter of Coventry*, ii, 268; *Rot. Litt. Claus.*, i, 578. Large numbers of royal letters in this period was attested by the king *coram* the justiciar and these two bishops.

[20] Matthew Paris, *Chronica Majora*, iii, 205–206,

[21] W.W. Shirley (ed.), *Royal Letters Illustrative of the Reign of Henry III* (London, 1862), i, 379–80.

[22] Luard, *Annales Monastici*, i, 79 and iii, 127; Matthew Paris, *Chronica Majora*, iii, 212.

[23] N. Denholm-Young, *Richard of Cornwall* (Oxford, 1947), pp. 10–12.

[24] R.F. Walker, 'Hubert de Burgh and Wales', *E.H.R.*, 87 (1972), 473–76; *Rot. Litt. Claus.*, i, 571b, 577, 580; *Close Rolls 1227–31*, pp. 582, 590; *Patent Rolls 1225–32*, p. 435; Matthew Paris, *Chronica Majora*, iii, 204–206. There may have been trouble with Richard of Cornwall (married to Richard's sister) at this time; Denholm-Young, *Richard of Cornwall*, pp. 19–20.

This was particularly unfortunate because if the justiciar was to have the support of an earl in 1232 Richard Marshal was, in some respects, the most likely candidate, despite possible conflicts of interest in Wales and Ireland. In the contention between the Marshall ally, Gilbert Basset of High Wycombe, and the bishop of Winchester's friend, Peter de Mauley, over the possession of Upavon manor, de Burgh had sided with Gilbert Basset. The Bassets, moreover, were confederates and kinsmen of Richard Seward of Headington, who was a former comrade-in-arms of Hubert de Burgh. In 1233, after the split between Richard Marshal and Peter des Roches, de Burgh and Marshal were brought together through the agency of Seward in time to rescue Hubert from imprisonment and (as he believed) from murder at Devizes, but too late, of course, to keep him in office.[25]

In the years before 1232, therefore, Hugh de Burgh became increasingly dependent on his friends within the royal administration and on the favour of the king. But the administration, at least under the pressure of events in 1232, was not united behind him. There is evidence that Ralph de Neville, bishop of Chichester, the prestigious and popular chancellor, took an independent line during the crisis,[26] and Hubert was followed as justiciar not by an outsider but by Stephen of Seagrave, the senior justice at the bench. In 1229, moreover, the king was enraged by the justiciar's failure to make adequate preparations for the projected expedition to Poitou. The breach was quickly healed, but de Burgh's prestige cannot have been enhanced by the indifferent success of the expedition when it did take place the next year.[27]

When, therefore, Peter des Roches, bishop of Winchester, returned to England in July 1231, after a five-year absence on crusade, which had magnified his prestige and stimulated his ambition, he found the justiciar, to adapt Powicke's words, 'isolated in his greatness'.[28] The bishop immediately journeyed to Wales to meet the king, who was rebuilding a castle at Painscastle (near Builth) in the hope of restricting the ravages of Llywelyn. Ominously enough, des Roches brought with him de Burgh's personal enemy, Peter de Mauley, who had been entirely absent from court since 1227.[29] Henry III spent Christmas 1231 as the bishop's guest at Winchester, and thenceforth des Roches was in fairly regular attendance on the king.[30] Roger of Wendover and Matthew Paris were clear

---

[25] *Curia Regis Rolls*, xv, pp. xxiii – iv; no. 131; Powicke, *Henry and Lord Edward*, i, 128–29; Matthew Paris, *Chronica Majora*, iii, 28–29; Luard, *Annales Monastici*, i, 91 and iii, 138.

[26] See below pp. 63–69.

[27] During the expedition, the king sought the appointment of a legate without consulting Hubert; Powicke, *Henry and Lord Edward*, i, 72–73; Walker, 'Hubert de Burgh and Wales', *E.H.R.*, 87, 485.

[28] Powicke, *The Thirteenth Century*, p. 47.

[29] The bishop first attested a royal charter on August 10, at Painscastle. De Mauley attested with him. He had last attested on December 12, 1227; PRO Charter Roll 15 Henry III, C.53 / 25, m.4; and 12 Henry III, C. 53 / 20, m. 11. See *Curia Regis Rolls*, xv, no. 131.

[30] Matthew Paris, *Chronica Majora*, iii, 211. Des Roches attested charters in January, February, April, May, and June. No charters were attested in March; PRO Charter Roll 16 Henry III, C. 53 /

that it was the bishop who, in the next year, worked Hubert de Burgh's down-fall.[31] The precise stages by which he did this are, however, unclear. Powicke believed that the justiciar's fate was determined between des Roches and the king as early as the Christmas feast of 1231. Thereafter it was simply a case of laying careful plans and awaiting a favorable opportunity.[32] But it may be argued that this view fails to appreciate how far Hubert's removal up to the last moment was the product of events – there was little about it that was planned – and how near Hubert came to surviving (at least for some time longer) in office.

During the course of 1231–32, Hubert de Burgh's position was progressively weakened by his failure to deal with two interrelated problems, the threat of Lleywelyn and the king's lack of money. The 1231 Welsh campaign ended without glory. 'While the king restored Paincastle, Llywelyn in the march of Wales destroyed ten castles' noted the Dunstable annalist sardonically.[33] Negotiations with the Welsh prince dragged on throughout 1232, controlled the king's itinerary, and emphasized Hubert's failure. Peter des Roches had many opportunities to complain (as Roger of Wendover says he did) about the king's helplessness in the face of the Welsh incursions.[34] The court (including des Roches) was at Shrewsbury for negotiations at the end of May, and another meeting there was fixed for August 4. In the meantime, the king decided to make a pilgrimage to Bromholm priory on the Norfolk coast, where supposed relics of the Holy Cross were preserved.[35] The king reached Bromholm on July 1, and then returned to London before setting out again for Shrewsbury. It was during this journey to Wales that Hubert was dismissed from court (probably at Woodstock on July 29).[36] It was while the king was negotiating with Llywelyn in August that Hubert was deprived of his royal castles.[37]

Failure on the Welsh border (as Henry pointed out) was closely linked to his poverty. In March 1232, at a great council, the justiciar failed to secure a tax on movables. The financial situation became desperate and humiliating. The crown jewels were pledged to the Duke of Brittany. No payments were to be made from the treasury save for necessary household expenses.[38] On June 7, the king

continued
26, mm. 18–7. All statements in this paper about attendance at court in 1232 come from the evidence of this roll. *Cal. Charter Rolls*, i, 142–87 omits the witnesses of the charters, but it serves to indicate the dates of the enrolled charters.

[31] Matthew Paris, *Chronica Majora*, iii, 220.

[32] Powicke, *Henry and Lord Edward*, i, 75, 77, 79; *The Thirteenth Century*, pp. 45, 47–50. The basic emphasis in the second account is the same, but it is less certain as to when Hubert's fate was 'determined'

[33] Luard, *Annales Monastici*, iii, 127; see, however, Walker, 'Hubert de Burgh and Wales', *E.H.R.*, 87, 490.

[34] Matthew Paris, *Chronica Majora*, iii, 219.

[35] *Close Rolls 1231–34*, pp. 66, 70.

[36] *Patent Rolls 1225–32*, p. 492.

[37] *Close Rolls 1231–34*, p.93, *Patent Rolls 1225–32*, p. 496.

[38] Matthew Paris, *Chronica Majora*, iii, 219, 211–12; *Patent Rolls 1225–32*, pp. 466, 490–91; *Close*

complained, 'We have at present no money with us and are in the greatest need'[39] The bishop of Winchester was at court around this time and in high favour.[40] The king must have listened with a ready ear to his plausible and far-reaching plans for financial reform, which Roger of Wendover describes.[41] The execution of these plans secured the first damaging breaches in Hubert's defences, for they involved a large part of the financial administration of the country being entrusted to Peter des Roches's nephew, Peter des Rivaux. Back at Painscastle in September 1231, Hubert de Burgh's protegé, Ranulf the Breton, had been ignominiously ejected from the treasurership of the royal household. It may be that the bishop of Winchester was behind this; certainly at some date before June 11, 1232 Peter des Rivaux was appointed treasurer in Ranulf's place. On that date (only four days after the king complained that he was penniless) Peter was granted the office for life, together with the keeperships of the king's wardrobe and chamber.[42] He was thus firmly installed in the area from which he had been expelled in 1223. Later, on June 28, as the king neared Bromholm, Peter was granted for life the custodies of wards and escheats; Jews; mint and exchange; and control over the king's purchases. These concessions were followed by life grants of the king's forest and of a large number of counties (July 7, 11).[43]

Despite these dangerous encroachments, Hubert de Burgh was far from beaten. He retained influence with the king and manoeuvred with courage and determination to strengthen his position and that of his friends. Between January 18 and June 4, his chaplain, Richard de St. John was promoted to be the king's chaplain. Hubert also managed (a hitherto unnoticed fact) to retrieve the fortunes of Ranulf the Breton. In September 1231, Ranulf had been ordered to leave the country. Two months later he was back in the king's favour, and in May 1232 he was once more about the court.[44] This was why it was so necessary for Peter des Rivaux to secure his household offices for life and why the June 11 life grants were such a blow to Hubert. The next day, Ranulf the Breton's brother was removed from the sheriffdom of Kent; but the justiciar countered immediately by having his own steward, Robert of Cockfield, appointed sheriff

---

continued

Rolls 1231–34, p. 140; see S.K. Mitchell, *Taxation under John and Henry III* (New Haven, 1914), pp. 199–200.

[39] *Close Rolls 1231–34*, p. 70.

[40] *Patent Rolls 1225–32*, p. 478. Peter attested on June 11.

[41] Matthew Paris, *Chronica Majora*, iii, 219–20.

[42] *Close Rolls 1227–31*, p. 599; *Cal. Charter Rolls*, i, 156; Matthew Paris, *Historia Anglorum*, Sir F. Madden (ed.), (London, 1866), iii, 265. The date of Peter's first appointment and of the life grant were sufficiently far apart for him to be given quittance for accounting for the interval; *Cal. Charter Rolls*, i, 164. But the precise date of his first appointment is unknown, Tout, *Chapters in Administrative History*, i, 200.

[43] *Cal. Charter Rolls*, i, 163; *Patent Rolls 1225–32*, pp. 488–89. After Hubert's fall, the king called him to financial account; Matthew Paris, *Chronica Majora*, iii, 220–21; Luard, *Annales Monastici*, iii, 129.

[44] *Close Rolls 1231–34*, pp. 2, 5, 7, 25, 57; *Patent Rolls 1225–32*, p. 466.

of Norfolk-Suffolk.[45] Hubert himself held the justiciarship of England for life under a charter of 1228. He now buttressed his own power by obtaining a grant, *de novo* and for life, of the justiciarship of Ireland (June 15).[46] It is probable that Hubert was also behind the life grant of the treasurership of the exchequer to the existing treasurer, Walter Mauclerc, bishop of Carlisle. This took place on July 2, shortly after the king's departure from Bromholm, when Henry was staying at Hubert de Burgh's home at Burgh. Mauclerc himself can hardly have inspired the concession, since he had been absent from court for more than a month.[47] The grant must have been particularly unpalatable to Peter des Rivaux, since he was already casting covetous eyes at the treasurer's place.[48] Until he obtained it with Mauclerc's dismissal and disgrace in January 1233, his control over the financial administration remained partial and insecure. Later des Rivaux described Mauclerc as his enemy.[49] At the same time as the life grant of the treasury to Mauclerc on July 2, Hubert achieved an even greater triumph. For a moment it appeared he had fought his opponents to a draw and that his hold and that of his allies in office was assured. On July 2, a series of charters were authorized in favour of Hubert de Burgh; his wife; Peter des Rivaux; Ralph de Neville (the chancellor); Walter Mauclerc (the treasurer of the exchequer); and Ralph fitz Nicholas and Godfrey of Crowcombe (the two senior stewards of the royal household). These stated that the king had taken a personal oath to maintain, on pain of papal excommunication, all the charters that he had granted to these high ministers. At the same time, a record was made of the fact that the justiciar, on the king's orders, had sworn to coerce the king to keep his oath should he ever think of violating it.[50] The charters granted to these ministers were for the most part concessions of lands and rights – Hubert's wife was included because many concessions had been made to them jointly – but they also included, for all but the two stewards, grants of central government office.[51] In these, therefore, the ministers were to become the more firmly entrenched. At the cost of accepting the position of Peter des Rivaux, Hubert had, it seemed, persuaded the king to keep him and his old colleagues and to affirm that decision in the most solemn way imaginable.

Powicke's interpretation of these events was rather different from that outlined above. For him the various grants to Hubert de Burgh, and perhaps also the oaths of July 2, were part of a plan carefully laid by des Roches and the king, and designed to secure Hubert's acquiescence to the elevation of Peter

---

[45] *Patent Rolls 1225–32*, p. 480; *PRO Lists and Indexes*, ix, 67.

[46] *Cal. Charter Rolls*, i, 74, 156.

[47] *Cal. Charter Rolls*, i, p. 165. The bishop had last attested on May 10.

[48] On June 15, Peter was allowed to have a clerk at the exchequer; *Cal. Charter Rolls*, i, 157.

[49] *Curia Regis Rolls*, xv, no. 1289.

[50] *Cal. Charter Rolls*, i, 164–65.

[51] The chancellor, Ralph de Neville, had charters that granted him for life the chancellorship and the custody of the great seal; *Cal. Charter Rolls*, i, 9, 156.

des Rivaux and to lull his fears before the final blow fell.[52] Precisely why it was necessary to indulge in such an elaborate and ingenious stratagem, unpopular as the justiciar was, is not clear. Hubert would have been naive in the extreme had he regarded the advancement of des Rivaux with anything but foreboding. In fact, examination of the circumstances out of which the oaths of July 2 emerged makes it fairly certain that they were devices of the justiciar (as Powicke admitted was possible) rather than 'traps' conceived by his enemies.[53] The oaths were, it should be stressed, authorized while the king was staying at Hubert's ancestral home of Burgh in Norfolk, a few miles from Bromholm. The implication of Powicke's account is that this has little importance. After a study of Henry's itinerary, he suggested that the oaths were conceived as early as June 25 when the king was at Chippenham in Cambridgeshire. Henry then decided to go to Bromholm (instead of returning to London as previously intended) in order to swear his oath before its famous Holy Rood. Having done this (on July 1), the oath was merely written down next day at Burgh.[54] Alluring though this view may be, it is at odds with the evidence. The king had in fact decided to visit Bromholm as early as June 7, long before the oaths can have been thought of.[55] And if the oaths were sworn at Bromholm, why were they not authorized there? This would have been quite possible, since one charter was authorized while the king was at the priory.[56] Delay seems unlikely in a mater of such importance. It is more probable, therefore, that the oaths were conceived and sworn at Burgh itself and owed a good deal to the special influence Hubert derived from his position as the king's host.[57] The court had, indeed, a strong Hubertian bias at this time. The charter rolls reveal the highly significant fact that Peter des Roches was no longer in attendance. (He departed sometime between June 16 and 21.) Present on July 2 were Hubert's son, John de Burgh, his stewards, Robert of Cockfield (sheriff of Norfolk-Suffolk) and William of Blockley, and his clerk, Philip of Eye. The rest of the party, apart from Peter des Rivaux and the chancellor, was composed largely of stewards, knights, and officials of the royal household. The senior steward present, Godfrey of Crowcombe, was included in the compacts. The household officials were the first to suffer from the advancement of Peter des Rivaux, and they probably were sympathetic to Hubert's cause. (Several, including Crowcombe, were dismissed during the 'Poitevin' ascendancy.)[58] Hubert's responsibility for the compacts is also

[52] Powicke, *Henry and Lord Edward*, i, 77, 79, 81; *The Thirteenth Century*, p. 48. See also Denholm-Young, *Richard of Cornwall*, p. 23.

[53] For Powicke's various hypotheses in respect of the oaths, see 'The Oath of Bromholm', *E.H.R.*, 56, (1941), 529–39; *Henry and Lord Edward*, i, 79–81; *The Thirteenth Century*, p. 49.

[54] Powicke, 'Oath of Bromholm', *E.H.R.*, 56, 530–34.

[55] *Close Rolls 1231–34*, p. 70.

[56] *Cal. Charter Rolls*, i, 164.

[57] Powicke felt that 'the fact that Hubert was the king's host is significant', but did not explain how this could be so if the oaths were conceived as early as June 25; 'Oath of Bromholm', *E.H.R.*, 56, 530.

[58] Tout, *Chapters in Administrative History*, i, 200–201. When des Rivaux attested his first charter

indicated by the fact that he alone swore to compel the king to keep his oath. The natural procedure would have been for all those involved to have sworn in common to do this. Indeed, Powicke stated erroneously that they had in fact done so.[59] In reality the justiciar's was the solitary oath, and two of the three witnesses of its record were his private servants, William of Blockley and Philip of Eye, who never attested royal charters.[60]

On July 2, 1232, then, the justiciar's light burned bright. Yet by the end of the month it was extinguished. The last day on which Hubert attested royal charters was at Oxford and Woodstock on July 28. On the next day on which charters were enrolled (August 2), his name had vanished from the witnesses. Roger of Wendover states that on July 29 Hubert was replaced as justiciar by Stephen of Seagrave.[61] In fact, Hubert was still styled justiciar in August, and Seagrave did not receive the office until September.[62] But it may well be that July 29 represents the day on which de Burgh was dismissed from court. What then happened between July 2 and July 29?

The oaths of Burgh were, of course, desperate and risky expedients. No earls were at court when they were concocted (apart from Hubert himself), and no bishops apart from the chancellor, Ralph de Neville. Neville, moreover, may have refused to take responsibility for the charters issued to the various beneficiaries of the king's undertaking.[63] The oaths were bound to evoke surprise and scandal once they became known. On the other hand, the king probably took his pledge seriously – otherwise he would not have sought papal absolution from it. True, when he did so he claimed that it had been exacted by fear.[64] But this was a fairly standard excuse where oaths were concerned. Among the many charges that Henry later brought against his fallen justiciar, he never included coercion at Burgh. It is more likely, perhaps, that the lingering exaltation of his devotions at Bromholm, the lavish entertainment in the justiciar's ancestral home, and the tone of the court dominated by Hubert's family and friends conspired to re-

---

continued

as keeper of the wardrobe (June 14) he was placed beneath the king's stewards in the witness list. In a charter of July 7 and in all those subsequent to that date, he was placed above them, which suggests that he was now the senior household official. The stewards cannot have welcomed this. Powicke's view that Crowcombe was an ally of the Poitevins is hard to accept; his extreme measures in arresting Hubert in September were taken 'out of fear of the lord king'; *Foedera*, I, i, 207; Matthew Paris, *Chronica Majora*, iii, 227; see also Peter des Rivaux's statement about Crowcombe; *Curia Regis Rolls*, xv, no. 1289.

[59] Powicke, *Henry and Lord Edward*, i, 81. Powicke was led into this error in part by his belief that all those involved in the compacts were present at court. In fact, both Walter Mauclerc and Ralph fitz Nicholas were absent.

[60] The other witness was Henry de Capella, usually the last witness to royal charters. The record was attested by the three in the presence of Peter des Rivaux and Godfrey of Crowcombe. (Peter and Godfrey could not act as witnesses since they were beneficiaries of the oath); PRO Charter Roll 16 Henry III, C. 53 / 26, m.4.

[61] Matthew Paris, *Chronica Majora*, iii, 220.

[62] *Curia Regis Rolls*, xiv, p.x.

[63] See below pp. 63–69.

[64] Shirley, *Royal Letters*, i, 551.

kindle the king's affection, and that he fell in easily enough with Hubert's plans. This being the case, the sudden shift in the king's mood points to some new accusation against Hubert (of powerful emotional significance for the king) rather than simply to criticism of the oaths. It is quite clear what this accusation was. Between July 2 and July 29, Hubert was charged with inciting riots against Italian clerks whom the pope had provided to English benefices. These riots had spread through many parts of England in 1231 and 1232. Henry III's own account (issued in November 1232) makes their instigation by the justiciar the sole reason for his dismissal.[65] Powicke took this to be no more than the justification offered for public consumption. Hubert's alleged involvement was 'not a cause so much as an excuse' for his dismissal.[66] Yet it seems an odd excuse to choose. Few issues stirred the passions of Englishmen more powerfully than papal provisions. Hubert's hostility to the Italians would be more likely to win than to lose him popularity. Henry III's account also indicates that it was only after receipt of papal letters of complaint that he learned from 'certain men of good faith' of the justiciar's complicity.[67] These letters (which required the king to punish the transgressors but made no charges against the justiciar) were dated June 7 at Spoleto, and could have reached England in the second or third week of July.[68] That it was around this time that accusations were first made against Hubert is suggested by a further piece of evidence. Apart from de Burgh, the most prominent royal official associated with the riots was Master Robert of Shardlow, a justice of the bench and former sheriff of Sussex. Until July 21, Robert remained innocent and undisturbed as a justice in eyre in Cambridgeshire. On July 22, his name disappeared from the list of justices; on the 26th he was given a safe-conduct with Robert Tweng, the chief leader of the rioters, to come and speak with the king.[69] As far as Shardlow was concerned, therefore, the scandal broke around July 20. Probably Hubert de Burgh was implicated about the same time. Until then he maintained his position. On July 7, when des Rivaux was conceded the forest of England for life, Hubert countered impressively and obtained a life grant of the Tower of London and the castles of Windsor and Odiham, which he had previously held during pleasure. On July 16, a favour was given to 'Simon, chaplain of Hubert de Burgh'.[70]

One may speculate about the identity of the 'men of good faith' from whom the king learned of the justiciar's disgraceful behaviour. Together with his letter of complaint of June 7 to the king, the pope commissioned inquiries of his own into the outrages. In the southern provinces, these were to be undertaken

---

[65] *Foedera*, I, i, 207.

[66] Powicke, *Henry and Lord Edward*, i, 79; *The Thirteenth Century*, p. 45.

[67] *Foedera*, I, i, 207.

[68] *Foedera*, I, i, 203–4; see also Luard, *Annales Monastici*, i, 239–43. For Powicke on this letter as giving the king his opportunity, see *The Thirteenth Century*, p. 50.

[69] *Curia Regis Rolls*, xiv, p. xvi; *Patent Rolls 1225–32*, p. 493.

[70] *Patent Rolls 1225–32*, p. 489; *Cal. Charter Rolls*, i, 163; *Close Rolls 1231–34*, p. 84. Between July 21 and 28 Ranulf le Breton was once more disgraced, either a symptom or an additional cause of Hubert's downfall.

by the abbot of Bury St. Edmunds and Peter des Roches, Bishop of Winchester. The pope, wittingly or unwittingly, had placed a devastating weapon in the hands of Hubert's greatest enemy. Roger of Wendover states it was precisely these inquiries, together with that of the king, that revealed the justiciar's guilt.[71] Des Roches and the abbot were still at work at the end of August, so their final report (which was sent to the pope) had no direct bearing on Hubert's fall.[72] But perhaps it was the 'evidence' so far collected that the bishop presented to the king, with all the authority of a papal commissioner, toward the end of July. (The bishop was in attendance at court from July 15 onwards.) According to rumours that reached both Roger of Wendover and the Dunstable annalist, Hubert protected those seizing the property of the alien clerks with his own and with royal letters patent.[73] Whether or not the 'men of good faith' had genuine evidence of this, they could certainly provide the justiciar with a convincing motive. The complaints of the late Archbishop of Canterbury, Richard Grant, in Rome in 1231, together with a general miscellany of scandalous rumour, had induced the pope (late in 1231 or early 1232) to set up an inquiry into Hubert's marriage on the ground that Margaret, his third wife, was related to his second. The justiciar was understandably furious. His marriage to Margaret, daughter of William the Lion, King of Scotland, was the chief prize of his career. The earldom of Kent was entailed on their joint issue. Hubert's anger was widely known and provoked a papal letter of rebuke (June 9, 1232). It was easy for the 'men of good faith' to suggest that he had encouraged the attack on the Italians to revenge himself on the pope. With his special devotion to the papacy, few allegations could have made more impact on the king. Henry revived the charge (along with others against Hubert) as late as 1239.[74] In 1232, the accusation was fatal to the justiciar. Next year the proceeds of several of Hubert's manors were assigned to provide the compensation the pope had demanded for the clerks.[75]

The attack on Hubert de Burgh in the summer of 1232 was led by Peter des Roches and Peter des Rivaux, but they were not responsible alone for the justiciar's removal. Several royal charters of July 28 (the last charters attested by Hubert) reveal who was at court at this time. Significantly, the bishop of Winchester had now been joined by two leading opponents of the 1223 changes,

---

[71] Matthew Paris, *Chronica Majora*, iii, 217–18; Luard, *Annales Monastici*, iii, 130. That the inquiries were commissioned at the same time as the letters to the king (which do not themselves order an investigation) is implied by Roger of Wendover. The instructions do not survive, however.

[72] *Patent Rolls 1225–32*, p. 498. Hubert claimed in 1239 that since the pope took no action on the report it must have cleared him; Matthew Paris, *Chronica Majora*, vi, 72.

[73] Matthew Paris, *Chronica Majora*, iii, 217–18; Luard, *Annales Monastici*, iii, 129.

[74] Matthew Paris, *Chronica Majora*, iii, 205 and vi, 72; Luard, *Annales Monastici*, iii, 128–29; Shirley, *Royal Letters*, i, 549; see the last paragraph of the pope's letter to the king; *Foedera*, I, i, 204. For Hubert's marriages, *Complete Peerage*, vii, 141–42; S.H.F. Johnston, 'The Lands of Hubert de Burgh', *E.H.R.*, 50 (1935), 429. Powicke does not mention the bishop of Winchester's inquiry or the question of Hubert's marriage.

[75] *Close Rolls 1231–34*, p. 188; *Foedera*, I, i, 203–4.

Ranulf, earl of Chester, 'unus de maximis hostibus [*justiciarii*]', and Brian de Lisle, who had been in attendance since July 15, and was soon to recover the custody of Knaresborough, which he had lost 1223.[76] But these were not the only interests represented. Stephen of Seagrave, the senior justice of the bench, had hurried to court from his unfinished eyre in Cambridgeshire.[77] More important, the king had also been joined, perhaps during the course of July 28th itself, by Richard, earl of Cornwall, and Richard Marshal, earl of Pembroke.[78] Both, as has been seen, had grievances against the justiciar. De Burgh's ultimate ejection was, therefore, instigated or at least agreed upon by a wider group than the bishop of Winchester and his immediate partisans. Further, though great magnates played little part in the war of attrition against Hubert during the course of the summer, since few were at court, three earls were present on the justiciar's last day.

In the months after July 1232, while Hubert was hounded and imprisoned, the bishop of Winchester and his supporters gradually extended their grip over court and government. Many of the established *curiales* suffered. The household officials Richard fitz Hugh and Henry de Capella disappeared from court shortly after Christmas 1232.[79] In January, an outraged Mauclerc was pushed from the treasury and forced to give a thousand pounds for various complaints against him to be dropped.[80] The steward, Godfrey of Crowcombe, after a struggle that extended from at least October 1232 was finally ousted in May 1233.[81] Hubert's old chaplain, Richard de St. John, and the former steward Richard de Argentan were both disgraced.[82] Meanwhile, some of the men of 1223 returned. Peter de Mauley was established at court in November 1232, and Engelard de Cigogné (as the bishop braced to meet the challenge of Richard Marshal) in April 1233. Two more foreigners began careers at court, which were to last into the 1258–65 period – Matthias Bezille, a connection of Engelard's, and John de Plessy, later earl of Warwick *iure uxoris*.[83] Des Rivaux himself became treasurer of the exchequer. His deputy was none other than Robert Passeleue, the envoy of the 1223 opposition to Rome, and probable author of Falkes's *querimonia*, who had been

[76] Matthew Paris, *Chronica Majora*, iii, 229; Norgate, *Minority of Henry III*, p. 291; *Patent Rolls 1225–32*, p. 504. Brian had been joint chief justice of the forest since 1229. After the forest was given to des Rivaux (July 1232) Brian became his chief coadjutor; *Close Rolls 1231–34*, p. 576.

[77] *Curia Regis Rolls*, xiv, p. xvi.

[78] The two earls attested at Woodstock but not at Oxford.

[79] They attested no charters after December 28, 1232. Both returned to court and favour after the collapse of the bishop's regime; *Close Rolls 1231–34*, p. 505; *Curia Regis Rolls*, xv, no. 1178. Evidence for changes at court between October 1232 and October 1233 may be obtained from PRO Charter Roll 17 Henry III, C. 53 / 27.

[80] *Cal. Pat. Rolls 1232–47*, pp. 7–8; PRO Fine Rolls 17 Henry III, C. 60 / 32, m.7; Matthew Paris, *Chronica Majora*, iii, 240, 248.

[81] See below, p. 164.

[82] *Close Rolls 1231–34*, pp. 202, 250, 327, 173; *Rot. Litt. Claus.*, ii, 139b; *Curia Regis Rolls*, xv, no. 1426. Both were rehabilitated after the bishop's fall. Crowcombe and Walter Mauclerc also returned to court at this time.

[83] John first attested in April 1233, Matthias in June.

totally out of government employ since his return to England in 1227.[84] Falkes de Bréauté's chief agent, Ralph de Bray, also was restored to the king's service, and was sent to Devizes to guard Hubert de Burgh.[85] Roger of Wendover's report that all the native *curiales* had been replaced by foreigners from Poitou was inaccurate, but probably reflects well enough the general reaction to the bishop of Winchester's regime by 1233.[86] Des Roches, moreover, proclaimed contempt for English custom and a dangerously exalted view of royal power – hence perhaps the spate of disseisins *per voluntatem regis* from which Hubert de Burgh and the Marshal ally, Gilbert Basset, suffered.[87] The disseisin of Basset (in favor of Peter de Mauley) in February 1233 provoked Richard Marshal's rebellion, and enabled him to stand as the upholder of the rights and customs of the realm.[88] Next year, the new Archbishop of Canterbury, Edmund Rich, and his fellow bishops intervened to force the removal of des Roches and effect a reconciliation between the king and his opponents.

But back in the summer and autumn of 1232 none of this could be foreseen. The removal of Hubert de Burgh (if not his subsequent treatment) raised no great issues and commanded general approval. Though Peter des Rivaux held many offices, Mauclerc retained the treasury, and no one could object to the choice of Stephen of Seagrave to replace de Burgh. Indeed, Seagrave's appointment, according to one annalist, had the sanction of a great council.[89] Richard Marshal, moreover, played a key role at court. Between August 1232 and the breach in February 1233 he attested more royal charters than anyone save the steward Ralph fitz Nicholas.[90] In September 1232, a great council voted the tax on movables that had been refused in March, the only time such a grant was made without a *quid pro quo* in the whole of Henry's reign.

Instead of the somewhat underhanded plotter of Powicke's picture, Henry III appears in 1232 as a man buffeted by rival influences and unable to exercise consistent control over events. In the flush of enthusiasm at Burgh on July 2, he entered into obligations quite inconsistent with the royal dignity. Yet it is important to put this instability into perspective. What emerges most forcibly from the events of 1232 is the king's reluctance to sacrifice his old minister. Probably on many occasions after 1227, Henry III could have dismissed de Burgh with more congratulation than complaint. Yet even in 1232, when many legitimate criticisms could be made of his administration and powerful voices clamoured for his removal, the king could not make a final decision. Early in July, he definitely

---

[84] *Cal. Pat. Rolls 1232–47*, pp. 7–8; Matthew Paris, *Chronica Majora*, iii, 240; *Patent Rolls 1225–32*, p. 137.

[85] *Close Rolls 1231–34*, pp. 332, 341–42; *PRO Lists and Indexes*, ix, 144.

[86] Matthew Paris, *Chronica Majora*, iii, 240. Des Roches, des Rivaux, and de Mauley were Poitevins. De Cigogné was from Touraine.

[87] Shirley, *Royal Letters*, i, 467–69; Powicke, *Henry and Lord Edward*, i, 75–76; *Curia Regis Rolls*, xv, p. 28 n.2; nos. 1426–27, 1475, 1895.

[88] Powicke, *Henry and Lord Edward*, i, 128, 132–33.

[89] Luard, *Annales Monastici*, ii, 311.

[90] *Curia Regis Rolls*, xv, p. xxiii n.2.

wanted to keep his justiciar, and Hubert might well have survived longer had it not been for the Italian riots. Doubtless the king recalled Hubert's faithful service during the war and minority, but there was more to the relationship between the two men than that. Created justiciar at Runnymede, and hence probably among the more moderate and acceptable of John's *curiales*, Hubert de Burgh's reassertion of royal rights after the war was tempered by caution, and limited by public acceptance of Magna Carta.[91] Captured at Chinon in 1205, and thus with personal experience of the disintegration of the Angevin empire, Hubert doubted whether it was possible to recover the lost lands in France. In Wales, with his experience of siege warfare (at Chinon and Dover), he concentrated on castle building. His policy was more a reaction to the aggrandizements of Llywelyn than a product of ambitious plans of his own.[92] Occasionally (as in 1229), Henry III was infuriated by the justiciar's inactivity. But the king, in Powicke's revealing words, 'lived spaciously from day to day, with little heed to the future'.[93] His own campaigns in Wales and France in the 1240s were hardly more vigorous than Hubert's. For much of the time Henry found the unambitious approach of the aging justiciar acceptable enough.

The chief actors in the conflict of 1232 were old servants of King John. In terms of personnel, it was only with Henry's marriage in 1236 that a new chapter opened. Hubert de Burgh and Peter des Roches were both justiciars of John. Peter de Mauley and Engelard de Cigogné (like Peter des Roches and Falkes de Bréauté) were among the hated foreigners whom John imported into England. Clause fifty of Magna Carta had stipulated that Engelard should be removed completely from office. (The St. Albans version of the charter optimistically added Falkes' name.) Brian de Lisle was another of John's protegés. The fathers of Richard Marshal and Gilbert Basset were among John's leading familiars. The alliance between the two families can be traced to the early years of the minority, and probably owed a good deal to common hostility to Falkes de Bréauté.[94] A large part of the political conflict between 1217 and 1234 was about power and its proceeds. Those ejected in 1223–24 burned with the desire to recover office and favour. Control over government was particularly desirable because of the number of conflicting claims to land, a problem not unique to this period of English history. Richard of Cornwall's demonstration in 1227 was the product of a dispute with the *curialis* Waleran the German over the possession of a manor. In 1233 the break between the king and Richard Marshal came when Henry preferred Peter de Mauley's claim to Upavon manor to Gilbert Basset's. Both these disputes originated in grants made by King John.[95]

[91] Norgate *Minority of Henry III*, pp. 201–02; Denholm-Young, *Richard of Cornwall*, pp. 12–13; see now D.A. Carpenter, *The Minority of Henry III* (London, 1990).

[92] This is the argument of Walker, 'Hubert de Burgh and Wales', *E.H.R.*, 87, 465–94.

[93] Powicke, *Henry and Lord Edward*, i. 302.

[94] D.A. Carpenter, 'Sheriffs of Oxfordshire and their Subordinates 1194–1236' (PhD thesis, Oxford University, 1973), pp. 118, 175–76.

[95] Denholm-Young, *Richard of Cornwall*, pp. 10–12; *Curia Regis Rolls*, xv, pp. xxiii – xxiv; no. 131, see also no. 1426.

This is not to say that the politics of these years lacked wider implications. The civil war of John's reign (like that of Stephen's) had left local office in the hands of great magnates and over-mighty *curiales*.[96] The changes of 1223–24 were needed to break the hold of these men (the last time it had to be done in English history), and clear the way for the renewed exaction of revenue above the farm – revenue that was largely incompatible with the tenure of sheriffdoms by great men. Hubert de Burgh and Stephen Langton, in effecting the redistribution, thus performed a valuable service to the crown. At the same time, Hubert cut the power of those who challenged his control of the king.

Peter des Roches probably grasped that the issue in 1223 was less changes in themselves than who should control them, himself or the justiciar.[97] But had the bishops been the controlling hand, the benefit to the crown would have been far less because the earl of Chester, Falkes de Bréauté, and others would probably have retained or recovered their offices. Falkes 'quasi rex in Anglia' would still have ruled in the midlands where he was sheriff of six counties.[98] The bishop's own achievements between 1232 and 1234 were small. It is questionable whether his view of royal power had much permanent influence on the king. The concentration of offices under Peter des Rivaux seems testimony to a radical approach to administration that was uncharacteristic of Hubert de Burgh. But little was actually achieved. Whatever the justification, the concentration of offices seems as much a stage in the attack on the justiciar as a means to financial reform. One obstacle to reform was that des Roches, des Rivaux, Engelard de Cigogné, and Brian de Lisle all returned to sheriffdoms on terms favourable to themselves.[99]

The politics of much of Henry III's reign before his marriage in 1236 were, therefore, dominated by struggles for power between the victors of the civil war, the former servants and supporters of King John. In that fact lies the real significance of the period, for it indicates how successfully the civil war had been brought to an end. There was no rump of recalcitrant rebels. This was partly because of the prudent terms of the treaty of Kingston, which closed the civil war, and partly because Magna Carta (in a revised version) was reissued in 1216, 1217, and (with the young king's consent) in 1225. Although, moreover, there was trouble over the forests in 1227, the predatory aspects of Henry III's administration in no way compared to those of John. Having healed the wounds of the war, and reestablished the position of the king, the government of England between 1217 and 1232 could claim a fair measure of success.

---

[96] Powicke, *Henry and Lord Edward*, i, 49.

[97] Norgate, *Minority of Henry III*, p. 200.

[98] For Falkes' sheriffdoms, see note 7. Hubert de Burgh quickly recovered the castles that he surrendered during the 1223–24 changes. He gave up the sheriffdoms of Kent and Norfolk-Suffolk in 1227; *PRO Lists and Indexes*, ix, 67, 86; Norgate, *Minority of Henry III*, p. 213.

[99] See below, pp. 163–5. Nicholas Vincent's new biography of Peter des Roches (Cambridge, 1996) provides the first scholarly account of Peter's extraordinary regime and the uprising which it provoked. Vincent shows that Peter came from the Touraine not Poitou.

4

Chancellor Ralph de Neville and Plans of Political Reform, 1215–58

Between 1215 and 1244 a transformation took place in plans of political reform.[1] In 1215 Magna Carta limited the operations of royal government without seeking to control the king's choice of ministers. The lay and ecclesiastical magnates at the parliament of November 1244, by contrast, demanded that *they* should select the king's justiciar and chancellor.[2] At the same time a more extensive plan of reform was drawn up, though perhaps not presented to the king. This, the so-called Paper Constitution, foreshadowed the Provisions of Oxford of 1258 by laying down a scheme for conciliar control of the king. Four men, chosen 'by common assent', were to be placed on the king's council and given powers to control certain appointments and supervise aspects of the running of government. Both the justiciar and chancellor were likewise to be chosen 'by all', and could be counted as two of these four elected councillors.[3]

Because there had been no justiciar since 1234, and no chancellor in day-to-day charge of the seal since 1238, what was being demanded in 1244 was, in effect, the restoration of these offices. Under the Angevins, their holders had been appointed by the king and had often become thoroughly unpopular in his service. By 1244, however, the reformers clearly felt that, provided the justiciar and chancellor were chosen 'by all', they could provide a check on the king and a form of open and equitable government. The purpose of this paper is to suggest that, in the formation of such a view, the career of Chancellor Ralph de Neville was of key importance.

[1] An early draft of this paper was read by two scholars who died in 1987, C.R. Cheney and E.L.G. Stones. I am also grateful for the comments of Pierre Chaplais and Mrs. Jeanne Stones, and for permission to consult the latter's thesis, written under her maiden name: J.M.B. Fradin, 'Ralph Neville, Bishop of Chichester and Chancellor to Henry III' (Oxford Univ. B. Litt. thesis, 1942). The Stones also allowed me to use their unpublished edition (complete with translations) of Neville's private correspondence. For this correspondence and a valuable discussion of Neville's career, see J. and L. Stones, 'Bishop Ralph Neville, Chancellor to King Henry III and his Correspondence: A Reappraisal', *Archives*, xvi (1984), 227–57.

[2] Matthew Paris, *Chronica Majora* (henceforth *CM*), ed. H.R. Luard (RS, 1872–83), iv. 362–3.

[3] Paris, *CM* iv. 366–8. For the date of the Paper Constitution, see C.R. Cheney, 'The 'Paper Constitution' Preserved by Matthew Paris', *EHR* lxv (1950), 213–21, which disposes of the argument that it belongs to 1238, for which see N. Denholm-Young, 'The 'Paper Constitution' Attributed to 1244', *EHR* lviii (1943), 401–23. However, in 1237 the proposals of 1244 were anticipated to the extent that three magnates were added to the king's council: Paris, *CM* iii. 383; see R.C. Stacey, *Politics, Policy and Finance under Henry III 1216–1245* (Oxford, 1987), 114–15.

In 1244, when the reformers looked back over past justiciars, they can have thought of only one man; that was Hubert de Burgh, who had been appointed justiciar in 1215 and had actually exercised the office from 1219 until his dismissal in 1232. Hubert, in the course of his career, had made many enemies, but his justiciarship was also remembered with approval, as we shall see. In 1244, however, the Paper Constitution was concerned more with the chancellor than the justiciar. In respect of the justiciar there were merely the regulations, cited above, regarding the method of his appointment. In respect of the chancellor there was also the stipulation that if, for any reason, the king took the seal from him, it should be returned and whatever was sealed in the interval be considered null and void. The further stipulation that 'writs sought against the king and the custom of the kingdom are to be wholly revoked' also dealt with the area of the chancellor's responsibilities. When the reformers looked back over past chancellors, they can likewise have thought of only one man, that was Ralph de Neville, bishop of Chichester. Neville had become keeper of the seal and effective master of the chancery in 1218, and chancellor itself in 1226. He remained in personal control of the seal until 1238; thereafter he retained the title of chancellor and received the emoluments of the office until his death in February 1244.[4]

Neville's career, as keeper of the seal and chancellor, thus spanned the years between Magna Carta and the Paper Constitution. It had several features which made it influential apart from its timescale. Matthew Paris repeatedly asserts that Neville 'received the seal by the common counsel of the kingdom'.[5] Probably, as Powicke surmised, this committal took place at the great council of November 1218, which inaugurated Henry III's first seal and, since the king was a minor, laid down regulations for its use.[6] Neville, therefore, had been appointed in precisely the manner demanded in 1244. He had also, on several occasions, acted in the responsible and independent fashion expected of one thus appointed. Of this the framers of the Paper Constitution were apparently aware, their proposals being influenced by specific incidents in Neville's career.

In 1236, according to Matthew Paris, Neville refused to surrender the seal to the king on the grounds that 'he had received it by common counsel of the kingdom, and therefore could not resign it to anyone without the common assent of the kingdom'.[7] This protestation paralleled almost exactly the statement in the Paper Constitution, in respect of the four elected councillors, that

[4] J. and L. Stones, 'Bishop Ralph Neville', 228–40. Until his death in 1226 the titular chancellor was Richard Marsh, bishop of Durham.

[5] Paris, *CM* iii, 74, 364, 491, 495; *Matthaei Parisiensis Historia Anglorum*, ed. F. Madden (RS. 1866–9), ii. 267, 337, 390.

[6] *PR 1216–25*, 177; F.M. Powicke, 'The Chancery during the Minority of Henry III', *E.H.R.* xxiii (1908), 227–9.

[7] Paris, *CM* iii. 364. Given that Matthew Paris is correct about both the dismissal of Ralph fitzNicholas in 1236, and the changes in the sheriffdoms, I am inclined to accept his testimony here about Neville; but for a different view, see Stacey, 100.

'as they are chosen by the consent of all, so none of them can be removed without common assent'. Similarly the Constitution insisted that both the justiciar and chancellor could only be replaced 'with the assent of all in solemn assembly'.

Another clause of the Paper Constitution laid down, as we have seen, that if the king, for any reason, took the seal from the chancellor, it should be returned to him, and whatever was sealed in the interval should be considered null and void. This may reflect the events of 1238 when the king, angered by Neville's refusal to withdraw his candidature for the bishopric of Winchester, at last took the seal from him, while allowing him, as we have said, to remain as titular chancellor and to receive the emoluments of the office.[8] The reformers may also have known of earlier incidents when the king, for a short time, had deprived Neville of the seal in order to authenticate charters of which the latter disapproved, charters which certainly deserved to be nullified, as the Paper Constitution required. In 1234, according to a story which Matthew Paris added to the account of Roger of Wendover, the notorious charter which promised to distribute Richard Marshal's lands in Ireland to his enemies (and thus conspired to bring about his death) was made 'after the seal had been taken from ... the bishop of Chichester, the chancellor, who did not consent to this fraud'.[9] This episode appears to show Neville performing a role which the 1244 reformers clearly expected of the chancellor – namely, that of preventing the issue of irregular royal letters and charters—the Paper Constitution stipulating that 'writs sought against the king and the custom of the kingdom' (or, if we accept Denholm-Young's emendation, 'the law and the custom of the kingdom') were to be 'completely revoked'.[10]

Most of the information we have used so far about Neville's career has come from Matthew Paris; perhaps Neville was himself the informant although Paris nowhere says so. It is fortunate that there is another incident, this time from 1232, where the evidence of the chancery rolls themselves suggests that Neville opposed the issue of a series of charters which he considered to be improper.

In the months before the fall of Hubert de Burgh at the end of July 1232, Hubert himself and his rival Peter des Rivaux, together with other ministers, extracted charters from the king which confirmed them for life in various offices and custodies.[11] These grants reached a climax during the king's tour of

---

[8] Paris, *CM* iii. 491, 525; *Ann. Mon.* i. 110; *CPR 1232–47*, 231–2.

[9] Paris, *CM* iii. 266. By a slip of the pen Paris wrote 'Hugh' rather than 'Ralph', bishop of Chichester. He was probably thinking of Hugh of Pattishall, who became treasurer in 1234: Paris, *CM* iii. 296. The charter rolls for 1233–4 do not survive so Paris's story cannot be checked.

[10] Denholm-Young, 'The 'Paper Constitution'', 422, the suggestion being that 'regem' should read 'legem'. The suggestion gains credence from the fact that the parliament of Nov. 1244 complained, according to Matthew Paris, about the issue of writs 'against justice': Paris, *CM* iii. 363. In 1240, however, again according to Paris, complaint was made about the king's desire to grant a charter 'against the crown of the king': Paris, *CM* iii. 629; v. 91.

[11] For much of what follows, see above, pp. 49–55.

East Anglia in late June and early July, and were supported on 2 July by an oath taken at Burgh, the ancestral home of the justiciar, in which the king swore, on pain of papal excommunication, to observe all the charters which he had granted to Hubert, des Rivaux and other chief ministers. At the same time Hubert, on the king's orders, swore to obstruct the king if he ever sought to violate these charters.

Neville had every reason to feel disquiet about the charters (tabulated on p. 67) issued in late June and early July, and the oaths which accompanied them. The charters of 28 June which conceded to des Rivaux, a foreigner and a clerk, life-custody of the coasts and ports and of all wards and escheats, even though he was to answer for their issues at the exchequer, touched vitally on both the kingdom's security and its system of patronage.[12] These charters were followed by life-grants of the treasurership of the exchequer to Walter Mauclerc, bishop of Carlisle, and of the Tower of London and the castles of Windsor and Odiham to Hubert de Burgh (2 and 7 July). There was, of course, nothing new about life-grants of office,[13] but those conceded by Henry on his East Anglian tour were made when he was surrounded largely by household officials.[14] On 2 July itself no earl was present save Hubert de Burgh, and no bishop save Ralph de Neville. In these circumstances the grants and oaths could easily be seen as irresponsible acts, totally inconsistent with the king's obligation to uphold the rights of the Crown. This was the view taken by the pope in 1233, when he allowed Henry to nullify the various gifts of 'liberties, possessions, offices and other things', and absolved him from his oath (apparently the oath of Burgh) not to quash them. This was on the grounds that they were contrary to Henry's coronation oath to preserve the rights and honours of the kingdom of England, and had been conceded 'against the foresaid kingdom and to the great prejudice and harm of the royal Crown'.[15] These words foreshadow the de-

[12] The port of Dover was excluded from the grant to des Rivaux as being held by Hubert de Burgh. Des Rivaux gained it after Hubert's fall. For the indignation of the magnates when they thought that des Rivaux had been granted Dover castle, see *Ann. Mon.* i. 86.

[13] Neville himself had been granted the office of chancellor for life in 1227; this charter was confirmed on 14 June 1232 and was buttressed by another specifically granting him custody of the seal for life: *CChR 1226–57*, 9, 156. King John had granted the chancery to Walter de Grey for life: *Foedera*, I. i. 93.

[14] The bishop of Norwich attested the charters on 28 June; the earl of Hereford attested the charter of 7 July. All statements about the composition of the court in this article are based on the witness lists to the royal charters enrolled on the charter rolls of 16 Henry III (C 53/26). (All subsequent manuscript references are to documents in the PRO.) The printed calendar omits the witnesses but serves to indicate the days on which charters were enrolled: *CChR 1226–57*, 142–69

[15] *Royal Letters*, i, 551. For the coronation oath and the rights of the king, see H. G. Richardson, 'The Coronation in Medieval England', *Traditio* xvi (1960), 151–61. Earlier, in June 1232, Neville had given the charters which granted the justiciarship of Ireland for life to Hubert de Burgh, and the custody of the king's wardrobe, chamber and small seal to Peter des Rivaux: *CChR 1226–57*, 156–7. There was less reason for anxiety here partly because people of more consequence were at court, notably the bishop of Winchester and the earl of Cornwall, and partly because the household offices granted to des Rivaux were peculiarly the king's personal concern.

mand in the Paper Constitution that letters sought 'against the king' (if that is the correct rendering) should be revoked. They likewise parallel the objection in 1240 of a later keeper of the seal, Master Simon the Norman, that a charter which sought to grant a tax on wool to Thomas of Savoy was 'against the Crown of the king'.[16]

That Neville did make some form of protest over these charters is suggested by their dating clauses. From the beginning of the reign of Richard I an elaborate dating formula, modelled on that employed by the papal chancery, was adopted as the concluding clause for English royal charters. The formula stated that the charter had been 'given by the hand', (*dat[a] per manum*) of the chancellor or some other official, at a specified place and date.[17] Between 1227, when Henry III began to grant charters, and 1238, when Neville was deprived of the great seal, Neville, as chancellor, almost invariably gave the charters himself. From 1238, however, the king became the normal giver, charters being 'given by our hand' (*dat[a] per manum nostram*).[18] During Neville's period in charge of the seal, the only occasions when this formula occurred, apart from those mentioned below, were when charters were issued in favour of Neville himself, or were connected in some way with the see of Chichester.[19]

It is, therefore, a remarkable fact that the charters (tabulated on p. 67) which were conceded between 28 June and 7 July to Peter des Rivaux, Walter Mauclerc and Hubert de Burgh, together with the charter embodying the king's oath at Burgh, were all given by the king. They thus form an absolutely unique series in the charter rolls of Neville's time. In each case, apparently, the authorization for the drawing up of the document came not from the chancellor but from the king.[20] This was not, initially at least, because Neville was absent from court for (as the table below shows) the charters given by the king were interlaced down to 3 July with charters (significantly ones of an innocuous nature)

---

[16] Paris, *CM* iii, 629; v. 91; for discussion of this episode, see Powicke, *Henry III*, ii. 780–2.

[17] For this formula, see R.L. Poole, *Lectures on the History of the Papal Chancery* (Cambridge, 1915), 38–9, 48, 55–6, 138–42; *The Memoranda Roll for the Michaelmas Term 1 John*, ed. H.G. Richardson (Pipe Roll Soc., new ser., xxi, 1943), lx-lxi; V.H. Galbraith, *Studies in the Public Records* (London, 1948), 127–30; C.R. Cheney, *English Bishops' Chanceries* (Manchester, 1950), 81–90; P. Chaplais, *English Royal Documents* (Oxford, 1971), 14–15; J.B. Edwards, 'The English Royal Chamber and Chancery in the Reign of King John' (Cambridge Univ. Ph.D. thesis, 1974), 118–32; see also above p. 5 and below p. 302.

[18] L.B. Dibben, 'Chancellor and Keeper of the Seal under Henry III', *EHR* xxviii (1911), 41–2, 50–1; Chaplais, 14–15. In 1230, when Neville stayed behind as regent during the king's expedition to Brittany, his brother, Nicholas de Neville, took over the 'giving' as the chancellor's deputy. In a fair number of enrolled charters between 1227 and 1238 the name of the giver is omitted, the formula being *dat' etc.*, followed by the place and date. Whenever it has been possible to check these enrolments against the original charters, or copies of them, the giver has proved to be Neville.

[19] I have only found one certain exception to this statement, the grant to the burgesses of Gloucester on 6 Apr. 1227: *CChR 1226–57*, 30.

[20] The evidence for this interpretation of the giving clause cannot be deployed here; but see Edwards, 'Chamber and Chancery under John', 124–5.

given by Neville. Nor was it simply the importance of the charters which caused the king to replace Neville as the giver, for, with the exception perhaps of that containing the king's oath, they were no more important than some given in the past by Neville – for example, the one which granted Hubert de Burgh the justiciarship for life in 1228. The difference was that the charter of 1228 commanded some sort of general consent.[21]

There are, therefore, strong indications that the reason why the king acted as the giver of various charters during his tour of East Anglia was that Neville himself refused to take responsibility for them.[22] When Master Simon the Norman made a similar stand in 1240 he was immediately dismissed.[23] In Neville's case, the immediate reaction to his *démarche* was an attempt to conciliate him. On 28 June, when the king gave charters in favour of Peter des Rivaux, he also gave a charter to Neville as bishop of Chichester.[24] However, it is possible that Neville subsequently withdrew from court and lost control of the seal. We can approach the evidence here by considering the extent to which Neville was involved in the oaths sworn by the king and justiciar at Burgh on 2 July.

In the printed *Calendar of the Charter Rolls* Neville's name does not appear in the list of those who received charters embodying the king's oath.[25] If, however, we consult the actual roll in the Public Record Office it is clear that two names have been erased from the list . In one case there is no clue to the name removed. But the other name, which stood at the head of the list, was almost certainly that of Neville – the shape and length of the erasure fits exactly with the frequent abbreviation 'R. Cycestr Ēpc', the places where the tails of the 'y' and 'p' have been removed being plainly discernible. What was going on? That Neville was *intended* to be a beneficiary of the settlement there can be no doubt, for his name also appears, in the record of Hubert's oath, as one of those whose charters Hubert swore to ensure the king would uphold. But this does not mean that he consented to his inclusion, any more than did the ministers who were

---

[21] *CChR 1226–57*, 74; there is a photograph of the charter in C. Ellis, *Hubert de Burgh: a Study in Constancy* (London, 1952), between pp. 120–1.

[22] Several of the charters given by the king on 28 June in des Rivaux's favour were not of overwhelming importance, e.g. that which conceded him life-custody of Guildford park and Kempton manor, and on 2 July Neville was prepared to give a different version of one of them in a form more favourable to des Rivaux. These charters were given by the king simply because they were dealt with in the same batch as those to which Neville was opposed. All the charters of 28 June in favour of des Rivaux have the same witnesses.

[23] Paris, *CM* iii 629; v. 91; Powicke, *Henry III*, ii. 780–2.

[24] It should be emphasized that it was not the practice, when the king gave a charter in favour of Neville, for him to take the opportunity to give charters in favour of other individuals. In other words, this is not the explanation for the charters of 28 June in favour of des Rivaux being given by the king.

[25] *CChR 1226–57*, 164–5; C 53/26, m.4. The enrolled charter recorded the king's oath to maintain the charters of Hubert's wife, the countess of Kent. There is then a list of those who received similar charters (*consimilem cartam habet*). The countess had to be included because many of the king's concessions had been made jointly to her and Hubert.

Table

Charters enrolled on Charter Roll 18 Henry III, 27 June – 15 July 1232
(C 53/26, mm.5,4)

Date	Giver	Beneficiary	Contents
27 June	Neville	Hubert de Burgh	quittance of accounts as justiciar of England and Ireland
28 June	king	Peter des Rivaux	six charters granting life-custody of the ports and coast of England, all wards and escheats, the exchange, Jews, and lesser items
1 July	Neville	men of Corfe	quittance of lawing of dogs
2 July	Neville	Peter des Rivaux	land of Gilbert de Laigle in hereditary right
2 July	king	countess of Kent (wife of Hubert de Burgh)	king's oath to maintain her charters
2 July	king	Godfrey of Crowcombe, bishop of Carlisle, Ralph fitzNicholas, Hubert de Burgh, Peter des Rivaux, countess of Kent [sic]; two names erased	note to effect that they have similar charters to that enrolled for the countess of Kent
2 July	king		letter (rather than charter) announcing that Hubert de Burgh has sworn to ensure that the king maintains the charters of Hubert and his wife, Neville, Peter des Rivaux, Ralph fitzNicholas and Godfrey of Crowcombe
2 July	king	bishop of Carlisle	treasurership of the exchequer for life
3 July	Neville	Godfrey of Crowcombe	quittance of military service
5 July	king	Peter des Rivaux	Lydmore castle and Dartmoor forest in hereditary right
?	?	lepers of Thetford	annual fair
7 July	king	Hubert de Burgh	life-custody of the Tower of London, and the castles of Windsor and Odiham
15 July	Neville	Osney abbey	confirmation

actually absent from the court.[26] Hubert, who was almost certainly the moving force behind the oaths, naturally wished to draw the chancellor into the settlement he was attempting to construct. In fact, however, it is pretty plain that Neville had nothing to do with Hubert's oath. That the king acted as giver may not be significant in this instance, for probably Neville could not act since he was one of the beneficiaries.[27] But in the case of the two other beneficiaries present at court, Peter des Rivaux and Godfrey of Crowcombe, who were likewise excluded from acting as witnesses, a unique formula was devised to indicate their involvement – the letter embodying the oath being witnessed 'in [their] presence'. No parallel formula was devised to indicate Neville's attendance.

If, however, Neville was included in the settlement at Burgh without his consent, how was it possible for his name to be recorded at all, as one receiving a charter embodying the king's oath, on the charter rolls, rolls over which, as chancellor, he had control.[28] The answer may be that the records of the oaths of 2 July were enrolled when Neville was absent from court. Neville gave a charter on 3 July and then another on 15 July, by which time the court was back in London. Between these dates only two charters with dating clauses (5 and 7 July) were enrolled. Both were given by the king. It may be that Neville refused to take responsibility for these charters, both of which he might have considered as 'against the Crown'.[29] But equally there is no evidence that Neville was present at all between 4 and 14 July. What may have happened, therefore, is that the oaths of Burgh were enrolled in his absence, and that Neville had his name (and that of an ally) removed once he had returned to court and recovered control of the chancery.[30]

An inspection of the charter roll lends support to this hypothesis. That the oaths of Burgh were enrolled in unusual circumstances is implied by the large number of slips found in their texts.[31] That they were enrolled before, rather

[26] Both Walter Mauclerc and the steward, Ralph fitzNicholas, were absent from court at this time.

[27] For the same reason the king would have given the charter which recorded his oath to uphold Neville's charters, but Neville could have given the charters conceded to the countess of Kent and the other beneficiaries. The charter in favour of the countess of Kent was apparently given by the king on a different occasion on 2 July to that in favour of Walter Mauclerc for the witness lists are different.

[28] For Neville's control over enrolments, see e.g. *CR 1227–31*, 118.

[29] At first sight the charter of 5 July, which granted des Rivaux in hereditary right Lydford castle and Dartmoor forest, looks comparatively unimportant. Perhaps the king gave this simply because Neville was now absent from court. On the other hand, Lydford was a royal castle and the grant represented the alienation of a possession of the Crown. The record of this charter was cancelled with the note that des Rivaux had returned it.

[30] As noted above, the shape of the second erasure affords no clue to the name removed. The most likely candidate is Stephen of Seagrave, with whom Neville had been joint regent in 1230 during the king's absence in Brittany.

[31] In the copy of the charter recording the king's oath to maintain the charters of the countess of Kent (see above, n. 25), the clerk at one point wrote 'foresaid bishop' instead of 'foresaid countess' (an error which he corrected), and superfluously, since her charter was the one written out in full, added the countess's name to the list of those who *consimilem cartam habet*. Although the name

than after, 15 July, by which time Neville had recovered control of the seal, is suggested by the fact that their enrolment plainly took place some time before that of the charter of 15 July given by Neville.[32] That Neville actually lost control of the chancery may be inferred from the singular nature of the enrolments of two of the charters issued between 4 and 14 July. The charter of 5 July, in favour of Peter des Rivaux, was recorded as given by the king at Thetford, but instead of a list of witnesses there is merely the statement that they were the same as in one of the charters issued to des Rivaux on 28 June. Next on the roll is not a properly written-out charter at all, but simply a bald note to the effect that the Leper hospital of Thetford had received a charter granting it the right to hold a yearly fair. No indication was vouchsafed of the giver, the place, the date or the witnesses. In their different ways these enrolments have no precedent in the charter rolls of Neville's time.[33]

There are, therefore, good reasons for thinking that in 1232 Neville resisted the issue of charters which he considered to be irregular, and that he temporarily lost control of the seal. According to Matthew Paris there was a similar episode in 1234. Such incidents may well have encouraged the belief in 1244 that a chancellor chosen 'by all' would help to prevent the issue of improper royal letters. They may equally have lain behind the stipulation in the Paper Constitution that if the seal was taken from the chancellor it should be returned to him, and that whatever was sealed in the interval should be cancelled. Neville's refusal in 1236 to surrender the seal to the king on the grounds that, appointed by common assent, it was only by common assent that he could be dismissed, was likewise echoed in the Paper Constitution. In 1244, therefore, the memory of Neville's career was a powerful argument in favour of establishing a chancellor and a justiciar appointed by common counsel. As important, however, in inculcating this lesson, as the specific incidents in Neville's career which we have discussed, must have been the general way in which he discharged his office in the twenty years between 1218 and 1238, when he

continued
of Walter Mauclerc figures on this list, it does not appear, in the letter recording Hubert's oath, as one of those whose charters Hubert swore to make the king uphold.

[32] After the oaths of Burgh there is a gap of 3 cms. before the next enrolled charter, that given by Neville on 3 July in favour of Godfrey of Crowcombe. Both the gap, which is highly unusual, and the hand and ink of the Crowcombe charter make it fairly clear that the latter was enrolled later than the oaths of Burgh. The Crowcombe charter is followed by that given by the king in favour of Mauclerc on 2 July, and then by the charter of 15 July given by Neville. These two charters have the appearance of being written at the same time and later again than the charter of 3 July. I would suggest that they were enrolled after Neville recovered control of the chancery on or shortly before 15 July. There is, incidentally, an erasure 4½ cms. long and ½ cm. deep (sufficient for, say, twenty – five letters) immediately below the record of the oaths of 2 July.

[33] One occasionally finds, in place of the complete record of a charter, the formula *consimilem cartam habet*, as indeed in the oaths of Burgh, but in these cases the implication is that the charter is the same, apart from the different beneficiary, as that given immediately above. That was clearly not the case with the charter conceded to the house of the Lepers at Thetford. (The charter given by the king in favour of Hubert de Burgh on 7 July has no unusual features in its enrolment.)

was in day-to-day charge of the seal. It is worth putting this in a more general context.

At the November parliament of 1244 the demand for the appointment of justiciar and chancellor by common consent was justified, according to Matthew Paris, by the complaint that Magna Carta had been infringed, the money received from aids misspent, and writs 'against justice' conceded thanks to the absence or failure (*defectum*) of the chancellor.[34] There may also have been anxieties provoked by government initiatives in 1244 over the forest, the 'lands of the Normans', serjeanties, distraint for knighthood, and liberties assumed without warrant.[35] More generally, however, the twenty-seven years of peace since the conclusion of the civil war of 1215–17 had seen a steady increase in the scope of the king's government, as the burgeoning size of the pipe rolls and curia regis rolls shows. More people than ever before, as litigators and debtors, were coming within the ambit of that government. The consequence was a corresponding increase in the number of petitions coming into the centre demanding justice, favour and the redress of grievances.

It was with such petitions, over many years, that Hubert de Burgh and Ralph de Neville dealt. 'You are justiciar of England, held to dispense justice to everyone', Falkes de Breauté told Hubert in 1219, as the latter commenced his active justiciarship.[36] Hubert's correspondence shows how seriously he took his responsibilities in this area, dealing carefully with a steady flow of letters full of complaints and requests.[37] Neville's responsibility for the issuing of royal letters meant that he coped with a similar type of business. It was he, in the last resort, who decided whether the writs out of course, which many petitioners sought, should or (because they were 'against justice') should not be granted.[38] In 1219, for example, Hubert de Burgh and Peter des Roches, bishop of Winchester informed Neville that, having heard the complaint of Roger fitzJohn, they thought a writ should be made out summoning before the justices of the bench the record of his case in Cornwall. But Neville was to hear Roger's complaint himself, discuss the matter with the judge Martin of Pattishall, and then do what he thought was 'most just and best'.[39] That Neville discharged his responsibilities in an even-handed fashion is suggested, for what they are worth, by the encomiums of Matthew Paris, who described him as a 'solitary column of truth and faith in royal affairs', and who averred that 'in the midst of the

---

[34] Paris, *CM* iv. 363.

[35] See Stacey, 250–2.

[36] *Royal Letters*, i. 5 (where misdated).

[37] An impression of this correspondence may be gained from *Royal Letters*.

[38] These were probably writs out of course which intervened in the judicial process by, for example, preventing cases from going to judgement or inventing *ad hoc* legal procedures; see *DBM* 260–3, 272–3. For other suggestions, see Denholm-Young, 'The 'Paper Constitution'', 422; Stacey, 216, n. 37.

[39] SC1/6/26. For a letter asking Neville for a judicial writ out of course, see *Royal Letters*, i. 68. For an analysis of Neville's correspondence, much of which deals with his private affairs, see J. and L. Stones, 'Bishop Ralph Neville', 243–4.

kingdom's many stormy disorders he stood upright, neither bending to right nor to left. He was not like a reed to be blown this way or that by any wind'.[40]

With the disappearance of Burgh and Neville all this came to an end. At the very time when the affairs of more and more people were encompassed by the king's government, so defined and navigable channels of communication with the centre of that government were closing down. After 1234 there was no longer a justiciar specifically charged with 'dispensing justice to everyone'.[41] Four years later there was no longer a chancellor or keeper of the seal, with an independent status, which helped him to oppose the concession of charters 'against the Crown', and to deal fairly with the numerous requests for writs out of course, resisting the issue of those which were 'against justice'. The household officials who kept the seal after 1238 might have had a sense of responsibility, but when Simon the Norman made trouble in 1240 he was immediately dismissed.[42] Equally, with the keepership of the seal now passing quickly from one relatively minor official to another, and sometimes being the responsibility of more than one official at the same time, the process of obtaining writs out of course, for those outside the circle of the court, was much more complex and obscure than in Neville's day.[43]

The measures in the Paper Constitution were essentially designed to open up and control a system of government which, while expanding in scope, had become more enclosed and remote, and for that very reason easier for those on the inside to manipulate and corrupt. The government was to be prized open through the creation of an elective justiciarship and chancellorship, and by the appointment by common consent of four councillors. Two of this group of elected officials (by implication they would frequently be the justiciar and chancellor) were to be always with the king 'so that they may hear the complaints of everyone and can speedily help those suffering injury', precisely the role which Hubert de Burgh had been expected to play as justiciar.[44] Other ministers too, in the first instance, were to be chosen by common consent –

---

[40] Paris, *CM* iii. 90, 206–7; see also 74, 90, 226, 266, 364, 491, 495, 525, 530. However, for Neville's private profit as chancellor, see *Chronicon Petroburgense*, ed. T. Stapleton (Camden Soc., old ser., 1849), 9.

[41] For some perceptive comments on the position of Hubert de Burgh, and the importance of the disappearance of the justiciarship, see W.L. Warren, *The Governance of Norman and Angevin England 1086–1271* (London, 1987), 176.

[42] Paris, *CM* iii. 629, asserts that Geoffrey the Templar, who was also involved in keeping the seal, protested with Simon and was likewise dismissed, but Powicke is sceptical about this: Powicke, *Henry III*, ii. 782.

[43] For the keepership of the seal after 1238, see Dibben, 'Chancellor and Keeper of the Seal', 42–3. Neville may have been in day-to-day charge of the seal on a few occasions before his death for charters were given by his hand in Nov. and Dec. 1243 but, apart from that, he did not in any real sense act as chancellor in 1242–3, as Dibben might seem to imply; see also J. and L. Stones, 'Bishop Ralph Neville'. 239.

[44] The reason given by the Paper Constitution for allowing the justiciar and the chancellor to be numbered among the four elected councillors was that both officials needed frequently to be with the king.

two justices of the bench, two barons of the exchequer and at least one justice of the Jews.[45] The aim of the Constitution was thus to exert common control over all the institutions of central government. As the Constitution observed, 'since [the justices of the bench, exchequer and Jews] deal with the affairs of all so everyone should assent to their choice'. There could be no more explicit acknowledgement of the range of English government in the mid-thirteenth century.

The reforms proposed in 1244, therefore, were designed to benefit 'everyone', not just the great magnates. Indeed, those great magnates who were prominent at Henry's court after 1234 were well placed to cope with the situation created by the disappearance of the justiciar and chancellor. In 1244 itself, as Dr. Stacey has argued, the policies which the king had pursued since 1239 may have isolated him from the earls and barons in a way untypical of the rest of his personal rule. That may be part of the background to the Paper Constitution.[46] But even in 1244 the earls of Cornwall and Leicester were prominent councillors, two of the household stewards, John fitzGeoffrey and William de Cantilupe, were great magnates, and the earls of Pembroke, Hereford and Norfolk all attested royal charters. Of course, great magnates with *entrée* to the court might still believe that the king would govern more sensibly and effectively if surrounded by responsible ministers with defined tasks and powers. They might regret in particular the loss of an independent chancellor who could check the king's feckless distribution of patronage and his consequent concession of charters 'against the Crown'. But the groups which had suffered most from the administrative changes since 1234, and had the strongest interest in the reforms in the Paper Constitution, were those with less influence at court, namely barons of local importance, county knights and esquires, freemen and the numerous religious houses whose claims to the chattels and amercements of their men were under challenge at the exchequer. The memoranda roll of 1243–4 shows no less than forty ecclesiastics and ecclesiastical institutions in this position; no wonder that the four elected councillors of the Paper Constitution were to be 'conservators of liberties'.[47]

There was nothing surprising in reforms being conceived in 1244 to meet the grievances of these groups. After all, the *quid pro quo* was to be taxation which they, indeed which 'everyone', would have to pay. When the king sought taxation again in the parliaments of the 1240s and 1250s, the demand that he appoint a chancellor and a justiciar by common consent was consequently reiterated.[48] Such plans of reform were not simply the product of some narrow conflict between the king and his 'barons'; they were the price required, by

---

[45] After this first election by common assent they were to be chosen by the four elected councillors.

[46] Stacey, 252–5; D.A. Carpenter, 'King, Magnates and Society: The Personal Rule of King Henry III', below pp. 93–6.

[47] See below, pp. 85–6; E 368/15, m.3.

[48] Paris, *CM* v. 5; *Ann. Mon.* i. 336.

political society beyond the great magnates, for the payment of taxation. In 1258 the great magnates appointed a justiciar and a chancellor both to secure their own control of central government and to meet the grievances of this wider political nation, thus winning support for their regime.[49] The demand for a responsible chancellor was justified in much the same way as it had been in 1244–as the statement drawn up for presentation to Louis IX in 1264 explained, the absence or failure (*defectum*) of chancellors before 1258 had led both to the concession of writs 'against right and the customary course of the chancery', and to the sealing of 'various excessive and unreasonable grants.'[50] Equally, the justiciar in 1258 was to 'uphold right to all persons', much as were the two councillors in 1244 and Hubert de Burgh before that.[51] By 1258, however, the increasing oppression of the sheriffs and justices in eyre, the lawless behaviour of the Lusignans, and their seeming monopoly over royal patronage, had intensified the need for such remedies and broadened their appeal.[52] They were, however, already out of date. The huge weight of petitions produced by the expanding apparatus of thirteenth-century government could no longer be dealt with merely by two officials, however responsible and conscientious. The real answer, grasped by Edward I, was to develop the process of petition to the king's council in parliament.[53]

---

[49] In 1258, although the king's keeper of the seal, Henry of Wingham (who was sometimes given the title chancellor), continued in office, he was in effect re-appointed, taking an oath about the custody of the seal 'in the presence of the barons of England': *CR 1256–9*, 315.

[50] *DBM* 260–3.

[51] *DBM* 102–3, 106–7.

[52] See below, pp. 171–81, 190–4; J.R. Maddicott, 'Magna Carta and the Local Community 1215–1259', *Past and Present*, cii (1984), 47–8; H.W. Ridgeway, 'The Politics of the English Royal Court, 1247–65, with Special Reference to the Role of the Aliens' (Oxford Univ. D. Phil. thesis, 1983), 266–8, 289.

[53] J.R. Maddicott, 'Parliament and the Constituencies, 1272–1377', in *The English Parliament in the Middle Ages*, ed. R.G. Davies and J.H. Denton (Manchester, 1981), 62–8.

5

King, Magnates and Society: The Personal Rule of King Henry III, 1234–1258

Between 1234 and 1258 King Henry III, having emerged from the tutelage of ministers inherited from his father, controlled the government of England himself.[1] Looking at this period of personal rule, it would be easy to gain the impression that Henry's kingship, in its theory, and also to some extent its practice, challenged the position of the magnates. M. T. Clanchy, for example, in a justly famous article has suggested that in the 1240s and 1250s Henry III evolved a theory of royal absolutism, a theory which had threatening implications for the magnates. He has also stressed the extent to which Henry was "the initiator both of the methods and of the theory" behind Edward I's *quo warranto* campaign, which questioned the liberties possessed by the magnates in the field of local government.[2] As for Henry's court, the impression has been given by R. F. Treharne that few English barons were present there, and that the king was largely surrounded by officials and foreign relatives — the latter being his wife's Savoyard uncles and his own Poitevin half-brothers of the house of Lusignan.[3] G. W. S. Barrow has written that Henry "appeared to be excluding the barons as a class from membership of his royal council."[4] The question whether Henry, like his father John, was pressing magnates to pay their debts has never been

---

[1] For the period down to 1234, see Frederick Maurice Powicke, *The Thirteenth Century* (Oxford, 1953), chs. 2, 3; David A. Carpenter, "The Fall of Hubert de Burgh," for which see above pp. 45–60.

[2] Michael T. Clanchy, "Did Henry III Have a Policy?," *History* 53 (1968), 207–19. Michael T. Clanchy, *England and Its Rulers, 1066–1272* (Glasgow, 1983), pp. 222–40, discusses Henry's high sense of his royal authority and argues that he became isolated by pursuing "sole royal power" (p. 240). However, Clanchy does not touch explicitly here on the question of absolutism.

[3] Reginald F. Treharne, *The Baronial Plan of Reform, 1258–1263* (Manchester, 1932), pp. 33–34. The chief laymen established by the king in England were the queen's uncle, Peter of Savoy, who was granted the honour of Richmond in 1240, and the king's half-brother, William de Valence, who came to England in 1247 and was married to the daughter of Warin de Monte Canisio, one of the heiresses of the earls of Pembroke. William was also granted many manors by the king. Peter of Savoy's brother, Boniface, became archbishop of Canterbury (1241). Of the other half-brothers, Aymer became bishop-elect of Winchester (1250). Guy and Geoffrey de Lusignan made frequent visits to England and were granted money fees and wardships. See Eugene L. Cox, *The Eagles of Savoy* (Princeton, 1974); Harold S. Snellgrove, *The Lusignans in England* (Albuquerque, New Mexico, 1950).

[4] Geoffrey W. S. Barrow, *Feudal Britain* (London, 1956), pp. 262–63.

investigated; but Matthew Paris's picture of the king as a "vigilant and indefatigable searcher after money" might indicate that the revolution of 1258, like that of 1215, was a "rebellion of the king's debtors."[5]

This paper will argue that an interpretation of Henry's personal rule along these lines would be misconceived. Henry did not hold a theory of royal absolutism; he did not challenge the liberties of his magnates; he did not foreclose on their debts; he did not exclude them from his court and council. Although the king's government bore heavily on sections of society through extortionate sheriffs and burdensome judicial eyres, magnates largely escaped these pressures. From their point of view, Henry's rule was characterized by lenity, not aggression. Indeed, many influential magnates benefited positively from the king's favour. If, as will be suggested, Henry's underlying aim in the treatment of his magnates was the maintenance of peace and stability, the policy was marred by the failure to reconcile his Lusignan half-brothers with other factions at court and by the consequent revolution of 1258. The significance of the king's policy, however, lies as much in its repercussions in the localities as in its relation to national politics. Henry's indulgence allowed both English magnates and his foreign relatives to encroach on the authority of the sheriff and make the power of their own courts and officials more pervasive, a development which helps to explain why there was pressure in 1258–59 for the reform of such private administrations. What had happened between 1234 and 1258, it may be suggested, was the emergence of a pattern of magnate rule in the shires similar to that which was to dominate England in the later Middle Ages.

1

It is difficult to sustain the argument that between 1234 and 1258 Henry III held a theory of royal absolutism. Henry might, on occasion, speak in high terms of the king's authority. In 1248, if Matthew Paris can be believed, he declared that "inferiors should be directed at the will (*arbitrium*) of the lord and the pleasure (*voluntas*) of the ordinary." However, the context of this remark was Henry's argument that the king, like any other lord, was free to choose his own servants and ministers.[6] A theory of absolutism would go far beyond this claim, which involved the king in a challenge to neither law nor custom. Its essence would be that the king was above the law — was, as the Roman law maxim used by the emperor Frederick II put it, *legibus*

---

[5] Matthew Paris, *Chronica majora*, ed. Henry R. Luard, 7 vols., Rolls Series 57 (London, 1872–83), 5:55, 274; James C. Holt, *The Northerners: A Study in the Reign of King John* (Oxford, 1961), p. 34.

[6] Paris, *Chronica*, 5:20; Clanchy, "Henry III," pp. 207–8 and n. 33, for the sense of "ordinary" as one who exercised jurisdiction *suo jure* and not by delegation. See also *The Song of Lewes*, ed. C. L. Kingsford (Oxford, 1890), pp. 16–17.

solutus.[7] In England such a theory might be employed to justify the king taking action against people by will, *per voluntatem,* in contravention of clause 39 of Magna Carta 1215, which forbad the imprisonment and disseisin of free men other than by the law of the land or by judgement of their peers.[8] It is true that in the years 1232–34 King John's former justiciar, Peter des Roches, bishop of Winchester, may well have brought absolutist ideas to Henry's court. The king, in this period, unquestionably proceeded *per voluntatem.*[9] But des Roches was dismissed in 1234, following the rebellion of Richard Marshal, and Henry denounced absolutism when he reproached the bishop for justifying, in the light of the "plenitude of royal power," the king's ability to do injury to his subjects "at his will" (*pro velle nostro*).[10]

After 1234 the evidence that Henry returned to absolutist theories is highly inconclusive. Such an accusation was not levelled by his opponents in 1258. The most that was claimed, in a speech to the pope by an envoy of the barons, was that the Lusignan half-brothers whispered to the king that he was above the law. But did the king himself take the same view as these supposed whisperings?[11] It is difficult to agree with Clanchy that a theory of royal absolutism can be found in *De legibus et consuetudinibus Angliae,* the great treatise on the laws of England which was produced in the 1220s and 1230s by the circle around the judge William de Raleigh and subsequently edited and revised by Henry de Bracton, a *coram rege* judge between 1247–51 and 1253–57. *De legibus* states that the king is under no man; one cannot bring legal actions against him or lawfully resist his acts. But this does not mean that the king's position licensed him to break the law. On the contrary, *De legibus* insists that the king is under the law and has a duty to govern in accordance with it. He must not rule *per voluntatem.* "The king ought not to be under man, but under God and under the law, since law makes the king.

---

[7] Ernst Kantorowicz, *The King's Two Bodies* (Princeton, 1957), pp. 106, 95. For a general discussion of ideas in the twelfth and thirteenth centuries as to whether the ruler was above or below the law see ibid., pp. 87–192. See also Brian Tierney, "Bracton on Government," *Speculum* 38 (1963), 295–317.

[8] For Magna Carta clause 39 see James C. Holt, *Magna Carta* (Cambridge, Eng., 1965), pp. 226–29, 326–27. In the 1225 reissue of the Charter it formed part of clause 29. For action *per voluntatem* under the Angevin kings, see John E. A. Jolliffe, *Angevin Kingship* (London, 1955), ch. 3, and compare James C. Holt, *King John* (London, 1963), pp. 10–11.

[9] *Curia Regis Rolls* (London, 1922–), 15:28, n. 2, and nos. 1426–27, 1475, 1895.

[10] *Treaty Rolls,* 1, ed. Pierre Chaplais (London, 1955), no. 15. I follow here the usual rendering of a passage in a letter of Henry III to Frederick II: see Frederick Maurice Powicke, *Henry III and The Lord Edward: The Community of the Realm in the Thirteenth Century,* 2 vols. in 1 (Oxford, 1947; repr. 1966), p. 145. However, the exact translation is open to some doubt. Henry also reproached the bishop for making him deviate from the observation of justice.

[11] *Annales monastici,* ed. Henry R. Luard, 5 vols., Rolls Series 36 (London, 1864–69), 1:463; compare ibid., pp. 457–60; Paris, *Chronica,* 6:406–9; *Documents of the Baronial Movement of Reform and Rebellion, 1258–1267,* ed. Reginald F. Treharne and Ivor J. Sanders (Oxford, 1973), pp. 76–91, 256–79. For a different view, Clanchy, "Henry III," p. 209.

. . . There is no king where *voluntas* rules rather than law." Thus, if the king acts unlawfully, *De legibus* feels there is no remedy, but it condemns rather than justifies a monarch wishing to indulge in such arbitrary conduct.[12]

Clanchy believes that Henry's "alleged absolutist theory is most fully documented in a particular application of it: his claim to be the ultimate interpreter of royal charters." This, however, was not a claim that the king was outside the law and could revoke charters at will. It was merely to say, as *De legibus* puts it, that "it is for him who establishes to explain his deed."[13] Clanchy goes on to quote Matthew Paris's report of a speech which Henry III made to the prior of the Hospitallers in 1252. Here the king threatened to imitate the papal practice of abrogating previously granted charters through the use of the clause "notwithstanding" (*non obstante*): that is to say, through stating that some new act or concession was made "notwithstanding" previously granted rights. This was not an explicit claim that the king was *legibus solutus*, but it was still an attempt to justify arbitrary conduct in direct contravention of Magna Carta clause 39. The sentiments attributed to Henry in 1252, however, have to be set beside an episode during which Henry referred to the papal use of "nothwithstanding" in a conversation with Matthew Paris himself. Indeed, we may suspect that the speech to the prior in 1252 was written up from Paris's own exchange with the king two years before. The background in 1250 was Henry III's grant to his knight, Geoffrey of Childwick, of rights which St. Albans Abbey believed impinged on its liberties. When challenged about this by Matthew Paris, the king declared: "surely the pope acts in a similar fashion, specifically subjoining to his letters 'notwithstanding any privilege or indulgence.' " Then, however, speaking "more modestly," Henry promised to think the matter over.[14] The result of these kingly cogitations can be seen in the judgement which Henry gave in person in the St. Albans v. Childwick case in 1251. Here the king, in effect, admitted that he had acted unjustly in making the grant to Childwick — a view in full accord with *De legibus*, which states that the king was not entitled to make new grants which infringed established rights.[15] Two years later

---

[12] Henry Bracton, *De legibus et consuetudinibus Angliae*, ed. George F. Woodbine, trans. and revised Samuel E. Thorne, 4 vols. (Cambridge, Mass., 1968–77), 2:33, 169, 305; Clanchy, "Henry III," pp. 208–9. In setting out the position of *De legibus* I follow closely Tierney, "Bracton on Government," p. 303; compare Kantorowicz, *The King's Two Bodies*, p. 147. For the authorship of *De legibus* see Thorne's introduction to *De legibus*, 3:xiii–lii. When Clanchy wrote it was generally assumed that the work was written by Bracton himself in the 1240s and 1250s.

[13] Clanchy, "Henry III," p. 209; see *De legibus*, 2:109. See also Michael T. Clanchy, "The Franchise of Return of Writs," *Transactions of the Royal Historical Society*, 5th ser., 17 (1967), 67. In practice the ruling meant that cases involving royal charters came before the court *coram rege*.

[14] Paris, *Chronica*, 5:129–30, 339; Clanchy, "Henry III," p. 209. Clanchy himself suspects that Paris embellished another part of the king's altercation with the prior of the Hospitallers (see p. 211).

[15] *Gesta abbatum Sancti Albani*, ed. Henry T. Riley, Rolls Series 28/4 (London, 1867), 1:318; *De legibus*, 2:169, where the judgement is cited. St. Albans lost the case, however, because it took direct action against Childwick instead of complaining about the grant to the king.

Henry specifically declared that he did not want the liberties which he had granted to William de Valence to harm those of the abbey of Bury St. Edmunds, thus carefully avoiding a repetition of the injustice in the Childwick case.[16] This was only what one would expect from a monarch who stressed in writs of the 1240s and 1250s that he wished to disseise no one of his possessions unjustly and without judgement.[17] Such sentiments were in full accord with the principles of Magna Carta clause 39. Writs of the king in this period also emphasized that he wished to deny justice to nobody, an aspiration in harmony with clause 40 of Magna Carta, which forbad the denial, delay, or sale of justice.[18] Indeed, the king's attitude to the Charter as a whole during his personal rule hardly suggests absolutist ideas. True, Matthew Paris implies that the king's aim was to deprive the *universitas regni* of its rights. But, in return for grants of taxation, Henry reissued the Great Charter twice, in 1237 and again, with apparent sincerity, in 1253. On many other occasions he stressed that he wished the charter to be upheld.[19] Although, as we shall see, Henry was sometimes guilty of contravening Magna Carta it does not follow that this conduct was inspired or justified by some political theory. Taking the evidence as a whole it is difficult to believe that Henry's considered position, during the period of his personal rule, was that he was in any way above the law.

2

If one looks in more detail at the actual practice of the king between 1234 and 1258, it rarely appears at odds with Magna Carta clause 39 in the sense that he deprived magnates, or anyone else, of possessions unjustly, *per voluntatem*. The disseisins consequent upon the reforms of 1236 were quickly reversed.[20] The number of people or institutions which suffered, like St. Albans, from grants made by the king which infringed their privileges was not large. Infringements of this kind could arise more from ignorance of existing rights than from any deliberate intention to breach them.[21] In practice, the king never used the "notwithstanding" clause to effect such breaches. Perhaps it might be said that the king and his council acted arbitrarily when they developed legal rulings to test claims to liberties. But,

[16] *Close Rolls of the Reign of Henry III, 1227–1272* [hereafter cited as *CR*], 14 vols. (London, 1902–38), *1251–53*, p. 462.

[17] *CR 1247–51*, pp. 49, 341; *1251–53*, pp. 103, 484; *1256–59*, p. 65; see *Foedera*, ed. Thomas Rymer, et al. (London, 1816), 1/1:408–9.

[18] For example, *CR 1251–53*, p. 228; *1254–56*, p. 418; see also *Foedera*, 1/1:408–9.

[19] Paris, *Chronica*, 5:514, 3:380–83, 5:375–78. For Paris's bias, see Richard Vaughan, *Matthew Paris* (Cambridge, Eng., 1958), pp. 139–43. For Henry and Magna Carta, see also below, pp. 80–81.

[20] For example, *CR 1234–37*, pp. 275, 281, 297, 302, 306.

[21] However, for the king's attempt to grant liberties to the abbey of Westminster which would infringe those of the city of London, see Paris, *Chronica*, 5:127–28; *Chronica maiorum et vicecomitum*, ed. T. S. Stapleton, Camden Society (London, 1846), pp. 14–17, 19; see also *Gesta abbatum Sancti Albani*, 1:361–66.

when the king demanded that warrant should be shown for such claims, he was inaugurating a judicial process, a process which would end in the final loss of the liberty only if a judgement against it was given in his court. Equally, whatever his initial impulses in moments of anger, Henry seems to have stayed within the law when he attempted to take punitive measures against, among others, Simon de Montfort, Peter de Mauley, Robert de Ros, and the Cistercians.[22] When, in an incident made much of by Matthew Paris, Henry unjustly deprived the countess of Arundel of a wardship, probably because he was misinformed of the facts, he quickly reversed his decision.[23] In 1256, the king's brother and leading councillor, Richard earl of Cornwall, considered it "most unfitting" for Henry's daughter to marry into the kingdom of Castile, where her husband might be deprived of his lands "by the sole will and pleasure of the prince." The implication was that things were very different in England.[24]

If, however, the king did not breach Magna Carta clause 39, his conduct stands up less well when set against Magna Carta clause 40, which forbad the refusal of justice. It was this clause, not clause 39, that Henry was accused of breaking by a manifesto of 1264.[25] Certain magnates, however, often had much to gain from this aspect of the king's conduct, since they were among those whom the king protected through his denial, or connivance in the denial, of legal redress. It was, indeed, the pressure of rewarding and managing such men, together with his foreign relatives, which made it impossible for the king to uphold clause 40, whatever the sentiments in his writs. It is true that on occasion the king showed a desire to restrain the malpractices of magnates. In 1250, in a speech at the exchequer to the sheriffs, Henry ordered them amongst other things to "diligently inquire how magnates behave towards their men" and to correct transgressions "as they are able." Three years later he sternly instructed the sheriffs to see that the magnates themselves observed Magna Carta. Again, in 1255, the sheriffs

[22] For the challenge to liberties, see below, pp. 85–8 and n. 51. Margaret W. Labarge, *Simon de Montfort* (London, 1962), pp. 119–24; *CR 1253–54*, p. 295; *1254–56*, p. 418; *Calendar of the Charter Rolls, 1226–1300* [hereafter cited at CChR], 2 vols. (London, 1903, 1906), *1257–1300*, p. 25; Paris, *Chronica*, 5:506, 569; *CR 1254–56*, pp. 329, 414, 444, 216; *Calendar of the Patent Rolls, Henry III, 1232–1272* [hereafter cited as CPR], 4 vols. (London, 1901–13), *1247–58*, p. 473.
[23] Paris, *Chronica*, 5:336–37; *CPR 1247–58*, p. 132; *CR 1251–53*, p. 357. The king also pardoned the countess a 30-mark amercement she had incurred in the course of the case. His only condition was that she should not repeat the *opprobria* she had said to the king at Westminster: C/60/51, m. 10; see Paris, *Chronica*, 5:336–37. Henry was sensitive about his reputation and disliked being accused of injustice. [Unless otherwise stated, all manuscript references are to documents in the Public Record Office, Chancery Lane. In the memoranda rolls and eyre rolls (E/368; E/159; Just/1) membrane references are to the numerals in ink. When citing receipt rolls (E/401) it is impossible to give membrane references since the membranes are unnumbered.]
[24] *CR 1254–56*, pp. 389–90.
[25] Treharne and Sanders, *Documents*, pp. 270–71. In the reissue of 1225 clauses 39 and 40 were run together as clause 29.

were ordered to have the Great Charter read in their county courts and to ensure, on pain of punishment, that it was upheld "both on the part of the king and on the part of all others in the kingdom."[26] Whether, however, the sheriffs were able to do much in response to these exhortations may be doubted, given their relative weakness in the period.[27] Nor, in practice, could they expect much backing from the king. Between 1250 and 1258 there appears to be only one instance of Henry intervening when a lord failed to observe Magna Carta, and in this case the complainant was the baron of the exchequer, John le Francis.[28] In 1255 Henry instructed the justices in eyre in Surrey and other counties to ensure that Magna Carta was observed both by the king and by everyone else.[29] Henry, however, never gave the eyre teeth in this area. It was left to Edward I to take the modest step of adding to the articles of the eyre a question on "those who are amerced without reasonable cause . . . and not by their peers," thus picking up one of the main ways in which private jurisdictions might breach the Great Charter.[30] Between 1246 and 1254 several new questions about the abuses of sheriffs and bailiffs were added to the articles of the eyre, but it was not made clear, as it was in articles in 1258, that these were to embrace the malpractices of private as well as royal officials, and they gave rise to few accusations against the former. Nor did King Henry exploit the easiest form of procedure by which lesser men could bring actions against their magnate oppressors: namely, a simple verbal complaint before justices in eyre. The complaint procedure was available during the personal rule. In the Gloucestershire eyre of 1248, for example, it was used successfully by the parson of Campden against the baron Roger de Somery. But it was left to the reformers of 1258 to bring this procedure to the front of the stage by setting up an eyre whose sole purpose was to enable men to act by complaint against both the officials of the magnates and those of the king.[31]

Before 1258 magnates did not merely gain from the king's failure to take new measures to protect the oppressed. They also influenced and sometimes corrupted in their favour the whole working of the judicial system. The

---

[26] Clanchy, "Henry III," p. 216; *CR 1251–53*, p. 482; *1254–56*, pp. 194–95. See also *CPR 1247–58*, p. 280.

[27] See below, pp. 102–3.

[28] *CR 1251–53*, p. 491; for an action by the government during the king's absence in Gascony, *CR 1253–54*, p. 39. For John le Francis, see Paris, *Chronica*, 5:320.

[29] Just/1/872, m. 9. This order paralleled that to the sheriffs in the same year.

[30] Helen M. Cam, *Studies in the Hundred Rolls*, Oxford Studies in Social and Legal History 6 (Oxford, 1921), p. 98. See clause 20 of Magna Carta 1215 and clause 14 of the 1225 reissue.

[31] *The Roll of the Shropshire Eyre of 1256*, ed. Alan Harding, Selden Society Publications 96 (London, 1981), introduction, pp. xxiv–xxvi; *Crown Pleas of the Wiltshire Eyre, 1249*, ed. Cecil A. F. Meekings, Wiltshire Archaeological and Natural History Society 16 (Devizes, 1961), pp. 31–32; Cam, *Studies in the Hundred Rolls*, p. 94; Ernest F. Jacob, *Studies in the Period of Baronial Reform and Rebellion, 1258–67*, Oxford Studies in Social and Legal History 8 (Oxford, 1925), pp. 34, 65–70, 341; Just/1/273, m. 8.

manifesto of 1264 alleges that no justice could be had in the king's court against certain aliens and some native *curiales*. It was difficult to get writs to begin legal processes against these men. If cases were brought, the judges would do no justice, either through fear of dismissal or because they were placed and maintained in office by the aliens and *curiales*, and were their *tributarii*. The aliens here were clearly the king's foreign relatives, but the manifesto goes on to specifically associate English magnates in the same abuses, stating that "after the power and pride of these aliens and *curiales* had grown so overweening that there was no one who would declare judgement in favour of *minores* against them and their excesses, nor could writs of common justice be obtained against them from the king's chancery, certain nobles and magnates of the realm . . . with equal injustice claimed this same right, or, rather, wrong, so that they would not permit justice to be done or writs to be executed against themselves and their bailiffs."[32] Although the 1264 manifesto is a partisan document, its allegations cannot be dismissed out of hand.[33] The king's favour certainly protected the Lusignans from legal actions, to such an extent that people felt that it was useless to bring cases against them. Some natives *curiales* and magnates (the two were often one and the same) were protected in a similar way. When disputes arose between the latter and the Lusignans, the king was faced with difficult choices. The belief that in such cases he often sided with his half-brothers was a major reason for their unpopularity. The king's denial of justice to the baron and *curialis* John fitz Geoffrey, when he complained of an armed attack by Aymer de Lusignan, bishop-elect of Winchester, precipitated the crisis of 1258.[34] But when such conflicts did not arise, when the potential victims were, as the 1264 manifesto says, *minores*, the king could protect aliens and English magnates alike. There is some confirmation that Henry may indeed have obstructed the issuing of writs. Matthew Paris states that in 1256 Henry ordered that no writs were to go out from the chancery which would harm the interests of two great native barons, the earls of Cornwall and Gloucester; the queen's uncle, Peter of Savoy; and the Lusignan half-brothers.[35]

A particularly striking example of the king's denial of justice at the instance of the earl of Gloucester occurs in a legal action which illustrates another complaint made in the 1264 manifesto, namely that the king "by his letters" prevented cases from going to judgement. In Somerset in 1255 an assize of novel disseisin came before the judge Henry de Bracton. The defendant, and thus the person who gained from delay, was the well-

---

[32] Treharne and Sanders, *Documents*, pp. 270–73.

[33] The manifesto was drawn up as part of the barons' statement of their case at Amiens in January 1264.

[34] Paris, *Chronica*, 5:708; *Annales monastici*, 1:458–59; Jacob, *Studies*, p. 61; Just/1/1187, m. 1.

[35] Paris, *Chronica*, 5:594. However, there is no further evidence concerning this order, and one cannot be certain about its precise intention or effect.

connected west country baron, William de Montacute. Montacute obtained a writ, authorized by the *coram rege* judge Henry of Bath, which told Bracton, after hearing the case, to adjourn it *coram rege* for judgement. Bracton apparently disapproved of this instruction so much that when recording it on his roll, he stated that it ordered the judgement to be put in respite "without any cause," and he strongly implied that since there was "nothing obscure" in the case, the king should send it back to Somerset for judgement. In fact, after Bracton adjourned the case *coram rege*, no judgement was pronounced, and the plaintiff, Andrew Wake, fined ten marks for a writ which commissioned Bracton to hear the assize again, this time with the *coram rege* judge Henry de Mara. Montacute, however, was now protected by the intervention of the earl of Gloucester. At his instance, the king simply ordered the assize not to be taken, and that, as far as is known, was the end of the matter. If this was the fate of Andrew Wake, who was later sheriff of Somerset and Dorset, one can imagine how hopeless was the situation of those beneath him in the social scale.[36]

In other cases Henry III eased the path of great men by acts of grace rather than of downright injustice. In 1257 the earl of Norfolk was convicted of disseisin before the justices in eyre in Suffolk. The king, on the earl's complaint that the case had proceeded "less than rightly," promised to correct what needed correction *coram rege*. Meanwhile, payment of damages by the earl was respited.[37] The 1264 manifesto, however, alleges that great men were frequently able to avoid hostile verdicts through their power over the king's judges. It is difficult to prove this charge. The judge Roger of Thirkleby proclaimed his own incorruptibility, and we have seen Bracton's protest.[38] However, the judges themselves admitted to the legal expert of St. Albans Abbey, William of Horton, that they dared not pronounce sentences against the earl of Cornwall and the clerk John Mansel, who was perhaps the king's most trusted *curialis*.[39] The king certainly tolerated close connections between nobles and leading judges. Henry de Mara, a *coram rege* judge between 1247–49 and 1253–56, was a tenant of both the Warenne

---

[36] Treharne and Sanders, *Documents*, pp. 272–73; *CR 1254–56*, p. 188; Just/1/1182, m. 7; *Somerset Pleas*, ed. Charles E. H. Chadwyck-Healey, Somerset Record Society 11 (1897), no. 1516 — see *De legibus*, 3:145–46; C/60/53, m. 21; C/66/70, m. 21d. In Bracton's roll (Just/1/1182, m.7) the parties were given a day *coram rege* "de audienda voluntate domini regis si velit quod procedat assisa in Som' et reddatur judicium cum nichil sit obscurum in predicto recordo [the record of the case set out above in the roll], eo quod idem Willelmus protulit quoddam breve domini regis quod judicium ponetur in respectum sine aliqua causa [*causa* interlined] post capcionem assise." Wake's fine of 10 marks to associate Mara with Bracton in the hearing of the assize (C/60/53, m. 21) was cancelled with the marginal note "postea rex ad instanciam comitis Glouc' mandavit ne assisa illa caperetur." I have been unable to establish the link between Montacute and the earl of Gloucester.

[37] *CR 1256–59*, p. 145; for the case see Just/1/567, m. 13.

[38] *Flores historiarum*, 1, ed. Henry R. Luard, Rolls Series 95 (London, 1890), pp. 450–51.

[39] *Gesta abbatum Sancti Albani*, 1:316.

earls of Surrey and the Longespees and is found in the service of both families before becoming a judge. His connection with William de Longespee, indeed, can be traced down to the latter's death in 1249. Between his spells *coram rege*, Mara served the earl of Cornwall, and it has been suggested that it was the earl's influence which brought him back to office in 1253.[40] The judge William Trussel was a tenant of Simon de Montfort. After he left the bench, but while still employed on numerous judicial and administrative commissions, he appears as Simon's attorney.[41] Another justice of the bench, Gilbert of Preston, was married to the step-daughter of the northern baron Thomas de Grelle.[42] The judge Henry of Bath had married into the Basset family of High Wycombe. Consequently Fulk and Philip Basset, together with their ally the earl of Cornwall, struggled to save Henry from dismissal and disgrace by the king in 1251 and probably had much to do with his recall to the court *coram rege* two years later. Bath's authorisation of the writ in favour of William de Montacute in 1255 is hardly surprising, since William was Fulk and Philip Basset's cousin and frequently attested their charters.[43] It may be that magnates were already retaining judges by granting them money fees. In 1259, while still a *coram rege* judge, Henry of Bath entered the service of the Lord Edward, the king's eldest son, and was granted an annual fee of £20. Perhaps the manifesto of 1264 was thinking of justices feed in this way when it styled them *tributarii*.[44]

The general picture of the breakdown of justice presented by the 1264 manifesto echoes the complaint of William of Horton in 1254 that "there are certain people in the land, like kings, against whom it is scarcely or not at all possible to have justice."[45] William may well have recalled an incident in 1251 when a servant of the abbot of St. Albans appealed Geoffrey of Childwick, who was the brother-in-law of John Mansel, of breach of the peace. When Henry III came to St. Albans, and the abbot saw the "tepidity

[40] These facts about Mara are taken from Cecil A. F. Meekings, "The King's Bench Justices 1239-58" (typescript at PRO, Chancery Lane), pp. 74-76, 111-13, 131-34; for the suggestion about his return to the court *coram rege*, see pp. 112-13.
[41] Trussel was a justice of the bench between 1252 and 1255; for his commissions thereafter see *CPR 1247-48*. He appears as de Montfort's attorney in 1257. His successor, Richard Trussel, died with Simon at Evesham: E/159/30, m. 18d; *Liber feodorum: The Book of Fees, Commonly Called Testa de Nevill (1198-1293)*, 2 vols. in 3 (London, 1920-31), 2:939; *The Victoria History of the County of Warwick* [hereafter cited as *VCH*], ed. L. F. Salzman and P. Styles (London, 1945), 3:60.
[42] *CR 1251-53*, p. 232.
[43] Paris, *Chronica*, 5:213-15; George E. Cokayne, *Complete Peerage of England*, ed. Vicary Gibbs, et al., 12 vols. (London, 1910-59), 9:77; *A Descriptive Catalogue of Ancient Deeds*, 6 vols. (London, 1890-1915), 3:nos. A4804, A5398; 4:nos. 6783, 7124.
[44] C/61/4, m. 5; Treharne and Sanders, *Documents*, pp. 272-73. For a discussion of the retaining of justices under Henry III, see John R. Maddicott, *Law and Lordship: Royal Justices as Retainers in Thirteenth and Fourteenth Century England*, Past and Present Supplement 4 (Oxford, 1978), pp. 4-13.
[45] *Gesta abbatum Sancti Albani*, 1:340.

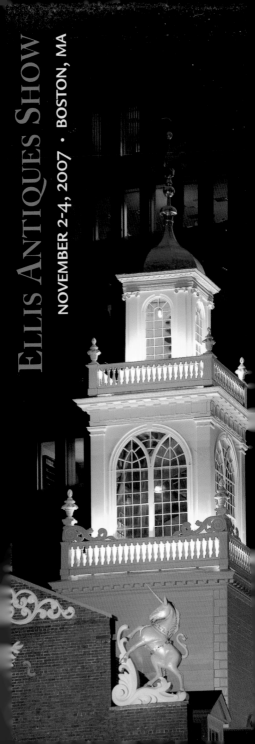

ELLIS ANTIQUES SHOW

NOVEMBER 2-4, 2007 · BOSTON, MA

Ellis Antiques Show

SINCE 1960

A Boston Tradition
NOVEMBER 2-4, 2007

~

GALA PREVIEW PARTY
Thursday, November 1

YOUNG COLLECTORS' EVENING
Friday, November 2

WINE TASTING
Saturday, November 3

SPECIAL BRUNCH AND LECTURE
Sunday, November 4

~

THE CASTLE AT THE BOSTON
PARK PLAZA HOTEL & TOWERS

FOR INFORMATION
WWW.ELLISANTIQUES.COM
OR 617-248-8571

A Benefit for
Ellis Memorial & Eldredge House, Inc.
and
Boston Health Care
for the Homeless Program at
Massachusetts General Hospital

Bookmark Sponsor
Cambridge Trust Company

Photo: Peter Vanderwarker

of justice and the slackness of the king," the appeal was withdrawn. Henry probably appeared equally tepid in other cases brought against aliens, *curiales*, and magnates. Like many later monarchs, he "would not offend his great men to secure impartial justice."[46]

3

The magnates, therefore, during Henry's personal rule were not threatened by absolutist theories. To some extent they profited from the king's arbitrary practice in impeding justice. They also had little reason to complain of a challenge to their liberties. It is true that Henry frequently spoke of maintaining the rights of the crown.[47] A vigorous effort to defend or recover these rights could have had serious implications for the liberties which many magnates claimed in the sphere of local government: for their right, for example, to hold the view of frankpledge, or to possess the franchise of return of writs and exclude the sheriff from their manors and hundreds.[48] A comparison between lay and ecclesiastical schedules of complaint in 1257–58, however, strongly suggests that Henry III's challenge to liberties was confined to those claimed chiefly by ecclesiastics. The Petition of the Barons of 1258 contains no indication that lay magnates felt their liberties to be under threat. On the other hand, the grievances of the church, drawn up in May 1257, state that the king's judges refused to allow liberties founded on ancient custom and insisted that charters make "express mention" of the rights which were claimed.[49] The explanation for this discrepancy is that the liberty most under pressure between 1234 and 1258 was the right to receive the amercements imposed by the king's judges on the liberty-holders' own men. This was a right to which many religious houses believed they were entitled. It was, by contrast, one associated with very few lay magnates. Until 1233–34, religious houses were allowed their amercements automatically when they produced at the exchequer the royal charters by which they claimed such amercements. In 1233–34 this practice was changed by a ruling of the king and council which laid down that no allowance of amercements was to be made without the specific sanction of the king. In the ensuing years this sanction was made dependent on the

[46] Paris, *Chronica*, 5:234; *Gesta abbatum Sancti Albani*, 1:316–17. The quotation is from Charles Ross on Edward IV — Charles Ross, "The Reign of Edward IV," in *Fifteenth Century England*, ed. Stanley B. Chrimes, Charles D. Ross, and Ralph A. Griffiths (Manchester, 1972), p. 62 — quoted by Maddicott, *Law and Lordship*, p. 82.
[47] For example, *Roberti Grosseteste Epistolae*, ed. Henry R. Luard, Rolls Series 25 (London, 1861), p. 338; *Foedera*, 1/1:290.
[48] For a brief summary of local government liberties, see Donald W. Sutherland, *Quo Warranto Proceedings in the Reign of Edward I* (Oxford, 1963), pp. 2–4.
[49] Treharne and Sanders, *Documents*, pp. 76–91; Paris, *Chronica*, 6:364–65; *Annales monastici*, 1:420–21. In 1251 Paris noted the "improper" insistence on "express mention": Paris, *Chronica*, 5:210–11.

"express mention" of a grant of amercements in a royal charter.[50] Since many religious houses based their title on vague, general clauses in their charters, by the early 1240s over thirty of them, together with some bishops and cathedral chapters, found their rights in question at the exchequer, and this continued to be the case down to 1258.[51] The complaints in the clerical schedule of 1257 are thus understandable; but the few magnates who had some claim to amercements seem to have been protected by the king from the rigours of the "express mention" rule.[52]

On the occasions when Henry III attempted a more general check on liberties his efforts probably placed very little pressure on his magnates. In a writ of 1244 and in the speech at the exchequer in 1250, Henry ordered the sheriffs to preserve the liberties, or rights, of the crown, and specified that they were to allow no one to hold the plea of replevin (1244), the view of frankpledge, the sheriff's tourn, or the franchise of return of writs or to take the sheriff's aid (1250) without warrant.[53] As we will see later, there are

---

[50] *Roll and Writ File of the Berkshire Eyre 1248*, ed. Michael T. Clanchy, Selden Society Publications 90 (London, 1972-73), introduction, pp. xxxv-xxxix; Sutherland, *Quo Warranto*, pp. 120-21, 205-7. The claim to amercements was usually linked to that for chattels of felons.

[51] Religious houses were able to get orders to sheriffs to respite collection of the disputed amercements, and these respites were recorded on the memoranda rolls of the exchequer; hence one can see the number of houses affected. In the 1240s and 1250s the houses receiving respites were grouped together in the memoranda rolls, eventually under the heading "common respite": for example, E/368/14, mm. 3, 3d, 9d, 20; E/368/15, m. 3; E/368/20, mm. 6d, 10. When the abbot of Bury St. Edmunds in 1255 told the king of a case concerning his liberties which "for a long time have been in demand at the exchequer because of their insufficient expression" (*minorem expressionem*), he was referring to the challenge to his title to amercements. When Merton Priory and Bec Abbey obtained new charters from the king in 1252-53 which clarified certain liberties in "express words," the first point elucidated was their right to amercements: *CR 1254-56*, p. 83; C/60/51, m. 9; E/368/29, m. 3; E/368/26, m. 9d; *CChR 1226-57*, pp. 381-82, 431. For references to "express mention" and judgements apparently depending on it recorded on the memoranda rolls from the late 1230s, see E/159/16, m. 5; E/368/13, m. 1d; E/368/27, mm. 1, 1d. See also *Select Cases in the Exchequer of Pleas*, ed. Hilary Jenkinson and Beryl E. R. Fermoy, Selden Society Publications 48 (London, 1931), no. 33; E/368/14, m. 4. However, it is probable that many cases were adjourned from term to term over a long period of time. This is one reason why the number of houses receiving the "common respite" remains so high. Another is that when the king allowed a house the amercements arising from, for example, a particular eyre, it did not clear the way for the future since the house would require a fresh sanction from the king for the next group of amercements to which it felt entitled; see Clanchy, *Berkshire Eyre*, introduction, pp. xxxvii-xxxix (compare *CR 1251-53*, pp. 424-25, 279-81). Even houses with new charters reappear receiving the common respite; see *CR 1256-59*, p. 427, *CChR 1226-57*, p. 382. For favoured ecclesiastics and ecclesiastical institutions, the king sometimes waived the "express mention" rule, instructing the exchequer to allow them their amercements "as before accustomed": *CR 1237-42*, pp. 157, 194, 304, 404, 448; *1247-51*, p. 128; *1251-53*, p. 275; *1254-56*, p. 79 (see *CChR 1226-57*, p. 129); E/368/20, m. 9; and see *CR 1251-53*, pp. 424-25, 279-81.

[52] See below, n. 141. The conflict over the liberty of amercements was ended by a concession of Edward I in 1290 which restored the position to what it had been before 1234; Sutherland, *Quo Warranto*, pp. 205-7.

[53] *CR 1242-47*, p. 242; Clanchy, "Henry III," pp. 215-16

good reasons for thinking these orders had a limited effect.[54] In 1255 Henry set up a county-by-county inquiry into those who had encroached on the rights of the king and assumed liberties without warrant. However, this inquiry had the power only to record, not to challenge, the usurpations which it uncovered. Nothing was done in response to its returns.[55] Under Edward I the vehicle used to challenge the liberties of magnates was the eyre. This was not the case under Henry III.[56] Admittedly, some new questions on the usurpation of liberties were put to the juries of presentment which appeared before the justices. For example, from 1239 they were to say who had withdrawn suit from the county and hundred courts without the king's assent.[57] Occasionally judges seem to have taken direct action in response to the replies of the juries. Some of those accused of usurping liberties in the counties visited by Henry of Bath in 1248–49 were placed "in mercy," and, if they had withdrawn suits, the sheriffs were ordered to distrain them to perform them.[58] But the justices were uncertain of the king's support in taking firm measures. In 1251–52, when they ordered Robert de Stuteville's gallows at Alton in Yorkshire to be pulled down, the king promptly set up an inquiry which found that they had acted "less than justly," and the gallows were restored.[59] Not suprisingly, therefore, the justices usually avoided measures which might be disowned. On the 1257 Norfolk eyre they periodically ordered the sheriff to produce usurpers before them in order to show warrant for their encroachments; but of over fifty people summoned, only one is recorded as turning up.[60] The commonest reaction of the judges in the eyres of the late 1240s and 1250s was to minute, against the juries' statements of usurpations, *loquendum* — "discuss": discuss, that is, with the king. The results of such discussions are unknown; probably there were few.[61] The contrast between the *loquenda* of the eyres of

---

[54] See below, pp. 102–5.

[55] *Annales monastici*, 1:337; Treharne and Sanders, *Documents*, p. 163; *Rotuli hundredorum*, 2 vols. (London, 1812–18), 1:20–34; 2:38–48, 55–86, 114–16, 230–42 (some of the 1255 returns).

[56] For a different view, see Maddicott, *Law and Lordship*, p. 9.

[57] Meekings, *Crown Pleas*, pp. 31–32; Cam, *Studies in the Hundred Rolls*, pp. 20–25. In 1246 a question was added on the plea of replevin.

[58] Just/1/232, m. 10 (Essex); Just/1/776, mm. 24d, 25, 26d, 29 (Hants.); Meekings, *Crown Pleas*, nos. 306, 429. Occasionally presentments of usurpations were annotated "to judgement": for example, Harding, *Shropshire Eyre*, no. 647.

[59] *CR 1251–53*, p. 169.

[60] Just/1/568, mm. 17d, 20d, 23d, 24d, 30, 32, 34, and see 29d. The number of those summoned was as high as it was because sometimes the tenants whose suits were withdrawn by their lords were named and summoned individually. One abbot, without being summoned, appeared and admitted he should make a payment to the sheriff. On several other eyres ecclesiastics came before the judges and offered some warrant, but there is never any pleading: for example Just/1/274, m. 12d.

[61] *Loquenda* are found on the following rolls: Just/1/nos. 952 (Warws., 1247), 56 (Bucks., 1247), 232 (Essex, 1248), 274 (Gloucs., 1248), 564 (Norfolk, 1250), 615 (Northants., 1253), 233 (Essex, 1254), 320 (Herts., 1255), 872 (Surrey, 1255), 361 (Kent, 1255), 778 (Hants., 1256), 568

Henry III and the massive number and length of the *quo warranto* cases in
the eyres of his son sums up the difference between the two reigns. Although the theories behind Edward I's *quo warranto* proceedings were present
under Henry III, Henry never anticipated the methods of his son by using
those theories in a sustained campaign to get the magnates to show warrant
for their liberties.[62]

4

King Henry III, then, did comparatively little to challenge the liberties of
his magnates. Indeed, on occasion he acted to protect or increase them.[63] He
also took a tolerant line towards their debts. In attempting to get these paid,
he failed to display the vigour and ruthlessness either of his father, John, or
of his son, Edward. Although Henry was often short of money, some of the
chief sources of revenue to which he turned — increments above the county
farm, the proceeds of vacant abbeys and bishoprics — could be exploited
without affecting lay magnates.[64] The latter, nonetheless, frequently owed

---

(Norfolk, 1257), 1109 (Yorks., 1257); and Clanchy, *Berkshire Eyre* (1248). See, for example,
Barbara English, *The Lords of Holderness, 1086–1260* (Oxford, 1979), p. 108.

[62] For Edward's proceedings, see Sutherland, *Quo Warranto*. They were not in the end
successful in resuming franchises on any considerable scale, but at least they "served the
purpose of establishing royal authority over the exercise of franchisal justice, emphasizing the
power of the crown": Michael Prestwich, *War, Politics and Finance under Edward I* (London,
1972), pp. 227, 225–27. Under Henry III there are some *quo warranto* cases on the *coram rege*
rolls of the 1240s and 1250s, but these rarely involve the liberties of great men. The only
initiatives connected with the franchise of return of writs in the period 1234–58 were in Henry's
speech at the exchequer in 1250 and in the inquiry of 1255. Any pressure on the franchise
seems to have been confined to its possession by boroughs: Clanchy, "Returns of Writs," pp.
64–69. It has been argued that in the 1240s and 1250s Henry III followed an assertive policy
which called into question the liberties of the Welsh marcher barons: Robert R. Davies, "Kings,
Lords and Liberties in the March of Wales, 1066–1272," *Transactions of the Royal Historical
Society*, 5th ser., 29 (1979), 56–60; Margaret Howell, "Regalian Right in Wales and the March,"
Welsh History Review, 7 (1975), 269–88. This thesis needs considerable qualification. For example, after 1243 the king appears to have dropped the case in which he was attempting to get the
earl of Gloucester to show what right he had to the custody of the temporalities of the see of
Llandaff during vacancies. In the vacancy of 1256 the custody of the temporalities by the earls
of Gloucester and Norfolk was probably quietly accepted by the crown: Howell, "Regalian Right
in Wales," pp. 286–87; Michael R. Altschul, *A Baronial Family in Medieval England: The Clares*
(Baltimore, 1965), pp. 273–75. In the Richard Siward case in 1247 the king and his council
accepted the earl of Gloucester's statement of his liberty and his suggestion as to the correct
procedure. Siward's appeal to the king availed him nothing: Davies, "Kings, Lords and Liberties," pp. 57–58; *Cartae et alia munimenta quae ad dominium de Glamorgancia pertinent*, ed. George
T. Clark (Cardiff, 1910), pp. 548–49; Altschul, *The Clares*, pp. 70–75.

[63] See below, pp. 103–4.

[64] For increments, see David A. Carpenter, "The Decline of the Curial Sheriff in England,
1194–1258," below pp. 171–73; for vacancies, see Margaret Howell, *Regalian Right in Medieval
England* (London, 1962), ch. 4; Treharne and Sanders, *Documents*, pp. 268–71.

large sums to the crown. These stemmed from a variety of sources: from judicial and forest amercements, from arrears of the feudal aids of 1245 and 1253, from proffers for concessions, from debts inherited from ancestors.[65] In addition, after 1248 the heirs of the Marshal earls of Pembroke, who included many of the greatest barons, together owed the king £400 annually for the money Henry was paying on their behalf to the countess of Leicester.[66] One of the problems in getting these debts paid lay in the relative weakness of the sheriffs. The memoranda rolls of the exchequer show how difficult they found it to distrain magnates effectively for their debts. As in the case of liberties, however, the king rarely countenanced the resort to stern measures.

To illustrate Henry III's approach to the debts of leading magnates, attention will be focused on the eleven laymen chosen in 1258 by the earls and barons to help draw up the plans of reform.[67] These men were at the forefront of the events of 1258, and their treatment by the king is thus especially significant. The most important members of the group were the four earls: Roger Bigod of Norfolk, Simon de Montfort of Leicester, Humphrey de Bohun of Hereford and Essex, and Richard de Clare of Gloucester and Hertford. Roger Bigod was the only member of the eleven against whose debts the king clearly attempted to take severe action. Yet that action, involving the king in personally arranging distraints for the debts after a quarrel in 1255, lasted for less than a month.[68] For most of the time Henry treated the earl with considerable leniency. Bigod maintained that he should answer for aids and scutages on only sixty fees. Between the earl's return from the Poitevin campaign of 1242–43 and his departure on the Gascon expedition of 1253, the exchequer regularly attempted to distrain him for money owed above these sixty fees from the scutage of 1230 and the aid of 1245, but it was constantly impeded by orders from the king giving Roger respites.[69] By 1256 Bigod had paid nothing above the sixty fees and consequently owed £217 16s 8d from the scutage of 1230, £102 15s from the aid

[65] For these aids, see Sidney K. Mitchell, *Studies in Taxation under John and Henry III* (New Haven, 1914), pp. 241, 254.
[66] This payment was to compensate the countess for not having received her full dower from the lands of her first husband, William Marshal earl of Pembroke.
[67] Treharne and Sanders, *Documents*, pp. 100–101. The one ecclesiastic who made up the twelve chosen by the earls and barons was the bishop of Worcester. The following section on debts is made in places necessarily tentative by the patchy survival of receipt rolls (E/401) from the 1240s and 1250s, and by the fact that payments were sometimes recorded in the pipe rolls (E/372) only years after they had been made.
[68] For this episode, see Paris, *Chronica*, 5:530; *CR 1254–56*, p. 238.
[69] C/60/41, mm. 9, 7; C/60/42, m. 6; C/60/43, m. 20; E/368/18, m. 10; C/60/43, m. 13; E/368/20, m. 14; C/60/45, m. 8; C/60/46, mm. 5, 1; E/368/23, m. 18d; *CR 1247–51*, p. 514; E/368/26, m. 16; C/60/50, m. 5; *CR 1253–54*, p. 196. The exchequer made such minutes as "he has respite till Hilary; afterwards distrain" (Michaelmas 1245), but when Hilary arrived it was not long before another order came from the king giving a further respite.

of 1245, and £235 16s 8d from the aid of 1253.[70] In the same year the earl owed the king a further 640 marks, as his share of the money which the king was paying to the countess of Leicester on behalf of the Marshal heirs. Since 1248 the earl had made no contributions towards the annual 80 marks which he owed the king on this score.[71] In February 1256 the king decided that Roger should pay off his debts at 200 marks annually;[72] in addition he was now to keep up to date with his 80-mark annual payment. All Bigod managed before 1258, however, was one 100-mark payment at Michaelmas 1256, while another 100 marks was pardoned by the king in return for a sum which the earl was owed by Aymer de Lusignan, bishop-elect of Winchester. Thus in January 1258 the exchequer, taking as yet no account of the 100-mark pardon, calculated that Bigod was 460 marks in arrears for payments he should have made in the years 1256 and 1257, and it ordered the sheriff of Norfolk to raise this sum by 3 February "as he loves himself and his possessions."[73] But the king soon intervened, and, in return for one payment of 150 marks, he informed the exchequer, on 10 March, that although the earl had not kept the terms of the agreement to pay 200 marks annually, he could nonetheless recover those terms, beginning his payments at Michaelmas 1258.[74] Instead of the 700 marks which had been due from Bigod in the two and a half years down to Easter 1258, Roger had cleared only 350 marks (£233 6s 8d).[75] Even if all this money was intended to reduce the arrears of Bigod's scutages and aids above the sixty fees (which is unlikely),[76] it contrasts starkly with the £893 which King John extracted from

---

[70] E/372/100, mm. 23, 24.

[71] E/159/34, m. 1; E/368/48, m. 27. Compare the earl of Gloucester, who also owed 80 marks annually and did much better in keeping his payments up to date: E/372/100, m. 9d; E/401/21, 23, 25, 28, 33.

[72] C/60/53, m. 18. The annual 200 marks were to pay Bigod's "clear" debts, that is, debts formally judged by the exchequer to be owed to the king. In November 1255 it had been arranged for Bigod's clear debts to be decided at the exchequer that December (*CR 1254–56*, p. 238). Unfortunately, there is no record of the decision, but it is probable that arrears of the scutages and aids and of contributions for the countess of Leicester were among the debts judged as clear: see *CR 1254–56*, pp. 426–27; E/368/31, m. 25.

[73] E/159/31, m. 8. For the basis of this calculation, and Bigod's payments, see below, n. 75.

[74] C/60/55, m. 8; *CPR 1247–58*, p. 620; E/372/127, m. 36. The 150 marks were given to a merchant to whom the king owed money.

[75] The annual payments of 200 marks and 80 marks were to be made in biannual instalments of 100 marks and 40 marks at Easter and Michaelmas. Thus, beginning at Easter 1256, by Michaelmas 1257 Bigod should have cleared 560 marks and by Easter 1258, 700 marks. For the payments of 100 marks and 150 marks and the pardon of 100 marks see E/401/28; *Calendar of the Liberate Rolls 1226–1272* [hereafter cited as *CLR*], 6 vols. (London, 1916–64), *1251–60*, p. 292; *CPR 1247–58*, p. 620. A full series of receipt rolls survives between Michaelmas 1256 and Easter 1258. The exchequer, in its calculation in January 1258, may have taken no account of Bigod's pardon because his debts had not yet been formally audited.

[76] Since Bigod's payments and pardon are not recorded in the pipe rolls until 1282–83, when the earl's debts from the time of Henry III had been amalgamated with others from the reign of Edward I, it is impossible to know what debts the 350 marks were intended to clear. However,

Bigod's grandfather between 1210 and 1212 to have a life respite of his arrears of scutages (totalling £179) and to answer henceforth for only sixty fees in his lifetime.[77] Edward I, too, was more successful than his father in getting money from the Bigods. Under Edward, Roger Bigod earl of Norfolk, nephew of the earl of the 1250s, was made to answer for nearly all the sums which had built up under Henry III. In 1275 Edward lost patience and forced him to surrender four manors until £300 had been raised from them as a contribution to these and other debts.[78] Later payments recorded in the pipe rolls were £120 (1283–84) and £860 (1295–96).[79] It is hardly surprising that the earl was one of the leaders of the opposition to the king in 1297.[80]

Henry III was equally tolerant towards the debts of the three other earls in the group. Between 1243–44 and 1257–58 only one substantial payment by Simon de Montfort is recorded on either the pipe or receipt rolls: £111 13s 4d at Michaelmas 1257, of which all but £6 repaid loans which had been made to him by the king. Meanwhile, on the pretext that he should answer for his half of the honour of Leicester at only one fee, Simon was allowed to leave the aids of 1245 and 1253 unpaid.[81] Humphrey de Bohun earl of Hereford had inherited large debts from his mother, who was the heiress of the Mandeville earls of Essex. In 1236–37 these were attermed by the king at £100 annually, and in 1239 at £50 annually; three years later the king decided that they should be set off against the £40 10s 10d which the king owed the earl each year for the third penny of the county of Essex.[82] In 1250 the various other Bohun debts amounted to £986 11s 6d. This sum included a forest amercement of £66 13s 4d; a £100-profit from the county of Kent, where Humphrey had been sheriff in 1239–41; and many debts which the earl had inherited from his ancestors. Between 1246 and 1250 the exchequer ordered Humphrey to be distrained for some of these items, but any concerted policy was prevented by a series of writs from the king giving respites.[83] Then, in April 1250, Henry decided that the debt should be paid off at 200 marks annually (£133 6s 8d), only to reduce the rate to an annual 100 marks in May 1253, and an annual 50 marks in that October. The earl's

---

since in March 1258 Henry did not say that Bigod was in arrears with his 80-mark annual payment, it may be that this had first call on the 350 marks. The 1282–83 account (E/372/127, m. 36) confirms that nothing came of the arrangements mentioned in *CR 1254–56*, pp. 426–27.

[77] *Pipe Roll 13 John*, p. 2; *14 John*, pp. 179, 172–73.

[78] E/372/127, m. 36; E/159/67, m. 19. However, only £142 16s 8d (from old fees) of the £217 16s 8d owed from the Poitevin scutage of 1230 were judged as "clear."

[79] E/372/128, m. 4d; E/372/141, m. 32d; E/368/48, m. 27.

[80] Prestwich, *War*, pp. 237, 248–52.

[81] E/401/33; E/372/101, m. 23d; E/372/103, mm. 3, 4; *CPR 1247–58*, p. 609; E/159/30, m. 19; Charles Bémont, *Simon de Montfort* (Paris, 1884), p. 335; Ivor J. Sanders, *English Baronies* (Oxford, 1960), p. 61.

[82] E/372/81, m. 7d; C/60/36, m. 9; E/368/21, m. 10d.

[83] E/372/94, m. 29; C/60/47, m. 10; E/368/19, mm. 11d, 6d; E/368/20, mm. 2, 6, 8, 13d, 15d; E/368/21, mm. 1, 10d, 3, 8d; *CR 1247–51*, pp. 49, 135; C/60/46, mm. 12, 5; E/368/23, m. 16; C/60/47, m. 13.

son and heir was to be allowed to continue repayments of 50 marks annually when he succeeded his father.[84] Had Humphrey kept these terms he would have cleared around £580 of his debt between 1250 and Easter 1258. In fact the most he cleared was £352 13s 4d, and it is likely that some of this money was paid between 1258 and 1271.[85] No contributions at all are recorded in the full series of receipt rolls surviving between Michaelmas 1256 and Easter 1258. The king treated the earl of Gloucester's debts with similar consideration. For at least six years he was allowed to leave unpaid £346 of arrears from the aid of 1245. The exchequer on several occasions attempted to distrain him for this money, but was held back by orders from the king.[86] Henry also pardoned the earl forest amercements of £100 (1250) and £10 (1256), plus amercements of 20 marks and 50 marks incurred respectively before the justices in eyre in Suffolk and the judges *coram rege*.[87]

The remaining seven lay reformers encountered few problems as a result of their financial relations with the crown. Peter de Montfort and Hugh Despencer owed little money at the exchequer. High Bigod successfully liquidated large debts arising from favours purchased from the king.[88] Richard de Grey's clearance of his debts as custodian of the Channel Islands (1252–54) was helped by having his annual fee, and that of his brother John, deducted from the money owed.[89] When the exchequer attempted to distrain Roger Mortimore for a 100-mark forest amercement imposed on his father, the king quickly pardoned the whole sum.[90] William Bardolph inherited large debts from his mother, the heiress of the Warennes of Wormegay; in 1246–47 these stood at £1,076. However, as in the case of the earl of

[84] C/60/47, m. 10; C/60/50, m. 9; *CR 1253–54*, pp. 179–80; *CPR 1247–58*, p. 245.

[85] Humphrey's debts were not audited until the pipe roll of 1270–71, where the payment of £352 13s 4d was recorded in seven tallies: E/372/115, m. 14d; E/401/21; E/368/31, m. 22d. In the pipe rolls the total debt is put at £928 14s.

[86] E/372/95, m. 17d; C/60/42, m. 6; C/60/43, mm. 19, 17, 13, 5; E/368/19, m. 9d; C/60/44, mm. 10, 7; E/368/20, mm. 2, 12; C/60/45, m. 12; C/60/46, m. 12; E/368/21, m. 13; E/368/23, mm. 17d, 18d; C/60/47, mm. 13, 5; C/60/48, m. 3; E/368/24, m. 14; E/368/26, m. 14d.

[87] C/60/47, m. 1; C/60/53, m. 19. The earl's clearance of his debts, as in the case of the earl of Hereford, was helped by their being set off against money owed him by the king, notably the annual £20 for the third penny of the county of Gloucester and an annual £40 19s 5d connected with Bristol. By 1260 the earl may have owed no more than £40 to the king: E/372/89, m. 8d; E/372/90, m. 14d; E/372/91, m. 23d; E/372/99, m. 34d; E/372/100, m. 9d; E/372/104, m. 30d; Altschul, *The Clares*, pp. 27–28.

[88] Between 1242 and 1254 Hugh cleared a £6,000 fine of his wife to have custody of the lands and marriage of the heirs of her first husband, Hugh Wake. Between 1254 and 1259 he cleared a fine of his own of £333 6s 8d for a grant to him and his heirs of the forest of Forendale: *Excerpta e rotulis finium* [hereafter cited as *ERF*], ed. Charles Roberts, 2 vols. (London, 1835–36), 1:364; E/352/47, r. 14; E/401/19; E/372/102, m. 39; E/372/103, m. 33d; E/372/95, m. 32d.

[89] E/372/98, m. 2d; E/372/99, m. 33d; E/401/30.

[90] E/372/100, mm. 15, 20d; E/368/30, m. 18. Between 1246–47 and 1249–50 Roger cleared a 2,000-mark fine for seisin of his lands before coming of age. By 1256, as one of the Marshal heirs he owed the king £142 4s 8d, but he did little before 1258 to reduce this debt: E/372/91, m. 10d; E/372/94, m. 27; E/401/30; E/368/32, m. 10d.

Hereford, the king allowed this debt to be paid off at increasingly easy rates: 50 marks annually in 1245; 20 marks annually in 1246–47; and finally 15 marks annually in 1254.[91] In 1242 John fitz Geoffrey's debts totalled £668 3s 2d, of which a large part derived from his arrears as sheriff of Yorkshire and Gloucestershire. The king then pardoned him £166 13s 4d and allowed him to pay off the remainder at £10 annually. When the barons of the exchequer objected to treating John's shrieval arrears in this lenient way, the king, in an angry letter, expressed astonishment at the difficulties they were making in executing his orders "for those serving us most laudably."[92]

King Henry's treatment of the eleven lay reformers was characteristic of his financial relations with his magnates. A study of a second group, the twelve men elected by the earls and barons in 1258 to represent them at the three annual parliaments, yields a similar pattern.[93] In this second group were individuals who had incurred large fines for transgressions or heavy judicial or forest amercements. But the burden of such penalties was often alleviated by the king. In general, the number of magnates whom the king pressured to pay their debts was small.

5

King Henry, therefore, did not challenge the liberties of his magnates, nor did he oppress many of them financially. Similarly, it was not part of his policy to surround himself with foreign relatives and low-born officials to the exclusion of English nobles. It is true that in the 1240s and 1250s the first place at court was often enjoyed by the queen's Savoyard uncles and the king's Lusignan half-brothers.[94] However, there was hostility between these two groups, and they never formed an exclusive party of alien *curiales*. It is probable that the queen welcomed the changes of 1258 in that they rid England of the Lusignans, and her uncle, Peter of Savoy, was one of the seven magnates whose confederation in April 1258 was the first step in

---

[91] C/60/42, m. 12; E/372/91, m. 6; E/368/30, m. 1.

[92] *Pipe Roll 1242*, p. 115; E/372/81, m. 10d; *CR 1237–42*, p. 516. The letter was subsequently toned down. Between 1251 and 1259 John cleared a £2,000 fine for the custody of the lands and marriage of the heirs of Theobald Butler: C/60/48, m. 4; E/372/105, m. 12d.

[93] For this group, Treharne and Sanders, *Documents*, pp. 104–5.

[94] Henry's patronage of these relations is in part explained by his continental ambitions. The role of the Savoyards in these is suggested by Clanchy, *England and Its Rulers*, pp. 232–35; see also Cox, *Eagles of Savoy*, pp. 47, 61–62, 112–20, 149, 151–52, 161–62, 241–43. As for the Lusignans, even after the disasters of 1242 the house retained significant power in Poitou. By binding the family to him Henry probably hoped to shore up the northern frontiers of Gascony. Thus the brothers were first invited to England in 1247 when there were rumours of a French move on Gascony: Paris, *Chronica*, 4:594, 627–28. For the possessions left the half-brothers by their parents, see *Layettes du trésor des chartes*, ed. Alexandre Teulet (Paris, 1866), 2:no. 3049. Within England, Henry wished to establish close family whom he loved and trusted, but this was not part of a policy to distance himself from his native barons. In the event, the Savoyards were settled in England with success. The Lusignans were not.

bringing about the revolution.[95] Alongside this foreign element there were many native magnates at Henry's court and on his council. Despite occasional tiffs, the king's leading councillor was often his brother, Richard earl of Cornwall.[96] After 1254 a central position at court was taken by Richard de Clare earl of Gloucester.[97]

In 1258 itself the twelve men chosen by the king to help draw up the plans of reform included three English magnates, all of whom were councillors: John de Warenne earl of Surrey, Henry son of Richard earl of Cornwall, and Fulk Basset, bishop of London, who was head of the Basset family of High Wycombe.[98] Although he eventually accepted nomination to the baronial panel instead, Henry also chose the earl of Gloucester.[99] Admittedly, Henry's other nominees in 1258 were three of his Lusignan half-brothers; the Poitevin John de Plescy, earl of Warwick *iure uxoris*; and five clerks and ecclesiastics.[100] But as a picture of Henry's court before the revolution the king's twelve are misleading .What happened in 1258 was that one group of courtiers, composed of English magnates, Simon de Montfort, and the Savoyards, turned on another group headed by the Lusignans. As a result, the king was left with a restricted number of *curiales* from which to choose his panel of reformers, while, conversely, the leaders of the opposition included many who were prominent at court. Thus, of the twelve reformers chosen by the earls and barons in 1258 — the eleven laymen whose debts were examined above, and one ecclesiastic — seven were *curiales*, namely the earls of Gloucester and Leicester, Hugh Bigod, John fitz Geoffrey, Peter de Montfort, Richard de Grey, and Walter de Cantilupe, bishop of Worcester.[101] The earls of Gloucester and Leicester, Hugh Bigod, the bishop of Worcester, and probably John fitz Geoffrey and Peter de Montfort were on the king's

[95] *Annales monastici*, 2:355; Bémont, *Simon de Montfort*, p. 327; Powicke, *The Thirteenth Century*, pp. 130–35. See Paris, *Chronica*, 5:348–54, 703; *CR 1259–61*, p. 265; *1256–59*, p. 276.

[96] For example, *CR 1254–56*, pp. 103, 113, 158, 211, 372, 389; *Annales monastici*, 4:118.

[97] *CPR 1247–58*, pp. 421, 423, 480, 500, 619; *Chronica maiorum et vicecomitum*, p. 33.

[98] Treharne and Sanders, *Documents*, pp. 74–75, 100–101.

[99] Clare is specifically stated to be among the king's representatives in a writ of 22 June 1258, *CPR 1247–58*, p. 637. However, in the draft of the Provisions of Oxford he appears amongst the baronial twelve, while the king's panel has only eleven names. The implication is that the earl deserted the king's twelve and was not replaced: Treharne and Sanders, *Documents*, pp. 100–101. It is indicative of Treharne's stereotyped picture of the division between an alien court and the baronage that he presumed, without any evidence, that Boniface of Savoy was the king's twelfth nominee, and rejected as an error the evidence relating to the earl of Gloucester: Treharne, *Baronial Plan*, p. 67, n. 5.

[100] Treharne and Sanders, *Documents*, pp. 74–75, 100–101.

[101] For the careers of these men see the chancery rolls passim. The earls of Gloucester and Leicester, Hugh Bigod, John fitz Geoffrey, and Peter de Montfort, together with Peter of Savoy, all *curiales*, were among the seven original confederate barons. The seventh baron was the earl of Norfolk: Bémont, *Simon de Montfort*, p. 327. Walter de Cantilupe, bishop of Worcester, was himself the member of a great baronial house; for him see David A. Carpenter, "St Thomas Cantilupe: His Political Career," below pp. 296–9.

council in the year and a half before April 1258. In the same period Richard de Grey's younger brother, William, was a steward of the royal household.[102] The king had granted nearly all these curial magnates such favours as money fees, wardships, and escheats.[103] Nor were the remainder of the twelve reformers remote from the court. The earl of Norfolk's brother was Hugh Bigod, and his brother-in-law was John fitz Geoffrey. Both Norfolk and the earl of Hereford made frequent appearances at court before 1258 and received a stream of gifts of game and timber from the king.[104]

Many baronial families were also connected with the court through marriages into the houses of Lusignan and Savoy. Warin de Monte Canisio's daughter married the king's Lusignan half-brother, William de Valence. John de Warenne, earl of Surrey, married Valence's sister. The heirs to the earldoms of Gloucester and Derby, Gilbert de Clare and Robert de Ferrers, married the king's Lusignan nieces, Alice and Mary. Meanwhile, the young earl of Lincoln, who died in 1258, and the northern baron John de Vesci were married to two of the queen's second cousins, daughters of Beatrice of Savoy and the marquis of Saluzzo, and the future earl of Devon was joined to the queen's first cousin, the daughter of Thomas of Savoy, sometime count of Flanders.[105] King Henry's purpose in arranging these unions was partly to do the best he could for his foreign relatives. But the marriages also reflected his desire to achieve a close and harmonious relationship with his native nobles. At his court Henry wished to bring together both his foreign relatives and his English magnates. This was how Matthew Paris saw matters. In 1255 he noted that the king had drawn foreigners round him, and he added that he had also "successively attracted to him and allied with him nearly all the *optimates* of England, for example the earls of Gloucester, Warenne (Surrey), Lincoln, and Devon and a great many other nobles."[106] Henry was happy to proclaim the closeness of his alliances with noble houses. When, in the 1250s, he gave a splendid sword belt to the count of

---

[102] *Annales monastici*, 1:395; *Cronica maiorum et vicecomitum*, p. 33; *CPR 1247–58*, pp. 563, 619, 458, 576, 607, 324; *CLR 1251–60*, p. 418.

[103] Bémont, *Simon de Montfort*, pp. 335, 338; *CPR 1247–58*, pp. 249, 273, 458, 610; *CChR 1226–57*, pp. 476, 132; *ERF*, 1:436; Altschul, *The Clares*, pp. 102–3; and see above, pp. 92–3 and nn. 88, 92.

[104] In 1257 Bigod attested royal charters on 28 May; 25 July; 14, 16, 18 August; 3, 12, 13–15, 24 September (during the Welsh campaign); 18, 27 October; 1 November. Bohun attested on 2 January; 26 March; 28 May; 24, 26 September; 28 December: C/53/47; C/53/48. For favours, *CR 1254–56*, pp. 98, 120, 126, 294, 297, 343, 349, 352; *1256–59*, pp. 3, 67, 78, 99, 166, 180; *CPR 1247–58*, pp. 465, 557. Both sons of the earl of Hereford, Humphrey and Henry, were granted annual fees during the 1253–54 Gascon campaign, and they remained in favour although the payments may not have been kept up: *CPR 1247–58*, pp. 245, 269, 529, 538; *CLR 1251–60*, pp. 207, 314; *CR 1256–59*, pp. 38, 40, 83. For favours to the other three reformers, William Bardolph, Roger Mortimore, and Hugh Despencer, see *CR 1254–56*, pp. 97, 300, 331, 342; *1256–59*, pp. 83, 92; *CPR 1247–58*, p. 449.

[105] Cokayne, *Peerage*, 9:422, 12/1:507, 5:707, 4:201, 12/2:279, 7:681, 4:320.

[106] Paris, *Chronica*, 5:514.

Champagne, his own arms, as donor, had the place of honour on the tongue; but the belt also displayed the arms of the earls of Cornwall, Gloucester, Surrey, Devon, Derby, and Hereford. Likewise, in the new choir of Westminster Abbey, which Henry rebuilt in honour of Edward the Confessor, Henry set up not merely the arms of the saint and himself, but also those of the earls of England. In the great hall of Dublin castle the king ordered a painting of a "king and queen sitting with their baronage."[107]

6

Henry's immediate aim in attempting to establish a good relationship with his magnates was, of course, to obtain their service and support. When the king intervened in the course of justice or made concessions over debts, he often did so to encourage or reward specific services. It was when the earl of Norfolk was setting out for the king's army in Wales that Henry promised to correct *coram rege* whatever had gone amiss in his case of novel disseisin. The debts of the earl of Hereford and William Bardolf were favourably attermed when the two of them participated in the 1253–54 Gascon campaign. Conversely, the only time that the king acted to collect the debts of Roger Bigod was when he quarreled with the earl in 1255. In the 1250s Henry wanted the support of his magnates above all for his crusade, for the 1253–54 Gascon expedition, and then for the Sicilian project. Whether, beyond that, as Matthew Paris seems to have believed, his aim was to construct a court party which would enable him to deprive the *universitas regni* of its rights may be doubted[108] There is, as has been seen, little evidence that Henry nourished such arbitrary ambitions. Rather, it may be suggested, the king's underlying purpose was altogether more benign: he wished to maintain peace and tranquility in England.

In a proclamation of 1261 Henry considered that the absence of "hostility and general war" was one of the chief achievements of his reign: "for the forty-five years in which we have held the government of our kingdom . . . , with our utmost desire and all our strength we have not ceased to study and labour . . . for the peace and tranquility of one and all." Five years later, Henry declared that "since the time of our youth, when God placed us to rule over the kingdom of England, we have always had it at heart to do with all our might those things which we knew to be conducive to the peace and tranquility of our subjects."[109] Such statements should not be dismissed as mere propaganda, produced by the political crises of 1261 and 1266.

---

[107] Bertha Collin, *The Riddle of a 13th Century Sword Belt*, Heraldry Society (East Knowle, 1955); John P. Neale and Edward W. Brayley, *The History and Antiquities of the Abbey Church of St Peter Westminster* (London, 1818), 2:26–28; *CR 1242–47*, p. 23. The Westminster shields cannot have been put up before 1259, but the heraldic scheme is likely to have been of an earlier date.

[108] Paris, *Chronica*, 5:514.

[109] *Foedera*, 1/1:408–9; *CR 1264–68*, pp. 242–43. The 1261 letter was to all sheriffs; that of 1266 to the sheriff of Yorkshire.

Chroniclers at Tewkesbury and Furness abbeys, as well as at the "house" monastery of Westminster, remembered Henry precisely as one who had desired peace and quiet for his kingdom.[110] Such an objective accorded well with the king's wish for a tranquil life. In contrast to his father's hectic itinerary, Henry lingered at his favourite palaces for weeks, sometimes months, planning building works and giving alms.[111] On several occasions he departed on pilgrimages rather than face political crises. In 1245 he preferred, as Matthew Paris noted, "the accustomed delights and rest" of Westminster to a campaign in Wales.[112] Although Henry had a fierce temper, he also appears as amiable, easy-going, and sympathetic towards petitioners.[113] Most of those with whom he clashed in the 1250s — for example, Simon de Montfort, the earl of Norfolk, and John de Grey — were quickly rehabilitated. Henry in effect pardoned all of John de Grey's fine of 500 marks for marrying without the king's permission.[114]

In his approach to kingship Henry may also have been influenced by the lives of his patron saint and hero, Edward the Confessor. The "official life" and the only one to achieve wide circulation was that by Ailred of Rievaulx. This formed the basis for the biography by Matthew Paris which Henry himself probably commissioned soon after 1236 for presentation to his new queen.[115] Both lives stressed the "glorious peace" of the saint's reign.[116] The

[110] *Chronicles of the Reigns of Stephen, Henry II and Richard I*, ed. Richard Howlett, 4 vols., Rolls Series 82 (London, 1884–89), 2:563; *Flores historiarum*, 3:15, 252. British Library Cotton MS Cleopatra A.VII, fol. 60v, has the Tewkesbury obituary, which was written in 1263; it styles Henry "pacis et quietis doctus reformator." For the obituary see "An Unknown Obituary of King Henry III from the year 1263", below pp. 253–60.

[111] Holt, *King John*, p. 13; "Itinerary of Henry III," ed. Theodore Craib (1923), typescript in PRO Round Room, Chancery Lane; Powicke, *Henry III and the Lord Edward*, pp. 302–3; *History of the King's Works*, ed. Howard M. Colvin (London, 1963), 1:94–95.

[112] *Foedera*, I/1:422; *CR 1251–53*, p. 433; Paris, *Chronica*, 4:385.

[113] This is, for example, the impression of the king one gets from his meetings with Matthew Paris: Paris, *Chronica*, 4:644, 5:129–30, 617–18; see also *Annales monastici*, 2:325–27.

[114] Paris, *Chronica*, 5:242, 282; *Annales monastici*, 3:182–83; E/372/98, m. 7d; *ERF*, 2:119, 167. In 1250 Matthew Paris was suitably impressed by the vast £1,000 fine (not as he thought 1,000 marks) imposed on Walter de Clifford for forcing a messenger to eat the seal of a royal writ. But by 1257–58 Walter had paid only £225 towards his debts (which totalled over £1,340), while the king had pardoned £200 and was allowing the balance to be paid at an annual £20: Paris, *Chronica*, 5:95; E/372/94, m. 25; E/372/100, m. 29; E/372/102, m. 22d; *CR 1256–59*, p. 34.

[115] *The Life of Edward the Confessor*, ed. Frank Barlow (London, 1962), introduction, p. xxxvii; Vaughan, *Matthew Paris*, pp. 173–76. I have accepted Vaughan's attribution of the life to Matthew Paris, but Dr. Nigel Morgan tells me that he has doubts about whether this is correct. The wording of the dedication to the queen suggests that the poem may have been written before the birth of the Lord Edward in 1239: *Lives of Edward the Confessor*, ed. Henry R. Luard, Rolls Series 3 (London, 1858), pp. 26–27, 180–81.

[116] "Glorious peace" is Paris. Ailred says, "since the pacific king reigned for a long time, all things met together within one bond of peace": Luard, *Lives of Edward the Confessor*, pp. 179, 198, 204, 25, 43–44, 50. For Ailred, *Historiae Anglicanae scriptores X*, ed. Roger Twysden (London, 1652), p. 375. For Henry as a *vir pacificus* see *The Chronicle of Walter of Guisborough*, ed. Harry Rothwell, Camden Society 89 (London, 1957), p. 201.

Confessor's peace, moreover, reflected his cordial relationship with his nobles. Ailred, describing how the Confessor brought back the "ancient happiness" to the English, declared that "in Edward the people recovered peace; the nobles glory; the church liberty." Matthew Paris expanded on this passage. Edward "loved his native-born barons and willingly advanced them." Once he ascended the throne,

> Then is the land in good estate,
> Count and baron and the prelate,
> There is none whom the king does not please,
> All are rich and all at ease.[117]

Of course, during his personal rule King Henry did a great deal more to "please" count and baron than he did the people. That was not, as we have seen, because he was unconcerned about the plight of the *minores*. The problem was that effective action to help them was likely to antagonize the magnates, and it was magnates, not *minores*, who could threaten the kingdom's general peace and stability. It was the magnates who needed most immediately to be appeased. The king never felt entirely secure. In 1256 he ordered the scene of "a king rescued by his dogs from sedition plotted against him by his men" to be painted in the wardrobe at Westminster where his head was washed.[118] Henry could not forget the 1215–17 civil war which had nearly deprived him of the throne. The 1261 manifesto precisely contrasted the peace of Henry's reign with the "wars and hostilities" before his time, that is, in the reign of John. The remembrance of the civil war was powerfully reinforced by the turmoil of the years 1233–34 when Henry was led astray by John's former justiciar, Peter des Roches. Once the crisis was over Henry ruefully reflected on what he had suffered from separating himself from "the hearts of our faithful subjects."[119] This political background provided the king with compelling reasons for eschewing arbitrary and aggressive policies like those which had brought his father to disaster.

7

King Henry's policy towards his magnates probably contributed to the internal peace in England between 1234 and 1258. From that point of view it paid dividends. On the other hand, it did not prevent the upheaval of 1258. Although Henry wished to create a harmonious circle at court, he was very much a *vir simplex* and lacked the political skill to achieve the aim. Above all, he failed to get his Lusignan half-brothers accepted in England, partly because of their own behaviour, partly because he was over-indulgent

[117] Luard, *Lives of Edward the Confessor*, pp. 50, 204; Twysden, *Historiae Anglicanae scriptores X.* p. 375.
[118] *CR 1254–56*, p. 326; see D. J. A. Ross, "A Lost Painting in Henry III's Palace at Westminster," *Journal of the Warburg and Courtauld Institutes* 16 (1953), 160.
[119] *Foedera*, 1/1:408; *Treaty Rolls*, 1:no. 15.

towards them. The immediate reasons for the revolution were hatred of the Lusignans and a general feeling, against the background of the Sicilian fiasco, that Henry was "useless and insufficient to dispose of the affairs of the kingdom."[120] The leaders of the opposition, as we have seen, were men close to the king. In that sense, the revolution was very much one within the court of Henry III. It was not engineered by outsiders whom the king had oppressed and excluded. Compared to the assertive kingship of John and Edward I, Henry's personal rule was a time of slack for the magnates. It was in the localities that the consequences were most profound. Here the way was cleared for lords to restore or increase the jurisdiction of their courts, to make inroads into the authority of the sheriff, and, in the case of the most powerful, to exercise their rule in the counties of England. At the heart of this activity were the earls of Gloucester and Cornwall and the king's foreign relatives, William de Valence and Peter of Savoy, the group whom Henry III in 1256, according to Matthew Paris's story, protected from hostile writs. But the movement involved many other magnates, together with bishops, religious houses, and some prominent members of the gentry.

The best-documented facet of these developments was the attempt by lords to force men to attend their courts, both honourial and manorial.[121] The 1264 manifesto, already referred to, alleged that before 1258, certain "aliens, *curiales*, and nobles and their bailiffs, in instances where their tenants from of old had not been accustomed to do any suit of court, unjustly constrained them to do such suits."[122] The weapon to enforce suits, as well as other "undue and uncustomary services" mentioned in the manifesto, was distraint, frequently distraint outside the lord's fee.[123] In December 1259, when the justiciar appointed under the Provisions of Oxford, Hugh Bigod, came to Chelmsford in Essex, he heard cases involving distraint outside their lords' fees by the bailiffs of Philip Basset, Peter of Savoy, and the earl of Gloucester. The earl's bailiffs had been attempting to enforce attendance at the honourial court of Clare; Peter's, at the manorial court of Fressingfield, which claimed the right to hold the sheriff's tourn.[124] The response to the

---

[120] *Annales monastici*, 4:118–19. For the reasons for the king's patronage of his half-brothers, see above, n. 94. I discuss the conflicts in which the Lusignans became involved in "What Happened in 1258?" in *War and Government in the Middle Ages: Essays in Honour of J. O. Prestwich*, ed. John Gillingham and James C. Holt (Woodbridge, Eng., 1984), pp. 106–19, below pp. 190–97.

[121] The manorial courts here were those to which their lords claimed local government liberties were attached. Few records of private courts survive from this period. What follows is based on evidence from statements in manifestos, royal proclamations, and chronicles and from reforming legislation and law cases.

[122] Treharne and Sanders, *Documents*, pp. 274–75.

[123] Treharne and Sanders, *Documents*, pp. 272–73.

[124] Just/1/1189, mm. 2d, 3, 4, 5, 5d, 6, 7. The Clare bailiffs were enforcing attendance at particular cases rather than regular suit at Clare court. For further cases involving suit of court or distraint outside the fee, see Just/1/873, m. 9, and Just/1/953, m. 7 (the defendants in these two cases were Robert Agylun and Peter de Montfort); Jacob, *Studies*, pp. 109, 361–64; Tre-

legislation of 1259, which placed restrictions on suit to the courts of magnates, reveals how widespread were grievances over the issue. Between 1260
and 1263, no fewer than twenty-three actions were brought under the terms
of the legislation. The defendants included the earl of Cornwall, the magnates Hugh de Neville, John fitz Alan, and William de Ros, the *curiales* Adam
of Jesmond and Nicholas of Lewknor, the county knights John de Scalariis
and William Marshal, and the bishop of Bath and Wells, the prior of Ware,
the abbess of Godstow, and the master of the Templars.[125]

This movement by "aliens, *curiales*, and nobles" to strengthen the jurisdiction of their courts had repercussions on the authority of the sheriff. Although the civil war of John's reign must have involved a setback to the
king's local power, some of the ground was probably recovered by the curial
sheriffs in office during Henry's minority and for some years thereafter.
The period of Henry's personal rule, however, saw a series of new or
renewed challenges to the sheriff's position. The king was clearly responding to these when he set up the 1255 inquiry and added new questions on
the usurpation of liberties to the articles of the eyre. The replies to these
questions in county after county tell of English magnates, the king's foreign
relatives, bishops, religious houses, and gentry withdrawing payments from
the sheriffs and suit of their men from the hundred courts. Instead, such
men were presumably subjected to the courts of their lords, where the
business of the hundred was then discharged. In addition, some of the
greatest men, notably the earls of Gloucester, Cornwall, and Leicester, Warin
de Monte Canisio, William de Valence, and Peter of Savoy, together with the
archbishop of Canterbury, the bishops of London and Worcester, the prior
of Merton, and the abbots of Westminster, Battle, Boxley, Netley, and
Reading, were accused of preventing the sheriffs from entering their lands
and liberties to make attachments and distraints.[126] In Essex in 1255, to take
one example, the earl of Cornwall, Peter of Savoy, the bishop of London, the
abbot of Westminster, and Nicholas Butler were presented, each in one
hundred, for preventing distraints. In Dengie hundred John de Grey, Wal-

---

harne, *Baronial Plan*, pp. 169–70. For the court at Clare, see Helen M. Cam, *The Hundred and the
Hundred Rolls* (London, 1930), pp. 207–9; *Court Rolls of the Abbey of Ramsey and the Honor of Clare*,
ed. Warren O. Ault (New Haven, 1928).

[125] Paul A. Brand, "The Contribution of the Period of Baronial Reform (1258–1267) to the
Development of the Common Law in England," Oxford University D. Phil. thesis (1974), pp.
105–9. Dr. Brand has provided me with additional information about these cases and the
defendants.

[126] These statements are based on the eyre rolls mentioned in n. 61 above. The usual form
was for the jurors to describe the encroachment and add that it was made "they do not know by
what warrant." It may be, of course, that some encroachments did have warrant from the king
(see below, p. 103). When describing the withdrawal of suits the jurors do not say what type of
lord's court men were withdrawn to. Large numbers of manorial courts claimed the right to
hold the view of frankpledge. The business of the hundred might also be discharged at great
honourial courts like those of Clare and Eye: see Cam, *Hundred and Hundred Rolls*, pp. 205–13.

ter fitz Robert, master Robert de Cantilupe, and Robert de Stamford were presented for withdrawing suit and sheriff's aid, as in Tendring hundred were Warin de Monte Canisio and John de Bovill. Meanwhile, in Uttlesford hundred, gallows and tumbrels had been erected *de novo* on the authority of the earl of Hereford.[127] Although on some of the eyres usurpations were dated to the king's minority, the great majority took place during his personal rule. This was true of all but one of the nineteen dated usurpations on the 1257 Norfolk eyre.[128] The losses to the sheriffs from such encroachments are most graphically illustrated in a document drawn up by Robert de Totehale, the sheriff of Bedfordshire and Buckinghamshire between 1256 and 1258. He claimed allowance in his farm for "suits, wards, view of frankpledge, and other issues of vills in Bedfordshire and Buckinghamshire of which his predecessors stood in seisin." He then listed twelve vills where "he does not dare to raise" a total of £9 16s 4d "because of the power of the earl of Gloucester." He was prevented from raising a further £9 4s 5d from nine vills "by the power" of William de Valence and of Richard earl of Cornwall, king of the Romans, and his wife Sanchia.[129]

The exaction of new suits and the encroachment on the authority of the sheriff formed part of a wider oppression exercised by the magnates over those below them. The picture of England in 1258 painted by the Waverley Abbey annalist was of a land where the *majores*, rising up against the *minores*, endeavoured to burden them with pleas, amercements, tallages, and exactions.[130] The manifesto of 1264, as we have seen, likewise described a situation where it was difficult to obtain writs to commence legal actions against certain aliens, *curiales*, and, by implication, certain nobles and magnates of the realm. If actions were commenced, *minores* could not obtain justice because the judges were either intimidated by, or *tributarii* of, these great men, who would not in any case permit writs against themselves and their bailiffs to be executed. "And thus," as the manifesto continued, "common justice being trampled underfoot, the stronger denied it to the weaker, without reason, and, making no distinction of tenure, any man who was stronger than his neighbour distrained him at will, and did as he saw fit, whether good or evil."[131] The social group which suffered from the oppressions of the magnates was probably wide. Perhaps the most numerous victims outside the villeinage were small free tenants, but in the eyres of

---

[127] Just/1/233, mm. 45, 50, 52, 53d, 41d. The earl of Hereford is here styled the "lord of the honour of Mandeville."

[128] Just/1/568, m. 1 onwards.

[129] E/101/505/9; see also Just/1/58; for the sheriff, *PRO Lists and Indexes*, 9:1. This document was brought to my notice by Dr. Robert Stacey. It was discovered by Dr. J. R. Maddicott.

[130] *Annales monastici*, 2:350. The special eyres of 1258–60 produced evidence of a wide variety of oppressions and exactions practised by lords and their bailiffs: see Jacob, *Studies*, pp. 55–56, 60–62, 106–16; Treharne, *Baronial Plan*, pp. 113–14, 149–56.

[131] Treharne and Sanders, *Documents*, pp. 272–73. See above, p. 82.

1258–60 complaints were also brought by knights.[132] Certainly the rising tide of complaint came from people of sufficient number and substance for the reforming barons in 1258–59 to take measures in response to it. In the Ordinances of February 1259 the council of fifteen, together with the twelve chosen by the community to represent it at parliament, promised that they would not obstruct the justiciar from hearing complaints against themselves and their officials. They also proclaimed that they would observe Magna Carta in dealings with their tenants and neighbours and agreed that their officials, both in their demesnes and in their liberties, should take the same oath to act justly as the king's sheriffs. In October 1259 the Provisions of Westminster dealt with the questions of suit and distraint. Suits to courts of magnates were limited to those required by charters of enfeoffment and those performed before 1230. At the same time magnates were forbidden to make distraints outside their fees.[133]

One means by which magnates developed their local power in this period was through their increasing use of professional officials. By the 1250s stewards such as William de Bussey, Hervey of Boreham, and Roger de Scaccario were prominent, sometimes notorious figures.[134] Such men gave magnates the ability to strengthen the jurisdiction of their courts and take over functions from the sheriff. Another factor was that during precisely the period of Henry's personal rule a change took place in the type of person who became sheriff. Between 1236 and the late 1240s the sheriffs ceased to be the great *curiales* who had so frequently held local office since the Conquest. They were more often minor royal servants or members of the local gentry.[135] There were persuasive reasons for the change, and in dealing with lesser men the new sheriffs were still formidable officials. But they lacked the financial resources, and the prestige and power derived from attachment to the court, to keep the magnates in check and uphold royal interests against them in the localities. Henry virtually admitted this when, in 1261, struggling to gain control of the country, he reappointed curial sheriffs, or, as he put it, sheriffs "of greater power than before." He explained to the people of the counties that he did so "because they will be able to provide you with justice and defence against the servitude and oppressions which magnates impose on you where sheriffs of lesser stature (*minores*) were

---

[132] Hugh of Coleworth, who was distrained to attend the earl of Gloucester's court at Clare, was a knight; so too was Gilbert of Elsfield, who complained of disseisin by the bailiffs of William de Valence. Both Hugh's grievances and Gilbert's dated from 1256: Just/1/1189, m. 3; Just/1/1188, m. 7; *CPR 1258–66*, p. 488; *VCH Oxon.*, 5:117; *VCH Bucks.*, 4:27–28, 342. Clearly knights and gentry, depending on the circumstances, could be either oppressors or oppressed.

[133] Treharne and Sanders, *Documents*, pp. 132–35, 138–41, 144 no. 11; see Treharne, *Baronial Plan*, pp. 169–70. See now Paul Brand's important article "Lordship and Distraint in Thirteenth-Century England", in his *The Making of the Common Law* (London, 1992), pp. 301–24.

[134] Noël Denholm-Young, *Seignorial Administration in England* (Oxford, 1937); Paris, *Chronica*, 5:737–39, 744; Just/1/1189, mm. 2d., 5, 5d. See also Maddicott, *Law and Lordship*, p. 10.

[135] See below pp. 166–82.

unable to do so." He added that the *tolerancia* of the previous sheriffs had also enabled the magnates to "occupy many things belonging to the king."[136] In 1261 Henry was thinking primarily of the sheriffs who had held office since 1258, but his remarks could have applied equally well to the sheriffs of the 1240s and 1250s. The ability of the latter to execute writs against magnates and their bailiffs, to protect lesser men from injustice, and to uphold the king's rights was limited. As Richard of Limminge, probably a bailiff of the king's half-brother, Guy de Lusignan, told a servant of the sheriff of Huntingdonshire around 1253–54, "he would do no more for the sheriff than he would for [the sheriff's] daughter."[137]

This replacement of the curial sheriff needs to be seen against the background of the king's general policy towards his magnates. Because the king intended to keep the peace through appeasement, he had less need of powerful local officials to control the magnates. He was able, therefore, to reap the very real benefits of non-curial sheriffdoms. Curial sheriffs might well give the king a strong local presence, but they had financial disadvantages. Traditionally, both to sustain themselves in the king's service and to help them maintain their power in their counties, they retained a large part of the revenue which they raised above the county farm. Non-curial sheriffs, on the other hand, were expected to give the king most of their surplus above the farm,[138] which remained substantial even allowing for the encroachments of magnates.[139]

Henry III's general policy, however, did more than permit the supersession of the curial sheriff — it greatly multiplied its consequences. The power of the sheriffs, as of other officials, was weakened by a series of royal concessions which protected or increased the liberties of both foreign relatives and English magnates. It is probable that some of the encroachments presented on the eyres had actually been authorized by the king, although of course this was never put to judicial test. Thus Henry sanctioned Peter of Savoy's exclusion of the sheriff from the bounds of Richmondshire. The only purpose of an inquiry into William de Valence's usurpations in Hampshire and Gloucestershire — again he had excluded the sheriff from his lands — was for the king to authorize these usurpations in a charter.[140]

---

[136] *Foedera*, I/1:408–9; Treharne, *Baronial Plan*, p. 263.

[137] KB/26/152, m. 8d; *CPR 1247–58*, p. 83.

[138] For discussion of this see below pp. 154, 155, 166, 182. Curial sheriffs also needed to be firmly controlled by the king; otherwise, as happened during Henry III's minority, their power might become a threat to the crown.

[139] To some extent what the sheriffs lost to magnates they could recover by additional pressure on those less well protected. See, for example, the conduct of the sheriff of Kent after the withdrawal of sheriffs' aid by the tenants of the archbishop of Canterbury: Just/1/361, m. 48.

[140] *Calendar of Inquisitions Miscellaneous* (London, 1916), I:nos. 131, 143, 164; *CR 1251–53*, p. 283; *Placita de quo warranto*, Record Commission (London, 1818), pp. 255, 765. There are no grants of liberties to the earl of Cornwall, but, without apparent challenge, he assumed or

Henry, meanwhile, intervened at the exchequer to protect the earl of Gloucester's claims to the amercements of his men within the *banleuca* of Tonbridge.[141] Other orders safeguarded the liberties of the earls of Leicester, Surrey, Derby, and Aumale and of the countess of Kent, Peter de Montfort, and Stephen de Longespee from the activities of sheriffs, judges, and exchequer.[142] In August 1248 when Henry confirmed to Simon de Montfort a charter which Henry I had granted to Robert earl of Leicester, he added the key concession, "nor shall any of these liberties be withdrawn because they have not so far been exercised." Thus the king exempted Simon from the legal rule that liberties could be lost if they were not used, leaving the earl free throughout his lands of the honour of Leicester to withdraw suits from county and hundred courts and take over from the sheriff the view of frankpledge. In Berkshire and Kent Simon also prevented the sheriff from entering his lands to make distraints.[143] Similar concessions on "non-usage" were made to the earl of Winchester in his half of the honour of Leicester.[144] The king also opened the way for the advance of Warin de Monte Canisio. King Henry was in seisin of the suit of Warin's men to the hundred and county courts down to 1247. In that year Warin's daughter married the king's half-brother, William de Valence, and Henry confirmed to Warin the charter Henry II had given to his ancestor, Ralph de Monte Canisio, which quitted the men of Ralph and his heirs of suit of county and hundred courts. On the strength of this confirmation, which the king ordered sheriffs, justices, and the exchequer to uphold, Warin withdrew his men from these courts in Kent, Essex, and Norfolk. In Norfolk indeed he went, like Simon de Montfort, even further than the king's concession justified, in that he prevented the sheriff from entering his lands to make distraints.[145]

King Henry meanwhile did little to sustain his position in the localities

---

continued very extensive liberties in manors granted him by the king: see *Placita de quo warranto,* pp. 200, 212–13, 805, 807–8.

[141] *CR 1256–59,* p. 196. See also *1254–56,* p. 414.

[142] *CR 1237–42,* p. 122; *1247–51,* pp. 188, 294, 378, 398, 400, 474; *1251–53,* pp. 120, 169; *CR 1254–56,* p. 357; *CPR 1247–58,* p. 305; but see *CR 1251–53,* p. 425. The 1234–58 period also saw large numbers of grants of free warren: *CChR 1226–57,* passim; Sutherland, *Quo warranto,* p. 2. For a writ "of grace" conceded to the earl of Norfolk which enabled him to bring legal actions to enforce suits and other customs within his hundred of Earsham, see *CPR 1247–58,* p. 506; C/60/53, m. 1. For his liberties at the exchequer, see *CR 1253–54,* p. 196.

[143] *CChR 1227–57,* pp. 333–34, 216; Clanchy, *Berkshire Eyre,* no. 756; Just/1/361, m. 58. See also Just/1/561, m. 42d, for Simon holding the plea *de namio vetito* without warrant known to the jury at Grendon (Buckinghamshire); for the rule that liberties could be lost through lack of use, see *De legibus,* 2:168.

[144] *CPR 1247–58,* p. 147.

[145] *Placita de quo warranto,* p. 336; *CChR, 1226–57,* p. 325; Just/1/564, m. 8; *CR 1247–51,* p. 249; Just/1/872, m. 17.

through the development of the eyre. The eyre was used neither to question the liberties of the magnates through *quo warranto* inquiries like those of Edward I nor to defend the oppressed through hearing complaints on the lines of the reforms of 1258. The king's general attitude, moreover, scarcely encouraged officials to stand up boldly for justice and the rights of the crown. We have seen how the exchequer was reprimanded when it tried to keep hold of John fitz Geoffrey's debts; how the justices in eyre were disowned when they pulled down Robert de Stuteville's gallows; how Bracton was prevented from giving judgement in the William de Montacute case. In 1250, in his speech at the exchequer, Henry told the sheriffs that if they were unable to correct the transgressions of magnates, they were to inform him.[146] He did not say what he would then do. The answer, if the offenders were great and powerful men, was that he would do nothing. Against such men it was difficult to obtain writs. Some of the king's judges were their *tributarii*. In these circumstances there was little that *minores* could do to escape "servitude and oppression."

For the magnates, therefore, Henry's personal rule provided ideal conditions for the development of their local power. The sheriffs were weak; the eyres ineffective; the judicial system corrupt; the king well disposed. In the long years of peace the magnates could build solidly, supervising the activities of their professional servants. Limited financial pressure from the crown helped them avoid the ephemeral expedients of hand-to-mouth finance. The years between 1234 and 1258 were followed by the weakness and collapse of the king's government during the period of reform and rebellion. The consequences were faced by Edward I. He chose to bully his nobles rather than show them benevolence, and preferred *quo warranto* inquiries to *loquenda*. Edward, however, was the last of the masterful kings, at least until Richard II. The benevolence of Henry III in some ways foreshadowed the conduct of Edward III. The diminution of the king's control over local government which began under Henry continued in the next century with the end of the general eyre, the annual appointment of sheriffs, and the development of the office of the justice of the peace.[147] These changes made it increasingly easy for magnates to control the government of the shires, not, as in the reign of Stephen, through holding earldoms and sheriffdoms, but by dominating those who did hold local office and corrupting the system of justice. This pattern of magnate rule was already apparent in England in the 1250s. Its development was greatly

[146] Clanchy, "Henry III," p. 216.

[147] For these developments, see Alan Harding, *The Law Courts of Medieval England* (London, 1973), ch. 3; Maurice H. Keen, *England in the Later Middle Ages* (London, 1973), pp. 157–59; Cam, *Hundred and Hundred Rolls*, pp. 64–65. See also Bertram Wolffe, *Henry VI* (London, 1981), pp. 117–18.

facilitated by the policies which Henry pursued in the years after 1234. That, perhaps, is the chief significance of his personal rule.[148]

[148] I would like to thank Dr. Paul Brand for commenting on a draft of this article and for helping me with numerous points of detail. After the article was completed and submitted to *Speculum*, there appeared J. R. Maddicott, "Magna Carta and the Local Community," *Past and Present* 102 (1984). Between pp. 48 and 61 this important and impressive paper covers some of the same ground as does my own article, although from a slightly different perspective. Another recent work is Huw W. Ridgeway, "The Politics of the English Royal Court 1247–65, with Special Reference to the Role of the Aliens," Oxford University D. Phil. thesis (1983). The thesis sheds altogether new light on the factional struggles within Henry III's court and on the reasons why the court "flew apart" in 1258.

6

The Gold Treasure of King Henry III

English medieval kings frequently strove to build up reserves of treasure. King Henry I, for example, in the words of the Anglo-Saxon chronicle, 'gathered a great amount of treasure – gold and silver – and no good to his soul was done with it'. The reasons for coveting a treasure are obvious. It gave the means to hire soldiers, buy support and meet emergencies, both foreign and domestic. Much of King Stephen's success, in the first years of his reign, was due to the possession of Henry's treasure. Once it was spent, his troubles began.[1]

The question of whether, in the years of his personal rule, King Henry III accumulated a financial reserve, has received little attention. In general, historians seem agreed that he lacked the necessary discipline and foresight.[2] But in fact, as this paper will show, between 1243 and 1258 Henry worked with success to build up a store of treasure. That treasure, for reasons which we will investigate, was in gold. By the 1250s, collection of gold had become central to the king's financial activities. The whole process throws new light on Henry's projected crusade, the Sicilian enterprise, the gold coinage of 1257, the Crown's financial predicament before the crisis of 1258, and, more generally, on the king's ability to save and live within his means in the period after 1237, when parliament denied him extraordinary taxation on moveable property. Henry's treasure is also relevant to a consideration of what has been called the 'European gold famine'. This meant that until the thirteenth century the currencies of Western Europe were in silver, whilst those of the East, where there was a dearth of silver, were largely in gold. During the course of the thirteenth century the situation was reversed. Whilst the East began to mint silver coinages, probably with silver coming from the West, gold, probably released by the East, moved westwards. The result was seen in western gold coinages,. In 1232 came Frederick II's augustales. Twenty years later both Florence and Genoa minted successful gold currencies, and 'touched off 'one of the greatest chain reactions in monetary history'. This was to end with the victory of gold in almost

---

[1] *English Historical Documents 1042–1189*, ed. D.C. Douglas and G.W. Greenaway, 2nd edn. (London, 1981), p. 210; J.O. Prestwich, 'War and Finance in the Anglo-Norman State', *TRHS*, 5th ser., iv (1954), 39–41.

[2] Sir J.H. Ramsay, *A History of the Revenues of Kings of England* (Oxford, 1925), i.262–365, see p. 359; idem, *The Dawn of the Constitution* (Oxford, 1908), 298; F.M. Powicke, *King Henry III and The Lord Edward* (Oxford, 1947), i.303–5; S.K. Mitchell, *Studies in Taxation under John and Henry III* (New Haven, 1914), 345; R.F. Treharne, *The Baronial Plan of Reform* (Manchester, 1932), 49–51.

every part of Europe by the middle of the fourteenth century'.[3] Was Henry III's ability to collect gold, and his gold coinage, testimony to the waning of the gold famine in England?

In uncovering Henry's gold treasure two major sources have been utilised, the first being the accounts of the king's Wardrobe enrolled on the Pipe Rolls. Henry's gold was largely collected in the Wardrobe, and its steady accumulation is revealed by the section of the accounts which detailed the amounts of gold, silver plate and jewels which the Wardrobe received each year. These accounts are not in print, and have been little used by historians; this is why the existence of Henry's gold treasure has hitherto been unknown. The second major source is the Fine Rolls. A considerable part of Henry's gold came in the form of fines which individuals and institutions made with the king for favours and concessions. From September 1251 onwards these were recorded on the Fine Rolls and thus we can see from whom Henry's treasure was obtained.

The story of Henry III's gold treasure begins on his return from Gascony in September 1243. Before that, the Wardrobe only acquired gold to fund the king's pious oblations.[4] Thereafter, Henry saved two separate gold treasures. The first, accumulated between 1243 and 1253, was spent financing the 1253–4 Gascon campaign. The second, gathered between the king's return to England at the end of 1254 and the political revolution of 1258, was largely sold in France in 1259–60 and in London in 1261. We will look at the two treasures in turn.

Between 1241 and his death in 1254, the whole period covered by the first gold treasure, the keeper of the Wardrobe was Peter Chaceporc. The appendix, on pp. 131–6, is based upon his annual Wardrobe accounts, and upon the special account which he rendered in June 1253 for all the gold which he had collected since 1242–3. The table shows the amount of gold received by the Wardrobe in each regnal year, the amount of that gold expended during the year, and the amount remaining at the end of it. Chaceporc's accounts for these 'remains' in June 1253 show that they were all kept. Together, they formed the whole of the Wardrobe gold treasure which, in June 1253, prior to the king's departure for Gascony, Chaceporc delivered to the treasurer and chamberlains of the Exchequer for deposit in the king's Treasury at Westminster.

According to the figure given in the accounts, the total amount of gold collected in the Wardrobe by 30 May 1253 was 2110 *mg.* 4*sg.*; that is, as we will see, the weight in pure gold of 2110 *m.* 4*s.* of silver.[5] There are grounds for thinking, however, that by June 1253 Henry's treasure was considerably larger than

---

[3] A.M. Watson, 'Back to Gold – and Silver', *EcHR*, 2nd ser., xx (1967) 7. The quotation is from R.S. Lopez, 'Back to Gold, 1252', *EcHR*, 2nd ser., ix (1956–7), 219.

[4] For the Wardrobe accounts prior to 1242–3, see E 372/79, m.21d; E 372/81, m.28; E 372/83, m.13. The numerous references to the acquisition of gold in the Liberate and Close Rolls before 1242–3 are concerned with the king's oblations. All manuscript references in this paper are to documents in the PRO.

[5] The total is given in *CLR 1251–60*, 134, and see *CR 1251–3*, 386. Throughout this paper *mg.* = marks of gold, *sg.* = shillings of gold, and *dg.* = pennies of gold, while *m.* = marks of silver.

the 2110 *mg.* collected in the Wardrobe. In June 1254, in Gascony, the king received 1632 *mg.* 5 *dg.* of treasure sent from England.[6] Before that, in return for loans in July 1253 and March 1254 of respectively 6000 *m.* and 4000 *m.*, 1207½ *mg.* had been pledged to Richard, earl of Cornwall. Since these loans were never repaid, this 1207½ *mg.* must have been separate from the money sent to Gascony. Although the king did not formally ratify the delivery of the gold to Richard until November 1256, from the start it had been placed in the latter's keeping.[7] If, then, we add together the sum sent to Gascony and the sum given to Richard, it makes the total gold treasure of 2839 *mg.* 7 *sg.* 1 *dg.* Since there is no evidence that gold was stored after 30 May 1253, all this was probably collected before that date.[8] The likelihood is that the 729 *mg.* 3 *sg.* 1 *dg.*, over and above the 2110 *mg.* 4 *sg.* of Chaceporc's Wardrobe treasure, came from a fund which the king had built up outside the Wardrobe. At 2839 *mg.*, Henry's gold weighed around 650 *kg.*, a little under two-thirds of a tonne, the equal of some 51 of the 28 lb. (avoirdupois) bars in which gold is currently stored in the vaults of the Bank of England. In terms of value, as we will see later, the treasure was the rough equivalent of some 28,390 *m.* of silver.

But at this point the reader may be sceptical. Did Henry's gold really exist or was gold perhaps a mere term of account? Anxieties on this score can be removed: there is no doubt that Henry's gold *was* gold. In Chaceporc's accounts the different forms in which the gold was received were often expressed. It was both in leaf, ingots and dust, (*in folio, cunio et palliola*),[9] and in various types of money: Byzantine bezants, a few of Frederick II's augustales and *oboli* and *denarii* of music, the latter being the dinars and double-dinars of the Almohade dynasty in Spain and North Africa (1130–1269).[10] Admittedly, in some years (1242–3, 1244–5, 1246–51) gold in money was distinguished from gold said

---

[6] Francisque-Michel, *Rôles Gascons* (Paris, 1885), i. no. 3874; *CPR 1247–58*, 314.

[7] *CPR 1247–58*, 236, 364, 373, 528; C 66/71, m.17; *CLR 1251–60*, 147; N. Denholm-Young, *Richard of Cornwall* (Oxford, 1947), 159.

[8] The Fine Rolls show that gold was still being received into the Wardrobe after 30 May. By the king's delayed departure in August, it amounted to some 61½ *mg.* 248 bezants; see C 60/50, m.8 onwards. Probably this gold was taken with the king Gascony. (There are no Wardrobe accounts for the period 30 May 1253–10 Jan. 1255.) After the king's departure, fines of gold virtually disappear from the Fine Rolls kept by the government in England, August 1253–Dec. 1254; C 60/50, mm.3–1; C 60/51; C50/52, mm.13, 12.

[9] *Aurum in palliola* is variously translated as gold dust, gold in spangles, and gold in ingots and satchels; for it see Lopez, 227.

[10] For the bezant, which may be identified with the hyperpyron of the Byzantine empire or with the hyperpyron of the Byzantine successor state of Nicaea, see P. Grierson, *Byzantine Coins* (London, 1982), 10–12, 215, 239–41. (Mr Grierson has kindly helped me with questions concerning the bezant.) For money of musc, see P. Grierson, '*Oboli de Musc*', *EHR*, lxvi (1951), 75–81; idem, 'Muslim coins in thirteenth century England', in *Near Eastern Numismatics. Studies in Honor of G.S. Miles*, ed. D.K. Kouymjian (Beirut, 1974), 387–91. Both papers are reprinted in P. Grierson, *Later Medieval Numismatics* (London, 1979). The king can be found buying bezants at between 22d. and 26d. each, and *oboli* of musc at between 14d. and 16d. each; see *CLR 1226–40*, 255, 478; *CLR 1240–50*, 113–14. See also below, n. 112.

simply to be in so many marks, but the accounts for 1243–4, 1245–6 and 1251–3 suggest the latter was made up of gold in leaf, or in leaf, ingots and dust.

How much then was Henry's treasure worth? It is clear that in both Chaceporc's accounts and the Fine Rolls, gold described as being of so many marks, shillings or pennies was pure gold to the weight of that number of marks, shillings or pence in silver.[11] When the king received gold which was impure a compensation was made for the degree of debasement. Thus, in Chaceporc's accounts 62 bezants were said to 'make' 1 *mg.*[12] If that was a calculation simply by weight then the bezant weighed 3.71 gm.[13] In fact, it weighed 4.5 gm., but because the bezant was a debased coin it took more than a mark's weight of bezants to make up a mark of pure gold.[14] Since, then, Henry's treasure was expressed in terms of pure gold, we can make a rough estimate of its value.[15] Although occasionally it did a little better, the most usual rate at which silver bought pure gold in this period was 10:1, that is 10 *m.* of silver bought 1 *mg.*[16] This ratio between gold and silver was also employed by the king when he priced fines in gold, when he received silver in place of gold which was owed him and when he fixed the value of his gold coinage in 1257.[17] This did not mean, of course, that Henry would necessarily find anyone to buy his gold at 10:1 if he suddenly wished to turn a large part of it back into silver, but if we take that ratio as a rough rule of thumb, then the Wardrobe treasure was the equivalent of some 21,110 *m.* of silver, and the treasure as a whole some 28,390 *m.* of silver.

Where did Henry's first gold treasure come from? Why did the King collect it? And what light does it throw on his financial situation?

It seems highly probably that initial contributions to the treasure – to the 65 *mg.*, whose source is not indicated, and the 198 *mg. de donis, finibus et perquisitis* saved in the years 1242–3 and 1243–4 – came from welcome-home presents to the king on his return from Gascony in September 1243. Both Matthew Paris

---

[11] In the Fine Rolls, when a fine in *mg.* was paid underweight, it was said to be underweight by so many (silver) pennies; C 60/49, m.3; C 60/54, m.5.

[12] See below, n. 112.

[13] I make this and other calculations on the basis that the mark used in London was 230 grammes, though it may have been a little more; see Grierson, '*Oboli de Musc*', 78.

[14] See Grierson, *Byzantine Coins*, 215, 241. It is equally clear that when in the accounts (see below, n. 112) 14 augustales were said to 'weigh' 3s. 6d. that was the weight of their gold content, not their gross weight.

[15] I assume that in the years, in Chaceporc's accounts, where totals were given in so many marks of leaf and money, a conversion into pure gold in respect, where necessary, of the money, has already taken place.

[16] For evidence of silver buying gold, including gold in *oboli* and *denarii* of musc, *aurum combustum* and gold in leaf at 10:1, see *CLR 1226–40*, 478; *CLR 1240–5*, 121; *CR 1247–51*, 418; *CR 1254–6*, 46, 76; C 60/52, m.11; and see *Cronica Maiorum et Vicecomitum Londoniarum*, ed. T.S. Stapleton (Camden Soc., old ser., 1846), 29–3, and below n.36. For gold being bought a little cheaper, see *CLR 1240–5*, 273–4; and below, p. 130. Money of musc was certainly pure gold or nearly so; Lopez, 225–7; Grierson, '*Oboli of Musc*', 75–81.

[17] *CR 1242–7*, 219, and see below, p. 125.

and the Dunstable annalist refer to these.[18] Since the regnal year ended on 27 October, such gifts could have got into the accounts for both 1242–3 and 1243–4. Also important were gifts and fines from the Jews: the Jews had always been a source of gold for the king.[19] But a heading of Matthew Paris, 'not a little gold extorted from the Jews', suggests that it was now being demanded from them on a new scale. The king was also, of course, keeping what he obtained. Paris adds that although the king allowed silver from the Jews to be collected on his behalf by others, he received the gold 'with his own hand', a clear indication that it came into the Wardrobe.[20]

After 1243–4, it will be seen that the rate of gold accumulation drops sharply for two years before beginning a steady ascent until, at 180 *mg.* in 1249–50, it is not far below the 1243–4 level. There is scattered evidence that much of this gold was still coming from Jewish gifts, fines and tallages.[21] In September 1249 the king was also employing a policy, which he was to develop more fully a little later, of using silver to buy gold; 380 *m.* of a Jewish tallage were set aside for that purpose.[22] It may also be that numbers of ecclesiastics and laymen were making fines of gold with the king. If these were paid cash down into the Wardrobe they would not need to appear on the Fine Rolls, whose chief purpose was to provide the basis for the Originalia Rolls which informed the Exchequer of money owed to the king.

Turning next to the period between 1250–1 and the end of May 1253, it will be seen that there was a sharp increase in the gold saved by the Wardrobe. Whereas 725 *mg.* were added to the treasure in the eight years between 1242–3 and 1249–50, the following two years and seven months, down to the end of May 1253, saw the collection of 1382 *mg.*

In 1250–1 itself some 434 *mg.* were added to the Wardrobe treasure. Of this, the 123 *mg.* 14 *dg.*, 339 bezants, 32 *denarii* and 13 *oboli* of musc *de donis, finibus et perquisitis*, probably came, as before, from the Jews and from unrecorded fines of ecclesiastics and laymen. The other major item in this year was the 288 *mg.* 3 *sg.* 4½ *dg.* 'bought with money received from the Treasury'. We know that 1299 *m.* 4s. 8d. of this money, which bought gold at almost exactly 10:1, stemmed from a royal order of January 1250 assigning to two Jews various issues from the Exchequer of the Jews to purchase gold 'as the king enjoined them'.[23]

---

[18] Matthew Paris, *Chronica Majora* (henceforth *Paris*), ed. H.R. Luard (RS, 1872–83), iv. 362–3.

[19] See, eg., *Ann. Mon.*, iii, 66.

[20] *Paris*, iv. 260; *CR 1242–7*, 130, 135, 156; and note the 12 augustales in the Wardrobe in 1243–4 of the gift of Aaron of York.

[21] Eg., *CR 1242–7*, 307, 317, 371; *CR 1247–51*, 249, 316; *CLR 1245–51*, 272; C 60/41, m.5; C 60/43 m.15; C 60/46, m.10.

[22] C 60/46, m.3. I have assumed that the new tallage, as well as the old, was to be used to buy gold although the wording is not quite precise on this point. For earlier purchased gold, see *CR 1242–7*, 277.

[23] *CR 1247–51*, 255–6, 418; *CLR 1245–51*, 338. For other orders between Oct. 1250 and July 1251 assigning money from the Jews for the purchase of gold, see *CR 1247–51*, 339, 374, 387, 425, 434, 473, and below, p. 119.

After 1250–1 the Wardrobe accounts indicate no further subventions from gold bought with money 'from the Treasury'. This does not mean that the king had given up using silver to buy gold. Rather, the gold thus purchased made up the 729 *mg.* which, we have suggested, were collected outside the Wardrobe.[24] As for the Wardrobe treasure, Chaceporc's accounts show that the large sums – the 447 *mg.* of 1251–2 and the 501 *mg.* of the seven months of 1252–3–came chiefly from fines of gold paid directly into the Wardrobe. In order to inform the Exchequer about the treasure, these fines now appeared on the Fine and Originalia Rolls.[25]They were still paid very quickly, either cash down or at least before the despatch of the Originalia Rolls where the payment into the Wardrobe was already noted.[26] Many of these fines were for the purchase of liberties. Chaceporc's accounts show that, between 18 February 1251 and 30 May 1253, 231 *mg.* 8 *sg.* 5½ *dg.* in leaf and money came from diverse people buying warrens, markets, fairs, respite of knighthood, 'writs' and 'other liberties'. The cost of a charter granting a free warren, or a market and fair, varied between ½ *mg.* and 2 *mg.*, with 1 *mg.* being the most common sum. The Fine Rolls show that, between 28 October 1251 and 30 May 1253, around 116 *mg.* 279 bezants came from 123 fines for warrens, markets and fairs, 25 being made by ecclesiastics, 97 by laymen and one by a town.[27] Chaceporc's headings of 'other liberties' and 'writs' probably included fines for exemption from jury service. The usual price for this liberty, frequently linked with exemption from office holding, was ½ *mg.* or 1 *mg.* Between 28 October 1251 and 30 May 1253, 115 of these fines brought in around 59 *mg.* 355 bezants and 10 talents. Much less lucrative were the 36 fines for respite of knighthood which produced, in the same period, around 3 *mg.* 4 *sg* 3 *dg.*, 240 bezants, 20 *oboli* of musc and 12 talents.[28]

Kings had, of course, long made concessions of these kinds. Two things now were new. In the first place, Henry III was mounting a deliberate selling campaign. Matthew Paris commented, in 1252, that the king

---

[24] For purchased gold which probably went to the treasure outside the Wardrobe, see *CLR 1251–60*, 48, 63; *CR 1251–3*, 70. After 1250–1, the only 'bought gold' contributing to the Wardrobe treasure came from fines in silver being used to buy gold. Between 28 Oct. 1251 and 30 May 1253, the Fine Rolls show some 306 *m.* earmarked in this way, nearly all from fines for quittance of jury service or for charters granting free warrens, markets and fairs.

[25] The relevant Fine Rolls are C60/49 (1251–2), and C 60/50 (1252–3). Excerpts from them (containing some fines of gold) are in *Excerpta e Rotulis Finium 1216–72*, ed. C. Roberts (London, 1835–6), ii. 120–74.

[26] The Originalia Rolls corresponding to C60/49 and C 60/50 are E 371/17 and E 371/18.

[27] These, and subsequent figures, are based on all the fines made between 28 Oct. 1251–30 May 1253 and stated to have been paid, provided that the payment was not attermed to a date outside the time span covered by the table. In fact nearly all this money would have come in after 17 Feb. 1252, for which division see below, n. 112.

[28] For exemptions and respites in Henry III's reign, see S.L. Waugh, 'Reluctant Knights and Jurors: Respites, Exemptions, and Public Obligations in the Reign of Henry III', *Speculum*, lviii (1983), 937–86.

caused it to be openly proclaimed in public places, namely markets, that those who wished to have warrens should speak to him, and, money having been given, they would be benignly heard.

This, Paris adds, 'many did'.[29] Probably, even before 1252, the king had encouraged people to come forward for such grants, since their number had been increasing before that year, as Table 1 indicates. (There was no similar increase in the grants of markets and fairs.) It is probable that the king adopted a similar policy of proclamation and encouragement in respect of grants of quittance of jury service. There were 14 of these on the Patent Rolls in 1249–50 and 121 in 1251–2.[30]

In the second place, of course, Henry increasingly insisted that these concessions should be paid for in gold. The insistence was not absolute. As Table 1 makes plain, considerable numbers of charters for free warrens, markets and fairs have no corresponding entry on the Fine Rolls. Gold may have been given for some of these grants, but others perhaps were paid for in silver or conceded free. But of the fines on the Fine Rolls, the great majority were made in gold. The same is true of letters conceding exemptions from jury service and office holding. In 1251–2, against the 40 fines in gold for this favour, there were 14 in silver. Next year, down to 30 May, there were 65 fines in gold and none in silver.

Table 1

Regnal year	A No. of charters granting free warrens in Charter Rolls	B No. of charters granting markets and fairs in Charter Rolls[31]	No. of A & B paid for in gold on Fine Rolls	No. of A & B paid for paid in silver on Fine Rolls
1247–8	27	11	–	14
1248–9	17	14	–	3
1250–1	52	18	3	33
1251–2	76	22	50	15
1251–30 May 1253	86	16	73	1

It was not, however, only fines for free warrens, exemptions and so forth that Henry was receiving in gold. He also required large numbers of miscellaneous fines, including some for further diverse liberties, to be paid in that medium. Between 28 October 1251 and 30 May 1253 there were, for example, 22 fines

[29] *Paris*, v. 356.

[30] *CPR 1247–58*, 117–55.

[31] *CChR 1226–57*, 327–434. I have included in Column A the few charters which conceded free warrens *and* markets and fairs.

made by monastic houses and cathedral chapters for confirmation of their liberties, bringing in over 70 *mg.* Towns, too, gave gold for the confirmation of old liberties or for the concession of new; 10 *mg.*, for example, came from the burgesses of Scarborough. Towns also paid for quittance of tallage, 20 *mg.* being given by the Londoners for this, an exaction noted by Matthew Paris.[32] In addition, up to 31 *mg.* were paid by 10 sheriffs for the pardon of various misdemeanours. Other kinds of concessions paid for in gold included pardons of homicide, and judicial favours such as the promise of speedy judgments, the appointment of particular judges, and the moving of cases to the court *coram rege.*[33] The gold from all these sources, together with around 65 *mg.* or 165 *mg.*, 395 bezants, 66 *oboli* of musc, and 26 talents from Jewish fines, contributed to the 568½ *mg.* 2 *sd.* 11½ *dg.* placed in Chaceporc's accounts under the heading 'fines' (at last separated from 'gifts and things acquired') between 18 February 1252 and 20 May 1253.[34]

Although we cannot be certain, it seems that the actual price charged in gold for concessions was the same as what the price would have been in silver, allowing for a conversion ratio of 10:1. Thus Peter de Roffa, having originally fined in 5 *m.* of silver for respite of knighthood, ultimately paid ½ *mg.* instead.[35] We will suggest later that most people, fining in gold with the king, bought the necessary gold from goldsmiths. That may have been a nuisance, but since there is evidence that even small amounts of gold could be bought on the 10:1 ratio in the 1250s, there was no direct financial loss involved in paying fines to the king in that metal.[36] If there had been, one may doubt whether Henry could have sold liberties on the scale that he did.

In general, therefore, the expansion of the treasure after 1249–50 was achieved by the king using silver to buy gold and by him receiving gold in return for the concession of liberties and other miscellaneous favours. The gold in the Fine Rolls came from four main sources: the Jews, ecclesiastics and ecclesiastical institutions, towns and laymen. Between October 1251 and 30 May 1253 the division was as follows in Table II.

---

[32] *Paris,* v. 333.

[33] The excerpts from the Fine Rolls give some impression of these miscellaneous fines. See *Excerpta Rot. Fin.,* ii. 124–67.

[34] In these years two fines of 50 *mg.*, from the community of the Jews, are not specifically stated as paid. The money from the liberties mentioned in this paragraph is too large to be included under Chaceporc's heading (1251–2) 'other liberties' and must therefore have been included under 'fines'.

[35] C 60/49, m.21. In Oct. 1256 and Jan. 1257, when there is evidence for some fines of gold being paid in silver, they were paid on the basis of a 10:1 conversion ratio. See C 47/3/7/48; C 47/3/5/14 (for the payments). Compare the fines themselves in C 60/53 and C 60/54.

[36] C 60/49, m.4., Edward of Westminster: 1 *mg.*, though see also m.3.; C60/52, m.11, Gregory le Paumer: 2 *mg.* in leaf etc; *CR 1254–6*, 76; the 100s in Chaceporc's accounts for 1252–3; and see *Cronica Maiorum et Vicecomitum*, 29–30.

Table 2

28 October 1251 to 30 May 1253	Gold paid into the Wardrobe according to the Fine Rolls	
	Amount	No. of fines
Jews	65 *mg.*, 395 bezants, 66 *oboli* of musc, 26 talents and perhaps 100 *mg.*	72
Ecclesiastical	160½ *mg.* 252 bezants	82
Towns	93 *mg.*	25
Laymen	292 *mg.* 1125 bezants, 20 *oboli* of musc. 22 talents[37]	370

Why, then, was this treasure collected, or, more exactly, why was it collected in gold? The only direct comment on this by a contemporary was made by Matthew Paris. Writing of the Christmas festivities of 1250, Matthew declared that Henry III reduced their scale in order to save money for his forthcoming crusade. Paris then added that

> since the king knew that he was to go to the eastern parts where gold is used as money and reward for stipendiaries serving on an expedition, he began to desire to collect gold . . . . Hence those who wished to expedite business at the king's court gave the king gold rather than silver.[38]

Paris's statement reflects exactly the way gold replaced silver in the fines made with the king. The link he makes between gold collection and Henry's crusade receives confirmation from the terms of the king's will made in 1253, before his expedition to Gascony. Here, Henry left all his gold, by now, as we have seen, a considerable sum – 'in subsidium Terrae Sanctae'. It was to be borne there, with the king's Cross, by men chosen by the queen and his executors.[39] Henry III had formally taken the Cross in March 1250. The probability, therefore, is that the great expansion in the gold treasure, seen in Chaceporc's accounts after 1248–9, is related to the king's projected crusade. What Henry was doing was exactly what Watson speculates that crusaders did. 'It seems likely', he writes, 'that the crusaders tried to take with them as much *gold* as they could secure, since gold was the basis of all currencies in the Arab East'.[40]

One might wonder, however, whether this policy was still valid in the thir-

[37] The amount of gold produced by the fines on the Fine Rolls was considerably less than that indicated as coming from fines in Chaceporc's accounts. Probably some fines were still escaping inclusion on the Fine Rolls.

[38] *Matthaei Parisiensis Historia Anglorum*, ed. F. Madden (*RS*, 1866–9), iii. 99, 320; see also, *Paris*, v. 274.

[39] *Foedera*, I, i. 496, where the will is misdated 1272. The significance of the will in this context was pointed out to me by Dr S.D. Lloyd.

[40] Watson, 7.

teenth century, when silver coinages were common in the East, and when the banking operations of the Templars and Italians were both reducing the need to transport large sums of specie and facilitating exchange between gold and silver.[41] Yet there are indications that in planning to take gold to the East, Henry was doing nothing unusual. Evidence for the composition of the treasure which accompanied Louis IX on his crusade in 1248 appears wanting.[42] But in 1250, according to Matthew Paris, a great amount of money was sent from France to Louis at Damietta. It consisted of 'gold and silver, namely talents, sterling and approved money of Cologne, and not unsatisfactory money, namely money of Paris and of Tours'.[43] As far as the gold was concerned, this statement cannot be dismissed as a combination of prejudice and hyperbole. An account roll from the same year, 1250, shows that gold worth 1684 pounds 12s. 6d. Tours, together with the silver worth 9719 pounds 12s. 11d. Tours was sent *ultra mare* to the crusading Alphonse of Poitiers.[44]

Many contemporaries doubted Henry III's sincerity as a crusader, and some later historians have echoed their scepticism. The story of Henry's gold treasure proves that the king's commitment was genuine.[45] Indeed, Henry was extremely reluctant to divert his treasure from the Holy Land to finance the unwelcome Gascon expedition of 1253. As we have seen, the treasure was not taken initially to Gascony. Instead, it was deposited in the Treasury and, if used, used at first only as a pledge for a loan from Richard of Cornwall. Plainly the king hoped to keep the treasure intact for his return. If he did not return, his gold and his Cross were to be taken to the Holy Land by others.

The gold treasure after March 1250, therefore, was related to the crusade. But how does one explain the smaller but nonetheless significant amount of gold amassed before that date? There seems little doubt that this treasure was deliberately collected. Between 1234 and 1242 virtually no gold had come into the Wardrobe in the form of gifts and fines. The flow of gifts and fines in gold thereafter must have been at royal instigation.[46] Equally, there can be little doubt that the gold the king received, he wished to retain. Year after year, as we have seen, the 'remains' were husbanded in the Wardrobe. When Henry was short

---

[41] Watson, 5–6; D.M. Metcalf, 'The Templars as bankers and monetary transfers between West and East in the twelfth century', in *Coinage in the Latin East. The Fourth Oxford Symposium on Coinage and Monetary History*, ed. P.W. Edbury, D.M. Metcalf (BAR International Ser., lxxvii, 1980), 1–17. I am grateful to Dr Edbury for discussing with me points arising from this volume. A. Sayous, 'Les mandats de Saint Louis sur son trésor', *Révue Historique*, clxvii (1931), 254–304.

[42] Sayous, 'Les mandats de Saint Louis', 262–5; see also W.C. Jordan, *Louis IX and the Challenge of the Crusade* (Princeton, 1979), 99–100, and ch. 4 as a whole.

[43] *Paris*, v. 116–17; Jordan, 99–100.

[44] *Layette du Trésor des Chartes*, III, ed. J. de. Laborde (Paris, 1875), no. 3911; E. Cartier, 'Or et argent, monnoyés ou non monnoyés, envoyés en Palestine à Alfonse, Comte de Poitiers', *Revue numismatique*, xii (1847), 121–50.

[45] For the fullest discussion of Henry's crusading vows, which likewise concludes that the crusade was seriously meant, see A.J. Forey, 'The Crusading Vows of the English King Henry III', *Durham University Journ.*, lxv (1973), 229–47.

[46] See *CR 1242–7*, 124.

of money in 1245 and 1247, instead of selling his gold, he pledged it to Richard of Cornwall for loans of 2000 *m.*[47] In 1248, when he needed money to finance Simon de Montfort in Gascony, he sold his silver plate rather than his gold.[48]

One reason for this early collection of gold can be ruled out. It had nothing to do with the king's oblations. Gold *de donis, finibus et perquisitis* was not used for these. Instead, the king's 'oblation gold', the bulk of it *oboli* of musc, was separately acquired and accounted for by Chaceporc. The only year in which the accounts were intermingled was 1243–4 and, even here, a separation was made between the *oboli* of musc *de donis* etc., which were all kept, and the *oboli* purchased and used for the king's oblations. What is a possibility, however, is that the beginning of the treasure had something to do with the new feretory of Edward the Confessor. Henry had begun this 'from purest gold' in 1241. Between 1243–4 and 1249–50, almost the only occasions on which gold *de donis* etc. was not stored was when it was given to the feretory.[49] Conceivably therefore, Henry, on his return from Gascony in September 1243, thought enthusiastically of the new feretory and declared that he would like gold for it. In the event, however, the king achieved a vast overshoot. More gold was quickly acquired than could actually be used on the feretory, which perhaps explains the sharp drop in the rate of collection in the years 1244–6. In all, between 1243–4 and 1248–9, while 32 *mg. de donis, finibus et perquisitis* were given to the feretory, 480 *mg.* were stored.[50] This gold, moreover, was not stored for use on the feretory at some future date for, in Henry's will of 1253, 500 *m.* of silver were thought sufficient to complete the work.[51] The feretory of St. Edward, therefore, may have provided the initial impetus behind the acquisition of gold, but it can scarcely explain why the king continued to save gold on the scale he did.

Perhaps Henry simply wished to have treasure in gold, the most prestigious of metals. We have seen that Henry I's treasure was both in gold and silver, and in 1216 King John probably held 60 *mg.* in Devizes castle.[52] But Henry III may also have had more tangible purpose, that of helping the crusading cause in the East. His brother, Richard of Cornwall, had gone to the Holy Land in 1241. Louis IX assumed the Cross in December 1244. In the next year, according to

---

[47] *CPR 1232–47*, 456; *CLR 1245–51*, 105. I assume that these were two separate loans of 2000 *m.*

[48] E 372/95, mm.12,13; *Paris*, v. 21–2.

[49] *Paris*, iv. 156–7; H.M. Colvin *et al.*, *The History of the King's Works* (London, 1963), i. 147. The only other substantial expenditure was 7 *mg.* used for two images in 1243–4. It is difficult, however, to distinguish gold offerings to the existing feretory (as perhaps in 1242–3) from gold for work on the new one.

[50] It is not suggested, however, that the gold indicated in Chaceporc's accounts was the total going to the feretory in these years.

[51] *Foedera*, I, i. 496.

[52] *RLC*, i. 602. For Henry I's gold, see also W.T. Reedy Jr, 'The Origins of the General Eyre in the Reign of Henry I', *Speculum*, xli (1966), 723–4; J.A. Green, '"Praeclarum et Magnificum Antiquitatis Monumentum": The Earliest Surviving Pipe Roll', *BIHR* lv (1982), 14 and n. 71.

Matthew Paris, Henry, explaining the parlous state of his kingdom surrounded by enemies, refused to allow the crusade to be preached in England.[53] But by 1247, although not taking the Cross himself, Henry accepted
that there should be an English crusade and tried to secure his half-brother,
Guy de Lusignan, as its leader.[54] Perhaps the steady raise in the gold treasure
from the year 1246–7 onwards should be seen against this background. Henry
was trying to build up funds to support the projected English expedition.

What light, then, does the gold treasure throw on the king's financial situation? The first point to establish is whether gold formed Henry's only treasure.
There can be little doubt that it did, at least by 1249–50. By that date there is
no evidence that the king either possessed or was accumulating a reserve of
silver. Certainly he had none in 1253 when the Gascon expedition was funded
by a 6000 *m.* loan from Richard of Cornwall (on the security of 700 *mg.*), a
5000 *m.* subvention from the Jews, and the timely arrival of 7750 *m.* of treasure
from Ireland. The 13,060 *m.* which followed in October 1253 were probably
the issues of the Michaelmas Exchequer.[55] Of course, the king always hoped
that a parliamentary aid might transform his situation; and in April 1250, having taken the Cross, he was granted by the pope a tenth of ecclesiastical revenues for three years. The prospect of this ecclesiastical taxation, however, did
not diminish the king's efforts to construct a gold treasure from his own ordinary resources. Henry was able to do this, moreover, without the burden of
old debts. In 1250, the king, according to Matthew Paris, 'prudently freed himself from the debts which he owed many merchants', a process which is confirmed by the Liberate Rolls.[56] Thereafter, until the king's departure for Gascony,
royal letters were free from the complaints of debt and shortage of money so
characteristic of other periods of the reign. After October 1249, therefore, Henry's collection of gold provides an accurate reflection of the surplus revenue
which the king could generate without help from extraordinary taxation.

The results which Henry III achieved in these circumstances were respectable. Between 28 October 1249 and 30 May 1253, if we use the 10:1 ratio between gold and silver as a rough guide, the equivalent of 15,620 *m.* of silver
were saved in the Wardrobe, a yearly average of 4363 *m.* If we take merely the
two years seven months between 28 October 1250 and 30 May 1253, the yearly
average rises to 5356 *m.* This, moreover, was only the Wardrobe treasure. If we
accept that between 28 October 1249 and the end of May 1253 a further 729
m. of pure gold were saved outside the Wardrobe, then the annual rate of collection becomes equal to some 6399 *m.* To save on this scale Henry, according
to Matthew Paris, reduced his household expenses in 1250.[57] But he still had
money for Westminster Abbey on which 3000 *m.* annually were probably spent

[53] *Paris*, iv. 488–9.
[54] *Les Registres d'Innocent IV*, ed. E. Berger (Paris, 1884), i. no. 4054.
[55] *CPR 1247–58*, 236, 216, 220; *CLR 1251–60*, 147, 150; *CR 1251–3*, 386.
[56] *Paris*, v. 114; *CLR 1245–51*, 279–80, 286, 307–8, 315–21.
[57] *Paris*, v. 199.

after 1245.[58] Had Henry continued to save at the rate of 6399 *m.* a year until June 1256, his projected date of departure, he would have had gold equalling some 47,587 *m* of silver to take with him to the Holy Land. The gold treasure would, then, have made a contribution to the crusade at least as large as the ecclesiastical taxation granted by the pope, which was expected to raise some 45,900 *m.*[59] Even the sum achieved by May 1253, if the equivalent of 28,390 *m.*, was only a little short of the 30,000 *m.* which Henry II is said to have assembled in the Holy Land for his own projected crusade.[60] As it was, the fact that Henry III had 2839 *mg.* to help fund his Gascon expedition in 1253–4 goes some way to explaining its relative success.

Powicke, therefore, was correct when he surmised that Henry III's underlying financial situation was sound.[61] Where he and other historians were wrong was in supposing that the king lacked the necessary discipline to take advantage of this. In fact, over some 10 years Henry displayed remarkable self-control in refusing to break into his gold treasure. In 1250, as we have seen, he also reduced the running expenses of his household. Several orders indicate the king's personal interest in the business of the treasure. In July 1251, when the treasurer, together with Edward of Westminster and Philip Lovel, were instructed to buy gold from the issues of the Jewry, the writ added that they were to do so 'as the kingly lately enjoined Philip'. In August 1252, Edward of Westminster was told to send the king 'the document concerning the receipt of gold and treasure during the time of the king, as the king, on his departure, ordered him by word of mouth'.[62] Two months later, by a writ which, incidentally, indicates where the treasure was kept, Edward of Westminster, Chaceporc and Lovel were despatched to the king's chest, *cista*, in the treasury at the New Temple where the royal *regalia* and jewels were deposited. They were to weigh the gold in Chaceporc's custody there, replace it securely and let the king know the weight without delay.[63]

Yet the king's gold treasure also reveals the weakness of his financial situation. First, we should not exaggerate its size. Although the 2839 *mg.* were a great help to the king in Gascony, by October 1254 he was borrowing heavily from the archbishop and citizens of Bordeaux, and he returned to England with

[58] Colvin, i. 134.

[59] I base this figure on the Valuation of Norwich which put the annual value of clerical income in England at around £102,000; W.E. Lunt, *Financial Relations of England with the Papacy to 1327* (Cambridge, Mass., 1939), 260.

[60] H.E. Mayer, 'Henry II of England and the Holy Land', *EHR*, xcvii (1982), 724. Of course, this only represented a portion of the money Henry would have assembled had his crusade taken place. Mr. J.O. Prestwich has kindly given me further information about Henry's treasure in the Holy Land.

[61] Powicke, i. 305.

[62] *CR 1247–51*, 473; *CR 1251–3*, 148.

[63] E 368/27, m.3. For an earlier indication that the gold was kept at the New Temple, see *CR 1242–7*, 277, 307.

many debts.[64] Henry's treasure seems small compared to his father's. Over a period of years, John had over 200,000 *m.* 'at call' in his various provincial treasuries.[65] Henry's gold also depended to an appreciable extent on the sale of liberties. Politically if money was obtained without causing discontent that had advantages. On the other hand, such a sale could not go on for ever; as the later 1250s were to show, there was a limit to the number of people who wanted to buy free warrens, and exemptions from jury service. The building up of the treasure was also a slow and painstaking process, averaging at best some 6399 *m.* a year. Although Henry could live within his means in time of peace, he required a long period of saving to build up a sufficient chest if he was to fight a war, or go on a crusade. Essentially, the history of Henry's gold treasure shows that there was no real substitute for extraordinary taxation. This was only partly a matter of size. At the equivalent of 28,390 *m.* of silver, Henry's treasure in May 1253 was dwarfed by the 60,000 *m.* of the fifteenth on moveables of 1225; but it did not compare unfavourably with the 24,750 *m.* of the fortieth of 1232, and the 33,750 *m.* of the thirtieth of 1237. The difference was that the bulk of these taxes came in within a year.[66]

When Henry III returned to England at the end of 1254 his gold treasure, nurtured over so many years, was totally expended. The king's reaction was immediate. He began to save gold all over again. The accounts of the new keeper of the Wardrobe, Artald de Saint-Romain, reveal that 390 *mg.* in leaf and money were collected in the Wardrobe between 10 January 1255 and 29 April 1256.[67] Of this sum 162 *mg.* 12 *sg.* 11½ *dg.* 'in leaf and money' were bought with 1583 *m.* of general Wardrobe receipts, a rate between gold and silver of 1:9.71. The second main source was 'gifts and fines', which produced 143 *mg.* 'in leaf', 13½ *mg.* in 'bezants and money', and a further 30 bezants, 4 *denarii* and an *obolus* of musc; a total of some 157 *mg.*[68] The Fine Rolls show that these sums derived, as before, from payments for liberties and other miscellaneous concessions. Thirdly, Saint-Romain's accounts recorded the receipt, besides other smaller items, of 34 *mg.* in leaf and bezants, 4 bezants and 12 *oboli* of musc from Jewish gifts and fines, and 13½ *mg.* in leaf from the issues of the seal.

King Henry's first gold treasure was related to his projected crusade. That crusade was no longer on the immediate agenda when Henry returned to England at the end of 1254. Instead, the king had accepted the papal offer of the throne of Sicily for his second son, Edmund, and was committed to sending an army to wrest the kingdom from its Hohenstaufen rulers. Since gold was the

[64] *CPR 1247–58*, 340–1, 344; *Paris*, v. 487–8.

[65] J.E.A. Jolliffe, 'The Chamber and the Castle Treasures under King John', in *Studies in Medieval History presented to F.M. Powicke*, ed. R.W. Hunt, W.A. Pantin, R.W. Southern (Oxford, 1948), 135.

[66] F.A. Cazel, 'The fifteen of 1225', *BIHR*, xxxiv (1961), 69–70; *The Red Book of the Exchequer*, ed. H. Hall (*RS*, 1896), iii. 1064.

[67] E 372/99, m.30d.

[68] The 157 *mg.* from gifts and fines probably included the gold bought with 245 *m.* silver from fines paid into the Wardrobe and designated for the purchase of gold. See C 60/52; C 60/53.

currency in Sicily, Henry's second treasure was presumably designed to fund his Italian army.[69] With this aim in view the king once again saw gold as his main financial reserve beyond what he could obtain from extraordinary taxation. Once again he tackled its collection with vigour. When Henry used silver to buy gold, he waited impatiently for the arrival of his purchases in the Wardrobe. He was also interested in the precise rates of exchange between gold and silver. Thus in April 1255, when he sent his goldsmith William of Gloucester 60 *m.* and ordered him 'to make us have without delay 6 *m.* of good smelted gold [*aurum combustum*]', he added,

> and since we understand that marks of this kind are not worth in all 10 *m.* of silver, make us have as much gold as you can from the excess of the gold [bought] from that money, so that we have the gold this coming Monday in the morning at Merton before we rise from our bed; and this omit to do on no account.[70]

What can Henry's second gold treasure tell us of his financial situation as the great crisis of 1258 approached? Unfortunately there are no Wardrobe accounts between 30 April 1256 and 7 July 1258. This gap makes it impossible to trace with any certainty the accumulation of treasure in this vital period. It is true that between 30 April 1256 and 7 July 1258 the Fine Rolls appear to show that 535 *mg.* 36 bezants and 6 talents were paid into the Wardrobe in the form of fines of gold.[71] But we cannot add this 535 *mg.* to the 390 *mg.* retained in the Wardrobe down to 29 April 1256 and say that the gold treasure, when the king bowed to reform at the end of April 1258, approached some 925 *mg.* First, there is evidence that some fines of gold were now being paid in silver.[72] Second, much of the gold coming into the Wardrobe was also going out again. Henry, as we shall see, was breaking into his gold treasure in a major way.

There are, however, some clues to the size of the king's gold treasure as the crisis of 1258 drew near. In the summer of 1257 Henry decided to mint his own gold coins. The task was entrusted to William of Gloucester who was sent, in all probability, a large part of the Wardrobe gold treasure. He may have also used gold in his own possession which he had bought with silver. A result of the minting was seen on 27 August 1257. On that day William delivered into the Wardrobe 466 *mg.* in the king's new money, together with a little over 103

---

[69] Lopez, 226–7.

[70] *CR 1254–6*, 178.

[71] Although many of these fines were attermed, they were all noted as paid either to Artald de Saint-Romain or his successor Peter des Rivaux. Thus there is no doubt that payment had been made by 7 July 1258 when des Rivaux was dismissed; C 60/53; C 60/54; C 60/55; see *Excerpta Rot. Fin.*, ii. 228–76, where examples of fines of gold may be found.

[72] See above, n.35. A few fines of gold in C 60/53; C 60/54 are specifically stated to have been paid in silver; see also *Excerpta Rot. Fin.*, ii. 326; C 47/3/5/26. However in 1257, as in March 1256, the Fine Rolls noted that gold proffered in payment of a fine was *debile*, C 60/53, m.15; C 60/54, m.5.

mg. in bezants and money of musc.[73] In August 1257, therefore, Henry's gold treasure was worth at least 569 *mg.* But how large was it nine months later, at the time of the political revolution of 1258? This question can be approached by looking at the fate of the treasure after the revolution. Although the evidence may not reveal the dispersal of all Henry's gold, we do know that in August 1258 100 *mg.* were sent as a pledge to the abbot and convent of Beaulieu. In 1259 these 100 *mg.* were used to expedite the king's affairs at the papal court.[74] Further, between 8 July 1258 and 27 October 1260, 529 *mg.* (335 *mg.* 3 *sg.* 10 *dg.* in the king's new money) were received by the keepers of the Wardrobe, much of it probably from the 'store' of the king which is mentioned in their accounts.[75] Taking these 529 *mg.* with the 100 *mg.* at Beaulieu, we have a total of 629 *mg.* If we then subtract from this sum around 130 *mg.*, which may be estimated very approximately as current gold receipts between 8 July 1258 and 27 October 1260, it leaves about 500 *mg.*[76] This represents, in all probability, the remains of the treasure which Henry had built up before the crisis of 1258.[77]

Henry III, therefore, was not exactly 'bankrupt' in 1258. At the time of the political revolution he probably held at least 500 *mg.* In addition, there was gold and silver plate in the Wardrobe worth over 1200 *m* of silver.[78] The king also had no problem in meeting his day-to-day expenses. Although most of the Issue Rolls for Henry III's reign are lost, they survive for the Michaelmas term of 1257 and for the Easter term of 1258, demonstrating that the king's writs of *liberate* were generally honoured.[79] Thus, for all the reformers' condemnation of the king's poverty, and their fierce talk of an act of resumption to cure it, there was no immediate need for them to press ahead with such unpopular schemes, and they did not do so.

---

[73] *CPR 1247–58*, 649–50; and see *CR 1256–9*, 90.

[74] *CPR 1247–58*, 643–4; *CPR 1258–66*, 15, 17.

[75] E 361/1, mm.1d,2,1; specifically between Oct. 1258 and Oct. 1259, the keepers received 462 *mg.*; 362 *mg.* 3 *sg.* in new money, 75 *mg.* 20 *dg.* in leaf, 30 *mg.* in musc, 24 *mg.* 4 *sg.* 4¾ *dg.* in bezants, 7 *mg.* 4 *sg.* 1 *dg. in cuneo* and diverse monies; between Oct. 1259 and Oct. 1260 they received 67 *mg.*; 31 *mg.* 3 *dg.* in leaf, 13 *mg.* 3 *sg.* ¾ *dg.* in musc, 14 *mg.* in bezants, 9 *mg.* 10 *dg.* in new money, and some small change.

[76] The current receipts included one major windfall. On 27 Oct. 1259 the Wardrobe obtained 85 *mg.* 40 *dg.* from the chattels of a disgraced Jew. See *CR 1256–9*, 459; *CR 1259–61*, 1; *CPR 1258–66*, 66, 48. Some 46 *mg.* from fines of gold appear to have been due to the king between July 1258 and Oct. 1260. Not all of this may have been paid, or paid in gold, but that compensates for our ignorance of the gold which the king received from gifts in this period, and for any fines not on the Chancery Rolls; C 60/55; C 60/56; C 60/57; *Excerpta Rot. Fin.*, ii. 318, 332; *CR 1256–9*, 386–7, 357, 448; *CR 1259–61*, 48, 84–5. I have assumed that the gold mentioned in *CLR 1251–60*, 485; E 403/18 came from the treasure saved before the revolution of 1258. It is impossible to say anything useful about either receipts or expenditure between 30 April and 7 July 1258.

[77] It will be noted that the keepers of the Wardrobe received steadily less gold as this reserve was exhausted; see above, n. 75. Between 25 July 1261 and 31 Dec. 1264, little more than 41 *mg.* entered the Wardrobe apart from what was acquired for the king's oblations; E 372/113, m.3d.

[78] E361/1.

[79] E 403 /15A; E 403/3114. The payments here may be compared with the writs of *liberate* for 1257–8 in *CLR 1251–60.*

If, however, Henry was not 'bankrupt' in 1258, his resources were tiny when set against his ambitions. A treasure worth some 5000 *m.* was negligible beside the cost of an expedition to Sicily or the money owed to the pope. It would not go far even for a campaign in Wales. Perhaps that was one reason why the new government concluded a truce with Llywelyn and claimed that the king's poverty placed the kingdom in danger if attacked by a neighbouring prince.[80] What is also clear is that by 1258 Henry's attempts to augment his gold treasure had run into the sand. This is reflected by its size in April 1258. Even if it was larger than the 500 *mg.* which we have postulated, equalling perhaps the 569 *mg.* which Henry possessed in August 1257, that still meant the treasure was only around 180 *mg.* larger than the 390 *mg.* in the Wardrobe in April 1256. It is possible to trace how this situation came about.

Henry III had returned from Gascony in 1254 burdened with debts. In the next three years his letters complained of poverty and 'extreme need' in a way they had not between 1250 and 1253.[81] Although Henry began at once to save gold, this was only possible because the household expenses were supported by a 10,000 *m.* loan from Richard of Cornwall.[82] Meanwhile the king faced the necessity of a campaign in Wales. Against this background he largely abandoned the practice of using silver to buy gold. Between April 1256 and April 1258, over 4800 *m.* of silver for this purpose may have been sent to William of Gloucester.[83] But, between November 1256 and July 1257, the king reluctantly instructed William to surrender either 4130 or 4430 *m.* of this sum. The money was now needed, amongst other things, to meet the expenses of the royal household and the costs of the 1257 Welsh expedition.[84]

At the same time as he ran into problems with the purchase of gold. Henry found it more difficult to collect it in the form of fines. As we have seen, there is evidence that some fines of gold were now being paid in silver. Conceivably, those making the fines were experiencing difficulties in obtaining gold. More probably, Henry needed silver to meet immediate household expenses and no longer insisted that payment be in gold. Another difficulty was that the sources from which the first gold treasure derived were drying up. After 10 January

[80] *DBM,* 91–2.

[81] *Paris,* v. 487–8; *CR 1254–6,* 28,74,88,113,157–61,242,425; *CLR 1251–60,* 271; *CR 1256–9,* 110.

[82] *CPR 1247–58,* 400–1, and 500–1, for the use of gold as a pledge for a loan; and see *Paris,* v. 488.

[83] 2110 *m.* from fines of silver paid into the Wardrobe and earmarked for the purchase of gold, C 60/63, C 60/54, C60/55; perhaps around 1500 *m.* from general Wardrobe receipts, a tentative conclusion from the perplexing accounts of William's executors in E 372/116, m.32d, partly printed in G.G. Scott, *Gleanings from Westminster Abbey* (Oxford, 1863), 113–14; perhaps 1255 *m.* from the Exchequer (prior to April 1256 William may have received 310 *m.* from this source), *CR1254–6,* 211–12; *CR 1256–9,* 208–9; *CLR 1251–60,* 278, 297, 431, 434; *CLR 1267–72,* no. 2299I; E 403/3114. It may be that further money was sent William of which we have no evidence.

[84] *CR 1256–9,* 6, 26, 38, 68; *CPR 1247–58,* 553, 558, 561, 570, this last involving 2000 *m.* which are given in the accounts of William's executors as only 1700 *m.*; E 372/116, m.32d. The failure of Henry's efforts to see that this money was returned to William is suggested by E 372/101, mm.8, 7d; see, however, *CR 1256–9,* 26; *CLR 1251–60,* 434.

1255 only 60½ *mg.*, 64 bezants and 6 talents came from the Jews.[85] This reflected the fact that in February 1255 the king had assigned the Jews to Richard of Cornwall in part payment of the 10,000 *m.* loan mentioned earlier.[86] In
addition, gold acquired through the selling of liberties was no longer so abundant. In the three years and six months between 10 January 1255 and 7 July
1258, according to the Fine Roll figures, fines for warrens, markets and fairs
were worth only 59½ *mg.* 12 bezants, little more than half the sum which they
raised in the one year and seven months between October 1251 and May 1253.
Similarly, the 52½ *mg.* 38 bezants from fines for quittance of jury service in the
second period were less than the 59 *mg.* 355 bezants and 10 talents produced
in the first.

For a while the decline in revenue from the sale of these liberties was offset
by a vast increase in the fines for respite of knighthood. In the Fine Rolls between April 1256 and 7 July 1258, there were 358 of these fines, producing, in
the same period, 256 *mg.* 20 bezants. Even if some of these fines were in fact
paid in silver, there was still a striking contrast with the 36 fines made between
27 October 1251 and 30 May 1253 which raised only 3 *mg.* 4 *sg.* 3 *dg.*, 240 bezants, 20 *oboli* of musc and 12 talents. The fines, for respite of knighthood were
produced by the king's order to the sheriffs in April 1256 to distrain all those,
holding by military service, with annual incomes of £15 or more, to take up
knighthood.[87] Although the king may genuinely have hoped to increase the
number of knights, his aim was also to make money. As he anticipated, large
numbers of people purchased respites from the doubtful honour. The king
now charged ½ *mg.* or, more rarely, 1 *mg.* for such favours, considerably higher
prices than those in force in the period of the first treasure when respites were
bought for 6 or 12 bezants. Nearly all the fines were now attermed, but only 38
had not been paid in full by 7 July 1258. These fines, then, were lucrative, but
they were probably a reason for the unpopularity of the king's government in
the shires in 1258. In addition, once they began to run out, Henry found nothing to take their place. Thus, although in 1257 gold was still flowing into the
Wardrobe from old fines, the number of new ones was steadily diminishing.
Between 28 October 1257 and 30 April 1258, new fines for respite of knighthood totalled only 4 *mg.*, new fines for warrens, markets and fairs came to 3½
mg., and those for exemption from jury service, 5½ *mg.* During the same period there were few fines in gold for the miscellaneous concessions we have
seen earlier. These concessions were still being made, but the fines for them
were in silver rather than in gold. As before, we may suspect that this reflected
the king's need for silver to meet his immediate expenses.

By July 1257, therefore, as he prepared for his campaign in Wales, Henry's
attempt to build up a second substantial gold treasure was beginning to col-

---

[85] Figures of fines in this paragraph are based on C 60/52 (1254–5); C 60/53 (1255–6); C 60/54
(1256–7); C 60/55 (1257–8).

[86] *CPR 1247–58*, 400–1; *Paris*, v 487–8.

[87] *CR 1254–6*, 293.

lapse.[88] The situation was further compounded by the decision the king now took to disburse a significant amount of the gold which he had collected since January 1255.

The medium for this disbursement was Henry III's gold coinage. On 16 August 1257, when the king was at Chester, he instructed the sheriff of London to proclaim that the 'gold money of the king' should run in the city and elsewhere throughout the kingdom, each coin being worth 20 silver pennies. This indicated an exchange rate between silver and gold of 10:1, since the coin was of pure gold and weighed two silver pennies.[89] In 1247, when Henry launched his new silver coinage, he borrowed the necessary silver from his brother, Richard of Cornwall. No loan was necessary from Richard or anyone else for the issue of 1257. What Henry did was to mint a large part of his gold treasure. If the coinage was launched in August 1257, minting had presumably begun somewhat earlier. We may doubt whether it continued long after the political revolution in April 1258.[90] Probably the 190 *mg.* in new money which William of Gloucester delivered into the Wardrobe in October 1258 had been coined considerably earlier.[91] This delivery, and the earlier one of 466 *mg.* in August 1257, establish a minimum mintage of 52,480 gold pennies.[92] It is not surprising, therefore, that the six surviving coins display the use of four different obverse dies, the minimum life of a die being perhaps 10,000 coins.[93] Just how much royal gold William minted in total can only be a matter for speculation. My own guess is that it was around 1000 *mg.*, the equivalent of some 80,000 pennies.

The new money was quickly put into circulation. By November 1257 the mayor and citizens of London were complaining that, in so many hands, it was bringing down the price of gold in leaf. Conceivably some individuals brought gold to William of Gloucester to have it turned into coin. But, if this had happened on any large scale, Henry's new money would have been more successful than

---

[88] However, in April 1258 itself, in three writs of *liberate*, the king ordered 203 *m.* to be given to William of Gloucester for the purchase of gold. The Issue Rolls show that two of these writs were honoured, producing 128 *m.*; *CLR 1251–60*, 431, 434; *CLR 1267–72*, no. 2299; E 403/3114; see also E 372/116, m.32d. The dwindling pace of gold collection prompted measures in 1257–8 to get in unpaid fines of gold, though it was admitted that some of the fines listed might in fact have been paid; an indication of the confusion into which affairs were drifting. See E 371/22, mm.14, 15.

[89] *CR 1256–9*, 88; *Cronica Maiorum et Vicecomitum*, 29–30.

[90] I can find no accounts for the mintage, but see *CPR 1247–58*, 576; *CPR 1258–66*, 4; *CR 1256–9*, 415; E 372/102, mm.9, 27; E 372/104, mm.3d, 4d; E 372/195, mm. 33d, 34d, 39, 40; E 372/107, mm.12, 11d; E 372/116, m.32d; E 372/141, m.19.

[91] *CPR 1258–66*, 4, which also shows that the 190 *mg.* were minted from the king's gold. The delivery formed part of the receipts mentioned above, n. 75.

[92] *CPR 1247–58*, 649–50.

[93] Sir J. Evans. 'The First Gold Coins of England', *The Numismatic Chronicle*, 3rd ser., xx (1900), 220–2, pl. xi; *Spink Coin Auctions Catalogue: the Norweb Collection of English Coins – Part 1* (Spink & Son, 1985), 36–8; D. Selwood, 'Medieval Minting Techniques', *The British Numismatic Journal*, xxxi (1963), 64.

it was. More likely, the king himself, having minted a large part of his treasure, put the coinage into circulation by using it to meet various debts and expenditures.[94] Had the Wardrobe accounts survived for this period they would probably show a large outflow of gold, in the form of the new money, to meet various household expenses. As we have seen, later than 7 July 1258, although the evidence may be incomplete, the king is only known to have possessed the 335 *mg.* which the keepers of the Wardrobe received in 1258–60, together with another 100 *mg.* if the sum deposited in Beaulieu Abbey was in new money.[95]

One reason why the king decided to mint his gold was the projected expedition to Sicily. We will suggest later that much of Henry's treasure was probably in leaf, *folium*, that is in thin strips of gold. It was not, therefore, in a particularly usable form. There is evidence that, as early as 1251, Henry reflected that it would be more helpful to have his treasure in coin, and perhaps he would have minted it before leaving on crusade.[96] In 1257 the king was clearly happy with the part of the treasure which was in money. This was why, that August, alongside the new gold pennies, William of Gloucester delivered bezants and musc into the Wardrobe. But it made sense to convert the treasure in leaf into coin. By doing so Henry also informed the Sicilians, aware of Frederick II's impressive augustales, of the power and authority of his own kingship. For Henry's gold coin boasted a new and splendid design. Whereas the silver pennies of 1247 merely presented a crude royal head, the gold coins of 1257 depicted Henry sitting elegantly on his throne, holding orb and sceptre.[97]

If Henry's main reason for collecting gold after 1254 was to fund his Sicilian expedition, why did he break into his precious store in order to launch the gold coinage in England? This was not simply because Henry wanted the English, like the Sicilians, to be struck by the golden aura of his kingship, though that may have been a factor. He also had little choice. By the summer of 1257, with the costs of the Welsh campaign looming, Henry saw no alternative to spending some of his gold treasure. If he had simply sold a large amount of it, he would probably have obtained a price worse than 10:1. It made more sense to mint his own coins, fix their value and insist, as he did, that they be accepted.

Another reason was more ambitious. Henry may have hoped that people would wish to change gold, in leaf and other forms, into his coinage. By charging for the change the king might make a considerable income. From this point of view the gold coinage was an expedient to raise money, an attempt to re-

---

[94] See *CPR 1247–58*, 576.

[95] See above, 75. Some of the money the king still possessed may itself have come back into his hands, having been in circulation. The 100 *mg.* at Beaulieu presumably ended in Italy since they were used to further the king's affairs at the papal court. Two of Henry's gold coins have been found in Italy. See *Spink Coin Auctions Catalogue: the Norweb Collection, Part 1*, 37.

[96] *CR 1247–51*, 509.

[97] For the design, *Spink Coin Auctions Catalogue: the Norweb Collection, Part 1*, 36–8; for augustales, see Lopez, 227.

place the now diminishing fines for knighthood with a new, and perhaps more permanent, source of income. In the event the king's hopes were dashed, for the coinage proved extremely unpopular.

In November 1257, clearly reacting to complaints, the king summoned the mayor and citizens of London to come before him at the Exchequer at Westminster. He charged them on oath to say whether the gold coinage was 'of use for the common benefit of his kingdom or not'. If Henry was hoping for reassurance he was disappointed. The mayor and citizens replied that the coinage would do 'great damage to his kingdom, and especially to poor people whose chattels were not worth one gold coin'. They then went on to say that the coinage had also reduced the price of gold, 'since the money had become dispersed in so many hands, which is evident from the fact that gold in leaf which always was accustomed to be worth 10 *m.* is now only worth 8 or 9'. After further unspecified reasons had been adduced as to why the coinage was useless, the king announced that he still wished the new money to run. However, no-one was to be compelled to take it and anyone could exchange it at the exchange for 19½d of silver.[98]

The king's concession acknowledged the unpopularity of his coinage and restricted his ability to put it any further into circulation. What had gone wrong? Lopez has suggested that Henry made the mistake of overvaluing his coin. Since, so Lopez avers, the price of gold was falling in the 1250s, by sticking to the 10:1 ratio Henry was expecting his coin to fetch more than it was worth.[99] The problem with this theory is that, as far as England is concerned, there is no conclusive proof that the price of gold was falling generally before 1257.[100] What is true, however, is that the sudden appearance of a large amount of gold quickly brought the price down. Consequently Henry found himself holding the value of his coin above what gold in other forms was fetching on the market. This can scarcely have inspired confidence in the new money.

The mayor and citizens pointed out another problem when they told the king that his coinage would harm poor people. They were probably appealing to Henry's celebrated concern for the poor, but it was true that many poor people would have little use for a coin worth as much as 20d. Its circulation was bound to be restricted. However, the chief reason for the failure of Henry's money lay in the fact that foreign gold coins, such as bezants and *oboli* of musc, had not prepared the way through any extensive circulation of their own. Although Henry would probably have preferred his gold in money, there are reasons for thinking that most fines were paid in leaf. According to Chaceporc's particularly informative account for 1243–4, gifts and fines produced in money only 110 bezants and 111 *oboli* of musc (less than 3 *mg.*), whereas 193 *mg.* 5 *sg.* 1 *dg.* came in 'leaf, ingots and dust'. The accounts of Artald de Saint-

[98] *Cronica Maiorum et Vicecomitum*, 29–30.
[99] Lopez, 234–9.
[100] For some of the evidence, see above, pp. 111, 114, 120; *CR 1254–6*, 46, 178, 76. C 60/51, m.11, Gregory le Paumer; C 60/54, m.5, Roger of Newcastle.

Romain show that between January 1255 and April 1256 gifts and fines brought 143 *mg.* in leaf and only a little over 13½ *mg.* in bezants and money. Elsewhere in Chaceporc's accounts, and most notably between 1251 and 1253, large amounts of gold from fines came both 'in leaf and money'. But that leaf preponderated here is suggested by the fines themselves on the Fine Rolls. Those in money, usually bezants, were both far less numerous and, in total, far less productive than those said simply to be in marks of gold. Two of the latter were specifically stated to have been paid in money, implying that the rest were paid in a different form which, as Chaceporc's accounts indicate, was leaf.[101] Money was regularly proffered only when the king demanded sums of less than ½ *mg.*, for example the 6 or 12 bezants for respite of knighthood. The conclusion is inescapable that large amounts of gold coin were not easy to come by. The situation was thus very different from that 80 years later when Edward III launched his successful gold currency. Then, great numbers of foreign coins were circulating in England.[102]

But if gold money was comparatively scarce in the 1250s, from where did people get the gold they paid the king? It is possible that some ecclesiastical institutions melted down objects which they possessed in gold. Yet this was a costly process, which lost one the value of the workmanship. Probably those fining in gold bought the necessary amounts from goldsmiths; the gold came in leaf since that was the form in which goldsmiths kept and sold it. No wonder that the mayor and citizens of London, amongst whom there was a strong goldsmith lobby, were concerned when the price of leaf began to come down.[103] They also faced the loss of what had been a roaring trade if men started to pay fines to the king in his own money rather than in leaf bought from goldsmiths. One conclusion from this situation was that a gold coinage was precisely what was required. Another, probably more correct, was that there was simply no need for one. Apart from when they made fines with the king, most people acquired gold only in the form of finished precious objects. Had Henry continued to demand gold on a large scale, that might have gone some way to support his coinage. But the king launched his new money at precisely the time when the demand for gold to buy warrens, exemptions and respites was coming to an end. In that sense the bonanza for the goldsmiths too was already over, whether or not the new coinage succeeded.

King Henry III, therefore, had miscalculated. He had been fooled by his own activity. Only his own hydropsical thirst for gold created the impression that it was in great demand and in wide circulation. The reality was different. Thus, instead of bringing him money, the new coinage was merely the medium for a substantial reduction in his gold treasure. By the end of 1257, spending rather

---

[101] C 60/49, mm.9, 6 (fines of Robert de Ros and of the abbot and covent of de Valle Sancti Salvatoris.) For the king's preference for money, see *CR 1247–51*, 509.

[102] M. Mate, 'The Role of Gold Coinage in the English Economy, 1338–1400', *Numismatic Chronicle*, 7th ser., xviii (1978), 127–8.

[103] G. Williams, *Medieval London* (London, 1963), 60.

than saving gold, Henry must have been painfully aware that his attempt to build up a treasure to fund the Sicilian enterprise had disintegrated. The stage was set for the crisis of 1258.

At the beginning of this paper we wondered whether Henry III's gold treasure was evidence for the easing of the European gold famine. Certainly the ability of English goldsmiths to respond to what must have been a sudden upsurge of demand in the 1250s is impressive. That demand may itself have served to draw gold into the country.[104] Although Henry I had kept gold in his treasury, we may doubt whether he could have collected it on the scale and at the rate of his great-great-grandson. On the other hand, the comparative scarcity of gold coins in England in the 1250s shows that there was still a long way to go before dearth turned to plenty.

As for the financial situation of the monarchy, the history of the gold treasure proves that, during his personal rule, Henry was able, without help from extraordinary taxation, to live within his means and generate a surplus, provided he lived in peace. This was one reason why, for the most part, live in peace was what Henry did. Appropriately, on his new gold coin, the king was portrayed holding not a sword, as on his seal, but a sceptre.

Henry, in collecting his gold, displayed both enthusiasm and self-discipline. But the story of its collection also reflects his misfortunes and miscalculations in the 1250s. Neither treasure was actually used for what it was intended. The first did not fund a crusade; the second did not support an expedition to Sicily. Nor did Henry get the best value from his gold when he did spent it. In acquiring much of his treasure he had accepted a 10:1 ratio between silver and gold. But this did not mean that, if he was forced to turn his gold back into silver, he would necessarily be able to sell it at that rate. Nor did he. We have seen that in 1253–4, 1207 *mg.* raised only 10,000 *m.* of silver from Richard of Cornwall, a rate of under 8.33:1. Similarly, in Paris and elsewhere in France in 1259–60, Henry sold 24 bezants and 383 *mg.* 6 *sg.* 6 *dg.* in musc, bezants and new money for only 3271 *m.* 6s. 8½d., a rate slightly worse than 8.5:1. In 1261 in London he secured a rate of just over 9.5:1 when he sold a further 87 *mg.* in leaf, bezants and new money.[105] In effect, Henry obtained much of his treasure at the rate of 10:1 between silver and gold and sold it at between 8.33 and 9.5:1. From that point of view the whole enterprise was a costly mistake. If there was logic in taking gold to the Holy Land or to Sicily, Henry might have done better to have acquired it at a later stage, once departure was certain.

Also open to criticism is Henry's policy of receiving a large amount of his gold in the form of small fines. In effect, this meant that his gold was obtained by numerous individuals making petty purchases. With little bargaining power they could not hope to better the 10:1 ratio and, as we have seen, Henry apparently accepted that ratio in pricing their fines. If, on the other hand, the king had saved his treasure in silver, and acquired his gold by making large

[104] See *CR 1251–3*, 70.
[105] E 361/1. m.1.

bulk purchases, he might have obtained a better rate of exchange. Although other explanations could be offered, this may account for the 9.71:1 rate of exchange when 1583 *m.* of silver bought gold between January 1255 and April 1256. One cannot help wondering, therefore, whether the method by which the king collected his gold lacked wisdom. Did it indeed owe something to Henry's sheer pleasure at seeing the gleaming metal accumulating day after day in the Wardrobe?

As for the gold coinage, here Henry had at least the consolation of being ahead of Louis IX. It was not until 1266, nine years after Henry's effort, that the French king minted his own gold coins, largely, it seems, as tokens of his Christian kingship.[106] But the issue of 1257 did little to enhance the prestige of the English monarch. Henry, majestic on his coins, was snubbed in his own Exchequer by the mayor and citizens of London, a disjunction between aspiration and reality which underlay much of the king's personal rule. The remark of the mayor and citizens that the coinage would do great damage to the kingdom also had a wider significance. Next year a similar charge was brought against Henry's governance as a whole. The days of gold were over.[107]

---

[106] Jordan, 206–7, 210–13.

[107] There is something compulsive about gold. I would like to thank my colleagues J.L. Bolton and J.B. Gillingham for fielding what must have seemed interminable questions on the subject. I am also most grateful to J. Brand, M. Archibald and Dr B. Cook for extensive help on the numismatic side and to Drs S.D. Lloyd and C.J. Tyerman for giving me considered advice in all matters connected with the crusades.

Appendix

Peter Chaceporc's Accounts for Henry III's Gold Treasure, 1242–53

Source: E 372/95, mm.12, 11d. (Chaceporc's account for the gold he received between 28 Oct. 1242 and 17 Feb. 1252); and E 372/96, mm.9d, 10d. (Chaceporc's account for the remains of the gold obtained between the above dates, and for the gold he received between 18 Feb. 1252 and 30 May 1253).

Notes: Each regnal year runs from 28 October to 27 October. The totals remaining at the end of each year I have calculated myself, using the rates of exchange employed in the accounts (see note 112). Small errors seemingly made by the Exchequer in its own calculations are incorporated, but they do not significantly affect the final total. Each total is given to the last whole mark. Throughout the table *mg* = marks of gold, *sg* = shillings of gold, *dg* = pennies of gold, for which see above p.110.

Year 27
1242–3

received
53 *mg.* 10 *sg.*
500 bezants
31 *dg.*
439 *d.* musc

expended
28 *sg.* 2 *dg.*   } in oblations of king at feretory
152 *d.* musc   } St Edward

remaining
51 *mg.* 8 *sg.* 6 *dg.*
500 bezants
31 *dg.*
287 *d.* musc

TOTAL REMAINING
65 *mg.*

Year 28
1243–4

received
193 *mg.* 5 *sg.* 1 *dg.* }
in leaf, ingots   }
and dust[108]   } from gifts, fines and *perquisitis*
110 bezants   }
110 ob musc   }

---

[108] *in folio, cunio et palliola.*

8 *mg.* 4 *sg.* 1 *dg.*
80 *d.* musc,   from William Hardel
36 pieces of gold,   weight 30s, as in roll of great purchases
215 ob musc,   as in roll of great purchases, year 28
12 augustales,   of gift of Aaron of York

expended
30 *d.* musc,   in oblations of king and queen
36 bezants
8 ob musc   }   to feretory St Edward
181 ob musc,   in oblations of king and queen in diverse places *extra capella sua*
36 pieces of gold,   in oblations king and queen
6 *mg.*,   to make one image in church of Christ, Canterbury
1 *mg.*,   for an image of St Edward

remaining
194 *mg.* 9 *sg.* 2 *dg.*
74 bezants
50 *d* musc
12 augustales
145 ob musc,   of which 34 ob were from the purchased *oboli* and were included next year in the king's oblation gold. The remainder (111 ob comprising all the *oboli* from fines and *perquisitis*) was retained amongst the remains.

TOTAL REMAINING
198 *mg.*

Year 29
1244–5

received   (down to 3 July)[109]
21 *mg.*,   from fines and *perquisitis*
150½ bezants
459 ob musc   }   from William Hardel
51 ob musc

expended
20 *sg.*
50 bezants   }   to feretory St Edward
306 ob musc

remaining
19½ *mg.*
100½ bezants
204 ob musc
28 ob musc

TOTAL REMAINING
23 *mg.*

[109] The account closes on 3 July, apparently because this was when the king set off for his campaign in Wales.

Year 30
1245–6

received
34½ *mg.* in money
and in leaf } from gifts, fines and *perquisitis*

expended
19 *mg.*   to feretory St Edward

remaining
15½ *mg.*
1 ob musc

TOTAL REMAINING
15 *mg.*

Year 31
1246–7

received
54 *mg.* 11 *sg.* 8 *dg.*
12 bezants } from gifts, fines and *perquisitis*

expended
5 *mg.*   to feretory St Edward

remaining
49 *mg.* 11 *sg.* 8 *dg.*
12 bezants

TOTAL REMAINING
50 *mg.*

Year 32
1247–8

received
67 *mg.* 3 *sg.* 4 *dg.*   from gifts, fines and *perquisitis*
2 augustales,   of the gift of Abergrattus

expended
nothing

remaining
all

TOTAL REMAINING
67 *mg.*

Year 33
1248–9

received
130 *mg.* ½ *dg.*
4 bezants   } from gifts, fines and *perquisitis*

expended
the weight of 32 *sg.*,   to feretory St Edward

remaining
127½ *mg.* 16½ *dg.*
4 bezants

TOTAL REMAINING
127 *mg.*

Year 34
1249–50

received
183 *mg.* 6 *dg.*
118 bezants   } from gifts, fines and *perquisitis*
15 ob musc

expended
3½ *mg.*
26 bezants   } to feretory St Edward
12 ob musc,   to feretory St Thomas the Martyr

remaining
179 *mg.*
92 bezants
3 ob musc

TOTAL REMAINING
180 *mg.*

Year 35[110]
1250–1

received
123 *mg.* 13 *dg.*
339 bezants   ⎫
32d musc   ⎬ from gifts, fines and *perquisitis*
13 ob musc   ⎭
288 *mg.* 3 *sg.* 4½ *dg.*,   bought from money received from the Treasury

---

[110] From this year onwards there is no expenditure.

11 *mg.*
27 bezants   } bought from money received from the Wardrobe
4 *d.* musc

4 *mg.* 10 *sg.*
14 *d.* musc   } bought from money received from Wibert[111]
1 ob musc

remaining
all

TOTAL REMAINING
434 *mg.*

Year 36
1251–17 Feb. 1252[112]

received
44½ *mg.*
10 bezants   } from gifts and fines

2 *mg.*,   bought from money from issues of the seal

remaining
all

18 Feb. –
27 Oct. 1252

received
273 *mg.* 4 *dg.*
in leaf and money   } from fines of diverse people

89 *mg.* 1 *dg.*
in leaf and money   } from diverse people to have warrens, markets, fairs and other liberties

18½ *mg.* 13 *dg.*
in leaf, money   } from diverse gifts
and dust

8 *mg.* in money of } from the issues of the seal by the hand of Wibert
musc and bezants

2½ *mg.* 4 *sg.* 7 *dg.*
in leaf and money   } *perquisitis* of the Justices of the Jews

3 *mg.* 5 *sg.* 1 *dg.*
in leaf and money   } from diverse people for respite of knighthood

---

[111] Wibert of Kent, the Chancery clerk.
[112] The division on 17 Feb. is because, in 1252, Chaceporc accounted for all the gold which he had received between 28 Oct. 1242 and 17 Feb. 1252. In his account, the sum of marks of gold was given as 1178½ *mg.* 22 *dg.* The sum of bezants was given as 1147, which were said to 'make' 18½ *mg.*, 'that is 62 bezants:1 mark'. The sum of *denarii* of musc was given as 418, which were said to 'make' 8 *mg.* and 2 *d.* musc, 'that is 52 *d.* musc:1 mark of gold'. The sum of *oboli* of musc was given as 304, which were said to 'make' 2½ *mg.* and 22 *d.* musc, 'that is 104 ob musc:1 mark'. 'The sum of these sums' was given as 1207½ *mg.*, and 22 *dg.* and 24 *d.* musc, which 'made' 8 *sg.*. Thus the final conclusion was 'Sum of all the gold in marks: 1208 *m.* and 16 *denarii* and 14 augustales which weigh 3*s.* 6*d'*

12½ *mg.* 4 *dg.*   ⎫
in leaf and money   ⎬   from diverse people to have writs
                    ⎭

3 *mg.* 22½ *dg.*   ⎫
in bezants and   ⎬   purchased
money of musc   ⎭

sum (18 Feb. – 27 Oct.)[113]
400½ *mg.* ½ *dg.*

TOTAL REMAINING
447 *mg.*

Year 37
1252–30 May 1253

received
295½ *mg.* 2 *sg.*   ⎫
7½ *dg.* in leaf   ⎬   from fines of diverse people
and money   ⎭

126½ *mg.* 3 *sg.*   ⎫
3½ *dg.* in leaf   ⎬   from diverse people to have warrens, markets and fairs,
and money   ⎭   respite of knighthood and writs

42 *mg.* 1 *dg.*   from gifts of diverse people

18½ *mg.* 16 *dg.*   ⎫
in leaf and money   ⎬   from issues of the seal

11 *mg.* 4 *sg.* 2 *dg.*
in money   *perquisitis* of the Justices of Jews

2 *sg.* 8½ *dg.*
in bezants   bought by P. Lovel

4 *mg.* 11 *sg.* 4 *dg.*   received from 10 cups sold by Henry de
in leaf   Frowick

1 *mg.* 3 *sg.* 7 *dg.*   from 2 cups sold to the abbess of Shaftesbury
in leaf

½ *mg.* 3 *sg.* 4 *dg.*   bought from 100s silver received from pannage of the
                     forest of Buckholt

Sum[114]
501 *mg.* 5 *sg.* 9½ *dg.*

TOTAL REMAINING
501 *mg.*

'Sum of preceding sums [from remains from year 27 inclusive] 2110 *m.* 4 *s.* of
gold all of which has been delivered to the treasurer and chamberlains to be
placed in the Treasury of the king at Westminster by a writ of the king which is
in forulo marescalli inter communia'.[115]

---

[113] This is the sum given in the accounts.
[114] This is the sum given in the accounts.
[115] This conclusion is quoted from the accounts. For the writ see, *CLR 1251–60*, 134.

7

Matthew Paris and Henry III's Speech at the Exchequer in October 1256

Every historian of the reign of Henry III confronts the massive fact of Matthew Paris. Down to 1234 Paris's greatest historical work, his *Chronica Majora*, was largely copied from the chronicle of his predecessor at St Albans, Roger of Wendover. Thereafter the *Chronica Majora* is entirely original. Alongside a great deal about Europe and the East, it covers in extraordinary detail the whole history of Henry's personal rule as well as the start of the subsequent political revolution. The printed text of the *Chronica Majora*, edited by H.R. Luard for the Rolls Series, runs to no less than 1738 pages between 1235 and 1259, when death at last ended Paris's labours. As a monk of St Albans, strategically placed on the north road out of London, Paris met all the chief actors of the day. He recorded information as it came in and wrote up a fair copy of the *Chronica Majora* within a few years of events. On the face of it, therefore, Paris's work should enable the history of this period to be written with almost unparalleled surety and detail. But does it? A great deal clearly depends on Paris's reliability, and the general view is that reliable Paris most certainly is not. Historians have admired his prolific output and the extraordinary range of his interests – what Galbraith called his 'humanity'[1] – but they have also felt his basic accuracy was undermined by a disastrous combination of carelessness, inventiveness and prejudice: the prejudice, of course, being a sulphureous hostility to papal and royal government and a passionate conviction that the king should banish foreigners and govern through native magnates. Galbraith considered Paris's additions to Wendover's account of the reign of King John 'not merely worthless, but very misleading'.[2] Holt has shown how, in dealing with the history and texts of Magna Carta, Paris 'distorted and fabricated history' and was 'confused by abundance [of his material] and by his own prejudices and preconceptions'.[3] Vaughan, in his classic study of the chronicler, concluded that he was 'basically unreliable as a historical source'.[4]

[1] V.H. Galbraith, *Roger of Wendover and Matthew Paris* (Glasgow, 1944), p. 38.

[2] Galbraith, *Roger of Wendover and Matthew Paris*, p. 37.

[3] J.C. Holt, 'The St Albans Chroniclers and Magna Carta', *Trans. Roy. Hist. Soc.*, 5th ser., 14 (1964), pp. 67–88, reprinted as chapter 12 of his *Magna Carta and Medieval Government*, from whence the quotations come (pp. 277 and 283).

[4] R. Vaughan, *Matthew Paris* (Cambridge, 1958), p. 134. A. Gransden, *Historical Writing in England, c.550–c.1307* (London, 1974), chapter 16 is rather milder. 'Matthew's critical powers are less remarkable than his wide range of interests and almost unlimited curiosity' (p. 361).

One fundamental problem in assessing Paris's accuracy is that he provides a large amount of information which it is impossible to control, or control in its entirety, by reference to other sources. This is particularly the case in respect of his numerous accounts of remarks and speeches made by King Henry III. It is at this point that the present essay seeks to make a contribution. It discusses one of the few cases where Paris's version of a speech made by the king can be checked in its entirety against the official government record. When this is done Paris emerges with more credit than the usual criticisms might lead us to expect. The essay will then go on to consider the light the speech throws on King Henry's aims and abilities.

The speech in question was made by King Henry at the exchequer in October 1256 and was recorded on the exchequer's memoranda rolls. To understand its purpose a word is necessary about its subject matter. Since the twelfth century each sheriff had been required to appear at the exchequer on the day after Michaelmas and the day after the close of Easter to make his 'proffer', that is to pay in the money which he owed both for the farm of his county and for all the debts (many arising from amercements) which the exchequer had summoned him to collect from individuals. The officials of the various cities, boroughs and manors, which answered directly to the exchequer, were required to appear with their proffer in the same way.[5] Henry's pronouncement dealt with this practice or rather with the breach of it. Matthew Paris's account is as follows.

What the King Did Then at the Exchequer

In the same year the lord king came to the exchequer on the fourth day before the day of St Edward [9 October], and sitting there with the barons, pronounced with his own mouth that each sheriff, who did not appear each year in the octaves of Michaelmas with his proffer of the king's money from farms, amercements and other debts, should be amerced on the first day at five marks, on the second day at ten, on the third at fifteen, and on the fourth, if still absent, he should be held to ransom. The king made a similar pronouncement against the cities which have liberties and answer at the exchequer through their own bailiffs; so namely that on the fourth day if they did not appear in the same way as the sheriffs they should lose their liberties.[6]

Here next is the official record on the memoranda roll of the exchequer.[7]

[5] The appearance of the sheriffs and other officials at the Michaelmas and Easter exchequers was desribed in the memoranda roll as the *Adventus Vicecomitum* (Appearance of the Sheriffs). See M.H. Mills '*Adventus Vicecomitum*, 1258–1272', *English Historical Review*, 36(1921), pp. 481–96. I am most grateful to James Collingwood (who is completing a thesis on English royal finance between 1255 and 1270), Paul Brand and David Crook for helping me with the problems of exchequer practice discussed in the following pages.

[6] *Matthaei Parisiensis . . . Chronica Majora*, 7 vols., ed. H.R. Luard (Rolls Ser., 1872–83), v, 588–89. For the Latin text see the Appendix.

[7] Each year there were two sets of memoranda rolls, one kept by the lord treasurer's remembrancer and one kept by the king's remembrancer, respectively Public Record Office (from which all manuscript references cited in this essay come) E 368 and E 159. In this period they are very

Provision of the Lord King

It has been provided by the Lord King that each sheriff of England shall come to the exchequer on the day after Michaelmas and the day after the close of Easter in his own person both with his farms and his summonses to make his proffer as he ought to according to the ancient custom of the exchequer. And unless they come, as aforesaid, within the fifth day on the foresaid terms they shall be amerced on the first day at £5, on the second day at £5, on the third day at £5, on the fourth day at £5 and on the fifth day at the king's will.

And all the sheriffs are ordered by the king to proclaim in their counties that all who ought to answer at the exchequer by their own hand for cities, boroughs and other demesne manors of the king shall be at the exchequer at the said terms in their own persons to answer for their farms and for other debts of the king for which they ought to answer by their own hand under the liberty conceded them by the king. And unless they are there as aforesaid, each mayor of each city and each keeper both of boroughs and other demesnes of the lord king, shall be amerced on the first day at five marks, on the second day at five marks, on the third day at five marks, on the fourth day at five marks, and on the fifth day the city, borough or other demesne shall be taken into the king's hands, not to be returned save by the grace and will of the king.

And if there is any other bailiff or keeper of the king who ought to answer at the exchequer for debts of the king by his own hand and has not come to the exchequer at the aforesaid terms to answer, then, as said before, he shall be amerced each day within the fifth day at £5 as with the sheriffs.

Matthew Paris's account is characteristically undiscerning in failing to explain either the background or the success of the king's pronouncement, points to which we will return. Here, however, the question is that of Matthew's factual accuracy. It is easy to point to the omissions and errors. He failed to note that the sheriffs were to appear at Easter as well as Michaelmas.[8] He said they were to be amerced five marks a day for the first three days whereas in fact it was £5 a day for the first four days.[9] He said the cities and boroughs were to be amerced at the same rate as the sheriffs whereas it was they who were to be charged the five marks. Yet though some of the details may be shaky, Paris has got the gist of the king's pronouncement absolutely right. He knows the ruling covered both sheriffs and cities; he knows the aim was to secure the personal appearance of the officials with their proffers; he has the size of the penalty nearly accurate and knows that it was to be repeated over several days until the sher-

---

continued

nearly identical. Henry's provision is found on both: E 368/32, m. 1d; E 159/30, m. 1d. For the Latin text see the Appendix.

[8] He also said the sheriffs were to appear in the octaves of Michaelmas rather than on the day after Michaelmas.

[9] Paris says that the sheriffs were to be amerced on the first day at five marks, on the second at ten and on the third at fifteen but he is probably here counting up the daily amercement of five marks.

iffs were amerced at the king's will[10] and the cities lost their liberties. More generally, it is impressive that Paris knows about the episode at all. No other chronicler mentions it. This confirms, what other evidence also shows, that Matthew was in close and unique touch with events at the exchequer.[11] Paris's tone, moreover, is sober, even though the episode touched on one of his main obsessions: the financial exactions of the crown.[12] Indeed, by making the monetary penalty five marks rather than £5 he actually made the level of those exactions rather less than they were.

What then of the two pieces of information Paris supplies which are not in the official record. The first is the date, namely 9 October, the second the priceless statement, if true, that Henry sat with the barons of the exchequer and made the pronouncement 'with his own mouth'. The date is precisely the type of detail one might expect Paris to get wrong, yet there is confirmation that he was right, or very nearly so. Having concluded his account of the king's appearance, Paris continued by saying that *on the same day* all the sheriffs were amerced five marks for disobeying an order to distrain all those with lands worth £10 a year to become knights. Again, we have an official record of this measure attached to a chancery roll which dates it to Tuesday before the feast of St Edward, that is Tuesday 10 October.[13] Either, therefore, the king's pronouncement took place on 10 October, not the 9th, or Paris was mistaken about it taking place on the same day as the measure about distraint of knighthood. Either way Paris has got the date very nearly right. We may be the more confident, therefore, that he was right about the much larger point, namely that Henry made the pronouncement in his own person. This was not, after all, the first occasion on which Henry had made a speech at the exchequer. The memoranda rolls themselves state that in October 1250 he issued a series of injunctions to the sheriffs *proprio ore*.[14] A study of the king's itinerary also supports the conclusion that Henry spoke for himself in 1256: it was precisely on 8 or 9 October that Henry reached Westminster on a journey back from Canterbury where he had been earlier in the month.

This impression of substantial accuracy mixed with the occasionally erroneous detail is confirmed by Paris's account, just mentioned, of the amercement of the sheriffs for disobeying the order for distraint of knighthood. Paris was wrong to say that all those with £10 a year were to be knights; the level was £15;[15] and, as we have seen, he may have been slightly out with the date. But

---

[10] Paris says that on the fourth day the sheriff would be held to ransom (*sit redimendus*). This was the equivalent of being amerced at the king's will.

[11] See Vaughan, *Matthew Paris*, pp. 14, 17–18.

[12] For a diatribe on this subject soon after his account of this episode: *Chronica Majora*, v, 594–5.

[13] C 60/53, schedule attached to m. 3.

[14] M.T. Clanchy, 'Did Henry III have a Policy', *History*, 53 (1968), pp. 203–16, with the text at pp. 215–6.

[15] *Close Rolls, 1254–6*, p. 293.

this time he was right about the size of the penalty – five marks – and he was right too about the story as a whole: all the sheriffs were indeed amerced.[16]

It would be wrong to extrapolate with total confidence from Paris's success on these occasions. There are other episodes where his narrative, tested against the records, appears far less satisfactory.[17] Yet Paris's reports of speeches, remarks and conversations must always be taken seriously. They may well be tolerably accurate. Indeed, his versions of Henry's speeches at the parliaments of 1244 and 1248, and his account of Henry's quarrels with the countess of Arundel and the earl of Norfolk, all find some confirmation from other evidence.[18] So does his story of the quarrel between Simon de Montfort and the earl of Gloucester in 1259 when Montfort upbraided the earl for not standing by his oath to the Provisions of Oxford, the first sign of the political stance which Montfort was to take over and over again.[19] In 1258, in a famous passage, Paris told of a meeting between Henry III and Montfort in a thunder storm: 'by God's head I fear you more than all the thunder and lightning in the world', cried the king. One would naturally dismiss this passage as written with blatant hindsight – were it not for the fact that within little more than a year Paris was dead.[20] Matthew Paris is, in short, a far better source than is often imagined. He was prejudiced and unperceptive. He rarely showed much insight into people and events. But he demonstrated both a range of knowledge and a factual accuracy rarely surpassed by a medieval chronicler.

Returning to the speech at the exchequer in October 1256, what light does it throw on Henry's kingship? At first sight, it is surely a favourable one. Henry appears very much a 'hands on' king, determined to control his local officials and increase his revenues. Admittedly one can devalue the fact that Henry spoke for himself. Perhaps he was pushed onto the stage by his councillors and halted through his part: the record on the memoranda rolls is thus very much the

---

[16] C 60/53, schedule attached to m. 3. The amercement is here described as being of a half mark of gold but that was the same as five marks of silver.

[17] See for example H. Summerson, 'The king's *Clericulus*: The Life and Career of Silvester de Everdon, Bishop of Carlisle, 1247–1254', *Northern History*, (1992), pp. 84–5.

[18] For the 1244 speech compare *Chronica Majora*, iv, 365–6 with the fuller version in Bodleian Library, MS Digby 11 f. 96v (an extract from a letter describing events at the parliament, a transcript of which was kindly sent me by Nicholas Vincent). The very close correspondence between the two accounts was pointed out to me by Suzanne Cawsey. For the 1248 speech compare *Chronica Majora*, v, 20 and *The Song of Lewes*, ed. C.L. Kingsford (Oxford, 1890), lines 489–526. For the episode concerning the earl of Norfolk, see *Chronica Majora*, v, 530; *Close Rolls 1254–6*, p. 238; for the countess of Arundel: *Chronica Majora*, v, 336–7; C 60/51, m. 10; D.A. Carpenter, 'King, Magnates and Society: The Personal Rule of King Henry III', above, p. 80.

[19] *Chronica Majora*, v, 744–5. Paris indicates that the cause of the quarrel was Gloucester's reluctance to extend reform to his own estates, precisely the issue being dealt with at this time by the Ordinance of the Magnates: *Documents of the Baronial Movement of Reform and Rebellion*, ed. R.F. Treharne and I.J. Sanders (Oxford, 1973), no. 10.

[20] *Chronica Majora*, v, 706. 'Like the lightning which Henry feared, this little scene illuminates, intensely and momentarily, the tensions and constraints in a relationship not wholly hostile but certainly full of ambivalence': J.R. Maddicott, *Simon de Montfort* (Cambridge, 1994), p. 150.

Hansard version. The story of Henry's gold treasure, however, shows his interest in both the strategy and detail of financial policy;[21] it seems unlikely that he did not, at the very least, have a major input into the provisions of October 1256. He may even have conceived them. Henry acted as soon as he arrived at Westminster from Canterbury, so there cannot have been lengthy discussion with the exchequer officials. Indeed, as we shall see, they may even have disapproved of the initiative, at least in the form it took. Nor, in fact, do either Paris or the official record refer to surrounding councillors, this in contrast to Henry's speech at the exchequer in 1250 when the memoranda rolls mention him coming 'with his council'.[22]

From one point of view there was every reason for Henry to take action. The ruling had two immediate objectives: first to make the sheriffs turn up on time on the day after Michaelmas and the day after the close of Easter; secondly, to make them turn up in person and not through deputies. With respect to punctuality, the memoranda rolls appear to suggest that nothing much was wrong. In 1256 virtually all the sheriffs are recorded as appearing, in person or by proxy, on the day after Michaelmas.[23] The pattern is much the same in previous years both at the Michaelmas proffer and the Easter one. There are reasons for thinking, however, that the record of appearances on the memoranda rolls was on some occasions fictional. According to the roll, the citizens of York appeared through a deputy on the day after Michaelmas 1256 and brought £23. Yet elsewhere on the roll, in fact immediately after the text of king's ruling, an entry states that the mayor and bailiffs of York had neither come in person nor sent deputies with money either on the day after Michaelmas or on the three subsequent days.[24] It is not till 7 October that the receipt roll records money received from the citizens.[25] The fact that only York was singled out for individual comment (and punishment) in 1256 might suggest that only York had failed to turn up. On the other hand, perhaps the Yorkists were made an example of because they were unlucky or because they had done nothing to palliate or excuse their offence. It may well be that the memoranda roll record was misleading in other cases also. Thus the proffers it records as brought on the day after Michaelmas (Saturday 30 September) do not begin to appear on the receipt roll until Monday 2 October and continue to come in over the next days and weeks.[26] Now it is possible that the sheriffs whose money was received on or soon after 2 October did indeed appear in person or through deputies on 30 September, for it would have taken some time for the money they brought

[21] D.A. Carpenter, 'The Gold Treasure of King Henry III', above, pp. 107–36.

[22] Clanchy, 'Did Henry III Have a Policy?', p. 215.

[23] E 159/30, m. 23.

[24] E 159/30, m. 1d. Printed in T. Madox, *The History and Antiquities of the Exchequer*, 2 vols. (2nd. edn., London, 1769), ii, p. 154 n.f.

[25] E 401/28.

[26] E 401/28. The receipts rolls officially recorded the money received day by day into the exchequer. The proffer section on the memoranda rolls merely recorded the sums the sheriffs said they had brought. See the next note.

to have been actually counted and thus formally received into the exchequer.[27] But can this still be true of the sheriffs, whose money was received as late as 14 and 17 October and indeed, in one case, on 4 November?[28]

Just how many sheriffs or deputies defaulted at Michaelmas 1256 is, therefore, impossible to say, but quite probably there were enough to make Henry feel there was a serious problem. Clearly the non-appearance of the mayor and bailiffs of York caused particular outrage. Henry could feel equally concerned about the use of deputies. At Michaelmas 1256, just before his démarche, eight sheriffs had appeared in person at the exchequer; sixteen sheriffs had sent deputies.[29] That made it difficult, on the face of it, if the proffer was inadequate to pin responsibility where it belonged. And the Michaelmas 1256 proffer was indeed inadequate, or so it appeared. It produced a mere £1447 as against £2486 the year before.[30] Henry's financial difficulties at this time were almost overwhelming.[31] He had every reason to get his money in on time and punish those responsible for delay and shortfall.[32] His action had plenty of precedent. In 1237 the exchequer had amerced sixteen sheriffs £5 each for failing to appear in person on the day after the close of Easter;[33] indeed the £5 a day penalty for

---

[27] The proffer is thus a record of the money the sheriffs *said* they had brought, not a record of the money actually received and counted by the exchequer. Thus, in the earliest surviving record of the proffer, that for Easter 1208, each individual sum of money brought by a sheriff is qualified by the statement *as he says: Memoranda Roll 10 John*, ed. R.A. Brown (Pipe Roll Soc., new ser., 31, 1955), pp. 31–3. This formula is still found in the memoranda rolls of Henry III's reign but gradually falls out of use. In 1235 the bailiff of Kingston appeared on the day after Michaelmas at the exchequer (of receipt), said he had brought £25 and caused it to be written down (it does indeed appear in the memoranda roll's record of the proffer) but he then went away without licence of the treasurer and paid nothing of the £25 in: E 159/14, mm. 4,1. In the record of the 1256 proffer some sheriffs are said to have come and brought no money, but money is later recorded as received from them on the receipt roll. This too suggests they may genuinely have appeared in person on 30 September, their money only arriving later. For the proceeds of the proffer see E.F. Jacob, *Studies in the Period of Baronial Reform and Rebellion, 1258–1267*, vol. 8 of *Oxford Studies in Social and Legal History*, ed. Sir Paul Vinogradoff (Oxford, 1925), table between pp. 248–9. See also Mills 'Adventus Vicecomitum'.

[28] The sheriffs were those of Oxfordshire, Lancashire and Cumberland although the money brought by the last two, according to the memoranda roll, does not match exactly with the money recorded on the receipt roll, a common problem for which see Mills, 'Adventus Vicecomitum', p. 491.

[29] E 159/30, m. 23.

[30] E 159/30, m. 23; E 159/29, m. 30.

[31] See above, p. 123.

[32] It should be stressed, however, that only a proportion of the king's annual revenue was expected every year at the formal proffers. The sheriffs were also summoned to pay in revenue at other times and individuals came with money throughout the Easter and Michaelmas terms. Hence the totals recorded on the receipt rolls were always much larger than those of the memoranda roll proffers.

[33] E 159/15, mm. 11, 12. According to the memoranda roll heading the amercement was for failing to appear on the day after the close of Easter, not for failing to appear in person, but it is noticeable that only those sheriffs who came through deputies were amerced. See also *Close Rolls, 1234–7*, pp. 438, 528.

non-appearance and the ultimate threat of direr penalties at the king's will were mentioned by the *Dialogus de Scaccario* in 1176.[34]

What then were the results of Henry's dramatic initiative? There were some immediately. The mayor and bailiffs of York were first amerced £20 for their failure to appear on the first four days after Michaelmas and then the city was taken into the king's hands.[35] The real test, however, would come at the Easter exchequer of 1257, the first at which the new ruling, requiring the sheriffs and bailiffs to appear on time and in person, would be in force. It was a test which was failed comprehensively. Just how many sheriffs did not appear on the day after the close of Easter itself we cannot know. But fail some almost certainly did if we may judge from the dates at which the money they brought was actually received into the exchequer. The day after the close of Easter was 16 April; it was not till 25/28 April that the proffers of the sheriffs of Lincolnshire, Bedfordshire-Buckinghamshire and Northumberland were received into the exchequer. Other receipts were later than that.[36] The continuation of deputies was even more blatant. Eight sheriffs appeared in person and fifteen sent deputies, almost exactly the same as at the previous Michaelmas.[37]

Now, then, was the moment for punitive action and the exchequer prepared to take it. 'Concerning the sheriffs who have not come personally to the exchequer on the day after the close of Easter as accustomed', wrote the clerk in the margin of the memoranda roll. Against this entry he added: 'The sheriff of Lincoln has not come on the first day, the second day nor the third. The sheriff of Bedfordshire and Buckinghamshire similarly'. The clerk then left about three inches blank and drew a bracket in the margin to embrace the names of the defaulters who would follow.[38] But none ever did. There is no sign that the sheriffs of Lincolnshire, Bedfordshire-Buckinghamshire or any one else were amerced for failing to turn up punctually and/or in person.[39] The whole scheme was abandoned. At the following Michaelmas proffer of 1257 eight sheriffs came

[34] *Dialogus de Scaccario*, pp. 79–80. In 1255 when the sheriff of Surrey failed to turn up to account, he was amerced £5 for each of the first three days and then at the king's will: E 368/31, m. 7d; see also m. 11 for the sheriff of Lincolnshire being treated in comparable fashion. An example from the 1230s is *Close Rolls, 1234–7*, pp. 385, 390; E 159/15, m. 16.

[35] E 159/30, m. 1d; E 368/32, m. 1d (Madox, *Exchequer*, ii, p. 154 n.f.). The monetary penalty is only mentioned in E 159 where it is cancelled apparently because of the order to take the city into the king's hands.

[36] E 401/30. Again the record of the proffer on the memoranda roll (E 159/30, m. 23d) has everyone coming on the day after Michaelmas.

[37] E 159/30, m. 23d.

[38] The bracket and gap is on the memoranda roll of the king's remembrancer only: E 159/30, m. 11d. It does not appear on the roll of the lord treasurer's remembrancer. E 368/32, m. 11d.

[39] This conclusion is based on an examination of the pipe rolls which have no sign of such amercements. By contrast, the amercements imposed on the sheriffs at Michaelmas 1256 for failing to distrain for knighthood do appear. Quite a number of sheriffs in the 1250s were amerced £5, and sometimes several lots of £5, for contempt *coram rege*, which probably means the court *coram rege*. The sheriff of Lincolnshire left office in the summer of 1257 but considerably later than Easter. The sheriff of Bedfordshire-Buckinghamshire remained in office till 1258.

in person and fifteen sent deputies, almost exactly the same as the year before.[40] The pattern of punctuality likewise seems much the same.[41] Nor is it
clear that the initiative had done much to improve the general efficiency of
the sheriffs and other bailiffs. The £1489 proffered at Easter 1257 was still some
£200 less than the previous Easter.[42] Admittedly, the Michaelmas proffer of 1257
raised £2722, £1275 more than at Michaelmas 1256, when the low amount may
have prompted Henry's initiative. But the figure in 1256 was explained neither by the use of deputies, whose numbers were much the same at Michaelmas 1255, 1256 and 1257, nor by the sheriffs' general delinquency. It was
explained by the way Henry had issued writs ordering the sheriffs to pay their
money direct into his wardrobe rather than into the exchequer, itself a reflection of the hand to mouth state of his finances. The exchequer was perfectly
aware of this and under its record of the Michaelmas 1256 proffer, recorded
for the first time the amount authorised by such writs alongside the amount
actually brought in cash.[43]

The trouble was that Henry was trying to reverse a very well-established practice. He claimed in his speech that the sheriffs were to appear on time and in
person with their proffers 'as they ought to do according to the ancient custom of the exchequer'. But the custom he referred to, if it had ever existed,
was so ancient that it had long since fallen into desuetude. The first chrono-
logical receipt roll to survive, that for Michaelmas 1236, already shows that the
shrieval proffers were paid in over a period of time.[44] Throughout Henry's reign,
the memoranda rolls of the exchequer show a good proportion of the sheriffs
making their proffers through deputies. The same had been true in the reign
of John. At the Easter proffer of 1208, the only one of which we have a record,
eight sheriffs came in person and fourteen through deputies.[45] True nine of
the fourteen had the best possible excuse: they were with the king, or so their
deputies claimed. But it would be wrong to conclude that absence from the
proffer was otherwise punishable in the way Henry had envisaged. The exchequer took no action against the five remaining absent sheriffs and also accepted that the others were with John on the sole say so of their deputies. In
other words, no formal writ from the king was required to excuse absence from

[40] E 150/31, m. 23. From one year to the next, the same sheriffs (the more distant ones) tended
to send deputies but this is not an invariable rule and the lists were never exactly the same. We
cannot tell how many sheriffs proffered acceptable excuses for failing to appear at the Easter and
Michaelmas proffers of 1257. Henry's provision, however, made no mention of excuses and was
surely designed to do more than secure them.

[41] This is to judge from a comparison of the memoranda roll and the receipt roll: E 159/31, m.
23; E 401/33.

[42] E 159/29, m. 31; E 159/30, m. 23d. These are the total proffers including the sums from the
cities, boroughs and manors.

[43] E 159/30, m. 23. E 159/31, m. 23. For examples of the writs: *Close Rolls, 1254-6*, pp. 417-8,
426.

[44] E 401/12; E 159/15, m. 13.

[45] *Memoranda Roll 10 John*, pp. 31-3. The number is actually fifteen but the master of one of the
deputies was actually present in his capacity as a baron of the exchequer (William Brewer).

the proffer. This was already established practice in 1176. In that year the *Dialogus de Scaccario* acknowledged that the sheriffs could excuse themselves on many grounds from personal appearance, provided they sent a deputy with the money. It was only if they wished actually to account through a deputy that they needed a writ of authorisation from the king.[46]

From one point of view Henry's attempt to overturn this long-established custom had some merit, for the shrieval office had changed a great deal since John's reign, making the personal appearance of the sheriff at the proffer far more important, or so it could be argued.[47] A considerable proportion of John's sheriffs were great men, close to the king, as the numbers with him at Easter 1208 showed. Their counties were usually run for them by under-sheriffs, at least eight of whom had turned up for their masters at the 1208 proffer. In effect, therefore, the exchequer was still dealing with the *de facto* sheriff. By the 1250s, by contrast, great men rarely held sheriffdoms, formal under-sheriffs had disappeared and the sheriff himself actually ran the county. Thus the deputies appearing at the proffers were no longer, as they had sometimes been in John's reign, the men actually responsible for the county. Many were simply sheriffs' clerks, although that trend too was already evident by 1208. It was, therefore, far more important to get the sheriffs to appear personally at the proffers in the 1250s, when they were really administering their counties, than in the 1200s when they were not.

Yet, looked at from another point of view, to do so was both impractical and pointless. There was one essential reason for this: the increasing time lag between the sheriff's proffer and the sheriff's account. In the early twelfth century, when the business of the exchequer was more limited, all the sheriffs could turn up for the Michaelmas proffer, remain around and render their individual accounts within the next few weeks. A hundred years later that was no longer possible. The hearing of the accounts lasted from Michaelmas through to the following summer. A few sheriffs could be dealt with in the days immediately after Michaelmas but the great majority would have to return home and come up again at later dates, dates which could not always be coordinated with the second compulsory personal appearance at the Easter proffer. Some sheriffs would have to make three journeys to the exchequer in the course of the year: twice to proffer, once to account.[48] With the administrative burdens of the office increasing by leaps and bounds, this was verging on the absurd especially when the sheriff had to come from outside the home counties.

This same delay also made it increasingly unnecessary for the sheriffs to come to the proffer. If they were there, perhaps Henry hoped to saddle them with responsibility when the proffer was inadequate. Certainly a grossly substandard performance would be detected; but, in many cases, adequacy or inad-

---

[46] *Dialogus de Scaccario* pp. 79–84.

[47] For the change in the nature of the office, see 'The Decline of the Curial Sheriff in England, 1194–1258', below, pp. 151–82.

[48] Four journeys if they had to come up separately for the *view* of their account after Easter.

equacy was something only the process of account, often months away, would establish. This was why, as the *Dialogus* already recognised, it was far more important to have the sheriff at the account than at the proffer. The person who brought up the money was little more than a postman. Nor was there much point in insisting he arrived on the day after Michaelmas and the day after the close of Easter. The amount of money brought mattered far more than the delay of a few days or even a few weeks.

If all this is true, however, how does one explain the exchequer initiative of 1237 when, as we have seen, it amerced sixteen sheriffs £5 each for failing to appear in person on the day after the close of Easter; or indeed explain a parallel action in 1290 when the exchequer amerced nine sheriffs five marks each for not arriving personally with their proffers that Easter.[49] If Henry was wrong in trying to enforce personal appearance he was in good company. Or was he? In 1237 and 1290 the exchequer made no grand pronouncements but took punitive action. In 1256 Henry pronounced grandly but took no action at all. He threatened penalties far more severe than in 1237 and 1290, but never executed them. Whether the earlier and later initiatives were really designed to secure personal appearance is an open question; if they were they were failures.[50] But what they did do was impress the sheriffs with the power of the exchequer and keep them on their toes. Henry's pronouncement had precisely the reverse effect. It showed that his threats would not be implemented. That was a lesson not lost on magnates and ministers alike as Henry's government stumbled towards the revolution of 1258.

Henry III was not, of course, the only king to make impossible financial demands and fail in attempts to get the sheriffs to pay money in more promptly. That often happened under Edward I.[51] Yet Edward, we may think, was grappling with problems on an altogether greater scale. Henry himself should have settled for something less grand and more practical. He could, following the advice of the *Dialogus de Scaccario*, have insisted that the deputies should not be clerks 'since it is improper for them to be arrested for matters of money or account';[52] he could have reinstated the practice of John's reign, revived briefly in the Minority, of recording on the memoranda roll the reasons for the sheriff's absence;[53] he could have anticipated the Cowick ordinance of 1323 which accepted that the proffer might last several days, maintained the principle of personal appearance but allowed excuses 'according to the usages of the exchequer', and solved the problem of not knowing how good the proffer was by

[49] E 368/61, m. 8 (Madox, *Exchequer*, ii, 155 n. i.).

[50] This is clear from the subsequent Michaelmas proffers: E 159/17, m. 12 (ink); E 159/64, m. 17 (ink).

[51] M. Prestwich, 'Exchequer and Wardrobe in the Later Years of Edward I', *Bull. Inst. Hist. Res.*, 46 (1973), p. 6.

[52] *Dialogus de Scaccario*, p. 81; the sheriff's clerk, however, long continued as his representative at the proffer.

[53] D.A. Carpenter, *The Minority of Henry III* (London, 1990), p. 163.

linking it, where necessary, to a preliminary 'view' of the sheriff's account.[54] A dramatic entrance and a grand pronouncement, however, appealed to Henry; actually forcing the policy through against hostile sheriffs and a tepid exchequer was another matter. By the time the exchequer opened at the close of Easter in 1257 Henry had left Westminster and withdrawn to the company of the emollient monks at Merton. He was still thinking about money but now another grand and improbable scheme filled his head: that of setting aside £13,333 a year (a far larger sum than required) for the expenses of the royal household.[55] Until the sum was collected the treasurer, poor man, was to resist Henry's orders for the diversion of money elsewhere even when given with Henry's own mouth! This scheme too was soon abandoned. So too was the gold coinage, launched later in the year, after the mayor and citizens of London had come to the exchequer and told Henry how useless the whole thing was. At least a few of the splendid gold pennies survive to show Henry, as he doubtless wished to be shown, sitting regally on his throne. Henry was certainly a king with ideas. What he lacked was the ability to judge their viability.

It would be wrong to be too critical, however. In his ruling at the exchequer, as in saving his gold treasure, Henry was grappling with the central problem of thirteenth-century kingship: the inadequacy of the ordinary revenues of the crown. The time it took to save the gold treasure out of ordinary revenues and the difficulty of increasing them through tighter control over the sheriffs both suggested the necessity of new solutions. It was Edward I who found them by securing general taxation from parliament. With all its constitutional consequences, that was the future for English kingship.

[54] *The Red Book of the Exchequer*, 3 vols., ed. H. Hall (Rolls Ser., 1896), iii, pp. 894–7. For actual practice after the Ordinance, see *Calendar of Memoranda Rolls, 1326–7* (London, 1968), nos. 1–57, 2118–197.
[55] *Close Rolls, 1256–9*, pp. 46–7.

Appendix

Henry III's Provision at the Exchequer, October 1256

1. Printed (with modernised punctuation) from the memoranda roll of the king's rembrancer, Public Record Office, London, 159/30, m. 1d. Save where indicated the text is virtually the same as that in the memoranda roll of the lord treasurer's remembrancer: E 368/32, m. 1d. It is this text which is printed in T. Madox, *History and Antiquities of the Exchequer*, 2 vols. (2nd. edn., 1769), ii, p. 154 n.f.

Provisio domini regis[56]

Provisum est per dominum regem, quod singuli vicecomites Angliae veniant ad scaccarium in crastino sancti Michaelis et in crastino clausi Paschae (in propria persona sua),[57] tam cum firmis suis quam summonitionibus, ad profrum suum inde faciendum sicut debent secundum antiquam consuetudinem scaccarii. Et nisi veniant sicut praedictum est infra quintum [diem][58] praedictis terminis, amercientur primo die ad centum solidos, secundo die ad centum solidos, tercio die ad centum solidos, quarto die ad centum solidos et quinto die ad voluntatem domini regis. Et praeceptum est per ipsum dominum regem singulis vicecomitibus quod clamari faciant in singulis comitatibus suis quod omnes firmarii qui debeant respondere per manus suas ad scaccarium tam de civitatibus, burgis quam aliis dominicis domini regis sint ad dictum scaccarium dictis terminis in propriis personis suis ad respondendum tam de firmis suis quam de aliis debitis domini regis de quibus debeant respondedendum per manus suas per libertatem eis a domino rege concessam. Et nisi sint sicut dictum est, quilibet maior cuiuslibet civitatis et quilibet firmarius tam burgorum quam aliorum dominicorum domini regis amerciatur primo die ad quinque marcas, secondo die ad quinque marcas, tercio die ad quinque marcas, quarto die ad quinque marcas et quinto die capiatur civitas, burgus sive aliud dominicum in manu domini regis, illud nullatenus rehabendum sine gratia et voluntate domini regis. Et si quis sit ballivus seu firmarius domini regis, qui debeat respondere [ad scaccarium de debitis domini regis per manum suam et non veniant ad scaccarium predictis terminis ad respondendum][59] inde sicut predictum est amerciatur quolibet die infra quintum diem ad centum solidos sicut esset vicecomes.

[56] This heading is in the margin. The E 368 version also has a hand pointing towards the provision.
[57] Interlined.
[58] Interlined.
[59] This section is omitted in E 368.

2. Matthew Paris's version printed from *Matthaei Parisiensis . . . Chronica Majora*, 7 vols., ed. H.R. Luard (Rolls Ser., 1872–83), v, 588–9.

Quid rex tunc faceret ad scaccarium

Anno quoque sub eodem, dominus rex venit die quarta ante diem Sancti Edwardi ad scaccarium, et sedentibus ibidem baronibus, ore proprio pronuntiavit, quod quilibet vicecomes, qui in octavis Sancti Michaelis non apparuerit singulis annis, cum ostensione pecuniae regis, tam de firmis quam amerciamentis, et aliis modis ei debitis, prima die sit amerciatus ad quinque marcas, secunda ad decem, tertia ad quindecim, et quarta sit redimendus, si absens fuerit. Similis quoque pronuntiatio facta fuit per eundem regem contra civitates, quae libertates habent et per proprios ballivos ad scaccariium respondent; ita scilicet quod quarta die amittant libertates suas, nisi comparuerint eo modo quo vicecomites debent comparere.

8

The Decline of the Curial Sheriff in England, 1194–1258

THE thirteenth century witnessed a great decline in the political status of the sheriff, and the end of the office as it had existed since the early Norman period. King John, like his brother, father and great-grandfather, placed many counties, sometimes for long periods of time, under those whom contemporaries naturally described as *curiales* or *familiares regis* since they were among the king's most trusted, exalted and rewarded agents and councillors.[2] Hubert de Burgh (chamberlain and justiciar); Hugh de Neville (chief forester); William de Cantilupe (steward of the royal household); William Briwerre (baron of the exchequer) together with many others of comparable stature were frequent sheriffs in John's time.[3] Later in the century the picture has been transformed. Despite the political and military exigencies of his reign, few of Edward I's most intimate servants controlled counties, though they acted as constables of castles, custodians of vacant bishoprics and commissioners of array. *Curiales* such as Robert Tiptoft, Otto de Granson, William Latimer and John de Vescy[4] never held shrieval office, nor (later than 1275) did stewards of the royal household.[5] In general, Edward's sheriffs came either from the expanding group of professional administrators, who moved easily from shire to shire, or from the important families of the county. Men of both types (and the line between them is often blurred) staffed the numerous judicial and administrative commissions of the time, and occasionally ascended into the higher reaches of the royal service. As sheriffs, they performed hard and

1. I would like to thank Mr J. O. Prestwich for help at every stage of my work on sheriffs. I have also profited in the preparation of this article from the suggestions of Professor J. C. Holt and Dr J. F. A. Mason.

2. W. A. Morris, *The Medieval English Sheriff* (Manchester, 1927), pp. 77–80, 84–87, 113–14, 137, 161–4; J. E. A. Jolliffe, *Angevin Kingship* (2nd edn., London, 1963), p. 63, and see ch. viii for the *familiaris regis*.

3. *Lists of Sheriffs for England and Wales* (P[ublic] R[ecord] O[ffice] Lists and Indexes, ix, 1898), pp. 6, 21, 34, 43, 54, 59, 78, 102, 107, 122, 141, 144, 152, 157.

4. For these and other *curiales*, see M. Prestwich, *War, Politics and Finance under Edward I* (London, 1972), pp. 43–44, 239, 41–66.

5. The fullest list of Edward's stewards is contained in *Handbook of British Chronology*, ed. Sir Maurice Powicke and E. B. Fryde (Royal Historical Society, 1961), p. 74.

responsible work in the provinces without enjoying the king's closest confidence or greatest favour.[1]

Although aware of these changes,[2] historians have neither been concerned to trace their precise stages, nor to investigate in any detail their immediate causes. As a consequence traditional views on the decline of the curial sheriff need testing and elaboration at several points. The tendency has been to imply that the change took place gradually over the century, but there are grounds for believing that it was in fact effected fairly abruptly and quickly. Furthermore, although the decline has been seen (rightly) as the consequence of general alterations in the nature of the shrieval office, it may directly have been the condition and the instrument of highly specific measures of financial reform; measures which, in the period 1194–1258, were dependent on political events and circumstances rather than the processes of their own inner logic.[3] Aspects of these reforms, and of exchequer policies generally, in the years up to 1241, have been investigated by Miss Mabel Mills, and a great debt is owed to her pioneering work[4]; but some of her conclusions may need to be modified or enlarged, while from 1241 to 1258 the whole trend of exchequer policy has yet to receive the attention it deserves. One problem of particular importance is that of the role of the curial sheriff, and here the view of Miss Mills and Sir Maurice Powicke which sees him as the instrument of financial reform[5] needs to be re-examined.

Towards the end of the twelfth century there began a progressive diminution in the sheriff's independent powers and a steady increase in his routine duties and responsibilities. These twin processes, the one commencing with the introduction of the justices in eyre and coroners, the other with the work deriving from the assizes of Henry II, continued in the thirteenth century,[6] and gradually made

1. There is no adequate study of the sheriffs of Edward I, but see H. M. Cam, *The Hundred and the Hundred Rolls* (London, 1930), pp. 62–64; Morris, p. 167; and for Cambridgeshire and Warwickshire, respectively, H. M. Cam, 'Cambridgeshire Sheriffs in the Thirteenth Century', *Liberties and Communities in Medieval England* (2nd edn., London, 1963), pp. 27–48; G. Templeman, *The Sheriffs of Warwickshire in the Thirteenth Century* (Dugdale Society Occasional Papers, vii, 1948). Biographies of many sheriffs are found in C. Moor, *Knights of Edward I* (Harleian Soc., lxxx–lxxxiv, 1929–32). The counties bordering Wales and those in the north were occasionally under *curiales* (e.g. Bogo de Knoville, Shropshire–Staffordshire 1274–8; Walter of Cambo, Northumberland, 1278–81), but even here the sheriffs were usually drawn from king's servants who were not of the highest rank, though they were often men of military experience.
2. See, Morris, pp. 167–8; Cam, *Hundred Rolls*, pp. 7–8; E. F. Jacob, *Studies in the Period of Baronial Reform and Rebellion, 1258–67* (Oxford, 1925), pp. 19–20.
3. Compare the view of Sir Maurice Powicke, *Henry III and the Lord Edward* (Oxford, 1947), i. 97, n. 2.
4. M. H. Mills, 'Experiments in Exchequer Procedure (1200–1232)', *Trans. Roy. Hist. Soc.*, 4th Ser., viii (1925), 151–70; 'The Reforms at the Exchequer (1232–1242)', *ibid.* 4th ser., x (1927), 111–33.
5. *Infra*, p. 162.
6. Morris, pp. 138–40, 238–9; Cam, *Hundred Rolls*, pp. 7–8, 244–5; for a view over a longer period see F. W. Maitland, *Justice and Police* (London, 1885), pp. 69–70 and *The Constitutional History of England* (Cambridge, 1908), pp. 233–4.

it less necessary for the shrieval office to be held by a major servant of the king. The curial sheriff would not, however, have disappeared in the way he did, nor as quickly, without the policy of extracting revenue above the county farm which was a favourite project of the exchequer after 1194. The sheriff, as is well known, was responsible every year at the exchequer for a fixed farm of his county which derived from various dues (like sheriff's aid); from the proceeds of the county and hundred courts; and from royal demesne manors.[1] These sources frequently produced a sum greater than the farm, and as the thirteenth century approached, and the king's financial predicament was aggravated by inflation, it became the urgent concern of the exchequer to secure accounts for some or all of this surplus. Two methods were developed. The first was to charge the sheriff with a fixed annual increment above the farm; the second to demand that he account for all the revenue which he received. The sheriff in this case was said to answer 'as a custodian', and the revenue in excess of that needed to meet the farm was charged to him on the pipe roll as a lump sum and called 'profit'.[2] There can be no doubt that profits (and presumably increments too) sometimes contained the surpluses of demesne manors remaining within the county farm,[3] and were thus related to the many expedients adopted in this period to get better value from the king's manors[4] – for although it has been rightly stressed that patronage was often the overriding factor governing the disposition of the demesne,[5] this did not preclude earnest endeavours to increase its revenue while it was in the king's hands. Probably the most effective way of doing so was to withdraw the royal manors from the sheriff, and lease them to their men or

1. *Dialogus de Scaccario*, ed. C. Johnson (London, 1950), pp. 64–65; Mills, *ubi supra* (1925), pp. 158–60; Cam, *Hundred Rolls*, pp. 88–95.
2. Mills, *ubi supra* (1925), pp. 159–60; B. E. Harris, 'King John and the Sheriffs' Farms', *EHR*, lxxix, 532–42; P. D. A. Harvey, 'The English Inflation of 1180–1220', *Past and Present*, no. 61 (1973), 9–11. Technically, a custodian sheriff did not answer for a farm but for all the revenues of his shire, and he made returns of these in a way a farmer did not; see *infra*, p. 171, n. 3. It was merely as a convenient method of account that the exchequer used these issues to clear the farm, and form the profits. There were probably different views at the exchequer throughout this period as to the respective merits of profits and increments. The custodian system enabled a closer control over the sheriff and his revenue, but for that reason was more troublesome to run.
3. B. P. Wolffe, *The Royal Demesne in English History* (London, 1971), p. 31 may take a different view. In 1227–8 the profits of Cumberland were said to be those of the county and its manors (which were within the county farm). Six years later the issues from various manorial items were accounted for separately, having previously been included in the county profits; *The Pipe Rolls of Cumberland and Westmorland 1222–1260*, ed. F. H. M. Parker (Cumberland and Westmorland Antiquarian and Archaeological Society, extra ser., xii, 1905), pp. 23, 54. In 1225–6 the profits of Nottinghamshire–Derbyshire were likewise stated to include those of manors (for which the sheriff was here replying outside the farm); P.R.O. Pipe Roll 10 Henry III (E. 372/70), m.21.
4. These included the sheriff replying for manors outside the farm at fresh valuations (as in Northamptonshire from 1213) or replying for all their issues as custodians (as for Bloxham in Oxfordshire, or Writtle and Newport in Essex in the 1220s); *Pipe Roll 16 John*, pp. 20, 21; Pipe Roll 9 Henry III (E. 372/69), ms. 10d, 30.
5. Wolffe, pp. 30–38, 46.

commit them to special keepers, as was done in individual cases from the reign of Henry II, and on a more general scale, with important consequences, in 1236.[1]

Curial sheriffs proved inappropriate or recalcitrant as agents of these increment and profit policies, despite the fact that they have sometimes been associated in the minds of historians with the implementation of programmes of financial reform.[2] In 1194, 1204 and 1236, the individual years in which such policies were developed most extensively, their executants were largely found outside the ranks of the king's familiars, among local knights and barons, or non-curial professional administrators. Indeed, in the two latter years, men of this stamp were appointed to carry out the exchequer's programmes after the removal or retirement of a large number of *familiares regis*; a retirement to which increasing incentive was given by the mounting exactions above the farm between 1236–58, and by the withdrawal of royal manors from shrieval control. There were several reasons why the *curialis* was an unsuitable sheriff from the exchequer's point of view. He was more troublesome in general to control than a man of less influence and favour; he frequently consigned the administration of the county to a deputy which created difficulties over the division of responsibility[3]; he harboured in the early years a dislike simply for the status of a 'custodian'[4] and, above all, he was reluctant to hold office on terms which deprived him of private gain. Thus, when the exchequer decided upon a rigorous exaction of profits or increments, which threatened to reduce the financial attraction of local office, it recognized that it must seek its sheriffs elsewhere.

All this is not to say that curial sheriffdoms served no useful purpose. Rather the period 1194–1258 saw two contrasting views of the sheriff's office. On the one hand there was that of the exchequer, outlined above, which wished to turn the sheriff into an efficient collector of revenue, who accounted realistically for the proceeds above the farm, and would be the type of man whom it could discipline. This view was closely associated with the schemes (in which Hubert Walter initially played an important part) to reduce the sheriff's responsibilities by the introduction of coroners, keepers of manors and escheats, constables of county castles and, later, commissioners of array, keepers of the peace and J.P.s. On the other

1. R. S. Hoyt, *The Royal Demesne in English Constitutional History* (New York, 1950), pp. 98–107, 136–40, 156–61.

2. *Infra*, p. 162.

3. See, *Memoranda Roll 1 John*, pp. 80, 5; *Lists of Sheriffs*, p. 43; for difficulty with two under-sheriffs of Hugh de Neville; and P.R.O. King's Remembrancer's Memoranda Roll 20 Henry III (E. 159/14), r. 6; *Close Rolls 1234–37*, pp. 248–9 for one between Stephen of Seagrave and his under-sheriff in Bedfordshire–Buckinghamshire.

4. S. Painter, *The Reign of King John* (Baltimore, 1949), p. 119. In the early days those answering as custodians were not considered (or appointed) as sheriffs; *Rot. Lit. Pat.*, p. 47; *Rot. Litt. Claus.*, i. 78.

hand there was the older view of the sheriff as a general-purpose regional governor, who might control several counties together with their castles, manors and escheats. Although certainly expected to account properly for the farms of his various custodies, he was beyond that entitled to his appropriate rewards. These rewards would help sustain him in his multifarious activities in the king's service. The extent to which sheriffs of this type, who were usually *curiales*, ran their counties in person depended on the strategic position of these counties and the political circumstances of the day.[1] In many cases it is clear that the routine administration was left to under-sheriffs,[2] and the almost complete disappearance of correspondence renders it difficult to estimate how far their activities were supervised.[3] The criterion by which such curial sheriffdoms were judged, however, was not so much the size of revenue raised above the farm as the strength of the shire contingent in the king's armies[4] and the general security provided for the county and its castle. Thus it may well be that the appointment of a number of relatively insignificant custodian sheriffs in 1204 produced next year Hubert Walter's scheme for a distinct military hierarchy in each county under chief constables.[5] In the same way, it was probably the comparative unimportance of the sheriffs which required the curial constables of county castles in the 1250s,[6] and the curial commissioners of array to whom Edward I eventually transferred the task of raising troops for his armies.[7]

Between 1194 and 1258, therefore, the king was faced with a series of difficult choices about the personnel and organization of local administration. On the one hand the need for increased revenue suggested the wisdom of removing *curiales* from the counties and

1. Thus Henry of Bath (sheriff of Yorkshire 1242-8), appointed when the king was preparing to leave the country, was initially closely involved in northern administration. From 1245, however, he combined the sheriffdom with the chief justiceship of the bench; *Crown Pleas of the Wiltshire Eyre 1249*, ed. C. A. F. Meekings (Wiltshire Archaeological and Natural History Society, Records Branch, xvi, 1960), pp. 128-9; *Close Rolls 1242-47*, p. 83.

2. For under-sheriffs in John's reign, see B. E. Harris, 'The English Sheriffs in the Reign of King John' (unpublished Nottingham Univ. M.A. thesis, 1961), ch. v.

3. For a letter to Philip Mark, sheriff of Nottinghamshire–Derbyshire, from his subordinates; *Royal Letters of Henry III*, ed. W. W. Shirley (Rolls Series, 1862), i, no. lxxxvi. The numerous letters in the same volume to Ralph de Neville, chancellor, and bishop of Chichester (1224-44) show how a great *curialis* was closely concerned with the administration of his own estates. For the curial role in the administration of ecclesiastical vacancies, see M. Howell, *Regalian Right in Medieval England* (London, 1962), pp. 63-66, 88-91. The few surviving private letters show that the picture of the relationship between the sheriffs and central government given by the official correspondence is highly inadequate; *Royal Letters of Henry III*, i, nos. ccxxv, ccxcix; P.R.O. Ancient Correspondence, i (SC. 1/1), nos. 155, 158.

4. Morris, pp. 151-2; I. J. Sanders, *Feudal Military Service in England* (Oxford, 1956), pp. 109-12, 114.

5. *The historical works of Gervase of Canterbury*, ed. W. Stubbs (Rolls series, 1879-80), ii. 96-97.

6. *Infra*, p. 177-8.   7. Prestwich, pp. 99, 100.

replacing them with those who could more easily be brought to answer for sums above the farm. On the other hand, the claims of political security, and the necessity of providing patronage for *familiares* argued for leaving numbers of shires under the latter and allowing them easy terms. The situation was further complicated by county society's hostility to the exaction of revenue above the farm for the obvious reason that sheriffs were then likely to recompense themselves for the loss in unpleasant ways. This did not mean, however, that the localities would welcome a curial sheriff holding at the ancient farm. Their ideal was a local knightly sheriff answering on these terms,[1] although later, as will be seen, this demand was moderated.[2] With the king thus forced to adjudge the conflicting claims of security, patronage, money and popularity, it is hardly remarkable that the terms of shrieval office were often matters of negotiation and dispute. The success of the exchequer's plans[3] for the sheriff depended on its ability to find men who would embrace office on conditions unacceptable to *curiales*. In fact, professional administrators and members of the county gentry (despite local society's antipathy to revenue above the farm) could often be induced or compelled to do this. They had less influence to escape the exchequer's exactions, and also less need since they ran their shires in person and enjoyed benefits which were not open to absentee *familiares*. The prestige of the office also counted for something with the local knight, while the professionals were usually unhampered by local connections and well versed in the expertise of exploitation. These men were of much the same type as those who had previously administered shires for *curiales* as undersheriffs; in this respect the decline of the curial sheriff was less significant than it appeared; yet the exchequer policies which caused it did much to shape the relationship between court and county, and prevent its reformation on more felicitous lines.

In 1194 the policy of extracting revenue above the county farm was developed extensively for the first time. After King Richard's return from captivity many counties were put up for sale to those who would offer the best terms. The result was that increments totalling 1,070 marks were imposed on ten sheriffdoms while three sheriffs made substantial fines to avoid them.[4] It was clear that *curiales* were

1. See the fine of Somerset-Dorset, *Pipe Roll 12 John*, p. 75. For the reasons why curial sheriffdoms might be unpopular, see, *infra*, p. 179.

2. *Infra*, p. 180.

3. A great deal of work needs to be done on the personnel, procedures and policies of the exchequer in the thirteenth century. There may well have been different views among the barons. In John's reign for example the outlook of the treasurer, William of Ely is unlikely to have been the same as that of William Briwerre; Painter, pp. 66–67, 71–78; H. G. Richardson, 'William of Ely, the King's Treasurer', *Trans. Roy. Hist. Soc.*, 4th ser., xv (1932), 45–90.

4. Harris, *EHR*, lxxix. 533; *Pipe Roll 6 Richard I*, pp. xvii–xx.

not the most suitable or willing undertakers of these new burdens. Of the thirteen sheriffs who accepted increments or fined to avoid them, nine came from outside their ranks.[1] They included four knights who were holding office in or near their home counties,[2] and two politically insignificant and inactive barons.[3] Meanwhile, of the ten sheriffdoms which avoided increments without conditions, eight were held by *curiales*,[4] and one by the justiciar's brother, Theobald.[5] Ten years later, at Michaelmas 1204, the government inaugurated a more ambitious policy and placed the majority of sheriffdoms under custodians who were to answer for all the issues of their shires and account for 'profits' above the farm.[6] To clear the way for this project, seven *curiales* were relieved of a total of thirteen sheriffdoms,[7] and in nine of these they were replaced by those whose

1. The exceptions were the chancellor, William de Longchamp, his two brothers (though neither had much personal connection with the king), and the professional judge, Simon of Pattishall. The chancellor and the archbishop of York also made offers of increments for various counties which came to nothing. *Pipe Roll 6 Richard I*, pp. 29, 30, 47, 127, 68, 69, xvii–xx.

2. *Pipe Roll 6 Richard I*, pp. 76, 43, 44, 183, 193, 102, 103. Reginald de Argentan (Cambridgeshire–Huntingdonshire); W. Farrer, *Honors and Knights' Fees* (London and Manchester, 1923–5), ii. 238–40; *Pleas Before the King or his Justices 1198–1212*, ed. D. M. Stenton (Selden Society, lxxxiii, 1966), iii, ccxcvi–vii; *Pipe Roll 3 & 4 Richard I*, p. 116. Reginald Basset (Warwickshire–Leicestershire); *V[ictoria] C[ounty] H[istory] Warw.*, vi 105–6; *Rot. Litt. Claus.*, i. 314, 413. William fitz Ralph de Cahaignes (Dorset–Somerset); L. F. Salzman, 'Sussex Domesday Tenants', *Sussex Archaeological Collections*, lxiii (1922), 193–8; *Red Book of the Exchequer*, i. 218; *Rot. Litt. Claus*, i. 131. Simon of Kyme (Lincolnshire); J. C. Holt, *The Northerners* (Oxford, 1961), pp. 55–59. That these men had no substantial connection with the court may be judged in part from the small number of royal charters they attest in L. Landon, *The Itinerary of Richard I* (Pipe Roll Soc., new ser., xiii, 1935).

3. Simon de Beauchamp (Bedfordshire–Buckinghamshire); and Henry d'Oilly (Oxfordshire); *Pipe Roll 6 Richard I*, pp. 203, 209; 89. For d'Oilly, see D. A. Carpenter, 'Sheriffs of Oxfordshire and their Subordinates 1194–1236' (unpublished Oxford Univ., D.Phil. thesis, 1973), ch. ii. The three other sheriffs were Hugh de Bosco (Hampshire); Herbert fitz Herbert (Gloucestershire) and Hugh of Chacombe (Shropshire–Staffordshire); *Pipe Roll 6 Richard I*, pp. 212, 219; 231, 232; 39. See once again the few references to these men in Landon, *Itinerary of Richard I*. Bosco and Chacombe were in the king's service; *Pipe Roll 5 Richard I*, p. 165; *Pleas Before the King or Justices*, iii. pp. xci, xcv, c.

4. William Briwerre; William fitz Aldeni; Hugh Bardolf; William de Braose; William earl of Salisbury; Robert of Thornham; William Marshal; *Pipe Roll 6 Richard I*, pp. 80, 251, 120, 132, 136, 195, 221, 226. See the many references to these men in Landon, *Itinerary of Richard I*.

5. *Pipe Roll 6 Richard I*, p. 123. The other sheriffdom (Kent) was held by Reginald of Cornhill. The counties of Devon and Cornwall which avoided increments, perhaps by making gifts that they might be treated 'benigne', have not been included in the above analysis; *Pipe Roll 7 Richard I*, pp. 130, 134.

6. Harris, *EHR*, lxxix. 535–6; Painter, pp. 118–20; Holt, pp. 152–3.

7. Geoffrey fitz Peter (4); Hubert de Burgh (3); William Briwerre; William de Cantilupe; Warin fitz Gerold; William Marshal earl of Pembroke; Peter de Stokes; and Robert of Thornham all one. For these men at court see the charters attested by them in *Rot. Chartarum*. The details of the changes are best followed in *Lists of Sheriffs*. It is misleading to think of Yorkshire as part of the new system. Roger de Lacy was never called a custodian, and the fine he made 'pro proficuo' in 1208–9 merely accounted for the sum he owed in respect of the increment he had agreed to in 1204–5; *Rot. de Oblatis et Finibus*, p. 273; *Pipe Roll 11 John*, p. 125.

connection with the court was far more tenuous.[1] Several of the new sheriffs were again local knights or minor tenants-in-chief.[2] One was an experienced non-curial sheriff.[3] The promotion of four under-sheriffs stressed the intention to pick men of less importance.[4] It is inconceivable that such drastic changes in personnel would have been brought about had *curiales* been seen as promising executants of the new policy[5]; indeed from the first this policy was restricted and reversed by the king's desire to maintain his familiars in local office. In 1204, King John had retained Thomas Basset, William Briwerre and William Marshal earl of Pembroke in three shrievalities as farmers,[6] although later figures show that these counties were capable of yielding reasonable profits. He likewise retained Robert fitz Roger in strategic Northumberland, having earlier decided that the demesne manors of this county should remain within the farm at their old valuation, instead of being transferred to their men at substantial increments.[7] By Michaelmas 1205, Peter de Stokes (steward of the royal household), and Robert of Thornham (a former seneschal of Poitou) had recovered the counties of which they had been relieved the previous year. To the exchequer's appreciable loss, and in Stokes's cases apparently against its opposition, they recovered them as farmers, not custodians.[8] Conversely, the only non-curial sheriff dismissed in 1204, John of Cornard, returned to Norfolk–Suffolk next year as a custodian.[9] Three other *curiales* who had retained office in 1204, but had become custodians, soon reverted to

1. Compare the small number of royal charters in *Rot. Chartarum* attested by those mentioned in the following notes. In the first year many of the custodians were given clerks as colleagues. The *curiales* appointed to new counties as custodians were William de Cantilupe (Herefordshire); William earl of Salisbury (Wiltshire); Robert de Vieuxpont (Nottinghamshire–Derbyshire) and Hugh of Chacombe (Warwickshire–Leicestershire). Hugh was only just establishing himself in the higher reaches of the king's service, and he did not survive there long. Cantilupe and the earl of Salisbury appear to have disliked their novel status; Painter, p. 119; *Pipe Roll 7 John*, pp. 271, 275–6.

2. Robert de Salceto (Northamptonshire); *Curia Regis Rolls*, iii. 13. William de Montagu (Somerset–Dorset); *Complete Peerage*, ix. 76; *Rot. Litt. Claus*, i. 131. William de Cahaignes (Sussex); Salzman, *ubi supra*, p. 195; Alexander of Dunham who followed John of Cornard, the only non-curial sheriff replaced, in Norfolk–Suffolk was also a local knight; *Curia Regis Rolls*, ii. 18, 136.

3. Robert of Tattershall (Cambridgeshire–Huntingdonshire); *Complete Peerage*, xii, part i, 647–8.

4. John of Wiggenholt (Berkshire); Robert of Braybrook (Bedfordshire–Buckinghamshire); Roger fitz Adam (Hampshire); Thomas of Erdington (Shropshire–Staffordshire); of the ninth sheriff, Richard de Maisy (Surrey) little can be discovered.

5. Compare the view of Painter who, looking at the changes from a slightly different angle, concluded 'in general there was no great revolution in personnel'; Painter, p. 118.

6. Oxfordshire; Devonshire; Gloucestershire. For other counties to escape see Painter, pp. 119–20.

7. *Rot. Chartarum*, pp. 86–87; *Pipe Roll 3 John*, p. 249.

8. *Pipe Roll 7 John*, pp. 152, 155, 255, 257; *ibid. 8 John*, pp. 115, 170, 172; *Rot. Litt. Pat.*, p. 54; *Pipe Roll 9 John*, p. 130; *Memoranda Roll 10 John*, p. 49; *Pipe Roll 10 John*, p. 173, n. 10 (Peter de Stokes died in 1206).

9. John passed his profit to the bishop of Norwich; *Pipe Roll 10 John*, p. 12.

being farmers[1]; and when four sheriffdoms were concentrated under William Briwerre in 1207-8 the custodian system was immediately abandoned in each, although it had by no means functioned ineffectively.[2] Briwerre, who reluctantly attended as a baron of the exchequer, having many more duties in the king's service, may well have been out of sympathy with the new policies of his colleagues.[3] If he was one of the most unpopular sheriffs of John's reign, this was not because he was raising large sums of money for the king above the farm, and the same is true of the detested foreigners, Engelard de Cigogné and Philip Mark, sheriffs respectively of Gloucestershire and Nottinghamshire-Derbyshire.

King John was, therefore, prepared to forego the receipt or control of a certain portion of revenue in order to maintain strong curial sheriffs in various counties, and to sustain such men generally in his service. This is not to say that *curiales* could not make efficient custodians. Gilbert fitz Reinfrey was a spectacular success in Yorkshire,[4] but usually their appointment did not facilitate financial reform, nor was it designed to do so. The most effective custodians of the reign over a long period were the promoted under-sheriffs of 1204, John of Wiggenholt, Thomas of Erdington and (best of all) Robert of Braybrook, who was later followed by his son, Henry.[5] Of these four, only Thomas of Erdington became a *curialis*[6]; and his utility as a custodian was then somewhat reduced by the 40 mark annual allowance for keeping his 'ballia' and its castles which his elevated station (with its many duties) helped secure.[7] John's reign, therefore, foreshadowed the decline of the curial sheriff should a policy of profits or increments ever be vigorously developed. Many years were to pass before this became possible. It required a stable

1. Reginald of Cornhill (Kent); *Pipe Roll 7 John*, p. 111; *ibid. 8 John*, p. 46. Gerard de Camville (Lincolnshire); *Rot. Litt. Pat.*, p. 53b; *Pipe Roll 7 John*, pp. 196, 197; William de Cantilupe (Worcestershire) who agreed to keep the king's castles at his own cost (a frequent stipulation when profit was conceded); *Rot. de Oblatis et Finibus*, p. 400.

2. Harris, *EHR*, lxxix. 539. Profits had been small or non-existent in Sussex and Dorset–Somerset, but reasonable sums were owed for Hampshire and Wiltshire; *Pipe Roll 8 John*, p. 182; *ibid. 9 John*, pp. 141, 201. The 40 mark annual 'profit' for which Briwerre answered in Dorset–Somerset was probably a sum agreed in return for his being pardoned the 100 mark annual increment; *Pipe Roll 10 John*, p. 105; *ibid. 12 John*, p. 70.

3. Painter, p. 72; *Rot. Chartarum*, p. 97; *Pipe Roll 2 John*, p. 191.

4. Holt, p. 154.

5. Harris, *EHR*, lxxix. 537; Painter, p. 122.

6. Roger of Wendover's placing of Robert and Henry of Braybrook in his list of John's evil councillors is shown to be misleading (even allowing for the rolls of several years being missing) by the fact that Robert attests few charters in *Rot. Chartarum*, and Henry none; *Matthaei Parisiensis Chronica Majora*, ed. H. R. Luard (Rolls Series, 1872–83), ii. 533.

7. *Rot. Litt. Claus.*, i. 78; *Pipe Roll 8 John*, p. 109; *ibid. 9 John*, pp. 7, 9. The timing of this grant should be noted. The size is erroneously stated as 500 marks in Harris, *EHR*, lxxix. 536. The strategic position of Erdington's counties of Shropshire–Staffordshire may also have been a factor in the concession. For a discussion of allowances see *infra*, p. 160, n. 5.

political situation in which the king could dispense with great curial sheriffs, and override the hostility of county society. In 1204, when profits were introduced, such a situation largely obtained but by 1207-8 the political outlook was more threatening, and this may well have led (as Sidney Painter suggested) to Briwerre's appointment to his four sheriffdoms, and the abandonment of the custodian system in each.[1] Later, in 1213, John decided to give up increments altogether, both as an act of political concession and a measure to strengthen his sheriffs,[2] although accounts continued to be rendered for profits in some shires till the civil war. Clause twenty-five of Magna Carta forbade increments by name, and profits by implication when it stated that the counties were to be held 'at the ancient farm'.[3] The clause was omitted from subsequent re-issues of the Charter, but it was not till the changes in the personnel of the sheriffs in 1223-4 that the custodian system was reimposed, and profits were demanded from nearly every shire.[4]

In the twelve years after 1224, however, the force of exchequer policy in regard to revenue above the farm was severely limited. Until 1229 the majority of sheriffdoms were under custodians, but the value of the profits was often corroded by the large allowances which they obtained for the keeping of their counties and castles. This had not been the case in John's reign. Although the theory that custodians had rights to allowances (as farmers had not) was then abroad, and was sensible since such sheriffs were supposed to account for all the revenue which they received, the evidence suggests that the actual concessions were neither as frequent in number nor as generous in size as they were between 1224-9.[5] After Michaelmas

1. Painter, pp. 122-3.
2. Harris, *EHR*, lxxix. 540-1.
3. For the sense in which a custodian sheriff did not answer for a farm, see *supra*, p. 153, n. 2.
4. Mills, *ubi supra* (1925), p. 167.
5. Dr Harris argues that the sheriff in John's reign 'became a paid official with an expense account'; *EHR*, lxxix. 536. In 1215 John certainly informed the exchequer that it was 'right' for the (curial) sheriff of Yorkshire, Peter fitz Herbert, to receive his reasonable expenses for keeping the county and its castles since he was answering for profits; *Rot. Litt. Claus.*, i. 187b; but, prior to this, the only discoverable allowance covering the 'ballia' and castles of a custodian sheriff is that conceded to Thomas of Erdington, which was considerably smaller than the equivalent allowance under Henry III; *supra*, p. 159; *infra*, p. 162. In the period from 1224 allowances regularly appear on the pipe rolls, the sums in question being deducted from the profits. (Miss Mills is incorrect in saying that there are merely 'traces' of them from 1227-8; *ubi supra* (1927), p. 121.) In a few isolated cases the concessions were in forms which did not appear on the pipe rolls, but it would be unsafe to assume that this is the explanation for their infrequent appearance under John, although see, *Pipe Roll 9 John*, p. 7. The exchequer was probably cautious and niggardly about granting allowances unless there was direct authorization from the king. Hence the orders in favour of Erdington and fitz Herbert, and the fact that after 1224 a large number of the concessions were sanctioned by royal letters. This obviously gave the *curialis* a great advantage over other sheriffs in securing one of generous size. The *Dialogus de Scaccario* (p. 124) actually denies that a custodian keeper of an escheat had a right to an allowance without a mandate

1229 ten sheriffs ceased to be custodians, and answered annually for fixed increments in place of profits.[1] These increments were small compared with those of the 1240s and 1250s.

There were probably two reasons for this moderation. The first was reluctance to antagonize county society, a reluctance which led to several government concessions in the 1220s.[2] The second was the number of sheriffdoms under *curiales* who used their influence to urge the utility or necessity of their enjoying easy terms which involved either large allowances or small increments. The removal of the over-mighty sheriffs of the minority in 1223–4 was a pre-condition for the reimposition of profits; Falkes de Breauté controlling six shires, and the earl of Chester three, owed considerable sums in respect of their county farms by the time they were dismissed,[3] and would scarcely have replied competently for revenue above them. But the turbulent circumstances of the changes did not permit a wide clearing of *curiales* from sheriffdoms as in 1204, and the pattern of that year was not in fact repeated till 1236. Thus the king's senior steward, Ralph fitz Nicholas, was sheriff of Herefordshire from 1223 to 1229, and of Nottinghamshire–Derbyshire for the whole period 1224–36, holding from May 1232 'tota vita sua, quamdiu regi bene servierit'.[4] Till 1229 the respective 100-mark and £100 allowances largely consumed the profits of these sheriffdoms[5]; thereafter in Nottinghamshire–Derbyshire Ralph was conceded all the profits (including those of the manors) in return for a 50 mark increment, half of that proposed in 1241[6] when the sheriff had lost most of the royal demesne.[7] The treasurer of the exchequer himself, Walter Mauclerc, bishop of Carlisle, who was sheriff of Cumberland from 1222 to 1233, was conceded all the substantial profits of the county and its manors from 1229, and he received a life grant on these terms in July 1232, during the competitions heralding the fall

---

from the king – otherwise 'he shall serve the king in these matters at his own expense' – but it is not clear whether the exchequer ever went as far as this in respect of custodian sheriffs. The subject merits fuller discussion than can be given here.

1. At Michaelmas 1229 five sheriffdoms remained under custodians, and five were already under farmers. These distinctions, however, are sometimes only formal since round sums were sometimes agreed in place of profits. The changes of 1229 had little effect on the revenue due to the exchequer and were probably made for reasons of administrative convenience.

2. Powicke, i. 67; *Close Rolls 1227–31*, p. 274. See also *infra*, p. 180.

3. Pipe Roll 8 Henry III (E. 372.68), ms. 2d, 3d, 5.

4. *Patent Rolls 1225–32*, p. 472.

5. Pipe Roll 9 Henry III (E. 372/69), m. 13; *ibid.* 10 Henry III (E. 372/70), ms. 17d, 21; *ibid.* 12 Henry III (E. 372/72), ms. 3, 24, 24d; *ibid.* 13 Henry III (E. 372/73), ms. 9, 10, 29, 30; *Cal. Lib. Rolls 1226–40*, pp. 98, 141; *Close Rolls 1227–31*, p. 411.

6. *Close Rolls 1227–31*, p. 282; P.R.O. Originalia Roll 25 Henry III (E. 371/8A), m. 4, sch. 2.

7. The profits of these demesne manors came to £17 2s. 8d. in 1228–9; Pipe Roll 13 Henry III (E. 372/73), m. 10.

of Hubert de Burgh.[1] Also in 1229 Stephen of Seagrave, then a leading justice at the bench, was allowed the profits of Bedfordshire–Buckinghamshire, Northamptonshire, and Warwickshire–Leicestershire,[2] counties which in July 1232 he was granted on the same terms for life.[3] Nine years later, long after Seagrave had been dismissed and his life grant nullified, they were expected to reply for increments of £313 6s. 8d.[4] Henry of Audley, as sheriff of Shropshire–Staffordshire (1227–32), was first permitted a 100-mark annual allowance (60 marks more than Thomas of Erdington's in John's reign) to keep the counties and the castles of Bridgenorth and Shrewsbury (1227–8)[5]; then conceded all the profit (1228–9); and finally after 1229 answered for a small 40-mark increment, which was to last for the duration of his tenure, and was itself fully pardoned in 1231 and 1232.[6] From the narrow exchequer point of view there were obvious advantages in the arrangements under Audley's predecessor, the versatile non-curial administrator, John Bonet, who without responsibility for Bridgenorth answered for 300 marks of profits over and above a 50 mark annual allowance, between Michaelmas 1224 and Michaelmas 1226.[7]

The concessions to Henry of Audley were probably related to the threat posed by Llywelyn, which burgeoned into war in 1228 and 1231. In other cases military and strategic considerations were less pressing, although the establishment of Stephen of Seagrave in 1229 was perhaps connected with the king's projected departure from the country to campaign in Brittany. It has been suggested that the purpose of *curiales* such as Seagrave, fitz Nicholas and Walter Mauclerc controlling sheriffdoms was to supervise programmes of financial reform, and tighten relations between the shires and the exchequer.[8] Yet the fact that they aspired to hold these offices for life, and on terms highly favourable to themselves makes this questionable. Indeed the specified purpose of the concessions to these men, beyond the keeping of the counties and castles, was to sustain them in the king's service,[9] much as in 1218–19 Engelard

---

1. *Close Rolls 1227–31*, pp. 264–5; *Cal. Chart. Rolls*, i. 165. *Cumberland Pipe Rolls*, pp. 18, 22, 23, 27, 28, 31.

2. *Close Rolls 1227–31*, p. 259.   3. *Cal. Chart. Rolls*, i. 166.

4. Originalia Roll 25 Henry III (E. 371/8A), m. 4, sch. 2. The farms of the Northamptonshire manors for which Seagrave replied had also increased considerably by 1241; *infra*, p. 169.

5. Pipe Roll 13 Henry III (E. 372/73), ms. 19, 20.

6. *Close Rolls 1227–31*, pp. 191, 561; Pipe Roll 13 Henry III (E. 372/73), ms. 29, 30; *Pipe Roll 14 Henry III*, p. 232; Pipe Roll 15 Henry III (E. 372/75), m. 17d; *ibid.* 18 Henry III (E. 372/78), m. 22.

7. Pipe Roll 9 Henry III (E. 372/69), ms. 28, 27d; *ibid.* 10 Henry III (E. 372/70), ms. 15d, 16d.

8. Mills, *ubi supra* (1927), 119, 112; Powicke, i. 95; F. West, *The Justiciarship in England* (Cambridge, 1966), p. 268.

9. *Close Rolls 1227–31*, pp. 259, 265, 282. The concession of profits to Seagrave was also to help him maintain the daughter of Llywelyn.

de Cigogné was promised either the county of Surrey or £100 p.a.
in escheats 'quod ei sufficienter provideretur pro magno servicio
suo'.[1] The store set on patronage of this kind is illustrated by the
endeavours of the king's second steward, Godfrey of Crowcombe,
to retain and profit from his custody of the county and castle of
Oxford, and the king's manor at Woodstock with which these were
linked. Godfrey had commenced in 1225 as a custodian with a £40
allowance – twice that received by the sheriffs after 1236 when they
no longer had manorial responsibilities.[2] He successfully resisted an
attempt to dismiss him in 1229,[3] and two years later obtained a life
grant of the castle, the county (at a 20-mark increment), and Woodstock (at its ancient farm). This concession probably meant his
private profit from the custodies was now double his old £40
allowance.[4] Whatever, therefore, the advantages of these curial
sheriffdoms, they were a great bar to any thorough exaction of profits
or increments; and their occupants neither wished to resign their
positions, nor to accept less favourable terms in the cause of
reform.

The regime of Peter des Roches, bishop of Winchester, and his
nephew, Peter des Rivaux, which secured full power in August 1232
after the dismissal of the last great justiciar, Hubert de Burgh, did
little to alter this situation, or in any way to improve the king's
position with respect to revenue above the farm. True, the bishop
and his nephew presented themselves as financial reformers, and
since the work of Miss Mills their claim to this distinction has been
widely accepted, and their measures are regarded as anticipating the
reforms of 1236–41.[5] It is possible that Peter des Rivaux (who became
treasurer of the exchequer in January 1233) tightened up on the
sheriff's collection and distraint for private debts, and secured more
efficient accountancy for the farm, although the evidence for this is
far from conclusive. It is possible, too, that the intention of des
Rivaux's brief control of twenty-one counties in 1232 was to enable
him to 'enquire into the state of local finances'[6]; yet there was no
attempt, as there was in 1236, to place the counties under custodians,
nor is there evidence of an enquiry into the local revenue through the
detailed lists of its constituents which the latter were required to
render.[7] The new sheriffs for whose appointments des Rivaux was
personally responsible around Michaelmas 1232 answered for
increments which were not as a whole more severe than those

1. *Rot. Litt. Claus.*, i. 403.
2. Pipe Roll 11 Henry III (E. 372/71), m. 19d; *ibid.* 20 Henry III (E. 372/80), ms. 27,
28.
3. *Patent Rolls 1225–32*, pp. 276, 313; *Close Rolls 1227–31*, p. 221.
4. *Patent Rolls 1225–32*, p. 455; Carpenter, p. 221. For Godfrey's later connection
with Oxfordshire, *infra*, pp. 164, 166, 167.
5. Mills, *ubi supra* (1927), pp. 111–19; Powicke, i. 98; *The Thirteenth Century* (Oxford,
1953), pp. 62–63.
6. Mills, *ubi supra* (1927), p. 119.   7. *Infra*, p. 171, n. 3.

undertaken by their immediate predecessors,[1] and were low by the standards of the 1240s and 1250s.

The number of counties under *curiales* would have continued to restrict the scope of reform even had it been seriously attempted.[2] If opponents of the new regime were ejected from local office, its members were quickly established within it. When, in May 1233, Godfrey of Crowcombe was ousted from court and from his offices in Oxfordshire after a fierce struggle, he was replaced, on the same easy conditions, by King John's old Poitevin sheriff and castellan, Engelard de Cigogné, whom the bishop's regime had summoned back to the king's side and favour.[3] The bishop himself had become sheriff of Hampshire in March 1232, and he answered for no sums above the farm till after his fall.[4] Peter des Rivaux, in the counties he controlled through under-sheriffs after Michaelmas 1232, scarcely set a more stimulating example. In Shropshire–Staffordshire he answered for a 60-mark increment, which was 20 marks higher than Henry of Audley's; but his under-sheriff, Robert de Hay, continuing alone as a custodian following Peter's fall, raised (Michaelmas 1234–Michaelmas 1235) over £115 of profit after the deduction of his allowance.[5] In Sussex, Peter answered for neither profits nor increments, the king having granted him the shire at the ancient farm.[6] In Yorkshire he continued on the terms of his predecessor until April 1233 when the county was granted for life, on the conditions in force in 1230, to Brian de Lisle, another leading supporter of the bishop of Winchester.[7]

However much it was the seizure of power, and then its retention against powerful and violent opposition, which invited and perhaps required this curial control of sheriffdoms, it cannot be said with certainty that the bishop's administration would have behaved differently had circumstances been more favourable. Many of the regime's chief members – Engelard de Cigogné, Brian de Lisle, Peter de Maulay, and Robert Passelewe, Falkes de Breauté's old clerk, who now became Peter des Rivaux's able deputy at the exchequer, had been deeply involved in the resistance to Hubert de Burgh's redistribution of the counties and castles in 1223–4. Peter des Rivaux had retired or been removed from the king's service

1. King's Remembrancer's Memoranda Roll 16 Henry III (E. 159/12), ms. 8, 15.
2. Another factor which may have slackened the impetus of reform was the success in obtaining a tax on movables in September 1232.
3. *Cal. Pat. Rolls 1232–47*, p. 16; Pipe Roll 17 Henry III (E. 372/77), ms. 17, 18; *Exc. Rot. Fin.*, i. 254. Godfrey had lost the county the previous October.
4. He was then asked to reply for the small increment borne by his predecessor, the household knight, Nicholas de Meulles; Pipe Roll 20 Henry III (E. 372/80), m. 19d.
5. Pipe Roll 17 Henry III (E. 372/77), ms. 9d, 10d; *ibid.* 19 Henry III (E. 372/79), ms. 29, 30d. The 60 mark increment was fixed in Michaelmas 1232, before war broke out in the Welsh march. However the situation was more stable by 1234–5.
6. *Patent Rolls 1225–32*, p. 489; Pipe Roll 18 Henry III (E. 372/78), m. 14.
7. Pipe Roll 17 Henry III (E. 372/77), m. 7; *ibid.* 18 Henry III (E. 372/78), m. 3; *Cal. Pat. Rolls 1232–47*, p. 15; *Pipe Roll 14 Henry III*, pp. 266–7.

following these changes. Peter des Roches, who lost the sheriffdom of Hampshire as a result of them, had sworn during the disputes that, if it cost him all he had, he would oust the justiciar from power.[1] When, eight years later, the bishop redeemed his pledge, and he and his followers returned to central and local office, their outlook was naturally conditioned by their fond memories of the minority with its great sheriffs, and freedom from profits and increments. Indicative of the conservative attitude of the regime was its dealing, or rather its failure to deal, with the royal demesne. There was no attempt to anticipate the reforms of 1236 which deprived the sheriffs of the king's manors,[2] and in some cases their responsibilities were rather increased. When Hubert de Burgh fell in August 1232, the royal manors granted to him and his relations (in heredity or during pleasure) were mostly committed to the relevant sheriffs,[3] and other manors returning to the king in the 1232–4 period were similarly treated.[4]

The collapse of the regime of Peter des Roches in 1234 did little to reduce the curial hold on sheriffdoms; if anything it increased it. At the Gloucester great council in May the king was reconciled to his opponents, and many of the counties and castles were redistributed; a redistribution which closely involved the king's household knights, and was probably organized by the steward, Godfrey of Crowcombe, who had returned to court in March.[5] This household involvement was not surprising. Peter des Roches and Peter des Rivaux were gone. Hubert de Burgh was restored to the king's grace but not to office. Indeed the justiciarship was now suspended. The household

1. *Annales Monastici*, ed. H. R. Luard (Rolls Series, 1864–9), iii. 84.

2. It is unsafe, therefore, to retain the view which gives des Rivaux the credit for these as recently in Harvey, *ubi supra*, p. 12. See Powicke, *Henry III and the Lord Edward*, i. 97, n. 2.

3. Cawston and Aylsham (Norfolk); Church Stretton (Shropshire); Archenfield and Wormelow hundred (Herefordshire); Essendon and Bayford (Hertfordshire); Pipe Roll 20 Henry III (E. 372/80), m. 7d; *ibid*. 17 Henry III (E. 372/77), ms. 9d, 10d, 5; *ibid*. 16 Henry III (E. 372/76), m. 27; *Patent Rolls 1225–32*, pp. 145, 500.

4. Alton (previously with the men of the manor), Selborne, and Tisted (Hampshire); Pipe Roll 16 Henry III (E. 372/76), m. 3; *ibid*. 17 Henry III (E. 372/77), ms. 13d, 4d; *ibid*. 18 Henry III (E. 372/78), m. 1d. In Oxfordshire, Engelard de Cigogné recombined the custody of the county with that of Woodstock (*supra*, p. 164 and n. 3), and became keeper of Wooton manor (as appurtenant to Woodstock) when it came into the king's hands. He also controlled Headington after the king ordered its seizure during the troubles of 1233–4; Pipe Roll 18 Henry III (E. 372/78), ms. 5, 6. A large number of escheats and wards in the 1232–4 period were committed to Peter des Rivaux (including other lands of Hubert de Burgh), and this has been claimed (probably rightly) as marking a new stage in their administration; Powicke, *Henry III and the Lord Edward*, i. 107; for Peter's accounts, see P.R.O. Minister's Accounts (SC. 6/1117/13). The stage was marked, however, by the centralization under one man, rather than the separation from shrieval control, which had long been a practice with such properties, particularly when they were large honors.

5. Godfrey authorized twenty-one writs in May. No one else authorized more than six; *Cal. Pat. Rolls 1232–47*, pp. 49, 51; *Close Rolls 1231–34*, pp. 414–39, 560. Ralph fitz Nicholas was away from court for most of the month on a mission, but his interests were represented by his knight, William of Pitchford; *ibid*. p. 560.

officials could, therefore, exercise power without the interference of a chief minister. Thus it was that Crowcombe recovered control of his old posts in Oxfordshire,[1] while transferring Engelard de Cigogné, who had succeeded in retaining the king's favour, to the sheriffdom of Berkshire, and the constableship of Windsor castle, the post in which he had won fame in 1216.[2] Ralph fitz Nicholas, the senior steward, added Warwickshire-Leicestershire to the counties of Nottinghamshire-Derbyshire which he had held since 1223, and his brother, Henry, moved from Dorset-Somerset to replace the bishop of Winchester in Hampshire.[3] The third steward, Amaury de St Amand became sheriff of Herefordshire, and Nicholas de Meulles,[4] Thomas of Hengrave[5] and William Talbot,[6] household knights frequently found attesting charters at court, went respectively to Devonshire, Norfolk-Suffolk and Gloucestershire. The terms on which these men held office were not stringent, and in several cases they were conceded for the duration of their tenures.[7]

In 1236 this curial hold on sheriffdoms was at last broken through a political revolution at court, and a subtly conceived reform of administration in the counties, which was designed to be popular with local society, and yet promised, as Miss Mills has shown, to increase the king's revenue both by relieving the sheriff of the royal demesne, and by making him account more realistically for the issues of his shire.[8] The development and exploitation of these reforms in the succeeding years deprived the sheriff of a large part of his private profit,[9] and were intimately linked with the retirement of the *curiales* from the counties which now commenced. Until 1234 the reign of Henry III had been dominated by issues and rivalries which stretched back to the minority, and by men who had come to prominence in the time of his father. In 1236, Henry married Eleanor of Provence and a new era opened. The marriage brought to England (early in 1236) the queen's uncle, William of Savoy, bishop elect of Valence, the first of those high-born foreigners whom Henry intro-

1. Godfrey's nephew and former ward, John le Brun, became sheriff, while Godfrey was granted the castle and Woodstock for life; *Cal. Pat. Rolls 1232-47*, p. 50; Pipe Roll 18 Henry III (E. 372/78), m. 6; P.R.O. Fine Roll 18 Henry III (C. 60/33), m. 6.
2. *Cal. Pat. Rolls 1232-47*, pp. 46, 49, 50.
3. For these and the following appointments, *ibid.* pp. 50, 48, 46.
4. *Patent Rolls 1225-32*, p. 243; P.R.O. Charter Roll 17 Henry III (C. 53/27), ms. 10, 4, 2; *Complete Peerage*, ix. 1-4.
5. *Cal. Lib. Rolls 1226-40*, pp. 77, 172; *Close Rolls 1231-34*, p. 233; Charter Roll 17 Henry III (C. 53/27), ms. 12, 11, 10, 4.
6. *Close Rolls 1227-31*, p. 33; Charter Roll 16 Henry III (C. 53/26), ms. 9, 4. For all these men, see *Exc. Rot. Fin.*, i. 213.
7. Thomas of Hengrave; Henry fitz Nicholas; John le Brun; Fine Roll 20 Henry III, part 1 (C. 60/35), m. 15; Pipe Roll 19 Henry III (E. 372/79), ms. 9, 31. The majority of the new sheriffs began as custodians but were given increments in place of profits at Michaelmas 1234.
8. Mills, *ubi supra* (1927), pp. 120-7. The following account differs from that of Miss Mills in points of detail, and also seeks to relate the financial and administrative changes to the political situation.   9. Mills, *ubi supra* (1927), p. 126.

duced to the country. It was on William's ambitions and his singular political circumstances that the events of 1236 hinged. He quickly established himself as the king's chief councillor,[1] and as a consequence some older *curiales* were dismissed from court, and others from their local offices. In itself this need not have cleared the way for reform because the outgoing curial sheriffs might have been replaced by supporters of William, enjoying much the same terms. But the bishop elect was new to England, and unlike Peter des Roches four years earlier had no party in the country eager to taste again the fruits of office. Thus it at last became possible to adopt ideas which had no doubt been cherished for years by elements at the exchequer, and replace the outgoing *curiales* as in 1204 with men of smaller political consequence, who were ready to undertake office on conditions less favourable than those enjoyed by their predecessors. At the same time these changes were cleverly packaged and proclaimed as reforms to meet the aspirations and grievances of county society so that in several respects the measures of 1236 anticipated the reforms of local government in 1258. William of Savoy, therefore, was able to secure his position with the king by sponsoring a financial programme which was far more effective than that of the bishop of Winchester, for all his propaganda; and was able to outmanoeuvre the opposition to his dominance at court by appealing to local society in a way, and with a success, that Henry III could never emulate or repeat.

When the elect of Valence arrived in England in 1236 he found a court where great influence was wielded by the stewards Ralph fitz Nicholas and Godfrey of Crowcombe. Entrenched in local office, these two were by far the most frequent authorizers of royal letters between 1234–6.[2] William, therefore, set about piercing the ring of the stewards and their allies.[3] By the end of March 1236 fitz Nicholas's position was collapsing, and he was dismissed from court shortly after 2 April. Godfrey of Crowcombe survived till January or February 1237,[4] but his standing and that of other *curiales* was weakened by their removal from local office. Between 15 April and 30 May there were changes in thirteen sheriffdoms involving seventeen counties.[5] Fitz Nicholas, of course, lost Nottinghamshire–Derbyshire and Warwickshire–Leicestershire, and his brother, Henry, lost Hampshire. Crowcombe surrendered control of Oxfordshire. Also dismissed were Nicholas de Meulles, Thomas of Hengrave, Engelard de Cigogné, Richard de Gray[6] and Peter de Maulay.

1. See, N. Denholm-Young, 'The "Paper Constitution" Attributed to 1244', *EHR*, lviii (1943), 409–14.

2. *Curia Regis Rolls*, xv, pp. lxi–lxii.

3. There was also an attempt to remove Ralph de Neville from the chancellorship.

4. *Curia Regis Rolls*, xv, pp. xxxviii–ix; *Chron. Maj.*, iii. 363.

5. *Cal. Pat. Rolls 1232–47*, pp. 141–5, 148. The change in Worcestershire is included for consideration, although the county was quickly returned to its hereditary sheriff.

6. For Richard as a household knight and at court, *Close Rolls 1231–34*, p. 131; Charter Roll 17 Henry III (C. 53/27), of ms. 12–10, 2.

The household settlement of the counties and castles made at the Gloucester great council in May 1234 was thus destroyed. The new sheriffs, as in 1204, were of reduced political importance. Not one had as yet a substantial connection with the court; not one had experienced the rain of gifts and favours which descended on the king's major servants; not one had attested even a solitary royal charter enrolled in Henry's reign. They seem to have come from that group of gentry and magnates which existed in every county, and which staffed the multitude of local commissions called into being by twelfth and thirteenth-century government.[1] Eleven had property in the shires to which they were appointed, and at least nine had played a part, and some a very large part in the local government of these counties, as escheators, tax collectors and assessors, judges, under-sheriffs and sheriffs.[2] The sheriffs of counties to which the reforms were extended in the next sixteen months were of similar background and experience.[3] William of Savoy can have had no personal responsibility for these appointments of men of whom he knew nothing. They were probably creations of the exchequer, and

1. The exceptions were Henry of Bath (Northamptonshire), and Walter of Bath who was promoted from under-sheriff in Devonshire. Henry was establishing himself in the king's service, and would soon be a justice at the bench. Walter remained a non-curial professional administrator.

2. Robert Brand (Berkshire); *Boarstall Cart.*, ed. H. E. Salter (Oxford Hist. Soc., lxxxviii, 1930), p. 306; *Cal. Pat. Rolls 1232–47*, p. 200; *V.C.H. Bucks.*, iii. 60, 98. Robert's manor at Goring was just outside Berkshire. His father was probably Matthew Brand, deputy constable of Wallingford. William of Dacre (Cumberland). Dacre is in Cumberland, and William was probably a county knight; *Cal. Chart Rolls*, ii. 124; *Cal. Pat. Rolls 1247–58*, pp. 434, 647. Peter de Thany (Essex–Hertfordshire); *Book of Fees*, i. 480; *Rot. Litt. Claus*, ii. 208b; *Close Rolls 1231–34*, pp. 131, 159. Geoffrey de Lisle (Hampshire); *Exc. Rot. Fin.*, i. 119; *Cal. Inq. Post Mortem*, i, no. 233; *Patent Rolls 1225–32*, p. 288. *Close Rolls 1231–34*, p. 158. Thomas of Ingoldisthorpe (in Norfolk) (Norfolk–Suffolk); E. Miller, *The Abbey and Bishopric of Ely* (Cambridge, 1951), p. 266; *Patent Rolls 1216–25*, pp. 384, 393, 394, 438; *ibid. 1225–32*, pp. 304–6; *Cal. Pat. Rolls 1232–47*, p. 119. Hugh de Bolebek (Northumberland); W. Dugdale, *The Baronage of England* (London, 1675), i. 452; *Patent Rolls 1225–32*, pp. 283, 284, 367, 513; *Cal. Chart. Rolls*, i. 390. There are references to Hugh in Holt, *The Northerners*. Hugh fitz Ralph (Nottinghamshire–Derbyshire); *Book of Fees*, ii. 976, 991, 992; *Patent Rolls 1225–32*, p. 448; *Close Rolls 1227–31*, p. 400; *ibid.* 1231–34, pp. 130, 157. Robert Damory (Oxfordshire); *V.C.H. Oxon.*, vi. 73. William de Lucy (Warwickshire–Leicestershire); *Book of Fees*, ii. 955, 956, 1340; *V.C.H. Warw.*, v. i, 35, 37, 38, 188. *Patent Rolls 1225–32*, p. 283. Hugh le Pour (Worcestershire); *Rot. Litt. Claus*, i. 280b; *Lists of Sheriffs*, p. 157; *Patent Rolls 1225–32*, p. 521; *Close Rolls 1231–34*, pp. 130, 157, 228, 576. Brian fitz Alan (Yorkshire); *Book of Fees*, ii. 1460; *Cal. Chart Rolls*, i. 278; *Patent Rolls 1225–32*, pp. 72, 160, 207, 219, 290. The most favoured of these men was Peter de Thany who enjoyed a £10 annual fee between 1227–30. Brian fitz Alan while sheriff of Northumberland (1228–35) made two substantial offers for wardships; *Cal. Lib. Rolls 1226–40*, pp. 12, 173; *Exc. Rot. Fin.*, i. 221, 290.

3. William fitz Gerebert (Wiltshire); *Book of Fees*, i. 420, 421; *ibid.* ii. 714, 731; *Close Rolls 1231–34*, p. 130. Thurstan Despencer (Gloucestershire); *V.C.H. Oxon.*, v. 50; *Close Rolls 1231–34*, p. 575; *Cal. Pat. Rolls 1232–47*, p. 163. Henry of Colne (Cambridgeshire–Huntingdonshire) was apparently a prosperous (and married) local clerk; Cam, 'Cambridgeshire Sheriffs in the Thirteenth Century', *Liberties and Communities*, pp. 37, 48; Miller, pp. 130–1; *Close Rolls 1231–34*, p. 573. Reginald of Whitchurch (Bedfordshire–Buckinghamshire) had a more elevated place in the king's service than the other sheriffs mentioned in this note.

the exchequer, given a free hand, turned to those who were county rather than court to carry out its programme.

This programme involved both the withdrawal of the royal demesne from the sheriff, and the general re-imposition of profits, accompanied by the revision of the system of allowances. The demesne was now placed under separate keepers who inquired into its value, and exacted fresh increments, or accounted in detail for its exits; later, around 1241, the practice began of leasing the manors (often to their men) at substantially increased values.[1] It is sometimes said· that so few manors remained under sheriffs by 1236 that the changes of that year were of limited significance.[2] Yet there were still a fair number of shires where the demesne contributed directly to the farm,[3] or where the sheriff retained manorial responsibilities outside it.[4] Sometimes, before 1236, the sheriff had already answered for all the issues of a manor,[5] but its loss remained important in that it diminished his area of responsibility, and deprived him of the hope of profit through securing more favourable terms on which to reply. In other cases, where manors were within the county farm, or were held outside it in return for unrealistic fixed sums, the changes of 1236 promised immediate gain to the exchequer, and loss to the sheriff. In Northamptonshire, for example, the sheriff had answered since John's reign for the manors of Abthorpe, Geddington and Kingsthorpe at an annual sum of £101 17s. Walter de Burgh, their keeper from 1236, established new increments, and in 1241 the manors were leased for £143 p.a.[6] It is true, of course, that before 1236 the sheriff may sometimes have used manorial surpluses to make up the increment of the county, or the profit if it was under a

1. Mills, *ubi supra* (1927), pp. 122–3.
2. Hoyt, p. 156; Powicke, *Henry III and the Lord Edward*, i. 102. Both Dr Hoyt and Miss Mills remark on the fact that after the withdrawal of the demesne, the county farm remained the same; Mills, *ubi supra* (1927), p. 126; *ubi supra* (1925), p. 159. This is not surprising, however, since in those cases where demesne which had contributed directly to the farm was withdrawn an appropriate allowance was made for its loss. See *Cumberland Pipe Rolls*, pp. 56, 62–63, 67, 72.
3. Cumberland (Langwathby; Penrith; Salkeld; Scotby, etc.); Herefordshire (Lugwardine; Marden); Lincolnshire (Torksey); Wiltshire (Melksham); Kent (Milton); Shropshire (Condover; Ford, Worfield); Staffordshire (Wigginton; Wolverhampton). Only the first four counties were effected by the reforms of 1236–7, Herefordshire and Lincolnshire without changes of sheriffs. For Kent, see *infra*, p. 175. For Shropshire-Staffordshire, *Close Rolls 1237–42*, p. 60; *Pipe Roll 26 Henry III*, pp. 2, 8–9, 13.
4. Gloucestershire (Barton Gloucester; Minsterworth; Newnham; Rodley; Slaughter), Hampshire (Alton); Hertfordshire (Essendon, Bayford); Norfolk (Aylsham); Northamptonshire (Abthorpe; Finedon; Geddington; Kingsthorpe); Nottinghamshire (Clipston, Darlton; Edwinstowe; Mansfield; Oswaldbeck; Ragnall); Oxfordshire (Bloxham); Yorkshire (the soke of Falsgrave; Pickering). Orford (Suffolk) with its castle, manors in Northumberland, and Linby in Nottinghamshire remained under shrieval control after 1236.
5. Alton; Essendon and Bayford; and the Gloucestershire manors.
6. Pipe Roll 22 Henry III (E. 372/82), ms. 5, 6; Originalia Roll 25 Henry III (E. 371/8A), m. 4; *Pipe Roll 16 John*, p. 21. As part of the policy explained below a £15 allowance in Kingsthorpe for keeping Northampton castle was also dropped after 1236.

custodian (like Northamptonshire). Yet the extent to which he needed to do so was limited either by the meagre size of the increments or the magnitude of the allowances. The second feature of the 1236 reforms was to deal with these. Increments were swept away. All the new sheriffs were custodians, and their allowances were considerably less generous than those hitherto conceded. A special schedule of the terms on which they were appointed was drawn up in order to record the reductions which had taken place.[1] The result was that in many shires after 1236 (despite the loss of any contributions from royal manors) more revenue was due to the exchequer from above the farm than before the reforms. Correspondingly less was available for the coffers of the sheriffs. This was either because the net profits after 1236 came to more than the previous increments,[2] or to more than the previous profits eroded as they were by larger allowances.[3] In Berkshire, for example, Engelard de Cigogné had answered for a £50 increment between 1234–6. In 1237–8, after deduction of the allowance, the profits were worth over £80 to the exchequer.[4]

The intention in 1236, however, was not simply to increase the king's revenue. The elect of Valence's ascendancy at court was quickly resented by the great magnates who had been happy enough with the familiar and unpretentious Godfrey of Crowcombe and, Ralph fitz Nicholas, a former steward of the earl of Derby.[5] William of Savoy and his advisers, therefore, attempted to counterbalance the opposition by seeking the support of county society, and, to judge from Matthew Paris's approval of the changes, they had some success.[6] Matthew welcomed the new sheriffs of 1236 on the grounds that they were less likely than their predecessors to take bribes since they were 'uberiores in tenementis, et abundantiores in thesauris, et genere nobiliores'. He had, of course, noticed or been informed of the consistent attempt to appoint sheriffs who came from the gentry and magnate society of their counties; sheriffs who could, in effect, measure up to the standard set by the Provisions of Oxford twenty-two years later, of 'a sound landholder' and a 'vavasour of the county'. Matthew Paris also recorded that the new sheriffs swore an oath not to accept bribes, and to be moderate in their demands for entertainment – just as did the sheriffs in 1258.[7] Finally all the 1236

1. King's Remembrancer's Exchequer Miscellanea (E. 163/24/14). Thus Brian fitz Alan in Yorkshire is to receive £100 annually 'ubi priusquam dari solent ducentae marcae'. Where the outgoing sheriff had not received an allowance, a comparison was sometimes made with one from some previous year.

2. Berkshire (see *infra*); Hampshire; Warwickshire–Leicestershire; Wiltshire.

3. Devonshire; Essex–Hertfordshire; Northamptonshire; in Norfolk–Suffolk the sheriff had answered for an increment, but had also enjoyed various allowances, and it was the removal of these which was decisive after 1236.

4. Pipe Roll 18 Henry III (E. 372/78), m. 17d; *ibid.* 22 Henry III (E. 372/82), m. 31d.

5. *Rot. Litt. Claus.*, i. 406; see *Close Rolls 1234–37*, pp. 562–3. See also *Cal. Chart. Rolls*, i. 188–9. 6. *Chron. Maj.*, iii. 363.

7. *Documents of the Baronial Movement of Reform and Rebellion*, ed. R. F. Treharne and I. J. Sanders (Oxford, 1973), pp. 120–1.

sheriffs were appointed as custodians with allowances, as they were to be in fulfilment of the clause of the Provisions of Oxford which stipulated that the king should pay the sheriff out of his own revenues so that he could administer the shire justly.[1] The reformers of 1258 may well have had the arrangements of 1236 in mind when they drew up their plans.

Within a few years, several counties affected by the 1236 changes were again under *familiares*, but the general development of policy in the ensuing years was not compatible with the continuance of curial sheriffdoms. Save in a few instances, the sheriffs remained bereft of royal manors, and where they were recovered, or retained, the terms did not permit much private gain.[2] The sheriffs had also to face an exchequer demanding money above the farm with increasing determination and power. Between 1236–41, as has been seen, the majority of sheriffs were custodians answering for profits and receiving allowances. In 1241, however, this system was altered; allowances and profits were abandoned, and the sheriffs were once again charged with fixed increments. There has been a tendency to regard the latter as the results of careful investigation into what each county could bear 'without overburdening the inhabitants', rather than (as is more probable) the product of the tightest bargains the exchequer was then able to drive.[3] The increments[4] rendered many sheriffs worse off than between 1236–41 because their size was such as to leave them a smaller proportion of the county revenue than that previously conceded by the allowances. Just how far the situation

1. *Documents of the Baronial Movement*, pp. 108–9; see also pp. 122–3; R. F. Treharne, *The Baronial Plan of Reform* (Manchester, 1932), pp. 98, 123–4; Meekings, p. 144.

2. Thus whereas the sheriff of Norfolk–Suffolk answered for Aylsham as a farmer between 1234–6, between 1249–54 he was a custodian. In 1255 the manor was leased to its men at nearly £20 above its 1234–6 farm; Pipe Roll 21 Henry III (E. 372/81), m. 24d; *ibid.* 38 Henry III (E. 372/98), m. 12; *Cal. Pat. Rolls 1247–58*, p. 448.

3. Mills, *ubi supra* (1927), pp. 125–6; Powicke, *Henry III and the Lord Edward*, i. 99; *The Thirteenth Century*, p. 62. The custodian sheriffs of 1236–41 returned annual lists of the constituents of their revenue (the *particulae proficui*); Mills, *ubi supra* (1927), pp. 123–4. Such lists had been rendered before by custodian sheriffs, although not in so much detail, and may have had antecedents in John's reign (*Pipe Roll 9 John*, p. 27). They provided information of particular value in 1236 because many counties had long been under sheriffs who did not make such returns since they were answering for farms and increments rather than for all the issues of the shire. In assessing the increments of 1241 it is unlikely that the exchequer used the information in the entirely benevolent way supposed by Miss Mills and Sir Maurice Powicke. Miss Mills did not appreciate that the *particulae proficui* were only rendered by custodians. Her statement that no figures for profits were given till around 1240 when there was a 'serious attempt to strike an average' for the preceding years appears to be based on the accounts of the sheriff of Cambridgeshire–Huntingdonshire – with which the exchequer were highly dissatisfied; T. Madox, *The History and the Antiquities of the Exchequer* (2nd edn., London, 1769), ii. 10, n. 4. In the majority of counties figures were entered annually or biannually. The increments of the 1240s and 1250s are often confusingly called 'profits', probably because they were sums rendered in place of profits.

4. They are set out upon Originalia Roll 25 Henry III (E. 371/8A), m. 4, sch. 2; *Red Book of the Exchequer*, ii. 771–2 contains an inaccurate copy. The terms in *Pipe Roll 26 Henry III* are in most cases the same.

had changed in twelve years may be gauged from the fact that the total due to the exchequer from the increments of 1241–2 was some £1,540, whereas the increments, and profits less allowances, of 1229–30 were worth around £750. After 1242 the pressure was intensified. So little account has been taken of this that Sir Maurice Powicke regarded shrieval abuse in the period before 1258 as something which 'outstripped the limits of exchequer control' without noting that it was also in considerable part the baleful product of exchequer demands.[1] By 1251–2 the increments imposed on every county but two had sizably increased over those of ten years before,[2] and the sum due to the exchequer was nearly £2,320. In the next five years the increments born by two sheriffdoms were reduced, but six suffered further increases, and the total for 1256–7 approached £2,500. The great improvement over 1229–30 was achieved despite the fact that in that year at least ten sheriffs held manors whose surpluses could have contributed to revenue above the farm – manors which were not held by 1241. The following table gives some individual examples of developments.[3]

Increments demanded above the farm

	1229–30 marks	1241–2 marks	1251–2 marks	1256–7 marks
Norfolk–Suffolk	90[4]	200[5]	300	400
Northants	profit allowed S. Seagrave	100	130	180
Shropshire–Staffordshire	40	90	150	190[6]
Yorkshire	300	200[7]	400[8]	470[9]

Against the background of these alarmingly escalating increments it is easy to appreciate some of the grievances of the period 1258–65 – the clause in the 1258 Petition of the barons, for example 'concerning

1. Powicke, *Henry III and the Lord Edward*, i. 99. Treharne likewise did not relate the corruption of local government to the size of the increments; Treharne, pp. 42–45.
2. The exceptions were Herefordshire; and Wiltshire; for which see Meekings, p. 143, where a different view is taken of the trend of exchequer policy.
3. The figures quoted above and below are largely obtained from *Pipe Roll 14 Henry III*; *Pipe Roll 26 Henry III*; and Pipe Rolls 36 and 41 Henry III (E. 372/96, 101). Occasionally they come from the rolls of succeeding years. It should be stressed that the sums are those due to the exchequer, not those for which the sheriffs actually obtained clearance. Variations in the size of a county's increment are occasionally influenced by changes in the sources from which revenue is derived. For example, a castle mill (or castle manor like Orford) may sometimes be accounted for within the shire increment, sometimes outside it. With the exception of Kent (*infra*, p. 175, n. 6), the figures given above have not been adjusted to take account of such factors. See *infra*, n. 5.
4. This sum is described as profit although the sheriff in fact returned profits of this size throughout his term.
5. It is probable (at least for the second half of the year) that the exits of Orford are included in this sum. They were certainly included in 1251–2 and 1256–7. In 1229–30,

the farms of sheriffs . . . who hold their counties at such high farms that they cannot recover these farms from them'[1]; and the more illuminating statement in the schedule of complaints presented to Louis IX in 1264, that 'whereas the shrievalities . . . were formerly let at a fixed and moderate farm, so that the sheriffs could properly answer for these farms without oppressing those subject to them, and without unlawful extortion, the treasurer of the exchequer and other councillors and hangers-on of the king, inflicted a heavier burden on the counties . . . exacting newly imposed increments in perpetuity as part of the fixed farm and increasing them successively.'[2] The expanding increments provided one motive for the sheriff's practice of subletting hundreds at higher individual farms which was a subject of such concern and grievance in and before 1258.[3] They were also responsible for the emphasis in the Provisions of Oxford, and in the oath taken by the new sheriffs in 1258, on the exaction of fees, gifts, bribes and entertainment.[4] What had happened between 1241–58 was that the increments had become so large that they often left, even after raising the farms of hundreds, insufficient revenue for the sheriff's sustenance, and thus he resorted increasingly to the imposition of fees and the exploitation of his traditional rights of hospitality.[5] The view of Miss Mills and Sir Maurice Powicke that after 1236 the sheriff was generally 'a collector of revenue entitled to a salary' is in conflict with the evidence, and makes the reforming proposals of 1258 unintelligible.[6] Between 1236–41 sheriffs had certainly received allowances, but from 1241, answering for increments instead of profits, they were neither entitled to them in theory, nor received them in practice. In 1258 the reformers attempted to remedy this situation by reverting to the 1236–41 system. The stipulation in the Provisions of Oxford that the king should sustain

---

after the allowance for keeping the castle, ten marks were due to the exchequer from this manor. See Madox, *History and Antiquities of the Exchequer*, ii. 207, n.f.

6. In Northamptonshire by 1241–2, and Shropshire–Staffordshire by 1251–2 the revenue available to meet increments was probably affected by the loss of manors. Madox, *History and Antiquities of the Exchequer*, ii. 207, n.f.

7. The reduction is probably explained by the loss of the manors and by the reluctance to impose harsh terms on the curial sheriffs in office in 1241–2. Pickering manor was restored to the sheriff mid-way through this year and remained under shrieval control till 1253. Separate accounts were rendered for it.

8. When the sheriff replied for this and next year's increment in the roll of 1252–3 he was pardoned 100 marks.

9. After 1253 the sheriff no longer had responsibility for Pickering or Scarborough castles.

1. *Documents of the Baronial Movement*, pp. 82–83.   2. *Ibid.* pp. 274–5.

3. *Ibid.* pp. 120–1; M. T. Clanchy, 'Did Henry III have a policy', *History*, liii (1968), 216; Meekings, p. 32. The hundred rolls have many complaints against the sheriffs of the 1250s on this score; *e.g. Rot. Hund.*, i. 247, 346.

4. *Documents of the Baronial Movement*, pp. 108–9, 120–1.

5. For fees see Morris, pp. 278–82.

6. Mills, *ubi supra* (1927), p. 126; Powicke, *Henry III and the Lord Edward*, i. 99; *The Thirteenth Century*, p. 62.

the sheriff from his own revenues was to be fulfilled by making him a custodian with an allowance.

In these circumstances of exchequer exploitation which saw many of limited political stature fining to be exempted from local office,[1] it is scarcely surprising that the *curiales* bade farewell to the shires. The age of the under-sheriff too was over. The new climate demanded a man who would run the county in person, since what private profit remained, obtainable only after assiduous if not corrupt administration, was insufficient to sustain both a sheriff and a deputy. The money above the farm which was necessarily a chief attraction to the absentee *curialis* now passed to the exchequer. He could derive little pleasure from the sheriff's rights of entertainment. The period 1236–42, therefore, constituted a watershed between curial and non-curial sheriffs in Bedfordshire-Buckinghamshire; Northamptonshire; Nottinghamshire–Derbyshire; Oxfordshire; and Warwickshire-Leicestershire.[2] Engelard de Cigogné in Berkshire; Thomas of Hengrave in Norfolk–Suffolk; and Nicholas de Meulles in Devonshire, all of whom lost office in 1236, were the last *curiales* in these counties before 1258. Counties retaining curial sheriffs after 1242 were Kent, Shropshire-Staffordshire and Yorkshire (till 1248); Hampshire (till 1249); and Gloucestershire (till 1250). In the 1250s only Dorset–Somerset remained, with Elias de Rabayne (1251–5), Henry's hated Poitevin protégé;[3] and Walter de Burgeis (1257–8), Elias's former under-sheriff, who was soon to become marshal of the king's household.[4] When Henry III left for Brittany in April 1230 ten sheriffdoms were headed by *curiales*,[5] each of whom had attested charters at court in the previous twelve months. Twenty-three years later when Henry set sail for Gascony, only Elias de Rabayne of all the sheriffs had witnessed more than a solitary royal charter.[6] This disappearance of *curiales* from the counties can be illustrated from the careers of several of Henry's chief servants. Robert Walerand became sheriff of Gloucestershire in 1246; resigned four years later, and held no sheriffdom in the 1250s. Ralph fitz Nicholas, continually in shrieval office before 1236, controlled no county between his return to court in 1243 and his death in 1257, although he recovered his constableship of Nottingham castle.[7] Indeed, not one of Henry III's

---

1. E.g. *Cal. Pat. Rolls 1247–58*, pp. 175, 184, 190–3.

2. Philip Marmion's place in the king's service dates from after his time as sheriff (1249–52); *Cal. Pat. Rolls 1247–58*, p. 267.

3. *Chron. Maj.*, v. 283; Elias attests royal charters during his sheriffdom.

4. *Lists of Sheriffs*, p. 122; *Cal. Pat. Rolls, 1258–66*, p. 57. Walter attests at court shortly before his appointment.

5. Stephen of Seagrave (three); Henry of Audley; Godfrey of Crowcombe; Walter de Envermeu (Lincolnshire); Ralph fitz Nicholas; Walter Mauclerc; Nicholas de Meulles (Hampshire); William de Stuteville (Yorkshire).

6. Reginald of Cobham (Kent) who witnesses once in 1247 was the only other sheriff to have attested. I am much indebted to Mr C. A. F. Meekings for allowing me to use his calendar of the witnesses to the royal charters enrolled in Henry's reign.

7. *Cal. Pat. Rolls 1247–58*, p. 89.

stewards is found in a sheriffdom between 1250 and 1258. The most prominent sheriffs of the 1250s, men such as Robert of Creepping (Yorkshire 1250–3), a former custodian of the king's northern manors and northern escheator; or William Heron, who combined for a time the custody of Northumberland (1246–58) with the justiceship of the northern forests, were highly responsible royal agents; yet neither enjoyed substantial rewards, and only Creepping attested a royal charter (a solitary one in 1237), for they stood outside the circle of the king's *familiares*.[1]

The decline of the curial sheriff enabled the exchequer, under its treasurer, to play an increasing part both in appointing sheriffs and in determining their terms[2] – hence the reference to the treasurer in the 1264 schedule of complaint. The exchequer had no desire to impede the retirement of *curiales* who might evade its control[3] and limit its exactions. A county to escape the measures of 1236 was Kent, which was largely under the household knight, Bertram de Criel, between 1232–48. It was not till Bertram's departure from the shrievality (while continuing as castellan of Dover), that it was possible to take the valuable demesne manor of Milton out of the farm and commit it to a separate custodian.[4] In 1241 the exchequer wished Kent to answer for an increment of £80, but Bertram brought a writ from the king which reduced this sum by half.[5] The sheriff who was appointed in 1249, the substantial but non-curial county knight, Reginald of Cobham, replied for an increment of £145.[6] In October 1241 the exchequer accepted that Hugh de Vivonne (a former seneschal of Gascony) should receive for keeping Corfe castle the 40 mark increment it wished to impose on Dorset-Somerset; it was either unable to understand or unwilling to admit the terms on which the king had in fact appointed him that February – namely that he should receive all the issues of the counties (both farms and profits) – and a succession of royal letters to the exchequer

1. Creepping caused the exchequer difficulties, however; *infra*, p. 176, n. 4.
2. E.g. *Cal. Pat. Rolls 1247–58*, pp. 430, 446–48; Madox, *History and Antiquities of the Exchequer*, ii. 68, n. v.
3. From the 1230s the exchequer was trying to tighten this by insisting on the overall responsibility of the sheriff, which it was much easier to do if he ran the county in person. In the 1240s several curial sheriffs account in person in the pipe rolls rather than through deputies as they would certainly have done earlier; *Close Rolls 1231–34*, pp. 276–7; *Cal. Lib. Rolls 1226–40*, p. 434; *List of Sheriffs*, pp. 54, 161.
4. *Cal. Pat. Rolls 1247–58*, p. 32; *List of Foreign Accounts* (P.R.O. Lists and Indexes, xi, 1900), p. 167.
5. Originalia Roll 25 Henry III (E. 371/8A), m. 4, sch. 2. These terms were not directly related to Bertram's position as castellan of Dover since he received a separate pension for this.
6. Pipe Roll 34 Henry III (E. 372/94), m. 22. This sum includes the increment imposed on Milton manor which had been returned to shrieval control. It is adjusted from the figure given on the pipe roll since that includes the ancient farm of Milton as well. Cobham's importance increased in 1255 when he became castellan of Dover.

were required for these terms to be implemented.[1] One such (in 1246) highlighted the loss of control a curial sheriffdom could threaten by stressing that Hugh was to be allowed all the profit since becoming sheriff even though he was ignorant of its sum.[2] The exchequer probably much preferred the arrangements made in 1255. Elias de Rabayne then gave up the counties, while remaining as constable of Corfe (with a £20 annual fee). He was followed within a few months as sheriff by the obscure Stephen de Ashton who answered for farm and profits at £110 p.a.[3] The exchequer could run into trouble even when it was left the choice of sheriff. In October 1253 it appointed the local knight, John le Moyne, to Cambridgeshire–Huntingdonshire, imposing upon him the same 85 mark increment which had been undertaken by his predecessor; an increment 25 marks higher than that of 1242. John, however, was beginning to ascend in the king's service and favour, and during the Gascon expedition of 1253–4, he complained to Henry that he had been made sheriff against his will, and that the increment was of such a size that he could not meet it without the sale or mortgage of his lands. The king ordered the barons of the exchequer to fix on a more reasonable sum, or to allow John to reply for all the issues as a custodian; and in the event the increment was reduced by 45 marks.[4]

The exaction of revenue above the farm had always implied the decline of the curial sheriff, but it was only after 1236 that the value set on this revenue outweighed the self-interest of *curiales*, and the advantages of curial sheriffdoms. This was so for a combination of political and financial reasons. In the 1240s and 1250s, poverty was constantly frustrating Henry III's ambitions and threatening his

1. Originalia Roll 25 Henry III (E. 371/8A), m. 4, sch. 2; *Pipe Roll 26 Henry III*, p. 326; *Cal. Pat. Rolls 1232–47*, p. 245; *Close Rolls 1237–42*, pp. 273–4; *ibid. 1242–47*, pp. 17, 282, 423, 428; *Cal. Lib. Rolls 1245–51*, p. 104.

2. *Close Rolls 1242–47*, p. 428.

3. *Cal. Pat. Rolls 1247–58*, pp. 416, 429. Vivonne's terms were continued under his successor, the *curialis* Bartholomew Pecche (1249–50). Then the Berkshire–Somerset knight, Henry of Earley replied for farm and profits at a 100 marks, terms which Elias de Rabayne also accepted. It may well have been Elias's reluctance to continue on them, or to accept more severe that led to his departure in 1255; *Close Rolls 1251–53*, p. 310.

4. Cam, 'Cambridgeshire Sheriffs', *Liberties and Communities*, pp. 40–41; *Close Rolls 1251–53*, p. 385; *Cal. Pat. Rolls 1247–58*, pp. 223, 245; *Close Rolls 1253–54*, p. 317; Pipe Roll 43 Henry III (E. 372/103), m. 30. For a previous Cambridgeshire sheriff securing from the king an alteration in his terms, see *Close Rolls 1247–51*, p. 502. For Robert of Creepping in Yorkshire (who was also pardoned part of his increased increment – *supra*, p. 172, n. 8) see, *Close Rolls 1254–56*, pp. 307, 371. It may be added that the grants of Cornwall and Lancaster to members of the royal family in the thirteenth century involved the concession of both farms and profits. Westmoreland was held in hereditary right by the Vieuxponts on similar terms. The Beauchamps who had a hereditary claim to Worcestershire rendered no profits between 1224 and 1258; Morris, pp. 179–82; and see, *Pipe Roll 26 Henry III*, p. 98. Such tenures cannot be used as evidence that the office of sheriff in general was a profitable one.

independence. He was denied, at least without conditions which he deemed unacceptable, the lucrative grants of taxation on movables which he had received in 1225, 1232 and 1237. There was thus a compelling incentive to secure the best possible value from sources of revenue such as the county farms and royal manors which could be tapped without the need for baronial consent. Political assumptions allowed the exchequer a clear run in the development of its policies. In 1261 when Henry was struggling for control throughout the country he again placed counties under his greatest servants,[1] but in the 1250s he clearly did not consider that the unpopularity of his government had created a type of opposition which necessitated a spread of curial sheriffdoms. The period 1236–58 was also one of fairly tranquil foreign relations. Henry was forced to go to Gascony in 1253–4 to quell trouble in the province, but apart from the war of 1242–3, relations with the king of France were largely governed by a series of truces – one of five years began in 1235. As far as Scotland was concerned, although Henry journeyed north in 1236, 1237 and, in some force, in 1244 and 1255, and was closely concerned in the problems presented by the minority of Alexander III, serious military operations along or north of the border were rarely contemplated.[2] The greater preoccupation was Wales; yet even here Henry was content in the 1250s for the marcher counties to be under men of lesser stature, until the development of open hostilities hurried Peter de Montfort into the sheriffdom of Shropshire–Staffordshire in 1257.

Increasingly it was found possible to combine the requirements of security and the policies of the exchequer by the separation of castles and counties. The former were placed under curial castellans; the latter under non-curial sheriffs, who could sometimes be charged with higher increments once they no longer had castle running costs to meet. In 1242 when Henry left for Poitou arrangements were still made involving the custody of the shires. Bertram de Criel was re-established in Kent; Henry of Bath was sent north to look after Yorkshire; Robert Passelewe became sheriff of Hampshire.[3] Eleven years later, when Henry was preparing to leave for Gascony, it was merely a question of transferring the castles of Oxford, Northampton, Bamborough, Pickering and Scarborough from the sheriffs to the curial castellans Imbert Pugeys, John de Gray, and John of Laxton.[4] Other castles passing out of shrieval control in the 1240s and 1250s included Hertford, Colchester, Corfe, Gloucester,

<hr>

1. Treharne, p. 263.
2. The northern sheriffs were, however, among the most important of the 1250s; *supra*, p. 175. Cumberland was under the great northern magnates, John de Balliol, and William de Forz, earl of Aumale (1248–55–60).
3. *Cal. Pat. Rolls 1232–47*, pp. 276, 284, 286, 287.
4. *Cal. Pat. Rolls 1247–58*, pp. 173, 193, 194, 195, 234.

Harestan, Nottingham and Porchester.[1] Several of the new curial constables were foreigners which helps explain the demand in 1258 that important castles should be in the hands of *fideles de regno Angliae natos*.[2]

The financial gains from the mounting increments in the 1240s and 1250s were probably considerable, and to achieve a complete picture of the value of developments since 1236 it would be necessary to follow the terms on which the manors taken from the sheriffs in and after that year were leased, although many of these passed out of the king's hands. The overall proceeds were reduced by occasional fees to castellans, and, in all probability, by an increasing number of annual fees to royal servants, who required some substitute for their lost shrieval patronage. In this respect what had occurred was simply a different method of financial arrangement in which tighter control was exercised over the distribution of the king's revenue than when there were large allowances (or small increments) designed to sustain *curiales* in the king's service as well as to enable them to keep the counties and castles. The policies of the 1240s and 1250s, however, had drawbacks, of which the most serious was that they helped to aggravate the endemic corruption of local government, and thus laid the foundations for the strident demands for its reform in 1258, which were partly met in the Provisions of Oxford and Westminster. In 1258 Henry found that he was alone, having alienated the church by his exactions; the barons by his foreign policy and their exclusion from influence and favour; and local society by acquisitive judicial eyres,[3] escalating county increments,[4] and the personally uncongenial sheriffs, with whom the increments were often linked. The new sheriffs of 1236 had been acceptable to the counties, but the standards of that year were not long maintained. True, there were probably as many local knights controlling shires in the 1240s and 1250s (some of whom yielded to none in the harshness or dishonesty of their administration),[5] as there had ever been before 1236 either as sheriffs

1. *Ibid.* pp. 1, 2, 46; 98, 417, 482; 416–17; 66, 89; *Cal. Lib. Rolls 1245-51*, p. 44; *Cal. Pat. Rolls 1247-58*, pp. 89, 166, 417, 449; 416–17, 459, 535.

2. *Documents of the Baronial Movement*, pp. 80–81, 112–13. William de Valence (Hertford); Elyas de Rabayne (Corfe); Matthias Bezille (Gloucester) though he was retained in 1258; Guy de Rochefort (Colchester; Northampton); Imbert Pugeys (Oxford); William de Chabanais (Porchester); Imbert Pugeys was also sometime constable of the Tower of London. In some cases the castellans were conceded the issues and appurtenances of their castelries in order to help sustain them in the king's service; in others they were given terms on which to answer, or were deprived of the issues and appurtenances and given annual fees which were kept as small as possible. In 1255 a particular attempt was made to secure better value from the appurtenances of the castles and reduce costs, and in some instances this involved transferring them back from curial castellans to non-curial sheriffs; *Cal. Pat. Rolls 1247-58*, pp. 46, 482, 98, 457, 449, 459, 416–17.

3. See, *Chron. Maj.*, iv. 186–7; *Ann. Mon.*, i. 387; Meekings, pp. 7–8.

4. For the comments of Matthew Paris on these, see *Chron. Maj.*, v. 577, 720.

5. *Chron. Maj.*, v. 577–81; see also *ibid.* 663.

or under-sheriffs. Thus the complaint of 1264 that sheriffs prior to 1258 were not 'prudent and knowledgeable knights of the counties as was old custom'[1] was somewhat misleading. Yet the exchequer was also turning in this period to outsiders[2] and men of obscure background,[3] who, ambitious and unconfined by local ties, were probably considered the most ruthless exactors of revenue above the farm. The famous stipulation in the Provisions of Oxford that the sheriff should be a substantial landholder and a vavasour of the county was directed against men such as these rather than the vanished curial sheriffs. As the 1264 schedule explained, the sheriffs had been 'men coming from far away and utter strangers in the counties'.[4]

In view of the consequential alienation of county society, Henry III's wisdom in allowing the appointments and increments policies to be pursued as they were in the 1240s and 1250s is questionable. An alternative would have been the maintenance of the 1224–36 system which gave the king the benefits of curial sheriffdoms, and attempted to conciliate the localities by the occasional concession of generous terms to local knightly sheriffs.[5] After the re-imposition of profits in 1224 the exchequer remained cautious in its dealings with the counties. The 1264 schedule perhaps recalled these years when it spoke of the shires being let at a fixed and moderate farm. Yet the arrangements were certainly not ideal, and the reforms of 1236 anticipated, as has been seen, those of 1258. In respect of the situation which may have developed in some curial sheriffdoms before 1236 (as in those where the terms were sterner) discontent was not altogether surprising. If a *familiaris* required a large proportion of the revenue above the farm for himself, his under-sheriff might be left in a position little better than the sheriffs after 1241 with their increasing increments. Equally, although local men were often employed by *curiales* as under-sheriffs, so were professional administrators of the type most disliked. When Matthew Paris declared that the new sheriffs of 1236 were more landed than their

1. *Documents of the Baronial Movement*, pp. 274–7.
2. Thus William of Englefield, sheriff of Devonshire 1251–4, under whom the increment was increased from 90 to 130 marks, arrived directly from being the escheator of his home county of Berkshire; *Close Rolls 1247–51*, p. 515. The increment of Norfolk-Suffolk was raised from 237½ marks to 400 marks between 1249 and 1255 under Robert Savage and William de Swineford. Swineford came from Northamptonshire. Savage had previously been sheriff of Surrey-Sussex (Sussex was his home county) and he left Norfolk-Suffolk in 1255 for the sheriffdom of Bedfordshire-Buckinghamshire; *Close Rolls 1253–54*, p. 41; *Lists of Sheriffs*, pp. 135, 86, 1; *Exc. Rot. Fin.*, ii. 345; *Cal. Pat. Rolls 1247–58*, p. 619; *Close Rolls 1256–59*, p. 200.
3. For example Adam of Nurstead (sheriff of Gloucestershire 1252–5) and the unpopular clerk, Hugh de Manneby, twice sheriff of Northamptonshire in the 1250s; Jacob, *Studies in the Period of Baronial Reform*, pp. 48–49. *Chron. Maj.*, v. 715–16.
4. *Documents of the Baronial Movement*, pp. 276–7.
5. Examples are Henry de Scaccario (Berkshire, 1229–32); and Herbert de Alençon (Norfolk-Suffolk, 1227–32).

predecessors 'et genere nobiliores' he was probably thinking not of the wealthy outgoing *curiales*, but precisely of their deputies who had been in day to day charge of the counties. Much would depend on the direction (or lack of it) given to his officials by the curial super-sheriff, and on the latter's own relations with the shire. In John's reign, for example, there are grounds for believing that Oxfordshire was reasonably content with the administration of Thomas Basset, scion of an old county family, and lord of Headington; but the same could not be said of Dorset–Somerset labouring under William Briwerre and his agents, or of Oxfordshire itself between 1215–23 when Falkes de Breauté was sheriff. A continuation of curial sheriffdoms into the 1250s might have appeased local society if the *curiales* had been such as John of Laxton and Ralph fitz Nicholas; but its effect would have been quite the opposite if the likes of Imbert Pugeys and William de Valence had acquired office.

Henry III had, however, an alternative to the restoration or maintenance of the curial system, an alternative which would placate county society, and constitute a medium between the small amount of revenue due above the farm before 1236 and the large amounts after 1241. Miss Mills saw the imposition of increments in 1241 as a natural completion of the reforms of 1236. There was certainly a case for reverting to this simpler system once the potential of the local revenue had been established from the returns of the custodian sheriffs. Yet the policy of 1241, in that it imposed harsher terms on many sheriffs, in reality represented a change of course, which involved, consciously or not, the rejection of the compromise with the counties achieved five years earlier; a change perhaps related to the appointment of William of Haverhill as treasurer of the exchequer in 1240 in place of Hugh of Pattishall who had been in office since 1234. The measures of 1236 had shown that the king could extract more revenue from the shires and yet conciliate local society as in the subsequent reforms of 1258 by appointing local men as sheriffs, and making them custodians with allowances. A compromise along these lines was possible because court and county were moving closer together. By 1258 the counties realized that the demand of 1215 for the shires to be at their ancient farms was unattainable, and were reconciled to profits provided the sheriff was a local knight and was given an allowance. (Soon after the re-introduction of profits in 1224, the men of Devon made an agreement with the king to have a custodian sheriff 'de se ipsis' who was to receive £30 p.a. for expenses).[1] It is probable that the concession of moderate increments would at one time have been as acceptable to the localities as profits and allowances, but by 1258 increments were tarred with the policies of the preceding seventeen years and

1. *Patent Rolls 1216–25*, p. 554.

the reformers not surprisingly demanded a return to the 1236–41 arrangements. There was also a substantial area of potential agreement around the personnel of the shrievality. The placing of a premium on revenue above the farm, and the consequent departure of *familiares* from the shires meant that the demand in 1258 for the sheriff to be a vavasour of his county no longer had the radical implications which it would have done in 1215. From the point of view of increased revenue the county knight was a better sheriff than the *curialis*, and he might also have advantages over professional administrators, if the latter lacked the resources to satisfy the exchequer for their debts.[1] During the last part of the thirteenth century questions concerning the person of the sheriff lost much of their contentious nature, and Edward I's concession in 1300 that the shire courts could elect their own was apparently little valued.[2] Between 1241–58, therefore, Henry III placed the financial needs of the crown above the possibilities of a compromise with the counties, and thus laid the foundation for the support given by local society to the cause of reform during the baronial wars. The consequences of the abandonment of the 1236–41 system were aggravated by the fact that after 1236 there was no wholesale dismissal of sheriffs, and no grand scale and well publicized inquiry into their activities. The addition to the articles of the eyre of several relating to shrieval abuse, the dismissal and disgrace of individual sheriffs, and the regional inquiries into their activities, were inadequate substitutes.[3] Henry lacked the determination or imagination to follow policies which, as it was put in 1262 when he was urged to make local men sheriffs, would 'draw the hearts of his faithful subjects and people to him in special affection'.[4]

The decline of the curial sheriff in England, foreshadowed in 1194 and 1204, was largely effected between 1236–50. Although permitted by the political situation, and connected with changes in the nature of the shrieval office, it was immediately produced by the implementation of policies designed to obtain better value from the county farm, of which curial sheriffs were unsatisfactory executants. In broader perspective it was made possible by developments in society and administration which created the experienced county knights and professional administrators from whom the king could increasingly draw his local officials. The period of disturbance and civil war beginning in 1261 when Henry III placed a considerable number of *familiares* into local office, and the years 1270–4 when Edward was away on crusade, saw the re-emergence of the curial

1. *Documents of the Baronial Period*, pp. 276, 277. For the indebtedness of sheriffs in 1258, see Jacob, pp. 9–12.
2. Morris, pp. 184–5; W. Stubbs, *Constitutional History of England* (3rd ed., Oxford, 1883), ii. 216.
3. Jacob, pp. 25–27; Meekings, pp. 27–33; Treharne, pp. 43, 44.
4. *Foedera*, I. i. 415. See Powicke, *Henry III and the Lord Edward*, ii. 425.

sheriff. But the situation for most of Edward's reign, at least in respect of the sheriff's connection with the court, was comparable to that found in the 1250s. Research into the terms on which the shrievalities were held in Edward's time would be necessary to determine how far this was due to a return to the high increments of the 1250s, and how far to the continuing diminution in the scope of the sheriff's authority.

9

What Happened in 1258?

Shortly after 7 April 1258 one of the most important parliaments of King Henry III's reign opened at Westminster. Its proceedings culminated in the king's oath, recorded on 2 May, accepting that the realm should be reformed by twenty-four men, twelve chosen by himself, and twelve by the magnates of the kingdom.[1] This concession opened the way for the ensuing period of baronial reform, rebellion and civil war. There was nothing new in 1258 about the demand for reform. It had been put at parliaments in 1244, 1248, 1249 and 1255.[2] Previously, the king had always refused to give way; not surprisingly because his control of policy, his choice of ministers, and his patronage of friends were thereby threatened. In 1258, however, Henry capitulated. Why? For R.F. Treharne the answer was clear. Henry surrendered in order to avoid papal excommunication and interdict. Treharne believed that these spiritual penalties were imminent because Henry had failed to find sufficient funds to fulfil an agreement with the pope concerning the throne of Sicily. In 1258 the only way to raise the money and escape the penalties was to secure an aid from parliament. When parliament refused to grant an aid unless there was reform of the realm, Henry had no alternative but to accept these terms. Aspects of this same interpretation are to be found in the work of Sir Maurice Powicke.[3] It is an interpretation which this paper will argue is misconceived. In reality, Henry was brought to surrender not by fear of the pope but by an armed demonstration of magnates. This use of force was largely overlooked by Treharne and Powicke. It grew out of events at the Westminster parliament, events which brought to a head the widespread hatred of the king's Lusignan half-brothers. Powicke believed that it was not until they resisted reform at the Oxford parliament in

---

[1] *Documents of the Baronial Movement of Reform and Rebellion*, ed. R.F. Treharne, I.J. Sanders, Oxford 1973, 73–7; R.F. Treharne, *The Baronial Plan of Reform 1258–63*, Manchester 1932, 65. The magnates were summoned to be in London for the parliament by 7 April; Treharne, Sanders, 73–4. However, the king's itinerary has him at Merton on 8 April and at Westminster only on 9 April; Treharne, 383. Probably the parliament opened on 9 April.

[2] W. Stubbs, *Select Charters and other Illustrations of English Constitutional History*, 9th edn. Oxford 1913, 326–9; Matthew Paris, *Chronica Majora*, ed. H.R. Luard, RS 1872–83, iv, 366–8. The specific demand at the parliaments mentioned was that the king should appoint a justiciar, chancellor and treasurer on the advice of his magnates. Also, in 1244, a general plan of reform was probably drawn up.

[3] Treharne, 62–6; Powicke, *Henry III and The Lord Edward*, Oxford 1947, 374–9.

June 1258 that the brothers were 'marked down'.[4] In fact, the movement against them was central to the decision taken at the parliament of Westminster to force reform upon the king.

Henry III's Sicilian entanglement had begun in 1254. In that year he accepted a papal offer of the throne of Sicily for his second son, Edmund. In return, Henry was to pay the pope 135,000 marks, and send an army to conquer the kingdom from its Hohenstaufen rulers. All this was to be done within a stated time limit. If the conditions were not fulfilled Henry would find himself excommunicated, England would be placed under an interdict, and the pope would be free to withdraw the offer.[5] Henry quickly found the greatest difficulty in raising the 135,000 marks, and, although a commander was picked for a Sicilian army, there were no troops for him to lead.[6] In 1257, after pope Alexander IV had waived one time limit, strenuous diplomatic efforts were made to persuade him to further modify the conditions of the agreement.[7] Powicke believed that Alexander's 'reply cost Henry his independence'.[8] Treharne wrote that 'Alexander showed no consideration for Henry's difficulties . . .Thus, far from securing the alleviation which they desired, [Henry's] envoys returned to inform the King . . . that 5,500 marks must be despatched at once, and that unless Henry immediately gave an undertaking to pay the rest of the huge debt of 155,000 marks very soon, he would inevitably be excommunicated by the implacable Vicar of God . . .This was the situation, which, at the end of 1257, made it certain that the English political deadlock would soon be broken. Alexander's ultimatum would precipitate a crisis quite different from the barren encounters with which the English magnates had grown contemptuously familiar since 1244. Henry dared not face Papal excommunication, while the vastness of the sum required, and the narrowness of the time-limit allowed by the Pope would prevent him from evading the political issue between himself and the magnates by the irregular finance of recent years. He would have no alternative to an appeal to the Great Council for military and financial aid . . .The barons, having the King at their mercy, would thus be able to demand their own terms'[9]

While features of Treharne's picture are correct, the whole is probably out

[4] Powicke, *Henry III*, 384; F.M. Powicke, *The Thirteenth Century*, Oxford 1953, 140 n. 1. The Lusignans were the offspring of the marriage between Henry III's mother and her second husband, the great Poitevin noble, Hugh le Brun, lord of Lusignan and count of La Marche. The half-brothers came to England in 1247; see below p. 190, and H.S. Snellgrove, *The Lusignans in England*, Albuquerque, New Mexico 1950, which recognises the importance of the family in the crisis of 1258.

[5] *Foedera*, I, i, 316–8; Powicke, *Henry III*, 371.

[6] *Foedera*, I, i, 359–60. For the financial side of the Sicilian affair see W.E. Lunt, *Financial Relations of England with the Papacy to 1327*, Cambridge Mass. 1939, 255–90.

[7] *Foedera*, I, i, 359. The time limit of the original agreement expired at Michaelmas 1256; see *Foedera*, I, i, 350.

[8] Powicke, *Henry III*, 376.

[9] Treharne, 62. Alexander's specific demands can be seen from Henry's replies to them drawn up after 2 May. One of the demands was that Henry should seek a 'common subsidy', that is an aid from parliament; *Close Roll Supplement 1244–66*, 29–30.

of focus. Certainly Henry was not like his father John; he would have regarded the excommunication of himself, and an interdict placed on the kingdom as horrific disasters. What is not clear, however, is that Henry felt that these penalties were imminent in April 1258. Alexander's letters, written in December 1257, which the papal envoy, Master Arlot, brought to England the following March, were friendly and re-assuring. 'The strength of papal charity' was not to be 'vanquished by lengthy periods of hoping, nor is our proposal in respect of you to be withdrawn so long as there are indications that hope may be revived'. Probably Alexander had been concerned by the possibility, raised by Henry's ambassadors, that the king would resign prematurely from the Sicilian enterprise, unless the terms were altered. The pope, therefore, sought to encourage the monarch. He wished the undertaking 'to arise in a state from which it might have a happy outcome'. More concretely, Alexander assured the king that he had not as yet incurred spiritual penalties, and he agreed to suspend them for another three months, that is until 1 June 1258.[10] According to Powicke, Alexander 'would go no farther'. This was not the case. In January 1258 the pope, 'wishing to help the affair forward, and so that it should not be destroyed for lack of time', gave Arlot the power, at his discretion, to extend the so-called deadline for another three months until 1 September. It is true that, after Arlot arrived in England, he probably delayed before conceding this extension, and he clearly made much noise about the prospect of excommunication and interdict. The Dunstable annals state that he 'threatened that he would excommunicate the king and all his magnates', while the annals of Tewkesbury record that Arlot brought papal bulls to place an interdict on the king's chapel and all the English church.[11] In a sense, however, this intimidation was aimed less at the king than at those from whom both king and pope hoped to extract money. Henry needed no coercion. He was the pope's greatest friend in England, and the chief enthusiast for the Sicilian project. Henry, as much as Arlot, must have hoped that the threat of penalties would induce parliament to grant money. Yet the king may well have appreciated that the threat was largely bluff and bluster.[12] Certainly this was shown to be the case when the time limit finally ran out in September. No spiritual thunderbolts hurtled down on England. The pope's response came in a letter dated 18 December. It was addressed to 'the illustrious king of England', a *rex Christianissimus*. The tone was more of sorrow than of anger. He could no longer hope that Henry would be able to fulfil his side of the bargain; he now held himself free to negotiate with

---

[10] *Foedera*, I, i, 358, 366.

[11] Powicke, *Henry III*, 376; *Foedera*, I, i, 369; *Annales Monastici*, ed. H.R. Luard, RS 1864–9, iii, 208; i, 163. That Arlot granted the extension is clear from *CR 1256–9*, 320, but there is no evidence as to precisely when he did this.

[12] It is interesting to note that, according to Matthew Paris, the king 'greeted Arlot with rapture on his arrival, since he was invested with the greatest powers and authority'; Paris, v, 673.

other candidates. As for the penalties, 'with our accustomed kindness, and through our special grace, we suspend them during pleasure'.[13]

Even if, in April 1258, Henry was seriously concerned about the possibility of excommunication and interdict, it is difficult to see why this should have forced him into the concession recorded on 2 May. By agreeing to reform of the realm, Henry lost his independence, and obtained no real prospect of financial aid. The king's concession, therefore, hindered rather than helped the Sicilian project, and, in that respect, made the penalties more, not less likely. The promise of financial aid made by the magnates needs careful inspection. The royal letter issued on 2 May, containing the terms of the agreement, states, that the king had negotiated with the great men of the realm about the furtherance of the Sicilian business, and 'they have replied to us that, if we should be pleased to reform the state of our realm by the counsel of our loyal subjects, and provided the lord pope would ameliorate the conditions which he had stated for the Sicilian affair in such a way that we might be able to take the matter up effectively, they would loyally use their influence with the community of the realm so that a common aid should be granted to us for that purpose'.[14] The magnates, therefore, did not say that they would grant an aid. They merely said that, on certain conditions, they would 'use their influence with the community of the realm' that one might be granted. This was no idle form of words. The day was passing when the barons could answer for the rest of the kingdom in the granting of taxation. Already in 1254 two knights from each county had been summoned before the king's council in order to say what aid 'all and each' in the shires were prepared to grant.[15] Perhaps some similar arrangement would have been necessary in 1258. There was thus no guarantee that the magnates would be able to obtain an aid from the community of the realm. Moreover, before they would even bring their advocacy to bear on the matter, they required the pope to alter the conditions of the agreement so that the king could prosecute the Sicilian project successfully. This stipulation made

---

[13] *Foedera*, I, i 379; Paris, vi, 416. When the king's clerk, Simon Passelewe, came to Waltham abbey in the middle of the Westminster parliament, he tried to persuade the monastery to stand surety for a loan to Henry from French merchants by lamenting that 'in three or four days his chapel will be placed under an interdict'. Simon went on to say much the same at the abbeys of St. Albans and Reading. It was largely bluff. The pope had warned Henry that his chapel would be placed under an interdict unless he allowed 5,500 marks, which the king's envoys to the pope in 1257 had obliged themselves to pay Siena merchants, to be given to the envoys from the clerical tenth then being collected in England. Henry was only too pleased to allow this. He also agreed, as the pope demanded, that another 4,500 marks should be raised for the same merchants from the tenth. Another threat to Henry's chapel could have arisen from an agreement which he made with Florentine merchants in June 1257, but it seems that this agreement was never completed; Paris, v, 682–8; *Flores Historiarum*, ed. H.R. Luard, RS 1890, iii, 349–52; *CLR 1251–60*, 434–5; *Foedera*, I, i, 368, 371; *Close Roll Supplement 1244–66*, no. 282; *CPR 1247–58*, 562, 625; Lunt, 270–80, 279, n. 1.

[14] Treharne, Sanders, 73–4.

[15] Stubbs, 365–6; but see J.C. Holt, 'The Prehistory of Parliament', *The English Parliament in the Middle Ages*, ed. R.G. Davies, J.H. Denton, Manchester, 1981, 27.

it virtually certain that no aid would ever be granted. It was for the magnates to judge on what terms the scheme might be practical, and since the Sicilian adventure was universally regarded in England as a monumental folly, they were almost certain to deem any papal concessions insufficient.[16] Alexander appreciated this. He simply ignored the magnates' offer to negotiate for an aid, and concluded that Henry was incapable of prosecuting the Sicilian venture any further.[17]

It seems unlikely, therefore, that Henry, in 1258, would have agreed to the reform of the realm because of papal threats which he probably suspected were empty, and in return for concessions which he must have feared were worthless.[18] But, if this is right, why did he capitulate? The answer is that he was forced to by his magnates. There are only two chronicle accounts of any length for the parliament at Westminster in April and May 1258; Matthew Paris's *Chronica Majora* and the annals of Tewkesbury abbey. Paris's version of the king's surrender is as follows. After numerous criticisms had been made of the king, Henry 'on reflection acknowledged the truth of the accusations, although late, and humbled himself, declaring that he had too often been beguiled by evil counsel, and he promised and made a solemn oath at the altar of the shrine of St Edward, that he would fully and properly amend his old errors, and show favour and kindness to his native-born subjects'.[19] Paris, then, provides no evidence of coercion, but equally he says nothing about a promise of an aid for Sicily. He seems, indeed, to be ill-informed about certain aspects of the parliament. His account of the king's oath is vague and inaccurate. Paris knows nothing about its most vital feature: the agreement to abide by the work of the twenty-four reformers. Indeed he nowhere mentions the twenty-four. The account in the Tewkesbury annals, on the other hand, is far more detailed.[20] Around the feast of St Vitalis (28 April) the demand was put for an aid for Sicily. It was agreed that the magnates should give their reply in three days time. The bishops, having obtained licence, departed lest they incurred the king's anger. Then 'on the third day, as the third hour approached, noble and vigorous men, earls, barons, and knights went to the court at Westminster, armed in excellent fashion, and girded with swords. However, they placed their swords at the entrance to the king's hall, and, appearing before the king, saluted him as their lord king in devoted manner with fitting honour. The king was immediately dis-

---

[16] For the unpopularity of the Sicilian enterprise, see Paris, v. 680–1; *Ann. Mon.*, i, 386–8.

[17] *Foedera*, I, i, 379, Paris, vi, 416.

[18] After 2 May the king drew up proposals for the pope as to how the terms might be modified, and the Provisions of Oxford named twenty-four men to 'negotiate an aid for the king'; *Close Roll Supplement 1244–66*, 29–30; Treharne, Sanders, 104–7. This does not mean, however, that Henry actually thought an aid would be granted. (There is no evidence the twenty-four ever met). The 'firm belief', expressed in a royal letter to the pope in August 1258, that assistance would be forthcoming if the terms were modified was probably a pretence to retain papal favour; *CR 1256–9*, 326.

[19] Paris, v, 689.

[20] *Ann. Mon.*, i, 163–5.

turbed in mind, and uncertain why they had come armed. He said, "what is this my lords, am I, wretched fellow, your captive?"' To this Roger Bigod, earl of Norfolk replied, 'No, my lord, no! But let the wretched and intolerable Poitevins and all aliens flee from your face and ours as from the face of a lion, and there will be "glory to God in the heavens, and in your land peace to men of goodwill"'. Bigod then went on to reveal the general demand that Henry should swear to adhere to 'our counsels'. When Henry asked what such adherence would involve, 'the baronage replied: "together with your son and heir Edward, swear on the gospels that, without the consent of twenty-four prudent men of England to be chosen, namely bishops, earls and barons, you will impose no . . . unaccustomed yoke [e.g. tax] . . . and that you will not delay handing your royal seal, through the counsel of the foresaid [twenty-four], to a discreet man whom they will provide"'. 'The king, therefore, seeing that he was not able to put the matter off any further, along with Edward his son and heir, although the latter was unwilling, swore on the gospels on 30 April 1258, and commended everything to their counsel [presumably the counsel of the twenty-four], and conceded and approved all things which they wished to be done'.

The Tewkesbury annals, therefore, make it plain that an armed demonstration forced the king to accept reform in 1258. There seems no reason for rejecting the substance of the account.[21] On the contrary, it has a special claim to belief not hitherto appreciated, namely the likelihood that it was written up from a news-letter received from an eyewitness of the parliament. This would explain why it has a wealth of detail, and a use of direct speech which is found nowhere else in the Tewkesbury chronicle.[22] Clearly the circumstantial nature

---

[21] In his list of grievances drawn up in March–April 1261 Henry did not complain of pressure brought on him in 1258; see Treharne, Sanders, 236–7, no. 26. However, when this list was drawn up, Henry was in a delicate political situation and had not formally rejected his oath of 2 May and the Provisions of Oxford.

[22] The Tewkesbury annals are in BL Cotton MS Cleopatra A VII, fos. 1–67v. They were edited for the Rolls Series by H.R. Luard in *Annales Monastici*, i, 1864, 43–180. The annals contain, in fact, two distinct chronicles: Tewkesbury I, the main chronicle of the abbey which commences before 1066 (the year in which Luard's printed text begins) and continues into 1263 after which it is lost; and Tewkesbury II which begins in 1258 with Tewkesbury I's account of events between the arrival of Master Arlot and the expulsion of the Lusignans, and then gives an independent history down to 1264 after which it too is lost; *Ann. Mon.*, i, 162 n. 5; A. Gransden, *Historical Writing in England*, London 1974, 405, n. 13, 416. The appearance of the manuscript of Tewkesbury I strongly suggests that by 1258 it was being written soon after the news of the events which it records came in. (For this point and further discussion of the Tewkesbury annals, see below pp. 253–9.) Tewkesbury II, by contrast, is unlikely to have been written before 1264, and its version of 1258 was thus copied from Tewkesbury I and not vice versa. Although roughly contemporaneous with the events which it describes, however, the Tewkesbury I account of the Westminster and Oxford parliaments in 1258, taken as a whole, is somewhat muddled. It is clear that before the account of the Westminster parliament begins with 'Circa festum Sancti Vitalis' (*Ann. Mon.*, i, 163) the chronicler had been writing about the parliament at Oxford in June. This confused the writer of Tewkesbury II, and he altered 'Oxford' to 'London'; *Ann. Mon.*, i, 163 n. 2. However, the reference to the bishops being at Merton makes it plain that Oxford is meant; see *Ann. Mon.*, i, 412. The author of Tewkesbury I may have tried to fit together his accounts of the Oxford and Westminster parliaments. Into

of the detail – the third hour of the day, the leaving of the swords at the entrance to the hall – suggests the testimony of an eyewitness. Other elements of
the account also carry conviction. Roger Bigod's emphasis in his speech on
the Poitevins, that is the Lusignans, is not surprising given previous events at
the Westminster parliament.[23] The swearing of the king's oath on 30 April is
consistent with the date, 2 May, given to the royal letter which recorded it, by
which time Henry had chosen his panel of twelve reformers.[24] Admittedly, the
chronicle says nothing about the promise concerning the Sicilian aid which
Henry must have obtained before swearing his oath, but this merely reflects
how insignificant the promise was felt to be. The demand that the king should
impose no tax without the counsel of the twenty-four, and hand his seal to someone decided by them was not embodied in the king's concession as recorded
on 2 May, yet these matters may well have been raised on 30 April. The Tewkesbury narrative grasps the vital point, namely the demand for the twenty-four
reformers, and its statement that the king 'commended himself and everything to their counsel, and conceded and approved all things which they wished
to be done' is not dissimilar from the passage in the oath, as recorded on 2
May, where Henry swore 'to observe inviolably whatever shall be ordained by
the twenty-four' in the reform of the realm.[25] If the chronicler's information
did indeed come from a news-letter, it is possible that the writer was the Tewkesbury monk, William de Bekeford. The Tewkesbury chronicle notes that in June
1258 Bekeford accompanied the eldest daughter of Richard de Clare, earl of
Gloucester, to Lyons for her marriage to the marquis of Montferrat. Perhaps
Bekeford was also present in the earl's retinue at the Westminster parliament,
where details of the marriage were settled. If that was the case, he may well

continued
the sentence, probably copied from the news-letter, about the bishops at the Westminster parliament excusing themselves and retiring there is a 'ut supradictum est'. This appears to refer to the
earlier statement that the bishops were absent from the parliament at Oxford, and was perhaps
inserted by the chronicler as a clumsy attempt to reconcile the two accounts. The nature of the
chronicle around this time shows that its author had little practice at writing a connected narrative, and he also admits that he is wholly ignorant of the names of two of the Lusignans (Geoffrey
and Guy); *Ann. Mon.*, i, 165. All this makes the coherent report of events between 28–30 April –
'Circa festum Sancti Vitalis . . . concessit et approbavit' – which it is suggested comes from the
news-letter, stand out the more sharply; *Ann. Mon.*, i, 163–4. (In Luard's text this section begins
and ends a paragraph, but in the MS there are no breaks of this kind.)
   [23] See below p. 192. Whether, however, Bigod denounced all aliens, as opposed to merely the
Lusignans, may be questioned since he was at this time in alliance with Peter of Savoy; see below p.
194. (He was, nonetheless, engaged in 1258 in a private dispute with Peter.) The Tewkesbury annals alone give the information that the aid demanded was a third on moveables and immove-
ables. The church was probably exempted from this demand since it was already making heavy
financial contributions for Sicily. Hence it was possible for the bishops to obtain licence to withdraw.
   [24] Treharne, Sanders, 74–5.
   [25] Treharne, Sanders, 74–5.

have sent back an account of proceedings there to his brothers at Tewkes-bury.[26]

If it is agreed that it was a menacing démarche by the barons, not any threats from the pope, which made Henry III accept reform, the question arises as to why in 1258 the king's critics took action, whereas previously they had de-manded changes but done nothing to compel them. By 1258 there were, of course, several reasons for what the barons called the *statum imbecillem* of the country. Throughout the counties of England there was discontent with the financial burden of the general eyre, the oppressions of the sheriffs, and the policies of the exchequer by which the latter were aggravated. All these mat-ters were subject to reform in the Provisions of Oxford, and Westminster, in 1258–9.[27] By themselves, however, such grievances would not have caused the revolution of 1258. Although doubtless made aware by their followers and sup-porters of the feelings in the counties, the great magnates who led the revolu-tion were amongst the least vulnerable to the abuses of the sheriffs, and the financial exactions of the justices in eyre. For events to come to a head in 1258 additional incitement was needed. In part this was clearly provided by the far-cical state of the Sicilian enterprise, underlining as it did both the king's in-competence and insolvency. These weaknesses were also exhibited in Henry's inability to meet the challenge of Llywelyn in Wales and the Marches. But per-haps the most important of the immediate spurs to action was the issue of the Lusignans. The king's Poitevin half-brothers had come to England in 1247. In that year, the second youngest, William de Valence, married one of the heir-esses of the Marshal earls, and obtained with her the county of Pembroke. The king also granted him Hertford castle and, over the ensuring years, a large num-ber of manors. In 1250 the youngest brother, Aymer, became bishop-elect of Winchester. The more senior brothers, Guy and Geoffrey de Lusignan, did not settle in England, but they made frequent visits, and were granted money fees and wardships by the king.[28] Henry III had also planted in England his wife's uncles, Peter of Savoy, who was granted the honour of Richmond in 1240, and Boniface who, in the next year, became archbishop of Canterbury.[29] The king, however, was far from being surrounded by a cohesive and exclusive party of foreign relatives. There were bitter quarrels between Lusignans and Sa-voyards. There were also many native barons prominent at court. In 1258 it was essentially a group of *curiales*, comprising native barons, Simon de Mont-fort, and Peter of Savoy, which turned on the Lusignans and their allies, and

---

[26] At the Westminster parliament on 2 May the king stood surety for money which the earl of Gloucester owed the marquis for the marriage; *CPR 1247–58*, 662. For Tewkesbury abbey and the earls of Gloucester, see *Ann. Mon.*, i, xvii, 159, 167; for Bekeford, *ibid*, 162.

[27] *Ann. Mon.*, i, 457; see above pp. 171–81. Treharne, Sanders, 108–9, 118–23, 140–3, 146–7.

[28] For the Lusignans, see Snellgrove.

[29] For the Savoyards, see E.L. Cox, *The Eagles of Savoy*, Princeton, 1974, and for both groups see now the fundamental works of Huw Ridgeway cited above p. ix.

imposed reform on the king. In that sense the revolution of 1258 was very much a revolution within the court of Henry III.

One reason for the unpopularity of Lusignans was the extent to which they monopolised the fruits of royal patronage.[30] Another was that their conduct was frequently arrogant and violent. The king's protection, moreover, seemed to place the brothers above the law. If, as seems the case, the Savoyards were far less unpopular in England than the Lusignans, it was because they behaved in a more circumspect and responsible fashion. When, for example, Archbishop Boniface came to St Albans in 1253 the monks were impressed by his moderation and civility. By contrast, the year before they had been outraged by Geoffrey de Lusignan's pride and contempt for others – his marshal had expelled all the horses from the abbey's stables to make way for Geoffrey's, although there was plenty of room.[31] The landed possessions in England which the king gave the Lusignans meant that many lesser men were exposed to the brutality and ruthlessness of their local agents. The unfortunate characteristics of the brothers could also be displayed in numerous disputes with great men over lands and rights. Aymer bishop-elect of Winchester came into conflict with Boniface of Savoy, archbishop of Canterbury, Roger Bigod earl of Norfolk, and the king's steward, Robert Walerand; William de Valence clashed with the earls of Leicester, Gloucester, and Hereford, with Humphrey de Bohun, Hereford's eldest son, and again with Archbishop Boniface. Meanwhile, Guy and Geoffrey de Lusignan offended Henry de Hastings and Geoffrey de Lucy.[32] A notorious example of the violence of the half-brothers occurred in a dispute between the bishop-elect of Winchester and Archbishop Boniface in 1252. 'A multitude of armed Poitevins from the *familia* of . . . the elect of Winchester, William de Valence and their brothers', as a jury of presentment put it, broke into the archbishop's palace at Lambeth, stole his money, jewels and silver plate, and dragged his servants off to the elect's castle at Farnham. Aymer appears to have escaped punishment for this incident. It was settled out of court on the strength of his oath disclaiming knowledge of the attack, and not all the archbishop's property was returned. In and after 1258 the complaint was frequently voiced that the king's protection had made it impossible to secure legal redress against the Lusignans and their followers. This belief was one reason

---

[30] See below p. 196.

[31] Paris, v, 344–5, 413–4; see also iv, 177; Cox 172–9, 233–6.

[32] Relations between the Lusignans and Richard de Clare, earl of Gloucester, were sometimes cordial, but there seems to have been a dispute between Richard and William de Valence over Roxhill manor in Bedfordshire, which ended with Richard ejecting William from the manor; M.R. Altschul, *A Baronial Family in Medieval England: the Clares*, Baltimore 1965, 66–7, 83; PRO E/163/2/30 (henceforth all manuscript references, unless otherwise stated, are to documents in the PRO); Just/1/9, m.39d; E.101/505/9. For the earl of Hereford and William de Valence, see R. Vaughan, 'The Chronicle of John of Wallingford', *EHR*, lxxiii, 1958, 76; see Paris, v, 442. For conflicts between the earl's son and William over their rights as respectively lords of Haverford and Pembroke, see KB/26/159, mm.1d,6; E/368/32, m.2d. For Guy and Geoffrey de Lusignan, see *CR 1256–9*, 20; Just/1/873, m.6d. The other cases are mentioned below in the text and in note 44.

why Henry III was accused of breaking the clause in *Magna Carta* which forbad the denial and delay of justice. In 1259 a Kentish knight alleged that he had been unable to obtain justice in the king's court against Roger of Leybourne because of the 'favour' which Roger had then enjoyed as one who 'stood' with William de Valence.[33] The king's protection of his half-brothers can be suspected in other cases. Perhaps it was why Archbishop Boniface, although disseized by William de Valence of the custody of a fee in Preston (Kent) around 1255, obtained redress only from the council of fifteen imposed on the king by the Provisions of Oxford in 1258.[34] Perhaps too it was why Robert Walerand abandoned a case of novel disseisin he brought against the elect of Winchester on the Hampshire eyre of 1256. Here, after the jury had given its verdict, plainly in Walerand's favour, Robert withdrew from his writ, and the elect went without day.[35] In another case on this eyre Roger Bigod earl of Norfolk accused the elect of deforcing him of the wardship of Richard son and heir of Richard de Bere. After the earl and Aymer had pleaded their cases, the earl sought judgement, and it is difficult to see, on the evidence of the pleadings, how this could have been other than in his favour. The judges, however, postponed their sentence for over two months until a later stage of their eyre. Unfortunately records of the case are then lost, but the whole episode may have left a legacy of ill feeling which influenced Bigod's actions in the crisis of 1258.[36]

By 1258, therefore, there was a great deal of pent up resentment against the Lusignans. Events at the Westminster parliament served to bring this to an explosive climax. An account of the parliament should begin with an episode which both Treharne and Powicke overlooked. At Shere in Surrey on 1 April 1258, little more than a week before the parliament opened, an armed band, allegedly on the orders of the bishop-elect of Winchester, attacked some servants of John fitz Geoffrey, the lord of the manor, and took them to the elect's castle of Farnham where one died of his wounds. All this was occasioned by a dispute between Aymer and John fitz Geoffrey over the advowson of Shere. When the parliament at Westminster opened John complained to the king about Aymer's attack, and sought redress. But Henry III, as the legal record made three months later stated, 'did not wish to hear him and wholly denied him

---

[33] Just/1/873, mm.3,18d; Paris, v, 348–54, 359, 738–9; *Ann. Mon.*, i, 458–9. The point about *Magna Carta* comes from a schedule of complaints against Henry III's government drawn up in 1263; Treharne, Sanders, 270–1.
[34] *CR 1256–9*, 276. The most numerous sufferers from the corruption of the judicial system were, of course, the lesser men who had no remedy against the abuses of the local officials of the Lusignans; see Treharne, Sanders, 270–3.
[35] Just/1/778, m.17; see *Cal. Inq. Post Mortem*, ii, no. 626. There is no sign that Aymer and Robert came to an agreement. For Walerand, see also *CPR 1247–58*, 537.
[36] Just/1/778, mm. 10,13. Later in 1256 Aymer is found owing Bigod 100 marks and perhaps this was in settlement of the dispute. Aymer, however, did not give the money to the earl but arranged with the king to have it deducted from the payments Bigod was supposed to make towards his debts at the exchequer; *CLR 1251–60*, 292. Whether Bigod welcomed this form of settlement may be questioned.

justice'.[37] Fitz Geoffrey was a dangerous man to offend in this way. The son of King John's justiciar, Geoffrey fitz Peter, he was a great baron who had risen high in the king's service. In 1237, in return for a grant of taxation, the magnates had insisted that John join the royal council. Subsequently he had served a long term as justiciar of Ireland; he was still a prominent figure at court.[38] Not surprisingly, therefore, John's experiences in April 1258 caused fury at the Westminster parliament. As a letter which the baronage wrote to the pope, complaining of Aymer's conduct put it, 'lately to John fitz Geoffrey, a noble and powerful man amongst us, we know that [Aymer] has committed the most atrocious injuries, so that the *majores* of the kingdom *vehementer scandalizati sunt contra eum*, recalling to their minds his earlier deeds'.[39] The incident at Shere, with its obvious echoes of the attack on Lambeth palace in 1252, seemed to typify the violence of the half-brothers.[40] The king's reaction illustrated in the most blatant fashion the way his protection placed them above the law, and supported the statement, made by the baronage in another letter to the pope, that, 'if anyone brought a complaint and sought judgement against [the Lusignans] . . . the king turned against the complainant in a most extraordinary manner, and he who should have been a propitious judge . . . became a terrible enemy'.[41] The king's failure as an impartial judge was one reason why the Provisions of Oxford in June 1258 re-established the office of justiciar. The first case the justiciar heard was that of John fitz Geoffrey.[42]

At the Westminster parliament this scandal concerning Aymer de Lusignan was quickly followed by angry scenes involving William de Valence. William, because of his possession of Pembroke, was especially interested in the debate about the situation in Wales where Llywelyn was spreading destruction, and he accused certain English nobles of treacherous connivance with the Welsh prince. These remarks infuriated both the earls of Gloucester and Leicester, and the latter would have come to blows with William had not the king intervened.[43] Later in the parliament de Montfort demanded justice against William. The issue here may well have been the claim which Simon's wife had to Pembroke.[44] According to Matthew Paris, one of the barons' final charges against

---

[37] Just/1/1187, m.1; Paris, v, 708.

[38] Paris, iii, 383; GEC, v, 433.

[39] Paris, vi, 409.

[40] For the Lambeth incident being recalled in 1258, see Paris, vi, 405–6.

[41] *Ann. Mon.*, i, 459.

[42] Just/1/1187, m.1; Treharne, Sanders, 260–1, 270–3.

[43] Paris, v, 676–7; Powicke, *Henry III*, 381.

[44] Paris, v, 689. In 1247 Simon and his wife Eleanor, the sister of Henry III, brought a case against the heirs of the Marshal earls of Pembroke for Eleanor's dower as the widow of William Marshal, earl of Pembroke, who had died in 1230. The Montforts' claim was for Pembroke (and thus one directed in the first instance against William de Valence) since Simon and Eleanor maintained that it was with Pembroke that Eleanor had been dowered. No judgement was given in the 1247 case, although, in 1260, Simon implied that one should have been; C. Bémont, *Simon de Montfort*, Paris 1884, 335; see, KB/26/159, mm.2d,3,3d. Eleanor was also in dispute with the Lusignans over their respective shares of their mother's inheritance in France; BN Clairambault 1188, fos.

the king also centred on the Lusignans. Henry had 'exalted his uterine brothers in a most intolerable fashion, as if they had been native born, contrary to the right and law of the kingdom, nor would he allow any writ to go out from the chancery against them'.[45]

It is against this rising tide of complaint against the half-brothers that the famous confederation formed at the Westminster parliament should be placed. In this, on 12 April 1258, the earls of Gloucester, Norfolk, and Leicester, Peter of Savoy, Hugh Bigod, John fitz Geoffrey, and Peter de Montfort, all save the earl of Norfolk *curiales*, swore to 'help each other, both ourselves and those belonging to us, against all people, doing right and taking nothing that we cannot take without doing wrong, saving faith to our lord the king of England and to the crown'.[46] The purpose of this alliance, therefore, was for the participants to provide each other with mutual aid.[47] Although that aid was to be against 'all people', it is likely that the pact was aimed chiefly at the Lusignans. Of the seven confederates, the earls of Leicester, Norfolk, and Gloucester had all quarrelled with them, as, of course, had John fitz Geoffrey. Hugh Bigod was the earl of Norfolk's brother; Peter de Montfort, though no relation, a close ally of the earl of Leicester.[48] Peter of Savoy doubtless shared the feelings of the archbishop of Canterbury and the queen about the half-brothers.[49] Probably the seven were already agreed on a reform of the realm, which would contain the reduction of the Lusignans as a major ingredient. The alliance was designed to meet the possibility that the brothers would defend themselves by force. Significantly, Matthew Paris records an alliance made precisely for 'safety' against,

continued

18–18v. It is interesting to note that the chronicle known as the Merton *Flores Historiarum* (for which see Gransden, 456–63) says that Simon de Montfort and John fitz Geoffrey were the leaders of the faction opposed to the king in 1258, stimulated by a 'common contention against the elect of Winchester and William de Valence'. It also implies that they resented their recall from respectively the seneschalship of Gascony and the justiciarship of Ireland; *Flores Historiarum*, iii, ed. H.R. Luard, RS 1890, 252.

[45] Paris, v, 689. The point about the writs was a reference to the way the king had obstructed legal actions against the Lusignans; see Treharne, Sanders, 270–3; Paris, v, 594.

[46] Bémont, 327. The translation is from, *English Historical Documents*, iii, ed. H. Rothwell, London 1975, 361.

[47] Powicke thought that the agreement was one 'to give each other aid . . . in the cause of right . . . and well doing'; Powicke, *Henry III*, 377; see *The Thirteenth Century*, 130. However, the 'doing right and taking nothing that we cannot take without doing wrong' were merely conventional phrases, designed to give a gloss of respectability to the nature of the help to be provided. I discuss the phraseology of agreements to provide mutual aid in 1258–9 in the essay which prints the Lord Edward's oath of October 1259 to aid Simon de Montfort above pp. 241–52.

[48] For Peter and Simon, see below pp. 227–9. It is also worth nothing that John fitz Geoffrey was the brother-in-law of Roger and Hugh Bigod.

[49] For the queen's relations with Aymer de Lusignan, see *CR 1259–61*, 265; the Waverley annalist says that she welcomed the changes of 1258 because they rid England of the Lusignans; *Ann. Mon.*, ii, 355; see also Paris, v, 703. It is significant that in 1258 the earl of Gloucester became connected to the house of Savoy through the marriage of his daughter to the marquis of Montferrat; see above p. 189; Cox, 275–6, 462.

by implication, the 'snares' of the Lusignans. Concluding his account of the Westminster parliament, he noted that, 'the nobles of England, for instance the earls of Gloucester, Leicester, Hereford, the earl Marshal [Roger Bigod earl of Norfolk], and other men of distinction, took precautions and provided for their safety by forming a confederation, and as they greatly feared the traps and snares of the aliens and had exceeding respect for the king's nets, they turned up at the Oxford parliament with horses and arms and the protection of an ample escort'.[50] Although Paris erroneously included the earl of Hereford among its members, it may be that he was here referring to the alliance of 12 April. Whether the half-brothers planned armed resistance may be doubted, but it was not difficult to suspect them. They had young and warlike allies in John de Warenne, earl of Surrey, Henry son of Richard of Cornwall, and, above all, the king's eldest son, the Lord Edward.[51] William de Valence's and Edward's preparations against Llywelyn could easily cover mobilization for civil war. On 17 April the king ordered the constable of St Briavels to deliver 2,000 cross-bow bolts to William. Around the same time William himself augmented Edward's means to raise troops by giving him a large sum of money in return for the lease of some manors.[52]

The Westminster parliament, then, opened with John fitz Geoffrey's complaint against Aymer bishop-elect of Winchester, and continued with angry exchanges between William de Valence and the earls of Gloucester and Leicester. On 12 April an alliance was formed, directed chiefly against the Lusignans. Meanwhile Arlot threatened the kingdom with an interdict, and the king, having refused justice to John fitz Geoffrey, begged for money to pursue his Sicilian dreams. The bishops, wanting no part of the extreme measures which they knew were afoot, withdrew from the parliament. The climax on 30 April seems hardly surprising. The occasion for the march on the king's hall was to reply to the request for the Sicilian tax; but the first demand that Roger Bigod put to Henry was: 'Let the wretched and intolerable Poitevins and all aliens flee from your face'.[53]

It is difficult to agree with Powicke, that after the concession of 2 May, the parliament ended with 'the king, his son, and his half-brothers . . . in agreement with the confederated barons', and that it was only at the Oxford parliament that the 'family party . . . broke asunder'.[54] In reality, between the two parliaments the magnates prepared at best for a show of force, at worst for civil war. Both the Burton abbey annalist and Matthew Paris state that the barons came to the Oxford parliament, which opened around 11 June, in arms, their excuse being that they were going on from Oxford to campaign in Wales. The truth, as Paris reported, was that 'they were in no slight fear that, in conse-

[50] Paris, v, 689–90.
[51] Treharne, Sanders, 92–3; Paris, v, 697.
[52] *CR 1256–9*, 210; Paris, v, 679.
[53] *Ann. Mon.*, i, 164.
[54] Powicke, *Henry III*, 378, 381.

quence of the disagreement of parties, civil war would break out between them, and that the king and his Poitevin brothers would call in aliens to aid him against his native born subjects'. The king was indeed bringing foreign knights into England, ostensibly for the campaign against Llywelyn. On 25 May he instructed eleven of them to be paid and sent on to the forthcoming parliament at Oxford.[55] At the parliament, having created Hugh Bigod justiciar, the reformers moved to appoint new castellans to the royal castles, thus depriving the king of the means of resistance.[56] That done, they turned their attention to the Lusignans. A letter which the barons wrote to the pope, explaining their actions, indicated that the offence of the brothers was to resist the programmes of reform at Oxford, and to try to get the king to renege on his oath of 2 May.[57] The brothers' conduct was scarcely unprovoked. Apart from the threat implicit in the justiciarship, another part of the reform programme was aimed directly at them – an act of resumption of 'all lands, tenements and castles alienated by the king from the crown'.[58] This measure could be presented as a public spirited attempt to restore the king's financial position. In reality, it was a partisan attack upon the Lusignans. The half-brothers, of course, were not the only potential victims of an act of resumption, but they knew that it would be enforced against themselves far more rigorously than against anyone else – in fact, once the proposed act had been used to intimidate the brothers it appears to have been quietly abandoned. William de Valence, moreover, was particularly vulnerable to schemes for resumption. Since coming to England in 1247 he had received far more land from the king than anyone else. Indeed, Henry had formally promised to give escheats to no one save his brother, Richard of Cornwall, until William's £500 annual pension was converted into land held in fee. An act of resumption would leave William with his wife's lands in Wales; but he would lose his chief base in England, Hertford castle, the royal demesne manors of Essendon, Bayford and Bampton, and, if the act extended to escheats, at least six other manors. His power in England would have been ended.[59] At the Oxford parliament, therefore, according to Matthew Paris, the brothers swore by the death and wounds of Christ that they would not surrender the castles, lands and wardships given them by the king. Simon de Mont-

[55] *Ann. Mon.*, i, 438; Paris, v, 695–6; *CR 1256–9*, 223–4.
[56] Treharne, Sanders, 90–1, 258–9; Treharne, 74.
[57] *Ann. Mon.*, i, 458.
[58] Treharne, Sanders, 92–3.
[59] *CChR 1226–57*, 339, 351; *CLR 1251–60*, 202, 396; *CR 1253–4*, 214–5. See Powicke, *Henry III*, 383–4. The only description of the proposed act of resumption is in a letter from an eye-witness of the parliament: 'it was provided that all lands, tenements and castles alienated by the king from the crown should be restored to him'; this is the passage quoted in the text above; Treharne, Sanders, 92–3. Paris (see below in text) adds the story of the oath of the half-brothers, and states that Simon de Montfort returned to the king *gratis* the castles of Kenilworth and Odiham (granted to him for life), although he had recently done much to improve them; Paris, v, 697. The lack of information about the act strongly suggests that it was never implemented. There is no evidence that the king ever took possession of Kenilworth and Odiham.

fort's riposte to William de Valence was 'either you give up your castles or you lose your head'. It was in this atmosphere, having refused to agree to the act of resumption, that the brothers fled from Oxford to Winchester; perhaps, as their enemies claimed, to make a stand at the elect's castle and call in foreign mercenaries, perhaps in pure desperation. The barons immediately broke up the Oxford parliament and followed them. They demanded that Guy and Geoffrey de Lusignan leave England *finaliter*, and that William and Aymer remain in custody until the reform of the realm was complete. Alternatively all the brothers were to leave England while reform was in progress. The Lusignans chose to depart together and crossed the channel on 14 July.[60] Fear and suspicion of them were now so great that when, later in the month, the deaths occurred of the abbot of Westminster and William de Clare, and the latter's brother, the earl of Gloucester, fell dangerously ill, it was widely believed that they were victims of a Lusignan poison plot.[61]

There was, of course, much more to the revolution of 1258 than the expulsion of the Lusignans. Whether, however, the movement would have begun without the hatred of the half-brothers, and the particular incidents which fanned this into flames at the Westminster parliament may be questioned. After April 1258 the king's opponents could never escape from the fact that their enterprise had commenced with the coercion of the king and an attack on his closest friends. They were bound to anticipate a royalist attempt to recover power. To prevent this it was imperative to make their movement as popular and as widely supported as possible. This need for support helps to explain perhaps the most striking feature of the reforms of 1258–9—the way they encompassed the courts and officials of the great magnates as well as those of the king.

---

[60] Paris, v, 697–8; Treharne, Sanders, 92–5. Reluctance to stand trial against John fitz Geoffrey and other complainants may have been a factor in the decision to depart; see *Ann. Mon.*, i, 459.

[61] Paris, v, 700, 702–5, 707–9, 747; *Ann. Mon.*, i, 165, 167, 460.

10

King Henry III and the Tower of London

During the course of his reign, King Henry III began the transformation of the Tower of London into the great concentric fortress which it remains today. Since he also embellished its living quarters, historians have naturally assumed that the Tower was a palace as well as a stronghold, a place where Henry frequently went to live and work. Thus the authoritative *History of the King's Works* lists the Tower as one of Henry's 'favourite residential castles', which he visited 'with some regularity'.[1] The purpose of this article is to demonstrate that such a view is false. Indeed, the truth is almost exactly the reverse. Henry virtually abandoned the Tower as a normal royal residence. One thing and one alone drove him there to stay – political crisis. He went to the Tower both to protect himself from his enemies and project power over them. This abandonment of the Tower as a residence reflected both the lengthy peace of Henry's reign and the increasing attractions of Westminster. It was a neglect which was largely continued by Henry's son, Edward I, a point perhaps obscured by the recent restoration of rooms at the Tower as Edward's royal apartments.

Henry III's works at the Tower, on which he spent over £9,000, may be briefly summarised.[2] When he came to the throne at the age of nine in 1216 the structure consisted merely of the Norman keep (the White Tower) and a surrounding wall. The latter ran uncomfortably close to the keep on its northern and southern sides and probably lacked towers along its length. A moat dug in the 1190s had proved a costly fiasco when it failed to flood. Building under Henry III was in two main phases. The first, in the 1220s, when the king was still a minor, saw the construction of a new water gate on the southern river wall, and alongside it a great round tower, now called the Wakefield Tower. The second phase, which began in 1238, a date whose significance will emerge later, witnessed the construction of a new curtain wall with eight towers, a large western gateway, and a moat this time with water. In circumference the new walls were considerably longer than those they replaced and thus a more extensive area

[1] R.A. Brown, H.M. Colvin and A.J. Taylor, *The History of the King's Works. The Middle Ages* [henceforth *HKW*], 2 vols (1963), i, 113–4; ii, 710. I am grateful to Dr Simon Thurley for letting me see in advance his paper 'Royal Lodgings at the Tower of London 1216–1327', *Architectural History*, 38 (1995), 36–57, which, although chiefly concerned with the architecture, comes to the same conclusions as myself about the political purposes of the Tower in the thirteenth century.

[2] *HKW*, ii, 710–5.

was enclosed within the bailey. From the military point of view the Tower had been thoroughly brought up to date.

Some of the reasons for these works were traditional. The Tower had always been intended less to protect London than to control it. Henry's own relations with the city were frequently tense. It had been the chief base for the rebels in the 1215–1217 civil war and its government was taken into the king's hands at least ten times between 1239 and 1257.[3] A powerful castle which could over-awe the city was vital. Not surprisingly the Londoners regarded the new wall begun in 1238 with hostility and alarm. When there was a fall of masonry in 1241 a priest told of a vision in which he had seen a scowling bishop come to the new walls and strike them with his episcopal staff, whereupon they collapsed. The bishop then revealed himself as Thomas Becket 'a Londoner by birth who considers these walls built not for the defence of the kingdom but only to oppress harmless citizens'[4] The Tower also served as a treasury, an arsenal and a prison. It was here that Hubert de Burgh was incarcerated in 1232, having been dragged from the chapel in Brentwood in which he had taken sanctuary. Here the Welsh prince, Griffin, was imprisoned between 1241–1244 before falling to his death in an attempt to escape, an incident vividly depicted by Matthew Paris.[5]

The grounds on which the Tower has been claimed as a major royal residence in Henry's reign are at first sight compelling. The king was certainly concerned to make it a more congenial and convenient place in which to live. In 1238 he ordered the construction of a screen between the chamber and chapel of 'the new tower' (probably the Wakefield tower) and the whitewashing of the walls of the queen's chamber and their adornment with points and flowers.[6] Two years later he had the queen's chamber wainscotted and painted with roses and the shutters of his own great chamber painted with the royal arms. He also ordered images and stained glass windows for the Chapel of St John the Evangelist in the White Tower and the placing of two large and handsome stalls for himself and the queen in the church of St Peter ad Vincula within the bailey.[7]

However suggestive of the royal presence, this evidence has to be set against the ascertainable facts of Henry III's itinerary. Apart from occasional information from chroniclers and the few surviving oblation and household rolls, this has to be reconstructed from the place and dating clauses of royal letters and charters which passed under the great seal and were recorded on the chan-

---

[3] G.A. Williams, *Medieval London. From Commune to Capital* (1963), p. 208. Henry's relations with London are best followed in the chronicle of the alderman Arnold fitz Thedmar: *De Antiquis Legibus Liber. Cronica Maiorum et Vicecomitum Londoniarum*, T. Stapleton, ed., (Camden Soc., 1846), 4–155.

[4] *Matthaei Parisiensis Chronica Majora*, H.R. Luard, ed., 7 vols. (Rolls ser., 1884–9), iv, 93–4,

[5] *Chronica Majora*, iii, 227, 230; iv, 295–6.

[6] *Cal. Liberate Rolls 1226–40*, pp. 315–16, 352 In general see *HKW*, ii, 713–14.

[7] *Cal. Liberate Rolls 1226–40*, pp. 444, 452–3.

cery rolls.[8] In the reign of Richard I these letters and charters were clearly dated for the first time; under John, for the first time, they were recorded centrally on the chancery rolls.[9] Since these rolls survive it is possible to construct the itineraries of thirteenth-century kings with a fair degree of confidence. This statement depends, of course, on the assumption that the typical dating clause of a royal letter, for example *Teste me ipso apud Wodestok xxiii Julii anno regni nostri xxxiii* ('witnessed by myself at Woodstock on 23 July in the thirty-third year of our reign') really does indicate that Henry III was present at Woodstock on 23 July 1249. This was certainly the theory: in 1272 Henry declared that if letters patent 'bore a place and date which did not agree with his itinerary they were undoubtedly forged'.[10] It was also, almost certainly, the general practice. True, in the fourteenth century, when the king was frequently separated from the great seal and the chancery, the *teste me ipso* clause on chancery letters became a mere formality in no way indicative of the royal presence.[11] But in Henry's reign no such separation had taken place and the chancery was usually with the king. Hence Henry made little use of a privy seal, the seal used by later monarchs when they were separated from the chancery;[12] hence too the royal itinerary from the chancery rolls marches closely with that revealed by the occasional oblation and household rolls. A complete run of the two last might well have added the odd day here and there to Henry's known stays at the Tower, but it is highly unlikely to have altered the basic picture revealed by the surviving chancery sources.[13]

That basic picture is striking. In the forty-five years between his full assumption of power in 1227 and his death in November 1272 Henry took up residence at the Tower on only eleven occasions, of which seven were in 1261. All but one of these visits, moreover, can be directly linked to the exigencies of the political situation. Henry went to the Tower to protect himself from and take action against discontented or rebellious magnates. The total time embraced by the eleven visits was some thirty-two weeks, largely because Henry's stays at the Tower in 1261, 1263 and 1272 were lengthy. If these years are excluded, Henry was at the fortress only twice in forty-two years for a total period of about a week. Between April 1238 and January 1261 he never took up residence at

---

[8] T. Craib, 'The Itinerary of Henry III' (1923), in typescript in the Round Room of the Public Record Office [henceforth PRO], Chancery Lane, reconstructs the itinerary essentially from the chancery rolls. A slightly revised version for the years 1234–42 is to be found in *Curia Regis Rolls*, xv, pp. lviii–lxi; xvi, pp. xliv–xlviii. Unless indicated, all statements about Henry III's itinerary come from these sources and from my own inspection of the chancery rolls. For other sources for the royal itinerary, see Appendix 1 and note 50 below.

[9] For the chancery see Sir H.C. Maxwell-Lyte, *Historical Notes on the Use of the Great Seal of England* (1926) and P. Chaplais, *English Royal Documents King John-Henry VI 1199–1461* (Oxford, 1971).

[10] Chaplais, *English Royal Documents*, p. 18.

[11] For this separation, see T.F. Tout,. *Chapters in Mediaeval Administrative History*, 6 vols. (Manchester, 1920–33), ii, 73–7; B. Wilkinson, *The Chancery under Edward III* (Manchester, 1929), pp. 9–11; Chaplais, *English Royal Documents*, pp. 18–19.

[12] For Henry's privy seal see Tout, *Chapters*, i, 206–13, 284–317 and especially p. 289.

[13] See Appendix 1.

all. All this is in clear contrast to Henry's sojourns at places which really were favourite residences. Winchester, Clarendon, Marlborough and Woodstock usually saw Henry at least once annually. Westminster and Windsor were always visited several times a year, in most years Henry's stays at Westminster totalled months. In 1241, for example, despite an expedition to Wales, Henry was 115 days at Westminster (five visits); forty-nine days at Windsor (seven visits); thirty-one days at Marlborough (four visits); nineteen days at Woodstock (two visits); and fourteen and four days respectively at Clarendon and Winchester (each one visit). In 1252 Henry was eighty-six days at Westminster (six visits); forty-three days at Windsor (six visits); forty days at Clarendon (three visits); twenty-one days at Marlborough (three visits); and twenty-six and nineteen days at Woodstock and Winchester respectively (both two visits).

The political purpose of Henry's residences at the Tower, tabulated below, may now be examined.

Jan. 1227 to Nov. 1272 Henry's Known Residences at the Tower

1236	a brief stay in late April
1238	23 February–2 March
1262	9 February–22 April; 14 May; 22 June–30 July; 5, 20, 23–5 August; 14 October–9 December.
1263	19 June–16 July
1272	13 January–7 February

In January 1236 Henry married Eleanor of Provence and quickly fell under the spell of her uncle, William bishop elect of Valence. At a parliament, which met at Westminster on 28 April, there was strident criticism of William's dominant role. Matthew Paris here takes up the story.[14]

> The king, however, on the first day of the council, taking up residence at the Tower of London, gave material for complaint to many about this . . . The magnates did not wish, either singly or in a body, to enter the Tower to see the king, fearing lest, influenced by irresponsible council, he might vent his rage on them . . . However, the king, restrained by the bridle of prudence, came from the Tower to his palace there to discuss current affairs more suitably with his [nobles].

This visit to the Tower has left no traces in the dating clauses of royal letters and thus was very brief, probably no more than a day. Clearly it was entirely determined by the political situation. By holding a great council at the Tower, Henry hoped to intimidate his recalcitrant magnates. The contrast which Matthew Paris draws between the Tower of London and the palace at Westminster is significant. The nobles did not consider the former a fitting place to hold a great council.

Two years later, in January 1238, another marriage took place. This was be-

---

[14] *Chronica Majora*, iii, 362–3.

tween the king's sister, Eleanor, and Simon de Montfort. Before a match of such consequence the great and wise of the land would normally have been consulted. Instead, anticipating opposition, Henry rushed through the wedding in secret in his own private chapel in Westminster palace. Even his brother, Richard earl of Cornwall, was kept in ignorance. Naturally there was an outcry. At a meeting with the king at Stratford-at-Bow on 23 February the magnates appeared in arms. Henry's reaction was immediate. He fled to the Tower. Dating clauses of royal letters show that he remained there from 23 February until 2 March when the crisis was ended by the buying off of Earl Richard.[15]

Henry's week at the Tower in 1238 was his first known stay there, apart from the brief visit in 1236, since he had entered full power in January 1227–since in fact the three days which he had spent there in March 1226. This is the best measure of how serious the crisis of 1238 was. The visit had important repercussions on the structure of the fortress. As he peered from the White Tower over an ancient largely unturreted curtain wall and over a moat which was dry, Henry must have been acutely aware that the defences were dangerously out of date. Hence this year saw the beginning of his most ambitious work, the construction of a new curtain wall with eight towers. Between 1238 and 1241 building operations were prosecuted with such vigour that over £5,000 were spent.[16] As has been seen, the Londoners resented the new walls and felt, rightly, that they were designed to control them; but the immediate reason for building was to make the Tower a place of safe retreat against baronial rebellion. In 1238, Henry had also experienced trouble with his personal quarters, hardly surprising since he had scarcely ever used them. Thus it was just after his departure from the Tower on 2 March that the screen to separate the chapel (probably in a window bay) from the chamber in the Wakefield Tower was ordered. Henry also instructed the chimney in the queen's chamber to be completed.[17]

After Henry III left the Tower on 2 March 1238 there is no evidence that he returned there to live for another twenty-one years. He did not do so even to supervise the hectic building of the years 1238 to 1241, thus behaving quite differently from his son, Edward I, who lived at the Tower for short periods in the 1270s in order to oversee his new works. But then Henry, in contrast to Edward, had little interest in the business of war. The Tower certainly had its attractions for Henry. As well as treasure and prisoners, it housed the fascinating animals of the royal menagerie: the three leopards sent by the Emperor Frederick II, a polar bear which went fishing in the Thames, and, the brief show piece of the collection before its untimely death, an elephant given by Louis IX of France.[18] Presumably, therefore, Henry did visit the Tower in these

[15] *Chronica Majora*, iii, 471, 475–9; *Patent Rolls 1232–47*, pp. 208–9. The political circumstances of Montfort's wedding have recently been clarified in J.R. Maddicott, *Simon de Montfort* (Cambridge, 1994), pp. 21–9.

[16] *HKW*, ii, 713.

[17] *Cal. Liberate Rolls 1226–40*, pp. 315–16.

[18] For other orders for building (notably for a privy chamber for the queen) see *Close Rolls*

years; the orders for the embellishment of the chapels and queen's chamber, issued at Westminster in 1240, were perhaps the result of one such tour of inspection.[19] But any idea that Henry was drawn by the improvements and the animals to take up residence for significant periods of time seems incompatible, as we have seen, with the surviving evidence.

King Henry's long absence from the Tower tells something about the level of political tension in the years of his personal rule. Between 1238 and 1258 there were numerous confrontations between king and magnates in parliaments at Westminster. Henry besought taxation. The magnates refused it and demanded the appointment, by common consent, of a justiciar, chancellor and treasurer. Yet criticism of the king remained within bounds. During these acrimonious parliaments, which frequently lasted for several weeks, Henry was content to live alongside his baronage in a palace unprotected by walls and moats. At no time did he retreat to the Tower as he had done in 1238. At no time did he seize the initiative, as in 1236, and try to hold a parliament there. When Sir Maurice Powicke wrote that the quarrels between the king and the baronage in this period were 'domestic, inside the great house of the king', he was correct in the literal, physical sense.[20] As a result, Henry gradually lost interest in the works at the Tower and the momentum of the years 1238 to 1241 slackened. The king's chamber in the Wakefield tower never received the stone vault once intended; in 1249 the queen's chamber was on the verge of collapse; and in 1253 there was still a gap in the new walls which had to be filled with palings.[21]

It was not till 1258 that the words of Henry's critics at last turned to deeds. A parliament met at Westminster on 9 April. On 2 May, after weeks of heated debate, Henry agreed to the appointment of twenty-four reformers who were to reorganize the government of the realm. The results were the Provisions of Oxford, which effectively took control of the realm from Henry's hands. That Henry did not move from Westminster to the Tower during April 1258 is strong proof that he offered no physical resistance to his opponents. In the event the failure to move proved fatal since it was precisely the openness and accessibility of Westminster which placed Henry at the barons' mercy. According to the Tewkesbury annalist, on 30 April, a large body of nobles, led by Roger Bigod earl of Norfolk, marched in arms to the king's hall at Westminster. Although they left their swords at the door, the king appreciated at once the novelty and menace of this demonstration. 'At once confused in mind and uncertain why

continued

1242–7, p. 534; *Cal. Liberate Rolls 1245–51* pp. 140, 154, 176, 218; *Close Rolls 1247–51*, pp. 300, 454. See *HKW*, ii, 714.

   [19] A.C.N. Borg, 'The Royal Menagerie' in *The Tower of London: its Building and Institutions*, ed. J. Charlton (1978), pp. 100–1.

   [20] F.M. Powicke, *King Henry III and The Lord Edward* (Oxford, 1947), p. 342.

   [21] P.E. Curnow, 'The Wakefield Tower, Tower of London' in *Ancient Monuments and their Interpretation. Essays Presented to A.J. Taylor*, ed. M.R. Apted, R. Gilyard-Beer and A.D. Saunders (1977), pp. 155–76 and esp. p. 171; *Cal. Liberate Rolls 1245–51*, p. 218; *HKW*, ii, 713.

they had come armed, he cried: "What is this my lords? Am I, poor wretch, your prisoner?"'.[22] Had the king been under the protection of the Tower, he could not have been pressurised in this way. Perhaps the peaceful complaints of the previous years had rendered Henry complacent. In 1258 the sudden show of force took him by surprise and brought his regime tumbling to the ground.

It was not till 1261 that Henry moved openly to free himself from the restrictions imposed in 1258.[23] He knew he would meet fierce and probably armed opposition. The Tower, therefore, became his headquarters. During 1261 he made three long stays there – from 9 February to 22 April; from 22 June to 30 July; and from 14 October to 9 December. Major building operations recommenced and over £1,000 were spent.[24] It was from the Tower in March that Henry began to retain a retinue of knights by the promise of annual fees; it was from there in July that he dismissed the baronial sheriffs and justiciar. And he hurried back there in October when the barons set up rival sheriffs in the counties and brought the country to the verge of civil war. Not till 7 December was Henry able to proclaim that all quarrels were settled.[25] He left the Tower two days later.

Henry III's bid for freedom in 1261 was carefully modulated. Not till his publication of papal letters in June 1261, did he formally and finally reject the Provisions of Oxford. But the extraordinary spectacle of Henry residing at the Tower warned the opposition from the first what was afoot. In February 1261 the barons repeated their refusal of 1236 and declined to go there for parliament. In the words of the Dunstable annalist, 'if it pleased the king they would come to Westminster where parliaments were accustomed to be held and not elsewhere'.[26]

Henry III's ultimate triumph in 1261 owed much to his great headquarters. The Tower had finally come into its own and justified his expenditure. More than at any other time in his reign, indeed more than at any other time in its history, the Tower had been a decisive factor in national politics. From its security, Henry had projected power and secured control of the whole country. For most of its history the Tower was like a fleet kept in being; its passive presence important for controlling London. In 1261 it at last came out of harbour and gave battle. Henry was not, however, reconciled to the Tower as a place to live, as his rapid departure after 7 December shows. Indeed, the martial activity only increased the domestic discomfort. Thus, whenever possible, during the course of 1261, Henry forsook the fortress for the bishop of London's pal-

---

[22] *Annales Monastici*, ed. H.R. Luard, 5 vols., (Rolls ser., 1864–9), i, 163–5. See D.A. Carpenter, 'What happened in 1258?', above pp. 187–8.

[23] The most detailed study of the politics of these years is in R.F. Treharne, *The Baronial Plan of Reform 1258–1263* (Manchester, 1932), but much new light is thrown on the whole period in Maddicott, *Simon de Montfort*.

[24] *HKW*, ii, 713.

[25] *Cal. Patent Rolls 1258–66*, pp. 194–5.

[26] *Annales Monastici*, iii, 217.

ace by St Paul's, which was still protected by London's walls. The palace at Westminster, by contrast, with no protection at all, was almost out of bounds. Between 11 January and 9 December 1261 Henry is known to have been there on only two days, of which one, significantly, was 13 October, the feast day of his patron saint, Edward the Confessor.

Henry III's recovery of power in 1261 lasted less than two years. At the end of April 1263 Simon de Montfort returned to England and placed himself at the head of a new party of rebels. They plundered the lands of the king's supporters and demanded the restoration of the Provisions of Oxford. Henry was taken by surprise and slow to react. He moved first from Westminster to the bishop's palace at St Paul's and, on 19 June, from there to the Tower. The situation was totally different from that in 1261. Then the king had been rich and the Tower well supplied. Now he was penniless and the Tower unstocked. Soon Henry's friends and family realised that the game was up. Having fled to the Tower, they now fled from it. The Lord Edward broke open the treasure chests at the Temple and departed for Windsor. John Mansel, Henry's chief councillor, sailed down the Thames and on to France. Finally, on 13 July, as Montfort approached London, the Queen herself took a barge upstream, hoping to join Edward at Windsor. At London bridge the angry populace pelted her with missiles and she was forced to return – an outrage for which Edward took sanguinary retribution from the Londoners at the battle of Lewes.[27] When Simon de Montfort at last arrived Henry had no alternative but surrender. On 16 July, a virtual prisoner, he left the Tower for Westminster.[28] To blame the Tower for this debacle would be unfair. No castle, however mighty, could be defended without funds and garrison.

The terrible weeks of June and July 1263 were almost the last occasions when Henry stayed at the Tower. He returned there only once for three weeks in January and February 1272, the year of his death. This is the only period of residence after 1226 which appears unconnected with the political situation. It is hard to explain. Perhaps there were problems with the royal quarters at Westminster. Perhaps (and this is the explanation which I favour) Henry was taken ill at or near the Tower and detained there till he recovered.[29]

Henry III, then, shunned the Tower as a place to live. This does not make

---

[27] *Annales Monastici*, iii, 223.

[28] The date is given in *De Antiquis Legibus Liber*, p. 55. There appears to be no evidence as to exactly where Henry lived in the Tower either in 1261 or 1263 although fitz Thedmar's chronicle gives a graphic picture of a meeting in 1261 in the king's chamber between Henry, his councillors and the mayor and citizens of London (*De Antiquis Legibus Liber*, p. 47). The fact that what appears to be the upper chamber of the Wakefield tower was called the king's chamber between 1279–81 (*HKW*, ii, 719) may reflect its use by Henry. On the other hand, during the crisis of 1263 it is possible he retreated to safer quarters in the White Tower.

[29] Henry's itinerary shows that he was returning from Winchester. The fact that he had spent the feast of Edward the Confessor there on 5 January, rather than at Westminster as normal, suggests that an earlier return had been prevented by ill health. Henry probably came into London over London Bridge.

his concern with its decoration inexplicable. The majority of orders of this type belong to the years 1238–40, and were inspired by Henry's enforced and unpleasant residence at the fortress in February and March 1238. The king could not know when further disturbances might force him back to the great castle. The king's absence, moreover, did not mean the Tower was unoccupied. It contained prisoners, arms and treasure. The rebuilding of the great hall (which took place in the 1230s) and the new images and windows for the chapels were as much for the benefit of the constable and garrison as the king. It was probably in the great hall that the justices in eyre for London held their sessions. If it is asked why these improvements did not tempt Henry back to the Tower, the answer lies in his growing attachment to the palace and abbey at Westminster to which we will return.

The Tower then was an abnormal residence during Henry's majority. Was the situation different in his minority and the reigns of his predecessors? Unfortunately, itineraries of twelfth century kings are sketchily known since royal letters were neither dated nor recorded. However, William fitz Stephen (writing in the reign of Henry II) described the Tower as *arx palatina*, which perhaps implies that it was a frequently used royal residence.[30] It certainly served that function under John and in Henry III's minority, in marked contrast with the situation which obtained after 1227. In the thirteen years between his departure from Normandy in December 1203, just prior to its loss, and his death in October 1216 (years largely spent in England) John made no less than twenty-eight visits to the Tower – as against Henry's eleven visits in forty-five years.[31] John's periods of residence were characteristically brief, some two or three days being normal. Unlike those of his son they do not seem related to the political situation. The total time of John's residence was just over ten weeks as against Henry's four weeks if the crises of 1261 and 1263 are omitted. During the minority of Henry III the fortress was in even greater use. Between the declaration of peace in September 1217 and the king's partial assumption of power in December 1223 the regency government made over forty visits to the Tower and stayed there for about twenty weeks. This extraordinarily high number of visits as compared even with John's reign was largely achieved by frequent movements backwards and forwards between the Tower and Westminster, with a few days being spent at either place. The extent to which Henry himself was with the government in this period is impossible to say. After December 1223, however, Henry himself attested nearly all royal letters and so his itinerary is known. Significantly, a decline in the use of the Tower is at once apparent. Between January 1224 and his assumption of full power in January 1227 he only took up residence twice, for a total of three days, in March 1226.

It would seem, therefore, that the rule of Henry III ushered in a sharp and

---

[30] *Materials for the History of Thomas Becket*, J.C. Robertson and J.B. Sheppard, eds., 7 vols. (Rolls ser., 1875–85), iii, 3.

[31] For John's itinerary, see *Rotuli Litterarum Patentium in Turri Londinensi asservati*, ed. T. Duffus Hardy (Record Commission, 1835) introduction.

decisive change in the role of the Tower, one which must have owed everything to his own personal wishes. The truth, in all probability, was that Henry deserted the Tower because he found Westminster a far more comfortable and congenial place to live, work, and worship; a feeling reinforced by various developments which took place there in the course of his reign.

Henry III gave much thought to the improvement and embellishment of his major palaces. He issued streams of orders for the wainscotting of walls, the tiling of floors and the glazing and enlargement of windows. Throughout his chambers and chapels there were new paintings and sculptures.[32] The Tower in this period must always have been a less pleasant place to live than Westminster. Fitz Stephen might describe the castle as the *arx palatina*, but Westminster was the *palatium regium*, the *aedificium incomparabile*.[33] William Rufus's vast hall had long secured Westminster pre-eminence. Until the new walls were begun in 1238, the bailey of the Tower must have been somewhat cramped. Its proximity to London made its immediate surroundings noisy, dirty and dangerous. At Westminster, on the other hand, the neighbours were the obsequious monks with their capacious monastic buildings, great church and royal saint. During Henry III's reign, these advantages were multiplied by the rebuilding of both the palace and the abbey. Between 1237 and 1239 a spacious chamber and chapel were built for Queen Eleanor. Likewise in the 1230s the king's great chamber, 80 feet long, 26 feet wide and 31 feet high, was transformed by the insertion of new doors and seven two-light lancet windows. Ultimately, in the splays of the windows Henry had painted large figures representing the virtues and the vices while behind his bed he commissioned a magnificent painting of the Coronation of Edward the Confessor.[34] It was devotion to the Confessor which tied Henry above all to Westminster and in fostering that devotion the 1230s were the decisive decade. Before 1238 Henry never managed to spend both the Confessor's feast days – 13 October and 5 January – at Westminster. From 1238 onwards he was always there, unless prevented by dire necessity, in which case elaborate services were carried out by proxies. Even in 1261, as we have seen, he braved the disorders to attend on 13 October. In 1245 Henry began his rebuilding of Westminster abbey in honour of the Confessor and thereafter nothing was closer to his heart. By the end of the reign he had spent over £40,000 and had created a church unequalled in Christendom.[35] With the triple magnets at Westminster of palace, abbey and saint it is hardly surprising that the Tower could not keep up.

The considerations which drew Henry to Westminster weighed little with his father, John. John was interested in Edward the Confessor but on nowhere near

[32] *HKW*, i, ch. iv. For what follows, see G. Rosser, *Medieval Westminster 1200–1540* (Oxford, 1989), Ch. I.

[33] *Materials for Becket*, iii, 3; *HKW*, i, 44–7, 491.

[34] P. Binski, *The Painted Chamber at Westminster* (London, 1986), pp. 33–45; *HKW*, ii, 494–504.

[35] *HKW*, i, 155–7; *Annales Monastici*, iv, 252.

the same scale as his son.[36] Nor, judging from the silence of his chancery rolls, so eloquent under Henry, did he give much attention to the improvement and decoration of his palaces. Here the difference with his son was related to a fundamental contrast in their pattern of movement. John tarried nowhere long. Only once did he remain in the same place for more than a month and that was at the siege of Rochester castle in 1215. 'Even a stay of a week's duration was uncommon. Usually after two or three nights, or frequently only one, he was off again'.[37] Henry, on the other hand, loitered at his favourite palaces for weeks and months. Nor surprisingly he was much more concerned than John to rebuild and adorn them. The disadvantages of the Tower meant little to the itinerant John; they were of consequence to the sedentary Henry. This contrast between the two kings was linked to very different approaches to the business of government. John was a 'hands on' king. Like the ministers in the minority he went to the Tower, one may suspect, to count the treasure, inspect the arsenal and impress by his immediate presence the citizens of London. Henry was not to be drawn there, or drawn for long, by such mundane considerations. The two kings also operated in very different political circumstances. If John was restless, he had much to be restless about. The Angevin empire imposed a life of ceaseless movement on its rulers and John never lost the habit. Henry, by contrast, could live largely in England and at his own pace. A magnificent court was a practicality for him in a way it was not for his predecessors. Under Henry II courtiers had 'sharp and bitter argument about a mere hut, and swords were drawn for the possession of lodgings which pigs would have shunned'.[38] Under Henry III a special two story chamber 'long and of good size' was built at Westminster to accommodate the knights of the royal household.[39] Henry II cared little for his personal appearance or the trappings of monarchy. Henry III had a porch constructed at Westminster palace so that he could descend from his horse 'with befitting dignity' (*ad honestam frontem*).[40]

Henry III, therefore, broke with the past in his use of the Tower. He also set a pattern for the immediate future. Although his son Edward I (1272–1307) carried out extensive work on the Tower, he hardly lived there once that work was securely under way.[41] During the thirteenth century, therefore, kings of England made the Tower of London a formidable stronghold yet abandoned it as a normal royal residence. They now lived almost exclusively at Westminster, where Henry rebuilt the abbey and commenced the transformation of the palace, a transformation completed by Edward I.[42] There was no conflict between work at Westminster and the Tower. The castle was a necessary adjunct

---

[36] For John's interest in English saints, see E. Mason, 'St Wulfstan's staff: a legend and its uses', *Medium Aevum*, liii (1984), 158–79.

[37] J.C. Holt, *King John* (London, 1961), pp. 135–6, 138.

[38] W.L. Warren, *Henry II* (London, 1973), p. 210.

[39] *Close Rolls 1242–7*, pp. 160, 167 (*HKW*, i, 504).

[40] Warren, *Henry II*, pp. 77–8, 80, 207, 245; *Close Rolls 1242–7*, p. 273 (*HKW*, i, 504).

[41] See Appendix 2.

[42] Binski, *The Painted Chamber*, ch. iii; *HKW*, i, 504–13.

of the palace, just as the majesty of kingship needed also might. At Westminster kings lived in splendour and were buried by their sainted predecessor. There they held parliaments and dispensed justice. The Tower stood for kingship's darker side, its need both for security and for coercive power. Westminster was insecure as the events of 1258 showed all too plainly. In the crisis of 1260, as the St Albans chronicler noted, Henry would not return 'to the palace of Westminster until he knew accurately the outcome of the discord'. In 1239 Simon de Montfort attended the festivities following the birth of King Henry's heir at Westminster. A few days later, when he fell from favour, Henry ordered him to the Tower.[43] In Henry's reign men did not like the Tower. The magnates would not go there for parliaments. The Londoners thought the new walls were designed to oppress them. Once the great fortress was deprived of its residential functions, its minatory role stood out all the more starkly. True, the deprivation was not to prove permanent. Both Edward II in the 1320s and later Edward III seem to have used the Tower as a normal residence.[44] Perhaps Westminster's very success as a seat of government ultimately rendered it uncongenial as a home. But for the Tower it was too late. Its grim reputation was not the product of the Tudor age. It had been set in the reign of the most pious and pacific of medieval kings, King Henry III.

[43] *Flores Historiarum*, ed. H.R. Luard, 3 vols. (Rolls ser., 1890), ii, 447–8. (Henry was at this time staying at the bishop of London's house at St Paul's); C. Bémont, *Simon de Montfort*, (Paris, 1884), p. 334.

[44] Between 1307 and 1320 Edward II took up residence at the Tower five times for a total of some seven days, a pattern of absenteeism similar to that under his father. Between 1321 and October 1326 he made fifteen visits and stayed for about twelve weeks: E.M. Hallam, *The Itinerary of Edward II*, (List and Index Soc., 211, 1984). (Hallam's work is a model of how an itinerary ought to be constructed). Although there was a great deal of tension in the years before Edward's deposition in 1327, many of his visits cannot be related to any immediate political crisis. Thurley, 'Royal Lodgings at the Tower of London 1216–1327' has a useful discussion of Edward II's relations with the Tower. For Edward III's apartments see *HKW*, i, 726; R.A. Brown, 'Architectural History and Development', in *The Tower of London*, ed. Charlton, p. 34.

Appendix 1

Henry III's Itinerary

There is only one piece of evidence which might seem to contradict the view that Henry III, in normal circumstances, rarely lived at the Tower. It comes from a roll recording the king's oblations between 28 October 1238 and the end of April 1239. Since the oblations in question included those given personally by the king at his daily mass or masses and since the roll gives each day a separate heading with place and date, the evidence provided about the king's itinerary is incontrovertible.[45] Headings in the roll show that between 3 and 29 January 1239 the king was at Westminster. Then, on Sunday 30 January, a heading states that he was at London. The following headings continue with him, 'in the same place' (*ibidem*) until Friday 4 February when he left for Sutton. During all this period, however, the *teste me ipso* clauses of the chancery letters have the king still at Westminster. A similar problem arises on 5 April when the oblation roll shows Henry travelling from Windsor 'to London' and staying 'in the same place' until 20 April when he left for Merton. During this time the *teste me ipso* dating clauses again have Henry at Westminster.

Might it not be argued, therefore, that both in January-February and April 1239 the king had left the chancery at Westminster and gone to live in London at the Tower? Might he not have done the same on many occasions when the chancery dating clauses appear to show long sojourns at Westminster? There are good grounds for rejecting these suggestions. The clerk, writing the oblation roll, could have been using 'London' either exactly or loosely. If exactly, he cannot have meant that Henry was at the Tower since he would have indicated that by saying so specifically, just as do the final clauses of royal letters: 'witness myself at the Tower of London'. If loosely (as I think was in fact the case), then it seems likely that Henry was still at Westminster. It was common in the thirteenth century to use 'Westminster' and 'London' almost interchangeably. It was equally common to speak of coming 'to London' when in fact one was coming to Westminster. In 1233, for example, Henry, in a royal letter, said he wanted new images to be ready in his chapels at Westminster 'on his first coming to London'.[46] It is precisely in this sense that the oblation roll is using

---

[45] PRO C 47/3/44. This roll was first brought to my attention by Robert Stacey. See R.C. Stacey, *Politics, Policy and Finance under Henry III 1216–1245* (Oxford, 1987), p. 124 n. 168.

[46] *Willelmi Rishanger Chronica et Annales*, H.T. Riley ed., (Rolls ser., 1865), p. 397; see also *Chronica Majora*, iii, 362–3; *Close Rolls 1231–4*, p. 207 and see pp. 9–10.

'London' on 5 April. As for the sudden appearance of 'London' in the heading of 30 January, probably the clerk was simply re-iterating the place where the king was (London, that is Westminster) as he occasionally did at the start of a week instead of simply continuing with the usual 'in the same place'.[47] There is proof, independent of the *teste me ipso* clauses of royal letters, that Henry was at Westminster at times between both 30 January–4 February and 5–20 April.[48] Indeed, the oblation roll itself mentions Henry's gift on 3 February to a monk of Westminster who was a recluse. This makes it all the more likely that the *teste me ipso* clauses of royal letters in this period genuinely reflect the king's presence. If they do, and yet the oblation roll still meant precisely what it said in stating that Henry was in London, then he must have been commuting from the city into Westminster nearly every day to work. It is difficult to see why he should have put himself to that inconvenience. Edward I, after all, frequently took the chancery with him on short visits to the Tower. There are only a few isolated days when he may have left it behind at Westminster.[49] It seems equally unlikely that there were more than isolated days when this happened under Henry.

In all the other cases where Henry's chancery itinerary can be checked against his oblation and household rolls, the chancery appears with the king.[50] The

---

[47] It should also be noted that the king's move from one place to another was specifically recorded in the oblation roll, it being the practice to give alms during such journeys: for example 'in journeying to Kenilworth 4s 2d in alms'. There is no indication of a journey from Westminster to the Tower.

[48] PRO C 53/32, m.6 (where a royal charter, dated 2 February, is given by the king's hand and witnessed at Westminster). On 11 April 'in the presence of the king at Westminster', a large gathering of nobles witnessed Amaury de Montfort's renunciation of the earldom of Leicester: *Cal. Charter Rolls 1226–57*, p. 243.

[49] See Appendix 2.

[50] There is only one other oblation roll, that for a period in 1264–5: PRO E 101/350/3. The household rolls in question are those recording expenditure on the household's daily food and drink. Other sources for the king's movements are the rolls (later books) which recorded daily payments by the wardrobe but these hardly survive for Henry III. It should be stressed that the sources from which royal itineraries are constructed are neither equal nor static in their value. The personal oblation rolls almost certainly indicate the actual presence of the king. Unfortunately, as just noted, only two survive for Henry III and their survival under Edward I is very patchy. (Later in the reign they may also have been reduced to more summary form.) Under Henry the chancery *teste me ipso* clauses were supposed to indicate the royal presence and may indeed have done so. Later, this gradually ceased to be the case and the dating clauses of privy seal letters give a more accurate picture of the itinerary. The king could become separated from the food and drink departments of his household, most notably when he was being entertained by someone else, although the rolls indicate when this happened (for example *Records of the Wardrobe and Household 1285–6*, B.F. and C.R. Byerly, eds., (1977), nos. 1373–1376). When the king was on the move the wardrobe spending department could lag a day or so behind him (for examples in 1278 see C 47/4/1, ff. 26v. 28). Under Edward II, there are occasional examples of longer separations between the king and parts of his wardrobe. See Hallam, *Itinerary of Edward II*, pp. 4–15 for a valuable discussion of these questions. For the household and wardrobe rolls in the thirteenth century, see *Lists of Documents relating to the Household and Wardrobe. John to Edward I* (PRO Handbooks No. 7 , 1964).

only clear qualification is that, when the king was on the move, the chancery occasionally lagged a day or so behind the household. In the process it might, for example, omit Henry's customary stay at Kempton on the journey between Westminster and Windsor. This is best studied in R.F. Treharne, *The Baronial Plan of Reform 1258–1263* (Manchester, 1932), pp. 384–6 where the itineraries from the chancery and household rolls for the year 1259–60 are set out side by side. This is the only year for which a complete household roll survives. Although it shows the household at Westminster and (between 1 and 15 May) at the bishop of London's house at St Paul's, it makes no mention of the Tower.

On the whole, therefore, there seems little substance in the view that Henry, for significant periods of time, established himself at the Tower while leaving the chancery at Westminster.

Appendix 2

Edward I and the Tower of London

In 1993, through a praiseworthy initiative, the Historic Royal Palaces Agency opened to the public the hall and great chamber built by Edward I in St Thomas's Tower at the Tower of London, the rooms, that is, above what is now called Traitor's gate. The great chamber was left unrestored but a model showing Edward standing by his bed there, talking to two councillors or servants, indicated its function. The hall and the adjoining upper chamber of the Wakefield Tower, meanwhile, were lavishly decorated to show their appearance as Edward's royal apartments, the Wakefield chamber becoming Edward's throne room complete with a chair of state based on the Coronation chair. It is natural to wonder, therefore, how frequently Edward actually used these rooms and whether the implication that they constituted important royal apartments is justified.

A word first about Edward's general relations with the Tower. One of his first priorities at the start of his reign was certainly to hugely strengthen the fortress.[51] The operations, which began in 1275, involved a second set of circuit walls, a new moat beyond them, a new land entrance, and a new river front with St Thomas's tower as its water gate. The total cost of the works, which lasted down to 1285, was at least £21,000. Edward's motives were much the same as those of previous kings, namely to intimidate and control the citizens of London. Between 1263 and 1267 the Londoners had insulted Edward's mother, provided matchless support for Simon de Montfort and harboured the rebellious Gilbert de Clare earl of Gloucester. Edward would now stamp on them once and for all.[52]

Edward also attended to the decoration of the new rooms in St Thomas's tower. They had tiled floors, stained glass windows and painted stone images above the roof.[53] And although there is no evidence, in the extensive account rolls, of any chair of state in the Wakefield Tower, a royal bed may well have been installed in the great chamber in St Thomas's.[54] Between 1281 and 1286

---

[51] *HKW*, ii, 715–23.

[52] Edward's determination to punish and dominate London is finely brought out in J.O. Prestwich, 'The Royal Household 1066–1307', *Medieval History*, I, no. 2 (1991), p. 46. For the whole reign see, of course, M. Prestwich, *Edward I* (1988).

[53] PRO E 372/ 121, m.43d (r.2d of the accounts section) (*HKW*, ii.719); C 47/ 3/ 47, mm.1–4.

[54] It is sometimes difficult, in the various rolls of expenditure and account in the 1270s, to separate items at the palace of Westminster from items at the Tower. However the king's 'seat' mentioned in E 372/ 121, m.43d (r.2d of the accounts section) was certainly at Westminster, as

the room was described as 'the great chamber of the king'.[55] Yet, despite all this, the facts of Edward's itinerary suggest that he hardly ever lived there. Edward's periods of residence at the Tower, according to the itinerary compiled by E.W. Safford, were as follows.

1274	5–11 October
1275	21–26 November
1276	18 July
1277	22 April
1278	2–18 January; 24, 25 February; 16 November
1280	7–9 December
1290	7 July
1293	6 November [?]; 13, 14 December
1294	3–9 November
1299	8–11 October[56]

What emerges from this table is that Edward's visits to the Tower were largely confined to the years between 1274 and 1280 when he was planning and executing his major building works. If we assume that the new rooms in St Thomas's tower were ready in 1280, then Edward can have resided in them for no more than eighteen days in the remaining twenty-seven years of his reign. Like his father, he had virtually abandoned the Tower as a place to live. Before we can be quite sure of this conclusion, however, we need to consider a little more carefully the sources from which Edward's itinerary is constructed. Safford made

---

continued

were the beds in E 101/467/6(2), mm.9,10 and E 372/121, m.43d, although that in E 372/ 121 is sometimes claimed for the Tower. A more likely candidate for the Tower is the bed the cost of whose timber, chains (presumably to hold the timber together) and transport is mentioned in C 47/ 3/ 47, m.2: *in meremio, bordis et tabulis de plano ad unum lectum ad opus domini Regis et ad ducendum per patriam xis []d; in octo paria parvarum catenarum ad eundem lectum xvid.* C 47/ 3/47 is described in *HKW*, ii, 719, n.1 as a roll of expenses subsidiary to the account in pipe roll 5 Edward I: E 372/ 121, m. 43d (r.2d of the accounts section). This may be right although it is difficult to match up exactly the items in the two rolls and the bed in C 47/3/47 does not re-appear in the pipe roll. Although its transport through the country (*per patriam*) is mentioned, it is not said where it was going. The expenses recorded on C 47/ 3/47 are very largely concerned with the Tower and some deal specifically with work on 'the great chamber above the water' and 'the new hall above the water', that is with St Thomas's Tower. It is possible, therefore, that this is where the bed was to go and perhaps the same is true of an altar referred to in the item next but one before the bed. (C 47/3/47, m.1 also refers to 'a little chapel above the water'.) It should be noted, however, that the 'four great tables' in C/47/3/47 are stated specifically as being 'for the new chamber' (m.1) in a way the bed is not.

[55] PRO E 101/ 467/ 10, m.1 (*HKW*, ii, 726 n.2).

[56] E.W. Safford, *Itinerary of Edward I*, 3 parts (List and Index Soc., 103, 132, 135, 1974, 1976–7). I have made a few minor alterations to Safford's dates. His itinerary is far more comprehensive than that in H. Gough, *Itinerary of King Edward the First . . . 1272–1307*, 2 vols. (1900) but Gough indicates the sources for each day whereas Safford does not. Safford follows Gough (who for once provides no reference) in having Edward at the Tower on 6 November 1293 but I have been unable to find the evidence for this and wonder if it is a mistake.

use of chancery, privy seal, wardrobe and household material.[57] The use of non chancery sources, now more plentiful than under Henry III, is important because there was a growing tendency during Edward's reign, and especially after 1292, for king and chancery to become separated.[58] Unfortunately, however, Safford does not indicate when he is relying solely on the *teste me ipso* clauses of the royal letters on the chancery rolls, and when the other sources come into play to confirm, amplify or contradict this material. There is a possibility, therefore, that if Safford only had chancery evidence for Edward's long stays at Westminster, the king had, in fact, left the chancery there while living himself in his new rooms at the Tower. In that case, as when we raised the same possibility with Henry III, the chancery *teste me ipso* clauses showing the king at Westminster were either fictional or Edward was travelling down to Westminster each day to work.

I have investigated this possibility and believe that it can largely be discounted.[59] First, Edward was perfectly ready to take the chancery to the Tower. The only certain visits on which he is not known to have done so are those on 22 April 1277 and 16 November 1278. Second, the surviving rolls concerned with the household's food and drink confirm the evidence of the chancery in suggesting that Edward spent both long and short periods at Westminster without ever going into residence at the Tower. Here are some examples:

Edward at Westminster from 1280 according to his household rolls

1286	9–27 February; 24–9 April
1289–90	23 December–19 February
1291	28 November–1 December
1291–2	24 December–5 February; 23 March–8 April
1293	19 April–1 July; 25 October–19 November
1302	23 May; 1 July–16 August
1303	3–10 March
1305	28 February–25 April; 24–25 September; 12 October–6 November.[60]

This evidence proves that during these periods Edward never set up court with his household at the Tower. Might he, none the less, have gone there to live with a small entourage, whilst leaving the bulk of his household, along with

---

[57] For the distinction between wardrobe and household material see above note 50. Safford appears to have missed the household roll for 1283–4: PRO E 101/351/ 13. Although I have checked Edward's few surviving daily oblation rolls for possible stays at the Tower, I have not checked to see how far they were used by Safford.

[58] See above note 11 and below , p. 415.

[59] Gough's itinerary (above note 56), which does cite sources, is helpful here.

[60] 1286: *Records of the Wardrobe and Household 1285–6*, nos. 1392–1409; 1466–71; 1289–90: PRO E 101/352/ 23; 1291, 1291–2: E 101/ 353/ 2 (a kitchen roll not used by Safford); 1293: (where there is both a household roll and a subsidiary pantry and buttery roll) E 101/ 353/ 10; E 101/ 353/ 17; 1302: E 101/ 361/ 10; 1303; E 101/ 364/ 27; 1305: E 101/ 368/ 3. Several of Edward's later visits may have been related to preparations for military campaigns. He was there in November 1294 before setting off for Wales and in October 1299 before proceeding north to Berwick.

the chancery, eating and drinking at Westminster? This would certainly have made the business of kingship rather difficult. Nor does it sit very happily with the evidence from the household rolls. There are only a small number of days when there is even a suggestion that the Westminster establishment was not catering for the king, and it seems highly unlikely that on all of them he was at the Tower.[61] For the rest of the time, if he was at the Tower, he must have been fed either by takeaways sent down river from Westminster or, more seriously, by a section of his domestic staff silently detached (as far as the rolls were concerned) and installed at the Tower. But although there was some separation between the kitchen of the king and the kitchen of the household, the daily rolls of expenditure on food and drink lump them together without distinction; it is hard to believe that, for any length of time, these rolls can have been dealing with two separate centres of operation, one at Westminster and one at the Tower.[62] The household's food and drink rolls were quite capable of recording even the briefest visit to the Tower: on 16 November 1278 they placed the king there while the chancery and wardrobe, according to their records, remained at Westminster.[63] If Edward had moved to the Tower during the periods tabulated above, the food and drink rolls would probably have shown it.

If we had the complete pattern of Edward's movements, we would doubtless find more days in which he was resident at the Tower but, in all probability, the basic picture sketched above would not alter, namely that, after 1280, he largely avoided it as a place to live. He did so for the same reasons as his father. It was at Westminster that Edward turned the king's great chamber into the famous painted chamber and built the chapel of St Stephen's.[64] The rooms at the Tower

---

[61] When the king was not catered for by the household departments because he was being entertained elsewhere, this was noted in the accounts, for example 'the king ate with the bishop of Durham' in PRO E 101/ 353/ 10 and see *Records of the Wardrobe and Household 1285–6*, nos. 1373–5. If we look at the accounts themselves, while the household was at Westminster, we find that on two consecutive days between 28 February and 25 April 1305 no expenditure was credited to the chamber and there are a few other days, as there are in some other rolls, when the expenditure was very low. No expenditure was likewise credited to the chamber on 10 November 1293. If we assume that the fact was not always noted in the accounts, the paucity of chamber expenditure could be taken to reflect the king's absence (see *Records of the Wardrobe and Household*, nos. 1373–5) and with a very small retinue for the overall level of expenditure usually remains at typical levels. Doubtless, during a long stay at Westminster, or anywhere else, the king sometimes went off for a day. It should be noted, however, that low expenditure by the chamber does not at all *prove* that the king was absent. There was no expenditure, as we have said, on 10 November 1293 but a subsidiary roll shows that the pantry and buttery provided bread and wine for both the king and the chamber on that day: E 101/ 353/ 10; E 101/ 353/ 17.

[62] See Tout, *Chapters*, ii 159; *Records of the Wardrobe and Household 1285–6*, p. xxxiii. In fact the split here was within the household with the senior members eating with the king, perhaps in his chamber, and the lesser eating in the hall.

[63] *Cal. Patent Rolls 1272–81*, p. 283; PRO C 47/ 4/ 1, f.49v; E 101/ 350/ 27. If the king did have only part of his kitchen establishment with him on this day, it shows the accounts indicated the whereabouts of the section serving the king rather than the section serving the rest of the household.

[64] Binski, *The Painted Chamber*, ch. iii; *HKW*, i, 504–13.

were certainly well decorated. Presumably Edward intended to use them if driven to the Tower by political crises, just as his father intended to use the chamber in the Wakefield tower. With Henry the crisis came; with Edward it did not; an accurate reflection of the very different political abilities of the two kings. The chamber of St Thomas's was 'the great chamber of the king' but it was usually occupied by the constable of the Tower or other royal officials and favourites. This continued to be the case after Edward's death since there is evidence that both Edward II and Edward III lived elsewhere in the fortress.[65] Above the watergate and with the portcullis actually rising into the hall, the new rooms in St Thomas's must always have been noisy and inconvenient.[66] To present them now to the public as rooms intended as royal apartments is perfectly reasonable; to imply, without any qualification, that they were actually used as such is misleading.[67] If Edward is saying anything in the little model of him by his bed in St Thomas's tower it is 'what a night; I'm not coming here again'.

Additional Note to Appendixes 1 and 2

In discussing the royal itinerary in these Appendixes, I raised the possibility that, if the chancery was separated from the king, it might date its letters by its own location rather than by that of the king, the *teste me ipso* clauses in the letters thus being fictional. This certainly was the practice in the later fourteenth century. However, I now realise from reading *Calendar of Chancery Warrants 1244–1326* (London, HMSO, 1927) that the chancery, under Edward I, when separated from the king, continued to date all its letters (and not just those warranted by the privy seal) by the king's location. This is, in fact, pointed out in Sir H.C. Maxwell-Lyte, *Historical Notes on the Use of the Great Seal of England* (London, HMSO, 1926), pp. 245–6. The chancery's practice in this regard strengthens the argument that Henry III and Edward I did not live at the Tower. Had they been there the dating clauses of the chancery letters would have said so. On the other hand, I was wrong to assume from the dating clauses that Edward I took the chancery with him on short visits to the Tower. The clauses may simply indicate that the chancery knew he was there.

---

[65] For Edward II, see Thurley, 'The Royal Lodgings at the Tower of London 1216–1327'; for Edward III: *HKW*, ii, 726; R.A. Brown, 'Architectural History and Development', in *The Tower of London*, ed. Charlton, p. 34.

[66] Even when Edward spent a few days in London in 1302, 1303 and 1305 (on his return from Scotland) he took up residence not at the Tower but at St Catherine's Hospital close by it. See Safford's itinerary and also *Chronicles of Edward I and Edward II*, 2 vols., W. Stubbs, ed., (Rolls Ser., 1882–3), i, 134 where III Kal. Feb. should probably be III Kal. Mar.

[67] A leaflet handed out to those visiting the rooms contains the following passages: 'You are standing in the Great Chamber . . . where nearly 700 years ago, the King would have slept'. 'While [Edward] was here at the Tower of London, the country was run from here.' This room was Edward's Hall . . . where he might have eaten and entertained, played chess and backgammon . . . Not only did the King live in these rooms but also part of his substantial household who were involved in court life and government'.

11

Simon de Montfort: The First Leader of a Political Movement in English History

'It happened on a certain night that there was a dispute between the brothers [of Peterborough abbey] about the earl; "some of them said that he was good, others that he was not and that he stirred up discord."'[1] The career of Simon de Montfort, earl of Leicester, was the subject of controversy in his own day and has remained so ever since. In recent times he has been portrayed by R. F. Treharne as a high-minded idealist, and by C. H. Knowles as a self-interested opportunist.[2] He has been described by Bishop Stubbs as 'one of the first to see the uses and the glories' of parliamentary government and by Sir Maurice Powicke as a 'dark' and destructive force.[3] My purpose, in this article, is not to approach these debates head-on, but to begin by examining another feature of Simon's career. What were the personal characteristics that made him the universally acknowledged leader of the great rebellion between 1263 and 1265?[4] The unprecedented nature of this position has rarely been stressed. Simon was both the first sole leader of a political movement in English history and the first political opponent of the king to seize power and govern the country in his name.

Simon was not the dominant figure from the start of the movement of reform. Between the initial revolution in 1258 and Henry III's recovery

This paper is based on a talk given to the inaugural meeting of the Simon de Montfort society in Evesham in 1988. I am most grateful to David d'Avray, David Crouch, John Maddicott and Michael Prestwich for their help and comments. Dr Maddicott has also kindly allowed me to see chapters from his forthcoming biography of Simon.

[1] *The Chronicle of William Rishanger: The Miracles of Simon de Montfort*, ed. J. O. Halliwell (Camden Soc., 1840) [hereafter *Rishanger*], p. 81. See St John's gospel, 7:12, for the quotation.
[2] R. F. Treharne, 'The Personal Rule of Simon de Montfort in the Period of Baronial Reform', *Proceedings of the British Academy*, xl (1954) [hereafter Treharne, 'Personal Rule'], 75–102, reprinted in the same author's *Simon de Montfort and Baronial Reform* (1986); C. H. Knowles, *Simon de Montfort, 1265–1965* (1965) [hereafter Knowles, *Simon de Montfort*], pp. 28–9.
[3] W. Stubbs, *The Constitutional History of England* (4th edn, 3 vols, Oxford, 1906), ii. 103–4 (a carefully measured judgement in some ways akin to Powicke's, however); F. M. Powicke, *King Henry III and The Lord Edward* (2 vols, Oxford, 1947) [hereafter Powicke, *Henry III*], i. 391.
[4] For a discussion relevant to this question, see Knowles, *Simon de Montfort*, pp. 20–5.

of power in 1261 he was one of several magnates who framed the Provisions of Oxford and attempted, often inharmoniously, to govern under their terms. The key moment in Simon's career came later, in 1263, when he returned to England after a period in France, took command of a new grouping of dissident magnates, and forced the king to reaffirm the Provisions of Oxford.[5] It was from this point onwards that his leadership stands out in all the contemporary sources. As the St Albans *Flores Historiarum* put it, 'the barons of England' 'adopted [Simon] as the leader [*dux*] by whom they were ruled'.[6] For a time in 1263, and then again between his victory at Lewes in May 1264 and his death at Evesham in August 1265, it was Simon who was effectively the ruler of England.[7]

In some ways Montfort was an unlikely person to have achieved this unique position. The period between 1258 and 1265 was one of increasing xenophobia. Simon was married to the king's sister and had inherited the earldom of Leicester; yet he was also a Frenchman, the younger son of the Simon de Montfort who had led the Albigensian crusade. The Melrose chronicler commented specifically on the paradox: Simon was 'the shield and defender of the English; the enemy and expellor of aliens although he himself was one of them by nation'.[8]

What then brought Simon to the fore in 1263? In trying to answer that question, one factor stands out above all others: Simon, more than anyone else, had been consistent in his political conduct. Having enthusiastically supported the Provisions of Oxford, he alone had refused to accept their overthrow. For contemporaries the 'Provisions of Oxford' covered the measures promulgated both at Oxford in June 1258 and at Westminster in October 1259.[9] To stand by them in the following years was to stand less by their precise details than by their general thrust, namely that the magnates, representing the community of the realm, should govern the king's choice of ministers, distribution of patronage and direction of policy; that there should be extensive reform of local administration, both royal and seignorial; and that England should be saved from domination by foreigners. If the king could endorse some

---

[5] The distinction between Simon's positions in 1258 and in 1263 has long been recognized; see, for example, Treharne, 'Personal Rule', pp. 323–4, 336. Treharne's *The Baronial Plan of Reform, 1258–1263* (Manchester, 1932) is the most detailed study of the politics of the period. The chief biographies of Simon are C. Bémont, *Simon de Montfort, comte de Leicester* (Paris, 1884) [hereafter Bémont, *Simon de Montfort*], of which a new English edition, translated by E. F. Jacob, was published by Oxford in 1930 (but without the appendix of original documents), and M. W. Labarge, *Simon de Montfort* (1962). Unless indicated all references are to the French edition of Bémont.
[6] *Flores Historiarum*, ed. H. R. Luard (3 vols, Rolls ser., 1890) [hereafter *Flores Hist.*], ii. 481.
[7] It should be noted, however, that Simon governed through the council, or members of the council, of nine set up after the battle of Lewes. It was only on a limited scale that he was directly concerned with day-to-day business. Probably he was often absent from court.
[8] *The Chronicle of Melrose*, ed. A. O. and M. O. Anderson (1936) [hereafter *Melrose*], p. 127.
[9] E. F. Jacob, *Studies in the Period of Baronial Reform and Rebellion, 1258–1267* (Oxford, 1925) [hereafter Jacob, *Studies*], pp. 122–4.

of the local reforms, he could never tolerate baronial control over appointments, patronage and policy. Hence the civil war.

In 1258 Simon had been one of the seven magnates whose confederation had begun the political revolution and one of the baronial twelve chosen to draw up the reforms at Oxford, in company with the twelve chosen by the king. He had then become a member of the council of fifteen, set up at Oxford, which governed England in the king's name. Thereafter a series of actions demonstrated Simon's commitment to the 'enterprise' of reform. He was determined to maintain control over appointments, patronage and policy. He also supported local reform including that of seignorial administration. On 23 July 1258 it was Simon, with Roger Bigod and John fitz Geoffrey, who went to the Guildhall and demanded that the Londoners accept the 'emendation of the realm'. Immediately afterwards, Simon almost certainly took a leading part as the reformers sat 'day after day' working on what was probably the *Providencia Baronum Anglie*, an early draft of the Provisions of Westminster which, amongst other things, limited the obligation to attend the private courts of magnates.[10] Next, in February 1259, as the barons debated the promulgation of 'salutary statutes', Simon, according to Matthew Paris, became 'enraged' when Richard de Clare, earl of Gloucester, seemed to be 'fluctuating in his support for their common purpose'. The issue here was almost certainly Clare's resistance to the Ordinance of the Magnates: the Charter in which the council of fifteen subjected themselves and their local officials to the process of reform.[11] In October 1259, under the terms of their alliance, Simon bound Edward, the king's son, to maintain the baronial enterprise.[12] Around the same time he told the count of Brittany that the king could not dispense patronage save on the advice of the council of fifteen. Then, early in 1260, Simon defended the attempt to hold a parliament at Candlemas (2 February), during the king's absence in France, on the grounds that the Provisions of Oxford had stipulated that three parliaments were to be held every year, of which one was to be at Candlemas. Later, when it seemed that the king would return to England with a band of mercenaries and reassert his independence, Simon, according to his own account, gathered men and made alliances to defend 'the common enterprise'. In October 1260, Simon's return centre-stage coincided with the magnates asserting their

[10] *Cronica Maiorum et Vicecomitum Londoniarium*, ed. T. Stapleton (Camden Soc., 1846) [hereafter *Cron. Maiorum*], pp. 38–9; *Documents of the Baronial Movement of Reform and Rebellion, 1258–1267*, ed. R. F. Treharne and I. J. Sanders (Oxford, 1973) [hereafter *DBM*], no. 9. I owe this point to Dr Paul Brand's article 'The Drafting of Legislation in Mid-thirteenth-century England', in *The Making of the Common Law*, pp. 325–67.
[11] *Matthaei Parisiensis Chronica Majora*, ed. H. R. Luard (7 vols, Rolls ser., 1872–83) [hereafter *Chron. Maj.*], v. 744; *DBM*, no. 10; Powicke, *Henry III*, i. 406–7. The twelve chosen to represent the community at the three annual parliaments also joined in this declaration.
[12] D. A. Carpenter, 'The Lord Edward's Oath to Aid and Counsel Simon de Montfort, 15 October 1259', below pp. 241–52.

right, under the Provisions, to appoint the king's chief ministers: a new justiciar, chancellor and treasurer all being foisted on Henry III against his wishes. The new justiciar, Hugh Despencer, was one of Simon's closest associates.[13] If, at the same time, the promises made in the Ordinance of the Magnates were watered down as the price for a reconciliation with Richard de Clare, Simon's continuing support for local reform can be deduced from the way Hugh Despencer, as justiciar, heard cases against lords and their officials.[14]

Between 1258 and 1260 there were also periods when Simon gave priority to his private affairs, a point to which I will return. None the less, he had clearly nailed his colours to the mast in defence of the Provisions of Oxford and the way was prepared for his conduct in 1261 which formed the watershed in his career. By the end of that year, he stood alone. All the other magnates, with greater or lesser degrees of reluctance, had accepted the king's overthrow of the Provisions and recovery of power. Rather than join them, Simon withdrew to France.[15] He returned to England only once in the next year when he put in a brief appearance at the October parliament and published papal letters commanding that 'the provisions made at Oxford be held in all things'.[16] In 1263, therefore, when the blunders of the king and his son had created a new party of dissidents, it was natural for them to turn to Simon, the leader across the water, the one man who, as the chronicler Rishanger later put it, 'had stood perseveringly like an immovable column ... while others had deserted, spurning their oath to maintain the Provisions of Oxford'.[17]

It was not simply consistency that made Simon a compelling leader, however. One can be consistent sitting in an armchair: Simon was also a man of action. That action, moreover, was frequently of a military nature. Simon did not merely stand by the Provisions; he also fought for them. Fundamentally he was a warrior, not a diplomat. When the odds were stacked against him, he might suggest negotiations and arbitration, but he preferred battle to surrender. There was nothing surprising about this. Again and again in his career Simon placed his trust in the use of force. If the king's opponents in 1263 wanted someone to lead them in war, as in effect they did, then Simon was the ideal man to do it.

[13] *DBM*, pp. 204–11, nos. 23, 31, 34 and pp. 222–3, no. 4[8]; H. W. Ridgeway, 'King Henry III's Grievances against the Council in 1261: a New Version and a Letter describing Political Events', *BIHR*, lxi (1988) [hereafter Ridgeway, 'King Henry III's Grievances'], 230–1; Treharne, *Baronial Plan*, pp. 244–5.
[14] Treharne, *Baronial Plan*, pp. 246–9; Jacob, *Studies*, pp. 109–15; Public Record Office [hereafter PRO] Just 1/911, 537. That the modification of the Provisions in the area of seignorial administration was Clare's price for his alliance with Montfort (for which see Ridgeway, 'King Henry III's Grievances', p. 231) is suggested in Dr Maddicott's forthcoming biography.
[15] *Annales Monastici*, ed. H. R. Luard (5 vols, Rolls ser., 1864–9) [hereafter *Ann. Mon.*], iii. 217; see also *Ann. Mon.*, iv. 129; *The Historical Works of Gervase of Canterbury*, ed. W. Stubbs (2 vols, Rolls ser., 1879–80) [hereafter *Gerv. Cant.*], ii. 213.
[16] *Gerv. Cant.*, ii. 217. The king at this time was in France.
[17] *Rishanger*, p. 6.

Simon had already distinguished himself in the fighting outside Saintes during the Poitevin expedition of 1242,[18] but it was as seneschal of Gascony, between 1248 and 1252, that he really made his reputation as a commander. He had been appointed to reduce Gascony to order, and from the first he saw his task as a military operation.[19] He hired mercenaries, took the castles and towns of Gramont, Fronsac, Mauléon and Castillon, and forced the vicomte of Béarn and his followers to submit. When these triumphs provoked only fresh disorders, he returned to Gascony with a force of mercenaries and, displaying considerable personal gallantry, defeated his enemies in a pitched battle which, according to Matthew Paris, lasted half a day.[20]

No earl in 1258 could rival Simon's experience of military command. He was a man, as Matthew Paris put it, 'powerful and expert in war'. Indeed, according to Paris, the king had called him 'a lover and inciter' of it.[21] No wonder, therefore, that in the political situation after 1258 Simon was so keen to move matters to the military plane. In October 1259, he bound Edward, in effect, to make war on those who refused to accept awards of the king's court. The next year, when, as I have mentioned, the king threatened to return to England with mercenaries and reassert his independence, Simon's reaction again took martial form. The men he assembled, he declared, would 'give [the mercenaries] such a welcome that others would have no great desire to follow them'. And then, in 1261, it was Simon above all who mobilized armed resistance to the king's recovery of power. Indeed, in so doing, he too tried to bring mercenaries into the kingdom.[22]

Of course, the use of force can often be counterproductive. 'He had set the whole Province in flames; and no proconsul could be justified in doing that', wrote Sir James Ramsay of Simon's time in Gascony.[23] The ultimate result of the earl's career in England was exactly the same. None the less, between 1263 and 1265 Simon's refusal to give in and his confidence in the use of force were often amply justified. More than anything else they sustained his leadership of the great rebellion. In this period, Simon proved himself a great general.

A crucial early moment had come at the end of June 1263 when Simon and his army were advancing southwards. The king's brother, Richard of Cornwall, had come to meet them, suggesting negotiations with a view to a settlement. Richard was a famous 'fixer', a man often called in to act as an arbitrator and diplomat. Since his election as King of Germany in 1257, he had enjoyed all the panoply and prestige

[18] *Chron. Maj.*, iv. 213; ibid., v. 290.
[19] Bémont, *Simon de Montfort* (English edn), p. 99.
[20] *Chron. Maj.*, v. 49, 77, 103–4, 193, 209–10, 222, 256, 314–15; *Royal and other Historical Letters Illustrative of the Reign of Henry III*, ed. W. W. Shirley (2 vols, Rolls ser., 1862, 1866) [hereafter *Royal Letters*], ii. no. cccclxxvi.
[21] *Chron. Maj.*, v. 313.
[22] Carpenter, 'The Lord Edward's Oath', pp. 248–9, 251; *DBM*, pp. 208–11, nos. 34, 38; see also no. 39; *Calendar of Patent Rolls* [hereafter *CPR*] *1258–66* (1910), p. 185.
[23] Sir J. H. Ramsay, *The Dawn of the Constitution* (Oxford, 1908), p. 135.

of a royal title.[24] Faced with his overtures, many less determined men would have called a halt and accepted the medieval equivalent of beer and sandwiches at No. 10. Simon's reaction was quite different. 'Yesterday ... we came to Cippenham, having heard that the earl of Leicester, with his followers, was at Reading', Richard reported to his brother in a letter of 30 June.

> We sent to him at once our messenger and letters, inviting him most urgently to come to meet us early this Saturday morning at Loddon bridge [near Twyford] to treat with us over peace. But [the earl], although our messenger reached him at daybreak on Saturday, replied that he was in no way able to meet us, nor to alter his previous plans, and I understand that, early this morning, moving camp with his followers, he will proceed today to Guildford where, having spent the night, it is said that he will continue on the morrow to Reigate.[25]

Simon had grasped the essentials of the situation, and was making for the Cinque Ports, aware that, once he had secured them, he would have no need to bother with the mediation of Richard of Cornwall. The king, isolated in the Tower of London, would be at his mercy. This appreciation proved correct. Having established an alliance with the Cinque Ports, and reached an agreement with the Londoners, Simon forced the king to surrender and reaffirm the Provisions of Oxford.

Simon's bravery and decision were equally evident as the king, later in 1263, began to recover power and the country slipped towards civil war. In December, when it seemed that Simon would be trapped in Southwark by superior royal forces, he prepared to fight rather than give in.[26] Early in 1264, he prepared to fight again rather than accept the verdict of the king of France, to whom both sides had submitted their quarrel, a verdict that condemned the Provisions of Oxford outright. Simon's initial situation, at the beginning of hostilities in March, was highly unfavourable since his forces were split between London and his midland bases at Kenilworth, Northampton and Leicester.[27] The king and Edward were placed in between at Oxford and almost at once were able to capture Northampton (5 April). Simon, leaving London, got no further than St Albans before he was forced to return by disturbances in the city. It was at this point that the earl demonstrated two essentials of generalship: he 'withstood the shocks of war' and seized the initiative, making his enemies dance to his tune.

After the initial defeat at Northampton, Simon shaped the course of events through three military decisions. First, he left London again,

[24] For Richard, see N. Denholm-Young, *Richard of Cornwall* (Oxford, 1947) [hereafter Denholm-Young, *Richard of Cornwall*].
[25] *Royal Letters*, ii. no. dcv; Denholm-Young, *Richard of Cornwall*, p. 120.
[26] *Ann. Mon.*, iii. 226.
[27] For more detail on what follows, see D. A. Carpenter, *The Battles of Lewes and Evesham, 1264/65* (Mercia Publications, Keele, 1987).

not this time for the north, but to lay siege to the royal garrison in Rochester. This had the effect, no doubt as intended, of bringing the king's army south, thus enabling Simon to unite his own forces. Then, second, with the king preparing to secure the allegiance of the Cinque Ports and blockade London, Simon marched out of the city on 6 May, determined to seek out the king's army and bring it to battle. He would fight 'with all for all', despite inferior forces and the hazards of battle which most medieval generals did everything to avoid. The armies finally met at Lewes where Simon again took the initiative. After the failure of desultory negotiations, he marched his army on to the Downs above the town during the night of 13–14 May, and, in the morning, caught the royalists at a decisive disadvantage.

Very much the same features can be discerned during the Evesham campaign in 1265 without, of course, from Simon's point of view, the same happy outcome. Again the beginning of hostilities found Simon badly placed, for the operations of Gilbert de Clare and the Lord Edward trapped him west of the river Severn. His initial attempts to cross the Bristol Channel from Newport were defeated. Again, however, Simon had an answer. He ordered his son, who had been besieging Pevensey castle, to march north to Kenilworth with all available forces. The idea was that this movement would force Edward back from the Severn and allow Simon himself to cross the river. One half of the strategy worked perfectly. On 2 August 1265 Simon was able to ford the Severn at Kempsey, just south of Worcester, unopposed. But meanwhile Edward had not merely been distracted by young Simon's advance; he had surprised him outside Kenilworth and captured a considerable portion of his army. Simon's response was to leave Kempsey and, during the night of 3–4 August, attempt a long circular march designed to skirt round Edward's army, which had returned to Worcester, and join up with young Simon and his remaining forces at Kenilworth. In the early hours of the morning of 4 August Simon crossed the bridge over the Avon at Evesham and paused at the adjoining abbey.

This was far from being the action of an exhausted and defeated man. Simon was no General Ritchie, so battered by Rommel in the Western Desert that he had lost the capacity to think and react. Rather, to the last, Simon was trying to outwit his enemies. He could leave Evesham by one of three routes. He could simply march north out of the town to Alcester and thence to Kenilworth. Alternatively, he could recross the bridge over the Avon and then either retreat south to London or march north along the east bank of the river, before recrossing it and reaching Kenilworth from that direction. The purpose of the delay at Evesham was to find out where Edward's army was. Simon knew that it was probably following him through the night. If he discovered that it was blocking the Alcester road, then he could take either of the two alternatives. It was here, however, that he was at last outgeneralled, for Edward, on the night of 3–4 August, saw beyond the facts and the rumours brought by his scouts and spies into his opponent's own mind and situation. Consequently he split his army into three parts so as to block all possible routes out of Evesham.[28]

Simon's campaigns between 1263 and 1265 amply demonstrate his prowess in the art of war. That prowess, allied to the consistency of his political conduct, made him a formidable leader. But these were not his only assets. Simon's financial resources, derived from land and money fees, were considerable. In the 1250s they amounted perhaps to over £2,200 a year. If this did not compare with the income of the earls of Cornwall or Gloucester, it still put Simon 'amongst the richest half dozen of the earls'.[29] Simon had also cemented an influential circle of personal followers who stood by him to the end. There was no parallel to the desertions from his immediate entourage suffered by a later baronial leader, Thomas of Lancaster.[30] Like those of other great magnates in the thirteenth century, there was nothing exclusively 'feudal' about Simon's affinity.[31] Some of its members, certainly, held from his half of the honour of Leicester,[32] but many others had, initially at least, no tenurial connection with him. Essentially the affinity was underpinned by the tie of neighbourhood, for it centred on Simon's great bases in the midlands, his borough of Leicester and his castle at Kenilworth. Simon had received Kenilworth from the king in 1244 and had turned it into one of the most impregnable fortresses in the country. It was there that he held court; there, after his death, that at least one miracle was performed 'at the place where the earl was accustomed to sit'.[33]

Reaching out from these bases, Simon was able to attract support through the glamour of his personality, the distribution of patronage and the use of force: several knights later complained that they were compelled to join his standard. Simon could also pick up the webs of existing alliances of kin and service so that his attraction of one

[28] For a very different version of events at the battle of Evesham, see D. C. Cox, *The Battle of Evesham: A New Account* (Evesham, 1988).
[29] This quotation and calculation of annual income come from J. R. Maddicott's forthcoming biography. See now his *Simon De Montfort* (Cambridge, 1994), pp. 44–59.
[30] J. R. Maddicott, *Thomas of Lancaster, 1307–1322* (Oxford, 1970), p. 295.
[31] In considering Simon's affinity I have been greatly helped by David Crouch, who has allowed me to see his collection of Montfort charters which overlaps with but is much larger than my own. All statements made below about attestations of Montfort charters (those in which he was either donor or donee) refer to charters noted by Dr Crouch and myself. The total is twenty-four. Simon's affinity would doubtless appear much larger were more charters known. Dr Simpson's study of the affinity of Simon's contemporary, Roger de Quincy, earl of Winchester, was based on eighty-one charters: G. Simpson, 'The *Familia* of Roger de Quincy, Earl of Winchester and Constable of Scotland', *Essays on the Nobility of Medieval Scotland*, ed. K. J. Stringer (Edinburgh, 1985) [hereafter Simpson, 'Roger de Quincy'], p. 123.
[32] The honour of Leicester had been split into two halves on the death of Robert earl of Leicester in 1204, his coheirs being his two sisters, who had married respectively Simon, lord of Montfort (Simon's grandfather) and Saer de Quincy, earl of Winchester.
[33] *CPR 1232–47* (1906), p. 419; *CPR 1247–58* (1908), pp. 5, 250; *Flores. Hist.*, ii. 489, 504; *Rishanger*, p. 87. Simon's midlands affinity was not apparently in place at the time of his crusade in 1240: S. Lloyd, *English Society and the Crusade, 1216–1307* (Oxford, 1988), p. 83.

family helped to bring others into his circle.[34] And he could exploit tenurial ties, for it was in the general vicinity of Kenilworth and Leicester that many of his knightly tenants held their lands.[35] Simon was helped in all this by the comparative absence of rival earls in the area.[36] True, Roger de Quincy, earl of Winchester, who held the other half of the honour of Leicester, retained a substantial following,[37] but he played little part in English politics and died without male heirs early in 1264. Simon, therefore, was able to draw into his circle from the Quincy affinity such knights as Saer de Harcourt, Peter le Porter and Arnold de Bois senior and junior.[38] Saer Harcourt, like other knights in Simon's following, was actually a tenant of the earl of Warwick, but from 1243 onwards that earldom was held by a Poitevin *curialis*, John du Plessis, who had merely a life interest in the right of his wife.[39] Simon's affinity was also drawn from families previously connected with the earls of Chester, not surprisingly since the last earl had died in 1237 and his lands had been split between numerous coheirs.

Operating in this favourable territory, by 1248 Simon had brought into his service Peter de Montfort (no relation), a major tenant of the earl of Warwick, and become a close friend of Peter's uncle, Walter de Cantilupe, the bishop of Worcester. The chief seats of the two men's families were respectively at Beaudesert and Aston Cantlow, four miles apart, and within twelve miles of Kenilworth.[40] By 1259 Simon could

[34] *Calendar of Inquisitions Miscellaneous*, i (1916) [hereafter *Cal. Inq. Misc.*], nos. 929, 930. For ties of kin, see below and nn. 40, 44, 46, 48, and for patronage n. 40 and *Cal. Inq. Misc.*, no. 930 (Peter le Porter).

[35] For the fees held from the earl of Leicester in the counties of Northampton and Leicester see *Book of Fees* (3 vols, 1920–31), ii. 939–40; *Feudal Aids* (6 vols, 1899–1920), iii. 97–8. Simon had, of course, important bases outside the midlands, for example at Hungerford in Berkshire: *CPR 1247-58*, p. 249; Jacob, *Studies*, pp. 231, 235, 292.

[36] This theme is developed in D. Williams, 'Simon de Montfort and his Adherents', *England in the Thirteenth Century*, ed. W. M. Ormrod (Harlaxton, 1985) [hereafter Williams, 'Simon de Montfort'], pp. 174–6.

[37] Simpson, 'Roger de Quincy', pp. 102–30.

[38] Ibid., pp. 108–9, 115–16, 118, 120–2, 130; J. Nichols, *The History and Antiquities of the County of Leicester* (4 vols, 1795–1811), i, part 1, Appendix, 35; ibid., ii, part 2, 637; *CPR 1258-66*, p. 418; Merton College Muniments, no. 2872; *Cal. Inq. Misc.*, no. 930; *Placita ... Abbrevatio* (Record Com., 1811), p. 183; *Feudal Aids*, iii. 101. For the de Bois, see below, n. 46.

[39] *Book of Fees*, i. 520; Williams, 'Simon de Montfort', pp. 174, 176; and see below and nn. 46, 47. The Harcourts also held from the earl of Winchester: Simpson, 'Roger de Quincy', p. 118. After John du Plessis's death in 1263 the earldom of Warwick passed to William Mauduit who was captured, along with Warwick castle, by Simon's forces in 1264: *Flores Hist.*, ii. 489.

[40] D. A. Carpenter, 'St Thomas Cantilupe: His Political Career', see below p. 298; *Book of Fees*, ii. 956. For Simon's grant of Ilmington to Peter de Montfort, see Bodleian Library, Dugdale MS 13, f. 256. The Cantilupe connection probably helped attract into Simon's movement another magnate with midlands interests, Henry of Hastings (one of the earl of Chester's coheirs). Henry had married a sister of the last Cantilupe of the main line and his son eventually inherited Aston Cantlow and much else besides: *The Complete Peerage*, ed. G. E. Cokayne, revised by V. Gibbs et al. (12 vols in 13, 1920–57) [hereafter *Complete Peerage*], vi. 346; *Cal. Inq. Misc.*, nos 928, 929.

also rely on the support of Richard de Grey, lord of Avington just by Leicester, and a Montfort tenant for a half fee at Byfield, nineteen miles south-west of Kenilworth.[41] Likewise he was very closely linked to Hugh Despencer of Loughborough, ten miles north of Leicester, whose forebears had been tenants and, like the Cantilupes, close associates of the earl of Chester.[42] These were all influential men. In 1258 Peter de Montfort, Richard de Grey and Hugh Despencer were among the baronial twelve chosen to draw up the plans of reform. Peter, Richard and Bishop Cantilupe were also members, with Simon, of the council of fifteen. In October 1260 Hugh Despencer became justiciar. All these men were loyal to the last. Grey was captured by Edward at Kenilworth; Montfort and Despencer were killed at Evesham; Bishop Cantilupe said mass to the trapped army before the battle.[43] Another important family, once linked to the earls of Chester, with which Simon enjoyed a long association, was that of Seagrave. (The place itself is eight miles north of Leicester.) Simon had granted a manor to Gilbert of Seagrave, who died in 1254. Nicholas, the latter's son, joined Simon in 1263 and was captured at Evesham.[44]

The Cantilupes, Montforts, Despencers, Greys and Seagraves were important families in their own right. Perhaps only Peter de Montfort was a member of Simon's inner circle on a day-to-day basis, judging from the witness lists of the latter's charters.[45] The most permanent fixtures in that circle, apart from Simon's steward, Richard of Havering, were two other midlands knights, Thomas of Astley (eleven miles from Kenilworth) and Ralph Basset of Sapcote (ten miles from Leicester). Both were Simon's tenants; both, like Peter de Montfort, went with him to Gascony in 1248. Both remained loyal: Thomas died at Evesham, while Ralph lost his lands for being 'with the earl of Leicester under

[41] *DBM*, pp. 200–1, no. 16; *Cal. Inq. Misc.*, nos. 644, 770; *Book of Fees*, ii. 940. Richard de Grey's chief seat was at Codnor in Derbyshire. He does not attest any Montfort charters.

[42] See Bémont, *Simon de Montfort*, p. 328, where Hugh appears as Simon's executor with Peter de Montfort and Arnold de Bois; *Complete Peerage*, iv. 259–60; *Patent Rolls 1225–32* (1903), p. 360. For two charters of Simon attested by Hugh Despencer, see Bodleian Library, Dugdale MS 13, f. 256, and PRO DL 42/2, ff. 49v–50r. For fish from the fishpond at Kenilworth being sent (in 1229) to stock the pond at Loughborough, see *Close Rolls 1227–31* (1902), p. 224.

[43] *DBM*, pp. 100–1, 104–5; *Cron. Maiorum*, p. 45; *Cal. Inq. Misc.*, nos. 927, 769, 770; *Ann. Mon.*, iv. 168. Grey, however, was an old man by the 1260s and did not play a leading role between 1263 and 1265.

[44] Gloucester Record Office D.225/T.7; see also *Feudal Aids*, iii. 97; *Cal. Inq. Misc.*, nos. 928, 929, 930, 769, 771. Gilbert of Seagrave, as the then constable, had delivered Kenilworth to Simon in 1244: *CPR 1232–47*, p. 419. The Seagraves were connected by the marriages of Stephen of Seagrave, Gilbert's father, to both the Despencer and the Hastings families. Stephen had had many links with the Montfort half of the honour of Leicester and attested two of Simon's charters, one in company with Gilbert: *Complete Peerage*, xi. 596–601; *Historical Manuscripts Commission: Hastings MSS* (1928), i. 335; Bémont, *Simon de Montfort*, p. 358.

[45] Peter attested five Montfort charters.

arms'.[46] Another knightly family in Simon's service before 1258 was that of Trussel. William Trussel, lord of Billesley, just by Aston Cantlow, and a Montfort tenant for a fee in Northamptonshire, became a justice of the bench and acted as Simon's attorney. His successor, Richard Trussel, died at Evesham.[47] Further midlands knights who were killed or captured at Evesham included William of Birmingham (Thomas of Astley's son-in-law), Robert of Hartshill (just by Astley), Thomas of Ardern (of Ratley, seventeen miles south-east of Kenilworth), Henry de Curzon (a Montfort tenant) and Ralph Basset of Drayton.[48]

Simon had, therefore, an influential affinity in England, an affinity which kept his cause alive during his absence abroad in 1262, and formed the nucleus around which allies could be grouped in the following year. In securing those allies two further characteristics were of paramount importance. The first was Simon's piety and passionate concern to aid the church in its mission, characteristics which help to explain the widespread ecclesiastical support for his regime.[49] This religiosity stands out above all in the correspondence (dating largely from around 1250) of the Oxford friar Adam Marsh, correspondence which reveals Simon's friendship both with Adam and with Robert Grosseteste, the greatest theologian and the most committed reforming bishop of the age. Simon did not merely entrust his sons' education to the bishop's care. He also enthused over his schemes to promote the salvation of souls. 'The earl of Leicester spoke to me', Marsh wrote to Grosseteste, 'about a most salutary proposal of triumphal magnificence for the saving of souls [perhaps some kind of crusading and preaching mission], which heaven has inspired in your heart. More than many would believe, he extols it, praises it and embraces it, as I can see, with ardent readiness for great conceptions and is firmly prepared, according to heavenly counsels ... to undertake it.'[50]

---

[46] *Book of Fees*, ii. 939; *Feudal Aids*, iii. 97–8; *CPR 1247–58*, p. 31; *Cal. Inq. Misc.*, i, nos. 928, 929. Astley itself was held from the earls of Warwick: *Book of Fees*, ii. 955. Ralph and Thomas attested respectively nine and seven Montfort charters. Thomas married the daughter of Arnold de Bois (d. 1255), the hereditary steward of the earls of Leicester, who attested four Montfort charters. Arnold, Arnold's son, was one of Simon's executors in 1259 but became an invalid and took no part in the politics of the period 1263–5. The de Bois held their lands from the earl of Winchester: Bodleian Library, Dugdale MS 15, f. 117; *Chron. Maj.*, v. 487; *CPR 1258–66*, p. 440; D. Crouch, *The Beaumont Twins* (Cambridge, 1986), pp. 109–11; Simpson, 'Roger de Quincy', pp. 108–9, 116; *Patent Rolls 1225–32*, p. 360.

[47] *Cal. Inq. Misc.*, nos. 927, 632; *Book of Fees*, ii. 939; PRO E 159/30, m. 18d. Billesley itself was held from the earl of Warwick although there was a mesne tenant between him and the Trussels: *The Victoria County History of Warwick*, ed. L. F. Salzman et al. (8 vols, 1904–68) [hereafter *VCH Warw.*], iii. 60.

[48] Bodleian Library, Dugdale MS 15, f. 111; *Cal. Inq. Misc.*, i, nos. 928, 930, 769, 771; *Book of Fees*, ii. 939. None of these men attested Simon's charters. The Astleys and Curzons were related through marriage: *VCH Warw.*, iv. 211. The Arderns held Ratley and other fees from the earls of Warwick: *Book of Fees*, ii. 956–7.

[49] See Powicke, *Henry III*, ii. 484.

[50] *Monumenta Franciscana*, ed. J. S. Brewer (Rolls ser., 1858) [hereafter *Mon. Franciscana*], p. 111; R. W. Southern, *Robert Grosseteste* (Oxford, 1986), pp. 289–90.

Marsh's picture is not without corroboration. Matthew Paris too referred to Grosseteste's influence upon Simon; indeed he was like the earl's 'father confessor'.[51] Nor was the connection forgotten after the bishop's death in 1253. By the early fourteenth century the chronicler Rishanger could believe that Grosseteste had inspired Simon with the cause for which he died.[52] Not surprisingly, therefore, reform-minded ecclesiastics rallied to Simon's support between 1263 and 1265, looking for the 'fitting rule' (*idoneum regimen*) in church and state which had been so lacking before 1258. Monastic and mendicant chroniclers sang the earl's praises.[53] Besides Cantilupe of Worcester, four bishops, all university graduates mitred since the revolution of 1258 – Berksted of Chichester, Gervais of Winchester, Gravesend of Lincoln and Sandwich of London – were suspended from office for supporting Simon in defiance of the pope.[54]

If Simon's religiosity earned him church support, a second characteristic helped him win backing from knights, gentry and those below them in the counties of England. There seems little doubt that Simon had the ability to recognize popular issues and turn them to his advantage. Fidelity to the Provisions of Oxford was itself a powerful slogan. Even the king acknowledged that the war was caused by his refusal to obey them.[55] Simon also exploited popular items within the Provisions. Take, for example, the reform of local government, the question that above all exercised the men of the shires. The process had begun in 1258 with making the sheriff a prominent local knight and giving him a salary or allowance, but there were strong feelings that it should also deal with seignorial administration.[56] That Simon aligned himself with these views is clear from the way he upbraided Richard de Clare when Richard appeared to resist the Ordinance of the Magnates in which the leaders of the new regime accepted that they and their bailiffs must be subject to the reforms.[57] When Simon finally attained power after Lewes he did not forget the reform of local government. The new sheriffs he appointed held office on the financial terms intro-

---

[51] *Chron. Maj.*, v. 416.
[52] *Rishanger*, p. 7. See also *Melrose*, p. 131. Posthumous stories of Simon's piety reach a climax in *Melrose*, pp. 132–44.
[53] See the references to Simon in A. Gransden, *Historical Writing in England, c. 550 to c. 1307* (1974).
[54] There are biographies of these bishops in the *Dictionary of National Biography*.
[55] *CPR 1266–72*, pp. 201, 219, 222. It is not suggested, however, that more than a minority of knights became actively involved on Simon's side: even in Warwickshire and Leicestershire, of the forty-five knights who appear on grand assize juries on the eyre of 1262 (PRO Just 1/954, mm. 1, 3, 4, 7, 10d, 13, 43) only thirteen (according to printed sources) were involved in the rebellion between 1263 and 1265. Knights and others who did participate often did so under pressure from great lords or as part of their affinities; for the role of John fitz John in Buckinghamshire and Northamptonshire, see Jacob, *Studies*, pp. 234–5; *Cal. Inq. Misc.*, nos 628, 834, 835, 838. For the support given to Simon, see Jacob, *Studies*, pp. 276–307. I have not discussed here Montfort's power-base in London.
[56] D. A. Carpenter, 'King, Magnates and Society: The Personal Rule of King Henry III', above pp. 98–106.
[57] See above p. 221.

duced by the Provisions of Oxford, being once again entitled to salaries or allowances.[58]

Equally significant was Simon's skill in exploiting the question of the aliens. By 1258 the unpopularity of the king's foreign relatives, and in particular of his Poitevin half-brothers, had become a major factor in politics. Great magnates resented the amount of patronage given to the brothers; the populace suffered from the extortions of their local officials. Both groups were affected by the way that the king's protection seemed to place them above the law.[59] Simon had early seen the issue's emotive power. In 1252, when he heard of the king's plans to have him condemned as a traitor, he exclaimed, according to Matthew Paris, 'I know well that, having despoiled me, he will enrich some Provencal or Poitevin with my earldom.' In 1260, on his own admission to a commission investigating his differences with the king, Simon made precisely the same kind of point: the king, in attempting to import foreign mercenaries, 'seemed to put his trust more in foreigners than in the men of his own land'.[60] In the abortive negotiations before the opening of the Lewes campaign in 1264, it was precisely the subject of the aliens that Simon made his final sticking-point. He was prepared to reach a settlement provided the king would remove them from the country and govern through natives.[61] The same call was made in the Song of Lewes, the poem written soon after Simon's great victory in May 1264, probably by a friar in the entourage of his closest ecclesiastical associate, Stephen Berksted, bishop of Chichester. Indeed, the danger posed to England by aliens was one of the Song's major themes. 'The earl was eager to obviate this evil', it declared.[62] That eagerness was one of the major factors binding Simon's movement together and giving it popular appeal.

At first sight Simon's understanding of such issues seems remarkable. In the 1240s and 1250s, he often appears as a member of the 'jet-setting' international aristocracy, utterly remote from the concerns of local England. Yet, as we have seen, Simon's ecclesiastical friends and knightly affinity meant that this was only part of the story. Grosseteste himself could instruct Simon about both the salvation of souls and Magna Carta, for the bishop excommunicated transgressors of the Charter and took special pains to see that its provisions concerning the holding of local

[58] PRO E 371/28, m. 3; D. A. Carpenter, 'The Decline of the Curial Sheriff in England, 1194–1258', above pp. 172–4.
[59] J. R. Maddicott, 'Magna Carta and the Local Community, 1215–1259', *Past and Present*, cii (1984) [hereafter Maddicott, 'Magna Carta'], 54–61. How justified the reputation of the Lusignans was is another matter: see H. W. Ridgeway, 'Foreign Favourites and Henry III's Problems of Patronage, 1247–58', *EHR*, cix (1989), 590–610.
[60] *Chron Maj.*, v. 338; *DBM*, pp. 208–9, no. 38.
[61] *Chronicles of the Reigns of Edward I and Edward II*, ed. W. Stubbs (2 vols, Rolls ser., 1882, 1883), i. 61.
[62] *The Song of Lewes*, ed. C. L. Kingsford (Oxford, 1890) [hereafter *Song of Lewes*], l. 311, and see ll. 955–8.

courts were upheld.[63] Likewise Peter de Montfort, for one, could tell
Simon of the concerns of a wide body of midlands knights. Peter's
pledges for fines in 1260 and 1262 included six knights who appeared
on Warwickshire and Leicestershire grand assize juries. One of these,
Thomas de Clinton, on the special reforming eyre of 1260, complained
of a sheriff of the 1250s, William Mansel, who had been bribed to deny
him justice.[64] Simon, therefore, was well placed to appreciate the pressure for the reform of local government in 1258. Indeed, the year before
he had been one of those appointed by the king to investigate the crimes
of the sheriff of Northampton. He was also, as his remark in 1252 shows,
perfectly aware of the unpopularity of the Poitevins. In 1257 the two
issues had come together in his own experience when the local agents
of the king's Poitevin half-brother, William de Valence, had invaded
his lands and seized his goods.[65]

Several factors, therefore, conspired to make Simon de Montfort the
leader of the 'common enterprise': his staunch adherence to the Provisions of Oxford; his readiness to support the Provisions by military
force; his influential affinity; his religiosity; and his ability to exploit
issues of key importance. In all this, it was his adherence to the Provisions
which, by 1263, had made him unique. It is also the most difficult feature
of his career to explain, raising the questions about his idealism and
self-interest which have always troubled historians.

Simon himself had the clearest possible explanation for this aspect
of his conduct. Running through a variety of sources is the same defence:
he had sworn an oath in 1258 to uphold the Provisions and he would
not break it, whatever others might do. 'For these things about which
we debate we have promised and sworn', Simon told Richard de Clare
in 1259, according to Matthew Paris. Next year, according to Simon's
evidence to the investigating commission, it was 'to keep his oath' to
the Provisions that he had attempted to hold a parliament in the king's
absence. At the end of 1261, rather than accept the king's recovery
of power, he declared, according to the Dunstable annalist, that 'he
preferred to die without land than be a perjurer and depart from the
truth.'[66] The Song of Lewes took up the same theme: 'woe to the wretched
perjurers ... for the earl had formerly pledged his oath [to preserve
the Provisions of Oxford] ... and because he had sworn, they were
to be stoutly maintained ...'.[67]

Simon's defence, however, only takes one so far. He never explained

[63] Maddicott, 'Magna Carta', p. 35.
[64] PRO Just 1/953, mm. 1d, 7; Just 1/954, m. 23d. Another Warwickshire knight, Jordan
of Whitacre, had grievances against Peter de Montfort: Just 1/953, m. 7.
[65] *Chron. Maj.*, v. 580, 634.
[66] Ibid., v. 744; *DBM*, pp. 206–7, no. 31; *Ann. Mon.*, iii. 217.
[67] *Song of Lewes*, ll. 221, 227–38. In the account of the friar, Richard of Durham, the oath
was invested with even more significance, through a tale that initially Simon had been reluctant
to take it: *Chronicon de Lanercost* (Bannatyne Club, 1839) [hereafter *Lanercost*], p. 67; see
also *Chronica Johannis de Oxenedes*, ed. H. Ellis (Rolls ser., 1859) [hereafter *Oxenedes*],
p. 204.

why the oath was so important or how it retained its force after its abrogation by the pope in 1261. His enemies, of course, had a very clear explanation for his conduct, one which the Song of Lewes felt obliged to rebut: 'if it was his own advantage which had moved the earl, he would have had no other zeal [but his] ... own advancement alone, and he would have set before himself the advancement of his own friends and the enrichment of his sons, and would have neglected the safety of the community.'[68] But did the Song of Lewes protest too much? Was not Simon's conduct, in truth, designed to secure his own advantage?

Simon was a younger son with his fortune to make. His hopes centred on King Henry and turned to bitter resentment when they were disappointed. The two men had quarrelled for the first time in 1239 when Simon, somewhat cavalierly, named Henry as the pledge for money that he owed Thomas of Savoy. In his rage Henry accused Simon of seducing his sister before their marriage.[69] In the early 1250s the two had quarrelled again over Simon's conduct as seneschal of Gascony. Quite apart, however, from these spectacular explosions, there was almost continuous tension over the king's failure, as Simon saw it, to provide him with land and money.

In many respects Simon had done well out of the king. In the 1230s he had gained possession of the earldom of Leicester; in 1238 he had married Eleanor, the king's sister; and in 1244 he had received, as her marriage-portion, an annual fee of £333 (500 marks). Next year, when Simon fined in £6,666 for the wardship of the lands of Gilbert de Umfraville, payable at £333 a year, he exchanged the fee for the pardon of the annual payment. Then, in 1253, trying to secure the earl's support once more in Gascony, Henry pardoned the whole of the Umfraville fine, and started to pay the £333 annual fee again. Indeed, he did even better, for he increased it to £400, entailed it on Simon and his heirs, and made it payable from the royal revenues of the midlands counties.[70] By the 1250s, as we have seen, Simon was among the wealthier of the English earls. Yet it was easy for him to see another side to the king's apparent generosity: the earldom of Leicester was no more than his right; the marriage-portion of the king's sister had been long in coming, and Henry had done nothing to fulfil his promise to convert the eventual £400 fee into land.[71] That failure highlighted the central problem with Simon's wealth, one which must have haunted almost his every moment. He was worth over £2,200 a year, but of that considerably less than

---

[68] *Song of Lewes*, ll. 325–32.
[69] *Chron. Maj.*, iii. 566–7; Bémont, *Simon de Montfort*, pp. 333–4.
[70] Of the original £333 fee only £200 was entailed on Simon, Eleanor and their heirs. The king promised to convert both fees into wardships or escheats: *Calendar of Charter Rolls* [hereafter CChR] *1226–57*, p. 278; Bémont, *Simon de Montfort*, pp. 335, 338; *Excerpta e Rotulis Finium*, ed. C. Roberts (2 vols, 1835), i. 436–7; *Calendar of Liberate Rolls* [hereafter CLR] *1245–51* (1937), p. 2; *CPR 1247–58*, pp. 249–50.
[71] Bémont, *Simon de Montfort*, pp. 333–5.

half was in hereditary land which he could pass on to his heirs. Eleanor's marriage-portion had not been converted into land. Eleanor's dower as the widow of William Marshal, earl of Pembroke, from which he derived a large part of his resources, Simon only held for her life. The bulk of the lands that he could pass on to his heirs were those inherited with the earldom of Leicester, which were worth perhaps £700 a year.[72] If Simon was an army commander, his eldest son would be no more than a divisional general; and there were three more sons to provide for!

This situation made it vital for the Montforts to exploit the life interest in Eleanor's dower to the full, but here too they ran into frustrating problems. The dower was partly in land and partly in the form of another £400-a-year money fee for the payment of which the king himself was surety. The Montforts, however, believed that the £400 undervalued by no less than £1,066 a year the sum to which Eleanor was entitled. They also thought that the dower should have been in land rather than in money. Since they blamed Henry for forcing Eleanor to accept such disadvantageous terms from the Marshals in the first place, they wanted him both to extract the full dower from the numerous Marshal heirs (the last earl having died in 1245), and to provide compensation for the losses suffered. By 1259 these amounted to £24,266.[73]

If the king could deny the responsibility for this huge sum, there were other debts which he did acknowledge. These had arisen from his apparent failure to keep up to date with the dower payments once the Marshal heirs defaulted after 1245, from the financial compensations that he owed Simon for his time as seneschal of Gascony, and from the mutual entanglement of the two men in the county of Bigorre. In June 1257 the exchequer put the grand total of these debts to the earl at £1,200.[74] Early in 1258 Simon extracted £600 from the exchequer, nominally for arrears of the dower payment, but he may still have been claiming substantial sums at the time of the political revolution a few months later.[75]

Simon, therefore, had many grievances against the king. Was not his enthusiasm for reform explained by the hope of doing better under the new regime? His conduct certainly fuelled such suspicions. On 5 May 1258, three days after the king accepted that the realm should

[72] I owe this figure to Dr Maddicott's forthcoming book.
[73] Carpenter, 'The Lord Edward's Oath', p. 246; *CPR 1258–66*, pp. 25–6; see *CPR 1232–47*, pp. 415–16. The king's reaction to the Montforts' complaint was to suggest that they brought a legal action against the Marshal heirs for the full dower. Such an action had been commenced in 1247 (not 1256 as I have said elsewhere), but no verdict was reached: PRO KB 26/159, mm. 2d, 3, 3d; Bémont, *Simon de Montfort*, p. 335. There were also suggestions that the £333 fee granted the Montforts in 1244 was intended as compensation for Eleanor's dower losses, or for the release of her claims against the king, rather than as her marriage-portion: Bémont, *Simon de Montfort*, p. 335; *CPR 1258–66*, p. 26.
[74] PRO E 159/30, m. 19, and see mm. 4d, 15.
[75] PRO E 403/15A; *CLR 1251–60* (1959), p. 285. When the king paid his debts to Simon in full in 1259, up to £636 had been owed from before the time of the 1258 revolution: PRO E 403/3115; *CPR 1258–66*, p. 26; *CLR 1251–60*, pp. 459–60.

be reformed by twelve men chosen by the barons and twelve by himself, Simon extracted a promise that these twenty-four should decide about the lands to be given to him 'for the yearly fee and debts' that he was owed by the king. Next year, the debts were settled in full while, in place of the £400 annual fee for Eleanor's marriage-portion, being paid from the revenues of the midlands counties, Simon and his heirs were granted a number of manors 'in tenancy'. If investigations showed that the manors were not ancient demesne of the crown, then the grant was to be converted into one outright.[76]

In 1258–9 Simon also made strenuous efforts to settle the question of Eleanor's dower. By refusing the renunciations required from Eleanor and himself by King Louis IX, he endeavoured to hold up the ratification of the Treaty of Paris until she received satisfaction. All this left Simon open to the charge that he was placing his own interests above any concern for the 'common enterprise'. Indeed, if he played an important part in the initial work behind the Provisions of Westminster, the subsequent progress of reform in 1259, as Matthew Paris implied, was hampered by his absences in France. He was even absent from the Westminster parliament when the Provisions were promulgated, for, pursuing the question of the dower, he seems to have left to see King Louis almost as soon as proceedings opened.[77]

Simon's subsequent conduct gave support to the same suspicions. His appearance at the parliament of October 1262 was not simply a high-minded attempt to restore the Provisions, for it was provoked by the collapse of Louis IX's efforts to settle his personal quarrels with Henry III.[78] And later, once he had attained power, Simon looked after both himself and his sons, whatever the Song of Lewes said. Indeed, was it not the crude fact that unless Simon sat in control at the centre and pulled the levers of patronage, there was no way he could provide for all his offspring? In the event, he secured grants in hereditary right of the county, castles and honour of Chester, the castle and honour of the Peak and the castle of Newcastle-under-Lyme. His second son was given the lands of John Mansel and the hand of the richest heiress of the day, Isabella de Fors. A hostile letter drawn up towards the end of 1263 drew attention to such aggrandizements and observed that the earl's 'followers [*sui*] ought not to devote themselves to spoils or gain, if he laboured for the common good'.[79]

If, alongside all this, Simon pushed forward projects for local reform and stood fast against foreigners, was that not merely opportunism?

[76] *CPR 1247–58*, p. 627; *CPR 1258–66*, p. 26; *CLR 1251–60*, pp. 459–60; PRO E 403/3115; *CChR 1257–1300* (1906), pp. 18, 20; PRO E 368/35, m. 3; see E. M. Hallam, *Domesday Book through Nine Centuries* (1986), p. 50.
[77] Carpenter, 'The Lord Edward's Oath', below pp. 244–6; *Chron. Maj.*, v. 745.
[78] *Foedera* ... , ed. T. Rymer, new edn (3 vols in 6, Record Com., 1816–30), I. i. 422. I owe this point to Dr Maddicott.
[79] *CChR 1257–1300*, p. 54; *CPR 1258–66*, p. 273; Jacob, *Studies*, p. 210 n. 3; *Ann. Mon.*, i. 179–80.

He thus won support, and embarrassed enemies like Richard de Clare and William de Valence.[80] Indeed, since Clare had a uniquely large network of local courts and officials, he had far more to lose from the extension of reform to seignorial administration than had Simon himself. And yet, if Simon, during the period of reform and rebellion, was in part out for himself, it is impossible to explain his actions entirely in such terms. 'Behold! Simon, obedient, scorns the loss of property, subjecting himself to penalties that he may not let go the truth', wrote the author of the Song of Lewes.[81] Simon had made the same point when he left England at the end of 1261: 'he preferred to die without land than be a perjurer and depart from the truth.'[82] Ultimately Simon's conduct surely went beyond any narrow calculation of material loss and gain. In 1261, at the time of his withdrawal to France, he could never have foreseen the *bouleversement* which brought him to the fore in 1263. On any rational calculation of the possibilities, he should have acquiesced in the king's recovery of power and extracted the highest price that he could in return.

It is possible, therefore, while not denying his pursuit of his own interests, to approach Simon's career from a different angle: it can be argued that his political stance was also informed by political theory and made ardent by religious zeal. In 1251 Adam Marsh, while staying with Simon, sent back to Robert Grosseteste 'that brief account which you have written *de principatu regni et tyrannidis* as you sent it sealed with the seal of the earl of Leicester'. This was, in fact, the text of the speech Grosseteste had made before the pope the previous year, arguing against the archbishop of Canterbury's right to exact procurations.[83] It had begun with a series of quotations from Aristotle about the differences between a king and a tyrant: 'a tyrant devotes himself to his own interests, a king to those of his subjects'; 'all things connected with rule [*regiminis*] should be directed by reason, the guardian of justice and equity.'[84] Of course, Adam's words do not prove that Simon had studied the tract, even if Grosseteste intended him to do so. He may have sighed 'Not more from the bishop!', and got Marsh to return it as soon as decently possible. On the other hand, it is clear that comparable ideas were abroad later in Simon's circle. In 1258, the letter of explanation to the pope sealed by Simon and other members of the council of fifteen declared that the realm should be 'ruled by the governing hand of reason' in a way very similar to that put forward in Grosseteste's tract. Again, the Song of Lewes argued that the king was subject

---

[80] *Chron. Maj.*, v. 634, 676–7, 689. The Montforts claimed that Eleanor had, in fact, been dowered with Pembroke, which William de Valence had obtained through his marriage: PRO KB 26/159, mm. 2d, 3, 3d.

[81] *Song of Lewes*, ll. 217–18.

[82] *Ann. Mon.*, iii. 217.

[83] *Mon. Franciscana*, p. 110; Southern, *Robert Grosseteste*, pp. 287–90.

[84] S. Gieben, 'Robert Grosseteste et the Papal Curia, Lyons 1250. Edition of the Documents', *Collectanea Franciscana*, xli (1971), 378.

to the law and must govern not for himself but for the benefit of his people.[85]

If Simon thought about such principles before 1258, he could certainly feel that they were relevant to the actual situation in England. He had intimate knowledge of events at Henry III's court. He was also well informed, as I have suggested, about the situation in the localities. Simon could easily believe that Henry had ruled for himself rather than his subjects, placing his half-brothers above the law and allowing his people to be oppressed by sheriffs and seignorial officials. He had hardly stood forth as a monarch governed by reason, a guardian of 'justice and equity'. If that was the case, what could be done about it? Grosseteste had merely implied that no obedience was due to a tyrant. But Simon would also have known of the constitutional remedies propounded in the abortive Paper Constitution of 1244 and at numerous parliaments thereafter. It was such remedies that the Song of Lewes sought to justify, arguing that if the king failed in his duties – if, in particular, he was over-indulgent to foreigners – then it was the task of the magnates and the community of the realm to place limits upon him.

It is possible, therefore, that before 1258 Simon had begun to think about the theory and practice of political reform, just as he had also contemplated the concerns of the church. His commitment to the common enterprise would thus have had deeper roots than some sudden conversion in 1258. That commitment may also have had an element of religious enthusiasm. When preparing to fight at Southwark in 1263, Simon ordered his followers to don crosses 'in the name of God'. He thus proclaimed that they were fighting in a holy, crusading cause.[86] Did Simon regard the common enterprise as something similar to the projects for the salvation of souls that he had discussed with Grosseteste and Marsh in the early 1250s? 'O most benevolent earl, what purity, what renown, what sanctity will you receive by divine reward in the kingdom of God, for the happy care with which you struggle indefatigably to purify, enlighten and sanctify the church of God by a fitting government [*idoneum regimen*].' *Idoneum regimen*. That was as necessary in the 1250s in secular as it was in ecclesiastical affairs, and, of course, the two were closely connected. Marsh himself linked together the 'honour of God' and the 'public utility' [*utilitatem publicam*] on which the salvation of souls depended. The earl of Leicester, he declared, 'burned with an ardent desire' for both.[87] The religious light in which Simon indeed looked on one of the major concerns of the reform movement, that of how magnates treated those subject to their own courts and officials, is clear from his will, drawn up in January 1259. There he expressed anxieties lest he might have oppressed 'the poor people

---

[85] *Ann. Mon.*, i. 459. See Powicke's eloquent comments in *Henry III*, i. 390–1.
[86] *Ann. Mon.*, iii. 226; *Lanercost*, p. 74; see also *Oxenedes*, p. 201. The crusading element in the baronial movement is the theme of a forthcoming paper by Dr R. C. Stacey.
[87] *Mon. Franciscana*, pp. 264, 225; Bémont, *Simon de Montfort* (English edn), pp. 44–5.

of my land' and ordered reparations to be made through the counsels of Adam Marsh and Richard Gravesend, bishop of Lincoln.[88]

There is no simple way, therefore, to explain the extraordinary force of Simon's commitment to the common enterprise. It certainly contained elements of self-interest and opportunism. It may equally have owed something to political ideas and religious zeal. That Simon himself saw any inconsistency between his personal aims and adherence to the enterprise seems doubtful. It was the purpose of the movement to do justice to him, just as much as to anyone else. But perhaps there was also one further factor. Was not Montfort, in the last analysis, more like Becket than Grosseteste? All three displayed a righteous inflexibility in matters which most concerned them. But it is with Becket and Montfort that this seems inseparable from arrogance, pride and personal animosity. Simon's relations with the king are a case in point. The two men possessed piety in common, but little else. Henry had a heart of wax, Simon one of steel. 'It would be well if he [Henry] was taken and kept apart as was done with Charles the Simple.' The terrible and prophetic words which Simon hurled at Henry during the débâcle at Saintes in 1242 exposed the nature of relations between the two men. They were words recalled bitterly by the king nearly twenty years later.[89] Simon had a basic contempt for Henry's limited abilities and perverse policies. It must have been immensely frustrating to be dependent on such a man, and immensely humiliating to suffer defeat at his hands. Here was a king who had insulted Simon in 1239, failed to support him as seneschal of Gascony and, instead of giving him patronage, had bestowed it on those far less close and deserving. No wonder Simon was passionately attached to a form of government which kept control of affairs out of Henry's hands.[90]

Simon had an equally self-righteous contempt for those who faltered in support of the common enterprise. 'I do not care to live amongst people so fickle and deceitful', he told Richard de Clare in 1259. Likewise in 1263 he declared that he would 'never surrender to perjurers and renegades'. The chronicler Thomas Wykes reported similar sentiments: 'he considered the magnates of the kingdom vacillating and easily changeable and did not shame to call them inconstant.'[91] From this point of view, Simon was out to demonstrate one thing: whatever others might do, *he* would not give way. This was a rectitude in which pride and principle were inseparable.

Simon de Montfort was a man apart. Most politicians in the thirteenth,

[88] Bémont, *Simon de Montfort* (English edn), pp. 277–8. This passage was kindly drawn to my attention by Dr Maddicott.
[89] Bémont, *Simon de Montfort*, p. 341. For good measure, Simon added that the houses with barred windows at Windsor would be good for keeping the king in.
[90] It was doubtless the embarrassment of being with the king and the restrictions placed upon his own style by the protocol of the court which explain Simon's absence from court in 1264–5; see above, n. 7. Much the same pattern reappeared with Thomas of Lancaster and Edward II: Maddicott, *Thomas of Lancaster*, pp. 331–2.
[91] *Chron. Maj.*, v. 744; *Ann. Mon.*, iii. 226; ibid., iv. 160.

as in other centuries, were prepared to compromise and change course, often for the best of reasons. Simon was not for turning. There was no dapple about him, only bright light. While he retained the support of his closest followers, he lost that of the majority of the magnates. It was never easy to work with him for long. At the root of Simon's fiery tenacity lay a basic contempt for those less resolute and principled than himself, a boundless confidence in his own ability, especially as a soldier, and a consequent readiness to carry matters to the extreme of war. People of this stamp do not enter English politics very often. When they do, one admires the power of their will but deplores the discord that often results from it.

12

The Lord Edward's Oath to Aid and Counsel
Simon de Montfort, 15 October 1259

MORE THAN A hundred years ago the French scholar Charles Bémont published his celebrated biography of Simon de Montfort. In an appendix, Bémont printed the texts of over fifty documents connected with Simon's career.[1] Many of these came from a volume preserved in the Bibliothèque Nationale in Paris, Clairambault 1188. This was put together in the early eighteenth century by the historian Pierre Clairambault, and contains both copies and originals of many documents concerned with Simon and his family. One document from this collection, surviving as a copy, which Bémont did not print, was the letter of 15 October 1259 in which the Lord Edward swore to give aid and counsel to Simon de Montfort, earl of Leicester. Edward's oath throws light on the careers of both Simon and himself at an important moment. Bémont, however, confined himself to a partial summary of the contents of the letter and a short quotation from it.[2] He made no reference at all to significant parts of Edward's oath, and these appear to be unknown to historians. The brevity of his summary has given rise to other confusions.[3] The purpose of this note is to publish the text for the first time. Opportunity is also taken to print a related document from the same period: a writ of the Lord Edward of 21 August 1259.[4]

Since Bémont in his biography gave a long description of Clairambault 1188 little need be said about it here.[5] A note by Clairambault against the first document copied on folio 2 states: 'Cet extrait fait sur les originaux communiquez par Monseigneur le duc de Chevreuse au mois de janvier 1708'.[6] The scribe who worked on folio 2 was responsible for all the documents copied between folios 2 and 16v, 18 and 26v, and 29 and 34v, including the oath of 15 October which is on folio 13.[7] Probably, therefore, the text of the oath and most of the other records copied by the scribe had come from the duke de Chevreuse, who

---

[1] C. Bémont, *Simon de Montfort* (Paris, 1884), pp. 263–380.

[2] The summary and quotation are in the second, English edition of the biography: C. Bémont, *Simon de Montfort*, trans. E. F. Jacob (Oxford, 1930), p. 173 and n. 3.

[3] Thus R. F. Treharne, *The Baronial Plan of Reform, 1258–63* (Manchester, 1932), p. 164 n. 4 states that Henry of Almain, John de Warenne and Roger of Leybourne swore with Edward, whereas in fact they merely sealed the letter with him. For comment on Edward's oath, see F. M. Powicke, *King Henry III and the Lord Edward* (1 vol. in 2, Oxford, 1947), pp. 407–8; *idem, The Thirteenth Century* (Oxford, 1953), p. 154; M. W. Labarge, *Simon de Montfort* (1962), pp. 178–9.

[4] The reference to this document, British Library, Additional MS. 35179 fo. 89v, was brought to my notice through the kindness of Dr. J. R. Studd.

[5] Bémont, *Simon de Montfort* (1930), pp. xiii–xvi.

[6] *Ibid.*, p. xv n. 3. It should be noted that the words Bémont quotes as preceding 'Cet extrait . . .', 'Liasse cotée Prieuré de Montfort', are on fo. 1 and are thus quite separate from the passage beginning 'Cet extrait . . .' which is on fo. 2.

[7] The oath of the seven confederates of 12 Apr. 1258 (Bémont, *Simon de Montfort* (1884), p. 327) is in the hand of this scribe.

then held the lordship of Montfort and had entered, so Bémont tells us, 'as a matter of course into possession of its archives'.[8] At some point the documents taken out of England in 1265–6 by Simon de Montfort's sons and widow had clearly passed into the hands of the senior branch of the family and had thereafter descended with its muniments. In respect of the oath of October 1259 Clairambault's scribe makes clear that he is working from the original document.[9] However, it is likely that he made several errors in his transcription and these are indicated in the notes to the text which is printed in the Appendix.

Bémont revealed only the part of Edward's oath in which the prince swore to aid and counsel Montfort, his heirs and friends in their needs against all, and was held to maintain the enterprise made by the barons of the land, and not to make war on anyone involved in it.[10] The clause concerning the enterprise of the barons has been seen, probably rightly, as an attempt by Simon de Montfort to bind Edward to the movement for reform of the realm which the barons had begun in May 1258, and which Edward had accepted with great reluctance.[11] Bémont, however, made no reference at all to the fact that Edward's promise not to make war on those involved in the enterprise was immediately qualified. He was not to make war on anyone 'tant cum il voudra ester al esgart de la court le Roy etee [*rectius* et en] droit fesant et droit prenant'. And, the text continues, 'si null vousist en aucune manere estre encontre lesgart de lavant dite court ou destorber que droitture ne fust tenue de soi meismes ou dautre par cel saremant somes tenus de efforcier celui ou ceus a tenir cel esgart et ce sans nul esparnier'.

It is difficult to be certain about the meaning and intention of this part of Edward's oath. Perhaps that is why Bémont did not mention it. The sentiment that one should 'do justice and accept justice' ('droit fesant et droit prenant') is found in other oaths of alliance in 1258–9.[12] But there are no parallels to these words being expanded into a long passage which allowed the oath-taker to make war on anyone involved in the enterprise of the barons who refused to accept the

---

[8] *Ibid.*, p. xv. Bémont makes some rather confusing remarks about the connections between Clairambault 1188 and Clairambault's contemporary, the collector Roger Gaignières (*ibid.*, pp. xv n. 3, xiii n. 2, facing pp. 37, 285–7). The point cannot be discussed in detail here, but the present writer suspects that the only parts of Clairambault 1188 associated with Gaignières are fos. 1–1v, 90–96v which were once numbered consecutively. The documents copied here are in hands found in other volumes in the Bibliothèque from the Gaignières collection. In respect of the documents from the duke de Chevreuse, there seems no reason why these should not have come to Clairambault direct from the duke. Probably the originals in Clairambault 1188 are those Clairambault acquired from the duke (copies and originals are mutually exclusive). For Gaignières and Clairambault (normally spelt thus rather than Bémont's 'Clairembault'), see L. Delisle, *Le Cabinet des Manuscrits de la Bibliothèque Impériale (Nationale)* (3 vols., Paris, 1868–81), i. 335–56, ii. 18–25.

[9] See below n. 67.

[10] Bémont, *Simon de Montfort* (1930), p. 173 and n. 3. For Bémont's actual words, see below n. 62.

[11] Bémont, *Simon de Montfort* (1930), p. 173; Powicke, *Thirteenth Century*, p. 154. The words in Edward's oath describing the enterprise made by the barons of the land 'al onor de Dieu et au profit du Roy et de ses hoiers et du Royaume' echoed those in the oath taken under the Provisions of Oxford by the 24 *fideles* chosen to reform the state of the realm, who swore to reform the realm 'al honur de Deu, e a la lei le rei, e al profit del reaume' (*Documents of the Baronial Movement of Reform and Rebellion, 1258–67*, comp. R. F. Treharne, ed. I. J. Sanders (Oxford, 1973), p. 100; Powicke, *Thirteenth Century*, p. 154 n. 2 (where this is pointed out).

[12] In the oath taken by the earl of Gloucester in March 1259 to aid and counsel the Lord Edward, the phrase is exactly the same: 'dreit fesant e dreit pernant [*sic*]' (Hist. MSS. Comm., *Middleton MSS.*, p. 68). In the oath to be taken by all men in Oct. 1258 it is 'droit fesant et prenant' (*Documents of the Baronial Movement*, p. 116 (mistranslated on p. 117)). In the oath taken by the seven confederate barons in Apr. 1258 there is 'droit feisant' followed by 'et prenant kanke nos porrons, senz mesfeire' (Bémont, *Simon de Montfort* (1884), p. 327; see also *Documents of the Baronial Movement*, p. 100).

esgart (award, decision, judgment)[13] of the king's court, and which, indeed, committed him to use force to secure the implementation of such *esgarts*. The wish to state platitudes about respect for justice can hardly explain these unusual clauses, clauses after all which indicated disrespect for the proper legal procedures for the enforcement of *esgarts* of the king's court.

One hypothesis might be that the *esgart* passage should be seen simply as a saving clause appended to Edward's promise not to make war on anyone involved in the enterprise of the barons. He may still make war on anyone who refuses to accept the *esgart* of the king's court. This qualification makes sense against the background of Edward's private affairs. By October 1259 it is probable that Edward was seriously at odds with one leading member of the baronial enterprise: Richard de Clare, earl of Gloucester. In March 1259 the two had come to terms when Gloucester had sworn to help Edward secure possession of his lands and castles. Any disputes arising from the agreement were to be decided by *l'agard* of named arbitrators.[14] If, as seems likely, this agreement quickly collapsed, by October 1259 Edward may have anticipated some *esgart* of the king's court, rather than of the March arbitrators, to settle his differences with Clare. (One of these arose from the latter's claim to Edward's castle of Bristol.)[15] Simon wished to hold Edward in check until such an *esgart* was pronounced, but then, if Clare resisted it, Edward might make war. There is, however, a problem with this hypothesis as an explanation of the whole *esgart* section. We need to link the permission given to Edward to make war with the next sentence which goes on actually to compel him to enforce *esgarts* of the king's court. If the *esgarts* in question were solely those in Edward's favour this seems an unnecessary stipulation since it did no more than compel Edward to act on his own behalf. The clause makes much more sense if the *esgarts* which Edward was bound to enforce were to be in favour, not of himself, but of Simon de Montfort or some third party.

A case could be made for saying that *esgarts* in favour of third parties were indeed envisaged. In 1258–9 there were strong feelings that the enterprise of the barons should be concerned with the abuses of the magnates in the administration of their own estates and liberties. This issue came to a head at the Westminster parliament in October 1259, at the very time that Simon and Edward were negotiating their agreement in London. On 13 October, at the parliament, 'the community of the bachelry of England', probably an *ad hoc* group of knights and gentry, protested that the barons had looked after only their own interests. It then pressed successfully for the promulgation of the Provisions of Westminster which, amongst other things, imposed restrictions on the jurisdiction of the magnates' private courts, and inaugurated a new eyre of justices with power to hear and determine complaints against the magnates and their officials.[16] There were, however, grounds for fearing that some magnates

---

[13] For the use of *esgart* in these senses, see *Anglo-Norman Dictionary*, ed. L. W. Stone and others, fasc. i (1977), p. 16; fasc. ii (1981), p. 260; for the Latin version *awardum* see *Revised Medieval Latin Word List*, ed. R. E. Latham (1965), p. 40; see also *Royal and other Historical Letters Illustrative of the Reign of Henry III*, ed. W. W. Shirley (2 vols., Rolls Ser., 1862–8), ii. 68; *Britton*, ed. F. M. Nichols (2 vols., Oxford, 1865), i. 291. I would like to thank Dr. Ian Short of Westfield College, and Dr. Richard Sharpe of the Medieval Latin Dictionary for help with the meaning of *esgart*.

[14] Hist. MSS. Comm., *Middleton MSS.*, pp. 67–9.

[15] Treharne, pp. 193, 164, though the reconstruction here is to some extent conjectural; M. Altschul, *A Baronial Family in Medieval England: the Clares, 1217–1314* (Baltimore, Md., 1965), pp. 26–8, 77. For an indication that Edward and Gloucester had quarrelled by July 1259, see below.

[16] *Annales Monastici*, ed. H. R. Luard (5 vols., Rolls Ser., 1864–9), i. 471; E. F. Jacob, *Studies in the Period of Baronial Reform and Rebellion, 1258–67* (Oxford, 1925), pp. 106–21, 126–34.

might obstruct the execution of the *esgarts*, the judgments, being passed against themselves and their officials in the courts of the king. Suspicions of this kind had already prompted the Ordinances of the Magnates of February 1259 in which the fifteen councillors set up by the Provisions of Oxford proclaimed that they would not hinder the justiciar, or anyone else appointed by the king, from redressing the wrongs which they and their bailiffs had committed.[17] There is evidence that Montfort was an enthusiastic protagonist of this measure, and the earl of Gloucester, protective of his uniquely large network of private courts and officials, its opponent. When, according to Matthew Paris, Simon furiously rebuked Gloucester for wavering in his support of proposed plans of reform, the plans in question were probably the Ordinances of February 1259.[18] The phraseology of Edward's oath has echoes of that of the Ordinances: both use the word *destorber* in the context of the obstruction of justice.[19] Conceivably, then, in October 1259 Simon de Montfort was thinking of the judgments which had been and were to be passed against magnates and their officials. Aware that the execution of such judgments might be resisted, he enlisted Edward to help enforce them.

It is impossible, however, to feel confident that this is the correct explanation of the *esgart* clauses. Did Simon really envisage Edward executing judgments against magnates like some extra arm of the law? The concept seems both bizarre and impractical. Was, moreover, the issue of magnate behaviour at the forefront of Montfort's mind in October 1259? The earl of Leicester may have advocated the Ordinances of the previous February, but for the next seven months he was out of England.[20] He can have played little part in the discussions which paved the way for the legislation passed at the Westminster parliament in October.[21] Although Montfort was probably present at the beginning of this parliament he is not mentioned in connection with the incident of the community of the bachelry; the latter's protest was made to Edward, Gloucester and other unspecified members of the council; the protest was taken up by Edward.[22] After Montfort had finalized his agreement with Edward—the letter containing the prince's oath was 'made' in London on 15 October—he must have left England immediately. He was, therefore, absent when the Provisions of Westminster were finally promulgated on 24 October.[23] The fact is that at this time Simon seems chiefly preoccupied with his private affairs. In all probability the *esgart* clauses are best seen against that background. There is a pointer to this conclusion in the form of Edward's oath. Simon binds the prince to enforce *esgarts* of the king's court. As we have seen, this makes it unlikely that the *esgarts* in question were those in favour of Edward. It also makes it unlikely that they were to be those given on behalf of a third party. For, if Simon was concerned about such judgments the oath might well have stressed that he would act with Edward to secure their implementation, just as Edward was held to maintain the enterprise of the barons 'ensemblemant aveques l'avant dit Conte et aveques ses hoiers et aveques ses amis'. Instead, when it comes to *esgarts* of the king's court, Edward is

[17] *Documents of the Baronial Movement*, pp. 130–5. The twelve appointed by the community to represent it at parliament joined with the council of fifteen in making this proclamation.
[18] *Matthaei Parisiensis, monachi sancti Albani Chronica Majora*, ed. H. R. Luard (7 vols., Rolls Ser., 1872–83), v. 744; Jacob, pp. 84–6.
[19] *Documents of the Baronial Movement*, p. 132.
[20] Bémont, *Simon de Montfort* (1930), p. 173.
[21] I owe this point to Dr. J. R. Maddicott.
[22] *Annales Monastici*, i. 471.
[23] Treharne, p. 167; compare *Documents of the Baronial Movement*, pp. 205, cl. 26, and 151, cl. 4 (a reference I owe to Dr. J. R. Maddicott).

alone. If, then, he is not swearing to enforce *esgarts* delivered either in his own favour or in that of some third party, he can only be swearing to enforce *esgarts* pronounced in favour of Simon himself.

This conclusion is strengthened if we now turn to consider Simon's private affairs. The fact is that in October 1259 the earl of Leicester had a pressing personal interest in an *esgart* of the king's court to whose execution there might indeed be considerable resistance. Simon and Eleanor, his wife, sister of Henry III, had longstanding grievances against the king. During 1259 they tried to extract a settlement from Henry by withholding Eleanor's consent to clauses in the treaty of peace being negotiated with the king of France, clauses in which Eleanor renounced her claims to the lands to be ceded by the king of England. Since Louis IX of France was reluctant to conclude the treaty without this renunciation, the Montforts' bargaining position was strong.[24] In July 1259 Henry and the Montforts submitted their dispute to arbitrators, who were to declare their award ('mise') by 1 November.[25] From Simon's point of view, it was important that Louis IX continued to demand Eleanor's renunciation. Otherwise there was little pressure on the arbitrators to proceed with their task. In October 1259, however, Montfort found himself in difficulties on this point. On 13 October in London a letter was 'given' in which Henry III's councillors, including Simon, announced that they had sworn, in the presence of the envoys of the king of France, to accept a form of the peace treaty which omitted the clauses in which the countess of Leicester renounced her claims. On the face of it Louis IX was no longer insisting on her renunciation: Montfort had lost his powerful lever.[26] Simon, however, now moved with speed. Having concluded his pact with Edward on 15 October he hurried from England, although parliament remained in session at Westminster. On 19 October Simon was with Louis IX at Evreux in Normandy.[27] Doubtless he brought the news that the treaty in its new form had been ratified. He also ensured that Louis still required the quit claim from the countess. To that end he may now have made clear that he was indeed claiming Eleanor's share in all the overseas territories of King John, a claim that made it essential for Louis to obtain her renunciation.[28] Certainly the French king continued to demand it. Although the renunciation clauses remained out of

[24] Labarge, pp. 40–3, 156–8; P. Chaplais, 'The making of the Treaty of Paris (1259) and the royal style', *Eng. Hist. Rev.*, lxvii (1952), 235–53, here 244–7; *Documents of the Baronial Movement*, pp. 195–203.

[25] *Treaty Rolls in the Public Record Office*, i, ed. P. Chaplais (1955), nos. 113–15; B.N., MS. Clairambault 1188 fo. 15.

[26] *Layettes du Trésor des Chartes*, iii, ed. J. de Laborde (Paris, 1875), no. 4555; Chaplais, p. 246. During the summer Henry, trying to get round the Montfort problem, sent Louis IX a draft of the treaty without the renunciation clauses (*ibid.*, pp. 244–5). In October Louis IX's envoys probably indicated that their master was ready to accept the treaty in this form. Montfort, in his capacity as a councillor, could not refuse to accept this offer.

[27] *Recueil des Historiens des Gaules et de la France*, xxiii (Paris, 1894), p. 467. It has been questioned whether Simon was really in London on and before 15 Oct. However, it is difficult to believe that the pact with Edward could have been arranged without his presence, which is also suggested by the fact that he is named with the other councillors as swearing to the treaty of peace in the letter 'given' on 13 Oct. He also sealed this letter (Powicke, *Henry III and the Lord Edward*, p. 408; Labarge, pp. 178–9; *Layettes*, iii, no. 4555).

[28] This possibility was suggested to me by Dr. J. R. Maddicott. In his complaints against Montfort in 1260, Henry III appears to distinguish between (i) Montfort 'putting it into the mind' of the king of France that a renunciation should be asked from the countess, and (ii) Montfort's demand for his wife's share of all the overseas territories of King John. Henry alleged that Simon made the latter demand from the envoys of Louis IX. These may have been the envoys in whose presence in Oct. 1259 was sworn the form of the treaty without the renunciation clauses (*Documents of the Baronial Movement*, pp. 194, cl. 5, and 204, cl. 22; *Layettes*, iii, no. 4555).

the treaty, Louis neither published it nor received Henry III's homage until he received, in a separate letter, Eleanor's quittance of her claims.[29]

At the time, therefore, when the Lord Edward swore his oath, the earl of Leicester was looking forward to the settlement of his complaints against the king. He was determined to maintain his bargaining strength in order to secure it.[30] It would not be surprising if, in Edward's oath, he anticipated the difficulties of executing such a settlement once it was pronounced. These difficulties were formidable. By July 1259 the chief complaint of the earl and countess was that the latter had never received her full dower from the lands of her first husband, William Marshal, earl of Pembroke.[31] As a result, they asserted she had suffered, and was suffering, an annual loss of 1,400 marks. The Montforts' demand, as put to the arbitrators in July, was that the king should compensate Eleanor for the arrears of her dower, which amounted to the vast sum of 36,400 marks. As for the future, the king should either render the countess so much that she should have 1,400 marks annually or Henry should 'cause the dower to be delivered to her' ('ou que il lur face le devant [dit] doeyre deliuerer').[32] Two suggestions may be offered as to how a mise of these arbitrators was related to the *esgart* of the king's court described in Edward's oath.

One form of mise might be that in which the king was told to give the Montforts a sum in lieu of the arrears of the dower, and an annual pension for the future, which could perhaps be converted into land from wardships or escheats. Such an award could be executed only with the counsel and consent of the council of fifteen imposed on the king by the Provisions of Oxford in 1258. These councillors had indeed taken an oath to accept the mise of the July arbitrators, and cause it to be 'held and accomplished'.[33] Acting in a quasi-judicial capacity in carrying out the mise, as they had agreed, the king and

---

[29] Eleanor made her renunciations on 4 Dec. and the treaty was published and Henry's homage taken on the same day (Chaplais, pp. 246–7; *Documents of the Baronial Movement*, p. 202, nos. 19–21). For the future of the Montforts' award, see below n. 30.

[30] Since the arbitrators were supposed to declare their award by 1 Nov. Simon may have wished to let them know by then that Louis IX was still demanding Eleanor's renunciation. That it was recognized in England that Simon still could make trouble is suggested by a concession to him on 20 Oct. and the tone of the king's letter on 24 Oct. (*Calendar of Patent Rolls 1258–66*, p. 46; *Close Rolls 1256–9*, p. 456 (I owe this point to Dr. J. R. Maddicott)). Nonetheless, according to Henry III in 1260, although the arbitrators were ready to make their award by 1 Nov., they were persuaded by Montfort's friends (Simon himself having remained in France) not to do so: presumably the friends thought Simon would not like the contents. (For some explanation of this, see below n. 40.) After 1 Nov. the authority of the arbitrators expired, and it was necessary to renew it or make a fresh start. Simon must now have realized that he could not delay the French peace any longer. He therefore settled for a compromise in which Eleanor made her renunciation in return for a different means of putting pressure on Henry III to reach a settlement: Louis IX kept back 15,000 marks due to Henry under the treaty until the Montforts' complaints had been satisfied (*Documents of the Baronial Movement*, pp. 200–2, nos. 14–16, 19–21; Chaplais, p. 247). For later attempts to reach a settlement, see Bémont, *Simon de Montfort* (1930), p. 196 n. 3. Although Powicke did not know of the *esgart* clauses in Edward's oath, he commented of Simon that: 'His main object at this time [in Oct. 1259] was to link the recognition of his wife's claims to dower with the ratification of the peace with King Louis, and his alliance with Edward undoubtedly had this object in view' (Powicke, *Henry III and the Lord Edward*, p. 408).

[31] By July 1259 a partial settlement had been reached of Montfort's other major grievance, namely the king's failure to transform his annual pension into land held in fee (*Charter Rolls*, ii. 18, 20).

[32] *Treaty Rolls*, no. 120; see also *Cal. Pat. Rolls 1258–66*, pp. 25–6.

[33] *Documents of the Baronial Movement*, p. 102, no. 7; *Treaty Rolls*, nos. 113–15. The grants of manors to Montfort in July 1259 in place of his annual pension were made by the counsel and consent of the magnates of the council who all witnessed the charters embodying the grants (*Charter Rolls*, ii. 20; B.N., MS. Clairambault 1188 fo. 13).

his council could well be called the court of the king.[34] Their consequent award of money or land to the Montforts seems aptly described by the word *esgart*. Montfort, however, knew that it was one thing for the king's court to pronounce such an *esgart*, quite another to get it implemented. If the grant of arrears approached anywhere near 36,400 marks it would have to be paid in instalments over several years. The payment of the annual 1,400 marks stretched out for the rest of Eleanor's life. If it was to be converted into wardships or escheats, the Montforts could monopolize much of what the king had to offer for some time to come. At any point, Simon must have feared, a hostile group on the council might turn off this tap of patronage, thus reneging on the *esgart* of the king's court.

Another form of mise would be that in which the arbitrators adopted the alternative suggested by the Montforts, and decided that Henry should 'cause the dower to be delivered' to Eleanor. For the king this would be a far less expensive award, but one very difficult to put into effect. The last Marshal earl had died in 1245 and his lands were divided amongst co-heirs who included many of the greatest barons in England.[35] Henry could not simply disseize these men of land to make up Eleanor's dower. Instead, he would have to begin a legal process against them, a process which, if completed, would end precisely in a judgment, an *esgart*, of the court of the king. Such an *esgart* would equally be the conclusion if the arbitrators decided that Simon himself, rather than the king, should sue the heirs for Eleanor's dower. This is what the king had told him to do before 1258, and Simon had brought cases on two occasions against the heirs, though on neither was judgment passed: with the pressure which he could now exert, Simon could hope for better results.[36]

If, however, the Marshal heirs were ordered to disgorge land and money to the Montforts would they do so? Simon was bound to anticipate resistance, resistance which could come precisely from those involved in the enterprise of the barons. There were two Marshal heirs, the earl of Winchester and Humphrey de Bohun, eldest son of the earl of Hereford, amongst the twelve chosen to represent the community of the realm at parliament. There were three Marshal heirs on the council of fifteen, the earl of Gloucester, his ally the earl of Norfolk,[37] and Roger Mortimore, later at any rate one of Montfort's fiercest enemies.[38] Perhaps above all Montfort expected trouble from the earl of Gloucester. Quite apart from their quarrel over the plans of reform in February

---

[34] Although in Henry's reign a staff of professional judges developed to hear cases *coram rege*, judgments and decisions in such cases were frequently given by the king and his council (see *Curia Regis Rolls*, xvi, nos. 8, 83, 1625; Public Record Office, KB 26/146 m. 10d and KB 26/152 m. 1; Jacob, pp. 378, 208–9, 220–1). For the later history of the council as a court, see *Select Cases before the King's Council*, ed. I. S. Leadam and J. F. Baldwin (Selden Soc., xxxv, 1918), pp. xv–xx.

[35] *Cal. Pat. Rolls 1364–7*, pp. 263–75.

[36] Bémont, *Simon de Montfort* (1884), p. 335; P.R.O., KB 26/159 mm. 2d–3d.

[37] *Middleton MSS.*, p. 68.

[38] However, William de Valence, a Marshal heir in right of his wife Joan de Monte Canisio, was outside the enterprise of the barons. In 1247–8 the Montforts had claimed that it was with lands in Pembroke, the Monte Canisio share of the Marshal inheritance, that Eleanor had been dowered (P.R.O., KB 26/159 mm. 2d, 3, 3d). Since neither William de Valence (though expelled from England) nor his wife had been sentenced to forfeiture in 1258, the other Marshal heirs would have had to compensate them if Eleanor's dower had been formed exclusively from their lands. How strong the Montfort claim to lands in Pembroke was we cannot say. There was bound to be opposition to Montfort's establishment as a power in South Wales. Simon probably thought a more likely verdict was that all the heirs should contribute directly to the dower, thus giving the Montforts a scattering of estates. In the summer of 1259 Simon had accepted a scattered collection of manors in place of his annual money pension.

1259, Gloucester had been enraged by Simon's refusal of Eleanor's renunciation.[39] Whatever, therefore, the precise form of the arbitrators' award, Montfort had reason for engaging Edward to compel compliance with *esgarts* of the king's court.[40]

What then can we glean from Edward's oath about Montfort's attitudes and ambitions in October 1259? Certainly his commitment to the enterprise of the barons is clear. In the accord of March 1259 between Edward and Gloucester there is merely a perfunctory clause at the end stating that the agreement was made saving the oath taken by the original twenty-four reformers in 1258.[41] By contrast, in Edward's oath of October 1259, Simon positively bound the prince to maintain the enterprise made by the barons of the land. In addition, Edward was not to disrupt the movement by making war on anyone involved in it, unless that person disregarded *esgarts* of the king's court. Up to that point, far from encouraging Edward to attack the earl of Gloucester or other members of the enterprise, Simon was holding him back. Edward's oath, therefore, may be taken with Montfort's dispute with Gloucester the previous February as evidence that as early as 1259 Montfort was strongly attached to the baronial enterprise. Against that background his subsequent emergence as its leader falls into place.

At the same time, however, the oath reveals Simon's preoccupation with his private affairs. Indeed, if we are right in thinking that the *esgarts* that Edward was bound to enforce were those in Montfort's own favour, the earl is open to the charge of placing his private concerns above the common good of the baronial enterprise. That might be even clearer had we the text of the oath which Simon swore to Edward. If, as is not unlikely, this was the exact counterpart of Edward's, then Simon too was allowed to make war on anyone involved in the enterprise who refused to accept *esgarts* of the king's court. Montfort, therefore, was impatient of the proper legal procedures for the enforcement of such decisions—in the first instance distraint by the sheriff—and emancipated both himself and Edward from them. The consequence had he and Edward acted under the terms of their agreement, and made war on, for example, the Marshal heirs, would surely have been the utter destruction of the enterprise of the barons.

We may be sure, however, that if the charge of setting private above public good had been put to Simon, he would have rejected it with contempt as he rejected every other accusation: 'il fere nul tort' he would have said. He might well have argued that for him and Edward to make war in support of *esgarts* of the king's court was perfectly compatible with the baronial enterprise. Under the terms of the common oath devised at Oxford in June 1258 everyone was to swear to 'do justice': anyone contravening the 'common oath' was to be treated as a 'mortal enemy'.[42] Someone, therefore, who refused to accept justice in the shape of *esgarts* of the king's court was surely a 'mortal enemy' on whom one might make war. But Montfort may have appreciated that his agreement with Edward could leave him open to criticism, and perhaps this explains its curious vagueness.[43] In Edward's oath the measures that he may take are open and

[39] *Chronica Majora*, v. 744–5.

[40] The interests likely to be disturbed by any award decisively in Montfort's favour may help to explain why, even with the pressures he could bring to bear in Oct. 1259, he was unable to obtain one (see above n. 30). Since the arbitrators were the earls of Norfolk and Hereford, and Philip Basset, the Marshal heirs were well represented (*Treaty Rolls*, no. 120).

[41] *Middleton MSS.*, p. 69.

[42] *Documents of the Baronial Movement*, p. 100, no. 4, and p. 116.

[43] The failure of Edward's oath to specify Montfort's needs and interests was pointed out to me by Dr. P. A. Brand.

naked: he may make war, but the occasions when he may, or indeed must do so, are hidden behind the meaning of the *esgarts* of the king's court. This contrasts with the agreement between Edward and Gloucester in March 1259. There the occasions on which Gloucester is to help Edward are specific: he is to help him recover his lands and castles, but the means he will use to do so are left vague. There is no talk of his making war: Gloucester merely promises to aid Edward 'a tut nostre poer'.[44] Simon, with typical extremism, wanted more than that from Edward, and for himself; but aware that he might be charged with destroying the enterprise for the sake of his private interests, he was careful not to specify the latter in the text of the oath. Instead they were camouflaged by the *esgarts* of the king's court. Simon de Montfort's agreement with Edward, therefore, illustrates several of the major characteristics of his career: his commitment to the enterprise of the barons; his cultivation of his private interests; his concern for his public reputation; and his confidence in the use of force.

Looking at the agreement from Edward's point of view, what did he expect from his alliance with Montfort?[45] Assuming that Simon's oath was the counterpart of Edward's, then Edward, on his side, bound Montfort to enforce *esgarts* of the king's court. As we have seen, Edward may particularly have anticipated an *esgart* to settle his differences with the earl of Gloucester. Beyond this, Edward wanted Simon's aid to free him from the fetters of the enterprise of the barons. By 1259 that meant above all freedom from the control which the council of fifteen was exercising over Edward's appointments.[46] This was, in all probability, what the earl of Gloucester was promising in March 1259 when he swore to help Edward have his castles and lands 'in his hands and in his power'.[47] However, in July 1259 there is evidence that the council, led by the earl of Gloucester, forced Edward to appoint Robert Walerand to the custody of Bristol.[48] With the backing of Montfort and his party on the council, Edward hoped to be rid of such restraints.[49] Some of the mutual interests which brought Simon and Edward together will be clear from the previous discussion. Both had differences with the earl of Gloucester; both may have anticipated his resistance to *esgarts* of the king's court. Next year the divisions between Montfort and Edward on the one side and Gloucester and the king on the other brought the country to the brink of civil war. In addition, both Simon and Edward, for different reasons, were making difficulties over the peace with France.[50] As for

[44] *Middleton MSS.*, p. 68.

[45] The best analysis of Edward's position in 1259–60 is contained in H. W. Ridgeway, 'The politics of the English royal court, 1247–65, with special reference to the role of the aliens' (unpublished University of Oxford D. Phil. thesis, 1983), pp. 336–61.

[46] For this control, see *Cal. Pat. Rolls 1247–58*, p. 654; *Close Rolls 1256–9*, p. 330; *Cal. Pat. Rolls 1258–66*, p. 1 (see also T. Rymer, *Foedera*, ed. A. Clarke, F. Holbrooke and J. Caley (4 vols. in 7, 1816–69) i. i. 374; *Close Rolls 1256–9*, p. 350).

[47] *Middleton MSS.*, p. 68.

[48] *Joannis Lelandi Antiquarii de Rebus Britannicis Collectanea* (2nd edn., 6 vols., 1770), i. 243–4 (a reference given to me by Dr. J. R. Maddicott); *Cal. Pat. Rolls 1258–66*, pp. 29, 32, 63–4; P.R.O., C 53/49 m. 4 which shows that Gloucester and ten other members of the council of fifteen attested a royal charter on 20 July and were thus at court; P.R.O., C 61/4 m. 4 for Edward's dismissal of Walerand on 7 Dec. 1259 and his replacement by Roger of Leybourne.

[49] Simon had at least three allies in the council: the bishop of Worcester, Peter de Montfort and Richard de Grey (*Documents of the Baronial Movement*, p. 200, no. 16).

[50] This point was suggested to me by Dr. J. R. Maddicott. For Edward see *The Historical Works of Gervase of Canterbury*, ed. W. Stubbs (2 vols., Rolls Ser., 1879–80), ii. 209–10 where it is said that Edward blamed Gloucester for procuring the peace treaty. Probably Edward feared that the treaty would enable the king of France to interfere in Gascony.

the enterprise of the barons, Simon accepted that its supervision of Edward's appointments should cease. In return, Edward swore to maintain the enterprise:[51] that meant above all supporting the conciliar control of the king imposed by the Provisions of Oxford. Edward and Simon could also agree that the enterprise should be concerned with the way magnates ran their private administrations. Montfort had supported the Ordinances of February 1259; Edward backed the community of the bachelry in October. They thus won popularity with county society, and perhaps embarrassed the earl of Gloucester.

In co-operating with the community of the bachelry, however, Edward had a problem. Before 1258 he and his followers had been notorious for their arrogant and lawless conduct.[52] The interest of the second document printed below is that it shows Edward's answer to this situation.[53] By August 1259 the prince was clearly anxious to cleanse his evil reputation, aware of the damage which it could do to his power and popularity. In the writ of 21 August Edward instructed his justiciar of Chester to ensure that 'common justice' was done in an assize of novel disseisin brought by R. de Orrebi and R. de Kautona.[54] What is striking is the preamble. It may be translated:

If, on account of the influence of any person, common justice is denied to any one of our subjects by us or by our bailiffs, we lose the favour both of God and man, and our lordship is belittled. We wish therefore that common justice shall be exhibited to everyone.

This statement probably indicated the standards of conduct that Edward inculcated throughout his private administration in the summer of 1259. He was already responding to the issue he took up with the community of bachelry in October. In so doing he exhibited the ability to react to grievances and the concern for good local government which were to be marked features of his kingship. The years 1258–60 were perhaps the most formative of Edward's life. The revolution of 1258, with its novel threats to his power and independence, forced him to cast around for support. The two documents printed here reveal different sides of this process. On the one hand, Edward made allies amongst the magnates.[55] On the other, he cultivated knights, gentry and freemen. For the first time in his life he considered his own duties and reputation. He had entered the business of winning the favour of God and man.

---

[51] Two days before his oath to Montfort Edward had told the community of the bachelry that he was ready to stand by the oath he had taken in 1258 to accept reform of the realm (*Annales Monastici*, i. 471).

[52] *Chronica Majora*, v. 539, 593–4, 598, 646.

[53] The provenance of the document is described in n. 68 below.

[54] R. de Orrebi may be the Richard de Orrebi who, in 1260, is found as Edward's chamberlain of Chester (P.R.O., C 61/4 m. 1). I have found nothing more about the assize brought by Orrebi and R. de Kautona. However, on 18 July 1259 Edward had ordered his justiciar of Chester to hear favourably the complaints of R. de Orrebi and R. de Kautona on certain transgressions done them in 'ballia vestra', and do them speedy justice, so that Edward should hear no further complaints on account of default of justice (Brit. Libr., Add. MS. 35179 fo. 89v).

[55] The three 'dear friends'—John de Warenne, earl of Surrey; Edward's cousin, Henry son of the king of the Romans; and Roger of Leybourne, who sealed the letter of 15 Oct. with Edward—were among the prince's allies whom the earl of Gloucester agreed to aid in March 1259 (*Middleton MSS.*, p. 68).

APPENDIX

1. *Bibliothèque Nationale, Paris, Clairambault 1188 fo. 13v*[56]

A tous ceus qui cest escrit ouvunt[57] ou verrunt Edward[58] fiuz einsnez le Roy de Angleterre, sachez que nos avons jure sur seinz evangiles et promis en bone foy que nos de tot nostre poer loialmant serons eidans et conseillanz a nostre cher et feal Simon de Montfort[59] Conte de Leycestre et a ses hoiers et tous ses amis de Angleterre de totes lor besognes que il ont et auront encontre tote gens a droiture sauve la foy le Roi de Angleterre et par celui meismes saremans sumes tenus ensemblemant aveques l'avant dit Conte et aveques ses hoiers et aveques ses amis a meintenir l'emprise qui est fete par les Barons de la terre al cuor[60] de Dieu et au profit du Roy et de ses hoiers et du Royaume a tot nostre poer et que nos ne surquerrons[61] ne ne guerroierons nul del emprise[62] tant cum il voudra ester al esgart de la court le Roy etee[63] droit fesant et droit prenant. Et si null vousist en aucune manere estre encontre lesgart de lavant dite court ou destorber que droitture ne fust tenue de soi meismes ou dautre par cel saremant somes tenus de efforcier celui ou ceus a tenir cel esgart et ce sans nul esparnier. Et en tesmognage de ceste chose a cest escrit avons mis nostre sael ensemblemant avec les saeus nos chers amis monsegnur Henry[64] fiuz le Roy dAlemagne et Monsegnur Jehan Conte de Warenn[65] et monsegnor Rogier de Leyborne.[66] Ceste letre fu fete a Londres le quinsime jour de Octobre l'an del regne le Roy nostre peire quarante tierz.[67]

2. *British Library, Additional MS. 35179 fo. 89v*[68]

Edwardus illustris **Regis Angliae** primogenitus dilecto et fideli suo domino R. de Monte Alto justiciario suo **Cestriae** vel eius locum gerenti salutem. Si ob favorem alicuius per nos aut ballivos nostros ius commune subditis nostris denegetur, sic a deo et ab homine gratiam amitteremus, et nostrum parvipenderetur dominium. Volentes igitur unicuique communis iusticia exibeatur, vobis mandamus firmiter et districte, iniungentes quatinus, non inpediente aliquo mandato nostro prius vobis directo, R. de Orrebi et R. de Kautona

---

[56] The spelling, punctuation and capitalization of the copyist have been retained. The comments on the text in the footnotes owe much to the advice of Dr. Ian Short.

[57] *ouvunt* should probably read *orrunt*, 'will hear'.

[58] *Edward* in large letters in MS.

[59] *de Montfort* in large letters in MS.

[60] As Powicke suggested, *cuor de Dieu* should probably read *onor de Dieu*, as in the oath of the 24 reformers in June 1258 (Powicke, *Thirteenth Century*, p. 154, n. 2).

[61] *surquerrons* means 'to make too great demands on', and by extension 'to pick a quarrel with'.

[62] Apart from mention of the sealing clauses Bémont's summary ended here: 'prince Edward swore to give [Simon de Montfort] and his heirs aid and counsel, against all men, saving their fealty due to the king. More, he promised to uphold the barons' enterprise "al cuor de Dieu et au profit du roy et de ses heiers et du royaume", and not to make war on any involved in the coalition' (Bémont, *Simon de Montfort* (1930), p. 173, Bémont's rendering of the spelling and capitalization of the MS.).

[63] *etee* should perhaps read *et en*: hence the sense 'both as regards the doing of justice and the accepting of it'.

[64] *Henry* in large letters in MS.

[65] *de Warenn* in large letters in MS.

[66] *de Leyborne* in large letters in MS.

[67] Having completed his transcript the copyist notes: 'Original en parchemin scelle de quatre sceaux'. He then describes the seals of the Lord Edward, Henry son of the king of Germany, John de Warenne, earl of Surrey, and Roger of Leybourne. There are also fine drawings of these seals.

[68] Brit. Libr., Add. MS. 35179 is a volume, written in the second half of the 13th century, containing English law codes and other legal material. These end on fo. 86. The remaining folios (86v-90v) are either blank or have miscellaneous material. On fo. 89v, in a 13th-century hand, there are copies of two writs of Henry III, the writ here printed of the Lord Edward, and another of Edward's writs referred to in n. 54 above. There are indications besides the two writs of Edward of a connection between the volume and Chester (*Catalogue of Additions to MSS. in the British Museum, 1894-9* (1901), pp. 200-2). In this edition of the letter of 21 Aug. punctuation and capitalization have been modernized, but spelling is as in the original. Dr. D. L. d'Avray has kindly helped me with the transcription.

super assisa sua nove desseisine quam arramdaverunt [?][69] per breve nostrum versus H. de Pulford' et alios de quodam molendino prostato in Crosleg' communis juris fieri faciatis complementum, nulla interveniente cavillacione[70] assisam illam capientes, et secundum recongnitionem eiusdem assise racionabile judicium exequamini et compleatis; et hoc in fide qua nobis tenemini nullatenus omittatis. Data apud Wariwic, xxi die Augusti anno regni regis patris nostri xliii.[71]

[69] The text here reads *arramd* with the *d* being followed immediately by three minims under a dash. It is difficult to see how this could be expanded into *arramdaverunt*, but that is what the context appears to require. I am grateful to Dr. Richard Sharpe for discussing this problem with me.

[70] *cavillacione* interlined in MS.

[71] I would like to thank Dr. J. R. Maddicott for reading a draft of this article. As will be evident from the footnotes I have made considerable use of his comments and suggestions. I am also grateful for the comments which were made when the article was read as a paper at Mr. J. L. Bolton's seminar at the Institute of Historical Research.

13

An Unknown Obituary of King Henry III
from the Year 1263

Once when Mark Twain was staying in London a false report spread of his death; a journalist came to his house to learn the date of the funeral. The author himself opened the door and made the now celebrated declaration, 'the report of Mark Twain's death is greatly exaggerated'. In the year 1263 King Henry III would have had the opportunity, if not perhaps the wit, to make a similar remark. Henry died on 16 November 1272. Yet in the annals of Tewkesbury abbey, under the date 23 March 1263, we find the entry 'Obiit Henricus rex Anglie, filius regis Johannis' followed by a rhyming obituary penned in different coloured inks.[1] At Tewkesbury the writing of the obituary was presumably accompanied by the tolling of bells and singing of requiem masses. The embarrassment and confusion when it was learnt that the king was still alive may be imagined. The obituary itself was crossed out and the word 'vacat', 'it is void', was placed in the margin. This curious episode has been hitherto unknown due to an inexplicable oversight by H.R. Luard when he edited the annals of Tewkesbury abbey for the Rolls Series (they were published in 1864).[2] Luard neither printed the obituary nor in any way referred to it. The text is thus published for the first time at the end of this article.

Although obituaries must always be read with caution, one of Henry III from March 1263 has a particular interest. It gives a picture of the monarch just prior to a great crisis of his reign; a month that is before Simon de Montfort, earl of Leicester, returned to England and took command of the movement which, in July, compelled the king to re-affirm the Provisions of Oxford. It was to be more than four years until peace and order were restored to the country. Before, however, we can consider the content of the obituary we must demonstrate that it was indeed occasioned by a fallacious rumour of the king's death.

The origin of the rumour may be explained without difficulty. In the summer of 1262 Henry III was seriously ill in France.[3] He returned to England in December, but for the next three months remained at Westminster in poor

---

[1] In the annals the notice of Henry's death is placed in the year 1262. However, since it is clear that Tewkesbury began the year on 25 March, this is the year 25 March 1262–24 March 1263. Henry 'died', therefore on 23 March 1263.

[2] *Annales Monastici*, ed. H.R. Luard (Rolls Ser., 1864–69), i. xv-xvii, 43–180.

[3] *Close Rolls 1261–64*, pp. 174–6; *Flores Historiarum*, ed. H.R. Luard (Rolls Ser., 1890), ii. 475. The king's illness gave rise to rumours in England about the state of his health.

health.[4] The king's illness and the uncertainty of the political situation prompted measures to secure oaths of fealty to the Lord Edward as Henry's successor. On 22 March the patent rolls record that Henry III issued a letter which ordered all and sundry, when Edward came into their area, to swear in his presence that they would faithfully adhere to the king. In addition, on Henry's death they were to maintain Edward as the king's heir and help him obtain coronation.[5] It is highly likely that in this letter of 22 March we have the origin of Tewkesbury's belief that the king died on 23 March. If a garbled version of the contents reached the abbey it would not be difficult to conclude that the king had expired. If, as seems likely, several copies of the letter were made for dispatch to different sheriffs, some may well have borne the date 23 March.

The chronicler must, of course, have written the obituary almost as soon as he heard of the king's demise. Otherwise his pen would have been stopped by the arrival of true intelligence. An inspection of the only manuscript of the Tewkesbury annals – British Library Cotton MS Cleopatra A VII, ff. 1–67v – is perfectly compatible with this thesis. The manuscript was almost certainly produced at the abbey.[6] Down to near the end of 1253 it looks like a fair copy. The same neat hand runs largely throughout.[7] After 1253 the appearance of the chronicle changes. By 1258 (that is the Tewkesbury year 25 March 1258–24 March 1259) there is an interval of at least a line between each new item, which is usually written in a different ink and in a hand of different size from those in the preceding item. The implication is that the information was being entered at different times, and comparatively soon after news came in.[8] If, by contrast, the chronicle had been drawn up at the end of the year, everything could have been written 'in one go' in one fair hand.

After March 1259 the chronicle retains the same basic appearance, but entries become less frequent and there are no items of information datable to the period between January 1261 and June 1262 inclusive.[9] We will return to

[4] *Annales Monastici*, iii. 220; *Close Rolls 1261–64*, pp. 281, 295.

[5] *Calendar of Patent Rolls, 1258–66*, pp. 285–6; *Foedera . . .*, ed. T. Rymer (Record Commission edn., 1816), I, i. 425.

[6] British Library Cotton MS Cleopatra A VII, ff. 1–67v, contains in fact two distinct annals, Tewkesbury I, the main chronicle of the abbey which has the obituary, and Tewkesbury II, for which see below, note 30. The chronicles are discussed in A. Gransden, *Historical Writing in England, c. 550–c. 1307* (London, 1974), p. 405, n. 13, and pp. 416–7. (Dr Gransden's work should be consulted for all the chronicles mentioned in this article.) The MS of the Tewkesbury annals has three separate sets of numbers. That used here is the set adopted by Luard in his Rolls Series edition.

[7] The hand is somewhat irregular between ff. 34v–40v.

[8] Cotton MS Cleopatra A VII, ff. 57–58v. For a similar view see Gransden, *op. cit.*, p. 405, n. 13. Nevertheless the Tewkesbury account of 1258 is somewhat confused and the Westminster parliament in April and May is placed after the Oxford parliament in June; see above, pp. 188 n. 22.

[9] It should be noted that all the datable items under 1260 (March 1260–March 1261) in fact belong to the year March 1259–March 1260, and the datable items under 1261 (March 1261–March 1262) belong to the years March 1260–March 1261: *Annales Monastici*, i. 168–9. It may be that the year headings were only added later in order to given an appearance of continuity, perhaps when the chronicle was recommenced in July 1262.

the significance of this later. The reason why the chronicle recommenced in July 1262 is easy to discern. The entry records an event of special significance to Tewkesbury, namely the burial at the abbey of its patron, Richard de Clare earl of Gloucester. This is followed by notes of deaths on 18 November and 24 November, and, under the date 10 March (1263), by the record of the birth of a daughter to Richard de Clare's son, Gilbert de Clare. This is the entry which immediately precedes the obituary of Henry III.[10] Again there are indications that these entries were made not long after the information which they record was obtained. Thus the death of the prior of Cranbourn on 18 November was quite probably written up before it was known of the death of Henry of Banbury on 24 November since the latter's obituary was set down in a different shade of ink. That the birth of Clare's daughter was recorded soon after it occurred is suggested by the fact that the chronicler was ignorant of the girl's name and left a gap for it which was filled in later.[11] There would seem, therefore, to be no difficulty with the hypothesis that Henry III's obituary was written shortly after news of his 'death' arrived.

Turning now to the content of the obituary its most obvious feature is unreserved praise of the king. Henry is commended both for his piety and, more surprisingly, for his political talents. The king is on the one hand 'ecclesie sancte verus amator et ornator', 'religiosorum tutor et consolator', 'elemosine indigentibus copiosus condonator', 'viduis et orphanis pius semper auxiliator', and, on the other hand, 'regni strenuus gubernator', and 'pacis et quietis doctus reformator'. What is said of the king's piety coincides with comments made by other chroniclers both during Henry's lifetime and after his death in 1272. The records of his government amply confirm the truth of their statements. In the 1240's, for example, Henry's practice was to feed 500 paupers every day.[12] In 1250, in a speech at the Exchequer recorded on the memoranda rolls, Henry urged the assembled sheriffs, amongst other things, to give protection and speedy justice to widows and orphans.[13] This part of the Tewkesbury obituary, therefore, reflects both an accurate appraisal of the king, and one which most contemporaries would have accepted.[14]

Where the Tewkesbury obituary is unique is in its praise of the king's politi-

---

[10] *Annales Monastici*, i. 169. The entry after the obituary is the record of the death of the prior of St James, Bristol on 22 June 1262. This is followed by the note of the election of the prior of Cardiff on 27 June 1262. These entries belong to the period before the chronicle was recommenced with the death of Richard de Clare on 15 July 1262, and were presumably added to the chronicle as afterthoughts.

[11] Cotton MS Cleopatra A VII, f. 60v. The record of the Clare birth is in red ink as, in part, is the obituary of Henry III. However, the hand of the king's obituary is slightly smaller than that in the Clare entry which precedes it.

[12] *Close Rolls, 1237–42*, p. 497; see H. Johnstone, 'Poor Relief in the Royal Households of Thirteenth-Century England', *Speculum*, iv (1929), 149–67.

[13] M.T. Clanchy, 'Did Henry III have a Policy?', *History* liii (1968), 215–6.

[14] I do not propose to discuss here how Henry was able to maintain this reputation while at the same time his government challenged many of the liberties claimed by the Church.

cal skills and achievements – 'regni strenuus gubernator; pacis et quietis doctus reformator'. No chronicler writing during Henry's lifetime was as positive as this. One of the reasons for the revolution of 1258 was the belief that 'regem Angliae regni sui negotiis disponendis inutilem et insufficientem'.[15] After Henry's death many obituaries, while commending his piety, were either silent or critical of his political abilities and conduct. The Oseney abbey chronicler wrote, 'iste super omnes reges qui fuerunt ante ipsum dilexit decorem domus Dei et obsequium divinum. Iste super omnes Anglicos dilexit alienigenas, et eos innumerabilibus ditavit donariis et possessionibus'.[16] Walter of Guisborough described Henry as a 'vir religiosus et pius, et licet simplex in administracione temporalium, tamen magne deuocionis in deum'.[17] This view was echoed by Nicholas Trevet, 'iste rex quantum in saeculi actibus putatur minus prudens, tanto majori devotione apud Deum pollebat'.[18]

How far then can the sentiments of the Tewkesbury chronicler be taken seriously? Are they merely the effusions of someone who wished to speak well of a pious man after his death? A case can be made for thinking that they are rather more than this.[19] In particular, it may be suggested that the writer was influenced by the king's conduct and declarations in 1261, the year in which Henry threw off the restrictions imposed on him by the Provisions of Oxford in 1258 and recovered unfettered power. In 1261, more than in any other year of his reign, Henry must indeed have appeared 'strenuus'. He established his base in the Tower of London, he dashed down to Dover and forced the surrender of the castle, he dismissed the 'baronial' sheriffs and placed the counties under loyal *curiales*, he defied his opponents, and he won through. By the end of the year all the leading barons, save Simon de Montfort who left England, had accepted the king's recovery of power and the nullification of the Provisions of Oxford.[20] In 1262, moreover, as far as Tewkesbury was concerned, Henry's conduct in some ways continued to be 'strenuus'. After the abbey's patron, Richard de Clare earl of Gloucester, died in July, Henry refused to allow his son, Gilbert, who was under age, to succeed to his father's estates. As a result the borough of Tewkesbury, which was part of the Clare inheritance, came into the king's hands.[21] It is true that, in other respects, Henry's conduct in 1262 became the very reverse of 'strenuus'. Even when over the worst of his illness, he lingered in France visiting shrines, and ignored pleas to return to En-

[15] *Annales Monastici*, iv. 118–9.

[16] *ibid.*, iv. 254.

[17] *The Chronicle of Walter of Guisborough*, ed. H. Rothwell (Camden, 3rd ser., lxxxix, 1957), pp. 212–3.

[18] *Nicholai Triveti Annales*, ed. T. Hog (English Historical Society, ix, 1845), pp. 279–80.

[19] However, it should be noted that the chronicler is full of praise for Richard de Clare when recording his death in July 1262–'vir nobilis et omni laude dignus': *Annales Monastici*, i. 169.

[20] R.F. Treharne, *The Baronial Plan of Reform, 1258–1263* (Manchester, 1932), pp. 250–79.

[21] M.R. Altschul, *A Baronial Family in Medieval England: The Clares* (Baltimore, 1965), pp. 95–6; *Close Rolls, 1261–64*, p. 284.

gland.[22] In the early months of 1263 the Welsh marches were in tumult, and the party which was to re-impose the Provisions of Oxford in July was beginning to form.[23] But in March when the king 'died' the disasters of July were in the future. Admittedly Tewkesbury's geographical position made it sensitive to events in the Welsh march, yet a swift descent from the new king, Edward I, might well restore matters there to order. When Henry 'died', the fruits of his great victory in 1261 were still intact. He died very much 'regni strenuus gubernator'.

Tewkesbury's second comment 'pacis et quietis doctus reformator' is a further indication that the obituarist was influenced by what happened, or more exactly what was said, in 1261. In 1261 there had been peace in England since the rebellion of Richard Marshal in 1233–34. Indeed, if one excludes the events of those years, when the military operations were of limited extent, and the siege of Bedford castle in 1224, there had been peace since the close of the Magna Carta civil war in 1217. In 1261 when Henry was struggling to win the hearts of his subjects throughout England, he drew attention to these long years of peace, and claimed them as his greatest achievement. In August he issued a manifesto which declared that for the forty-five years 'quibus, volente Domino et eius cooperante gracia, regni nostri gubernacula tenuimus, studium nostrum et labores circa universorum ac singulorum tranquilitatem et pacem, toto desiderio totisque viribus per nos et nostros, ponere non destiterimus'. As a result, Henry continued, his reign had been free from 'hostilitas aut guerra generalis'. This letter was sent to all the sheriffs and was probably read in the county courts.[24] It may well be the immediate origin of the Tewkesbury obituarist's picture of the king as 'pacis et quietis doctus reformator'. This is suggested by the very phraseology. One who 'circa universorum ac singulorum tranquilitatem et pacem' had devoted so much 'studium' might well be called a 'doctus reformator pacis et quietis'.

This thesis that the political part of the obituary expresses genuine opinions is compatible with the views previously expressed in the Tewkesbury chronicle. The account of 1258 is plainly favourable to the enterprise of the barons. The king's Lusignan half-brothers are stigmatised as Pharisees and their expulsion from England is applauded.[25] After this, however, events are recorded without judgement being passed upon them. The chronicle itself was not kept up between January 1261 and June 1262. No reference, therefore, was made to the king's recovery of power in 1261. This suggests that the chronicler was perplexed rather than outraged by the course of events. His reforming sympathies may well have been diminished by the king's victory in 1261. When Henry

---

[22] *Foedera*, I, i. 442.

[23] Treharne, *op. cit.*, pp. 291–308.

[24] *Foedera*, I, i. 408–9.

[25] *Annales Monastici*, i. 165.

'died' in March 1263 the chronicler wrote the obituary in the light of the monarch's success two years before.[26]

If then the Tewkesbury obituary was seriously meant it becomes a useful pointer to political feeling in March 1263. Henry III's own dealings with Tewkesbury abbey gave it no peculiar reason to think well of him. He was rarely there and his last recorded gift to the house was back in 1241.[27] Others besides the Tewkesbury writer, therefore, may well have been impressed by the king's conduct and declarations in 1261. We have suggested the further possibility that the obituarist was influenced by the king's firm treatment of Gilbert de Clare in 1262, but, if so, he would not have been alone in that.[28] If the positive view of the king expressed in the obituary was more widely shared, it may help to explain the difference between the movements against the king in 1258 and 1263. Montfort's party in 1263 was but a fraction of that which had supported reform in 1258.[29] Clearly, the more one regarded the king as 'regni strenuus gubernator' and not 'regni sui negotiis disponendis inutilem et insufficientem', the less one was likely to call for the re-imposition of the Provisions of Oxford. Equally, the more one valued the peace which Henry stressed in 1261, the less one would welcome the return of Simon de Montfort and the beginning of civil war.

Since the Tewkesbury annals are lost after 1263 we cannot know whether the disastrous events of the years 1263–67 modified the view of the king, and prevented the re-employment of the obituary in 1272.[30] Certainly no chroni-

<hr>

[26] The need to explain the change of view depends, of course, on the assumption that the obituary was composed by the same person who was responsible for the Tewkesbury chronicle in 1258, which may not have been the case. The handwriting is inconclusive on this point. The entries in the chronicle between 1258 and the obituary appear to be in two hands of slightly different appearance, that of 1258, which usually employs a small 'a', and that of the obituary which prefers an 'a' in a more elaborate style. Whether, however, these are the hands of two different scribes is an open question, and one which is only important if we believe that the scribes were also the authors of what they wrote rather than mere copyists. I would like to thank Dr Andrew Watson for giving me his comments on the handwriting in the Tewkesbury chronicle.

[27] *Close Rolls, 1261–64*, p. 284. Little is known about the abbot of Tewkesbury in 1263, Abbot Thomas de Stoke: see W. Dugdale, *Monasticon Anglicanum* (London, 1817–30), ii. 55

[28] From the point of view of Gilbert de Clare, this treatment was a reason for thinking ill of the king and explains his alliance with Simon de Montfort in 1263. The king's obituary is not the only place where the Tewkesbury chronicle does not reflect the views of the house of Clare. For example, it records the quarrel between the Lord Edward and Richard de Clare in 1260 without comment: *Annales Monastici*, i. 168–9. For Tewkesbury II, see Gransden, *op. cit.*, pp. 416–7.

[29] Treharne, *op. cit.*, pp. 302–3.

[30] Tewkesbury II (for which see above note 6) may represent a further change of heart at Tewkesbury or a different strand of political opinion within the abbey from that represented in Henry III's obituary. Tewkesbury II incorporates Tewkesbury I's account of the events of 1258 and then gives an entirely independent history down to 1264 in which year (before the battle of Lewes) it breaks off abruptly. Probably it was written in 1264. The tone of Tewkesbury II after 1258 is entirely different from that of Tewkesbury I, being passionately pro-baronial. Far from ignoring the king's recovery of power in 1261 it stigmatises in the most vitriolic terms the barons whose desertion to the king made it possible. In Luard's view (and mine) Tewkesbury II is in a different hand

cler writing after Henry's death approached Tewkesbury's claim that Henry
was 'regni stenuus gubernator'. On the other hand, Henry's reputation as a
'rex pacificus' persisted. The obituary in the chronicle of Hailes abbey spoke
of Henry as 'iustus, pacificus, clemens et carne pudicus'.[31] Walter of Guisborough described Henry as 'vir simplex, pacificus non bellicosus'.[32] At Furness
abbey Henry was remembered as 'clementissimus populi rector, pacisque, aequi-
tatis executor et amator', a passage which should perhaps read 'pacisque, et
quietatis executor et amator'. The chronicler went on to claim that 'fuit in Anglia omnibus diebus vitae eius abundantia pacis atque laetitiae'.[33] The continuation of the *Flores Historiarum* which was possibly produced at Westminster abbey
likewise emphasised how Henry 'regnum ejus diutius siluit, et quieverunt fines
ejus'.[34] Such sentiments were appropriate. Henry's propaganda in 1261 was
effective because it had some basis in fact. His reign had indeed witnessed a
long period of peace, a peace to which the king's policies had contributed.[35]
Henry himself would have welcomed Tewkesbury's declaration that he was 'pacis et quietis doctus reformator'. It was in those terms that his patron saint Edward the Confessor was remembered. As the 'official' life by Ailred of Rievaulx
said of Edward 'quoniam diu rege pacifico regnante, in uno vinculo pacis omnia convenirent'.[36]

continued
from the one or more found in Tewkesbury I: *Annales Monastici*, i. 170–80; see Gransden, *op. cit.*,
pp. 416–7.

[31] M.N. Blount, ' A Critical edition of the Annals of Hailes (MS Cotton Cleopatra D. iii, ff.
33–59v) with an examination of their sources' (Manchester University M.A. thesis, 1974), p. 81. It
is worth remarking in passing that this chronicle appears to be the source for some of the material
on the reign of Henry III in *The Metrical Chronicle of Robert of Gloucester*, ed. W.A. Wright (Rolls Ser.,
1887).

[32] *The Chronicle of Walter of Guisborough*, p. 201.

[33] *Chronicles of the Reigns of Stephen, Henry II and Richard I*, ed. R. Howlett (Rolls Ser., 1884–89),
ii. 563, n. 3. The surviving MS of the Furness chronicle (British Library Cotton MS Cleopatra A I)
is 'an ignorantly written copy' made in the late thirteenth century: see *ibid.*, ii, p. lxxxviii.

[34] *Flores Historiarum*, iii. 252.

[35] See above, pp. 96–8.

[36] *Historiae Anglicanae Scriptores X*, ed. R. Twysden (London, 1652), p. 375; *The Life of Edward the
Confessor*, ed. F. Barlow (London, 1962), p. xxxvii.

Appendix

Annals of Tewkesbury Abbey

(British Library Cotton MS Cleopatra A VII, f 60v.) Under the heading 1262 [25 March 1262–24 March 1263][37]

[Red Ink]	X kal Aprilis [23 March]
[Black Ink]	Obiit Henricus rex Anglie, filius regis Johannis; ecclesie sancte verus amator et ornator;
[Red Ink]	religiosorum tutor et consolator; regni strenuus gubernator; pacis
[Black Ink]	et quietis doctus reformator; elemosine indigentibus copiosus condonator;
[Red Ink]	cat[38] viduis et orphanis pius semper auxiliator.

[37] The following transcription retains the lines of the original. In the MS, save between 'X kal Aprilis' and 'Obiit Henricus rex . . .', a gap is left between each line. The passages in red ink are faint. I would like to thank Dr David d'Avray for helping me decipher them.

[38] 'cat' (which is not in red ink) is on the extreme edge of the page. A trimming of the margin has removed the preliminary letters 'va'. The obituary is also crossed out by two diagonal lines running from corner to corner.

14

King Henry III's 'Statute' against Aliens: July 1263*

IN January 1264, in his famous Mise of Amiens, King Louis IX condemned the Provisions of Oxford outright. He also quashed 'the statute made declaring that the realm of England should in future be governed by native-born men, and that aliens must depart, never to return, save those whose stay the faithful men of the realm might in common accept'.[1] This statute has puzzled historians. It has been assumed that no text survives; it has also been suggested that the statute was promulgated in 1258 as part of the reforming programme known loosely as the Provisions of Oxford, a programme which both set up a council of fifteen to govern the country and introduced extensive reforms of local administration.[2] Since the decisions taken at Oxford and Winchester in the June and July of 1258 only survive in draft form, it is not impossible that a statute against the aliens has been lost.[3] But, in fact, as this Note will show, the text of the statute does survive, and forms an addition to the confirmation of the Provisions of Oxford which Simon de Montfort forced on Henry III in July 1263. It thus marks an important stage in the development of the anti-alien movement in England during the years of 'baronial' reform and rebellion.

By the mid-thirteenth century there was already a history of hostility to foreigners who held land and office in England. To be English in this period was first and foremost to be native-born: to be, as it was put in 1258, *de regno Angliae natus*; hence the affection contemporaries expressed for their 'native country' or 'native soil'.[4] The great bulk

* I am most grateful to John Maddicott, John Prestwich and Huw Ridgeway for commenting on a draft of this article.

1. R. F. Treharne and I. J. Sanders (ed.), *Documents of the Baronial Movement of Reform and Rebellion, 1258-1267* (Oxford, 1973 [hereafter *DBM*]), pp. 288-9, cap. 15. I employ the term 'statute' throughout this Note although Louis IX was not using it in any technical sense.

2. D. R. Clementi, 'The Documentary Evidence for the Crisis of Government in England in 1258', *Parliaments, Estates and Representation*, i (1981), 104; M. Prestwich, *English Politics in the Thirteenth Century* (London, 1990), p. 88; and see R. F. Treharne, *The Baronial Plan of Reform, 1258-1263* (Manchester, 1932), p. 80. For contemporaries the 'Provisions of Oxford' could mean all the reforms of 1258-9 (including those promulgated at Westminster in October 1259) or just some part of them.

3. *DBM*, pp. 96-113; H. G. Richardson and G. O. Sayles, 'The Provisions of Oxford', *Bulletin of the John Rylands Library*, xvii (1933), 291-321. Clementi, 'Documentary Evidence', is an attempt to reconstruct the reforms of 1258 without even the help of the drafts.

4. *DBM*, pp. 80-1, caps. 4-6; *Patent Rolls, 1216-25*, p. 113; *The Shorter Latin Poems of Master Henry of Avranches Relating to England*, ed. J. C. Russell and J. P. Heironimus (Cambridge, Mass., 1935), p. 125. For more general discussion of the development of English national feeling in the reign of Henry III, see M. T. Clanchy, *England and its Rulers, 1066-1272* (Glasgow, 1983), pp. 241-4; D. A. Carpenter, *The Minority of Henry III* (London, 1990), pp. 261-2, 394-5; Prestwich, *English Politics*, ch. 5.

of the knightly class, the lords of one or a few manors, who formed the bedrock of local society, had been native-born for well over a century by 1258. So, of course, had the majority of monks, who produced the chronicles in which anti-alien sentiments were so frequently expressed. After the loss of Normandy in 1204, the great barons too would always be native-born and England their only country. Against this background the king's bestowal of land and office on foreigners was bound to cause increasing resentment, especially when those foreigners seemed to behave in an arrogant and oppressive fashion. Chroniclers ascribed a great deal of the political turmoil in England between 1199 and 1234 to the aliens introduced by King John; and great magnates, when they were native-born, could share that antipathy. There was also antagonism to foreign churchmen, especially 'the Romans' provided by the pope to English livings, and to foreign merchants, especially those from Cahors involved in money-lending. In 1232 there were serious riots against 'the Roman' clergy in England.[1]

In many ways King Henry III shared the increasing Englishness of his subjects. He was native-born and indeed was known as 'Henry of Winchester' after his birthplace;[2] he lived almost exclusively in England, and regarded it as his homeland; he named his sons after Anglo-Saxon saints. And yet, as the chronicler of Osney Abbey sadly remarked, 'he loved aliens above all Englishmen, and enriched them with innumerable gifts and possessions.'[3] There were two groups of foreigners, in particular, who enjoyed Henry's favour. The first was headed by the Savoyard kinsmen of his wife, Eleanor of Provence; the second by his own Poitevin half-brothers of the house of Lusignan.[4] The Savoyards had come to England following Henry's marriage in 1236. The most important were Peter of Savoy, who was given the honour of Richmond, and Boniface, who became Archbishop of Canterbury. The Poitevin influx began in 1247. Of the half-brothers, William de Valence was married to the heiress of the county of Pembroke; Aymer became bishop elect of Winchester; and Guy and Geoffrey de Lusignan were given wardships and money fees. All told, Huw Ridgeway has calculated that some forty Savoyards and twenty-eight Poitevins received annual revenues of 100 marks or

---

1. Carpenter, *Minority of Henry III*, pp. 394–5; W. W. Shirley (ed.), *Royal ... Letters Illustrative of the Reign of Henry III* (2 vols., Rolls ser., 1862–6), i. 221; H. MacKenzie, 'The Anti-Foreign Movement in England in 1231–2', *Anniversary Essays in Mediaeval History by Students of Charles Homer Haskins* (Boston, 1929), pp. 183–203; N. Denholm-Young, 'Merchants of Cahors', in his *Collected Papers* (Cardiff, 1969), pp. 290–7.

2. H. Rothwell (ed.), *The Chronicle of Walter of Guisborough* (Camden Soc., lxxxix, 1957), p. 201.

3. H. R. Luard (ed.), *Ann[ales] Mon[astici]* (5 vols., Rolls ser., 1864–9), iv. 254.

4. For these groups, see H. W. Ridgeway, 'King Henry III and the "Aliens", 1236–1272', in *Thirteenth Century England, II. Proceedings of the Newcastle upon Tyne Conference 1987*, ed. P. R. Coss and S. D. Lloyd (Woodbridge, 1988), pp. 81–92, and id., 'Foreign Favourites and Henry III's Problems of Patronage, 1247–1258', *EHR*, civ (1989), 590–610.

more from Henry III, although the number who actually lived for any time in England was much smaller.[1]

At first sight there seem compelling reasons for locating in 1258 the statute subsequently condemned by Louis IX. The revolution had begun in April with Roger Bigod's demand that 'the wretched and intolerable Poitevins and all aliens' should flee from King Henry's face.[2] In June the Petition of the Barons called for royal castles to be committed to the custody of men 'born in the kingdom', and asked the King not to marry women to those who were not 'true-born Englishmen'.[3] A little later, a newsletter, describing events at the Oxford and Winchester Parliaments, told how the now contrite King 'has often begged [the barons] that none but Englishmen shall stay around him, and so it will be'. The newsletter went on to declare that the barons would soon 'make provision ... on many matters touching aliens, both Romans and merchants, money-changers, and others', an intention which reflected the hostility to the Roman clergy beneficed in England and to the Cahorsin money-lenders [the 'money-changers'], against whom, indeed, there was complaint in the Petition of the Barons.[4] These demands and prophecies were accompanied by action. The King's Lusignan half-brothers were expelled from England, together with their fellow Poitevins, William de Sancta Ermina, the King's Chamberlain, Elyas de Rabayne, the castellan of Corfe, and Guy de Rochford, the castellan of Colchester.[5] In addition, 'all the castles of the lord king', in the words of the newsletter quoted above, 'were entrusted ... to certain Englishmen, nearly all of them having previously been in the hands of foreigners.'[6] It is hardly surprising, therefore, that several chroniclers assumed or affirmed that a provision expelling the aliens had indeed been part of the reforms of 1258. The Burton annalist believed that it was under the terms of the Provisions of Oxford that the ejection of aliens was demanded in 1263. Likewise, the Tewkesbury annalist, recalling the work of the reformers at Oxford, declared that 'such was their counsel, namely that

1. Ridgeway, 'Henry III and the "Aliens"', pp. 81-2. Thirty-nine Savoyards obtained land from the King, but there were only eight Poitevin landholders.

2. *Ann Mon.* i. 164. Bigod's speech is recorded in the Tewkesbury annals, which may well have written it up from a newsletter. Whether Bigod meant to include the Savoyards amongst those to be dismissed may be questioned: see D. A. Carpenter, 'What Happened in 1258?'; above, pp. 188-9 and n. 23.

3. *DBM*, pp. 80-1, caps. 4-6. For marriages, see D. A. Carpenter, 'King, Magnates and Society: The Personal Rule of King Henry III, 1234-58', above p. 95.

4. *DBM*, pp. 94-7, and pp. 86-9, cap. 26. The widespread animosity to foreign clergy between 1258 and 1265 has been suggested to me by John Maddicott.

5. H. R. Luard (ed.), *Matthaei Parisiensis Chronica Majora* (7 vols., Rolls ser., 1872-83), v, 702, 725; *Close Rolls, 1256-9*, pp. 339, 352; Ridgeway, 'Henry III and the "Aliens"', p. 84.

6. *DBM*, pp. 90-1; cf. the terms in which this was later recalled in the baronial presentation to Louis IX at Amiens: ibid., pp. 258-9. In the 1250s such major royal castles as Colchester, Corfe, Gloucester, Hadleigh, Hertford, Montgomery, Oxford, Sherborne, Tickhill, the Tower of London and Windsor spent time under alien control: see the list in H. W. Ridgeway, 'The Politics of the English Royal Court 1247-65, with Special Reference to the Role of the Aliens' (D. Phil. thesis, Oxford, 1983), pp. 21-7.

aliens of whatever nation, Romans and others, possessing, devouring and dissipating the greatest part of the goods of England, and behaving by the King's side as second kings, should be removed as exiles from England'.[1] Most specifically of all, the chronicler Walter of Guisborough, describing a series of reforms promulgated at Winchester in July 1258, included one stating that 'all aliens, of whatever condition or nation, shall immediately return home, on penalty of loss of life and limb'.[2]

Examined more closely, however, this evidence proves less conclusive. The Burton and Tewkesbury annalists were both writing in, or soon after, 1263, and were influenced by the events of that year. Guisborough was writing much later still, at the end of the century, and, as Treharne pointed out, clearly antedated several of his Winchester provisions.[3] Nor do the actual events of 1258 suggest that there was any general proscription of foreigners along the lines of the statute condemned by Louis IX. While the Lusignans and their satellites departed, the Savoyard party of the Queen remained in place. Indeed, spurred by antagonism to the Lusignans, it helped bring about the political revolution. Peter of Savoy was one of the original seven confederate barons, and later he and Archbishop Boniface were elected to the council of fifteen, along with another foreigner, John du Plessis, Earl of Warwick.[4] Meanwhile, the Queen's steward, Matthias Bezill, remained as castellan of Gloucester, and the Savoyard, Imbert Pugeys, continued as one of the stewards of the King.[5] All of this would have been in clear breach of the statute nullified by Louis IX, which banned foreigners absolutely from any role in government. It was more or less congruent with the statute's call for the expulsion of foreigners, given the qualification that those accepted 'in common' by the faithful men of the realm might stay or return; but there is no evidence that the survival of the Savoyards in 1258 had to be sanctioned formally in this way.

Apart from the expulsion of the Lusignans, the only anti-alien measure in 1258 for which there is incontrovertible evidence was the decision to place the king's castles in the hands of native-born men. This, of course, fell a good deal short of the statute quashed by Louis IX. Nor was it implemented in any blanket fashion, for two foreigners figured in the list of castellans appointed by the reformers: Matthias Bezill, who was confirmed as castellan of Gloucester, and John du Plessis, who

1. *Ann. Mon.* i. 500, 174-5. See also H. R. Luard (ed.), *Flores Historiarum* (3 vols., Rolls ser., 1890), iii. 256; W. A. Wright (ed.), *The Metrical Chronicle of Robert of Gloucester* (2 vols., Rolls ser., 1887), ii, lines 11060-5.
2. *Walter of Guisborough*, p. 186.
3. Treharne, *Baronial Plan of Reform*, p. 80. For Guisborough, see A. Gransden, *Historical Writing in England, c. 550 to c. 1307* (London, 1974), pp. 470-6.
4. See above pp. 93-4; H. W. Ridgeway, 'The Lord Edward and the Provisions of Oxford (1258): A Study in Faction', in *Thirteenth Century England, I. Proceedings of the Newcastle upon Tyne Conference 1985*, ed. P. R. Coss and S. D. Lloyd (Woodbridge, 1986), pp. 89-99.
5. *DBM*, pp. 112-13, cap. 24; *Close Rolls, 1256-9*, p. 356. For these men, see Ridgeway, 'Politics of the English Royal Court', pp. 36-7, 42.

received Devizes.[1] In 1258, therefore, there was certainly some general hostility to foreigners; the Lusignans were expelled from England; and the royal castles were placed very largely in the hands of native-born men. All this encouraged later chroniclers to think that there had been more general measures against the aliens; but it is far from clear that there was any statute of the type condemned by Louis IX. The final proof of this lies in the statute itself. It is, in fact, quite certain that Louis was referring to a statute of 1263. It is equally clear that, as introduced in 1263, the statute was something new, an addition to the original Provisions of Oxford. It was necessary in 1263 because there had been nothing like it in 1258.

In 1261 Henry III overthrew the Provisions of Oxford and recovered unrestricted power. In 1263 a party of dissidents brought Simon de Montfort back to England as their leader, and decided to fight for the Provisions' reimposition, which meant, above all, the reimposition of some form of conciliar control over the King.[2] According to the chronicle of the London alderman, Arnold fitz Thedmar, 'before Pentecost' [20 May], these dissidents sent a letter to the King, under the seal of Roger of Clifford, asking him (*petentes ipsum*) to keep the Provisions.[3] They next defied and began to attack their enemies, violence which began in the first week of June.[4] Fitz Thedmar goes on to say that around 24 June the barons sent a letter to the citizens of London, sealed by Simon de Montfort, asking 'if they wished to observe the said ordinances and statutes [made at Oxford]'. Fitz Thedmar then continues: 'And know that such was the petition of the Barons' ['Et sciendum, quod talis fuit petitio Baronum'], the actual text of a petition to the King being transcribed.[5] That *petitio* called for the King to accept the Provisions, but added the demand that the realm be governed solely by native-born men. This is the first indication that such a measure was on the political agenda. The *petitio* was evidently not the same as the letter of c. 24 June, sealed by Simon de Montfort, which simply asked the Londoners if they would observe the Provisions; but it may well have been conveyed to them at the same time. If, however, the *petitio Baronum* (as we will call the document transcribed by fitz Thedmar) was thus in being by c. 24 June, it may well have been drawn up considerably earlier. Indeed, it is possible

1. *DBM*, loc. cit. There is no evidence of measures in 1258 against foreign clergy or merchants.
2. I say 'some form' because in 1263 it was no longer possible to revive exactly the council of fifteen of 1258. I say 'above all' because by 1263 the King had spontaneously accepted at least some of the local reforms propounded in 1258-9. It was conciliar control at the centre which he resisted before anything else. Treharne, *Baronial Plan of Reform*, contains the most detailed account of the politics of these years.
3. T. Stapleton (ed.), *De Antiquis Legibus Liber. Cronica Maiorum et Vicecomitum Londoniarum* (Camden Soc., 1846), p. 53.
4. *Close Rolls, 1261-4*, p. 512; *Cal. Close Rolls, 1272-9*, p. 333.
5. *Cronica Maiorum et Vicecomitum*, p. 54. The text of the *petitio* is printed in full in the Appendix to this Note.

that similar demands were made in the original letter sealed by Roger of Clifford before 20 May.

The precise contents of the *petitio Baronum* were as follows. It demanded that the Provisions of Oxford 'be firmly and inviolably observed', but promised that anything within them found prejudicial to the King and kingdom would be withdrawn, and that things needing correction would be corrected. It then went on to require that security be provided for the observance of 'other good and useful things', and concluded with a separate demand not apparently covered by the Provisions of Oxford:

> Item, they seek that the kingdom in future be governed by native-born men, faithful and useful under the lord king, and not by others, as is done in common in all other kingdoms of the world. ['Item, petunt quod regnum de cetero per indigenas, fideles et utiles sub Domino Rege, gubernetur, et non per alios, sicut fit communiter in omnibus aliis mundi regnis'.][1]

The *petitio Baronum* embodies, down to some of the same words and phrases, the bulk of the terms accepted by the King three weeks later. The passage, just quoted, restricting office to native-born men, was itself adopted very closely. The *petitio*, however, said nothing about aliens having to depart from the country. This stipulation first appears in a later document, based in part on the *petitio*, namely 'the form of peace' (*forma pacis*) with which the bishops of Lincoln, London, and Coventry and Lichfield were sent to the King and the Lord Edward, *ex parte baronum*, on, or shortly before, 29 June 1263: on that day the Bishop of Worcester, Walter de Cantilupe, wrote to Henry III's Chancellor, Walter de Merton, urging him to persuade Henry and Edward to accept the *forma*.[2] Its demands, as found in what may be a slightly later version belonging to early July, are summarized by the *Flores Historiarum* of St Albans Abbey as follows:[3] that Henry of Almain be freed by the King and Queen;[4] that the King's castles be placed in the custody of the barons; that the Provisions of Oxford be 'firmly and inviolably observed' both by the King and by others; and that the kingdom hence-forth be governed by native-born men, faithful and useful under the

---

1. *Cronica Maiorum et Vicecomitum*, p. 54.

2. T. Rymer (ed.), *Foedera, Conventiones Litterae ...* (new edn., 3 vols. in 6, Record Comm., 1816-30), I, i. 427. The significance of the *forma pacis* in representing a separate stage in the evolution of Montfortian demands was pointed out to me by John Prestwich.

3. *Flores Historiarum*, ii. 482. The text of the *forma pacis* is printed in full in the Appendix to this Note. For the date see next note.

4. Henry of Almain, the son of the King's brother, Richard, Earl of Cornwall and King of Germany, was at this time a leading dissident. According to the Dunstable annalist, he had been taken prisoner at Wissant by Ingram de Fiennes, a kinsman of the Queen acting on the orders of John Mansel who had just arrived in Wissant, having fled overseas from the Tower of London. The St Albans *Flores Historiarum* says that Henry of Almain was arrested by Ingram at Boulogne having pursued John Mansel across the sea, but this is contradicted by the Canterbury/Dover annalist who says that Henry crossed before John Mansel, although in this version Mansel does go to Boulogne. If Henry's arrest was in some way connected with John Mansel's flight, the version of the *forma pacis* in the *Flores Historiarum* must be later than 29 June, the day Mansel crossed the Channel: C[alendar of] P[atent] R[olls], *1258-1266*, p. 269; *Ann. Mon.* iii. 223; *Flores Historiarum*, ii. 481; W. Stubbs (ed.), *The Historical Works of Gervase of Canterbury* (2 vols., Rolls ser., 1879-80), ii. 222.

lord king ['et quod regnum de caetero per indigenas, fideles et utiles sub domino rege, gubernetur'].

This last stipulation followed exactly the *petitio Baronum*, but the *forma pacis* now concluded with what was explicitly a new, additional demand, for it began with the word *insuper*, 'in addition':

> In addition, that aliens must depart from the kingdom never further to return, save those whose stay the faithful men of the realm might with unanimous assent accept. ['Insuper, quod exeant alienigenae a regno, ulterius non reversuri, exceptis illis quorum moram fideles regni unanimi assensu acceptarent'.]

This demand too was embodied almost exactly in the terms finally accepted by the King.[1]

On or shortly before 29 June, as Walter de Cantilupe's letter shows, the bishops of Lincoln, London, and Coventry and Lichfield, were sent to the King and Edward with the *forma pacis*. On 4 July, the King empowered these three bishops, together with John of Darlington and William of Wilton, 'to make peace with the barons'.[2] The results were finally proclaimed in a letter patent of 16 July, printed for the first time in the original Latin in the Appendix to this Note. (An English translation appeared in the *Calendar of Patent Rolls, 1258-1266*.) In this letter, the King explained that he had given power to the bishops of Lincoln, London, Coventry and Lichfield, and Exeter, together with John of Darlington and William of Wilton, to arrange peace with the barons. He then set out the settlement which they had agreed. This was derived from the *petitio Baronum* and the *forma pacis*.[3] The section on aliens followed the *forma pacis* very closely, beginning with its restriction of office to native-born men, first found in the *petitio Baronum*, and then continuing with the extra clause in the *forma* under which aliens, with certain qualifications, were to be expelled from the kingdom. This time the whole section began with the word *insuper* ('in addition'), thus indicating that it was something new, over and above the original Provisions of Oxford.

> And, in addition, that the realm of England should in future be governed by native-born men, faithful and useful under us, and that aliens must depart, never to return, save those whose stay the faithful men of the realm will in common accept.

1. After this passage the *Flores* continues: 'But those who had been introduced into the noble castle of Windsor, the foresaid aliens, numbering about a hundred strenuous knights and many more satellites, fortified it and munitioned it exceedingly well, laying waste and devastating the countryside everywhere': *Flores Historiarum*, ii. 482. This is clearly a comment by the chronicler, prompted by the reflection that the *forma pacis* had been breached. It does not form part of the *forma* itself. However, when Rishanger came to copy this part of the *Flores* he altered it so as to make the comment part of the *forma*: 'and those who had been introduced into the noble castle of Windsor ... should be similarly expelled': J. O. Halliwell (ed.), *The Chronicle of William de Rishanger* (Camden Soc., 1840), p. 13.

2. *Foedera*, I, i. 427; *CPR, 1258-66*, p. 268. See *Ann. Mon.* iii. 223-4. The Bishop of Exeter was soon joined to the other three bishops (see below), although there is no evidence as to exactly when.

3. The letter of 16 July made no mention of the first two points in the *forma pacis*, since these were dealt with separately. A royal letter of 10 July ordered the release of Henry of Almain; letters of 18 July appointed new castellans to the King's castles: *CPR, 1258-66*, pp. 269, 271.

268 The Reign of Henry III

That Louis IX had the text of this July 1263 letter before him when he drew up the Mise of Amiens, is shown conclusively by a comparison of the two texts in their original Latin:[1]

16 July 1263
ac, insuper, quod regnum decetero per indigenas, fideles et utiles sub nobis gubernetur, necnon ut exeant alienigene, non reversuri, exceptis illis quorum moram fideles regni communiter acceptabunt.

Mise of Amiens, cap. 16
Item, retractamus et cassamus illud statutum factum, quod regnum Anglie de cetero per indigenas gubernetur, necnon ut exirent alienigene, non reversuri, exceptis illis quorum moram fideles regni communiter acceptarent.

The statute against aliens condemned by Louis IX, therefore, was introduced in 1263, not 1258. This is perfectly understandable because, as Ridgeway has observed, in the intervening years anti-alien feelings had rapidly become both less discriminating and more intense.[2] One reason for this was the growing hostility to the Queen and the Savoyards. In 1258 they had largely escaped attack. Although more numerous than the Poitevins,[3] the chief sufferers in that year, they were then also less unpopular. They had been established in England a decade earlier, when the King's resources were more plentiful and competition for patronage less severe;[4] they had behaved with greater tact and moderation;[5] and they had formed alliances with English magnates through controlling appointments to the household of the Lord Edward. When that control seemed threatened by the Lusignans in 1258, the Savoyards could make common cause with the English magnates demoted from Edward's entourage.[6] But if the courtier allies of the Savoyards distinguished between them and the Lusignans, there were others who were already lumping all foreigners together. Matthew Paris thought that the patronage given in 1258 both to the Queen's uncle, Thomas of Savoy, and to the Poitevin, William de Sancta Ermina, was equally reprehensible; and that such views were shared by some of the reformers is shown by the demands over castles and marriages in the 1258 Petition of the Barons, which attacked foreigners without distinction.[7] If the Savoyards welcomed the fall of the

---

1. The letter patent of 16 July was itself based on the *forma pacis*, but a comparison of all three texts shows that it was the former, not the latter, which Louis saw. Louis' judgement imitates the *forma pacis* in having 'acceptarent' rather than the 16 July letter's 'acceptabunt', but follows the letter in having 'necnon', 'communiter' (rather than 'unanimi assensu') and in omitting 'ulterius'. However, in a talk to the London Society of Medieval Studies in 1984, John Prestwich rightly drew attention to the close similarity between the *forma* and Louis' judgement.
2. Ridgeway, 'Henry III and the "Aliens"', pp. 90–1.
3. See *supra*, pp. 263–4 and p. 264, n. 1.
4. Ridgeway, 'Foreign Favourites and Henry III's Problems of Patronage, 1247–1258', 590–610.
5. See above p. 191; Ridgeway, 'Henry III and the "Aliens"', pp. 88–9.
6. Ridgeway, 'The Lord Edward and the Provisions of Oxford', pp. 92–3.
7. *Chronica Majora*, v. 677–8; see *Calendar of Liberate Rolls, 1251–60*, p. 432. Cf. *supra*, p. 263.

Lusignans, they must have viewed the accompanying xenophobia with acute unease. By 1263 they too were engulfed by it.

Just as Lusignan and Savoyard enjoyment of royal patronage could be condemned in the same breath, so increasingly could the harshness of their stewards and bailiffs, placed, as they seemed to be, above the law by the King's protection. Whether this local tyranny had really provoked widespread resentment before 1258 has been questioned.[1] But what is certain is that the Lusignans were subjected in 1258 to such charges,[2] charges which were quickly believed[3] and to some extent supported by the cases brought against them on the eyres of the period of reform. Here again dangerous currents of anti-alien feeling were released, for the eyres also seemed to show that in the localities the Savoyards had been just as oppressive as the Lusignans. As early as August 1258, before the new justiciar, High Bigod, Matthias Bezill was sentenced to gaol when a Wiltshire jury of twenty-four men refused to reverse his conviction for reducing a fee tenant to serfdom.[4] Later chroniclers, therefore, made no distinction between Lusignans and Savoyards. They had both, 'wherever they held dominion, behaved unbearably like kings and tyrants.'[5] While the Savoyards were damaged in this way, they also lost ground at the centre when Peter of Savoy, in 1260, either resigned or was removed from the king's council. The growing threat to her own party turned the Queen against the Provisions of Oxford, and in 1261, with Peter of Savoy, she played an important part in masterminding their overthrow. This was a large nail in the Savoyards' coffin. It was, in the popular mind at least, as destroyers of the Provisions that they were attacked in 1263.[6]

By that time there were other factors in the growing xenophobia. The collapse of the Provisions in 1261 revived the fortunes of the Lusignans,

1. Ridgeway, 'Henry III and the "Aliens"', p. 86; contrast J. R. Maddicott, 'Magna Carta and the Local Community, 1215-1259', *Past & Present*, cii (1984), 54-61.

2. The charge appears in the baronial letter of explanation to the pope probably written in July 1258, a letter which received wide circulation: *Ann. Mon.* i. 172, 458-9; *Chronica Majora*, vi. 402-3. The newsletter describing events at the Oxford and Winchester Parliaments already mentions the setting aside of the Lusignans' revenues 'to satisfy all who complain against them and their bailiffs': *DBM*, pp. 91-2. See Maddicott, 'Magna Carta and the Local Community', 56. The essence of the charge is also found in Matthew Paris's comments on William de Valence and his brothers in 1257: *Chronica Majora*, v. 634.

3. *Ann. Mon.* iii. 209 (the annals of Dunstable); H. M. Cam and E. F. Jacob, 'Notes on an English Cluniac Chronicle', *ante*, xliv (1929), 100 (the chronicle of the priory of St Andrew's, Northampton). Both these chronicles in 1258 were being written soon after events.

4. Ridgeway, 'Henry III and the "Aliens"', p. 87; Maddicott, 'Magna Carta and the Local Community', 54-61; E. F. Jacob, *Studies in the Period of Baronial Reform and Rebellion, 1258-1267* (Oxford, 1925), pp. 109-15, 355-64; P[ublic] R[ecord] O[ffice], Just 1/ 1187, m.24d. The eyres also revealed the malpractices of English magnates, notably the Earl of Gloucester.

5. A. Gransden (ed.), *The Chronicle of Bury St Edmunds, 1212-1301* (London, 1964), p. 23; cf. *Ann. Mon.* i. 174-5.

6. *DBM*, pp. 206-7, cap. 33; *Ann. Mon.* i. 175, ii. 355, iv. 128, 135; *Robert of Gloucester*, ii, lines 11046-53; *Chronicle of Bury St Edmunds*, pp. 26-7. Ridgeway, 'Politics of the English Royal Court', pp. 396-400, contains an important analysis of the events of 1263, focusing particularly on the unpopularity of the Queen and her party.

and William de Valence, Elyas de Rabayne, William de Sancta Ermina and Guy de Rochford all returned to England.[1] Even more, a whole new dimension was given to anti-alien feeling by the introduction of foreign mercenaries into the country. This enabled the King's opponents to play on the fear of foreign invasion and conquest, just as the young King himself had done when faced by Prince Louis and his Frenchmen in 1216–17.[2] In April 1260, fearing the plots of Edward and Simon de Montfort, Henry III had come back to England with a large body of foreign troops. Although they had not stayed for long, as late as August 1261 Henry was having to explain, in a proclamation circulated to all the counties, that he had acted merely to preserve the peace of the realm. It was nonsense to suggest that 'we intended to trample upon the native-born of our realm and introduce aliens to the damage and injury of the native-born'. Although the proclamation was careful not to say so, Henry's protestations were also relevant to the situation in 1261 itself, for, in his bid to recover power, he once again imported foreign knights and serjeants.[3]

By 1263, therefore, there was a great deal of smouldering resentment against Savoyards, Lusignans and foreign mercenaries. Up to a point, however, these resentments were felt by the men in the counties, those whom Henry had hoped to reach by his August 1261 proclamation, rather than by magnates at the centre of politics. It took a detonation at the centre for all the combustible material to ignite. This was finally provided by the actions of the Lord Edward. Indeed, an upheaval within Edward's household helped provoke the crisis of 1263, just as it had that of 1258. During the course of 1262 the Prince had quarrelled with one of his closest associates, Roger of Leybourne, being turned against him, according to the Canterbury/Dover Annals, by the machinations of the Queen. Just as she had resented Edward's alliance with the Lusignans in 1258, and had supported the ensuing revolution which drove them from England, so again in 1262 she conspired to rid her son of undesirable company. In so doing she provided another reason for the attack upon herself and her Savoyard friends in the following year. For Leybourne did not stand alone: others who had been close to Edward down to 1260 sympathized with him and had grievances of their own. Consequently, when Edward left England in 1262, not merely Leybourne was absent from his train. So too were such old familiars as Roger of Clifford, John de Warenne, Earl of Surrey, Henry of Almain, John de Vaux and Hamon Lestrange. All these men threw in their lot with Simon de Montfort

1. *Gervase of Canterbury*, ii. 211, 213; CPR, *1258–66*, pp. 148–50; *Close Rolls, 1261–4*, pp. 12, 32, 65, 199. On their return in 1261, the Lusignans were reconciled to the Savoyards.

2. Carpenter, *Minority of Henry III*, pp. 29, 394.

3. *Foedera*, I, i. 408–9; *Ann. Mon.* iii. 214; CPR, *1258–66*, p. 69; DBM, pp. 208–11, caps. 37–9; CPR, *1258–66*, pp. 152, 191; *Close Rolls, 1259–61*, pp. 487–8; *Flores Historiarum*, ii. 472; *Gervase of Canterbury*, ii. 213.

in the spring of 1263.[1] By that time their existing discontents had been inflamed by the nature of Edward's return, for he landed, on 24 February, surrounded by foreign knights and serjeants. The claim that these imported troops were needed for a campaign against Llywelyn rang hollow when the operation ended in complete failure.[2] Instead, Edward's new alien entourage underlined the fall of his old companions and gave them a second reason for an assault on foreigners: they thereby punished the Queen for plotting their eclipse and assailed the aliens who had replaced them at Edward's side.

The crucial role played by Edward's ousted followers in the events of 1263 was recognized by the Westminster *Flores Historiarum*. Indeed, the *Flores* links their grievances (though the chronicler here confuses various groups of foreigners) directly with the call for Simon de Montfort to return to England:

> The Burgundians, Frenchmen and Champagnois, whom the Provisions of Oxford had exiled, having been recalled to England, the eldest son of the King honoured them above his English familiars. ... On account of which certain strenuous knights, once his familiars, vehemently indignant, having made an alliance with all those whom the royal power had once offended, recalled the Earl of Leicester to England.[3]

The part assigned here to Edward's former companions is confirmed by one striking fact. The initial demand for the restoration of the Provisions of Oxford in 1263 was made, as we have seen, in a letter to Henry III sealed by Edward's erstwhile associate, Roger of Clifford.[4] The call for office to be restricted to native-born men may well have been made at the same time. Certainly Edward's conduct, in the view of the Burton Abbey annalist, was connected with the wider cry for aliens to be expelled altogether from the country. In his words,

> The Lord Edward ... having brought knights from overseas, immediately after Easter went to the borders of Wales to subjugate the Welsh to his dominion without the aid of the English. Accordingly, the indignant English, not only did not wish to help him, but also excited all the more for this reason, hastened with one mind to expel aliens according to the Provisions of Oxford.[5]

This 'expulsion' of aliens took the form of attacks on individual foreigners and provided the final impetus behind the statute. The assaults began in the first week of June, the first victims being the Savoyards, Peter de Aigueblanche, Bishop of Hereford, and Mathias Bezill, castellan of

1. Ibid. ii. 214, 220–1; *CPR, 1258-66*, p. 222; M. Prestwich, *Edward I* (London, 1989), pp. 37–8; Ridgeway, 'The Lord Edward and the Provisions of Oxford', p. 97. Leybourne and the rest seem equally to have been absent when Edward went abroad in 1261.
2. *Flores Historiarum*, ii. 478, iii. 256; *Ann. Mon.* i. 500, ii. 100.
3. *Flores Historiarum*, iii. 256. I owe this reference and my argument about the importance of Edward's return in 1263 with a following of aliens to John Maddicott's forthcoming biography of Simon de Montfort.
4. *Cronica Maiorum et Vicecomitum*, p. 53; cf. *supra*, p. 265.
5. *Ann. Mon.* i. 500; see also ii. 100.

Gloucester. They then spread to the properties of the Queen, the Lusignans, foreign clerics (shades of 1232), Cahorsin money-lenders, and natives accused of opposing the Provisions of Oxford. Many of the clerics, fearful for their safety, fled the country. Meanwhile, Edward's alien soldiers continued to focus attention. Around 24 June the Londoners told the prince and his father that 'they wished to allow no alien knights and serjeants to stay in the City since through them all the discord had arisen between the King and the barons'. At the end of the month these alien forces, put at 100 knights and 'many more satellites' by the St Albans *Flores Historiarum*, and described as 'all the aliens of his household' by the Dover annalist, left the city and went with Edward to garrison Windsor Castle, from where they promptly devastated the surrounding countryside.[1]

The statute against the aliens, therefore, was promulgated in July 1263, events over the previous three years having magnified hatred of foreigners many times over. The statute had effectively two clauses, which were probably conceived at different times. The first clause, confining office to native-born men, appeared in the *petitio Baronum*, which was in being around 24 June, but may have been drawn up considerably earlier, indeed perhaps as early as Roger of Clifford's initial letter written before 20 May. This, then, was the original demand, a demand which obviously served the purposes of Edward's fallen associates, and of other magnate enemies of the Lusignans and the Savoyards. It was only later that the second and more radical requirement emerged – that which called for the expulsion of all aliens, 'never to return', save those accepted 'in common' by the faithful men of the kingdom. This clause, as we have seen, appears not in the *petitio Baronum*, but in the somewhat later *forma pacis* of late June/early July, where it was explicitly stated to be something new. Its implication was that the Savoyards, Lusignans and Edward's entourage were not merely to leave office, but also to vacate the kingdom. So too were foreigners in general, the particular targets presumably being the 'Roman' clerics and Cahorsin money-lenders who had been subject to attack in June 1263. Essentially, the new clause was produced by the actual events of that month. It marked the decision of the Montfortians to sanction and exploit the popular tide of xenophobia in the hope of winning wide support for their cause.

The original demand banning foreigners from office represented hard, practical politics. A demand for the expulsion of Edward's soldiers from the country would have come into the same category. But the decision to go for something wider and call for the ejection of *all* foreigners was

1. *Robert of Gloucester*, ii, lines 11060–125; *Ann. Mon.* iii. 222, iv. 134–5; *Cronica Maiorum et Vicecomitum*, pp. 53–5; *Gervase of Canterbury*, ii. 221–2; *Flores Historiarum*, ii. 479–82, iii. 256–7; *The Chronicle of Bury St Edmunds*, p. 27; *Ann. Mon.* ii. 100; *Close Rolls, 1261–4*, pp. 308–9. The attack on Peter de Aigueblanche took place on 7 June: *Close Rolls, 1264–8*, p. 512. For the link between the *forma pacis* and the Windsor garrison made by the *Flores Historiarum*, see *supra*, p. 267, n. 1.

to move from the realm of practicalities into that of propaganda.[1] The very language of the *forma pacis* and the letter patent of 16 July was emotive: the aliens were 'never to return'. Good care was taken to give the contents wide publicity, for the Dunstable Annals as well as the St Albans *Flores* knew the terms of the *forma pacis*.[2] That the Montfortians, in practice, had reservations about the new clause is shown by the way they qualified it: aliens accepted 'in common' by the faithful men of the kingdom might stay. Thus the door was to be left open for the more acceptable of the King's foreign favourites, and for foreign clergy with English livings, the assaults on whom, in 1263, could not be condoned by Montfort's episcopal supporters.[3] In addition, of course, the country would be impoverished if barriers were placed in the way of foreign merchants. Indeed, the reluctance of merchants to visit the kingdom because the King failed to pay for their goods had been one of the original complaints in 1258, and was repeated before Louis IX at Amiens in January 1264.[4] For purposes of propaganda, however, these reservations were easily played down or forgotten. The Dunstable annalist, in his summary of the *forma pacis*, did not mention them at all. The King and Queen, he stated, were to 'cleanse England entirely of foreigners'.[5]

If, then, the statute against aliens owed a good deal to Edward's former entourage and the general wave of anti-alien violence in June 1263, was Simon de Montfort pushed into it against his own inclinations? For Simon, of course, was himself a foreigner. He had been born in France and was the son of a great French noble.[6] Nothing could make him native-born. On the face of it, under the terms of the statute, he was disqualified from any role in the governance of England, and even his residence in the country needed the unanimous sanction of the faithful men of the realm. Simon, moreover, just as much as the King, could be charged with bringing foreign soldiers into England. He had done that in 1260, 1261,[7] and quite probably in 1263: hence, at the end of 1263, a letter written by a supporter of Gilbert de Clare, then floating ambiguously between the two camps, warned against Simon since, although he persecuted and expelled some aliens, he protected others.[8]

1. I owe this point and the general perspective in this and the preceding paragraph to the suggestions of John Prestwich.

2. *Ann. Mon.* iii. 223-4.

3. *Cronica Maiorum et Vicecomitum*, p. 70.

4. *DBM*, pp. 86-7, cap. 23, pp. 274-5, cap. 5. It is significant that when the Montfortians presented their case to Louis IX at Amiens, they concentrated on the malpractices of certain curial foreigners rather than on those of aliens as a whole: ibid. no. 37C, caps. 2, 4, 7. No mention was made of the statute.

5. *Ann. Mon.* iii. 224.

6. The chief biographies are C. Bémont, *Simon de Montfort, comte de Leicester* (Paris, 1884), of which an English translation, by E. F. Jacob, was published at Oxford in 1930, and M. W. Labarge, *Simon de Montfort* (London, 1962). A new biography is being prepared by John Maddicott.

7. *DBM*, pp. 188-9; *Foedera*, I, i. 406 (*CPR, 1258-66*, p. 185).

8. *Ann. Mon.* i. 180.

Later, in 1265, Gilbert criticized Simon for placing important castles in the hands of foreigners and declared it was 'ridiculous' for Simon, an 'alien', to dominate the kingdom.[1] And yet, for the most part, Simon was able to shrug off these charges. Indeed, by the most extraordinary paradox of his career, far from hesitating over the statute of July 1263, he almost certainly urged its introduction. Nor was this the result of some sudden conversion, for he had long exploited hostility to foreigners, both to defend himself and to blacken the reputation of the King.[2] In 1252, when Simon was threatened by the King with disinheritance as a traitor, he burst out, according to Matthew Paris: 'I know well that, having despoiled me, [the King] will enrich some Provençal or Poitevin with my earldom.'[3] Eight years later, in 1260, Simon dragged in the same point when defending his resistance to the King's importation of foreign mercenaries: the King, he averred, 'seemed to put his trust more in foreigners than in the men of his own land.' This statement was far from being the wishful thinking of some chronicler: it came from Simon's own evidence to a commission investigating his dispute with the King.[4]

For Simon, therefore, antipathy to aliens was a two-edged sword, but one which he generally kept pointing in his opponents' direction. In part this was because Englishmen simply accepted the paradox. Simon was 'the shield and defender of the English, the enemy and expellor of aliens, although he himself was one of them by nation', declared the Melrose chronicler.[5] Yet it was also because Simon was regarded as the nearest thing to an Englishman. Indeed, in 1252, Matthew Paris actually described him as *naturalis*, 'native-born'.[6] Simon, after all, could claim to have inherited the earldom of Leicester – 'my earldom' – through his grandfather's marriage to the sister of Robert, Earl of Leicester, who had died childless in 1204.[7] Thus when Simon married the King's sister in 1238, he already had his own stake in the realm. He was not, like William de Valence, brought landless to England and foisted at once on a rich heiress. If, moreover, Simon himself was not English, his eldest son certainly was, having been born at Kenilworth in 1238.[8] And then Simon, far from surrounding himself with foreigners, like some other aliens, had gathered a substantial affinity of Midlands knights. His friend

---

1. The sources for these statements, however, respectively the chronicle of Robert of Gloucester and that ascribed to Rishanger, were compiled in the late thirteenth/early fourteenth centuries: *Robert of Gloucester*, ii, lines 11450–2; H. T. Riley (ed.), *Willhelmi Rishanger ... Chronica et Annales* (Rolls ser., 1865), p. 32.

2. For what follows, see also D. A. Carpenter, 'Simon de Montfort: The First Leader of a Political Movement in English History', above pp. 231, 235–6.

3. *Chronica Majora*, v. 338.

4. *DBM*, pp. 208–9, cap. 38.

5. A. O. and M. O. Anderson (ed.), *The Chronicle of Melrose* (London, 1936), p. 127.

6. *Chronica Majora*, v. 289.

7. *Complete Peerage*, vii. 536–7; *Chronica Majora*, v. 338.

8. Ibid. iii. 518.

and spiritual adviser was that most English of intellectuals, Robert Grosse-teste. Simon was at least an honorary Englishman.[1]

In 1263 itself, the first victims, following the promulgation of the statute, were Edward's foreign soldiers, who were given safe-conducts out of the realm after his surrender on 26 July.[2] Paradoxically, their expulsion helped undermine the restoration of the Provisions of Oxford achieved in July, since the way was cleared for Edward's reconciliation with Ley-bourne, Clifford, Warenne, Vaux, Lestrange, and Henry of Almain, all of whom, in the autumn of 1263, deserted Simon de Montfort to rejoin their old master. But there was no question of the July 1263 statute being abandoned once this had happened. On the contrary, Simon held on to it before everything else. In January 1264, as we have seen, Louis IX quashed both the Provisions of Oxford and the statute. In the abortive negotiations in March 1264, just before the outbreak of civil war, Simon and his followers offered to accept Louis' verdict if the condemnation of the statute was excepted from it: they 'begged the King humbly and devotedly that at least he would give up one article [in Louis' judgement], and that, aliens having been removed from England, he would govern through natives, and then they would accept all the statutes, provisions and ordinances of the King of France.'[3] The statute of 1263 thus became Simon de Montfort's final rallying-point. It was cunningly chosen, for it linked the irreducible minimum of the Provisions of Oxford – some restriction on the King's choice of councillors and ministers – to the popular cry of 'down with the aliens'.

After Simon's great victory at Lewes in May 1264, the Provisions of Oxford were reaffirmed.[4] But the statute of July 1263 was significantly modified. In his Constitution of June 1264 Simon set up a council of nine, chosen by three 'electors', to govern the country. In August, in a series of additions to the Constitution (the new form became known as the Canterbury peace), he laid down that the councillors and electors (although one was Simon himself), together with the king's castellans and other bailiffs, should always be natives: aliens at no time were to be appointed 'to any office or bailiwick in the realm or in the king's household'.[5] The ban on foreigners having any role in the government of the country was thus to remain absolute. The second part of the statute of July 1263, however, which had laid down that aliens must leave unless accepted by the faithful men of the kingdom 'in common', was effectively abandoned. It was now stated that

1. See above pp. 226–9; Ridgeway, 'Henry III and the "Aliens"', pp. 86–7; R. W. Southern, *Robert Grosseteste: The Growth of an English Mind in Medieval Europe* (Oxford, 1986), pp. 246, 289–90. Ridgeway, however, observes (p. 87) that the followers of William de Valence too were 'overwhelmingly English'.

2. *CPR, 1258–66*, p. 272; *Gervase of Canterbury*. ii. 223; and see *supra*, p. 272.

3. W. Stubbs (ed.), *Chronicles of the Reigns of Edward I and Edward II* (2 vols., Rolls ser., 1882–3), i 61.

4. J. R. Maddicott, 'The Mise of Lewes, 1264', *EHR*, xcviii (1983), 588–603.

5. *DMB*, pp. 298–9.

aliens may peacefully come, stay, and go away again, both laymen wishing to live on their possessions and clergy wishing to reside in their benefices, and merchants and all others may freely come to conduct their business and may stay in peace, provided they come peacefully, and not in arms or in suspiciously large numbers, and provided that none of them may be at any time appointed to any office or bailiwick in the realm or in the king's household.[1]

The immediate reason for this change was that Simon was under pressure. The Queen, with Louis IX's connivance, was gathering an army in Flanders and threatening to invade the kingdom. The papal legate was likewise threatening the Montfortians with excommunication. Simon therefore persuaded both Louis and the legate to come to Boulogne (where they arrived in August) to preside over attempts to find some new political settlement. The Canterbury peace was the document concocted for their inspection and approval, the pill of conciliar control of the King being sugared by the abandonment of part of the July 1263 statute.[2] There were also good practical reasons for this modification. The call for aliens to leave the country had been essentially propaganda, designed to garner support. In reality, the Montfortians themselves had recognized the undesirability of blanket expulsions, hence the qualification that aliens accepted by the faithful men of the kingdom 'in common' might remain. But the impossibility of all foreign magnates, merchants and clergy being vetted efficiently and harmoniously in this way must have been obvious. By abandoning the provision, Simon appeased his critics and showed himself a practical man of affairs. His regime was to be no short-term expedient; he intended it to survive.

At the same time, however, as Simon hushed the call to expel foreigners from the kingdom, he reiterated, as we have also seen, that part of the July 1263 statute which excluded foreigners from office. Such a ban had always been the main political objective of the Montfortians, and upon its retention, at least in some form, they remained immoveable. The Canterbury peace found no favour in Boulogne. The legate denounced the three electors and nine councillors for usurping royal power; Louis IX declared that 'he would prefer to break clods behind the plough than have a rule of that kind'.[3] On 11 September, therefore, Simon's party named arbitrators to modify the Canterbury peace and reach a fresh settlement. They were given full power to do so with one restriction: they were to agree to nothing 'by which the kingdom of England might be governed through others than natives; nor shall the custody of castles

1. Ibid.

2. Ibid., pp. 50, 294, n.2, 298, n. 9; Close Rolls, 1261-4, pp. 390-1; J. Heidemann, 'Papst Clemens IV: das Vorleben des Papstes und sein Legationsregister', in Kirchengeschichtliche Studien, ed. A. Knöpfler et al. (Münster, 1903), pp. 202, 211, 214. The register of the legate, Gui de Foulquois, soon to become Pope Clement IV, is printed ibid., pp. 194-248. This source was drawn to my attention by John Maddicott. The term 'Canterbury peace' derived from the fact that the document was drawn up at Canterbury, where the court stayed so as to be close to Louis IX and the legate at Boulogne.

3. Heidemann, 'Papst Clemens IV ... Legationsregister', p. 230; Foedera, I, i. 446.

or other bailiwicks in the kingdom be committed to others than natives.'[1] This scheme also failed, and on 26 September the Montfortian proctors, in what was to be their final effort, presented an entirely new *Forma compromissi* to the legate, which was recorded in his register. The compromise involved here was indeed substantial, for the Canterbury peace was jettisoned and the power of choosing the king's councillors was placed in the hands of five arbitrators of whom one was the legate. Again, however, it was laid down that the councillors were to be chosen 'from English and natives only' ('de Anglicis et indigenis tantum').[2] And, significantly, in the official version of the *Forma compromissi*, that found on the Patent Rolls, the councillors themselves were to choose only English and natives as important officials and bailiffs ('officialibus magistris et ballivis suis de Anglicis et indigenis tantummodo creandis et constituendis').[3]

Simon's refusal to abandon the July 1263 statute in its entirety was related in part to the situation which he faced in the late summer of 1264. While he tuned down the anti-alien rhetoric in the hope of getting Louis IX and the legate to prevent the Queen's invasion, he also tuned it up in order to resist the invasion, should it take place. Thus in response to emotional orders which warned of 'a great multitude of aliens' threatening everyone's 'perpetual confusion and disinheritance', 'innumerable people gathered on horse and foot from all the counties of England' eager, as the Annals of Dunstable put it, to preserve 'the English from total confusion and destruction'.[4] By this time, resistance to foreigners was seen as central to Simon's cause. It was a major theme of the Song of Lewes, the great political tract written to celebrate his victory, probably by a friar in the entourage of Stephen Berksted, Bishop of Chichester.[5] Likewise, monastic chroniclers came to explain the revolution of 1258 almost exclusively in terms of rescuing England from the oppression

---

1. Ibid.
2. Heidemann, 'Papst Clemens IV ... Legationsregister', pp. 235-7; *Foedera*, I, i. 447.
3. PRO, C 66/ 81, m.4d (*CPR, 1258-66*, pp. 370-1, where the translation of 'indigena' as 'denizen' is misleading). See also ibid., p. 347. Another variant text of the *Forma compromissi* is found in *The Chronicle of William de Rishanger*, pp. 37-8. Since the *Forma* shown to him was not absolutely explicit on the point, the legate asked the bishops among the Montfortian proctors if they agreed with the barons that the King should be compelled to follow the counsel of his councillors. Each of them said yes: Heidemann, 'Papst Clemens IV ... Legationsregister', p. 238. A large part of the conflict in England between 1258 and 1265 was summed up in that exchange. For the negotiations of August-September 1264, see F. M. Powicke, *Henry III and The Lord Edward* (2 vols., Oxford, 1947), ii. 478-82; N. Denholm-Young, 'Documents of the Barons' Wars', in his *Collected Papers*, pp. 159-62.
4. *Cronica Maiorum et Vicecomitum*, pp. 67-9; *Ann. Mon.* iii. 233. Simon may have used much the same propaganda in 1263: see *Gervase of Canterbury*, ii. 223. Likewise in 1264, according to the story in the hostile chronicle of Thomas Wykes, when the piracy of the Cinque Ports prevented foreign merchants entering the country and thus pushed up the price of goods, Simon 'in order to charm plebeian ears with frivolous diversions, declared and caused it to be proclaimed throughout the kingdom that natives could be perfectly well sustained from their own goods without the supplies of foreigners: *Ann. Mon.* iv. 158.
5. C. L. Kingsford (ed.), *The Song of Lewes* (Oxford, 1890), lines 281-324.

of the aliens.[1] What gave the issue such potency was that it appealed across the classes and divisions of English society. Magnates could resent the patronage given to foreigners; knights, freemen and peasants could suffer from the extortions of their local officials; the English as a whole could feel exploited when aliens, lay and clerical, grew fat on their resources; and the whole race was threatened if foreign mercenaries and armies invaded the country. Simon de Montfort had rightly made the question of the aliens his final sticking-point both before the outbreak of the civil war in March 1264 and during the Boulogne negotiations the following September. More than anything else, anti-alien feelings solidified his movement and broadened its popular appeal.

It is not surprising, therefore, that the statute was the one part of the reform programme which Gilbert de Clare sought to preserve when he finally deserted Simon in May 1265 and made his alliance with Edward. We have already seen how Gilbert had tried to turn the alien issue against Simon. Now he made Edward swear to induce the King 'to remove aliens from the kingdom and his council, and to prevent them from having custody of castles or any kind of administration in the kingdom, so that affairs are ruled by the council of natives faithful to him'.[2] Gilbert was still standing by this programme after the Battle of Evesham for, in January 1267, he demanded that Henry III should remove aliens from his council (a reference perhaps to William de Valence). A similar demand was made by the Disinherited in the Isle of Ely.[3] In fact the country was still awash with anti-alien sentiments. The King himself, in January 1266, tried to silence rumours that he had conferred the lands of the Earl of Norfolk 'and other of his lieges on aliens ... contrary to justice', while next year the clergy at Bury St Edmunds accused the legate of wishing 'to exile the native-born progeny of the land so that aliens can freely conquer it'.[4]

Of course, however strong these feelings, and whatever promises Edward made to Gilbert de Clare, no statute banning foreigners from holding office in England was ever introduced. Increasingly the issue lost importance. While Edward I and his successors sometimes had foreign ministers and favourites, these never formed groups and parties as they had done in the middle of the thirteenth century. Even Gaveston was a provocative individual, not the head of a family network. Hostility to foreigners continued, but it was channelled into external wars, not internal political strife. In one sense the huge importance attached to the issue of the aliens in mid-thirteenth-century England was due to the misguided practices of a particular king. In a broader perspective, it

1. *Ann. Mon.* i. 174-5, ii. 349-50, 335; *Flores Historiarum,* iii. 252-4; *Chronicle of Bury St Edmunds,* p. 23.

2. *Ann. Mon.* iv. 164-5.

3. *Chronicle of William de Rishanger,* pp. 60, 64; *Willelmi Rishanger ... Chronica et Annales.* pp. 47, 55: references I owe to John Maddicott.

4. *Foedera,* I, i. 467; *Chronicle of William de Rishanger,* p. 62, a reference I owe to John Prestwich.

marked a stage in the 'making' of England, when political society was almost completely Anglicized, but monarchy still retained vestiges of the imperial outlook of the Angevin kings.

Appendix

The *petitio Baronum* of May/June 1263: printed from T. Stapleton (ed.), *De Antiquis Legibus Liber. Cronica Maiorum et Vicecomitum Londoniarum* (Camden Soc., 1846), p. 54. MS: Corporation of London Record Office, Custumal 1, fols. 84b–85. For the date, see *supra*, pp. 265–6.

Et sciendum, quod talis fuit petitio Baronum.
Petunt Barones a Domino Rege humiliter et devote, quod ordinationes et statuta apud Oxoniam facta, et juramento firmata, tam Domini Regis quam et Magnatum, et subsequenter omnium et singulorum totius regni Anglie, firmiter et inviolabiliter observentur. Ita, tamen, quod si aliqua in eis, per considerationem bonorum virorum ad hoc electorum, inveniantur Domino Regi vel regno prejudicialia vel dampnosa, illa penitus subtrahantur; et si que fuerint obscura vel corrigenda, declarentur vel corrigantur; et provideatur securitas de aliis, videlicet, bonis et utilibus, imperpetuum firmiter observandis. Item, petunt quod regnum de cetero per indigenas, fideles et utiles sub Domino Rege, gubernetur, et non per alios, sicut fit communiter in omnibus aliis mundi regnis.

The *forma pacis* of late June/early July 1263: printed from H. R. Luard (ed.), *Flores Historiarum* (3 vols., Rolls ser., 1890), ii. 482. MS: British Library, Loan 94 (Chetham Library, Manchester, MS 6712), fo. 232. For the date, see *supra*, p. 266, n. 4.

De pacis forma inter regem et barones facta.
Et haec fuit forma pacis, concepta tunc temporis inter regem et barones suos; videlicet, quod Henricus filius regis Alemanniae per regem et reginam liberetur, et quod castra regis custodiae baronum committantur. Item, quod provisiones et statuta Oxoniae firmiter et inviolabiliter tam a rege quam ab aliis observentur, et quod regnum de caetero per indigenas, fideles et utiles sub domino rege, gubernetur. Insuper, quod exeant alienigenae a regno, ulterius non reversuri, exceptis illis quorum moram fideles regni unanimi assensu acceptarent.

Letter patent of 16 July 1263: printed from the patent role of 47 Henry III (part I), Public Record Office C66/ 79, m.7 (ink), m.6 (pencil). Punctuation modernized. Printed in English translation in *Calendar of Patent Rolls, 1258–1266* (London, 1910), pp. 269–70.

Rex omnibus etc. salutem. Cum nuper plenam dederimus potestatem per nostras patentes litteras venerabilibus patribus Ricardo Lincolniensi, H. Londoniensi, R. Coventrensi et Lichefeldensi et W. Exoniensi episcopis, fratri Johanni de Derlington' et Willelmo de Wilton' tractandi de pace necnon et pacem ineundi ac pacem firmandi inter nos et barones nostros super questionibus et contencionibus habitis de constitucionibus et statutis factis apud Oxoniam, et dicti episcopi, frater Johannes et Willelmus vice nostra et auctoritate concesserint Baronibus predictis quod ordinaciones et statuta apud Oxoniam facta, et iuramento nostro ac magnatum et aliorum singulorum regni nostri Anglie firmata, inviolabiliter et firmiter observentur, et statu providenciarum in pristina seisina prout poterit reformato, ex tunc si aliqua in eis per consideracionem bonorum virorum per regni fideles ad hoc electorum nobis et regno nostro preiudicialia vel dampnosa inveniantur, penitus subtrahantur, et obscura quoque vel corigenda si qua fuerint declarentur et corigantur; securitate provisa de istis et aliis bonis videlicet et utilibus nobis et regno nostro imperpetuum firmiter observandis; ac, insuper, quod regnum decetero per indigenas, fideles et utiles sub nobis, gubernetur, necnon ut exeant alienigene, non reversuri, exceptis illis quorum moram fideles regni communiter acceptabunt; nos premissa omnia grata habentes et accepta, ea concedimus ac firmiter et inviolabiliter volumus observari, omnibus impetratis et impetrandis a quibuscunque curiis vel personis per que effectus presencium impediri possit aut differri penitus et plene renunciantes. In cuius rei testamentum sigillum magnifici principis et fratris nostri dilecti R. Regis Romanorum illustris una cum sigillo nostro presentibus procuravimus apponi. Teste Rege apud Westmonasterium xvi die Julii.

15

Simon de Montfort and the Mise of Lewes

IN A RECENT article in the *English Historical Review*, Dr. J. R. Maddicott has shed important new light on the terms of the Mise of Lewes, the settlement drawn up between King Henry III and Simon de Montfort immediately after Simon's victory at Lewes on 14 May 1264.[1] Maddicott has shown that both the chronicle of Furness abbey and the London chronicle, probably written by the alderman, Arnold fitz Thedmar, give the same account of the Mise. Both state, in virtually identical words, that, on the night after the battle, the king and the barons agreed that the Provisions of Oxford should stand unbroken ('inconcusse'). However, if anything in the Provisions needed correction, it was to be wholly ('penitus') corrected by four of the more noble bishops or magnates of England. If there was disagreement between these four arbitrators, then the verdict was to be accepted ('staretur veredicto') of Charles of Anjou and the duke of Burgundy, provided the majority of the barons would agree to this. Henry III and his brother, Richard king of Almain, meanwhile, were to give their eldest sons, Edward and Henry, as hostages for the observance of this settlement, and it was stipulated that a parliament should meet in London on 8 June, presumably to approve the terms of the Mise.[2] On the basis of this, and other supporting evidence, Maddicott successfully rebuts the view of N. Denholm-Young that the Mise said nothing about the Provisions of Oxford, but submitted the question of the future constitution of the kingdom to a committee to be chosen by six Frenchmen, a committee which is mentioned in other references to the Mise. Rather Maddicott shows that the central feature of the Mise was the reimposition of the Provisions, with the concession to the king that they could be revised by a panel of English bishops or magnates. It was, in all probability, only the secondary question of how to settle grievances arising from the depredations and spoliations of 1263–4 which was referred to the committee nominated by the Frenchman.[3]

Maddicott has, therefore, brought us closer to what was actually in the Mise of Lewes. He has also opened up for debate the whole question of why Simon de Montfort, after his great victory, was prepared to concede that the Provisions of Oxford might be revised. Maddicott stresses Simon's 'reverence' for the Provisions: hence their reimposition in the Mise. The offer of arbitration, he

---

[1] J. R. Maddicott, 'The Mise of Lewes, 1264', *Eng. Hist. Rev.*, xcviii (1983), 588–603.
[2] The Furness account is in *Continuatio chronici Willelmi de Novoburgo* in *Chronicles of the Reigns of Stephen, Henry II and Richard I*, ed. R. Howlett (4 vols., Rolls Ser., 1884–9), ii. 544. For the London chronicles see *De Antiquis Legibus Liber: Cronica Maiorum et Vicecomitum Londoniarum*, ed. T. Stapleton (Camden Soc., 1846), p. 63. For fitz Thedmar see A. Gransden, *Historical Writing in England, c. 550–c. 1307* (1974), pp. 509–11. For both accounts see Maddicott, pp. 593–4, 602–3.
[3] Maddicott, pp. 592–601; N. Denholm-Young, 'Documents of the Barons' Wars', *Eng. Hist. Rev.*, xlviii (1933), 558-75. For the proposed committee of six Frenchmen see Maddicott, pp. 591-2, 596–600.

suggests, needs to be seen in terms of the 'political constraints on Montfort's position'. The fact was that Simon's defeat of the king

had given him no firm basis for his government; rather, it had made that government more difficult. A régime based merely upon coercion, upon the military victory of rebels in a civil war, was likely to be neither stable nor permanent, for it lacked both legitimacy and the consent of the defeated. It was the earl's awareness of these weaknesses that largely explains both the terms of the Mise and his other actions immediately after the battle. The Mise itself was a moderate settlement, designed to attract support. If the Provisions were once again resurrected (and no less could have been expected), the proposal to amend their details suggests that Montfort may have been less obdurate in their defence than is sometimes thought.[4]

There are, however, difficulties with an hypothesis which seeks to explain Simon's concessions along these lines. If the Mise was indeed 'a moderate settlement, designed to attract support', Simon would surely have given it as much publicity as possible. With the entire apparatus of the state in his hands after 16 May he had ample means to do so. He could, for example, have embodied the terms in royal letters patent, and sent them to the sheriffs to be read in every county court. But, as far as is known, nothing like this was done. Accurate information about the Mise reached only the Furness and London chroniclers, both of whom, as Maddicott plausibly suggests, probably derived their information from an unofficial news-letter written immediately after the battle.[5] Consequently it has needed Maddicott's ingenuity over 700 years later to unravel the terms of the settlement. If, moreover, Simon was indeed less than obdurate in his attachment to details of the Provisions, and was prepared to emend them in the search for much needed support, he would surely have set the process of arbitration speedily in motion. But again, as far as is known, absolutely nothing was done about this.[6] Instead, in June 1264 at a parliament in London, Simon imposed his own constitution on the king: an *Ordinatio* which, although it differed in its form, embodied all the principles of the Provisions of Oxford. It is true that this *Ordinatio* was to be superseded once the Mise of Lewes was fulfilled, but no indication was given as to when that might be.[7] And when, shortly before 15 August 1264, the *Ordinatio* was re-issued, it was laid down that it was to last throughout the lifetime of Henry III until an undetermined date in the reign of his son. Although this duration was still conditional on the non-fulfilment of the Mise of Lewes, the implication was that the *Ordinatio*, rather than a version of the Provisions revised by arbitration, was to form the long-term basis for Simon's government.[8]

Maddicott, of course, is aware that nothing was done to emend the Provisions, and he offers two possible explanations for this, the first being that the Mise was 'aborted by circumstance'. 'Within two months of its drafting', he writes, 'the threat of invasion, the combined hostility of the French king, the pope and the papal legate, war in the Marches and disorder throughout the country, made the implementation of reform impossible'.[9] Yet even if it were accepted that these

---

[4] Maddicott, pp. 592, 601. He also suggests that Montfort devised the terms of the arbitration so as to place it in the hands of those likely to be friendly to the Provisions (*ibid.*, pp. 596, 601).

[5] *Ibid.*, p. 594.

[6] *Ibid.*, p. 601.

[7] *Documents of the Baronial Movement of Reform and Rebellion, 1258–67*, comp. R. F. Treharne, ed. I. J. Sanders (Oxford, 1973), pp. 294–301.

[8] *Ibid.*, pp. 294–5; see also Denholm-Young, pp. 562–3 ('Simon is struggling to make his constitution permanent').

[9] Maddicott, p. 600.

pressures rendered Simon less rather than more likely to consider reform,[10] it is difficult to see why he could not have put the Provisions to arbitration before his political situation deteriorated. After all, as early as 26 May he had appointed the six Frenchmen who, under the terms of the Mise, were probably to deal with the question of the spoliations of 1263-4.[11] Had he wished, he could surely have made the parallel appointments of the bishops or magnates who were to decide about the Provisions of Oxford. Maddicott's second explanation is to question how far Simon de Montfort was sincere in conceding that the details of the Provisions might be emended.[12] But if he was insincere, if he had little intention of executing what he had promised, it is hard to understand how he thought the offer of arbitration would bring him legitimacy and support. Certainly the value of that concession would have been very short term. Once its non-fulfilment was apparent, it was more likely to harm than enhance Simon's credit, since he would be open to charges of bad faith. The London chronicle probably hinted at such a charge when, having recorded the Mise, it added that it 'nunquam pervenit ad effectum', while the Merton *Flores Historiarum* stated specifically that the barons drew up the June *Ordinatio* 'compromissi Lewensis et praestiti juramenti . . . immemores'.[13]

There is a final difficulty with Maddicott's thesis, namely that, leaving aside for the moment the Mise of Lewes, it is far from clear that Simon at any time agreed that the Provisions of Oxford might be revised merely to gain general political support. Consequently to have done so in the Mise would have been uncharacteristic. Montfort's proposals for revision were all made in difficult or critical political situations. But he seems to have been concerned less to win general popularity than to make acceptable offers to the king or his supporters, thereby inducing them to alter course. Montfort's first proposal for revision was part of the settlement in July 1263 when Henry III reaffirmed the Provisions. The vagueness of the plan, which committed Simon to virtually nothing and was never developed further, tells against the view that it was intended to bring him support. More probably it was a concession to the king, designed to ease and expedite his agreement to abide by the Provisions.[14] After July 1263, apart from

---

[10] It will be argued below that, in fact, when Simon came under pressure he became more prepared to make concessions.

[11] *Close Rolls 1261-4*, pp. 385-6; Maddicott, p. 596.

[12] Maddicott writes, 'With what sincerity the proposal [of arbitration] was made is hard to gauge: the apparent failure to go ahead with their amendment [the amendment of the Provisions], in July 1263 as well as in May 1264, leaves room for doubt' (Maddicott, p. 601).

[13] *Cronica Maiorum*, p. 63; *Flores Historiarum*, ed. H. R. Luard (3 vols., Rolls Ser., 1890), iii. 261; Denholm-Young, p. 560. For the Merton *Flores* see below nn. 34-6.

[14] In July 1263 Henry III agreed that the Provisions of Oxford should be observed 'inviolabiliter et firmiter' and should be brought back as far as possible to their 'pristina seisina'; and, if things in the Provisions were found to be 'prejudicialia vel dampnosa' to the king and the kingdom 'per consideracionem bonorum virorum per regni fideles ad hoc electorum' then 'penitus subtrahantur'. Obscurities and things needing correction were also to be clarified and corrected. This proposal, therefore, gave no indication as to the identity or number of the arbitrators, what was to happen if they disagreed, or when they were to be chosen. The statement that the arbitrators were to be nominated by 'faithful men of the kingdom' settled nothing save the obvious point that the king could not choose the arbitrators himself. Who were to be the 'faithful men of the kingdom'? These proposals were far less specific in their terms than those in the Mise of Lewes (which is discussed below), and Simon had consequently much less to worry about accusations of bad faith when the arbitration was not proceeded with. The July 1263 settlement was enrolled on the patent roll (Public Record Office, C 66/81 m. 6; *Calendar of Patent Rolls 1258-66*, pp. 269-70), but it is unclear whether Simon took steps to publicize his concession over arbitration, which is mentioned only by the Dunstable annals (*Annales Monastici*, ed. H. R. Luard (5 vols., Rolls Ser., 1864-9), iii. 224). The political background to this period is most easily followed in Sir J. H. Ramsay's splendid work, *The Dawn of the Constitution* (Oxford, 1908), chs. xiii, xiv.

the Mise of Lewes, there were three occasions on which Montfort countenanced
further schemes for arbitration. In December 1263, having lost control of the
king, deserted by many of his followers, and anxious to avoid the doubtful issue
of a civil war, Simon agreed to submit the Provisions to the arbitration of Louis
IX of France.[15] Similarly, in the days before 14 May 1264, hoping to escape a
battle in which he would be heavily outnumbered, he offered to accept the
arbitration of learned ecclesiastics.[16] Finally in September 1264, with invasion
by the queen's army gathered in Flanders imminent, he referred the future
structure of the kingdom's government to named French and English magnates
and churchmen.[17] Once the queen's army had dispersed in October 1264,
however, little more is heard of arbitration, and in the parliament of March 1265
the *Ordinatio* of June 1264 was solemnly reaffirmed.[18] This pattern of conduct
does not suggest that Simon de Montfort would have made the concessions in
the Mise simply to secure political backing and favour. Rather, one would
expect them to have been made directly to the king and his son in order to
influence their actions. What, however, could those actions have been?

In order to answer this question it is necessary to look at the battle of Lewes
and its immediate aftermath. All the historians who have written about the battle
have assumed that Simon's victory was complete and overwhelming. I have
myself spoken of Simon's 'stupendous victory', which left both 'Henry and his
son, the Lord Edward, prisoners in his hands'. Similarly Maddicott states that 'at
Lewes Montfort won a great victory, capturing not only Henry III but also the
Lord Edward'. Thus the earl was able to 'impose' the terms of a settlement.[19] But
were Henry and Edward Montfort's prisoners when the Mise of Lewes was being
negotiated? There are good reasons for thinking that they were not.

It is true that the St. Albans abbey *Flores Historiarum*, the monastic chronicles of
Worcester, Waverley, Battle, Furness and St. Benet of Hulme, a London
chronicle and the chronicle of Robert of Gloucester, all state that while the Lord
Edward was engaged in the pursuit of Montfort's contingent of Londoners, the
king was taken prisoner. The impression left by all these accounts is that the
king's surrender took place on the field of battle.[20] The chronicles of Worcester,

[15] T. Rymer, *Foedera*, ed. A. Clarke, F. Holbrooke and J. Caley (4 vols. in 7, 1816–69), I. i. 434;
Ramsay, pp. 209–10.
[16] Maddicott, pp. 588–90.
[17] *Cal. Pat. Rolls 1258–66*, pp. 347–8; Denholm-Young, pp. 564–5; Ramsay, pp. 231–2. It is
indicative of the weakness of Montfort's position at this time that he was unable to return to the
scheme of arbitration in the Mise of Lewes, which confined the arbitrators, in the first instance, to
Englishmen (see below), but had to accept a joint panel of Englishmen and Frenchmen.
[18] *Foedera*, I. i. 451–2; Ramsay, p. 236.
[19] D. A. Carpenter, 'St. Thomas Cantilupe: his political career', *St. Thomas Cantilupe, Bishop of
Hereford: Essays in his honour*, ed. M. Jancey (Hereford, 1982), p. 58; below p. 294; Maddicott,
p. 591. For the views of other historians see below n. 42.
[20] *Flores Historiarum*, ii. 496; *Annales Monastici*, iv. 452 (Worcester, based on a Winchester annal);
ibid., ii. 357 (Waverley); C. Bémont, *Simon de Montfort* (Paris, 1884), p. 377 (Battle); *Chronicles of Stephen,
Henry II and Richard I*, ii. 543 (Furness); *Chronica Johannis de Oxenedes*, ed. Sir H. Ellis (Rolls Ser., 1859),
pp. 223–4 (St. Benet of Hulme); *Annales Londonienses* in *Chronicles of the Reigns of Edward I and Edward
II*, ed. W. Stubbs (2 vols., Rolls Ser., 1882–3), i. 63 (this is not the London chronicle attributed to fitz.
Thedmar, for which see below n. 32); *The Metrical Chronicle of Robert of Gloucester*, ed. W. A. Wright (2
vols., Rolls Ser., 1887), ii. 750. For these chronicles, see Gransden, pp. 402, 508–9, and ch. xviii. A
similar account is found in the Dunstable annals, but without referring to Edward when describing
the flight of the Londoners (*Annales Monastici*, iii. 232). A large number of other chronicles mention
the king's capture without placing it in the context of the episode of the Londoners, some of them
giving no details at all about the battle (for example, *Annales Monastici*, ii. 101 (annals of Winchester);
The Chronicle of Bury St. Edmunds, 1212–1301, ed. A. Gransden (1964), p. 28; *The Chronicle of the Abbey of
S. Werburg at Chester*, ed. R. C. Christie (Lancs. and Cheshire Record Soc., xiv, 1888), p. 88; *Chronicon*

Waverley, Battle, Furness and Robert of Gloucester, moreover, agree that Henry submitted to Gilbert de Clare, earl of Gloucester.[21] There is, however, another group of chronicles, those of Thomas Wykes, Walter of Guisborough, Dover abbey and that known as the Merton *Flores Historiarum* which tell a different story, namely that Henry escaped from the field and returned to the Cluniac priory of St. Pancras in which he had been staying before the battle.[22] There is some divergence of view about what happened next. Wykes says that Henry fled into the priory church, but was compelled to give himself up through the prevarication of those who should have given him protection. All this happened before Edward's return to Lewes after his destruction of the Londoners.[23] There are, however, some grounds for treating Wykes's story of the king's rapid surrender once in the priory with suspicion. Wykes alleges that Henry's brother, Richard king of Almain, fled there with him. But it is a well attested fact that Richard took refuge and was compelled to capitulate in a windmill, an episode which caused much amusement at his expense.[24] Wykes was closely associated with Richard, and he may well have doctored his account of the battle of Lewes to conceal the king of Almain's humiliation.[25] The chronicler, Walter of Guisborough, moreover, gives a version of events very different from that of Wykes, a version which needs to be set out in some detail.[26]

According to Walter, while Edward was engaged with the Londoners, the barons attacked the division ('aciem') of the king of Almain and took him prisoner. They also attacked the king's division and killed his war-horse. Henry's attendants ('sui'), therefore, seeing that the battle was going badly, 'reduxerunt regem in abbatiam[27] unde prius exierat, claudentes portas et custodiam adhibentes cum multis militibus'. The barons, then, having obtained victory on the field, entered the town, and for a long while there was confusion, the number of wounded making it difficult to see who were barons and who royalists. On Edward's return from his pursuit of the Londoners, a fierce fight ensued between him and the barons, and an important contingent of royalists, including the earl of Surrey, Hugh Bigod, William de Valence and Guy de Lusignan, took flight. After this, Edward circled around the town as far as the castle (which was still in royal hands) 'et ibi non invento patre reversus est ad eum in abbatiam'. The barons then attacked the castle, but the garrison defended it with vigour.

de Lanercost, 1201–1346, ed. J. Stevenson (Bannatyne Club, lxv, 1839), p. 75; H. M. Cam and E. F. Jacob, 'Notes on an English Cluniac chronicle', *Eng. Hist. Rev.*, xliv (1929), 102; British Library, Cotton MSS. Nero A. ix fo. 72, Cleopatra D. ix fo. 54v, Faustus B. vi fo. 75).

[21] *Annales Monastici*, iv. 452, ii. 357; Bémont, p. 377; *Chronicles of Stephen, Henry II and Richard I*, ii. 543; *Chronicle of Robert of Gloucester*, ii. 750.

[22] *Annales Monastici*, iv. 151 (Wykes); *The Chronicle of Walter of Guisborough*, ed. H. Rothwell (Camden 3rd ser., lxxxix, 1957), p. 195; *The Historical Works of Gervase of Canterbury*, ed. W. Stubbs (2 vols., Rolls Ser., 1879–80), ii. 237 (Dover); *Flores Historiarum*, iii. 260. The king also escapes to the priory in Nangis's history of the reign of St. Louis, *Recueil des Historiens des Gaules et de la France*, xx (Paris, 1840), p. 414. The chronicle of Lewes priory mentions the king's escape but does not say where he escaped to.

[23] *Annales Monastici*, iv. 151.

[24] *Ibid.* It is difficult to believe that the incident of the windmill is an invention; for the story see *Chronicle of Robert of Gloucester*, ii. 750; Bémont, p. 377; *The Chronicle of Melrose*, ed. A. O. Anderson and M. O. Anderson (1936), p. 128; *The Political Songs of England*, ed. T. Wright (Camden Soc., 1839), p. 69.

[25] For Wykes and Richard king of Almain see N. Denholm-Young, 'Thomas de Wykes and his chronicle', *Eng. Hist. Rev.*, lxi (1946), 160.

[26] *Chronicle of Walter of Guisborough*, pp. 194–6.

[27] Guisborough speaks throughout of 'abbey' rather than 'priory'.

Quod videntes barones retraxerunt se et ad abbathiam diverterunt, et illuminata est ecclesia telis eorum sed tamen post modicum ignis ille extinctus est. Videns autem filius regis eorum audaciam et recollectis multis ex suis, cum remansissent adhuc plures viri strenuissimi, disposuit iterato exire ad pugnam. Quo cognito miserunt barones mediatores pacificos qui diem differentes in crastinum promiserunt quod in crastina die loquerentur de plena pace cum effectu . . . . Sequenti vero die Jovis |15 May| discurrebant inter regem et barones bini et bini de ordine predicatorum et minorum portantes verba pacifica et sic cum quibusdam aliis interponentes partes suas quod sequenti die veneris |16 May| tradidit se filius pro patre, Edwardus scilicet pro rege et pro ceteris commilitonibus suis et Henricus filius regis Alemannie dedit se pro patre suo, et hoc sub spe pacis et quietis ut cum deliberacione tractarent inposterum que provisionum et statutorum essent pro utilitate regni tenenda et que rationabiliter recusanda, et quod hinc inde captivi libere et absque ullo dato redderentur.

There are good reasons for accepting the substance of this account. Walter of Guisborough began writing his chronicle about the year 1300. For the period 1264–7, however, as Professor C. H. Lawrence has recently shown, 'there are . . . strong indications that . . . Guisborough was using a contemporary narrative of the Barons' Wars', a narrative which for the battle of Lewes displays a marked degree of 'independence and detailed knowledge'.[28] None of the chronicles which state that Henry was taken prisoner while Edward was giving chase to the Londoners can compare with Guisborough in the amount of detail given either about the battle or the negotiations after it from which the Mise of Lewes emerged.[29] The Guisborough version, moreover, is supported by the Dover chronicle, which, as Maddicott says, is 'not only contemporary, but also particularly well-informed about events in south-east England'.[30] The Dover annalist, having mentioned the capture of the king of Almain and Philip Basset, continues

Rex vero Angliae reversus est in prioratum, et Eadwardus filius eius, et Henricus filius regis Alemanniae; et comes Simon cum exercitu suo prioratum obsedit. Tandem rex, timens sibi et suis, ad comitem venit licet invitus, et statuta Oxoniae juravit.[31]

This account, then, confirms that Henry escaped to the priory, and that Edward was with him there.[32] Its reference to the priory being besieged recalls Guisborough's narrative about the barons going to the priory, and setting its church on fire with their arrows. The Dover annalist, however, does not say, any

---

[28] C. H. Lawrence, 'The university of Oxford and the chronicle of the Barons' Wars', *Eng. Hist. Rev.*, xcv (1980), 102, 104–5. For the influence of Guisborough's account on other historians, see below n. 42.

[29] None of the chronicles which place Henry's surrender during the battle gives any detail about how the Mise of Lewes was negotiated. Apart from a brief remark in the annals of St. Benet at Hulme (*Chronica Johannis de Oxenedes*, p. 222), none of them says anything about how the rival armies were divided up. Guisborough, on the other hand, goes into great detail about the various divisions and gives the names of the commanders (*Chronicle of Walter of Guisborough*, pp. 193–4).

[30] *Works of Gervase of Canterbury*, ii. 237; Maddicott, pp. 592–3; Gransden, p. 423.

[31] *Works of Gervase of Canterbury*, ii. 237.

[32] The Battle chronicle, which places Henry's surrender on the field, has the king returning to the priory afterwards, but, of course, as a prisoner (Bémont, p. 377). Another chronicle, the St. Albans *Flores Historiarum*, states that the Lord Edward, on his return, went to the priory, ' and deferred vengeance till better times'. Whether the chronicler believed that Edward surrendered on entering the priory is not clear (*Flores Historiarum*, ii. 498). Two chronicles, however, say that Edward returned to the house of the Franciscan friars (*Annales Monastici*, ii. 357 (Waverley); *Chronicle of Robert of Gloucester*, ii. 750). A London chronicle says that Edward entered the 'church' of Lewes (*Chronicles of Edward I and Edward II*, i. 63). It is worth noting that the London chronicle, probably by Arnold fitz Thedmar, mentions the capture of the king of Almain, but not that of Henry III or the Lord Edward (*Cronica Maiorum*, p. 63).

more than Guisborough, that this siege brought Henry's immediate surrender. His statement that 'tandem' the king came to Montfort and swore to the Provisions is perfectly compatible with the negotiations which Guisborough describes.

The king's escape from the field is also implied by a further chronicle, and one which was probably well informed since it is that of Lewes priory. Although the surviving text was not written till the early fourteenth century, it was based for the reign of Henry III on annals roughly contemporaneous with the events which they describe. The Lewes chronicle states that 'rex bene verberatus gladiis et de maciis et duo equi sub eo [mor]tui ita quod vix evasit, et frater suus R[icardus] rex alemannie confestim captus'.[33] Finally, the Guisborough version is corroborated by another independent chronicle, the Merton *Flores Historiarum*. This was written in the thirteen-hundreds, and, unlike Guisborough, has a pronounced royalist bias, being possibly produced at Westminster abbey. However, its author had access to convincing information, for example in what he says about the Mise of Lewes, which is found in no other source.[34] In the *Flores* account of the battle, after Richard king of Almain and Philip Basset had been taken prisoner, 'reversus est . . . rex Angliae ad prioratum Lewensem, raro satellite sociatus'. The barons then entered Lewes and captured and plundered those whom 'extra castellum et prioratum poterant invenire'. When Edward returned with the Marcher lords, and other warlike 'familiares' who were more than double the number of their adversaries,

ipsisque viriliter se parantibus ad congressum, omnes et singulos dicti comitis Leycestriae calliditas circumvenit. Per quosdam enim fratres Minores dicto regi Angliae et eius filio nunciavit, quod pacem et benivolentiam dicti regis et suorum affectantes, ne plus humani sanguinis funderetur, causam suam supponerent libenter arbitrio quorumcumque, quos idem rex duxerit eligendos. Et si dicti rex et eius filius, oblivionis huiusmodi moderamine non contenti, vellent congredi cum eisdem, ipsi . . . regem Alemanniae, Johannem Comyn, Philippum Basset, et caeteros captos in praelio trucidarent, capitibus eorum levatis in lanceis pro vexillis. Quamobrem dicti rex et eius exercitus, moti visceribus pietatis, a suo proposito destiterunt, et habito tota nocte sequente de pace tractatu, tandem in formam subscriptam fuit a partibus in fine consensum.[35]

This account may be exaggerated in certain of its details. It seems unlikely that Edward's forces on his return greatly outnumbered those of the barons. Equally the terms of the Mise do not suggest that Montfort offered to let the king choose the arbitrators. But the Merton and Guisborough narratives agree well enough on the vital points, namely that the Mise was negotiated while Edward still had a considerable body of troops, and while the king was in the priory, not yet a prisoner in Montfort's hands.[36]

[33] Brit. Libr., Cotton MS. Tiberius A. x. fo. 170. The manuscript of the chronicle is damaged. I have supplied the portions within square brackets. The passage is printed (with emendations) in W. H. Blaauw, 'On the early history of Lewes priory, and its seals, with extracts from a MS. chronicle', *Sussex Archaeol. Collections*, ii (1849), 28.

[34] Gransden, pp. 456–63; Denholm-Young, p. 560; Maddicott, p. 595. Although the account of the battle in the Merton *Flores* is similar to that of Guisborough it appears to be independent of it. For example, it places the flight of the earl of Surrey, Hugh Bigod and William de Valence at an earlier stage of the battle (*Flores Historiarum*, iii. 260). For the Merton chronicle and the Mise of Lewes see n. 35.

[35] *Flores Historiarum*, iii. 259–60. The agreement which the *Flores* sets out contains the details of the committee of six Frenchmen (Denholm-Young, p. 560; Maddicott, pp. 592, 595).

[36] The Merton account does not state specifically that Edward joined his father in the priory, although nothing that is said contradicts this.

Guisborough's narrative of the actual negotiations is itself consistent with what we know of them from other sources. The Furness and London chronicles state that the Mise was 'provisum et ordinatum' 'nocte illa', that is the night of 14–15 May. The Merton *Flores*, which like Guisborough mentions the role of the friars as intermediaries, says that 'habito tota nocte sequente de pace tractatu tandem' agreement was reached.[37] The difference between these testimonies and that in Guisborough, which indicates that negotiations began on the 14 May but were then postponed until the morrow, is small. That the Mise was completed by 15 May is confirmed by a royal letter of that date which declares that 'peace has been made between the king and his barons, oaths taken on both sides, and all things are settled in peace'.[38] Guisborough does not say specifically that peace was agreed on 15 May, but a settlement by then is compatible with his account. What he does say is that it was on the next day, the Friday (16 May), that Edward and Henry of Almain gave themselves up as hostages. It may well be that, although the Mise was finalized on 15 May and oaths were sworn, the hostages were not formally delivered until the 16th. Guisborough concludes his account by saying that on the Saturday (17 May) the king gave permission for those in the castle and church of Lewes to depart. This seems likely since the dating clauses of royal letters show that Henry himself moved from Lewes to Battle on 17 May.[39]

If the Guisborough version of events is fundamentally correct, however, how does one account for the widespread belief among chroniclers that the king did indeed surrender, and surrender to the earl of Gloucester? One also needs to explain a royal letter of 6 October 1264 which says that at Lewes Edward and Henry of Almain became hostages for the preservation of peace and for the 'deliverance' ('deliberatio') of the king, Roger Mortimore, James de Audley (two great Marcher barons) and Roger of Leybourne.[40] There are, however, no real difficulties here. It may well be that after negotiations were completed on 15 May, Henry formally surrendered to the earl of Gloucester. Edward then became a hostage for his father's 'deliverance'. It was easy for ill-informed or over-enthusiastic chroniclers to assume that the king's surrender took place during the battle. Two of these chroniclers, however, give details which imply that it did not. The Battle annalist says that Henry called for the earl of Gloucester so that he could surrender to him, and the Waverley annalist says that Henry, because he disliked Simon de Montfort, gave up his sword to Gloucester.[41] It might well have been possible during a period of negotiations

---

[37] Maddicott, pp. 602–3; *Flores Historiarum*, iii. 260. The St. Albans *Flores* says that peace was arranged 'nocte sequenti' (*ibid.*, ii. 498). Although the Guisborough narrative correctly places the battle on a Wednesday, it errs in saying this was the feast of St. Dunstan (19 May). However, as Prof. Lawrence suggests, this is probably a mistake by a copyist. The text should have read that the battle was fought on the Wednesday before the feast of St. Dunstan, that is 14 May (Lawrence, p. 105).

[38] *Cal. Pat. Rolls 1258–66*, p. 318.

[39] *Chronicle of Walter of Guisborough*, p. 196; *Calendar of Liberate Rolls 1260–7*, p. 136; *Cal. Pat. Rolls 1258–66*, p. 318. One small further point may be cleared up here. Robert of Gloucester mentions that after the battle Alan la Zouche was captured in the priory in the dress of a monk (*Chronicle of Robert of Gloucester*, pp. 753–4). This sounds like an authentic detail. But how can it be reconciled with Henry and Edward holding out in the priory with a considerable body of men? Robert of Gloucester tells us, however, that Zouche had been captured in the battle. Although his captor, William Maltravers, had let him go, he had presumably done so on certain conditions. Probably Zouche was to take no further part in the fighting, and give himself up when it was over. Zouche was, therefore, in a different position from the other royalists in the priory. When the latter went out on 17 May, he may well have attempted to conceal himself in order to avoid surrendering to William Maltravers.

[40] P.R.O., C 66/81 m. 2d (*Cal. Pat. Rolls 1258–66*, p. 374).

[41] Bémont, p. 377; *Annales Monastici*, ii. 357. Another factor which may have led the St. Albans *Flores* and a Winchester chronicle to think that Henry was taken in the battle was their knowledge that the king's horse was killed under him (*Flores Historiarum*, ii. 496; *Annales Monastici*, iv. 452). By the 14th

for Henry to insist that he wished to surrender to Gloucester. It seems unlikely that he could have done so during the heat and confusion of a battle.

On the evening of 14 May 1264, therefore, Simon de Montfort faced a difficult situation. He had achieved victory on the field, but his triumph was incomplete. The chief prize, the surrender of the king and his son, had yet to be won. Simon could not entirely impose the terms of a settlement.[42] The king and the Lord Edward were in the priory. This lay just outside the town of Lewes, and was surrounded by its own wall.[43] The gates were shut and guarded 'cum multis militibus'. Edward retained 'plures viri strenuissimi', including Henry son of the king of Almain, and several Marcher barons.[44] The Winchester chronicle says that there were over 500 men in the priory.[45] The king's forces also held the castle, having resisted one baronial assault.[46] Of course, the cards remained stacked heavily against the royalists. Otherwise they would not have agreed to terms which involved the reimposition of the Provisions of Oxford and which placed the Lord Edward and Henry of Almain in Montfort's hands as hostages, But, albeit at cost to themselves, they still had the power to damage Montfort's position. If a sally from the priory ended in a bloody imbroglio in the vicinity of Lewes, or if the priory had to be taken by starvation or attack, Simon might face accusations of brutality, his victory at Lewes might no longer appear so God-given and miraculous, the power and prestige of his régime might be dealt a considerable blow. Thus although Montfort's archers set the priory church on fire with arrows, the earl drew back from ordering an all-out assault. When Edward, according to both Guisborough and the Merton *Flores*, prepared to go out again to fight, Montfort suggested negotiations. Clearly he was eager to bring matters to a conclusion as quickly and as peaceably as possible.

To achieve such a conclusion Simon threatened, if hostilities were recommenced, to execute his prisoners. Perhaps there were also hints that the priory might be burnt down. Thus Henry, according to the Dover annalist, swore to the

century the belief that Henry was captured on the field was so entrenched that the chronicler Nicholas Trevet altered Guisborough's account, which otherwise he copies or summarizes, so as to have Henry made a prisoner there, and then brought back and kept in custody in the priory. This makes nonsense of the subsequent narrative in which Edward joins his father in the priory and wishes to continue the fight (*F. Nicholai Triveti . . . Annales*, ed. T. Hog (English Hist. Soc., 1845), p. 260). For further elaboration see *Willelmi Rishanger . . . Chronica et Annales*, ed. H. T. Riley (Rolls Ser., 1865), pp. 27–8.

[42] Nineteenth and 20th-century historians, in their accounts of Lewes, divide into those who believe that the king was taken during the battle, those who, usually with variations, follow Guisborough, and those who take an independent line of their own. Even those who follow Guisborough most closely, however, do not appreciate the significance of his narrative for the situation that Montfort faced on the evening of 14 May. All historians appear to accept that by then the earl's victory was complete. Those who have Henry captured during the battle include Bémont, p. 213; M. W. Labarge, *Simon de Montfort* (1962), p. 235. Those who follow Guisborough include W. H. Blaauw, *The Barons' War* (2nd edn., 1871), pp. 199–200, 205, 207–8, still the best account of the battle; Ramsay, pp. 223–4, although with nothing said about an attack on the priory, and with Edward returning to the house of the Franciscans (see above n. 32); A. H. Burne, *More Battlefields of England* (1952), pp. 106–7. Sir Maurice Powicke's version was as follows: 'the king took sanctuary with the Cluniacs, Edward in the house of the Grey Friars or Franciscans' (F. M. Powicke, *King Henry III and the Lord Edward* (1 vol. in 2, Oxford, 1947), p. 467; idem, *The Thirteenth Century* (Oxford, 1953), p. 190).

[43] Blaauw, pp. 199–200.

[44] For the Marchers, see below n. 50; for Henry of Almain, *Works of Gervase of Canterbury*, ii. 237.

[45] *Annales Monastici*, ii. 102. In the chronicler's view, during the battle some were killed, some fled and over 500, not wishing to go out to fight, remained in the priory.

[46] *Chronicle of Walter of Guisborough*, pp. 194–6; *Flores Historiarum*, iii. 260. There is no evidence that the garrison in the castle surrendered before Henry gave them licence to come out on 17 May (*Chronicle of Walter of Guisborough*, p. 196).

Provisions of Oxford, 'timens sibi et suis'.[47] On the other hand, Simon made concessions. One of these was his agreement to let the Marcher barons go free.[48] On the face of it this was a remarkable blunder. Simon and Roger Mortimore were already sworn enemies. After Roger and his fellows departed from Lewes they played a major part in the events leading up to Simon's defeat and death at the battle of Evesham.[49] The decision to let the Marchers go, however, becomes explicable when it is seen as something forced upon Montfort by the necessity of achieving an immediate and peaceful settlement. To that end it was a logical and perhaps a necessary move because while the Mise of Lewes was being negotiated the Marchers were not Simon's prisoners. Instead they were with Henry and Edward in the priory.[50] Edward was unable to secure his own freedom since Montfort insisted that he remain as a hostage. But in return the king's son obtained the free departure of his Marcher allies.

Simon also made the concession over the Provisions of Oxford. Both the Merton *Flores* and Guisborough narratives are absolutely clear that the promise of revision was the bait that Simon offered Henry and Edward in order to bring hostilities to an end. As the *Flores* noted, Montfort prevented a renewal of the conflict both by threatening the prisoners, and by suggesting that the dispute be referred to arbitration. Similarly, according to Guisborough, Edward and Henry of Almain became hostages for their fathers, 'sub spe pacis et quietis ut cum deliberacione tractarent inposterum que provisionum et statutorum essent pro utilitate regni tenenda et que rationabiliter recusanda'.[51] In negotiating the terms of the arbitration, therefore, Montfort had to ensure that they were generous enough to induce the royalists to give up the fight. Thus in the two Frenchmen who were to decide disputes between the four English bishops or magnates, royal and baronial interests were evenly matched. The duke of Burgundy was 'notable for his loyalty to Louis IX', and thus was likely to be hostile to the Provisions of Oxford. Charles of Anjou, by contrast, although a brother of Louis, was said to favour the party of Montfort, and to be bound to the earl by oath.[52] This balance between the two Frenchmen at least gave the impression that it would be repeated when it came to choosing the four Englishmen. The Mise also gave some indication that the process of arbitration would quickly get under way in its stipulation that parliament was to meet as early as 8 June. The implication was that the assembly was both to approve the terms of the Mise, and perhaps to help choose the four English bishops or magnates. Of course, Henry and Edward were well aware that once Simon controlled the government the chances of his proceeding with revision were slim. But the concessions which they secured still had some value. The more they could pin Montfort down on the arbitration, the more his failure to go through with it would appear in a bad light and weaken

---

[47] *Works of Gervase of Canterbury*, ii. 237; *Flores Historiarum*, iii. 260 (for the threat to the prisoners).

[48] *Cal. Pat. Rolls 1258–66*, p. 374; *Annales Monastici*, iii. 232.

[49] Labarge, pp. 221, 223; Ramsay, pp. 212, 233–4, 239, 245–6.

[50] That the Marchers were with Edward on his return to Lewes is stated by the Merton *Flores* (*Flores Historiarum*, iii. 260). Significantly the Dunstable annalist does not include the Marchers in his list of those captured in the battle, but adds that they were allowed to go free (*Annales Monastici*, iii. 232). The St. Albans *Flores* confirms that Roger Mortimore and the other Marchers were not taken prisoner, though it believes they fled from the battle (*Flores Historiarum*, ii. 498). The treatment of the Marchers contrasts sharply with that of royalists who were taken prisoner. The Mise of Lewes probably laid down that the latter 'were to be controlled by their captors, who were entitled to ransom their prisoners' (Maddicott, p. 591). Given the good relations which Montfort was able to achieve with Llewelyn, it is unlikely that Simon let Roger and his fellows go in order to protect the March from the Welsh prince.

[51] *Flores Historiarum*, iii. 260; *Chronicle of Walter of Guisborough*, p. 196.

[52] Maddicott, p. 596; *Flores Historiarum*, ii. 502.

the legitimacy of any constitution which he imposed. Hence, as we have seen, the comment of the London chronicle that the Mise of Lewes 'nunquam pervenit ad effectum', and that of the Merton *Flores* that the barons drew up the June 1264 *Ordinatio* 'compromissi Lewensis et praestiti juramenti ... immemores'.[53]

For Simon de Montfort, therefore, the essential purpose of the concession over arbitration was to prevent a messy and bloody conclusion to the battle of Lewes. The offer was designed to get Henry and Edward out of the priory and into his hands. Once it had done that it had served its purpose. With the king and his son in Montfort's custody, control of the outstanding royalist castles quickly followed, and 'ex tunc', as the chronicler Nicholas Trevet put it, Simon 'ad tractandum de pace secundum formam praemissam [the form in the Mise of Lewes] difficiliorem se exhibuit, eo quod regem et regnum totum in sua habuit potestate'.[54] Simon's problem, of course, was that failure to carry out the Mise left him open to charges of duplicity. But the spread of such accusations could be contained. Far from publicizing the promise of arbitration, Montfort kept as quiet about it as possible. This was why accurate details reached only two chroniclers. Both before and after the battle of Lewes Simon de Montfort's political skills were used to win support for the cause of the Provisions. He would not alter the Provisions to win support. In that respect there was little that was flexible about the great earl.[55]

---

[53] *Cronica Maiorum*, p. 63; *Flores Historiarum*, iii. 261.

[54] F. *Nicholai Triveti Annales*, p. 261. Trevet (for whom see Gransden, pp. 501–7) was here developing a passage in Walter of Guisborough (*Chronicle of Walter of Guisborough*, pp. 196–7).

[55] A draft of this article was read as a paper in 1983 at Mr. J. L. Bolton's seminar at the Institute of Historical Research. I hope that it has profited from the criticisms which were made in the subsequent discussion. Readers should now consult D. W. Burton, '1264: Some New Documents', *Historical Research*, 161 (1993), 317–328, where a contemporary newsletter about the battle is printed and discussed.

16

St Thomas Cantilupe: His Political Career

Thomas Cantilupe's tomb, erected not long after his death, survives in the north transept of Hereford cathedral. In niches around its sides are carved a series of weepers. Each represents a knight in full armour. A monument of this kind might seem more suitable for a baron than for a bishop who was to be made a saint. Yet it was perfectly appropriate. As Richard de Swinfield, Thomas' friend and successor, remarked during the canonization proceedings, it was 'well known throughout the kingdom' that Thomas came from 'the noble stock of the barons of England'.[1] The Cantilupes had risen through the service of kings. Thomas' grandfather William de Cantilupe I (ob. 1239), a Norman by birth, was King John's steward of the household. William de Cantilupe II (ob. 1251), Thomas' father, held the same position under Henry III. Both Williams were richly rewarded for their royal service, and gained extensive lands in England.[2] Thomas was proud of his lineage. The fleur-de-lis of the Cantilupe arms were prominently displayed on both sides of his episcopal seal.[3] The weepers on the tomb would doubless appear as his kinsmen, had the blazons once painted on their shields survived. Family connections were of crucial importance in moulding Thomas Cantilupe's political career. That career was brief but significant. Apart from a sequel as a councillor of Edward I, it was confined to the years 1263–5 when Thomas emerged as a leading supporter of Henry III's great opponent, Simon de Montfort, earl of Leicester. For a few months in 1265, when Montfort was controlling the government of England, Thomas was chancellor of the realm. This chapter will consider the factors which led Thomas to embrace the cause of Simon de Montfort; it will examine his term as chancellor, which has not previously been studied; and it will look at the relationship between Thomas' Montfortian phase and his subsequent career as Edwardian councillor and bishop of Hereford.

To understand Thomas Cantilupe's role between 1263–5 it is necessary to glance briefly at the course of English politics in the preceding years.[4] 1258 in

---

[1] *Acta Sanctorum* (Antwerp-Brussels, 1643 sqq.), Octobris, 1 (hereafter AA.SS), 599.

[2] For the Cantilupes, see Sir William Dugdale, *The Baronage of England* (London, 1675), I, 731; the *Dictionary of National Biography; Victoria County History of Warwickshire*, III, 36.

[3] See *Rolls of Arms Henry III*, ed. T.D. Tremlett (Harleian Soc., CXIII-IV, 1961–2), 119–20.

[4] For politics in this period see R.F. Treharne, *The Baronial Plan of Reform* (Manchester, 1932); F.M. Powicke, *Henry III and The Lord Edward* (Oxford, 1947); *The Thirteenth Century* (Oxford, 1953).

England was a year of revolution. Exasperated by many aspects of his government, the great magnates forced King Henry III to accept the Provisions of Oxford. These laid down that Henry must govern with the advice and consent of a council of fifteen. The great magnates were to have a major role in determining the personnel of the council and in controlling the king's choice of ministers. These restrictions lasted until Henry III's recovery of power in 1261. However, two years later a coalition, which included Gilbert de Clare, the young earl of Gloucester, revived the cause of the Provisions of Oxford, and summoned Simon de Montfort back to England to act as its leader. Montfort, an enthusiastic protagonist of the reforms of 1258, had retired to France in 1261, rather than accept their overthrow. In July 1263 he and his friends forced Henry to re-affirm the Provisions. The political situation was, however, very different from that in 1258. Many of those who had supported reform then, now stood aside, or were actively hostile to the earl of Leicester's party. When some of Montfort's allies deserted, Henry III was able to re-assert his independence. By December the country stood on the brink of civil war. All that could be agreed was to refer the dispute to the arbitration of Louis IX, the widely respected king of France. It is at this point that Thomas Cantilupe made his first appearance. In December 1263 Montfort sent him, with several colleagues, to plead the cause of the Provisions before Louis IX.[5] Their advocacy was to no avail. Louis' judgement, the mise of Amiens of January 1264, condemned the Provisions outright, and declared that the king could appoint and dismiss ministers 'at his own free will'. Since Montfort and his followers would not accept this verdict the result was civil war. This culminated in Simon's stupendous victory at Lewes in May 1264, which left both Henry III and his son, the Lord Edward, prisoners in his hands. Montfort had now to devise a constitution for the governance of England. The council of fifteen set up by the Provisions of Oxford had been broken up by death and defections. Instead, in the parliament of June 1264, three 'electors' were chosen (Simon himself; Gilbert de Clare, earl of Gloucester; and Stephen de Berksted, bishop of Chichester), who were to nominate a king's council of nine. On the advice of this council the king was to select his ministers and 'settle the affairs of the realm'. One of the councillors chosen by the 'electors' was Thomas Cantilupe.[6] The euphoria of Lewes soon evaporated. By early 1265 Simon's government was torn by dissension with Gilbert de Clare, earl of Gloucester; was defied by the lords of the Welsh March, who had been set free after Lewes; and was condemned by the papacy, which had ordered the excommunication of Simon and his supporters. It was at this point, on 25 February 1265, that Cantilupe was elected 'by the king and

---

[5] *Gervase of Canterbury*, ed. W. Stubbs (Rolls Series, 1879–80), II, 232; *The Chronicle of William Rishanger*, ed. J.O. Halliwell, (Camden Soc. 1840), 122.

[6] *Documents of the Baronial Movement of Reform and Rebellion*, ed. R.F. Treharne, I.J. Sanders (Oxford, 1973), (hereafter *DBM*), 295–9. One of the council of three was always to be at court, and collectively they had power to dismiss the nine. In practice the government was run by Simon de Montfort and members of the nine.

the magnates of the council' to the chancellorship.[7] His predecessor, John of Chishill, had been appointed by the king in December 1263, and was probably politically neutral.[8] In February 1265 a more convinced Montfortian was required.

Thomas Cantilupe, then, entered politics at a time of crisis, and as a partisan of Simon de Montfort. How can we explain Thomas' political allegiance? The most central and controversial feature of Montfort's programme was the demand that the great magnates, representing the community of the realm, should regulate the appointment of the king's councillors and ministers. The documents which Cantilupe and his colleagues took to Louis IX in December 1263 justified this claim on the simple grounds that the king had ruled badly before 1258 and must be controlled. Henry's heedless liberality, especially to his foreign relatives, had made him bankrupt; these relatives and other courtiers had placed themselves above the law, and 'justice was shut out from England'; the sheriffs had been corrupt; the church oppressed. In 1258 these indictments had secured wide support for the Provisions of Oxford. By 1263, and even more by 1265, great magnates had become increasingly aware of the difficulties and dangers of conciliar rule. Many were also antagonised by the personal ascendancy of Simon de Montfort. Yet, while others wavered, Thomas remained committed to the cause of reform and its controversial leader. In seeking to explain the strength of Thomas' attachment, the role of various influences may be considered: Thomas was a teacher at Oxford university: an ecclesiastic: and above all, a Cantilupe.[9]

Thomas Cantilupe's political convictions may have been reinforced by likeminded colleagues at Oxford. Cantilupe had been there since at least 1255, and in 1261–2 was chancellor.[10] An issue like conciliar control of the king, first demanded at a parliament in 1244, must have been eagerly discussed in university circles. Of course, Oxford is unlikely to have taken a uniform view of politcal matters.[11] Henry III had been a generous benefactor, and there is no evidence that the University was in disfavour after his recovery of power in 1265. Many of Henry's clerks were Oxford graduates. Cantilupe would not, however, have been alone in sympathising with Montfort and his cause. Two of the bishops closest to the earl of Leicester in 1264–5 were Berksted of Chichester, one of the three 'electors', and Sandwich of London, who was with Thomas on the council of nine. Both, like Cantilupe, were fresh from the University where

---

[7] *Calendar of Patent Rolls* (hereafter *CPR*) *1258–66*, 410.

[8] T.F. Tout, *Chapters in the Administrative History of Mediaeval England* (Manchester, 1937), I, 297, 299, 307–9.

[9] *DBM*, 257–67. (The documents of December 1263 are here dated – with equal validity – January 1264). In the absence of any writings it is impossible to know whether Cantilupe justified his politics in the light of some political theory.

[10] *CPR 1247–58*, 412; A.B. Emden *A Biographical Register of the University of Oxford to 1500*, (Oxford, 1957), I, 347–8.

[11] For Oxford in this period, see C.H. Lawrence, 'The University of Oxford and the Chronicle of the Barons' Wars', *English Historical Review* (XCV, 1980), 99–113.

'they had spent most of their adult lives . . . before they were mitred in 1262'. When the king besieged Northampton in 1264, at the start of the campaign which ended at Lewes, clerks of the University fought against the royal army under their own banner.[12]

Thomas Cantilupe's views, and those of masters and students at Oxford who thought like him politically, were probably coloured by the predicament of the church in England. Of all the groups in English society the church was the most solidly behind Simon de Montfort in the years 1263–5. Monastic chroniclers eulogised the great earl.[13] At the parliament of March 1265 nine bishops gave their support to his regime. Five of these bishops-Berksted of Chichester, Sandwich of London, Cantilupe of Worcester (Thomas' uncle), Gravesend of Lincoln and Gervais of Winchester-were later suspended from office by the papacy for being 'especial favourers' of the earl.[14] Only four bishops between 1263–5 were clearly on the king's side, and two of these were foreigners.[15] Ecclesiastical enthusiasm for Montfort derived from Henry III's subjection of the church before 1258 – the manipulation of elections; the extortions during vacancies; the encroachments on jurisdiction; and the heavy taxation brought by Henry's misguided scheme to place his second son on the throne of Sicily.[16] Simon de Montfort's religiosity helped him benefit from these grievances. He cultivated the friendship of churchmen, and encouraged, to a degree unusual for a lay magnate, ecclesiastical reform. Robert Grosseteste, bishop of Lincoln, the greatest reforming bishop of the age (ob. 1253), had been 'a close personal friend of Simon's, perhaps in some sense his spiritual director'.[17] In 1264–5 Montfort did not disappoint the hopes of ecclesiastics. Several were given high office in his government, which showed itself continuously sympathetic to the claims and rights of the church.[18]

Thomas Cantilupe, then, may well have been drawn towards Simon de Montfort in much the same way as were other conscientious clerics. There was also, however, a more personal, and probably more potent bond between the two men. Thomas' early career had developed under the wing of his uncle, Walter de Cantilupe, a son of William de Cantilupe I, and strong links remained between them. Walter, as the royalist chronicler Wykes put it, was a 'brave and intimate' adherent of the earl of Leicester.[19] Unlike the other bishops close to

[12] *ibid.*, 111, 100.

[13] A. Gransden, *Historical Writing in England* (London, 1974), 415–35.

[14] Powicke, *op. cit.* (1947), II, 490; Lawrence, *op. cit.*, 111; *Annales Monastici*, ed. H.R. Luard (Rolls Series, 1864–9), IV, 156; hereafter *Ann. Mon.*

[15] The archbishop of Canterbury, and the bishops of Hereford, Rochester and Norwich; all were closely connected with the court; M. Gibbs, J. Lang, *Bishops and Reform 1215–72* (Oxford, 1934), 189–91.

[16] *DBM*, 268–71, 278–9.

[17] *Robert Grosseteste*, ed. D.A. Callus (Oxford, 1955), 205–6.

[18] Powicke, *op. cit.* (1947), II, 484–5.

[19] *Ann. Mon.*, IV, 180. There is a good account of Walter's career in the *Dictionary of National Biography.*

Montfort in 1263–5, Walter de Cantilupe was an old stager. He had been elected to the bishopric of Worcester in 1236, and was by far the most prominent ecclesiastical champion of the Provisions between 1258–61. His relationship with Simon de Montfort can be traced from at least 1248, when the Franciscan, Adam Marsh, remarked in a letter to the earl, 'the bishops of Lincoln [Grosseteste] and Worcester [Cantilupe] amongst all mortals are most favourably linked to you in special friendship'.[20]

The association between Walter and Simon de Montfort probably rested, in part, on similar views about the problems of church and state. Cantilupe was a committed churchman, and had quarrelled with Henry III on several occasions over ecclesiastical matters. In 1250 he defied the king's prohibition, and defended the jurisdictional rights of his see against the sheriff of Worcester by prosecuting a plea at the papal court. In 1255 he opposed the taxation of the church for the Sicilian venture.[21] These differences were the more likely to cement a political coalition with Simon de Montfort because Walter was not only a reforming bishop. He was also a councillor of the king. Both his family's connection with the court, and his own early career as a royal clerk pushed him in this direction. Dismissed from the king's council in 1255 for his opposition to Sicilian taxation, he was re-appointed two years later, and sent to negotiate peace with the king of France.[22] The experiences of Simon and Walter before 1258 were not dissimilar. Both were councillors of Henry III; both had felt the king's displeasure.

It has not, hitherto, been fully appreciated that this connection between the bishop and Simon de Montfort, was part of a wider alliance which embraced Walter's nephew, Peter de Montfort and perhaps another nephew, the son of William de Cantilupe II, William III. Peter de Montfort, who was no relation of Simon, had spent at least fifteen years as the ward of Walter's father (1216–31). In 1242 he journeyed to Gascony in the company of his cousin William de Cantilupe III. The tradition of the Cantilupe family was of loyal service to the crown, but when William III, by marriage a great Marcher lord, succeeded in 1251, his relationship with Henry III became strained. On his death in 1254 Peter de Montfort and Walter de Cantilupe judged money which was owed his executors. Simon de Montfort laid his body in the grave. Two years before, when Simon was on trial at Westminster for his conduct as seneschal of Gascony, only Peter de Montfort, Bishop Cantilupe and Peter of Savoy (the queen's uncle) stood by him. In 1258 Walter, Simon and Peter de Montfort were among the twelve representatives elected by the great magnates to assist in the drawing up of the programme of reform. In June all three became founder members of

[20] *Monumenta Franciscana*, ed. J.S. Brewer (Rolls Series, 1858), 270, 277–8; C. Bémont, *Simon de Montfort* (Paris, 1884), 19, n. 4.

[21] *Close Rolls* (henceforth *CR*) *1247–51*, 525; *Ann. Mon.*, I, 143, 145; IV, 102, 440; *Chronica Majora Matthaei Parisiensis*, ed. H.R. Luard (Rolls Series, 1872–83), V, 525, 326; hereafter *Chron. Maj.*

[22] Cantilupe was certainly on the council in 1255. His dismissal may be inferred from his re-appointment in 1257; *CR 1254–6*, 160; *Ann. Mon.*, I, 395; *CPR 1247–58*, 594.

the council of fifteen. The following year Simon named Peter as one of his executors. In 1261 both Peter and Walter were his representatives in the process of arbitration which was to settle his differences with the king.[23] About this time Peter de Montfort told the king's clerk Walter of Merton, 'whatever you do to favour [our uncle Bishop Walter] we will count it wholly done for us'[24] In 1264 the bishop absolved Simon's army before the battle of Lewes. After the battle Peter was elected to the council of nine. The next year Peter de Montfort died with the earl of Leicester at Evesham. The bishop of Worcester had said mass for the doomed army before the battle.[25]

The two Montforts and Walter de Cantilupe saw each other at court. They must also have met in the country. The chief seat of the Cantilupes was at Aston Cantlow in Warwickshire; that of Peter's family was at Beaudesert. The two places were but four miles apart. Simon de Montfort's great base in England was at Kenilworth: twelve miles from Aston Cantlow and nine from Beaudesert.[26]

Walter de Cantilupe, then, enjoyed a longstanding personal and political friendship with Simon de Montfort. The friendship also encompassed Thomas Cantilupe's cousin, Peter de Montfort, and perhaps his brother, William de Cantilupe III. There seems little doubt that Thomas was drawn by his uncle Walter into the same circle. Thus, as bishop of Hereford, one of Thomas' most trusted clerks was his 'kinsman', master William de Montfort, a son of Peter de Montfort of Beaudesert.[27] From the first, Walter de Cantilupe exercised a decisive influence on Thomas' career. The story that he prophesied that the infant Thomas would become an ecclesiastic may be apocryphal, but there seems no reason to doubt the evidence of Richard de Kimberle, who had spent ten years in Thomas' household and whose father had served Bishop Walter. 'He had heard it said that his uncle Walter brought Thomas up, kept him in the schools and beneficed him'. One of those in Thomas' *familia* in Paris was master Thomas de Buttevilt, who was later steward of Walter de Cantilupe. Thomas held several livings in the Worcester diocese which were of the bishop's gift. In 1255 he was pardoned a small offence connected with the royal forest on his uncle's 'prayers'. When Walter died in February 1266, Thomas was his executor, and was left that most personal of possessions, his hair shirt. Thomas' servants probably reflected the view of their master when they described Walter as a man of

---

[23] *Complete Peerage*, IX, 123; Dugdale, *op. cit.*, I, 404, *Pipe Roll 26 Henry III*, 341; *Chron. Maj.*, V, 224–5; *CPR 1247–58*, 348; *Ann. Mon.*, III, 192; *Monumenta Franciscana*, 123; Bémont, *op. cit.*, 328, 196 n. 1. See Powicke, *op. cit.* (1947), 229, n. 2.

[24] Public Record Office (hereafter PRO) SC/1/7/20.

[25] *Ann. Mon.*, IV, 168, 174; *DBM*, 295.

[26] *Victoria County History Warwickshire*, III, 32, 36, 45–6. Beaudesert was situated in a hundred held by the bishop of Worcester.

[27] *AA.SS*, 555; *Reg. Cantilupe*, 111, 221, xix; *Reg. Swinfield*, 71, 101; *Roll of the Household Expenses of Richard de Swinfield*, ed. J. Webb (Camden Soc., 1855), cxxx; *Complete Peerage*, IX, 128 n.a. One of Thomas' benefices was at Aston Cantlow.

learning and of saintly and austere life, for whom, after his death, God worked many miracles.[28]

Thomas Cantilupe's politics, therefore, probably owed a great deal to his uncle Walter and to the company in which Walter moved. The same connections doubtless facilitated his elevation both to the council of nine and to the chancellorship. Thomas, however, was well known in his own right by 1263. On one occasion, while in Oxford, he had invited the Lord Edward and many earls, barons and justices of the king to a feast in London. His prestige and training as a scholar, and his familiarity with Louis IX, whom he had met whilst studying in Paris, made him an ideal choice to promote the cause of the Provisions at Amiens. In the period 1258–65 outsiders were quite frequently given charge of the chancery and treasury, but they had usually proved their administrative ability in other fields. Here Thomas' term as chancellor of Oxford may have been important. That he exercised a firm rule over the turbulent masters and students is suggested by his conduct during his second term of office in the 1270s, and by his complaint that another chancellor of Oxford was insufficiently 'stern and attentive in the administration of justice'. It was necessary, in Thomas' own words, to be a 'terror to fools'.[29]

Thomas Cantilupe kept the king's seal from 25 February to 7 May 1265.[30] The chancellor was responsible for the writing and sealing of all royal letters and thus held a pivotal position in the government of England. Apart from a couple of stories told during the canonization proceedings, the sources for Thomas' term in office are the rolls of the chancery itself. The chancery recorded the royal letters which it issued, according to their type, on the close, patent, liberate and fine rolls. Charters were entered on the charter roll. All five rolls survive for the period of Cantilupe' keepership.[31] Although this comprised less than three months Thomas clearly took vigorous hold of his office. He rejected gifts and accepted a rise in the chancellor's salary. He refused to consent to at least one royal letter, and took more responsibility than his predecessors in the 'giving' of royal charters. He probably instituted the large increase in the number of notes on the chancery rolls indicating on whose authority royal letters were issued. It is difficult to be certain whether a common theme runs through all this activity. The interpretation of chancery practice has many pit-

---

[28] *AA.SS*, 544, 555; *Reg. Cantilupe*, xix, 134; *CR 1254–6*, 197; *CPR 1258–66*, 596.

[29] *AA.SS*, 558; *Cal. Ancient Correspondence concerning Wales*, ed. J.G. Edwards (Cardiff, 1935), 38. For the firm discipline during Thomas's second term as chancellor, see *AA.SS*, 545.

[30] *CPR 1258–66*, 410; *CR 1264–8*, 54.

[31] Each chancery roll ran for a regnal year. Thus Cantilupe's term was included in the rolls for 28 October, 1264–27 October, 1265, Henry III's 49th year. The close roll for 49 Henry III is printed in full in *Close Rolls 1264–8* (H.M.S.O., 1937). The patent, liberate, and charter rolls are calendared in *Cal. Patent Rolls 1258–66*; *Cal. Liberate Rolls 1260–7*; *Cal. Charter Rolls 1257–1300* (H.M.S.O., 1910, 1961, 1906). Excerpts from the fine roll are in *Excerpta e Rotulis Finium*, II, ed. C. Roberts (Record Commission, 1836).

falls for the historian.[32] Nonetheless, a good case can be made for saying that Cantilupe was influenced by criticisms made of chancellors in office before 1258; criticisms like those found in the documents of December 1263. He wished to avoid the failures of these officials, and run the chancery in the spirit of the Provisions of Oxford and reform. Cantilupe's predecessor, John of Chishill, appointed by the king before Lewes, probably felt no such commitment.

Under the Provisions of Oxford, the council's control of the king rested upon the stipulation that the chancellor should seal no writs, other than those which were routine, without its orders. That stipulation was not repeated in the constitution of June 1264, but the king was to dispose of the affairs of the kingdom on the advice of the council of nine. The implication was that the chancellor should take instructions from king and council, and refuse to seal anything important on the sole authority of the king.[33] There are signs that Cantilupe did not think the king should be reduced to a mere cipher. He was clearly concerned to record that Henry had admitted him to office 'willingly'-*gratanter*.[34] Nonetheless, a story told by Cantilupe's nephew and former clerk, William de Cantilupe appears to show Thomas refusing to seal a letter on the king's orders: 'He had heard it said' that Thomas 'returned his seal to the king on a certain occasion when the king ordered him to seal a letter which Thomas thought should not be sealed'.[35]

The constitution of June 1264 followed the Provisions of Oxford in requiring officials to swear that they would take 'no reward, beyond food and drink commonly brought to the table'.[36] Cantilupe zealously upheld this oath, judging from an incident which Richard de Swinfield personally witnessed in 1265. Some monks, having business to transact at the king's court, offered Thomas a precious jewel. He refused the gift civilly but rebuked the monks for offering it, 'as if they thought him pliable and corruptible'.[37] Cantilupe's stand against 'rewards' may explain the question of his salary. The Provisions of Oxford made clear that the purpose of a salary was to prevent the acceptance of 'presents'. 'It is right that the king should pay . . . his servants sufficiently so that they have

---

[32] For the chancery, see P. Chaplais, *English Royal Documents* (Oxford, 1971); H.C. Maxwell-Lyte, *The Great Seal* (London, 1926).

[33] *DBM*, 102–3, 106–7, 296–7. In practice it is clear from the authorisations of royal letters that the chancellor received orders from the council of nine, or members of it, and from Simon de Montfort. The king later complained that Simon used the seal 'at his will'; *CPR 1258–66*, 436.

[34] PRO C/ 66/ 83, m.18. This is said in the writ dealing with Thomas' salary; *CPR 1258–66*, 416; the statement (for which see below) that the king folded this writ with his own hands is another example of Thomas' concern for the position of the king. It is not impossible that Thomas was personally acceptable to Henry; see below pp. 305–6.

[35] *AA.SS*, 547. William's story does not fit the circumstances of Thomas' departure from court on 7 May when there is no evidence of any disagreement, and he handed the seal to Ralph of Sandwich, not the king; *CR 1264–8*, 54. Presumably on the occasion mentioned by William the king gave away and Thomas recovered the seal. It may be, of course, that William's details are inaccurate, and that in fact Thomas' argument was with the councillors rather than the king.

[36] *DBM*, 106–9, 296–7.

[37] *AA.SS*, 547, 607; from the canonization proceedings.

no need to accept anything from anyone else'.[38] On 26 March 1265 Cantilupe was granted 500 marks p.a. for the upkeep of himself and his staff. Since 1261, when a salary was first introduced, chancellors had probably only received 400 marks p.a. Perhaps the extra 100 marks was granted to Cantilupe because he took a more rigid view of gifts than his predecessors. His concern to demonstrate his honesty is seen in the matter of the salary itself. A memorandum noted that the king had caused the writ, which granted the 500 marks, to be sealed in his presence and that of various ministers. It also stated that Henry had folded the writ with his own hands – an action otherwise unrecorded in his reign. Thus Cantilupe showed, in the plainest way possible, that he had not authorised his own increase in salary.[39]

According to the complaints of December 1263 one consequence of the failure -*defectum* – of chancellors before 1258 was the concession of writs 'against right and the customary forms of the chancery'.[40] The inference was that the chancellor should watch over the letters he issued, and resist those he considered irregular. That Cantilupe took this view is suggested by a statement of disavowal, without parallel in the reign of Henry III, which was added to a writ of 7 March, 1265 enrolled on the patent rolls. This writ was *per*, that is authorised by, the justiciar (Hugh Despencer), Peter de Montfort, Adam of Newmarket and Giles de Argentan, all members of the council of nine. The record of authorisation then continues *tamen magister Thomas de Cantelupo cancellarius non consensit illi litterae;* 'however the chancellor did not consent to that letter'.[41] The root of Thomas' objection is not easy to uncover. He did not, perhaps, consider the matter to be of prime importance, otherwise he would presumably have resigned. The letter stated that the citizens of Lincoln had complained to the king that whereas they had been accustomed to pay a toll of 6s 8d p.a. at Boston fair, over the last seven years, the lords of the vill (Peter of Savoy and John de Vaux) had extorted £10 p.a. The king, therefore, 'wishing to be more fully informed of the truth of these matters', commissioned two judges to inquire into them. The writs 'against right and the customary forms of the chancery' complained about in December 1263 were probably those which initiated new and *ad hoc* legal procedures. The writ of 7 March was not of this type since it only ordered an inquiry. Perhaps Cantilupe had reservations because the investigation affected, in his absence and while his lands were in the king's hands, the rights of the queen's uncle, Peter of Savoy. Perhaps Cantilupe thought the writ should have been authorised by the whole council rather than four members of it. The next entry on the patent rolls ordered an inquiry

[38] *DBM*, 68–9.

[39] *CPR 1258–66*, 416; *Cal. Liberate Rolls 1260–7*, 169; L.B. Dibben, 'Chancellor and Keeper of the Seal under Henry III', *Eng. Hist. Rev.*, XXVIII (1911), 48.

[40] *DBM*, 260–3.

[41] PRO C/ 66/ 83, m.21d; *CPR 1258–66*, 481–2.

into a complaint of the prior and canons of Koketon park. This writ was authorised by all the council, *per totum concilium.*[42]

'Excessive and unreasonable grants' by the king were another result of the failure of chancellors before 1258, according to the complaints of December 1263.[43] Many of these grants had been made by royal charters; the most solemn instruments which the chancery issued, since they conferred rights in perpetuity. Cantilupe consequently may have felt a special responsibility regarding the concession of charters, and perhaps this explains why they were sometimes 'given' by him as chancellor, rather than being 'given' by the king as was normal, or being left without a 'giving' clause at all. Between 1227, when Henry III began to issue charters, and 1238, when he deprived his chancellor, Ralph de Neville, of the seal, nearly all charters were 'given' by the chancellor, that is they ended with a clause which stated that they were *data per manum*, 'given by the hand', of the chancellor at a specified place and date. After Neville lost the seal in 1238, charters were 'given' by the king himself — *data per manum nostram*. Apart from a few charters issued in 1243 and 1261 no other 'giver' appears until Cantilupe's appointment in 1265.[44] On the charter roll for 49 Henry III, before Thomas received the seal, charters were either 'given' by the king, or ended with a highly unusual clause which stated that they had been 'witnessed' by the king. The latter form appears on the first two charters of Cantilupe's keepership, which are dated 27 February, and on charters of 5 March and 14 April. The other four charters belonging to Thomas' term were all 'given by the hand of master Thomas de Cantilupe, chancellor of the king'.[45] Thus Cantilupe indicated that he had authorised, or had in some way taken responsibility for these grants.[46] His successor as keeper did not shoulder the same responsibility. After Thomas left court on 7 May the king resumed as 'giver'.[47]

---

[42] *ibid.*. I would like to thank Dr Paul Brand for discussing this writ with me. The responsibility for the interpretation, however, is my own.

[43] *DBM*, 260–3.

[44] Dibben, *op. cit.*, 50, 43. The charters of 1261 were the last issued during the chancellorship of Nicholas of Ely.

[45] *ibid.*, 50; PRO C/ 53/ 54, ms. 6, 4–3. On the charter roll the charters of 27 February; 5 March; and 14 April (a duplicate with different witnesses of one 'given' by Cantilupe on 1 March) end *T[este] R[ege.]*. This form, which the present writer has discovered only once outside the roll for 49 Henry III, appears on several charters before Cantilupe's appointment, and on one after Evesham, that of 18 October. The form implies that the original charters ended *Teste me ipso*, the usual conclusion for royal letters but not for charters. However it is impossible to be certain how the originals ended since none survive. The question is made the more puzzling by a fourteenth-century copy of an otherwise unknown charter which is date 3 March and is 'given' by Cantilupe. In its text and witnesses this charter is identical with the enrolled charter of 5 March which ends *Teste Rege*, PRO C/ 53/ 133, m.3. The original of the enrolled charter of 20 March (to Montfort) 'given' by Cantilupe, survives in Bibliothèque Nationale, Paris, Clairambault 1188, f. 79. (The second grant to Simon de Montfort on 20 March is by letter not charter).

[46] For discussion of the 'giving' clause, J.B. Edwards, 'The English Royal Chamber and Chancery in the Reign of John' (unpublished Cambridge Univ. D.Phil. thesis, 1974), 118–32; see also C.R. Cheney, *English Bishops' Chanceries* (Manchester, 1950), 81–90; Chaplais, *op. cit.*, 14–15.

[47] One might wonder whether one reason for Cantilupe taking over the 'giving' of charters

Under the Provisions of Oxford the chancellor was to hold office for a year, and answer for his term before the king and council. These regulations are not found in the constitution of June 1264, but the chancellor, like other officials, was to be appointed by the council of nine. If officials 'behaved badly' the council could dismiss them.[48] Cantilupe, unlike his predecessor, was appointed by the nine and perhaps he felt answerable to them. Conceivably, a marked feature of Cantilupe's chancellorship – the sharp increase in notes which indicated on whose authority royal letters were issued – should be seen against this background. The increase coincides exactly with Cantilupe's assumption of the seal and thus was probably ordered by him. If Cantilupe felt accountable for his term it was sensible to record on whose orders he had acted, the more especially as the political outlook was uncertain. Cantilupe received the seal on 25 February, 1265. In the close roll of October 1264-October 1265 about 200 letters were issued before his appointment, of which twenty-three were authorised. Of about 170 letters for which Thomas was responsible between 25 February and 7 May authorisations were appended to 108.[49] Before Cantilupe's appointment no letter on the face of the roll had been authorised since 12 February, leaving ten unauthorised letters. After Cantilupe received the seal there was a run of twenty-seven letters until 9 March of which only two were unauthorised.[50] A similar pattern can be seen on the fine rolls. In the roll of October 1264-October 1265 not a single letter was authorised before Cantilupe's appointment. After 25 February authorisations began at once.[51] There was also an increase in authorisations on the patent and liberate rolls.[52]

A final indication of Thomas' sense of the chancellor's responsibilities may be discovered in the regulations which were issued on 7 May, 1265 for the use of the seal while he was away from court. Since it is, on balance, unlikely that Thomas' departure on 7 May was connected with any challenge to his authority as chancellor, he probably played a large part in devising these rules. Nor-

continued
was that Henry III was making difficulties over doing it. Is this the explanation for the appearance of the *Teste Rege* clause (note 45 above)? Henry must have resented the charter of 20 March which gave the honour of Chester to Simon de Montfort. However, other charters 'given' by Cantilupe seems no more important than ones which Henry 'gave' after Thomas' departure. The king 'gives' all seven charters between Thomas' departure and Evesham, save the last which is merely 'given at Hereford'.

[48] *DBM*, 106–7, 296–7.

[49] *CR 1264–8*, 1–54, 78–116.

[50] *ibid.*, 22–41. The colour of the ink and the shape of the hand suggest that the first eight authorisations were added later than the entries to which they belonged. It seems that the clerk initially continued with his old practices, and then was pulled up; PRO C/ 54/ 82, m.9.

[51] PRO C/ 60/ 62, m.7.

[52] During Cantilupe's term, in the patent rolls *circa* 1 in 7, and in the liberate rolls *circa* 1 in 5.5 letters were authorised, as against *circa* 1 in 13 and 1 in 8 respectively between 28 October-25 February, 1265; *CPR 1258–66*, 385–423; 473–86; *Cal. Liberate Rolls 1260–7*, 145–74. After Thomas' departure, in all the rolls, there is a gradual falling off in the rate of authorisations. In Henry III's reign generally there are great fluctuations in the frequency with which letters were authorised. The whole subject needs further study.

mally, when the chancellor left court, the name of the keeper of the seal in his absence was recorded in the briefest of notes on the chancery rolls.[53] On this occasion, by contrast, it was laid down that, until Thomas' return, Ralph of Sandwich was to keep the seal in the king's wardrobe under the seal of Peter de Montfort, or Roger de St John, or Giles de Argentan, all members of the council. Ralph could only seal writs, other than those which were routine, in the presence and with the consent of one of these three councillors. Cantilupe, it seems, was determined to prevent irresponsible use of the seal during his absence.[54]

Thomas Cantilupe, therefore, gives every appearance of having been an active and conscientious chancellor. Why did he hand over the seal on 7 May? The court at this time was at Gloucester, engaged in abortive negotiations through Walter de Cantilupe and others for a settlement with Gilbert de Clare. T.F. Tout wondered whether Thomas departed because he was 'weakening in his support for the revolutionary government'.[55] Evidence could be brought to support this case. According to the story of Cantilupe's nephew, Thomas had clashed once with Henry III and had returned the seal to him. He had certainly disagreed with councillors over the Boston fair inquiry. Perhaps such episodes left Cantilupe disillusioned with conciliar rule. Hence his reconciliation with Henry III after the battle of Evesham. A somewhat different theory might be that Cantilupe's colleagues had become frustrated by difficulties which he had made over the issue of letters, and he was 'advised to leave', as Sir Maurice Powicke put it, because the council wished to be 'more certain' about the use of the seal.[56]

There are, however, problems with such hypotheses. Thomas' career after Evesham can only throw uncertain light on his attitudes in April and May 1265.[57] More concretely, there is no evidence of a breach between Thomas and his colleagues at the time of his departure on 7 May. Cantilupe was no place man. A well-attested story tells how he sought leave to retire from the council of Edward I when he was opposed to one of the king's decisions. Yet in May 1265 he did not resign as chancellor, and Sandwich was to hold the seal merely till his return. On 7 May itself Thomas joined with Hugh Despencer and Peter de Montfort in authorising a royal letter. On 30 May when the court was at Hereford a letter was sent which ordered officials to collect a tallage on the Jews and to 'do it with master Thomas de Cantilupe our chancellor if he is still staying in London'.[58] Clearly Thomas was still recognised as chancellor and considered a loyal member of the government. References to Thomas' return seem more

[53] *e.g. CR 1256–9*, 220, 225, 342, 368, 403.

[54] *CPR 1258–66*, 423; *CR 1264–8*, 54. There were precedents both for the seal being kept in the wardrobe, and for its keeper being a layman, as was Ralph of Sandwich; Tout., *op. cit.*, 287–8; compare *Ann. Mon.*, IV, 168.

[55] Tout., *op. cit.*, 311, n. 2.

[56] Powicke, *op. cit.* (1947), II, 492, n. 5.

[57] This point is discussed below.

[58] *CR 1264–8*, 55, 62.

than a polite fiction. The conditions for Ralph of Sandwich's use of the seal tied one of three councillors permanently to court. No arrangements were made for replacements or deputies. These conditions cannot have been intended to endure for long. In the event the political situation soon made Thomas' return impossible. On 28 May the Lord Edward escaped from custody. He quickly formed an alliance with the earl of Gloucester. In June the two broke down the bridges over the river Severn, and Montfort and the court became trapped on the Welsh side of the river. Thomas, who had been staying in London, was powerless to rejoin his friends.

If, then, there was no cleavage between Cantilupe and the Montfortians, why did he depart? It was not uncommon for chancellors to hand over the seal and spend time away from court. May 1265, however, seems an unlikely time for a vacation. Perhaps Thomas left to perform some special mission. The fact that he went to London, and that the court knew this, are pointers in that direction.[59]

If Cantilupe had hopes of resuming as chancellor, they were crushed by Montfort's defeat and death at the battle of Evesham on 4 August, 1265. Cantilupe returned to academic life until his election to the bishopric of Hereford in 1275. According to one story, impossible to authenticate, Walter de Cantilupe confessed on his death bed that he had erred in favouring Montfort's party.[60] There is no clear indication from his career after 1265 that Thomas took this view. Evesham had killed the cause of the great earl. Cantilupe could not avoid the new world. He had soon to act in it as his uncle's executor. How far Thomas' past conduct as chancellor affected his position after Evesham is difficult to say. Personally, at the time of his appointment, he may have been acceptable to the king; in some ways he had treated his monarch with respect. On the other hand, there had probably been disagreements over individual letters and charters. Within three weeks of Evesham Thomas was granted letters of safe conduct to go where he wished in England; but he did not have a clean bill of political health, and in February 1266, as 'sometime chancellor', he obtained a writ which admitted him to grace, and forgave, in the conventional words of the time, the king's 'rancour and indignation'.[61] By the following year he had apparently fully recovered or acquired a place in the king's esteem, since he is

---

[59] A badly damaged letter to King Henry from '. . . Cantilup . . ', who was in London, may have been written by Thomas at this time; PRO SC/ 1/ 3/ 3; *PRO Lists and Indexes*, LX (1968), 36. It was chiefly concerned with a request which the king had made to the Dean and chapter of St. Paul's. However, it refers to 'when I will come to you'. It also states that 'it is believed that the messengers of the king of France in a short time are about to come to England'. Louis IX's messengers were eagerly awaited by Montfort in May 1265, and one wonders whether Cantilupe was sent to meet them and conduct them to court. There are, however, problems with this hypothesis; see *CR 1264–8*, 120–1.

[60] *Flores Historiarum*, ed. H.R. Luard (Rolls Series, 1890); III, 9.

[61] The admission to grace was on 10 February, 1266, only two days before Walter de Cantilupe's death; *CPR 1258–66*, 443, 459, 596. Another member of the council of nine, Giles de Argentan, who was captured at Evesham, was admitted to grace in the same month.

found with the style 'king's clerk' (August 1267).[62] Perhaps their common piety had always been a bond between the two men. There was nothing inconsistant about Thomas becoming a 'king's clerk'. He thereby acknowledged a personal association with Henry. He did not necessarily condone his government. The title was probably honorary, and there is no evidence that Thomas was active in the king's service. In 1267 or 1268 he left England for the university of Paris.[63] The accession in 1272 of Edward I, a far abler and wiser man than his father, must have made schemes for conciliar rule seem irrelevant. Cantilupe was one of many former Montfortians to rise high in Edward's service. Nonetheless the memory of the great earl may have been cherished in Thomas' circle. Both Thomas' steward and hawk were said to have been cured of illness through the earl's miraculous intervention. The compilers of Cantilupe's own miracles were happy to preserve the statement that Thomas was 'as much a saint as Simon de Montfort who is buried at Evesham'.[64]

The second phase of Thomas' career outside the schools confirms the impression of a strong and vigorous personality given by the first. He returned to the king's council not simply because he was bishop of Hereford. Edward would never have chosen him, had he not thought highly of his abilities and wanted him as a councillor. In 1279 Thomas was appointed one of the regents during the king's absence from the kingdom – a position that his father had held in 1242.[65] The one substantial story preserved of Cantilupe as an Edwardian councillor seems utterly characteristic of a man who in 1265 had refused to consent to a royal letter. When Edward proposed to give a converted Jew the right to bear witness against Christian forgers, Thomas rose up in tears and sought leave to withdraw from the council. The king gave way.[66]

Thomas Cantilupe was bishop of Hereford for a comparatively short time- seven years. He was chancellor of Henry III for only a few months. Yet he made a significant impression in both offices. In 1265 Thomas may well have been fired by the desire to run the chancery in the spirit of the reforms which the Provisions of Oxford had brought to England. He rejected bribes; he refused consent to a royal letter; he recovered the 'giving' of royal charters from the king; he increased the notes of authorisation to writs. As bishop of Hereford, Cantilupe's 'zeal and love for his church and for the conservation of its rights'

---

[62] *CR 1264–8*, 326, 332; *CPR 1266–72*, 300.

[63] Emden, *op. cit.*, I, 347–8.

[64] *Chronicle of Rishanger*, 70–1; *AA.SS*, 671. It has been suggested that, whilst bishop of Hereford, Thomas' former politics influenced him in his proceedings against the relatives of his predecessor, Bishop Peter de Aqua Blanca (1240–68), the hated foreign minister of Henry III; N. Yates, 'Bishop Peter de Aqua Blanca', *Journal of Ecclesiastical History*, XXII (1971), 314. However, Cantilupe's register does not suggest any particular hostility to the family; nor does it show he had a 'dislike of foreigners'; *Reg. Cantilupe*, 13, 135, 188, 192, 247, 195, 294, 197, 199, 214–5, 233–4, 248–50.

[65] Thomas was on the council bv February 1276; *Cal. Close Rolls 1272–9*, 288; *CPR 1272–81*, 309.

[66] *AA.SS*, 547–8. The judge Ralph of Hengham witnessed this scene.

made him a conscientious diocesan, and plunged him into law suits against the mightiest in the land.[67] Thomas had a fertile and ordered mind. It is no accident that two of the most unusual entries in the chancery rolls in the thirteenth century belong to his period as chancellor – the statement that the king folded a writ with his own hand, and the rules laid down for the use of the seal in his absence. The same type of mind is seen at work in Thomas' episcopal register; for example, in the detailed instructions Cantilupe issued to his steward.[68] Probably the greatest influence on Cantilupe's political career was his uncle Walter. The two made similar bishops. Both were personally austere. Both worked hard in their dioceses in the cause of reform. Both were also political bishops, and sat on the king's council. Robert Grosseteste perhaps would have worried whether such activity was compatible with diocesan duties. The Cantilupes might have replied that it helped them defend the interests of their sees and the rights of the church. They might also have rejected any narrow distinction between affairs of church and state. Prelates who contributed as councillors and diplomats to their country's peace and well-being surely helped the cure of souls.[69] Bishops like the Cantilupes, active at court and in the diocese, were an important 'hinge upon which the social order turned'.[70] The more one studies Thomas Cantilupe's career as an academic, as a chancellor of Henry III, and as bishop of Hereford, the more the impact which he made on contemporaries becomes explicable. In the discharge of his duties, Thomas instructed his steward to display 'an open heart and a vigilant mind'–*cor directum et animum vigilantem.*[71] It was these which Cantilupe brought to every field of his activity.

---

[67] *Reg. Cantilupe*, 215.

[68] *ibid.*, 108–11.

[69] Grosseteste would have acknowledged the force of this point; see his letter to Walter de Cantilupe, *Roberti Grosseteste Epistolae*, ed.H.R. Luard (Rolls Series, 1861), 302–4. See also *Robert Grosseteste*, ed. Callus, 181.

[70] *ibid.*, 182; Powicke, *op. cit.* (1947), II, 716.

[71] *Reg. Cantilupe*, 110.

17

English Peasants in Politics, 1258–1267

On 8 August 1265, four days after the battle of Evesham, an esquire of the royalist captain Peter de Neville, who was leading a cart through the village of Peatling Magna in Leicestershire, was intercepted by some of the villagers "wishing to arrest" the cart and horses. In the ensuing mêlée, the villagers wounded the carter and accused Neville and his men of "treason and other heinous offences because they were against the welfare of the community of the realm and against the barons".[1]

This famous incident demonstrates that ideas about the community of the realm had percolated down to the level of the village. Indeed some of the peasants of Peatling Magna clearly saw themselves as part of that community, and felt that "the barons" were acting in its interests.[2] The incident also reveals peasants involved at the sharp end of politics, taking physical action in support of the baronial cause. It is these aspects of peasant attitudes and conduct which this article seeks to explore. While historians have appreciated the significance of the Peatling Magna incident, they have never explained why the peasants there took the view that they did.[3] In general the movement of

* I am most grateful to Paul Brand for commenting on a draft of this article. Earlier versions were read to the Anglo-American Conference of Historians in 1985, and to a seminar at the University of Leeds. I have been helped by the points made in the subsequent discussions.

[1] "Inponentes ipsi et hominibus suis seditiones et alia opprobria, eo quod fuerunt contra utilitatem communitatis regni et contra barones": *Select Cases of Procedure without Writ under Henry III*, ed. H. G. Richardson and G. O. Sayles (Selden Soc., lx, London, 1941), p. 43. The villagers' statement was recorded in Peter de Neville's plea, in January 1266 in the court *coram rege*, which sought to justify his taking of hostages from the vill in response to the offence perpetrated against him and his men. The hostages themselves did not deny Peter's story. A jury stated that certain "foolish men" (*fatui*) wounded the carter "wishing to arrest" the cart and horses, which seems to confirm that the villagers were engaged in some misguided political act rather than simple robbery.

[2] I say "some of the peasants" deliberately, since the pleadings in the case show that Peatling Magna was far from being a united village community: *ibid.*, pp. 42-5.

[3] For comment, see *ibid.*, p. clxx; F. M. Powicke, *Henry III and the Lord Edward*, 2 vols. (Oxford, 1947), ii, pp. 509-10; H. M. Cam, "The Community of the Vill", in her *Law-Finders and Law-Makers* (London, 1962), pp. 81-4; S. Reynolds, *Kingdoms and Communities in Western Europe, 900-1300* (Oxford, 1984), pp. 149, 272. Both

(cont. on p. 310)

"baronial" reform and rebellion has been thought irrelevant to
the peasant condition. If peasants had a "political" role in the
thirteenth century, it has been seen to lie rather in the activities
first diagnosed by R. H. Hilton, namely in the struggles of both
individual peasants and peasant communities to resist the impositions of their lords.[4] This article aims to show that in fact there
was nothing isolated or surprising about the Peatling Magna
incident. On the contrary, during the period of civil war between
1263 and 1267, there was widespread peasant involvement in the
physical "fighting" side of politics. Peasants, moreover, had
reason to side with the baronial movement, since it had given
them some redress against the oppressions of both their lords and
the king. It had done so, at least in part, because the peasantry
belonged to the community of the realm of thirteenth-century
England, and were thus the concern of a movement publicly
dedicated to that realm's reform.

The peasantry constituted by far the most numerous class in
thirteenth-century England. It was divided between peasants who
were free, many of these coming into the category of tenants
called sokemen, and those who were unfree, who were called
villeins.[5] If a peasant had customarily performed labour services,
had given merchet (a payment to marry a daughter) or had been
tallaged at the will of his lord, then he might be deemed unfree.
The consequence was that he could not sue his lord in the king's
courts about the terms of his tenure, and the lord could, in law,
impose whatever services and requirements he liked.[6] The

(n. 3 cont.)

Helen Cam and Susan Reynolds perceptively place the incident within the context of
the community and collective action at the village level.

[4] R. H. Hilton, "Peasant Movements in England before 1381", *Econ. Hist. Rev.*,
2nd ser., ii (1949), pp. 117-36; repr. in R. H. Hilton, *Class Conflict and the Crisis of
Feudalism* (London, 1985), pp. 122-38.

[5] Sokemen might be obliged to perform labour services, although these were usually
comparatively light. For a useful general survey, see J. L. Bolton, *The Medieval
English Economy, 1150-1500*, 2nd edn. (London, 1985), pp. 21-3, 109-18. The peasants
of Peatling Magna were very concerned to stress that they were "free men of free
condition": *Select Cases of Procedure without Writ*, ed. Richardson and Sayles, p. 43.

[6] For the relative advantages of freedom and unfreedom, and the argument that in
thirteenth-century conditions it was in some respects better to be unfree since —
whatever the legal theory — in practice manorial custom provided more protection
for the unfree against the increasing exactions of lords, see J. Hatcher, "English
Serfdom and Villeinage: Towards a Reassessment", *Past and Present*, no. 90 (Feb.
1981), pp. 3-39; see also the criticisms offered by C. Dyer, *Standards of Living in the
Later Middle Ages: Social Change in England, c.1200-1520* (Cambridge, 1989),
pp. 137-8.

amount of land held by peasants varied greatly. The scale ran down from tenants of a whole virgate (which could be as much as thirty acres) through a large group of half-virgaters down to peasants with little or no land at all. During the thirteenth century peasants suffered from the increasing exactions of their lords.[7] The rising population and the consequent scarcity of land also resulted in at least half the class becoming smallholders possessing less than ten acres — ten acres being the very rough minimum, according to some calculations, necessary for a peasant family's subsistence.[8]

The tumult of the years of reform and rebellion, therefore, took place in a period when the material position of the peasantry was under increasing threat. That tumult had begun in 1258 when a group of magnates, claiming to act for the "community of the realm", both took control of central government from Henry III and (in 1258 and 1259) carried through wide-ranging reforms of local administration. In 1261 Henry had recovered power only to lose it again in 1263 to a movement lead by Simon de Montfort, which ravaged the lands of the royalists and reimposed the "Provisions of Oxford" (as the reforms of 1258-9 were loosely known).[9] Montfort, however, was unable to maintain his political control and, by the end of 1263, with the country an armed camp, the two sides referred their quarrel to the arbitration of Louis IX of France. His verdict, the Mise of Amiens (January 1264), quashed both the Provisions of Oxford and related measures introduced in 1263 against foreigners. It was consequently rejected by the Montfortians, and the result was a violent civil war. Montfort's extraordinary victory at Lewes (14 May 1264) meant that he controlled central government, with the king a puppet, until his own defeat and death at the battle of Evesham

[7] R. H. Hilton, "Freedom and Villeinage in England", *Past and Present*, no. 31 (July 1965), pp. 3-19; repr. in R. H. Hilton (ed.), *Peasants, Knights and Heretics* (Cambridge, 1976), pp. 174-91. For the measures taken by Richard de Clare, earl of Gloucester, in 1251 to increase the burdens on his villeins, see *Annales monastici*, ed. H. R. Luard, 5 vols. (Rolls ser., London, 1864-9), i, p. 146.

[8] J. Z. Titow, *English Rural Society, 1200-1350* (London, 1969), pp. 78-80; Dyer, *Standards of Living*, pp. 118-19, 124-7. For a recent discussion of how far smallholders could supplement their income, for example by wage labour, and whether co-operation within the village community alleviated the lot of the poor, see *ibid.*, pp. 133, 185-7.

[9] In practice the restoration of the Provisions of Oxford in 1263 meant the restoration of baronial control over central government. For surveys of the politics of these years, see R. F. Treharne, *The Baronial Plan of Reform, 1258-1263* (Manchester, 1932); Powicke, *Henry III and the Lord Edward*, chs. 10-12.

(4 August 1265). Evesham, however, did not conclude the strife. The king's seizure of the lands of his enemies created a large group of "Disinherited", who established themselves in Kenilworth Castle and in the Isle of Ely. The Dictum of Kenilworth (October 1266) replaced disinheritance with redemption, the Disinherited being allowed to repurchase their estates at up to seven times their annual value, according to the gravity of their offences. But these terms were harsh, and it was not until the summer of 1267, when they were slightly modified, and the Isle of Ely was taken, that peace returned to England.

It has long been recognized that during this period of profound "shaking" the political community in England was far wider than that of the great barons. The reforms of local government and the proliferating propaganda were designed to appeal, at the very least, to knights and gentry: a well-known article by R. F. Treharne was even entitled "The Knights in the Period of Reform and Rebellion, 1258-67: A Critical Phase in the Rise of a New Class".[10] The political role of the peasants in the same period is less easy to divine since the evidence, while voluminous, bears mostly on the role of lords. There is, however, one source which reveals activities further down the social scale, namely the rolls of the special eyre held between 1267 and 1272 in order to enforce the terms of the Dictum of Kenilworth. Since part of the eyre's business was to fix the redemption fines of those involved in the rebellion — the fines by which they bought back their property — it often recorded the value of a rebel's lands or chattels. Unfortunately in the case of the unfree peasant the interest was usually confined to the chattels: the king frequently imposed fines of half their value, but, with some exceptions, he ignored the land since that was the concern of the lord.[11] There are, however, two areas — Cambridgeshire and a small part of Buckinghamshire — where the evidence from the eyre about a peasant's social and material position can be supplemented by the much greater detail

---

[10] R. F. Treharne, "The Knights in the Period of Reform and Rebellion, 1258-67: A Critical Phase in the Rise of a New Class", *Bull. Inst. Hist. Research*, xxi (1948), pp. 1-12; repr. in R. F. Treharne, *Simon de Montfort and Baronial Reform: Thirteenth-Century Essays* (London, 1986), pp. 269-80.

[11] E. F. Jacob, *Studies in the Period of Baronial Reform and Rebellion, 1258-67* (Oxford, 1925), p. 321 n. 2; see also below, p. 316; *Documents of the Baronial Movement of Reform and Rebellion*, ed. R. F. Treharne and I. J. Sanders (Oxford, 1973), pp. 326-7 (cap. 14). Sometimes the fine may have been assigned to the villein's lord: see Jacob, *Studies in the Period of Baronial Reform and Rebellion*, p. 321 n. 3.

found in the Hundred Rolls, the village-by-village survey of landholding in England carried out in 1279.[12] The section which follows, therefore, begins by looking at evidence from Buckinghamshire and Cambridgeshire for the physical involvement of the peasantry in activities associated with the rebellion.

I

Buckinghamshire boasted some leading Montfortians, of whom the most important was John fitz John, the lord of Waddon, Aylesbury and Wendover. Other Montfortians in the county included Robert fitz Nigel of Salden and Mursley, killed at Evesham, John Passelewe of Drayton Parslow, Richard le Vache of Shenley and Eustace fitz Thomas of Westbury. These men engaged in a series of raids on the property of the leading royalists in the shire, the principal sufferers being the *curialis* John de Grey and his tenant and associate Richard Grosset of Morton.[13]

Similarly, it was in raids on the property of loyalists that peasants became involved. Among those convicted on the special eyre of despoiling the property of John de Grey, for example, was William Popping. His land was valued at 7s. 6d. a year, and he was compelled to redeem it at twice that sum. In the Hundred Rolls Popping appears again. He was a cottager at Westbury owing his lord, the former rebel Eustace fitz Thomas, a rent of

[12] For the Cambridgeshire eyre, see Public Record Office, London (hereafter P.R.O.), Just 1/83, partly printed in *Rotuli selecti ad res Anglicas et Hibernicas spectantes*, ed. J. Hunter (Record Comm., London, 1834), pp. 231-46; the pleas for Cambridge itself printed in Jacob, *Studies in the Period of Baronial Reform and Rebellion*, pp. 395-406. See also *Liber memorandorum ecclesie de Bernewelle*, ed. J. W. Clark (Cambridge, 1907), pp. 124-5. Cambridgeshire's Hundred Rolls are printed in *Rotuli hundredorum temp. Hen. III & Edw. I in turr' Lond' et in curiae receptae scaccarii West. asservati* [ed. W. Illingworth], 2 vols. (Record Comm., London, 1812-18; hereafter *Rot. hund.*), ii, pp. 356-590. For Buckinghamshire's eyre, see P.R.O., Just 1/59, from which there are extracts in Jacob, *Studies in the Period of Baronial Reform and Rebellion*, pp. 406-13; for its Hundred Rolls, covering the hundreds of Mursley, Stodfeld, Bonestowe (Newport) and Mucha (Buckingham), see *Rot. hund.*, ii, pp. 334-55. For the Dictum of Kenilworth eyre, see Jacob, *Studies in the Period of Baronial Reform and Rebellion*, pp. 162-201; C. H. Knowles, "The Disinherited, 1265-80" (Univ. of Wales, Aberystwyth, Ph.D. thesis, 1959), pt. iv, pp. 18-123.

[13] P.R.O., Just 1/59, mm. 1, 9, 13, 15, 15d, 17, 18d, 20 (all membrane references in this roll are to the typed numbers on the dorse of each membrane); *Cal. Inq. Misc.*, i, nos. 628, 633-4, 636; *Close Rolls Suppl., 1244-66*, no. 398; P.R.O., KB 26/175, mm. 19d, 20d. For fitz John, see also Jacob, *Studies in the Period of Baronial Reform and Rebellion*, pp. 223, 234-5, 291, 296. For Grey and Grosset, see *Cal. Pat. Rolls, 1258-66*, p. 395. For manorial spoliation in general during this period, see Jacob, *Studies in the Period of Baronial Reform and Rebellion*, pp. 223-39.

2s. 8d. a year or labour services of the same value.[14] One peasant
accused of despoiling the property of Richard Grosset at Morton
was Thomas *prepositus* of Salden, almost certainly the predecessor
of the Geoffrey *prepositus* of Salden who appears in the Hundred
Rolls as a serf holding a virgate of land in villeinage from Robert
fitz Nigel, the son of the Robert killed at Evesham. Since Thomas
was accused of acting with four named men from Salden and
Mursley, as well as others unnamed, it seems likely that he led a
small band of villagers on an expedition to Morton.[15]

The individuals mentioned so far were all involved in local
activities, but peasants could equally be drawn further afield. One
of those convicted of being with the Montfortians in Kenilworth
Castle was Richard Borre of Steeple Claydon. He had no land,
and his chattels were worth 10s.; another was John le Franc (the
Free) of Great Horwood, who was condemned to redeem his land
at five times its annual value, placed at 13s. 4d. The Hundred
Rolls show that John held half a virgate of land in Great Horwood
from the prioress of Newton Longville in return for a rent of
16½d. a year, suit of court, "ward" and relief.[16] Peasants were
not only active individually or in small groups. The vills of
Aylesbury (where John fitz John was lord), Dorton and Walton
were charged with sending men against the king and generally
preaching and working against him. The vill of Wendover
(another fitz John property) was similarly charged with disloyalty
to the king and with plundering the lands of his supporters.[17]

[14] P.R.O., Just 1/59, m. 15; *Rot. hund.*, ii, p. 334. Under the Dictum of Kenilworth
(cap. 26) a two-year redemption fine was fixed for those who had laboured to win
supporters for Montfort. In practice it was also used for a variety of other offences:
Documents of the Baronial Movement, ed. Treharne and Sanders, pp. 332-3; Knowles,
"Disinherited", pt. iv, pp. 61-2. The valuations of land and/or chattels cited in this
article would have placed their holders near the bottom of the material scale indicated
by the 1242 Assize of Arms, which distinguished between those with land worth £15,
£10, £5, £2 (40s.) and below £2 per annum, and those with chattels worth £40, £26,
£13, £6 and £2. In the 1250s land worth £15 or £20 a year qualified one for knighthood.
"No poor man" had to pay the tax on movables of 1237 unless he had chattels worth
more than 40d. (3s. 4d.). See *Close Rolls, 1234-7*, p. 546; *Close Rolls, 1237-42*, p. 483;
Close Rolls, 1254-6, pp. 135, 293.

[15] P.R.O., Just 1/59, m. 19; *Rot. hund.*, ii, p. 336.

[16] P.R.O., Just 1/59, mm. 19, 11; *Rot. hund.*, ii, p. 337.

[17] Jacob, *Studies in the Period of Baronial Reform and Rebellion*, pp. 410, 291-2. The
men of Aylesbury, Dorton and Walton said that they had letters from the Lord
Edward testifying to their fidelity, and that they had merely sent contingents to the
sea (that is to Montfort's army gathered to resist invasion in July 1264) on the king's
orders. The men of Wendover, part of whose defence was to allege coercion by fitz
John, were acquitted by a local jury. The lord of Dorton was the rebel knight, William
of Birmingham. See *Cal. Inq. Misc.*, i, no. 631.

In Cambridgeshire, too, peasants became involved in the process of raid and counter-raid. When, for example, the prominent Montfortians Richard de Argentan, Ralph Perot and Ralph fitz Fulk of Shepreth raided the queen's properties at Caxton and Comberton and did damage to the value of £100, they were accompanied by "a certain Hebbe of Meldreth who has land in the same vill and holds nothing save in villeinage". When the knight and former sheriff of the county Philip of (Long) Stanton attacked the property of his neighbour Philip of Croydon at Croydon, he had with him Thomas the Reaper of Stanton, whose land was valued at 5s. a year, and William de Bridecote, whose chattels were valued at the same sum.[18] Peasants could also feature in the bands of the royalists. When Sir Baldwin de Akeny (who was in the service of the Lord Edward) attacked the properties of the Montfortian sheriff of Cambridgeshire, John de Scalariis, he took a band of nineteen named individuals. On the basis of the Hundred Roll evidence four of these men were villeins holding from Baldwin at his manor of Whittlesford.[19]

Since the Scalariis manors plundered by Baldwin's men were at Thriplow and Cheveley, respectively two and seventeen miles from Whittlesford, his villeins had limited distances to cover. But, as in Buckinghamshire, Cambridgeshire peasants sometimes ventured further afield. Thus the jury of Radfield hundred declared that "William Corbet of Burgh [Burrough-Green] was with Henry of Hastings [the great Montfortian captain] at Kenilworth as a crossbowman against the king. He has land in Burgh which Thomas his brother now holds worth 5s.".[20]

If the pattern in Cambridgeshire was in some ways similar to that in Buckinghamshire, it was given an extra dimension by the presence between 1265 and 1267 of the Disinherited in the Isle of Ely. As many as fifteen peasants from Staine hundred were accused by the Dictum eyre of having been with the rebels "in the Isle".[21] One was Geoffrey Cripa. On the eyre his solitary acre

[18] P.R.O., Just 1/83, mm. 19d, 16d, 28d (in this roll the membrane numbers cited are those written in ink in arabic numerals). There is no Hundred Roll survey of Armingford hundred in which Meldreth was situated. Christopher Lewis of the Victoria County History has kindly helped me with many points concerning Cambridgeshire.

[19] The four were Thomas and Reginald atte Asse, Jakelin atte Hacche and Walter Springald: *ibid.*, mm. 30d, 30, 22; *Rot. hund.*, ii, p. 575.

[20] P.R.O., Just 1/83, m. 21. A jury agreed with Thomas's contention that William had never had seisin of the land.

[21] For the presentments of Staine hundred, see *ibid.*, mm. 25d, 26.

in Bottisham was said to be worth 2s. per annum; in the Hundred Rolls he appears as holding one "little messuage" there from the knight Simon de Mora in return for a rent of 6d. a year.[22] More substantial was Peter fitz Ranulf of Swaffham Prior. The jurors on the Dictum eyre declared that he had land in villeinage and chattels worth 40s., which he recovered by giving half their value to the king. The Hundred Rolls took a more elevated view of Peter's status, making him one of the prior of Ely's sixteen "free sokemen" in Swaffham, each of whom owed rents of 5s. a year and various labour services. Another of the prior's free sokemen in the Isle was Richard *ad portam ecclesie*, who was made to pay a fivefold redemption fine for his land, valued at 3s. per annum.[23] There was also a recruit from the adjoining village of Swaffham Bulbeck, namely the son of Geoffrey *prepositus* of Swaffham, whose chattels were valued at 2s. In the Hundred Rolls Geoffrey appears as a "villein" holding half a virgate of land in return for 6s. 4d. a year and labour services.[24]

Staine was one of the northern Cambridgeshire hundreds, almost adjoining the Isle of Ely. But men were also drawn to the Isle from the centre and south of the county. The jurors of Wetherley hundred, for example, stated that Simon Barliwey of Orwell harboured his son who was in the Isle "against the king". Simon was compelled to give the king 20d., half the value of his "goods". In the Hundred Rolls three Barliweys appear in Orwell, each holding ten acres in villeinage from John de Camoys, son of the prominent Montfortian, Ralph de Camoys.[25] Having gone into the Isle, Cambridgeshire peasants also came out of it on plundering raids. Thus the person accused of leading the malefactors who pillaged the vill of Toft was a peasant, Roger Blancpain of Madingley.[26] Other predators from the Isle included

---

[22] *Rot. hund.*, ii, p. 490. There appears to be no evidence as to Simon de Mora's activities during the war. The same is true of the lords mentioned below, nn. 24, 27, 29.

[23] *Rot. hund.*, ii, p. 485; see also *Cal. Inq. Misc.*, i, no. 330. I assume that the Dionisia *ad portam ecclesie* in the Hundred Roll survey was Richard's widow or descendant. After the Isle surrendered in July 1267, its garrison was included among those subject to redemption fines of five years: *Documents of the Baronial Movement*, ed. Treharne and Sanders, pp. 324-5, 325 n. 16.

[24] *Rot. hund.*, ii, p. 494. In 1279 Geoffrey's lord was the knight Roger de Walesham.

[25] P.R.O., Just 1/83, m. 19d; *Rot. hund.*, ii, p. 558; G. E. C[okayne] (ed.), *Complete Peerage of England, Scotland, Ireland, Great Britain and the United Kingdom*, rev. V. Gibbs *et al.*, 13 vols. (London, 1910-59), ii, p. 506.

[26] For Roger, see p. 322 below.

Geoffrey Pricke, probably a member of the Pricke family of *customarii* in Croxton; William Tugge, a "cotar" with a messuage in Swavesey, worth 2s.;[27] John de la Dale of Sawston, a villein of the Montfortian Sir Ralph Perot (who was himself in the Isle), with chattels worth 2s.;[28] and William Little of Babraham. William was said by the eyre to have a messuage and two acres worth 12d. a year, and his redemption fine was fixed at 5s. He survived the disaster, however, for he appears again in the Hundred Rolls in Babraham, holding an acre for 1d. a year and sharing with four others a half acre and three messuages in return for a rent of 12d.[29]

There is no reason to think that this evidence from Cambridgeshire and Buckinghamshire is unique. In Norfolk and Suffolk peasants, both free and unfree, engaged in robberies and were drawn into the Isle. Few peasants anywhere can have done better than the Suffolk villein Harvey Todding, who, with unnamed colleagues, imprisoned Richard le Hoppere of Walberswick and forced him to pay a ransom of 100 marks.[30] Up to a point, moreover, in other parts of England major castles like Windsor and Wallingford, where local peasants probably formed a good part of the garrisons, played the same role as the Isle of Ely.[31]

Peasants were also present in the armies of the civil war. Indeed they probably formed the largest element among both the combatants and the casualties. The number of dead at Lewes in May 1264 was almost certainly very great: in 1810 three pits, discovered near Lewes gaol (the fulcrum of the battle), contained "by estimate quite 500 bodies in each". Yet one would be hard pressed to put names to more than a dozen of the fatalities. The reason, of course, is that virtually the only deaths revealed by chronicle and record sources are those of knights, and the number of

[27] P.R.O., Just 1/83, m. 17d; *Rot. hund.*, ii, pp. 509, 471. Geoffrey Pricke had nothing, but the chattels of his father and brother (valued respectively at 12d. and 20s.) were taken into the king's hands. Tugge's fine was 20d. He was particularly accused of raiding the house of William of Hilton (a neighbouring village to Swavesey). Tugge's lord in 1279 was John fitz Henry Benet.

[28] P.R.O., Just 1/83, m. 30; *Rot. hund.*, ii, p. 578.

[29] P.R.O., Just 1/83, m. 29; *Rot. hund.*, ii, p. 414. In 1279 William held from a subtenant, John of Babraham.

[30] Jacob, *Studies in the Period of Baronial Reform and Rebellion*, p. 321; see also *ibid.*, pp. 313-28, for an analysis of the presentments made before the justices of the Dictum of Kenilworth eyre in Suffolk. Only fragments of the Dictum eyre in Norfolk survive, but see P.R.O., Just 1/569B, esp. mm. 1, 2.

[31] P.R.O., Just 1/59, mm. 17d, 18d; Just 1/42, mm. 1d, 10, 14, 15, 16, 16d. The social status of the men involved here cannot be determined precisely.

knights killed at Lewes was very small.[32] The other casualties, apart from the Londoners in Montfort's army slaughtered by the Lord Edward, were almost certainly peasants. The pattern of fighting at Lewes, like that in many medieval battles, was one of heavily armoured knights on horseback killing lightly protected peasant footsoldiers. Thus the Canterbury/Dover chronicle, in its account of Lewes, observed that "many footsoldiers on the side of the barons were killed". Likewise the Furness Abbey chronicle, having given the names of the great men who died, noted that "the others who were killed in that battle were ordinary people from the masses (*mediocres exstiterunt de vulgo*)".[33]

The presence of "ordinary people from the masses" was even more pronounced in another army of 1264, that mustered by Montfort in Kent to meet the threatened invasion by the queen. This had numerous peasant contingents raised on a communal basis. In July 1264 the Montfortian government sent writs to each shire, addressed to the bishops, abbots, earls, knights, freemen "and all the community of the county". The letters explained the danger of invasion and ordered each vill to provide "four to eight men, according to the magnitude of the vill, from the best and most upstanding footmen well equipped with suitable arms, namely lances, bows, arrows, swords, crossbows and axes".[34] The response to this mandate was overwhelming. The men of Aylesbury, Dorton and Walton in Buckinghamshire admitted that they had sent their contingents. The chronicle of the London alderman, Arnold fitz Thedmar, recorded that "innumerable people" came to the army "on horse and foot from each county of England". The Winchester chronicle similarly noted that the army contained "the people of the land of diverse conditions and ages".[35] Indeed the government ultimately took steps to thin the ranks. In

[32] For a discussion of the numbers of combatants and casualties at Lewes, see D. A. Carpenter, *The Battles of Lewes and Evesham, 1264/65* (Keele, 1987), pp. 22-3.

[33] *The Historical Works of Gervase of Canterbury*, ed. W. Stubbs, 2 vols. (Rolls ser., London, 1879-80), ii, p. 237; *Chronicles of the Reigns of Stephen, Henry II and Richard I*, ed. R. Howlett, 4 vols. (Rolls ser., London, 1884-9), ii, p. 544. The Furness chronicler adds "and especially from the Scots", but this was probably no more than a reflection of his bias as a northerner.

[34] T. Rymer, *Foedera*, ed. J. Caley and F. Holbrooke, 3 vols. (Record Comm., London, 1816-30), i.1, p. 444.

[35] *De antiquis legibus liber: cronica maiorum et vicecomitum Londoniarum*, ed. T. Stapleton (Camden Soc., old ser., xxxiv, London, 1846), p. 69; *Annales monastici*, ed. Luard, iv, p. 453; see also *ibid.*, iii, p. 233. For Aylesbury, Dorton and Walton, see Jacob, *Studies in the Period of Baronial Reform and Rebellion*, pp. 410-11, 291-2; above, n. 17.

October, in response to the complaints of "the poor men" of Suffolk, it declared that there was no intention of burdening "poor men, weak and needy without lands and tenements by which they can be sustained". Instead the army was to be confined to "knights, free tenants and all others who are able to bear arms and have tenements by which they can be sustained". The distinction between "free tenants" and "all others" indicates that the army was still expected to retain an unfree peasant element.[36]

There is nothing surprising about the appearance of peasants in the armies of the civil war. For both the individual knight, bringing his "power" to an army, and the government facing invasion, the most obvious place to look for footsoldiers was in the manors and villages — the vills of the writ of July 1264. Thus at the end of 1263 a letter preserved in the Tewkesbury annals gave the following advice about how to resist a rumoured invasion by Louis IX: "from each vill let the freemen and the reeve and the strong men (*liberi et praepositi et potentes*) be prepared for war to defend the land and their own heads, and by such means a great army may grow without damage". Here again the distinction between the *liberi* and the *praepositi et potentes* shows that the army was to contain significant numbers of unfree peasants.[37] The truth was that village society was highly militarized: the peasants of England were armed, indeed they were armed by government decree. The Assize of Arms made no distinction between the free and the unfree: in 1225 the "arms" to which villeins were sworn were specifically excluded from the chattels to be assessed for the taxation on movables.[38] The obligation to bear arms was, in fact, virtually universal. By the Assize of Arms of 1242 all those with land worth less than 40s. a year were to have "scythes, halberds, knives and other small arms". All those who were able ("qui possunt") living outside the forests were to have bows and arrows. These were the minimum requirements. Prosperous peasants needed to be considerably better armed. Under the 1230 assize men with chattels worth 40s. were to have an iron cap, a doublet and a lance.[39] This was no doubt the position of Adam de Kenteis, claimed by his lord as a villein,

[36] *Close Rolls, 1261–4*, p. 409.

[37] *Annales monastici*, ed. Luard, i, p. 180. I am grateful to John Maddicott for reminding me of this evidence.

[38] *Pat. Rolls, 1216–25*, p. 560. See H. G. Richardson and G. O. Sayles, *Law and Legislation from Aethelbert to Magna Carta* (Edinburgh, 1966), pp. 137–8.

[39] *Close Rolls, 1237–42*, p. 483; *Close Rolls, 1227–31*, pp. 398–9.

who, returning from the siege of Bedford in 1224, was robbed of the lance and helmet to which he was sworn under the assize. Again, 40s. was the value put on the chattels of Peter fitz Ranulf of Swaffham, one of the prior of Ely's free sokemen accused of being "in the Isle" with the Disinherited.[40]

II

Peasants, therefore, were active in the plundering bands and armies of the civil war. But what was the basis of their involvement? Did they simply take part because they were made to by their lords or by the dominant military forces in the area, or did they sometimes act independently? Were they ignorant of the political issues, or did they sometimes identify their interests with those of one or other party? This section will suggest both that peasants did take independent action and that they had reasons for supporting — as did the villagers of Peatling Magna — the baronial cause.

Of course peasants taken on raids by Cambridgeshire lords, like Baldwin de Akeny and Philip of Stanton, can have had little choice about whether or not to go. Equally, although the Dictum eyre does not mention the lords of such raiders as William Popping, Thomas *prepositus* of Salden and John de la Dale of Sawston,[41] it is surely significant that they were, in fact, Montfortians. In some cases coercion was specifically alleged.[42] When the jurors from Lambourn in Berkshire accused three men of a robbery in Wiltshire, the men replied that they were *nativi* of John fitz John, and had been distrained to take part by his bailiffs.[43] Another Berkshire jury agreed that the men of Hungerford, Holt and

---

[40] P. R. Hyams, *King, Lords and Peasants in Medieval England: The Common Law of Villeinage in the Twelfth and Thirteenth Centuries* (Oxford, 1980), pp. 158-9; P.R.O., Just 1/83, m. 25d; *Rot. hund.*, ii, p. 485. For peasants in later armies, see J. R. Maddicott, "The English Peasantry and the Demands of the Crown, 1294-1341", *Past and Present*, supplement no. 1 (1975), pp. 34-45.

[41] See above, pp. 313-4, 317.

[42] The Dictum of Kenilworth, cap. 27, fixed a one-year redemption fine for those who, under coercion, had gone on plundering raids or otherwise aided the rebels: *Documents of the Baronial Movement*, ed. Treharne and Sanders, pp. 332-3.

[43] P.R.O., Just 1/42, m. 1d. Again, one of two "men of John fitz John" accused of despoiling the vill of Walton in Buckinghamshire said that "he held his tenement in order to do the will of the seneschal and he was there by distraint of Richard le Vache, then seneschal" (of John fitz John), an excuse upheld by a jury: Just 1/59, m. 15d. The men of Wendover also alleged coercion by fitz John and his bailiffs: Jacob, *Studies in the Period of Baronial Reform and Rebellion*, p. 410.

Kintbury had been "driven" to the siege of Marlborough "by threats of death and arson".[44]

This is not, however, the whole story. In some cases peasants had freedom of manoeuvre because their immediate lords were ineffective. Perhaps this was the situation at Peatling Magna, where the lord of the manor was the abbot of St. Evroul in Normandy.[45] Juries, moreover, did not always uphold pleas of coercion. In Northamptonshire thirteen men, accused of being present at the siege of Fotheringhay and burning and robbing the houses of John de Balliol, replied that they had been forced to go by "the barons making transit through the [royal] manor of King's Cliffe". The jurors agreed that this was true of four of them. The rest had gone "with a good will", although only three had taken part in the robbery.[46] Here then we find, at the peasant level, the same diversity of conduct characteristic of other sections of society.

Even where peasants were following their lords, they may well have done so with enthusiasm. In Berkshire, when John de Musson was accused by the vill of Hungerford of being in the garrison of Wallingford and despoiling the surrounding country, he replied that he was a man of Simon de Montfort (who was lord of Hungerford) and had acted under compulsion. A local jury disagreed; John had acted "willingly".[47] In some cases peasants clearly sided against their lords. This was true of Richard Oxfoot of Reach, in the Staine hundred of Cambridgeshire, who was

[44] P.R.O., Just 1/42, m. 3; Jacob, *Studies in the Period of Baronial Reform and Rebellion*, p. 235.

[45] For the lords of Peatling Magna, see J. Nichols, *The History and Antiquities of the County of Leicester*, 4 vols. (London, 1795-1811), iv, pt. 1, p. 327, although the statement about Simon de Montfort appears mistaken. The abbot's overlord was the earl of Winchester. After the death of the last earl in April 1264, without male heirs, the overlordship passed to the Zouches of Ashby la Zouche (hence perhaps Peatling's seizure by Eudo la Zouche after the battle of Evesham: *Select Cases of Procedure without Writ*, ed. Richardson and Sayles, p. 42). A separate tenancy in Peatling Magna was held from the earls of Winchester by Arnold de Bois, an executor of Simon de Montfort in 1259, but an invalid and non-participant during the civil war: C. Bémont, *Simon de Montfort Earl of Leicester, 1208-1265*, new edn., trans. E. F. Jacob (Oxford, 1930), p. 277; *Cal. Pat. Rolls, 1258-66*, p. 440. Another tenancy was held by the Muschet family from the Bassets of Weldon: *Liber Feodorum: The Book of Fees Commonly Called "Testa de Nevill"*, 3 vols. (London, 1920-31), ii, p. 949; P.R.O., Just 1/455, m. 12; see also *Select Cases of Procedure without Writ*, ed. Richardson and Sayles, p. 42.

[46] P.R.O., Just 1/618, m. 7.

[47] P.R.O., Just 1/42, m. 1d. John was sentenced to a fivefold redemption fine, but no value was given for his properties.

convicted of being in the Isle and condemned to redeem his one
acre of land, worth 12d. a year, at five times its value. In the
Hundred Rolls, where his holdings are slightly larger, Richard
appears as the tenant of two royalist lords, Gilbert de Peche and
William de Kirketot.[48] Similarly Roger Blancpain of Madingley,
who led the gang from the Isle which pillaged Toft, held a
messuage and one-and-a-half acres in villeinage in Gretton from
the royalist knight Roger of Trumpington, and in Madingley
itself a messuage and thirteen acres (for a rent of 6s. 6d.) from
the equally loyal prior of Barnwell. Perhaps Roger was influenced
by other lords, for the rebel knight John de Burdeleys was
a neighbour, but he would hardly have headed a party of
malefactors had his heart not been in it.[49]

That peasants acting against the king were sometimes beyond
the control of their lords was stated explicitly, and from personal
knowledge, by the chronicler of Battle Abbey. As the royal army
made its way through Sussex in the days before the battle of
Lewes, Master Thomas, the king's cook, riding out in front, was
killed "by a certain pleb". In revenge the king ordered the
execution of "very many men of the country", loosely suspected
of involvement in the crime. Then, arriving at Battle, he gave
the abbot a frosty greeting and demanded payment of 100 marks.
The royalists alleged that some of those executed were the abbot's
men and directed by him. "As to the first", the chronicler of the
abbey commented, "they were saying the truth, but as to the
second they were very far from doing so, for at that time it was
not in the power of lords to restrain their men (*suos*) from such
things". Nor was the murder of Thomas the cook an isolated
incident. After the battle of Lewes, the Battle Abbey chronicler
described how the royalists, "dispersed through flight, were
everywhere slaughtered by villeins living in the countryside".[50]

Peasants could, of course, kill and pillage without political
motive or understanding. Although the robberies revealed by the
Dictum eyre were ostensibly political, in that they were committed "in the time of disturbance", many may have been robberies
pure and simple. Lords might certainly be of the opinion that

[48] P.R.O., Just 1/83, m. 25d; *Rot. hund.*, ii, pp. 485-6; Cokayne (ed.), *Complete Peerage*, x, p. 335; *Cal. Inq. Misc.*, i, p. 186, nos. 716-17.

[49] P.R.O., Just 1/83, mm. 21d, 19, 10; *Rot. hund.*, ii, pp. 465-6, 459, 446-8; *Liber memorandorum ecclesie de Bernewelle*, ed. Clark, pp. 308, 121-3.

[50] "A vilanis patriam incolentibus trucidantur": C. Bémont, *Simon de Montfort comte de Leicester* (Paris, 1884), pp. 375-7.

those lower down the social scale should have no political views. Take the case of Nicholas Tonney, who served "with the king at his wages" in Windsor Castle under the *curialis* Drogo de Barentin and was then dismissed when the Montfortian John fitz John took over in 1264. After a while, fitz John's *ministri* sought Tonney out in the vill of Windsor, where he had gone to live, and asked him to return to the castle, "having taken an oath according to the fashion of the enemies of the king". Tonney refused; he would take no oath save "for the benefit of the king and his sons". The reply to this was brusque: "matters of this kind have nothing to do with a sergeant".[51] Doubtless the same remark would have been made about a peasant. Indeed there was clearly an element of astonishment and contempt in the way Peter de Neville related the sentiments of the villagers of Peatling Magna.

It is important, however, not to underrate the awareness and acuity of individual peasants. One of those convicted on the Dictum eyre of being in the Isle was John Wapurnet. He was said to hold three acres in Swaffham worth 3s. a year, and was compelled to redeem them for 15s. But if he was at the bottom of the social scale, he was far from ignorant either of legal niceties or political realities. On the eyre he was accused of robbing the Shelford house of the royalist castellan Alan de Kirkebi "in the time of the disturbance". Despite pleading through an attorney, Alan was apparently unaware that, under the terms of the Dictum of Kenilworth, he had no case against John Wapurnet since anyone who had paid a redemption fine was not liable for damage done to those "who fought in the time of the disturbance". They were only answerable to those who had remained neutral and joined neither side. Wapurnet saw his chance. He "came [before the judges] and said that he ought not to answer [Alan] since he says that in the war he [John] was against Alan because Alan was on the side of the king and he [John] was on the side of the barons". "And", the judges recorded, "Alan cannot deny this and so the foresaid John Wapurnet is quit".[52]

John Wapurnet of Swaffham, therefore, was perfectly aware of whose side he was on and might well, in his own mind, have

---

[51] "Responderunt quod nichil habuerunt agendi de huiusmodo serviente": P.R.O., Just 1/42, m. 15. For Tonney, see *Close Rolls, 1264-8*, p. 72.

[52] P.R.O., Just 1/83, mm. 11, 25d; *Documents of the Baronial Movement*, ed. Treharne and Sanders, pp. 334-7 (cap. 35). For Alan de Kirkebi, see *Cal. Pat. Rolls, 1266-72*, p. 134. Clive Knowles has kindly helped me with the interpretation of Wapurnet's pleading. No one else in Cambridgeshire made the same defence.

linked the cause of the barons with that of the community of the realm. Indeed, if he was a tenant of the prior of Ely at Swaffham, he had every reason to make the connection since, as we shall see, the reforming legislation of 1259 had dealt explicitly with one type of grievance which those tenants harboured against their lord.[53] However, before going on to look at the way the "common enterprise" (as Simon de Montfort described the movement of reform) appealed to peasants, it is important to put that appeal into context. For peasants did not become politically aware all of a sudden in 1258.

In the years before 1258 peasants had suffered from the oppressions of both their lords and the king, but they had not been totally outside the political system. If they were burdened by Angevin government, they also helped to run it. They were sworn to bear arms, as has been seen. They were also involved in local administration. Coroners' inquests had to be attended either by the reeve and four men from each of the four vills nearest to the place where the body was found, or by everyone over the age of twelve from those vills, which often meant in practice everyone in a tithing, the groups of ten men and upwards into which the peasant population was arranged in order to provide collective security for lawful behaviour.[54] Similarly the reeve and four men of each vill, or the heads of the tithings, provided the information for the juries of presentment which appeared both before the justices in eyre and the sheriff's tourn, the especially well-attended biannual meetings of the hundred court.[55] The juries of presentment themselves included peasants, indeed occasionally unfree peasants, as well as more substantial landholders.[56] These activities, however lowly, had a significant educative effect, put-

[53] See below, pp. 334-5.
[54] P. A. Brand, "The Contribution of the Period of Baronial Reform (1258-1267) to the Development of the Common Law in England" (Univ. of Oxford D.Phil. thesis, 1974), pp. 262-3; see below, p. 334. The tithings were largely, but not exclusively, composed of the unfree. The situation varied with local custom. However, few with significant freehold property would be included because that property provided sufficient security for observance of the peace: see W. A. Morris, *The Frankpledge System* (London, 1910), pp. 75-8, 85-6.
[55] H. M. Cam, *The Hundred and the Hundred Rolls* (London, 1930), p. 120; see *Documents of the Baronial Movement*, ed. Treharne and Sanders, pp. 126-9 (cap. 16); Brand, "Contribution of the Period of Baronial Reform", pp. 276-7.
[56] For an example of a villein on a jury of presentment, see the case of Hubert of Stapelford below, p. 327; see also the suggestions in J. R. Maddicott, "The County Community and the Making of Public Opinion in Fourteenth-Century England", *Trans. Roy. Hist. Soc.*, 5th ser., xxviii (1978), p. 33.

ting peasants in touch with the processes of royal government and administration. The very business of providing answers to the articles of the tourn and the eyre presented the opportunity, in theory at least, to reveal the malpractice of royal and seigneurial officials.

It was in struggles against their lords that peasant protest was most marked.[57] Manorial records suggest that peasants waged continual guerilla actions against attempts to increase services. They also brought cases against their lords in the king's courts. Frequently these cases turned on the question of freedom. If the lord could prove that his tenants were unfree, then, as we have mentioned, they could bring no action against him about their customs and services. Peasants, on the other hand, often claimed that they were free sokemen, or had title to the fixed services and conditions derived from living on a manor which had once been part of the king's "ancient demesne".

The period of reform and rebellion is bounded by cases of this kind. One striking example is the struggle at North Ashby (now Mears Ashby) in Northamptonshire, a village some twenty-two miles south-east of Peatling Magna. In 1242 the king gave the manor (which had escheated into his hands and was not ancient demesne) to Robert de Mares, a much favoured huntsman, esquire and ultimately household knight. For seven years Robert accepted the sokeman status of his tenants, the most substantial of whom were virgaters. Then he attempted to reduce them to villeinage, demanding the payment of merchet and the right to tallage them as he pleased. In response the men sued Robert before the justices of the bench at Westminster and forced him to make an agreement in which he largely admitted defeat. Robert died in December 1256 and was buried, at the king's request, in Salisbury Cathedral. His widow, Sibyl, a determined woman who also enjoyed the king's favour, was given custody of North Ashby during the minority of her son. Almost at once she reneged on the agreement and renewed the struggle. This time both sides went to law and cases came before the court *coram rege* during the Oxford and Winchester parliaments of June and July 1258, thus plunging the men of North Ashby into the midst of the political revolution of that year. Lengthy proceedings followed

[57] For what follows, see Hilton, "Peasant Movements in England before 1381"; R. H. Hilton, *A Medieval Society: The West Midlands at the End of the Thirteenth Century* (London, 1966), pp. 151-61; R. H. Hilton, *Bond Men Made Free: Medieval Peasant Movements and the English Rising of 1381* (London, 1973), pp. 85-91.

before the justiciar set up by the reformers, Hugh Bigod, his successor, Hugh Despencer, and the judge Gilbert of Preston when he visited Northamptonshire in March 1261. On this last occasion six of the villagers "followed for themselves and for the other men of North Ashby in common". Finally in June 1261, before the itinerant justices in Northamptonshire, Sibyl and the men set out their differences in comprehensive detail, and Sibyl at last backed down. In return for a payment of 4½ marks she agreed that the sokemen could hold by the customs and services which they acknowledged until her son came of age. In fact the men maintained their victory, for a survey of North Ashby on the death of Sibyl's son in 1282 described the twelve virgates which she had claimed to be villeinage as "held in free socage".[58]

With the involvement in Angevin government and the struggles against their lords as a "training ground", it is difficult to believe that peasants were incapable of taking a view about the great conflict in England between 1258 and 1267. But what would that view have been? The regime of a peasant's lord and the claims of the contesting parties could give conflicting signals. Perhaps the peasants of Swaffham Prior were encouraged to join the Montfortians in the Isle by the exactions of their royalist lord, the prior of Ely. But, of course, as lords of manors, Montfortians could be just as aggressive as anyone else. The Montfortian custodian of Northamptonshire in 1264, William Marshal, for example, had been accused in 1258 of forcing his men to perform services "against the custom of the manor". At North Ashby itself the situation was complex. Sibyl de Mares's second husband (she married again between 1261 and 1264) was William Marmion, a Montfortian who fought at Lewes and Evesham. When, as a consequence, Sibyl's property at Ashby was plundered by neighbouring royalists on 12 August 1265 (within a week of the Peatling Magna incident), whose side did her peasants take?[59] Nor was the king's case without its appeal. Henry III had spoken

---

[58] *Cal. Charter Rolls, 1226-57*, p. 267; *Cal. Liberate Rolls, 1251-60*, p. 346; P.R.O., KB 26/158, mm. 10d, 15d; Just 1/1187, m. 11d; Just 1/1192, m. 2 (a reference I owe to Paul Brand), printed with a few omissions in *Placitorum in domo capitulari Westmonasteriensi asservatorum abbreviatio* [ed. W. Illingworth] (Record Comm., London, 1811), p. 150; P.R.O., Just 1/616, m. 20d; C 133/29, no. 7 (*Cal. Inq. Post Mortem*, i, no. 425); see Hilton, "Peasant Movements in England before 1381", p. 126; Hilton, *Bond Men Made Free*, p. 88. For other disputes over peasant services in the court *coram rege* in 1258, see P.R.O., KB 26/158, mm. 2, 4.

[59] P.R.O., KB 26/158, m. 2; *Rotuli selecti*, ed. Hunter, pp. 197-8; *Cal. Pat. Rolls, 1258-66*, p. 142; *Cal. Inq. Misc.*, i, nos. 925, 833.

of his concern for peasants, and had heard cases brought by them in the court *coram rege*.[60] His stand for peace and order might appeal to those threatened by the burning and pillaging of crops. On the other hand there were also powerful reasons why peasants could believe themselves encompassed by the movement of baronial reform, and could think that it had served their interests. To these reasons we will now turn.

One of the first actions of "the barons" in 1258 was to expel the king's Lusignan half-brothers from England. Here both the greatest baron and the smallest peasant could have a mutual interest. The former resented the Lusignans because they monopolized the king's patronage and behaved in an arrogant and lawless fashion. The latter experienced directly the oppressions of their local officials.[61] In Surrey, investigations set on foot by the Provisions of Oxford revealed that Geoffrey de Lusignan's steward, William de Bussey, had increased the tallage paid by the men of Byfleet, Weybridge and Bisley from 40s. to 100s., and that as a result "the tenants were wholly destroyed". At Walton he had extended the manor at twice its value and forced its "free tenants" to give 13 marks "to have peace from being unduly tallaged".[62] The incident that Matthew Paris fastened on above all others to illustrate Bussey's brutality occurred at Trumpington in Cambridgeshire. There he and his agents had caused the death of a young man through harsh imprisonment and then hung his dead body. That this created as much scandal in the local community as in the monastery of St. Albans is clear from the terms in which the incident was reported on the 1261 eyre by the presenting jury of Thriplow hundred, a jury which included Hubert of Stapelford, a *custumarius* holding fifteen acres of land from the bishop of Ely, and later accused of aiding and abetting those in the Isle. According to the jury the young man had died

---

[60] See below, p. 344; above, n. 58. In January 1263 Henry had also, of his own free will, confirmed the Provisions of Westminster of October 1259, although coming when it did the impact of this was possibly limited.

[61] For these oppressions, see J. R. Maddicott, "Magna Carta and the Local Community, 1215-1259", *Past and Present*, no. 102 (Feb. 1984), pp. 54-61. However, Huw Ridgeway doubts whether there was widespread hostility in the localities to the Lusignans before 1258, and has suggested that much of their unpopularity was due to the propaganda of their enemies at court: H. Ridgeway, "King Henry III and the 'Aliens', 1236-1272", in P. R. Coss and S. D. Lloyd (eds.), *Thirteenth-Century England*, ii (Woodbridge, 1988), pp. 86-7, 90-1.

[62] P.R.O., Just 1/873, mm. 6-9; Maddicott, "Magna Carta and the Local Community", p. 57. Geoffrey de Lusignan was also accused of oppressing the men of Effingham.

as a result of "the cruel punishment and most harsh imprisonment" inflicted on him by Bussey's agents, "and before he had
been convicted of any felony they hung him dead". Asked
whether all this took place on Bussey's orders "they say yes".[63]

Of course, however notorious, the activities of the Lusignans
only affected a tiny number of peasants in proportion to the
whole. But there were other ways in which peasants more generally could feel embraced by the movement of reform. Under the
oath of "the commune of England", conceived by the Oxford
parliament in June 1258, "all faithful men" (not simply all free
men) swore to observe the statutes of reform, aid each other
against all men, and treat opponents as "mortal enemies". It is
probable that this oath was widely taken by the peasantry since
a suitable forum was provided by the sessions of the hundred
courts convened after Michaelmas to hold the view of frankpledge — to check whether the peasant population was pledged
together in its tithings. It was at such meetings that oaths of fealty
to the king were sworn by those newly admitted to tithings. The
wide circle of those intended to take the 1258 oath explains its
proclamation in letters issued in English as well as French and
Latin.[64] When Simon de Montfort described the movement of
reform as "the common enterprise", he meant that everyone "in
common" was involved in it.[65]

The reformers indeed quite explicitly claimed that everyone
should benefit from their measures. According to the Ordinance
of the Sheriffs of October 1258, another proclamation issued in
English as well as Latin and French, the sheriffs were to swear
to "do justice in common to all people . . . as well and as quickly
to the poor as to the rich". In the Ordinance of the Magnates of
February 1259, the council of fifteen and the twelve elected to
represent the community at parliament promised that their officials would take nothing unjustly from anyone "cleric or layman,
freeman or villein, house of religion or vill".[66] All this was more

---

[63] *Matthaei Parisiensis . . . chronica majora*, ed. H. R. Luard, 7 vols. (Rolls ser.,
London, 1884-9), v, p. 739; P.R.O., Just 1/82, mm. 24d, 36; Just 1/83, mm. 13, 22;
Rot. hund., ii, p. 543.

[64] *Documents of the Baronial Movement*, ed. Treharne and Sanders, pp. 100-1,
116-17; Cam, *Hundred and the Hundred Rolls*, pp. 185-6; B. Dickins and R. M.
Wilson, *Early Middle English Texts* (Cambridge, 1952), pp. 8-9.

[65] *Documents of the Baronial Movement*, ed. Treharne and Sanders, pp. 208-9 (cap.
34).

[66] *Annales monastici*, ed. Luard, i, p. 453; *Documents of the Baronial Movement*, ed.
Treharne and Sanders, pp. 120-1, 134-5.

than mere rhetoric. A major plank in the programme of reform was the restoration of the office of justiciar with the intention of sending him on eyre around the country. The aim of his visitation, and of the inquiries by four knights in each county which preceded it, was to see that "speedy justice be done throughout our realm, no less to the poor than to the rich", as the king explained in his October proclamation. The four knights, on a hundred-by-hundred basis, were to enquire through juries into "all excesses, trespasses and acts of injustice . . . by no matter what persons, done to anyone whatsoever". As Matthew Paris put it, they investigated "the number and kind of wrongs with which the strong had oppressed the simple".[67] At the same time the justiciar summoned "all men" to come before him to complain against whomsoever they wished — a complaint (*querela*) which they could make verbally, thus enabling the poor to ventilate their grievances without the bother and expense of obtaining writs. Bigod and his fellow judges, according to the St. Albans *Flores historiarum*, were sworn to give justice "to rich and poor, serf and free, stranger and relation".[68]

That peasants really did bring their grievances before Hugh Bigod's eyres, and those subsequently commissioned by the Provisions of Westminster, is confirmed by the eyre rolls themselves. Indeed peasants may have imagined that the jurisdiction of the eyres was wider and more revolutionary than it actually was. Thus the men of Bampton in Oxfordshire, on the Provisions of Westminster eyre of January 1260, presented several articles against their lord, the knight Roger de Oilly, accusing him of distraining them to perform services "which they ought not and were not want to do, and of tallaging them so heavily that they are unable to support their tenure". Roger's answer was simple: his men were villeins not sokemen, and so he could tallage them as he pleased. The men then came before the judges and freely acknowledged their villein status, whereupon they were placed in mercy for a false plaint and Roger was acquitted. In other words there was no question of the eyre breaching the great legal

[67] *Documents of the Baronial Movement*, ed. Treharne and Sanders, pp. 118-19, 114-15; Matthew Paris, *Chronica majora*, v, p. 714.
[68] *Flores historiarum*, ed. H. R. Luard, 3 vols. (Rolls ser., London, 1890), ii, pp. 426-7; *De antiquis legibus liber*, ed. Stapleton, p. 40; Jacob, *Studies in the Period of Baronial Reform and Rebellion*, pp. 65-70. For the justiciar's oath, see also *Documents of the Baronial Movement*, ed. Treharne and Sanders, pp. 102-3 (cap. 6); *Annales monastici*, ed. Luard, iii, p. 209.

rule which barred the unfree from suing their lords over their tenements and services. But it is testimony to the hopes aroused by the eyre that the villeins of Bampton believed that they could do so.[69]

The hopes of peasants were not entirely misplaced, however. The London chronicler, Arnold fitz Thedmar, observed that when Bigod heard pleas for Surrey (at Bermondsey in November and December 1258) he imprisoned and amerced "several bailiffs and others" convicted of "transgressions against their subjects".[70] This was no more than the truth. As many as five lords and/or their bailiffs were sent to gaol,[71] as were six more bailiffs when Bigod heard pleas for Kent in January 1259.[72] In fact the maintenance of the rule which stymied the peasants of Bampton did not mean that the eyres were entirely closed to the unfree. They were perfectly entitled to commence actions (as they had been before) against their lords for such things as serious physical assault and (although this was something of a grey area) false imprisonment.[73] Thus one villein complained that he had been falsely imprisoned and maltreated against the king's peace by Peter of Ashridge, the earl of Cornwall's bailiff at Wallingford. He lost his case and was sent to gaol with the bleak observation "pauper est". On the other hand a Leicestershire villein complained successfully about two bailiffs of the honour of Peverel who had unjustly imprisoned him.[74] On the Cambridgeshire eyre in 1261, a jury found that Richard fitz Richard Herbert had assaulted William le Brid and stolen the doors of his house at Quy. The verdict was that Richard should be imprisoned, amerced and pay William 2s. damages.

---

[69] *Select Cases of Procedure without Writ*, ed. Richardson and Sayles, p. 106. For the operation of the rule on Hugh Bigod's eyres, see, for example, P.R.O., Just 1/1187, m. 2d; Just 1/873, m. 2d.

[70] *De antiquis legibus liber*, ed. Stapleton, p. 39.

[71] P.R.O., Just 1/873, mm. 5, 6, 8d. The Lord Edward's bailiff in Southwark was one of those arrested. Hugh Bigod's first two eyre rolls have been edited by Andrew Hershey, and I have been greatly helped by his analysis of the cases in them: A. H. Hershey, "An Introduction to and an Edition of the Hugh Bigod Eyre Rolls, June 1258-February 1259: PRO Just 1/1187 & Just 1/873" (Univ. of London Ph.D. thesis, 1991).

[72] P.R.O., Just 1/873, mm. 18d, 19d, 20, 23, 23d. The six included three royal bailiffs of the hundred of Milton Regis.

[73] See Hyams, *King, Lords and Peasants*, pp. 124-51, for the villein as litigant; for false imprisonment, see *ibid.*, pp. 138-9, 139 n. 69.

[74] P.R.O., Just 1/1188, m. 7; *Select Cases of Procedure without Writ*, ed. Richardson and Sayles, pp. 100-1. In these cases the fact that the plaintiffs were in tithings makes it likely that they were villeins: see above, n. 54.

"Afterwards", a note adds, "the judges remitted the amercement as William was one of Richard's villeins". But William apparently kept his damages. The Hundred Rolls of 1279 show two Brids each holding ten acres at Quy in villeinage.[75]

For free peasants, of course, and those with ancient demesne status, the eyre could be used to bring forward a wider range of grievances. Thus nine peasants from Coleby in Lincolnshire came before Bigod and won actions of novel disseisin against their lords, Bartholomew and Herbert Pecche, who had attempted to force them into villeinage. On Bigod's Surrey eyre William of Burhurst, having shown that he was a free man and held his land as a sokeman of the king's ancient demesne, brought a successful *querela* against his lord, who had distrained him to perform the "customary services of a villein". Both the lord and his agent were sent to gaol before promising 60s. in return for being pardoned for their transgressions. The men of Dwelly and Leigham in Surrey, having successfully asserted their ancient demesne status, were victorious in a *querela* brought against their lord, the prior of Bermondsey, who had tallaged them *pro voluntate sua*. Equally successful were "the men of the king's ancient demesne of Walworth and Newington" who brought a *querela* against Master William, parson of Newington Church, who had taken the manors at farm and compelled the men to "perform other customs than those which were customary". William too was sent to gaol.[76]

Complaints by men of manors and vills were indeed a feature of Bigod's first eyres in 1258-9. On his Surrey and Kentish eyres, apart from the cases mentioned above, they were brought by the king's men of Norbiton; by the vills of Birling, Burham and "part" of Larkfield hundred; by the men of Hamo de Crevequor and Robert de Barbling of the tithing of Yalding; by the men of the tithings of Hale Bridge and Tiffenden, Milstead and Hyldeston; and on behalf of "the whole community of the country of Lossenham and Maytham".[77] Earlier in August 1258 Bigod had

<hr/>

[75] *Select Cases of Procedure without Writ*, ed. Richardson and Sayles, p. 121; Hyams, *King, Lords and Peasants*, p. 141; *Rot. hund.*, ii, p. 497.

[76] P.R.O., Just 1/1187, m. 21; *Select Cases of Procedure without Writ*, ed. Richardson and Sayles, pp. 90-1; P.R.O., Just 1/873, m. 8d. For the failure of the peasants of Witley to prove their ancient demesne status, see *Select Cases of Procedure without Writ*, ed. Richardson and Sayles, pp. 91-2, clxvii.

[77] *Select Cases of Procedure without Writ*, ed. Richardson and Sayles, p. 92; P.R.O., Just 1/873, mm. 7, 18d, 19, 21, 22, 23d. In Kent the custom was for the men of a whole vill or district to form a single tithing: Morris, *Frankpledge System*, p. 88.

heard complaints from the men of Walthamstow and Chingford in Essex and from the sokemen of the royal demesne manor of Brill in Buckinghamshire. Eighteen of the latter, acting together, brought no less than seventeen complaints against the king's bailiffs running the manor. The jury both confirmed the charges and added new ones of its own.[78]

Bigod heard these complaints from the men of Brill at Woodstock. Perhaps it was the Brillites' success which inspired the men of Bampton and Hardwick, manors five miles apart and within fifteen miles of Woodstock, to bring *querelae* against their respective lords, Roger de Oilly and Walter de Grey, on the Provisions of Westminster eyre in Oxfordshire in January 1260. The failure of the men of Bampton has already been noted, but those of Hardwick did rather better. In the Hundred Rolls of 1279 (which shows that most of them were half-virgaters) they were described uncompromisingly as serfs. None the less on the 1260 eyre their ancient demesne status went unchallenged. As a result they presented a huge *querela*, running to twelve separate items, about the novel exactions of Walter de Grey and his bailiffs. Although the jury rejected most of their charges, the men did recover an annual payment of 8s. 4d., with five years' worth of arrears, which they had customarily received in place of food when they mowed their lord's meadow. The jury also decided that their beasts had been unjustly driven by Walter's bailiffs from Hardwick to Cogges.[79]

In all these examples individuals or village communities presented their complaints directly to the eyre. In addition Bigod also heard cases brought before him by the inquiries of the four knights. It was the four knights in Surrey who revealed the malpractices of the bailiffs of Geoffrey de Lusignan mentioned above. In Kent they exposed the grievance of the men of the manor of Birling: their lord's bailiff, William de la Green (who was sent to gaol), had appointed fourteen reeves in four years, each of whom exacted fresh sums from the villagers.[80] The way

[78] P.R.O., Just 1/1187, m. 5d; Jacob, *Studies in the Period of Baronial Reform and Rebellion*, pp. 344-9, 44-7.

[79] *Select Cases of Procedure without Writ*, ed. Richardson and Sayles, p. 106; P.R.O., Just 1/713, m. 1d; *Rot. hund.*, ii, p. 701.

[80] Jacob, *Studies in the Period of Baronial Reform and Rebellion*, pp. 352-3, 61-2. In Surrey the four knights brought to light the grievances of the vill of Guildford and of the men of Chilberton and Merstham; in Kent those of the tithings of Aylesford, and of Binney and Moriston: P.R.O., Just 1/873, mm. 5d, 18d, 24. More generally, the four knights said that every vill in Surrey complained of increased shrieval

(cont. on p. 27)

that the knights took cognizance of peasant grievances can also be seen from the one surviving record of their investigations, that for the Loes hundred of Suffolk. Here they recorded that the bailiff of the earl of Norfolk had taken a new payment from thirteen vills (or lordships within them) so that one man could answer for all at the view of frankpledge and "that they should not be fined in their replies in the renewal of the pledges".[81] Lords were entitled to hold the view of frankpledge either at specially privileged manorial courts or, as here at Loes, where they controlled the court of a hundred.[82] What the earl of Norfolk's bailiffs were doing was to impose the fine of *beaupleder*, a fine paid by tithings so as to avoid amercements for slips and omissions when giving their evidence.[83] Similar grievances about *beaupleder* may well have been raised on the 1260 Oxfordshire eyre. There the jury of Ploughley hundred complained that seven vills had suffered from the increased exactions either of the sheriff or the earl of Cornwall at the view of frankpledge; they also complained of a new park at Newington which harmed the men of the vill "both free and villein".[84]

The legislation promulgated in the Provisions of Westminster in October 1259 formed another aspect of the reforms carried through by "the common enterprise". While some clauses in drafts of the Provisions, relevant to the peasantry, were dropped in the final published version,[85] others remained. One of these

(n. 80 cont.)
exactions at the tourn: *Select Cases of Procedure without Writ*, ed. Richardson and Sayles, pp. 92-3; P.R.O., Just 1/873, mm. 5, 8; Jacob, *Studies in the Period of Baronial Reform and Rebellion*, p. 55.

[81] Jacob, *Studies in the Period of Baronial Reform and Rebellion*, pp. 341-2, 34-5. The earl's bailiff appears to have gone quit on the charges against him.

[82] For the private hundred, see Cam, *Hundred and the Hundred Rolls*, pp. 137-45.

[83] The fine of *beaupleder* is fully discussed in Brand, "Contribution of the Period of Baronial Reform", p. 266-9. See above, p. 328.

[84] P.R.O., Just 1/713, mm. 3, 4.

[85] The first omission was the section in clause 16 of the *Providencia baronum* (*Documents of the Baronial Movement*, ed. Treharne and Sanders, pp. 126-9) which limited the obligation to attend the sheriff's tourn to those from each vill who were needed to make the inquisition (into the articles of the tourn): see Brand, "Contribution of the Baronial Movement", pp. 276-7. The implication was that large numbers of villagers would no longer be forced to attend or be amerced for failing to do so. Secondly, the clause in the French draft of the Provisions which limited amercements, imposed on vills for failing to follow the hue and cry, to occasions where it had been raised for a reasonable cause, was omitted: *Annales monastici*, ed. Luard, i, p. 476. Thirdly, there was a clause, also in the French draft, which laid down that vills were not to be amerced by coroners, sheriffs and other bailiffs for failing to come to inquests; this was to be a matter for the justices in eyre: *ibid.*, i, pp. 475-6. These

(cont. on p. 28)

laid down that the justices in eyre were to cease amercing vills because not everyone over the age of twelve had come before the coroners for inquests or for other things pertaining to the crown. The aim here was to abolish a practice which the justices had greatly extended in the late 1240s, and return instead to the customary procedure of allowing a vill to be represented by a reeve and four men.[86] Another clause in the legislation concerned the *murdrum* fine. This was the fine the justices imposed on a hundred when it was unable to prove that a dead man was English. Under the Provisions of Westminster the fine was abolished in cases of death by misadventure and confined to those of genuine felony.[87] The burden of the *murdrum* fine was usually divided between the vills of the hundred, and was then paid by the peasantry. Indeed in some parts of the country the fine was paid only by the unfree.[88]

In all the legislation discussed so far, peasants gained protection chiefly from royal officials. But at least one clause in the Provisions of Westminster could also protect them from their lords. This was the clause which abolished the fine *beaupleder*. We have already seen this fine being levied by the earl of Norfolk's agents in Loes hundred, and it was probably widely imposed by lords when they held the view of frankpledge in manorial and hundred courts.[89] That peasants were aware that they should benefit from

(n. 85 cont.)

clauses would have restricted the profit of the king's local officials and of lords with private hundreds. For the argument that the French text of the Provisions (*ibid.*, i, pp. 471-6) is the penultimate draft prior to the published Latin version (*Documents of the Baronial Movement*, ed. Treharne and Sanders, pp. 137-49), see P. A. Brand, "The Drafting of Legislation in Mid-Thirteenth-Century England", *Parliamentary Hist.*, ix (1990), pp. 269-70, (ch. 16 of his *The Making of The Common Law*).

[86] *Documents of the Baronial Movement*, ed. Treharne and Sanders, pp. 146-7 (cap. 21; see also cap. 14 of the Petition of the Barons, *ibid.*, pp. 82-3); Brand, "Contribution of the Period of Baronial Reform", pp. 262-3. The age of twelve was the age for entry into a tithing. On the Essex eyre of 1254 the coroners of Colchester testified that inquests should be held by "all those who were in tithing": P.R.O., Just 1/233, m. 58.

[87] *Documents of the Baronial Movement*, ed. Treharne and Sanders, pp. 146-7 (cap. 22); Brand, "Contribution of the Period of Baronial Reform", pp. 246-52.

[88] *The 1235 Surrey Eyre*, ed. C. A. F. Meekings and D. Crook, 2 vols. (Surrey Rec. Soc., xxxi-xxxii, Guildford, 1979-83), i, p. 107; F. Pollock and F. W. Maitland, *The History of English Law before the Time of Edward I*, 2nd edn., 2 vols. (London, 1898), i, p. 547 n. 5. In Northamptonshire the *murdrum* fine was "to be paid and collected by the heads of the tithings but not equally from all": "Estate Records of the Hotot Family", ed. E. King, in *A Northamptonshire Miscellany*, ed. E. King (Northants. Rec. Soc., xxxii, Northampton, 1983), p. 58.

[89] The fine of *beaupleder* was abolished in the Provisions as imposed in the eyres of justices, in shire courts and in the "courts of barons" (*in curiis baronum*): *Documents*

(cont. on p. 29)

the new legislation is suggested by the declaration of the free sokemen of Swaffham Prior, at least two of whom had been with the rebels in the Isle. The Hundred Rolls of 1279 recorded a long list of new exactions and services which the prior of Ely had imposed on the sokemen, one being that he had levied the fine of *beaupleder* at the view of frankpledge "against the statute of the king". The statute referred to by the sokemen was the 1267 Statute of Marlborough, but, in fact, the relevant clause there was based on the Provisions of Westminster of 1259.[90] The Swaffhamites, therefore, had good grounds for looking favourably upon the "common enterprise", since it had tackled directly one of their own grievances.

The legislation in the Provisions of Westminster indeed became widely known in the localities, and was at least partly obeyed. Paul Brand has shown that the clause limiting the incidence of the *murdrum* fine was usually observed on the eyres held between 1259 and 1263.[91] The counties of Cambridgeshire, Buckinghamshire and Oxfordshire specifically drew the judges' attention to the legislation.[92] As for the legislation limiting the numbers having to attend inquests, this too seems to have been upheld on the eyres, and the judges were reminded of it when they visited Oxfordshire. None the less the concession was effectively withdrawn by the Statute of Marlborough in 1267.[93] What the

(n. 89 cont.)
of the Baronial Movement, ed. Treharne and Sanders, pp. 142-3 (cap. 5). The clause was thus more specific than its precursor in the Petition of the Barons (cap. 14), which only referred to the eyre: *ibid.*, pp. 82-3 (where slightly mistranslated). The Statute of Marlborough added hundred courts to the list, but it is probable that the relevant clause in the Provisions of Westminster had intended to abolish the fine comprehensively including its imposition in the hundred. It was certainly thus interpreted: *Statutes of the Realm*, ed. A. Luders *et al.*, 11 vols. (Record Comm., London, 1810-28), i, pp. 22-3; *Select Cases of Procedure without Writ*, ed. Richardson and Sayles, pp. 105-6; Jacob, *Studies in the Period of Baronial Reform and Rebellion*, pp. 354-5; Brand, "Contribution of the Period of Baronial Reform", pp. 265, 270-1; see also *Documents of the Baronial Movement*, ed. Treharne and Sanders, pp. 128-9 (cap. 17). The legislation built on clause 42 of Magna Carta 1217, which forbade sheriffs from taking *occasiones* at the view of frankpledge.

[90] *Rot. hund.*, ii, p. 485; *Documents of the Baronial Movement*, ed. Treharne and Sanders, pp. 143-4 (cap. 5); *Statutes of the Realm*, ed. Luders *et al.*, i, pp. 22-3 (cap. 11).

[91] Brand, "Contribution of the Period of Baronial Reform", pp. 252-5. How far hundreds really gained financially from the restrictions on the fine is unclear, however. For the 1261-3 eyres, see D. Crook, *Records of the General Eyre* (London, 1982), pp. 126-33.

[92] P.R.O., Just 1/82, m. 23; Just 1/58, m. 20; Just 1/701, m. 19.

[93] P.R.O., Just 1/701, m. 19; Brand, "Contribution of the Period of Baronial Reform", pp. 264-5.

reformers of 1258-9 were prepared to do for the peasantry, the king in 1267 was not. The legislation concerning *beaupleder* also became well known. On the Oxfordshire eyre of 1260 the "men" of Bloxham hundred complained that the sheriff, "after the provision was made", had exacted what amounted to fines for *beaupleder* "but they [the men of the hundred] did not then know about the provisions made by the barons". Since the Provisions of Westminster referred to here had been promulgated in October 1259 and the Oxfordshire eyre took place in January 1260, news of the legislation had in fact travelled quite fast.[94]

By 1263 constructive reform had given way to violent ravaging of royalist estates. But this too shaped the peasantry's political ideas. It was justified by the Montfortians under the terms of the oath taken by "the community of England" in 1258, which stated that anyone who was "against" the oath (and thus by extension against "the community" which had sworn it) should be treated as a "mortal enemy".[95] Hence the estates of the royal knight Geoffrey de Childwick were seized, so the king was made to explain, "because he stood against the community of our realm".[96] This was precisely the reason the peasants of Peatling Magna adduced for their own actions: Peter de Neville was "against the welfare of the community of the realm". It may well be, therefore, that it was in part through the violence and the way it was justified that the concept of "the community of the realm" percolated down to the level of the village. There it was grasped all the more easily because of its kinship to the emerging concept of the "community of the vill". In 1261 the six sokemen of North Ashby acted "for themselves and the other men of North Ashby in common"; the villagers in the Peatling Magna case pleaded specifically for "the community of the vill". As early as 1250 a charter was issued by four named individuals "and all the community of the vill of Wellow" (in Nottinghamshire) and sealed with the seal of that "community".[97]

[94] *Select Cases of Procedure without Writ*, ed. Richardson and Sayles, pp. 105-6; Brand, "Contribution of the Period of Baronial Reform", pp. 270-1.

[95] *Annales monastici*, ed. Luard, iii, p. 221, iv, pp. 119-20, 134; *Documents of the Baronial Movement*, ed. Treharne and Sanders, pp. 100-1 (cap. 4), 116-17.

[96] *Close Rolls, 1264-8*, pp. 45-6. John Maddicott kindly drew this reference to my attention, and pointed out the parallel with the statement by the villagers of Peatling Magna. In 1258 the Lusignans were said to have been "against the community of the realm concerning the provisions of the barons": *Documents of the Baronial Movement*, ed. Treharne and Sanders, pp. 92-3.

[97] *The Registrum Antiquissimum of the Cathedral of Lincoln*, ed. C. W. Foster, 3 vols. (Lincoln Rec. Soc., xxvii-xxix, 1931-5), iii, pp. 311-13, cited by Cam, "Community

There was also another political dimension to the violence: it was portrayed from its start in 1263 as intended to save the English race from destruction by foreigners. The anti-alien feelings present in 1258, when the Lusignans were expelled from England, had intensified in the following years. The queen and her party of Savoyards were widely blamed for overthrowing the Provisions of Oxford in 1261. In the same year the Lusignans returned to England. Henry and Edward meanwhile were stigmatized for bringing foreign troops into the country. All of this was cleverly exploited by the Montfortians to give their movement popular appeal. In July 1263 the king was even forced to promulgate a "statute" which banned foreigners absolutely from office and, with certain qualifications, expelled them from the country "never to return".[98] Chroniclers began to see the movement of reform almost exclusively in terms of preserving the English people from the oppressions of foreigners, a view with which peasants could naturally identify, having suffered from the harsh lordship of both Lusignans and Savoyards. The St. Albans

n. 97 cont.)
of the Vill", p. 77; *Select Cases of Procedure without Writ*, ed. Richardson and Sayles, pp. 42-5; see also "Estate Records of the Hotot Family", ed. King, pp. 13, 56-7. This early use of the Latin "communitas" in a village context makes it highly likely that the word was readily transferable into spoken English, most probably by the use of the French equivalent "commune" (Sir James Holt has pointed out to me that there was no exact English equivalent). The earliest appearance in an English text of the French "commune" or "communaute" is in the life of Thomas Becket in the Laud version of the South English Legendary. This manuscript dates from *c.* 1290-1300, but the original may have been begun *c.* 1270-80, probably in the diocese of Worcester. Its purpose was to provide easier and more popular readings for saints' days: *Middle English Dictionary*, ed. H. Kurath *et al.* (Ann Arbor, 1954-), i.1, p. 436; *The South-English Legendary or Lives of Saints, I: MS. Laud, 108, in the Bodleian Library*, ed. C. Horstmann (Early English Text Soc., London, 1887), p. 143 l. 1282; M. Görlach, *An East Midland Revision of the South English Legendary* (Heidelberg, 1976), p. 8; see also M. Görlach, *The Textual Tradition of the South English Legendary* (Leeds Univ. Texts and Monographs, new ser., vi, Leeds, 1974). It is true that when the chancery clerk Robert of Fulham rendered the king's proclamation of 18 October 1258 into French and English, the French "la commune de nostre reaume" became the English "þæt loandes folk on vre kuneriche". But since Robert's task was precisely to write in English (Treharne, *Baronial Plan of Reform*, p. 120 n. 1) he may well have shied away from "loan" words, only one of which ("seel") appears in his text. I owe this point and much else in this note to Rosamund Allen. For the text of the October proclamation, see *Documents of the Baronial Movement*, ed. Treharne and Sanders, pp. 116-17; Dickins and Wilson, *Early Middle English Texts*, pp. 8-9; A. J. Ellis, "The Only English Proclamation of Henry III", *Trans. Philol. Soc.* (1868-9), pp. 1-135.
[98] Ridgeway, "Henry III and the 'Aliens'", pp. 90-1; D. A. Carpenter, "Simon de Montfort: The First Leader of a Political Movement in English History", see above, p. 231. See also D. A. Carpenter, "King Henry III's 'Statute' against the Aliens, July 1263", above pp. 261-80.

chronicler caught the flavour of this popular xenophobia in 1263 when he noted that "whoever did not know the English tongue was despised by the masses (*a vulgo*) and held in contempt".[99]

The same anti-alien sentiments were used to mobilize the villages to resist the army of foreign mercenaries gathered by the queen for her projected invasion in the summer of 1264. The aliens, so Montfort's government proclaimed, threatened "everyone in the kingdom" with "perpetual confusion and disinheritance"; they thirsted after blood and would spare neither sex nor age a cruel death.[100] If some peasants thought merely of the inconvenience and expense of coming to the army, others must have found the experience instructive and exhilarating. Montfort's miraculous victory at Lewes had taken place only two months before. It had been agreed that the Provisions of Oxford should stand "unbroken". But now it was up to everyone to defend the victory and save the English race from death and destruction at the hands of foreigners. If friars and chaplains went through the ranks preaching this message, the peasant contingents took it back to their villages. Perhaps above all this was how rural society got to know about the heroism of Simon de Montfort and the merits of his cause.

The oath which began the movement of reform, the legislation of 1259 and participation in the great army of 1264 were all, in intention at least, to apply to the country as a whole. But Montfortian feelings were clearly at their most extreme in particular regions. Much of Simon's knightly support came from the midland counties, notably Warwickshire and Leicestershire. There were also important centres of rebellion in Northamptonshire, Buckinghamshire and Berkshire.[101] Later the focus was the Isle of Ely. Doubtless it was in such areas that Montfortian propaganda spread most easily. In Northamptonshire, according to the Dictum eyre, the chaplain of Hemington "publicly preached concerning Simon earl of Leicester against the king". So did

[99] *Flores historiarum*, ed. Luard, ii, p. 481. For the Savoyards, see Ridgeway, "Henry III and the 'Aliens'", pp. 86-7. On Bigod's eyre in September 1258 a jury of twenty-four refused to reverse the conviction of the queen's steward, Matthias Bezill, for reducing one of his free tenants to villeinage: P.R.O., Just 1/1187, m. 24d.

[100] Rymer, *Foedera*, i.1, p. 444; see also *Annales monastici*, ed. Luard, iii, p. 233, iv, p. 453.

[101] See above pp. 226-9; see also D. Williams, "Simon de Montfort and his Adherents", in W. M. Ormrod (ed.), *England in the Thirteenth Century* (Harlaxton, 1985), pp. 166-77; above, pp. 315, 320-1. The civil war began in April 1264 with the king besieging the Montfortians in Northampton.

another ecclesiastic, Master Walter de Hyldeborw, the rector of
Little Billing. When, so it was testified on the eyre, William
Marshal, the Montfortian keeper of the shire, "gathered the
community of the county of Northampton at Cow Meadow under
Northampton, Walter [de Hyldeborw] was William's accomplice,
and when William encouraged preaching to the people on behalf
of the earl of Leicester, Walter himself preached on behalf of the
earl".[102] Probably the same happened in other Montfortian areas.
It is no coincidence that Peatling Magna is only eight miles south
of Montfort's borough of Leicester.

Within this favourable environment, information and ideas
spread by the villagers themselves could be all the more potent.
The men of North Ashby, only four miles from Walter de Hyldeborw at Little Billing and seven miles from Northampton, must
have talked eagerly to their neighbours about the events they had
witnessed at the Oxford and Winchester parliaments in 1258 —
the revival of the justiciarship, for example, and the expulsion of
the Lusignans. Likewise the men of Dorton in Buckinghamshire,
having returned from the great army of 1264, must have spoken
of Simon de Montfort to their neighbours, none being closer than
the villagers at Brill. In 1258 the Brillites had brought a successful
action before the justiciar against the bailiffs of the manor, and
thus had already benefited from the "common enterprise".[103]
Later, after Evesham, the whole vill testified that two of its
members had been cured of illness through Simon de Montfort's
miraculous power. Nothing could show more graphically the
passion with which peasants viewed politics in the period of
reform and rebellion.[104]

III

Peasants, therefore, had some reason for thinking that they could
benefit from the reforms propounded in 1258-9, and thus that

[102] *Rotuli selecti*, ed. Hunter, pp. 207, 194-5; P.R.O., Just 1/618, m. 10; Jacob,
Studies in the Period of Baronial Reform and Rebellion, p. 229 n. 2; *Rotuli Ricardi
Gravesend*, ed. F. N. Davis *et al.* (Oxford, 1925), p. 103. See also *Royal and Other
Historical Letters Illustrative of the Reign of Henry III*, ed. W. W. Shirley, 2 vols.
(Rolls ser., London, 1862-6), ii, p. 158.

[103] See above, p. 314, n. 17, p. 332.

[104] *The Chronicle of William de Rishanger of the Barons' Wars: The Miracles of Simon
de Montfort*, ed. J. O. Halliwell (Camden Soc., old ser., London, 1840), p. 88; for
Brill's rebellious mood, see also Jacob, *Studies in the Period of Baronial Reform and
Rebellion*, pp. 290-1. The educative effect of peasant participation in later armies is
discussed in Maddicott, "English Peasantry and the Demands of the Crown", p. 45.

they too were caught up in the "common enterprise". But why did the barons stoop to include them? Part of the answer here is easy to supply, for the reforms of 1258-9 were conceived against the background of an economic crisis, a crisis which bore above all upon the peasantry and brought matters concerning them to the forefront of the public mind.

With the proliferation of peasant families living on the edge of subsistence, a bad harvest in the thirteenth century could lead to widespread famine. The harvest of 1257 was disastrous. "Owing to the shortage of food", wrote Matthew Paris of the spring and early summer of 1258, "an innumerable multitude of poor people died; and dead bodies were found everywhere, swollen through famine and livid, lying by fives and sixes in pigsties, on dunghills, and in the muddy streets".[105] This testimony is confirmed both by other chroniclers and by the record evidence. The London alderman, Arnold fitz Thedmar, noted that "the men from the vills flocked to the city to acquire food", but, the famine worsening, "many thousands" perished. On 9 April, with the "men from the vills" perhaps crowding around the palace and the abbey, the parliament which began the movement of reform opened at Westminster. On 16 April the king acknowledged that so many poor people had "died miserably through famine in places and fields" in Norfolk, Suffolk, Essex and Lincolnshire that they could not be viewed by the coroners and were being left unburied. He thus allowed them, if there were no suspicious circumstances, to be buried without a coroner's inquest.[106] Such mortalities were clearly the immediate background to the abolition of the *murdrum* fine in cases of misadventure. The Petition of the Barons of June 1258 specifically linked the two, complaining that many men, travelling around the country on account of the famine and dying of hunger, "the coroners hold inquest with the four neighbouring vills; and when the vills say that they know nothing of the men who have died in this way . . . the country is amerced before the justices in eyre as for *murdrum*". Clearly the large number of mortalities also made more burdensome the judges' practice of imposing heavy amercements when all over the age of twelve did not attend inquests, a procedure about

---

[105] Matthew Paris, *Chronica majora*, v, pp. 690, 673-4.
[106] *De antiquis legibus liber*, ed. Stapleton, p. 37; *Close Rolls, 1256-9*, p. 212. For other chroniclers, see *Annales monastici*, ed. Luard, iii, pp. 207-8, iv, p. 118.

which there was complaint in the Petition of the Barons, and legislation in the Provisions of Westminster.[107]

The acknowledgement of this background, however, only takes us so far. The famine made everyone aware of the plight of the peasantry, but awareness alone did not ensure action. Apart from pity for their "misery", which there certainly was, other reasons may be canvassed why account was taken of the peasant predicament.

An obvious starting-point here is the interest that every lord possessed in preventing his peasants being exploited by anyone other than himself. This explains why Magna Carta in 1215 protected the villein from excessive amercements imposed by the king, but said nothing about amercements imposed by his lord.[108] In 1258-9, it is true, peasants were not discriminated against quite so pointedly. We have seen how they complained against their lords on the reforming eyres, and were protected against them by some of the legislation, notably the abolition of the fine *beaupleder*. Even measures apparently directed at royal officials might place some lords under threat. Thus a few great magnates, along with many ecclesiastical institutions, could lose from the abolition of the *murdrum* fine in cases of misadventure since they claimed such fines when imposed on their own men. It may well be that the clauses benefiting the peasantry, which appeared only in drafts of the Provisions of Westminster, were dropped from the final version at least in part because they threatened the private profit of lords.[109]

This, however, is not the whole story, for if some lords were threatened by the legislation, probably a greater number stood to gain from it. When fines for *beaupleder* at the view of frankpledge were taken in the hundred court by the bailiffs of the king or of a magnate, the lords of the manors with peasants attending that view cannot have welcomed seeing their tenants thus penalized.[110]

[107] *Documents of the Baronial Movement*, ed. Treharne and Sanders, pp. 84-5 (cap. 21), 82-3 (cap. 14), 146-7 (cap. 21). See above, p. 334.

[108] Cap. 20 in the 1215 charter: "villanus . . . amercietur salvo wainagio suo, si inciderint in misericordiam nostram". The slightly confusing plural of *inciderint* was altered to a singular in the 1216 and subsequent charters: *Statutes of the Realm*, ed. Luders *et al.*, i, p. 15. In the 1217 charter the king's own villeins were excepted from the concession.

[109] D. A. Carpenter, "King, Magnates and Society: The Personal Rule of King Henry III, 1234-1258", above pp. 85-6, 104. See above, n. 85.

[110] The returns from Loes hundred state in three cases that the earl of Norfolk's bailiffs took money at the view of frankpledge from the men of a particular lord: Jacob, *Studies in the Period of Baronial Reform and Rebellion*, pp. 341-2.

Hence one *querela* heard by the justiciar, Hugh Despencer, at the end of 1260, was brought by the lord and later rebel William Marmion, who complained that he and "his men" of Berwick (in Sussex) had been forced by the bailiff of Peter of Savoy to give 40s. at the hundred court for *beaupleder* contrary to the Provisions of Westminster. The great majority of peasants who paid the *murdrum* fine or were amerced for failing to come before inquests must have been tenants of lords who did not have the right to receive the resulting proceeds themselves.[111]

It could be argued, therefore, that the peasants came under the wing of the reform programme not for their own sake, but for that of their lords. Yet it is impossible to feel certain that this is the only explanation. On 2 May 1258 the king had agreed that "the state of our realm" should be "put in order, corrected and reformed".[112] There was no basis for excluding the peasantry from that process for, in important respects, in both practice and theory, they were just as much part of the realm as anybody else. This is not to deny that the relationship between lord and peasant was "conflictual". Examples of that conflict have been cited abundantly in this article. The lord's coercive power was ultimately guaranteed by the state, and in particular by its law which denied the unfree peasant any remedy against many types of abuse. Lords also believed that the peasant condition was immutable. Peasants should know their place and not seek to transform it:

> What can a serf do unless serve, and his son?
> He shall be a pure serf deprived of freedom.
> The law's judgement and the king's court prove this.

Thus ran Leicester Abbey's triumphal poem of 1276 celebrating the failure of its villeins of Stoughton (seven miles from Peatling Magna) to prove that they were sokemen.[113] And yet alongside such sentiments, there were others which gave a very different picture of how the relationship between the lord and the peasant

[111] *Ibid.*, pp. 354-5; *Cal. Inq. Misc.*, i, nos. 925, 833. This was the same William Marmion as above, p. 326. For the same man bringing a case on behalf of one of his villeins against a bailiff of Peter of Savoy, see P.R.O., Just 1/537, m. 1d. For the *murdrum* fine, see, for example, "Estate Records of the Hotot Family", ed. King, pp. 13, 58.

[112] *Documents of the Baronial Movement*, ed. Treharne and Sanders, pp. 74-5.

[113] R. H. Hilton, "A Thirteenth-Century Poem on Disputed Villein Services", *Eng. Hist. Rev.*, lvi (1941), pp. 90-7; with the transcription of the penultimate line slightly emended in Hilton, "Freedom and Villeinage", p. 19.

ought to function. According to *Walter of Henley* and other thirteenth-century treatises on estate management, the ideal was for
lords to be wealthy and powerful *without* committing wrongs and
trespasses. *Walter* stated that a lord should take nothing wrong-
fully from any man, should allow his free and unfree tenants to
be amerced by their peers, should moderate the amercements if
his conscience told him they were too high, and should look after
the poor. According to the *Seneschaucy* the lord was to command
his auditors to hear the complaints of everyone on the manor
against the steward, bailiff and reeve "so that full justice be done
to free and customary tenants".[114]

These ideals were not those of a self-contained manorial world
where there was no external pressure on a lord to uphold them.
On the contrary, the idea that peasants should be treated justly
was stressed by the king, by lawyers and by churchmen. It is
these ideas which help to explain the reforms in favour of the
peasants in 1258-9.

"The villein as subject", it has been said, "was created out of
the needs of Angevin government".[115] The Angevin kings were
keen to stress that peasants owed them allegiance and must bear
public burdens along with everyone else. In 1176 the Assize of
Northampton instructed the justices in eyre to take oaths of fealty
to the king "even from rustics".[116] The 1205 Assize of Arms was
probably the first to include both free and unfree in its obligations.[117] Coroners' inquests and the replies to the articles of the
eyre and the tourn, as we have seen, depended on the co-operation
of the peasantry. Similarly free and unfree paid the great taxes
on movable property levied by King John and his successors. The
extent to which royal clerks felt that this made peasants part of
the political community is reflected in the writ which ordered the
collection of the fortieth of 1232: the tax had been conceded, so
it stated, "by the archbishops, bishops, abbots, priors, clerks . . .
earls, barons, knights, freemen and villeins of our kingdom".[118]

[114] *Walter of Henley and Other Treatises on Estate Management and Accounting*, ed.
D. Oschinsky (Oxford, 1971), pp. 310-11, 294-5.

[115] Hyams, *King, Lords and Peasants*, p. 152; see ibid., pp. 151-60, for a discussion
of the villein as subject. See also Hatcher, "English Serfdom and Villeinage", pp. 35-6;
Richardson and Sayles, *Law and Legislation*, pp. 138-49.

[116] *Gesta regis Henrici secundi Benedicti abbatis: The Chronicle . . . of Benedict of
Peterborough*, ed. W. Stubbs, 2 vols. (Rolls ser., London, 1867), i, p. 110.

[117] Richardson and Sayles, *Law and Legislation*, pp. 137-9.

[118] *Close Rolls, 1231-4*, p. 155. In 1237 the earls, barons, knights and freemen were
said to concede the tax "for themselves and their villeins": *Close Rolls, 1234-7*,

(cont. on p. 344)

If the peasants thus shouldered the burdens of citizenship, they were by no means excluded from its benefits, at least in theory. Kings were very ready to proclaim that in some respects villeins were equal with everyone else. "We are all to obtain one reward in Christ, whether of servile or free condition, without distinction before Him", declared a royal letter personally authorized by Edward I in 1303. In 1250, in his famous speech at the exchequer, Henry III had instructed his sheriffs to ensure that "no rustic" was distrained for the debt of his lord so long as the lord had sufficient to be distrained by. The king's "general care of his subjects", as the *Dialogus de Scaccario* put it, embraced free and unfree alike.[119] Thus "the common law", Paul Hyams has observed, "had no intention of attributing to lords absolute power over their villeins' lives".[120] As far as criminal law was concerned there was no distinction between free and unfree. The murder of a villein was as much an offence punishable by the king as that of a freeman. "Be it remembered", declared the judges on the London eyre of 1244, "that earls, barons and free tenants may lawfully put their serfs in the stocks, but not in irons; and if they may sell their serfs like oxen and cows, they may not kill them, maim them or wound them because the bodies and members of the serfs belong only to the king".[121]

The king's judges, moreover, or at least some of them, took the view that the maltreated peasant did have some legal remedies available. The essence of theory found in the great law book, *Bracton*, was that "the villein was free against the whole world except his lord". Thus while a villein could not bring an assize of novel disseisin against his lord, he could do so against a third party who had granted him a free tenement.[122] *Bracton* also believed that a villein had some rights of action against his lord. He could proceed against him for violence and injury done in

---

(n. 118 cont.)
p. 545. For the burdens shouldered by the vill, see Cam, "Community of the Vill", pp. 71-4.

[119] *Cal. Pat. Rolls, 1301-7*, p. 118; M. T. Clanchy, "Did Henry III Have a Policy?", *History*, liii (1968), pp. 215-16; *Dialogus de Scaccario*, ed. C. Johnson (London, 1950), p. 101.

[120] Hyams, *King, Lords and Peasants*, p. 125; see also *ibid.*, p. 261.

[121] *The London Eyre of 1244*, ed. H. M. Chew and M. Weinbaum (London Rec. Soc., vi, 1970), no. 346.

[122] Hyams, *King, Lords and Peasants*, pp. 91, 95-6; *Bracton on the Laws and Customs of England*, ed. G. E. Woodbine, trans. and revd. S. E. Thorne, 4 vols. (Cambridge, Mass., 1968-77), iii, pp. 88, 98.

breach of the king's peace and perhaps for false imprisonment.[123] He could proceed too if his lord deprived him of his "wainage", his means of livelihood. Here the king and his lawyers exploited the clause in Magna Carta which included villeins in the protection afforded against extortionate amercements: a free man was to be amerced by his peers and according to the gravity of his offence, "saving his livelihood . . . and a villein is to be amerced in the same way saving his wainage". In respect of villeins this clause, as we have said, was intended to relate only to amercements imposed by the king.[124] But since, as the king stressed repeatedly in the years after 1225, and as the reformers in 1259 acknowledged must be the case, "all the people of the kingdom" were to observe the Charter towards their own men, it could equally be taken as applying to the activities of lords in their own courts.[125] Hence the sentiments of *Walter of Henley* about how unfree tenants should be amerced by their peers; hence too the statement in *Bracton* that peasants had rights of action against their lords when "the wrong is an insufferable one, as where their lord so strips them that their wainage cannot be saved them".[126]

The theories in *Bracton*, of course, were just that. In practice the legal remedies open to villeins were far fewer than it suggested. The general view, for example, at least after the minority of Henry III, was that a villein could not lawfully hold a free tenement, and thus could not bring an assize of novel disseisin even against someone who was not his lord.[127] Even the few legal remedies which were available "exceeded any real chance of success". Peasants, as Hyams has remarked, "were very vulnerable to a repeat dose of the treatment which had induced them to come before the justices in the first place".[128] But in the context of the reforms of 1258-9, the practice was less important than the theory. The original text of *Bracton* was put together in the

[123] *Bracton*, ed. Woodbine, ii, pp. 34, 438. For the whole subject of the villein as litigant, see Hyams, *King, Lords and Peasants*, pp. 125-51. For unlawful imprisonment note also the declaration of the judges on the 1244 London eyre, quoted above, which is cited *ibid.*, p. 139 n. 69.

[124] See above, n. 108.

[125] D. A. Carpenter, *The Minority of Henry III* (London, 1990), pp. 387-8; Maddicott, "Magna Carta and the Local Community", pp. 52-3; *Documents of the Baronial Movement*, ed. Treharne and Sanders, pp. 132-3; *Annales monastici*, ed. Luard, iii, p. 209.

[126] *Bracton*, ed. Woodbine, ii, p. 34; Hyams, *King, Lords and Peasants*, pp. 143-4.

[127] Hyams, *King, Lords and Peasants*, pp. 98-102.

[128] *Ibid.*, pp. 143, 134.

1220s and 1230s by the legal circle around the judge William Ralegh. Then, about the time of the great crisis of 1258, it was edited and revised for publication, gaining the form in which it survives in around forty manuscripts. The theory of villeinage in *Bracton* sought to make the villein "free and equal in public but an unfree serf to his lord".[129] Even against his lord he had certain rights of action. There is some reason to think that these ideas, or ones like them, influenced legal developments during the period of reform. It is precisely in a register of writs dating from the 1260s that the common-law remedy for the breach of Magna Carta's clause on amercements first appears. It was a remedy which applied to the courts of lords, and was apparently open to villeins, for the writ which initiated the action, in referring to the clause in the Charter, mentioned the stipulation that a villein was to be amerced "saving his wainage".[130]

The influence of lawyers and the law was not the only one bearing on the reformers of 1258-9. There was also that of churchmen. An impression of their ideas is gained from the writings of John of Wales, a friar who probably lived in Oxford throughout the years of reform and rebellion. In describing the state (*respublica*), John employed "the well-worn physiological simile" whereby it was likened to a body. Within that body the workers had a place along with everyone else. If the "prince" was the head, the "labourers" were the feet. Since, moreover, the "labourers" were of great service to the body, they must be protected and guarded. Judges must particularly give justice to "the poor". The "village bailiffs" must be careful not to abuse their authority. These were the reverse of private sentiments, for John's works were intended as preaching aids for friars.[131] The reformers of 1258, therefore, may well have heard sermons along such lines, perhaps reinforced in private conversations if there were friars in their households. Simon de Montfort, of course, was closely linked with the regent of the Oxford friars, Adam

---

[129] *Ibid.*, pp. 86, 160. For the authorship and dating of Bracton, see S. E. Thorne's introduction to *Bracton*, ed. Woodbine, iii.

[130] *Early Registers of Writs*, ed. E. de Haas and G. D. G. Hall (Selden Soc., lxxxvii, London, 1970), p. 63, nos. 99, 99a, pp. xliv-xlv.

[131] J. Swanson, *John of Wales: A Study of the Works of a Thirteenth-Century Friar* (Cambridge, 1989), pp. 3, 66-8, 83, 85-6, 94-5, 98; see also Hyams, *King, Lords and Peasants*, pp. 261-2.

Marsh, one of whose sermons is known to have upset Henry III.[132]

That such ideas were indeed present in reforming circles is proved by the well-publicized letter addressed to the pope in 1258, which justified the political revolution. This was sealed on behalf "of all the community" by the justiciar (Hugh Bigod), Simon de Montfort and ten other members of the council of fifteen. Again the *respublica* was compared to a body, a body whose limbs had been pulled apart by the activities of the king's half-brothers. Remarkably, in describing those activities, the letter dwelt upon the local oppressions of the brothers: " 'the clamour of the poor ascended to the skies against them'. For their ministers and officials, or rather partners in crime and robbers, despoiled the poor, attacked the simple, favoured the impious, oppressed the innocent . . . rejoicing in the sufferings of the subject people". Did Simon de Montfort, as Sir Maurice Powicke speculated, influence the content of this letter?[133] Certainly, in his will, drawn up a few months later, he expressed concern for the "poor people of my land . . . namely the tillers (*les gaaneuors*)", whom he might have oppressed, and ordered reparations to be made through the counsels of Adam Marsh.[134]

The reforms of 1258-9, therefore, alleviated the lot of the peasantry in part because this served the interests of their lords. But they did so too because the idea that peasants should be treated justly was integral to contemporary thought. There could be no genuine reform of the realm if they were excluded.

*   *   *

There was nothing unusual or isolated about the action of the villagers of Peatling Magna. During the civil war peasants engaged in plundering raids, soldiered in the armies, and joined the Disinherited in the Isle of Ely. Some were forced to take part. Others did so with a will, often acting independently of their lords. As

---

[132] *Monumenta Franciscana*, ed. J. S. Brewer and R. Howlett, 2 vols. (Rolls ser., London, 1858-82), i, p. 275; Bémont, *Simon de Montfort* (1930), pp. 42-6.

[133] *Annales monastici*, ed. Luard, i, pp. 457-60; for other copies of the letter, see *ibid.*, pp. 170-4; Matthew Paris, *Chronica majora*, vi, pp. 400-5; Powicke, *Henry III and the Lord Edward*, i, p. 390.

[134] Bémont, *Simon de Montfort* (1930), pp. 277-8. John Maddicott kindly drew this passage to my attention.

the chronicler of Battle Abbey observed, "at that time it was not in the power of lords to restrain their men from such things". And yet, in all this, one thing is missing: the suggestion in any contemporary source of a peasants' revolt, a revolt, as in 1381, in which peasants fought for their own programme against their lords. There is no *communitas rusticorum Angliae* to match the *communitas bacheleriae Angliae*, the body broadly representing the knightly class whose threats precipitated the publication of the Provisions of Westminster in 1259.[135] If the movement of reform redressed peasant grievances it did so out of a mixture of self-interest and idealism, not from a fear of peasant revolt. Throughout the country there were pockets of peasant resistance and activity. The peasants of Bampton complaining about Roger de Oilly were four miles from those at Hardwick complaining about Walter de Grey. The peasants of North Ashby fighting Robert and Sybil de Mares were within eleven miles of those at Stanwick and Ringstead struggling against William de Waldis.[136] But nothing was ever co-ordinated. In part this was because economic conditions did not favour peasant revolt. The rising population and the dearth of land solidified the power of lords, just as the fall in the population and the abundance of land after the Black Death sapped it. There was also another factor. Peasants were caught up in the "common enterprise" which had begun in 1258. They had some reason for thinking, with the men of Peatling Magna, that "the barons" were working for "the welfare of the community of the realm", a community of which, in significant respects, the peasantry of thirteenth-century England were part.

---

[135] *Annales monastici*, ed. Luard, i, p. 471. By contrast, fear of unrest may have been a factor in the inclusion of peasant grievances in fourteenth-century plans of political reform: Maddicott, "English Peasantry and the Demands of the Crown", pp. 23-4, 64-7.

[136] At Stanwick and Ringstead the peasants had gained their freedom, but in return for rents they soon found intolerably high: see P.R.O., Just 1/616, mm. 7, 25.

18

Was There a Crisis of the Knightly Class in the Thirteenth Century? The Oxfordshire Evidence

DURING the thirteenth century 'the knightly class was passing through a period of economic crisis, a crisis that was both extensive and prolonged'.[1] In expounding this thesis in a recent article Dr P. R. Coss was developing in fuller form and with a fresh emphasis ideas first presented (independently) by Professor Postan and Professor Hilton.[2] The theories of these historians countered views which saw the thirteenth century as a period of stability or of rising prosperity for the knightly class.[3] They also offered a different explanation of the political prominence which the knights achieved in these years, a prominence seen in the concessions to the class in 1215 and 1258-9, in the summons of knights to parliament, and in the development in the shires of 'self-government at the king's command'. Coss, on the one hand, cites with approval the view of Postan that 'if what Simon de Montfort and Edward I tried to do was to win the support of the knightly class, they did so not by bowing to its new strength but by coming to its relief'.[4] Professor Treharne, on the other hand, saw the role of the knights between 1258 and 1267 against 'the greatly enhanced wealth of the mid thirteenth-century knight, and the much higher standard of living and civilization which he enjoyed'.[5] For Professor Holt, more recently, 'the political independence which men of knightly rank were showing [in the reign of John] had a secure basis in wealth and administrative

---

1. P. R. Coss, 'Sir Geoffrey de Langley and the Crisis of the Knightly Class in Thirteenth-Century England', *Past and Present*, lxviii (1975), 25. (Hereafter cited as Coss.)

2. M. M. Postan, *The Cambridge Economic History of Europe*, 2nd edn. (Cambridge, 1966), i. 590-5; *The Medieval Economy and Society* (London, 1972), pp. 158-65; R. H. Hilton, *A Medieval Society: The West Midlands at the End of the Thirteenth Century* (London, 1966), pp. 49-55. For important criticisms of Postan's views, see, E. King, 'Large and Small Landowners in Thirteenth-Century England', *Past and Present*, xlvii (1970).

3. R. F. Treharne, 'The Knights in the Period of Reform and Rebellion 1258-67', *Bull. Inst. Hist. Res.* xxi (1946-8), 1-12.

4. Coss, p. 29.

5. Treharne, *ubi supra*, p. 8. See also F. M. Powicke, *Henry III and The Lord Edward* (Oxford, 1947), i. 306.

experience' – an opinion which derived from biographical work on many individual knights.[1] The economic position of knightly families must also have had important (though as yet little discussed) repercussions upon those below them in the social scale. The worse the situation of their immediate knightly lords, the better perhaps that of the peasants and small free tenants since the lord (and Coss provides a good example of this) would lack the resources to buy up land and increase services.[2] The aim of the present paper is to take a fresh look at the crisis thesis, primarily as it has been presented by Coss. Attention will be focused on the chief question to which he addresses himself – 'were the difficulties of the smaller landowners sufficient for us to speak of a "severe social and economic crisis for the class as a whole"?'[3] The unqualified affirmative with which Coss answers this question, it will be argued, is hardly supported by a study of Oxfordshire knightly families in the thirteenth century.

A note first on the definition of the 'knightly' or 'gentry' class. Historians would probably agree, easily enough, on a description of an active member: a lord of one or a few manors; frequently a knight, although the number who assumed the honour was diminishing; a man busy in local government as a coroner, forest official, sheriff or under-sheriff. At any time in the thirteenth century there were men of this kind throughout the counties of England. A large part of local government depended on them.[4] To define the class itself, however, is more difficult. Contemporaries had no word for it. In the thirteenth and fourteenth centuries barons, knights, esquires and some laymen who held no military rank were all considered 'noble' or 'gentle'.[5] The class cannot be confined to those who were technically knights – that is, had been girded with the sword of knighthood – since this was a group of rapidly diminishing size which lacked any real unity. Early in the thirteenth century nearly all lords of manors (and some men of lesser consequence) were knights. A hundred years later, to make a broad generalization, the honour was becoming confined to those with two or three manors and above. Aware of this difficulty Coss decides to focus attention on 'all who' (presumably beneath the baronage) 'held by military tenure and were manorial landlords'. One need not cavil at this definition, although there are problems connected with it.[6] The knightly class thus defined covers a wide social and material spectrum. It embraces a few lords

1. J. C. Holt, *The Northerners* (Oxford, 1961), p. 55.
2. Coss, p. 16. Of course if a lord was forced to sell his manor the position of the peasantry might change for the worse.
3. Coss, p. 4. Coss is here quoting from Hilton, p. 50. Hilton, however, is concerned with the whole period 1150–1300, and his emphasis is rather different from that of Coss.
4. A. B. White, *Self-Government at the King's Command* (Minneapolis, 1932).
5. It was not till the fifteenth century that the term 'gentleman' was used in a more restricted sense; G. R. Sitwell, 'The English Gentleman', *The Ancestor*, i (1902), 58–77.
6. Coss, p. 5, n. 11. In material terms the definition provides no separation between the knightly class and the baronage since both were lords of manors. There is also the problem (not of great importance in Oxfordshire) of what constitutes a manor.

at the top of the scale who enjoyed incomes of baronial proportions. It also includes a group of lords who held single manors which contained well under 300 acres of land.

Coss is not primarily concerned with the extent to which his postulated crisis effected overall changes in the amount of property held by this knightly class. Rather he concentrates on the immediate hardships, the financial weakness and material collapse, which he believes overtook all sections of the class, and had important political repercussions. According to this grim picture 'large numbers' of knightly families 'became indebted, primarily to the Jews, and were ultimately forced to sell out'. 'Financial strain and the horrors of debt take us a long way towards explaining why the reformist earls [1258–65] received such widespread support from the knightly class'.[1] The cause of this crisis, Coss argues, lay in the inability of the knightly class to cope with the social and economic conditions of the thirteenth century.

When examined in detail these theories appear unconvincing. Take the alleged cause of the crisis – the oppressive social and economic climate. The main social phenomenon which affected the gentry was the rising cost of knighthood. But is it not true that many families escaped this expenditure by refusing to assume the honour? Coss considers that the chief cause of the crisis was economic – the rapid inflation of the years 1180–1220, which continued at a slower pace between 1220 and 1260. The best way to combat its effects was to develop a substantial demesne farm which would enable surplus corn to be sold and allow advantage to be taken of the rising market for agricultural produce. Great landowners with large demesnes could profit from these conditions. Smaller landowners, Coss argues (here developing a thesis of Postan) were often ill placed to do so 'the more so, in some cases, as they lived substantially, or even wholly, off rents and lacked the resources in land to shift to demesne farming'. 'This helps to explain why such a cross-section of the knightly class was affected' (by the crisis).[2] However, Coss bases this view on the study of only one family whose manor, he stresses, was in some ways untypical.[3] He makes no survey of the general size of gentry demesnes, and does not consider other ways in which income could be increased – for example, by acquiring new property, imposing heavier burdens on the peasantry, and holding local office.

The chief evidence for the material difficulties of the knightly class comes from the amount of gentry land acquired in the century by religious houses and *curiales*, and from the histories of knightly families which nearly or completely collapsed under the pressure of accumulated debt. Yet sometimes *curiales* were themselves either

1. Coss, pp. 27–29, 34.
2. Coss, pp. 27–28. See Postan, *Cambridge Economic History of Europe*, i. 593. For the inflation, P. D. A. Harvey, 'The English Inflation 1180–1220', *Past and Present*, lxi (1973), 3–30.
3. Coss, pp. 14–15, 27–28.

founders, or members and beneficiaries of gentry families. In
Oxfordshire when the Romillies of Steeple Aston stumbled into
oblivion in the 1290s their manor was bought by the clerk Thomas
of Adderbury. The heir to the properties on which Thomas spent
over £360 was his nephew Richard, an Oxfordshire esquire, sheriff
and M.P.[1] Or take the case of the *curialis* Geoffrey de Langley around
which Coss groups much of his thesis. Geoffrey was the son of a
Gloucestershire knight. His aggrandisements were split, after his
death, between heirs who formed knightly families in Gloucestershire and Warwickshire.[2] In this case, therefore, the distressed
families which succumbed to Geoffrey's attentions were quickly
balanced by his own descendants. This hardly suggests a crisis of the
whole class. Of course, it may be objected that few families could
hope to produce successful *curiales*. But if the Langleys were untypical, might not that equally be the case of the families which were
forced to sell up to them?

Few would dispute that the knightly class suffered an overall loss
of property to religious houses in the thirteenth century. This hardly
proves that there was a crisis in the fortunes of the *whole* class.[3] Many
families may have made no significant alienations. Not every alienation was necessitated by financial weakness or was part of a process
which culminated in a family's near or total ruin. Some grants to
religious houses were easily afforded pious gifts. Others were isolated
alienations, even though made under duress. Admittedly, the individual case histories analysed or mentioned by Coss show problems
escalating until families, burdened by debt, are forced to 'sell out'.[4]
But how representative are these histories? All are obtained from the
cartularies of individuals or institutions which were vigorously
acquiring property. Gentry who retained or increased their lands will
appear little, if at all, in such records.[5] To be at all representative
histories of knightly families need to be selected from quite different
sources.[6]

It is at this point that the present paper seeks to make a contribution. The families which feature in it are those of the knights who
appeared on commissions and grand assizes in Oxfordshire in the
1220s.[7] It will be seen that this group does not illuminate the position

1. P[ublic] R[ecord] O[ffice] CP 25(1)/188(12)/12, 39, 49, 70; CP 25(1)/188(13)/18,
35, 64. PRO *Lists and Indexes*, ix. 108; F. Palgrave, *P[arliamentary] W[rits]* (Record
Commission, 1827, 1830, 1834), II. iii. 420. R[eturn] M[embers of] P[arliament] (House
of Commons, 1878), i. 88; C[al.] I[nquisitions] P[ost] M[ortem], vii, no. 557.
2. P. R. Coss, *The Langley Family and its Cartulary* (Dugdale Society Occasional Paper,
Oxford, 1974), pp. 5–6, 21–22.
3. This point is well made by King, *ubi supra*, p. 50. See below p. 377.
4. Coss, pp. 5–17, 24–25, 33–34.
5. For the bias of the evidence obtained from cartularies see, King, *ubi supra*, p. 30:
J. Z. Titow, *English Rural Society 1200–1350* (London, 1969), p. 47.
6. See King, *ubi supra*, pp. 30–31.
7. It might be objected that this is a group of knights rather than of lords of manors.
However, few lords, even of small manors, had given up knighthood by this stage of
the century.

of lords of very small manors (under 300 acres). Nor does it give much opportunity to study new families which entered the ranks of the gentry. But with these qualifications and with some others which will be mentioned later, the group probably provides a reasonably representative sample of the middle and upper sections of the knightly class. Oxfordshire was a county where the 'typical' manor predominated.[1] It had its fair share of acquisitive *curiales* and men of affairs. Walter de Grey, archbishop of York; Laurence de Broke, the king's attorney; Walter de Merton, Henry III's chancellor; Roger de Meulant, bishop of Coventry, and Walter de Langton, Edward I's treasurer, were active in the county's land market in the thirteenth or early fourteenth centuries. Moreover after 1227 when the earl of Cornwall was granted the honours of Wallingford and St Valery, and became the lord of numerous Oxfordshire knights, the county was an important base for the richest lay magnate in the country. In terms of wealth Oxfordshire lacked a religious house of the first rank, but its medium sized houses were quite able to raise money to buy or secure claims to property. The wealthiest, Osney abbey, spent extensively in the thirteenth century.[2] The degree to which a great house (like Peterborough or Reading) would have transformed the local land market may be doubted.[3]

The group of knightly families chosen for study comes from the 1220s and is therefore composed of those which have already survived the worst of the inflation. But they had not thereby survived the worst of the supposed crisis. Coss believes that difficulties accumulated from the 1180–1220 period, and reached their height later, in the reign of Henry III.[4] The present paper does not, however, attempt to estimate the material well-being of its families at different times in the century. There is not the evidence for such an exercise. Rather the aim is to assess how families fared in material terms over the century as a whole – a century which had a certain economic unity since it probably coincided with the period when demesne farming was at its height. There are, of course, many difficulties involved in tracing the material fortunes of the chosen families. The evidence is incomplete, and at times inconclusive. The properties of some families cannot be identified at all. Few have left sufficient private records for their histories to be traced 'from the inside'. The first evidence for the internal structure of manors does not come until the hundred roll survey of 1279. Profitable use can be made of the vast array of records left by thirteenth-century central government. But the government's main legal and financial rolls (after 1241

1. E. A. Kosminsky, *Studies in the Agrarian History of England in the Thirteenth Century* (Oxford, 1956), pp. 126–30.
2. For Oxfordshire houses see, *Victoria County History of Oxfordshire*, ii. 64–164 (henceforth cited as *VCH*), and the cartularies listed in p. 354, n. 3 below. For the *curiales* see below pp. 363, 371, 375–6, 362, n. 1, 358, n. 7.
3. See below pp. 376–7.
4. Coss, p. 28.

and 1219 respectively) are treasured up in the Public Record Office, as yet unpublished and unindexed. The searcher can easily miss relevant evidence.[1] Oxfordshire is almost unique, however, in that its hundred rolls cover most of the county and are very detailed.[2] There is also abundant local material provided by private charters, cartularies of religious houses,[3] feet of fines, eyre rolls, and tax returns of the early fourteenth century.[4] In the great majority of cases it is possible, with the aid of these sources to establish with (it is hoped) tolerable accuracy a family's property in the early thirteenth century, and to say whether or not that family met with material collapse in the next hundred years.[5] Frequently a more detailed picture of acquisitions, alienations, and sizes of manorial demesnes can be obtained. When this evidence is analysed the material health of middle and upper knightly families in the thirteenth century emerges as rather less fragile, and the general social and economic climate rather less treacherous than the crisis thesis seems to suggest.

II

Names of Oxfordshire knights in the 1220s may be gathered from five grand assize juries; from nine panels of knights chosen to present the record of the county court or to 'view' those engaged in law cases; and from a jury of twenty-four knights which perambulated

1. Dr D. Crook of the P.R.O. has kindly allowed me to consult the texts of the forthcoming Curia Regis Rolls volumes xvii–xix (1242–50).

2. *Rotuli Hundredorum* (Record Commission, 1812, 1818), ii. 688–877 (henceforth *RH*); for surveys of fees in the county, [*The*] B[*ook of*] F[*ees*] (London, 1920, 1923, 1931), i. 445–57; *ibid.*, ii. 819–42. Work on Oxfordshire is greatly facilitated by the *VCH* volumes v–x.

3. C[*artulary of the*] A[*bbey of*] E[*ynsham*], ed. H. E. Salter (Oxford Hist. Soc., xlix, li, 1906–8); *The English Register of Godstow Nunnery*, ed. A. Clark (Early English Text Soc., cxxix–xxx, cxlii, 1905–11); *Cartulary of the Monastery of St. Frideswide at Oxford*, ed. S. P. Wigram (Oxford Hist. Soc., i–ii, 1895–6); [*The*] C[*artulary of*] O[*seney*] A[*bbey*], ed. H. E. Salter (Oxford Hist. Soc., lxxxix–xic, xcvii–viii, ci, 1928–9, 1933–4, 1936); [*The*] S[*andford*] C[*artulary*], ed. A. M. Leys (Oxfordshire Rec. Soc., xix, xxii, 1938, 1941); [*The*] T[*hame*] C[*artulary*], ed. H. E. Salter (Oxfordshire Rec. Soc., xxv–vi, 1943–4); *A Cartulary of the Hospital of St. John the Baptist*, ed. H. E. Salter (Oxford Hist. Soc., lxvi, lxviii–ix, 1914–16); also useful is I.[*uffield*] P[*riory*] C[*harters*], ed. G. R. Elvey (Northamptonshire Rec. Soc., xxii, xxvi, 1968, 1975). Private charters are found in [*The*] B[*oarstall*] C[*artulary*], ed. H. E. Salter (Oxford Hist. Soc., lxxxviii, 1930); *Cartulary of the Medieval Archives of Christ Church*, ed. N. Denholm-Young (Oxford Hist. Soc., xcii, 1931); White Kennet, *Parochial Antiquities of Ambrosden* (2nd edn. Oxford, 1818); *Oriel College Records*, ed. C. L. Shadwell, H. E. Salter (Oxford Hist. Soc., lxxxv, 1926); *Facsimiles of Early Charters in Oxford Muniment Rooms*, ed. H. E. Salter (Oxford, 1929); [*Calendar of Charters and Rolls in the*] Bod[*leian Library*], ed. W. H. Turner (Oxford, 1878).

4. F[*eet of*] F[*ines for*] O[*xfordshire 1195–1291*], ed. H. E. Salter (Oxfordshire Rec. Soc., xii, 1930); Oxfordshire Eyre Rolls 25, 31, 45, 52 Henry III, 13 Edward I – P.R.O. Just 1/695, 699, 701, 702A–C, 703, 710. The two earliest rolls are being edited for the Oxfordshire Record Soc. by Dr J. Cooper, who has kindly allowed me to use her transcripts.

5. One problem here is that evidence for holdings is, in some respects, more plentiful as the century advances. The tendency is to work back, particularly from the *BF* survey of 1242. But if for this reason one may underestimate alienations early in the century one may also underestimate acquisitions.

the county's forests. The total is seventy-one knights. For practical purposes the number is reduced to fifty-seven since the properties of fourteen cannot be traced. It will be argued later that the necessary omission of these families does not greatly prejudice conclusions derived from the remainder.[1] These fifty-seven knights may be divided into four groups according to the amount of property which, as far as can be judged, they or their predecessors held at the beginning of the century. These groups are as follows. Group one – five knights with four or more manors; group two – twenty knights with two or three manors; group three – twenty-five knights with one manor containing three or more hides of land; group four – seven knights with under three hides of land. (Most of these last were probably not lords of manors.) This categorization can be no more than rough. The difficulties implicit in the nature of the evidence have already been stressed. It should also be remembered that manors varied greatly in value, and that gentry might hold property outside them. Nevertheless the divisions broadly coincide with what might be deduced from other evidence concerning the wealth and status of the families.[2]

The history of each of these Oxfordshire families has been worked out as comprehensively as possible.[3] What sort of overall pattern

1. C[*uria*] R[*egis*] R[*olls*], viii. 173, 372; ix. 141, 344; xi, nos. 508, 1207, 1234, 1456, 2208; xii, no. 1859; xiii, nos. 242, 319, 899, 2449; P.R.O. C 47/11/1/19. For the unidentified see below p. 376.

2. Other studies suggest that in the thirteenth century most gentry in the west midlands held between one and three manors; Hilton, p. 58. The groups are set out below. Their properties may be worked out from the sources indicated on p. 354, and from the references given in the course of the article. Group one: Philip de Hastings; Reginald Basset (representing fitz Nigel); Ralph fitz Robert and his brother and heir Guy fitz Robert (fitz Guy); Peter fitz Oger; Ralph de Salceto. Group two: Robert Damory; William fitz Ellis; Robert Mauduit; Richard of Williamscot; Nicholas de Noers; Herbert Quatremain; Roger Golafre; Robert Purcel; William Wace; Henry of Wheatfield; Genteschiu le Poure; Stephen of Fritwell; William de Parles; Humphrey de Rokele; Jordan Forester; Reginald de Cruce; Hamon de St Fey; Matthew of Bigstrup; Ralph fitz Aumary; William of Hampton. Group three: Geoffrey Marmion; Roger Gernon; Roger de Lisle; Hugh of Whitehill; William of (Westcott) Barton; Richard Foliot of Rousham; William of Sarsden; Alexander of Coombe; Fulk of Rycote; Ralph of Sandford; Walter fitz Pain of Garsington; Robert Waundard; William of Fifield; William le Moyne; Bardolph of Chastleton; Guy of Wheatley; Gilbert of Finmere (see however p. 365, n. 1); Gilbert de Baseville; Walter of Wheatfield; Simon of Merton; Robert Pipard; Robert of Chilham; Fulk Basset; Robert of Thomley; William Fraxino. Group four: Hugh of Haddon; Henry of Lew; Richard of Chislehampton; Adam of Mountsorrel; Henry of Cassington; Richard Pirun; Ralph de Rosay. Unidentified: Henry of Horton; Gilbert de Hyda; William de Grenville; Roger de Bray; Ralph of Wootton; William of Chadlington; William de Sedesle; Geoffrey of Alwaldesbury; Roger fitz Ralph of Cassington; Robert of Deddington; William Marmion; Alexander of Milcombe; William de Romilly of Pudlicote not Steeple Aston); John de Hokeling. There is a good deal of material bearing on several of these knights, but insufficient to establish the size or the fate of their properties. In a few cases, in compiling these groups, properties (indicated hereafter by *) have been counted as manors although there is no evidence of their size, save as a proportion of a knight's fee, or no evidence of their internal structure.

3. Space forbids full references to these histories. They may be worked out from the sources indicated on p. 354 above.

emerges? Let us look first at the extent to which the acquisitive attentions of religious houses, barons and *curiales* undermined the material position of the families. The extent to which they did so was in fact limited. In the early thirteenth century about ninety manors were held by the knights of the 1220s or their predecessors. The following table indicates alienations in the period up to 1307.[1]

Number of manors acquired by religious houses	7[2] (two probably by pious gifts)
Number acquired by *curiales*	1[3]
Number acquired by barons	4[4]
Number leased to religious houses	1[5]
Number leased to or seized by ecclesiastics and *curiales*	4[6]

These losses, permanent or temporary, affected seventeen manors held by fifteen of the fifty-seven families. However, seven of these fifteen families also acquired property. Three of the seven actually increased their possessions over the course of the century or displayed others signs of prosperity such as private chapels.[7]

Apart from the alienation of whole manors, at least thirty families, in the late twelfth or thirteenth centuries, granted, confirmed or quitclaimed property of lesser consequence to religious houses. In many cases the motive may have been genuine piety.[8] The amount of property involved was usually comparatively small. There was enough 'slack' in the majority of manors to accommodate such gifts. In the hundred rolls of 1279 thirty-four manors which had been held by 1220s knights appear almost entirely free from the holdings of religious houses.[9] In five manors the latter held up to two vir-

1. See above p. 355, n. 2. This figure includes the chief properties (perhaps not manorial in form) of families in group four. Manors which came to *curiales* or religious houses after families failed through lack of male heirs are not included amongst the alienations; for these manors see below p. 358, n. 5, p. 362, n. 1.

2. Lyde* (Salceto); Wellow* (Hampton); Thornborough (Fraxino); Thomley; Chislehampton; Swalcliffe* (Wheatfield); Moreton* (Bigstrup); the last two probably pious gifts – see below p. 360, n. 5, p. 362, n. 1, p. 358, n. 1, p. 357, n. 6, p. 358, n. 3, p. 358, n. 2.

3. Great Rollright (Parles); see p. 362, n. 1.

4. Chesterton; Handsworth (Parles) – not sold however; Chilham; Goldor and Clare* (Pilun); see p. 362, n. 7, p. 358, n. 1, p. 357, n. 8.

5. Bucknell (Damory), see below p. 364.

6. Whitehill, Tackley (le Poure); Checkendon (Marmion); Arkesdon (Rokele); see 362, n. 1, 363, n. 6. Stoke Goldington of the Hastings was also leased but this was an acquired manor. Another Hastings manor (Yelford) was leased to an Oxford burgess; see below p. 364, n. 3.

7. Le Poure; Hampton; Parles; Rokele; Damory; Marmion; Bigstrup. The last three are the three mentioned; see 361, n. 9, 361, n. 10, 362, n. 1, 358, n. 2.

8. Grants couched as pious donations could, of course, conceal financial transactions. On the other hand, the passage of money does not necessarily show that a family was in financial difficulties.

9. These manors (and those mentioned in the next four notes) include those acquired by 1220s knights. Group one: Yelford, *RH*, ii. 698; Salden, pp. 335–6; South Weston, p. 817; Asterley, p. 734; Salford, pp. 728–9. Group two: Williamscot (where the

gates,[1] and in seven between two and three.[2] In only ten manors of which surveys survive did they hold a hide or more than a hide, and in half of these this still left two or more hides of manorial demesne.[3] In some manors the stake of the religious house demonstrably went back to the twelfth century.[4] Perhaps only at the small manor of Merton were alienations in the thirteenth century sufficient to threaten a family's position amongst the gentry.[5]

If one looks at the families individually, it is evidently those in group four which fared worst. Only one or two of the seven came successfully through the century. From the material point of view, however, there was a considerable gap between these families and the great majority of those in the other groups. Coss would probably exclude most of them from the knightly class. Only three seem to have begun the century as lords of manors. Of these, one was forced to dispose of its manor to a religious house[6]; one retained its property intact in the 1300s[7]; one failed of male heirs.[8]

---

holdings of the prior of Chacombe did not come from the lord), p. 707; Noke, p. 836; Ewelme, p. 760; Tythrop, pp. 784-5; Oddington, pp. 835-6; Whitehill, p. 858; Wheatfield, pp. 788, 817-18; Rofford, p. 755; Bucknell, p. 826; Woodperry, p. 717; Ascot, North Weston, pp. 821-2; Lyneham, p. 743; Swinbrook, p. 737; Tiddington, p. 714; Black Bourton, p. 695; Dornford, p. 865; Standlake, p. 702. Group three: Checkendon, Stoke Marmion, p. 779; Coombe Gernon, p. 716; Coombe, pp. 714-15; Whitehill, pp. 857-8; Rycote, p. 757; Clifton Hampden, p. 749; Brize Norton, p. 693; Wheatley, p. 718. Group four: Haddon, p. 691; Tythrop, pp. 784-5. It should be noted, however, that the impression that a manor escaped the attentions of a religious house can be misleading. At Brize Norton, for example, the virgate granted to Thame abbey by the Fritwells (1180s) was probably included in the separate description of Thame's holdings here – pp. 693-4; *TC*, pp. 67-68.

1. Group one: Mursley, *RH*, ii. 336. Group two: Broughton, p. 698. Group three: Westcott Barton, p. 853; Garsington, p. 721; Ewelme, p. 761.

2. Group one: Iffley, pp. 711-12. Group two: Bletchingdon, p. 830; Waterperry, p. 725; Newton Purcel, pp. 834-5. Group three: Chastleton, p. 729; Stoke Lyne, pp. 825-6; Rousham, p. 864.

3. Group one: Ardley, p. 833. Group two: Churchill, pp. 745-6; Sarsden, pp. 729-30; Tackley, p. 859; Great Rollright, p. 728; Hampton, p. 831; Wendlebury, p. 834. Group three: Fifield, p. 732; Sandford*, p. 722; Merton, pp. 38, 718.

4. *E.g.* Bletchingdon; Stoke Lyne; pp. 830, 825-6; *The Cartulary of Cirencester Abbey*, ed. C. D. Ross (Oxford, 1964), ii. nos. 652-3; *SC*, no. 464. At Fifield the bulk of the large alienations took place before 1205; *RH*, p. 732; *Rot. Chartarum*, p. 146b. At Rousham the alienations of the Foliots (which ultimately passed to Osney abbey) were made before 1214; *RH*, p. 864; *COA*, iv. 173-8, 210-12; *Pipe Roll 16 John*, p. 53.

5. One hide out of three; see below p. 358, n. 1.

6. Chislehampton. Dorchester abbey resold the manor and in the fourteenth century it was probably in gentry hands; *VCH*, vii. 9-10, 12. The following clarify the history and size of the manor – P.R.O. Just 1/702A, m. 3d; Just 1/710, m. 18; *RH*, p. 750; P.R.O. CP25 (1)/189(15)/21, 26, 40. For the Chislehamptons see also *CRR*, xvii (forthcoming), nos. 148, 263; *BF*, ii. 880.

7. Haddon; *RH*, p. 691. John of Haddon's tax assessment was 7s in Haddon (1306); 8s in Bampton (1316); see p. 358, n. 7 for these taxes; see also however P.R.O. CP 25(1)/189(14)/5. The other family which may have been successful was that of Lew; see *RH*, p. 690, and John of Lew's 5s 11d tax assessment (in Lew) in 1316.

8. Rosay; *VCH Bucks.*, iv. 96. For the Piruns see, *VCH*, viii. 156; and *FFO*, p. 208; *RH*, pp. 813-14, from which the size of the fee may be deduced. For the Cassingtons, *VCH*, v. 84; *RH*, pp. 712-13; for the Mountsorrels, *BF*, i. 315; *RH*, pp. 760-1. The

In the case of the fifty families in groups one to three the picture is different, as the following table shows.

	Groups:	I	II	III
	Number of families:	5	20	25
(i)	Number forced to sell out through financial weakness	–	–	2 or 6[1]
(ii)	Number which gave their properties to religious houses probably from piety	–	1[2]	1[3]
(iii)	Number extinguished by failure of male heirs	2[4]	5[5]	2[6]
(iv)	Number surviving beyond 1300 as lords of manors and possessors of substantial moveable property	3	14	14[7]

properties of the Piruns, Cassingtons and Mountsorrels seem to have consisted of demesne and free tenants.

1. 'Selling out' here means 'out' to the extent that the families were not possessors of substantial moveable property compared with the families mentioned in p. 358, n. 7 below. Thomley; Fraxino (where it is probably safe to infer financial pressure); *VCH*, v. 299-301; *LPC*, ii. pp. lviii, lxiii. In the other four cases either the extent of the decline is less certain or its process and circumstances are less clear. Pipard *BF*, ii. 829 (holding of Henry fitz Robert at Ewelme); *FFO*, p. 155; *Cal. Charter Rolls*, ii. 39; *C[al.] P[atent] R[olls 1247-58]*, p. 646; *RH*, p. 761; *FFO*, p. 211; *VCH*, vi. 317. Basset of Williamscot and Shutford*, *VCH*, x. 214, 232-4; *RH*, pp. 707-8; P.R.O. Just 1/702A, m. 6. Merton, *VCH*, v. 223-5. Chilham, *BF*, ii. 660; *C[al.] C[lose] [Rolls 1313-18]*, p. 84.
2. Bigstrup, *VCH*, vii. 176; *Bod*, p. 298; *CEA*, ii. 172-4; *Pleas Before the King or his Justices*, ed. D. M. Stenton (Selden Soc., lxxxiii, 1966), iii. pp. ccxcix-ccciii.
3. Wheatfield of Swalcliffe*; *SC*, nos. 375-80, 208; *VCH*, x. 235. The beneficiaries were the Templars.
4. Salceto; fitz Oger; see below p. 358, n. 5, p. 361, n. 9.
5. Most of the families were followed by other knightly families though these were not always resident in Oxfordshire. St Fey, *VCH*, vi. 340; *VCH Bucks*, iv. 24; Hampton, *VCH*, vi. 161-3; P.R.O. *Lists and Indexes*, ix. 108; Forester, *VCH*, vii. 126; *VCH Berks*, iii. 172. Cruce (and fitz Oger), *VCH Essex*, iv. 205; *CIPM*, ii. no. 248; iii. no. 515; *BF*, ii. 828, 829, 685; *RH*, p. 737; *F[eudal] A[ids]*, iv. 176. For leases to Walter Langton (c. 1300) see, *CIPM*, vi. no. 601; A. Beardwood, *The Trial of Walter Langton* (Trans. American Philosophical Soc., new ser., liv, part 3, 1964), p. 35. For the Chestertons see below p. 362, n. 1. It is probable that the male line of the Noers family failed after Nicholas de Noers (1250s). However the Noers have been included among the surviving families since Roger de Noers followed Nicholas de Noers immediately at Churchill and, like Nicholas, came to hold one other manor. It is thus possible to follow the later history of the family without the complications which in other cases follow from the failure of male heirs; see E. St John Brooks 'Nowers of Wymington' *Bedfordshire Hist. Rec. Soc.*, xiv (1931), 54-58.
6. Finmere, *VCH*, vi. 118-19; Baseville, *The 1235 Surrey Eyre*, ed. C. A. F. Meekings (Surrey Rec. Soc., xxxi, 1979), pp. 167-8. Two other families, the Wheatleys and Chastletons, disappear after 1279 for no discernible reason; failure of male heirs seems a more likely explanation than financial weakness. Their properties eventually passed to the Louches and Trilloes, important knightly families of the fourteenth century; *VCH*, v. 106, 110; *RH*, pp. 718-20, 733; P.R.O. CP 25(1)/188(12)/60; *RH*, p. 729; *FA*, iv. 161, 165, 184; *PW*, II. ii. 254; *COA*, iv. 324-9.
7. The Oxfordshire tax returns of the early fourteenth century are those for the thirtieth of 1306, the sixteenth of 1316, and the twentieth of 1327: P.R.O. E 179/161/10;

The nature of the evidence makes it impossible to give an exact number to the families which financial weakness, in Coss's words, 'ultimately forced to sell out'. Yet even by the illegitimate procedure of adding together the six families in the table's section (i) (several of them questionable examples of the phenomenon), the two families which gave their properties to religious houses, probably for reasons of piety, and the two which disappeared for no discernible reason,

---

E 179/161/8; E 179/161/9. All but five of the thirty-one families had representatives who answered, in one place, for sums of 6s or over for one of these taxes – (in two cases this is combining the assessments of brothers or mother and son). The highest assessments of two families (both with other properties) were 5s 2d and 5s, and of one 4s 1d (1327) – for the two other families (Parles and Rokele) see below. Many of the families from groups one and two answered for higher sums on individual properties than families in group three, or were taxed in more than one place. 1316 was a year of bad harvest and very high prices, which may help explain why the assessments of this year are sometimes much higher than those of 1327. However the analysis given above would not be greatly different if the 1316 figures were excluded from consideration. For the twentieth of 1327 an assessment of 5s would indicate moveable property worth £5. However the under-assessment of these taxes was notorious, and at times over fourfold. Great landowners had both more numerous, and often more individually valuable properties than these Oxfordshire lords, but the latter were still far more wealthy than the great bulk of the rural population. In many villages even an assessment of 4s–5s was well above that born by the great majority of tax-payers, who answered for sums of 2s and below. For example, in 1327 at Brize Norton the three lords paid between 6s and 7s 1d; four men paid between 3s and 4s 3d; five between 2s and 2s 11d; and twenty paid under 2s. (See also *VCH*, vii. 21; ix. 163.) For taxes on moveables, the property on which they were assessed, and under-assessment, see J. F. Willard, *Parliamentary Taxes on Personal Property* (Cambridge, Mass., 1934), pp. 73–81, 138–41; P. D. A. Harvey, *Cuxham: A Medieval Oxfordshire Village* (Oxford, 1965), pp. 105–9. For the assessments of the leading Worcs. knights for the twentieth of 1275 – several answered in only one place for sums of between 6s 8d and 10s – see Hilton, pp. 57–58. When no figure is given for a tax in the lists below it is because the returns for the vill are lost, or there is no reference to the family; two figures indicate assessments of two members of the family. Property outside Oxfordshire has only been indicated where an assessment for it has been discovered (there are few early Bucks. taxation rolls).

Group one: fitz Guy; Wigginton 7s 8½d (1306), 13s 4d (1316), 6s 4d (1327); South Weston 8s 6d (1316); Ardley 4s (1327); in Warw., Bubbenhall 4s (1327); Barnacle 4s 3d (1332); Shotteswell 4s (1332). (The 1327 and 1332 assessments are those of John of Seagrave who obviously held the fitz Guy property at this time, probably during a minority; a fitz Guy held all six manors later in the century; see the *VCH* accounts.) Fitz Nigel; Iffley 20s (1306), 17s 11d (1316), 16s (1327). Hastings; Yelford 5s 2d (1316), 4s (1327 in Brighthampton); Daylesford 5s (1327) – P.R.O. E 179/200/1.

Group two: Damory; Bucknell 8s 2d (1316), 10s (1327); Woodperry 6s 4d (1306), 8s 9d (1316), 4s (1327); Bletchingdon 5s 6d (1316), 3s 4d (1327). Fitz Ellis; Waterperry 26s 9d (1316), 5s (1327). Williamscot; Williamscot 7s 6d (1327); Asterley 7s 8d (1306), 7s 11d (1316); Kiddington 6s 6d, 2s 11d (1327). Mauduit; Broughton 10s (1316), 8s (1327); Standlake 5s 6d (1306), 12s 5d (1316); Black Bourton 5s 6d (1306); and in Wilts, Whitley 13s 1d (1327); Somerford 6s (1334), Fontel 3s 7½d (1327). Noers; Churchill 17s 9d (1316), 18s 4d (1327); Wymington 10s 9d (1316) – P.R.O. E 179/71/12. Golafare; Sarsden 10s (1306), 6s (1327); in Wilts., Blunsdon Bury 6s 6d (1334). Purcel; Newton 9s 9d (1306), 6s (1316), 5s (1327). Wace; Ewelme 8s (1327); Tythrop 4s 3d (1306), 4s (1327). Wheatfield; Wheatfield 9s (1316), 8s (1327). Le Poure, Oddington 10s 8d (1316). Quatremain; North Weston 9s 2d (1306), 7s (1327). Fritwell; Brize Norton 13s 9d, 7s (1316), 6s 8d (1327). Rokele; Astwood 3s 6d (1327) – *Early Bucks. Taxation Returns*, ed. A. C. Chibnall (Bucks. Rec. Soc., xiv, 1966), p. 117; for the Rokele manor in Essex, *Feet of Fines Essex* (Essex Archaeological Soc., 1913–49), ii. 226; iii. 272. For the Parles manor in Northants., *CPR 1307–13*, p. 176; *CIPM*, viii. no. 573.

though most probably because of failure of male heirs,[1] a total is reached of only ten families out of fifty; and the properties of four of these ten passed to other members of the gentry.[2] In fact the number of families which sold out in the manner envisaged by the crisis thesis was probably much smaller than ten; only two families come clearly into that category. Against these families may be set thirty-one which remained as lords of manors after 1300, and possessors of substantial moveable property. Over half of these families produced knights or esquires after 1300; one a peer summoned to parliament; nine produced fourteenth-century M.P.s.[3]

Just how many of these thirty-one families withstood crises in their material affairs in the thirteenth century is difficult to say. However, the table set out below goes some way to suggest that in the great majority of cases problems were of limited duration and severity.

Groups:	I	II	III
Number of families surviving beyond 1300	3	14	14
Number suffering overall loss of manors 1200s–1300s[4]	–(1)[5]	5(2)[6]	–
Number increasing number of manors[7]	2[8]	4(1)[9]	3(1)[10]
Number maintaining number of manors	1(1)[11]	5(2)[12]	11(3)[13]

Group three: Gernon; Coombe 3s 10d (1306), 9s 6d (1316); 10s (1327); in Wilts. Steeple Lavington 17s 9d (1327). Marmion; Checkendon; 4s 9d, 2s 2d (brothers) (1327). Barton; Tackley 8s (1316); Westcott Barton 4s, 1s 6d (1327). Foliot; Rousham 2s 3d – and 11d in Broughton – (1306), 5s, 3s (1316), 6s 2d (1327). Rycote; Rycote 6s 4d (1316, 1327). Coombe; Coombe 4s, 2s 1d (1306), 7s, 4s 4d (1316), 5s, 5s (1327). Sandford; Sandford 8s (1306, 1316), 5s 7d (1327). Fitz Pain; Garsington 1s 6d (1306), 6s, 4s (1316), 3s, 2s (1327). Le Moyne; Clifton Hampden 4s ½d (1306), 10s 1d (1327). Whitehill; Whitehill 1s 9½d (1306), 3s 6d, 3s (1316), 5s, 1s 8d (1327) (1316, 1327 mother and son). Sarsden; Sarsden 3s (1306, 1316, 1327); Balscott 1s 5½d (1306), 5s (1316), 4s 2d – in Showell – (1327). Fifield; Fifield 4s (1306), 2s 4d (1316), 9s (1327); these are the assessments of the guardian of the heiress of Thomas of Fifield (1306), and her probable husband John Murimouth – C[atalogue of] A[ncient] D[eeds], iii. D1149; FA, iv. 161, 165, 185. Waundard; Pillerton Hersey (Warw) 4s 1d (1327), 4s (1332), see below p. 363, n. 1. Lisle; Stoke Lyne 11s 4d (1316), 5s (1327) – these are the assessments of Richard Damory who had probably married a daughter of Giles de Lisle; P.R.O. CP 25(1)/189(14)/129, 130; VCH Bucks, iv. 207, 240; VCH, vi. 315–16. For Warw. taxes, see P.R.O. E 179/192/4; Lay Subsidy Roll for Warwickshire 1332, ed. W. F. Carter (Dugdale Soc., vi. 1926); for Wilts. taxes, P.R.O. E 179/196/7; E 179/196/8. For lordships see, FA, iv. 24, 161–72; i. 17, 109 (Lisle, see references above), 110; v. 208, 214. The only families which do not appear here are Wace, Pain, Coombe, for whom see FA, iv. 176, 198; and Waundard for whom see below p. 363, n. 1.

1. See p. 358, n. 6.
2. Shutford* (Basset); Ewelme (Pipard); see references in p. 358, n. 1 above Chastleton; Wheatley; see p. 358, n. 6.
3. See table below p. 365.
4. The figures in brackets in this table indicate the gains or losses of families extinguished by failure of male heirs before they were so extinguished.
5. Salceto, alienation of Lyde*; BF, ii. 803. See C[lose] R[olls] 1231–4, p. 391; C[al.] P[lea] R[olls] E[xchequer of the] J[ews], ed. J. M. Rigg et al. (Jewish Hist. Soc., 1905, 1910, 1929, 1972), i. 76–78, 100; CR 1247–51, p. 402.
6. Wheatfield; Fritwell; Parles; le Poure; Rokele; and (extinguished by failure of male heirs) Hampton; Chesterton. See below p. 361, n. 1.

7. The increase in question is that enjoyed by the senior branch of the family. Save where mentioned the manors were of three hides or more.

8. Hastings, Stoke Goldington (Bucks.), over 200 acres (half of the original manor); Lyneham for a life interest (1285–1305); *VCH Bucks*, iv. 467; *CCR 1279–88*, p. 315; *RH*, pp. 347, 350, 743; see also F. Blomefield, *Topographical History of Norfolk* (London, 1805), i. 338, 340. Fitz Nigel, Salden (Bucks), size uncertain; elsewhere six virgates and 104 acres of land, 100 acres of wood; *VCH Bucks*, iii. 404; P.R.O. CP 25(1)/284(22)/127; CP 25(1)/17(50)/3. See also *VCH Beds*, ii. 358; *VCH Bucks*, iii. 377; P.R.O. C 135/28/20 (*CIPM*, vii. no. 382).

9. Damory: Woodperry; *VCH*, v. 286, which could be amplified; the manor was inherited through the extinction of another branch of the family; Bucknell; *VCH*, vi. 75, *RH*, p. 826; Ubley (Som); *CRR*, vi. 387; *Somerset Pedes Finium*, ed. E. Green (Somerset Record Soc., vi. 1892), i. 28, 46, 48. Fitz Ellis: Tiddington; Oakley (Bucks) perhaps only two hides; Corton (Wilts), size uncertain. These manors were obtained after lengthy litigation on the grounds that they had been held by the ancestors of Emma mother of William fitz Ellis; *Rolls of the King's Court Richard I* (Pipe Roll Soc., xiv, 1891), pp. 25–26; *Rot. Curiae Regis*, ed. F. Palgrave (Record Commission, 1835), i. 22–23, 26; *Pipe Roll 6 Richard I*, p. 200; *7 Richard I*, p. 139; *10 Richard I*, pp. 15, 67; *1 John*, pp. 110, 118–19; *3 John*, p. 202; *4 John*, pp. 8–9; *CRR*, v. 316; R[ot.] L[itt.] C[laus]., i. 216b, 217; *Cal. Feet of Fines County of Buckingham*, ed. M. W. Hughes (Bucks. Archaeological Soc., iv. 1940), pp. 45, 60; *FFO*, p. 77; *BF*, ii. 724. Later in the century Tiddington and Corton were given to a junior branch of the fitz Ellis family; *Cat. Ancient Deeds*, iv. no. 7194; *RH*, p. 714; *VCH*, v. 10; *VCH Wilts*, ix. 55. Mauduit: Broughton; Black Bourton; Standlake; Dornford; all by Robert Mauduit's marriage to Beatrice Murdac, see below p. 374; *BF*, ii. 821–3, 830; *CIPM*, i. no. 842; H. M. Colvin, *A History of Deddington* (London, 1963), p. 31; *RH*, pp. 698, 695, 702, 865. See also *Pipe Roll 11 John*, p. 155; *BF*, ii. 735. The property of the Mauduits was split between brothers in the second half of the century but reunited through the extinction of the senior branch in 1303; see the references above and *CIPM*, ii. no. 684; iv, no. 161. Williamscot: Asterley; Kiddington; Salford; all by marriage to the heiress of Ralph de Salceto; Bickmarsh (Warw.), size uncertain, which was sold in 1307; *VCH*, x. 215–16; *VCH Warw*, v. 190; *BF*, ii. 828; *RH*, pp. 728, 734, 877. Forester (removed by failure of male heirs): Ascot; *VCH*, vii. 126.

10. Gernon: Easterton (Wilts.); *VCH Wilts*, x. 90. Marmion: probably what amounted to the manor of Stoke; *BC*, pp. 12–16; *RH*, p. 779; P.R.O. C 133/62/5. Lisle: halfs of manors at Bix Gibwen (size uncertain) and Marsh Gibbon (Bucks.), two hides; *Bracton's Note Book*, ed. F. W. Maitland (London, 1887), iii. no. 1189; *CR 1234–7*, p. 153; *COA*, vi. 178; *RH*, p. 38; P.R.O. CP 25(1)/189(14)/129; *VCH Bucks*, iv. 207. In the early fourteenth century Bix Gibwen was leased. Baseville (removed by failure of male heirs): Greatham; half a manor at Bepton (both Sussex); sizes uncertain; *1235 Surrey Eyre*, ed. Meekings, pp. 167–8; *VCH Sussex*, iv. 41–42. In addition Hugh of Whitehill held a manor for his wife's lifetime; *VCH*, v. 9.

11. Fitz Guy. Between 1236 and 1242 Shipton on Cherwell (frequently held by junior branches of the fitz Guy family) passed from Guy fitz Robert (a coroner, escheator and sheriff) to John de Peauton – John's descendants were Oxfordshire esquires. Guy had been in debt to the Jews but there is no indication that the loss of Shipton was the result of this. Guy probably offset the loss by his share of an inheritance in Devon which included the manor of West Portlemouth; P.R.O. E 159/11, m. 1d; *BF*, i. 448; ii. 834; *COA*, vi. 103 (Guy's elder brother Ralph was alive at this time); *FFO*, pp. 20–21; P.R.O. Just 1/185, m. 5; *Devon Feet of Fines*, ed. O. J. Reichel (Devon and Cornwall Rec. Soc., 1912, 1939), i, no. 626; ii, no. 832; P.R.O. Just 1/710, m. 15. For holdings of junior branches of the fitz Guy's in the second half of the century, see the references above and P.R.O. Just 1/702A, m. 1d; Just 1/710, m. 18d; *RH*, ii. 817, 843. The family removed by failure of male heirs was fitz Oger; see above p. 358, n. 4, and *CIPM*, ii, no. 327. The later history of the fitz Oger property in Devon has not been traced but Peter fitz Oger seems to have strengthened his hold upon it; *Devon Feet of Fines*, i, no. 387.

12. Noers; Quatremain; Golafre; Purcel; Wace; and, removed by failure of male heirs, Cruce; St Fey.

13. Whitehill; Barton; Foliot; Coombe; Rycote; Sandford; Pain; Fifield; Waundard; le Moyne; Sarsden; and, removed by failure of male heirs, Finmere; and (if they were so removed) Chastleton; Wheatley.

Only five of the thirty-one surviving families, therefore (and three more extinguished by failure of male heirs) suffered an overall diminution in the number of their manors. That diminution was not always the direct result of financial weakness. With the Wheatfields the cause was a family settlement. The Fritwells probably, the Parles certainly, were in financial difficulties; but the former lost their property at Fritwell through a law-suit; the latter their manor at Handsworth when William de Parles was hanged (unjustly, it was later claimed) for felony. William's descendants produced a line of fourteenth-century M.P.s, and were still trying to recover Handsworth in the reign of Richard II. Most of these less fortunate families acquired some new property, even if it did not entirely offset their losses. All retained at least one manor. All but one boasted fourteenth-century knights, esquires or M.P.s. The le Poures, who were still gentry in the seventeenth century, survived debts (uniquely large) of over £340 – an indication of the margin of safety which similarly endowed families from group two enjoyed but did not need.[1]

1. For Wheatfield property in the late twelfth century see *Feet of Fines Henry II Richard I* (Pipe Roll Soc., xvii, 1894), no. 130. It is not possible to trace the later history of all this property. Chadlington passed to a junior branch; Rofford to another knightly family (St Valery), but this loss was offset by the acquisition of a manor in Bucks.; *RH*, p. 747; *FFO*, p. 205; *The Topographer and Genealogist*, ed. J. G. Nichols (London, 1853), ii. 340–1; *VCH Bucks*, iii. 41; *VCH*, viii. 266. (In the 1190s both Chadlington and Rofford formed dower portions.) For litigation which ended in Stephen of Fritwell losing Fritwell*; *VCH*, vi. 137, 308; v. 311; see *CAE*, i. 135–7. Stephen also leased his manor at Brize Norton (recovered by his son) to a neighbouring knightly family (St Valery); *CRR*, xiv, nos. 1581, 1869. Other litigation may be found in *CRR*, xi–xiv. See also P.R.O. E 369/13, m. 1; *TC*, pp. 67–8. £100 of William de Parles's debts to the Jews were bought up by his lord Roger de Somery. However William acquired a manor through marriage, and a hundred from the king; *CR 1268–72*, p. 438; *CCR 1272–9*, pp. 328–9; *CPREJ*, ii. 190; *C[al.] I[nquisitions] M[iscellaneous]*, i, nos. 1161, 1176; *Placitorum Abbreviatio* (Record Commission, 1811), pp. 201, 204. After the hanging William's son granted Great Rollright to the judge Roger Brabazon; R. W. Jeffrey, *The Manors and Advowson of Great Rollright* (Oxfordshire Rec. Soc., ix, 1927), pp. 60–61. For later Parles, 'Extracts from the Plea Rolls of Edward III and Richard II', ed. G. Wrottesley, *Collections for the History of Staffordshire* (William Salt Archaeological Soc., xiii, 1892), pp. 51, 171; *CIPM*, xi, no. 173; *RMP*, i. 139, 265. Le Poure manors at Whitehill and Tackley were leased in the 1270s (to a kinsman Roger de Meulant, bishop of Coventry). They were sold in the reign of Edward II; *RH*, pp. 858–9; *CIPM*, iii. 252, 272; vi. 470–1; *CPREJ*, iv. 79; *CCR 1302–7*, p. 435; *VCH*, vi. 278; *COA*, vi. 70–72. For le Poure acquisitions and confirmations; *FFO*, pp. 2, 30, 166; *COA*, v. 419–20; *Rot. Ricardi Gravesend*, ed. F. N. Davis (Lincoln Rec. Soc., xx, 1922), p. 222; *VCH Berks*, iv. 422, 425; *VCH*, vi. 278 n. 56. For Rokele, who lost Wotton Underwood to the knightly family of Tothall, leased other property, and were in serious financial straits; *VCH Bucks*, iv. 132, 270–1; *Fines Bucks*, i. 83; *CR 1259–61*, p. 13; *CAD*, vi, no. C6980. For these families in the early fourteenth century see p. 365, n. 7, 358, n. 7. For the alienation of the Hamptons (ultimately removed by failure of male heirs), C. A. F. Meekings, 'The Early Years of Netley Abbey', *Journal of Ecclesiastical History*, xxx (1979), 9. See also *COA*, vi. 77–79; P.R.O. C 132/35/4; *CIPM*, i, nos. 62, 229, 670; *VCH*, vi. 161–3. Ralph of Chesterton (in debt to the Jews and lacking male heirs) sold Chesterton to the earl of Cornwall shortly before his death. However Ralph retained his second property at Coklescomb* (rents here were worth 18 marks p.a.). This was granted by his daughter to the Templars in return for spiritual benefits; *VCH*, vi. 94–96; *CPREJ*, ii. 270; iii. 226; *BF*, ii. 656; P.R.O. CP 25(1)/98(59)/77; E. Hasted, *History of Kent* (Canterbury, 1799), viii. 128.

Alongside these five families which suffered overall losses (and the small number selling out more completely), there were twenty-six families which, over the century, either maintained or multiplied their total of manors. (Eight of the eleven families which were removed by failure of male heirs did likewise.) Seventeen of the twenty-six families experienced no change in their number of manors. Since there is rarely evidence as to the condition of manors early in the century, nice calculations concerning their improvement or deterioration are impossible. However, the 1279 survey, the tax returns of the early fourteenth century, and sometimes other evidence, shows that these manors remained of considerable value.[1] Nine of the twenty-six families (and two extinguished by failure of male heirs) added to their total of manors and probably enjoyed increasing prosperity as a result.[2]

A few examples may show in more detail that resources were husbanded or increased. In 1200 the property of the Quatremains at their two manors of Ascot and North Weston amounted to twenty-seven virgates. Seventy-nine years later all but one and a half of these virgates can be traced. The manors were in good condition. Eleven virgates were in demesne, twelve held by villeins, and only two and a half in the hands of free tenants.[3] For the tax of 1306 Quatremain moveables were valued at over £13, a considerable sum given the prevalence of under-assessment.[4] Some families transformed their situations. The Mauduits and Williamscots each obtained four manors through marriages.[5] The Marmions had originally been enfeoffed in the 1170s with £10 of land in Checkendon. In the 1240s they spent 130 marks securing what was probably the neighbouring manor of Stoke in fee. By the 1270s their property at the two places could bring in well over £45 a year. In the 1300s John Marmion had the resources to defeat a ruthless and lawless attempt by the king's treasurer, Walter de Langton, to obtain his lands.[6] In the 1320s the

1. For the families see the table above p. 360; for their manors see p. 358, n. 7, and below pp. 369–70. Obviously the mere retention of a manorial lordship is small guide to a family's material situation since the manor may have been rendered valueless by alienations. Thus the Thomleys, though still lords of a manor in 1316, have been placed in the category of families who sold up; see above p. 358, n. 1. Apart from the fitz Guys (p. 361, n. 11) and the Noers (where there were complicated family settlements, p. 358, n. 5) all seventeen maintained the same manors throughout the century. The Waundards ran into serious financial difficulties in the reign of Edward II, and sold Shotteswell in 1319. However at precisely this time they acquired Pillerton Hersey manor through marriage; *VCH Warw*, v. 149, 133; see p. 358, n. 7, p. 369, n. 6.
2. Apart from those of the fitz Nigels (p. 361, n. 8) and Noers (below p. 371) most major new acquisitions came in manorial form. However, families might also transform their situations by a series of small acquisitions in and around their manors from free tenants; see below p. 370.
3. *FFO*, p. 17; *RH*, pp. 821–2; *VCH*, vii. 127, 173.
4. See above p. 358, n. 7.
5. See above *p.* 361, n. 9.
6. *BC*, pp. 12–16; *RH*, p. 779; *Account and Surveys of Adam de Stratton*, ed. M. W. Farr (Wiltshire Archaeological and Natural History Soc., Records Branch, xiv, 1958),

Williamscots, Quatremains and Marmions were listed amongst Oxfordshire's esquires, and the Mauduits amongst Wiltshire's knights.[1]

Of course, even some of the most successful families were sometimes short of ready cash, and leased or sold land to raise it. But their difficulties did not escalate relentlessly in the way Coss postulates. Coss acknowledges that 'the better endowed families survived for a time because they enjoyed some scope to alienate property without dire consequences'.[2] In these Oxfordshire examples the time of survival was the whole length of the thirteenth century and beyond. For a family with several manors a lease might be a safe and acceptable expedient. In the second half of the thirteenth century Miles de Hastings (group one) twice leased manors to raise money. He recovered both and died seized of six manors, two of which he had obtained through marriage.[3] Roger Damory (group two) mortgaged his chief manor of Bucknell to Osney abbey in return for a loan of £140. He repaid the money on time, recovered unfettered control of Bucknell (1271), and at about the same time acquired a neighbouring manor. In 1198–9 Emma fitz Ellis described herself as 'in great need' – a phrase which sometimes appears as the sombre prelude to a succession of alienations. In this case the need was for money to finance litigation, which turned out to be highly successful and secured the fitz Ellises three manors.[4] Families less amply endowed, like the Bartons and Finmeres, coped with debts to the Jews. In the 1190s William fitz Gregory of Finmere owed money to them, and leased or sold lands and rents to Biddlesden abbey in consequence. But his son Gilbert (1200s–1230s), a knight active in war and local

---

pp. 90, 99, xxi; see also below p. 370, and p. 370, n. 6; *Records of the Trial of Walter Langton*, ed. A. Beardwood (Camden Soc., 4th ser., xiv, 1958), pp. 166–8, 270–3 (see cl. 33 of the Ordinances of 1311). John owed Langton £40 (which he paid) and £52. These debts were hardly overwhelming given the value of Marmion properties; hence John's determination not to sell. For later Marmion history, *BC*, pp. 2–3, 8–9, 24–28; for some Marmion property in Gloucs., *CAD*, iii. D196; P.R.O. E 326/B8691.

1. The Williamscots were knights later in the century; see the references below p. 365, n. 8. There is no space to discuss in detail the histories of the surviving families in the fourteenth century; and to do so would have limited relevance to a crisis which reached its height in the reign of Henry III.

2. Coss, p. 25.

3. Leased were Yelford and Stoke Goldington; the latter had been acquired through marriage; Just 1/701, ms. 7, 8; *CCR 1279–88*, pp. 281, 488–9 (see also *RH*, p. 689); *CIPM*, iv, no. 309. For the manor of Miles's wife at Lyneham see above p. 361, n. 8. The senior Hastings line failed of male heirs in 1311; the line of Miles's second son continued at Yelford and Daylesford. In 1310 Yelford was apparently sold for £100; but it is certain that the Hastings retained the manor; P.R.O. CP 25(1)/189(14)/39.

4. Roger's grandsons, Richard and Roger Damory, became prominent at the court of Edward II, and were summoned as peers to parliament. Roger Damory died of wounds during the Boroughbridge campaign. The family suffered material collapse in the reign of Edward III: *Complete Peerage*, iv. 42–47; *COA*, vi. 35; *VCH*, p. 75 (see also p. 348); *RH*, p. 826; *Pipe Roll 1 John*, pp. 118–19; for fitz Ellis acquisitions see above p. 361, n. 9.

government, obtained two virgates in Finmere from one of his free tenants and by a concession of pasture rights recovered 122 acres of arable land and a mill which Biddlesden had previously held 'in firmam perpetuam'. It was failure of male heirs, not mounting debts, which finished this family.[1]

Among the richer families there are signs of the 'higher standard of living and civilization' of which Treharne speaks. John fitz Guy (ob. 1300s) afforded a military effigy in his local parish church. (So – in the 1340s – did Robert fitz Ellis, descendant of the Emma who lamented her great need in 1198–9).[2] Four families in the thirteenth century secured licences for highly prestigious private chapels.[3] As many as seventeen bore coats of arms.[4] On the other hand, all the one-manor families ceased to take up knighthood in the thirteenth or early fourteenth centuries.[5] Some continued as esquires; others (although they might hold local government office) bore no military title.

Groups:	I	II	III
Number of surviving families	3	14	14
Number producing knights after 1300	1[6]	9	–
Number producing esquires after 1300	–	3[7]	4[8]

1. *Starrs and Jewish Charters in the British Museum*, ed. I. Abrahams *et al.* (Cambridge, 1930, 1932), i, no. 1207; Brit. Mus. Harleian Charters 86, C.24; 85, D.51; *CRR*, ix. 95–96; *FFO*, pp. 65–66; *VCH*, vi. 118; the Finmeres also had an unidentified half fee in Devon; for Barton: *CR 1237–42*, p. 101; *FFO*, p. 85; *RH*, p. 853; P.R.O. CP 25(1)/189(17)/65; *PW* ii. iii. 487.

2. *VCH*, ix. 169. The armour of the effigy cannot be later than the early fourteenth century. There were no other families of importance in Wigginton. J. Todd, *Waterperry Church* (Eynsham, 1969), pp. 9–11.

3. Fitz Guy; fitz Nigel; Damory; Bigstrup; J. Nichols, *History and Antiquities of the County of Leicester* (London, 1815), i, ii. Appendix, 79 (this concession is dated too late in *VCH Warw*, vi. 51); *LPC*, i, no. 40; ii, pp. lxviii, 219; *CAE*, ii. 172–4.

4. Group one: fitz Nigel; Hastings; fitz Guy. Group two: Damory; Mauduit; fitz Ellis; Wace; le Poure; Wheatfield; Golafre; Noers; Quatremain; Williamscot. Group three: Gernon; Marmion; Rycote; Whitehill. Most of the evidence for these arms comes from the fourteenth century; *PW*, i, i. 411, 413; P.R.O. E 326/B8537 (seal of the 1220s) – these fitz Guy arms are also carved in an early fourteenth-century window in Wigginton church; *VCH*, viii. 266; W. F. Carter, 'Gresley and Gernon', *The Genealogist*, new ser., xxxv (1919), 176–7; *COA*, ii. 14 n.; B.M. Add. MS. 38133, fos. 139b–143; *Catalogue of Seals in the PRO* (London, 1978), nos. P876, P516. Westminster Abbey muniments, no. 15166; *The Visitations of the County of Oxford*, ed. W. H. Turner (Harleian Soc., v, 1871), pp. 18–19, 53–54, 71, 21–22, 104–5.

5. This can be demonstrated in nearly every case by evidence from witness lists of charters. Among two-manor families which ceased, at least for a time, to take up knighthood were Golafre and Wace; see above p. 364.

6. Fitz Guy; W. A. Shaw, *The Knights of England* (London, 1906), i. 119; also an MP; *RMP*, i. 29. The failure of the fitz Nigel and Hastings families to produce knights after 1300 is explained by failure of male heirs; see p. 364, n. 3, and *VCH*, v. 193.

7. Knights: Damory (also peers); Wheatfield (MP); Noers (MP); Mauduit (MP); Golafre (MP); Wace (MP); fitz Ellis; le Poure; Williamscot (MP). Esquires: Purcel; Quatremain; Rokele. The Parles were also MPs. See references in next note.

8. Gernon; Marmion (both now held two manors); Rycote; Whitehill. In addition

The surrender of knighthood, however, did not entail a serious decline in social status. In the early years of the thirteenth century the rank involved no high social distinction. How could it do so when some knights held less than three hides of land and were not lords of manors? In Oxfordshire it was rarely the practice (as it became later) to designate those who were knights in the witness lists of charters. Unknighted manorial lords at the end of the century were not, therefore, in a very different position from their knightly predecessors for whom the title had carried a limited significance. It is true that by 1300 social divisions were more defined. As knighthood became confined to the richer families, so it became a mark of distinction. But no social chasm yawned between those who were and were not knights. There was nothing irrevocable in ceasing to take up the honour. The Golafre pedigree happily put down Thomas Golafre (1297–1330) as 'esquire' when his father and son were knights.[1] Between 1264 and 1370 the Waces alternated between esquire, knight, lord with no military title, and knight.[2] Non-knights were employed in local government as coroners, forest officials,[3] and (by the late thirteenth and early fourteenth centuries) as commissioners of various kinds and sheriffs. They were also elected as M.P.s.[4] As esquires they could still be militarily active. The decline in the number of knights in the thirteenth century produced the rise of the squires in the next.[5] But 'esquire' still denoted a military rank which a lord (even if a local government official) might or (like one of the Waces) might not assume.[6] Lords of manors, especially manors of reasonable size and value, even if they held no military title, were firmly on the right side of the basic social divide between those who were and were not 'noble' or 'gentle'.

Can any conclusions be drawn from the evidence surveyed above? The lord at the centre of the crisis thesis, the lord who succumbed to his debts and sold off his properties, does appear in Oxfordshire.

Barton, Sarsden, le Moyne provided local government officials. Giles de Lisle was an MP (1305) but became a knight before 1300. Evidence for the squires usually comes from the lists of the 1320s; the rank may sometimes have been assumed before 1300; *PW*, II, ii. 589 (Rokele); 593, 654 (Bucks and Beds lists), 656–7 (Wilts and Berks lists); Shaw, *Knights of England*, pp. 115, 121; *CIPM*, xiii, no. 155; *RMP*, i. 90; *BC*, pp. 9–10, 39; B.M. Add. MS. 38133, fos. 139b–143; *Complete Peerage*, iv. 47; *RMP*, i. 19, 49, 96, 115 n., 139, 189; *CAE*, i. 365; ii. 211; *PW*, II, iii. 487 (see also pp. 856, 933, 1229, 1153, 1103, 1608).

1. B.M. Add. MS. 38133, fos. 139b–143; a fifteenth-century pedigree based on accurate earlier information.

2. *BC*, pp. 9–10.

3. R. F. Hunnisett, *The Medieval Coroner* (Cambridge, 1961), p. 173. Oxfordshire verderers were frequently not knights in the thirteenth century.

4. *The English Government at Work*, ed. J. F. Willard, W. A. Morris (Cambridge, Mass., 1940), ii. 51–53; G. Lapsley, 'Knights of the Shire in the Parliaments of Edward II', *EHR*, xxxiv. 34–42.

5. A. R. Wagner, *English Genealogy* (Oxford, 1960), pp. 104–6.

6. Sitwell, *ubi supra*, pp. 58–77.

But he was untypical. Given the size of the Oxfordshire group the number of families which 'sold out' was not 'large'. Even where there were serious debts and alienations one cannot assume that they were always caused by the distinctive economic conditions of the period, and were thus part of the crisis Coss envisages, a point which will be returned to. In this Oxfordshire survey the majority of families in groups one to three maintained or increased their number of manors, and probably retained these manors in reasonable condition. Just how prolonged and severe can the crisis have been? Certainly, if it did occur, a large proportion of the knightly class was able to deal with it. The underlying material position in the century of many families which began the period with upwards of three hides of land seems secure. These families beat off such problems as they encountered, and remained as gentry after 1300. This is not to deny that the thirteenth century saw both social definition and material polarization – although the latter was limited by the practice among successful families of dividing property among sons. The families which acquired the most extensive new possessions were those which began the century with two or more manors. It was these families which continued to assume knighthood. The one-manor families did less well. All of those which collapsed came from this group. Yet the majority remained as lords of manors and possessors of not inconsiderable moveable property.

What has been said above has depended on a survey of individual family histories. The crisis thesis also depends on deductions from the general social and economic climate of the thirteenth century as it affected the knightly class. It is suggested, in effect, that conditions were so malignant that they threw the whole class into prolonged crisis. However, an examination of how Oxfordshire families dealt with these conditions does not support this ugly view; rather, it sustains, as a working hypothesis, what has been suggested above – namely, that the underlying material position of many of the better endowed knightly families in the thirteenth century was sound.

III

The main social phenomenon of the thirteenth century – the rising cost of knighthood – cannot have created difficulties for the whole knightly class. As has been seen, one-manor families which could not afford the rank simply ceased to assume it. Coss himself recognizes that 'few families were prepared to jeopardize their position in an attempt to retain [knighthood's] benefits'.[1] In any case, the rising cost of knighthood was hardly confined to the thirteenth century. The necessary equipment became steadily more elaborate and

1. Coss, p. 27.

expensive throughout the Middle Ages.[1] The suggested economic
cause of the crisis was the rapid inflation of the years 1180–1220,
which thereafter continued at a slower pace. This necessitated the
generation of increased income just to stand still. Here Coss rightly
concentrates on the question of the demesne. The more a family had
a productive demesne farm, and derived its income from selling the
crops, the better protected it was against the inflation, since income
would rise with the rising price for agricultural produce. Yet just
how typical were manorial lords who, in Coss's words, 'lived substantially, or even wholly, off rents and lacked the resources in land
to shift to demesne farming'?[2] One difficulty in the way of answering
this question is that the value of demesne varied according to the
fertility of the soil and the efficiency of its exploitation. Moreover,
its extent was often estimated in hides, which themselves differed in
area according to the size of the virgate. For both these reasons the
value of one hide of demesne could sometimes equal that of two.[3]
The example Coss gives of a family which failed effectively to 'shift'
to demesne farming is that of the Nerbonnes of Stivichall in
Warwickshire. Here, before the manor was divided, the demesne was
a little less than a carucate.[4] However, if that carucate had been
properly exploited, it would hardly have condemned the Nerbonnes
to live, as Coss implies, 'substantially or even wholly off fixed rents' –
not, if the demesne income can be judged from villein rents in 1279.[5]
Allowing these difficulties of assessment, it is worth noting that
Walter of Henley (who may have had experience of Oxfordshire
conditions) gives his advice on the basis of 160 acres of demesne
between two fields, and 180 acres between three.[6] With the small
virgate most common in Oxfordshire, this would be the equivalent
of a demesne of about two hides.[7] Certainly this seems sufficient to

1. S. Harvey, 'The Knight and the Knight's Fee in England', *Past and Present*, lix
(1970), 40; C. Blair, *European Armour* (London, 1958). The initial capital cost of the armour
and horses was a major reason for postponing or declining knighthood – to take the
rank in the thirteenth century was usually styled to take 'arma militaria'. The desire to
escape local office was less important since such office was not confined to knights.
   2. Coss, p. 28.
   3. In Chadlington hundred in 1279, where valuations were given, they ranged
between £2 and £5 p.a. per hide, with £5 and £2 10s being most common; *RH*, pp.
725–47. Without account rolls it is impossible to assess the real value of demesnes of
knightly manors. The hundred roll figures are almost certainly underestimates. For the
'profit' from the demesne at Cuxham (in knightly hands till the 1260s) see Harvey,
p. 100.
   4. Coss, p. 14.
   5. Coss, pp. 14–16, 28.
   6. *Walter of Henley*, ed. D. Oschinsky (Oxford, 1971), pp. 314–15, 157, 189.
   7. In Oxfordshire the virgate ranged from fifteen to forty acres, with twenty to
twenty-five acres being most common. Kosminsky assumes an average of twenty-five
acres; Kosminsky, p. 126. The estimate of demesne in the hundred rolls is, of course,
only approximate, and no precise acreage figures can be deduced even when the size of
the virgate is known. Kosminsky believes that the hundred roll assessments are, if
anything, likely to be under-estimates; Kosminsky, pp. 29, 36, 92, 94. For the con-

leave considerable corn for sale. A family of villein half-virgaters had to subsist, and market a surplus to pay rent on a sixteenth of that land. Judged by the demesne of Walter many Oxfordshire families seem well placed. In the 1279 survey, of the forty families from groups one, two and three not yet removed by failure of male heirs (or pious gifts) twenty had manors with demesnes of two or more hides – perhaps as large or larger than those Walter envisaged. With several families there is other evidence of demesnes of respectable size. Only four families in 1279 were confined (like the Nerbonnes) to single properties with a hide or less in demesne. In group one, only the fitz Nigels had a manor with two hides in demesne.[1] But the fitz Guys had four manors each with one hide in demesne, and their chief manor, like most of the property of the Hastings, was not surveyed. Later evidence shows that all these families could derive substantial income from demesne farming.[2] In group two, of the fifteen surviving families, four had manors with two hides in demesne,[3] and eight had manors with three or more hides.[4] All told the Damories had seven hides of manorial demesne and the Williamscots nearly nine.[5] In group three, of the twenty-two families, seven had manors with two hides in demesne.[6] The smaller harvest of two or three hide demesne manors in

siderable under-assessment at Cuxham (where the virgate was twenty-four acres) compare Harvey, pp. 94–95, *RH*, p. 758. For the hundred rolls as a source see Kosminsky, pp. 20–42; *Oxfordshire Hundred Rolls of 1279*, ed. E. Stone, P. Hyde (Oxfordshire Rec. Soc., xlvi, 1969), pp. 10–11.

1. Salden (Bucks); *RH*, pp. 335–6.
2. Ardley; South Weston; Bubbenhall, Shotteswell (Warw); *RH*, pp. 833, 817; P.R.O. E 164/15/fos. 23–23ᵛ, 121ᵛ. For the fitz Guy chief manor at Wigginton where there was probably a large demesne; *VCH*, ix. 163. In the inquisition post mortem extents of 1305 there were 580 acres of demesne noted on the Hastings manors. There were also two hides of demesne (in 1279) at Lyneham, a manor of Miles de Hastings's wife; P.R.O. C 133/118/14; *RH*, p. 743. On the fitz Nigel properties in 1332 (excluding fourteenth-century acquisitions) over 1100 acres of demesne are mentioned; P.R.O. C 135/28/20.
3. Parles: Great Rollright; Golafre: Sarsden; Fritwell: Brize Norton; Quatremain: North Weston (where there were just under two hides; another hide was nearby at Ascot). The Parles manor was leased in 1279, but at a reasonable rent; *RH*, pp. 728–9, 693, 821–2; *CCR 1279–88*, p. 2.
4. Fitz Ellis: Waterperry; 'in demesne' is almost certainly omitted from the four hides here – compare the description of the Beaufeu manor; *RH*, p. 725; Noers: Churchill, p. 745; Wheatfield, p. 788; le Poure: Oddington, p. 835; Forester: Ascot – and two more hides at Lyneham – pp. 821, 743; Mauduit: Broughton, p. 698, and see pp. 865, 695, 702 for further manors. For the Damories and Williamscots see next note. Many of the families mentioned in this note and in p. 369, nn. 3, 5 had further demesne manors of which there are no surveys.
5. Damory: Bucknell (three hides); Bletchingdon; Woodperry; *RH*, pp. 717, 826, 830. Williamscot: Williamscot (three hides); Asterley; Kiddington; Salford; Noke; pp. 707, 734, 877, 728, 836. Of the remaining three families, there is no survey of Rokele manors. No demesne is mentioned at the Purcel manor of Newton Purcel, and the Wace manor at Ewelme; pp. 834, 760; *BF*, i. 316. Newton was probably valued at £20 p.a. in 1255; P.R.O. C 47/1(1), m. 31. For later tax assessments see above p. 358, n. 7.
6. Marmion: Checkendon and Stoke, *RH*, p. 779; Barton: Westcott Barton, p. 853; Foliot: Rousham, p. 864; Whitehill, p. 857; Chastleton, p. 729; Gernon, Coombe Gernon, p. 716; Waundard: Shotteswell (Warw), P.R.O. E 164/15, fo. 122.

this group, as compared with group two, is to some extent misleading. It is true that the Pipards, Thomleys, Mertons, and Bassets of Shutford, families placed in the category of those 'selling up', had small or non-existent demesnes.[1] The manor of John of Fifield at Fifield had only one hide in demesne, but John had other properties.[2] Of the manors of the remaining eight lords, one manor was not surveyed,[3] and in the others the area of demesne was not stated. This does not mean that it was small or non-existent. In two of the manors inquisition post mortem surveys (which were very prone to under-statement) mention or suggest demesnes of 127 acres (1273) and 160 acres (1302).[4]

With Oxfordshire knightly families, therefore, the size of the demesne might seem more frequently a source of strength than of weakness. It is difficult to know how these demesnes were created or maintained. There is evidence, however, which suggests that they owed something to acquisitions – many quite small individually – from freeholders. If this is right, knightly families were precisely able to 'shift' to demesne farming. They were not helpless against inflation. Private charters or cartularies for Ewell (Surrey), Wymington (Beds.) and Checkendon (Oxon.) show that Robert fitz Nigel (on a small scale), Roger de Noers I and II, and John Marmion increased the demesnes of these manors by acquisitions from free tenants in the second half of the thirteenth or the early fourteenth centuries.[5] John Marmion in his most important transaction acquired twenty-one acres of land from his only substantial tenant, Nicholas de Bendford.[6] At Wymington in 1279 there were only two virgates of manorial demesne. Eleven virgates were held by free tenants who paid around 17s in rent. Twenty-two years later there were 240 acres of arable

---

1. *RH*, pp. 761, 714, 707–8; *CIPM*, i, no. 627; for the other families in this category see *CCR 1313-18*, p. 84 (Chilham) and *LPC*, ii, lvii–viii, lxiii (Fraxino).

2. *RH*, pp. 732, 690, 693, 697.

3. Balscott of the Sarsdens; see P.R.O. CP 25(1)/189(16)/80; *RH*, p. 730.

4. Coombe and Rycote; *CCR 1272-9*, p. 67; P.R.O. C 133/104/11; *RH*, pp. 38–39, 714–15, 757. The other families were fitz Pain: Garsington, pp. 39, 720–1; Sandford, pp. 39, 722; Lisle, Stoke Lyne, pp. 825–6; Wheatley, pp. 39, 718–20; le Moyne, Clifton Hampden, p. 749. In 1255 the fitz Pain's Garsington was probably valued at £15 p.a.; P.R.O. C 47/1(1), m. 31 – 'filius Pagani' can be identified with Walter fitz Pain of Garsington. In 1265 Stoke Lyne was valued at £20 p.a.; *CIM*, i, no. 865. Although the situation is far from clear it is possible that the le Moyne's Clifton Hampden was largely leased in 1279. However the family must have recovered its position in the manor since John le Moyne, the then lord (he was also a regarderer) answered for a large tax assessment in the fourteenth century; *VCH*, vii. 18, 21; *CAE*, ii. 211; see p. 358, n. 7.

5. *Fitz Nells Cartulary*, ed. C. A. F. Meekings, P. Shearman (Surrey Rec. Soc., xxvi, 1968), pp. xciii–iv; nos. 9, 11, 14, 85; Bedfordshire County Record Office, County Hall Bedford, GA 95, nos. xxxix, lv–lx, lxiv–lxvii; see 'Cal. Feet of Fines Edward I', ed. G. H. Fowler, *Bedfordshire Historical Rec. Soc.*, xii (1928), 42; *BC*, pp. 16, 21–27.

6. *BC*, p. 23. Nicholas de Bendford is probably the Nicholas de 'Budiford' of *RH*, p. 779. The vigorous policies of the Marmions are reflected in the four hides of demesne at the two adjoining manors of Checkendon and Stoke in 1279; in the small number of free tenants; and in the very high rents paid by the villeins.

demesne and the rents of the remaining free tenants came to 51s 7d.[1] Roger de Noers had also obtained half the advowson and a half virgate of land from none other than Edward I's great minister, Robert Burnel.[2] At his second manor of Churchill, Roger spent 94 marks on two purchases which brought him 156 acres of land, and two and a half virgates of meadow (1278, 1286).[3] Other families known to have made acquisitions in or near their manors were the fitz Guys at Shotteswell (group one); the Golafres at Sarsden and Blundsden Bury; the Mauduits at Dornford; the Purcels (1314) at Newton Purcel (all group two); the Finmeres at Finmere; the Waundards at Shotteswell; and the Gernons at Coombe and Easterton (all group three).[4] The small number of freeholders found on many manors in 1279 may well testify to the successful pursuit of such policies. Fewer than three virgates of land were held by free tenants (or by religious houses) in as many as twenty-two manors, held by seventeen of the families.[5] Merton College charters suggest that Sir Ralph de Chenduit – father of the feckless and improvident Stephen who sold up to Walter de Merton – was an 'active improving landlord' who reorganized the demesne of Cuxham into a contiguous area, and increased its extent by purchases from freeholders.[6] Other knightly families, in Oxfordshire and elsewhere, probably carried through similar programmes.[7]

It might be argued that demesne farming was itself an uncertain and exacting way of producing income. The running of the demesne required close supervision. Revenue varied from year to year according to the state of the harvest. Yet lords of a few manors, who lived largely on their farms, absorbed the rules of estate management with the revolution of the seasons. They might possess considerable expertise. In 1311 when Robert fitz Nigel inherited Ewell manor in Surrey a detailed extent was drawn up of its demesnes and rents. In 1295 the single manor lord, Fulk of Rycote, employed a steward,

1. *RH*, p. 330; P.R.O. C 133/85/1.
2. Bedfordshire County Record Office, GA 95, no. liii.
3. *FFO*, pp. 209, 224.
4. *Warwickshire Feet of Fines*, ed. F. C. Wellstood (Dugdale Soc., xi, 1932), i, nos. 782, 864; *FFO*, p. 216; compare the holdings of Hugh the Franklin between *ibid.*, p. 144 and *RH*, p. 730; P.R.O. CP 25(1)/189(14)/132 – compare *RH*, pp. 834–5; *ibid.*, p. 865; P.R.O. Just 1/710, m. 8; *Feet of Fines relating to Wiltshire Edward I and Edward II*, ed. R. B. Pugh (Wiltshire Archaeological and Natural History Soc., Records Branch, i, 1939), p. 45. For the Finmeres see above pp. 364–5.
5. Group one: South Weston (fitz Guy), *RH*, p. 817; Yelford (Hastings), p. 698. Group two: Kiddington, Salford (Williamscot), pp. 877, 728–9; Ascot, Lyneham (Forester), pp. 821, 743; Waterperry, Tiddington (fitz Ellis), pp. 725, 714; Ewelme (Wace), p. 760; Wheatfield, pp. 788, 817–18; Bucknell (Damory), p. 826; Oddington, Whitehill (le Poure), pp. 835–6, 858; Ascot, North Weston (Quatermain), pp. 821–2, Dornford (Mauduit), p. 865. Group three: Rycote, p. 757; Stoke (Marmion), p. 779; Wheatley, p. 718; Stoke Lyne (Lisle), p. 825; Whitehill, pp. 857–8. Group four: Haddon, p. 691.
6. Harvey, pp. 4–5, 21, 113–15.
7. See P. Spufford, *Origins of the English Parliament* (London, 1967), p. 10.

and a clerk who wrote his letters and perhaps also his account rolls.[1]
Men like Fulk were often baronial stewards, sheriffs, coroners and
local judges and commissioners. They did nòt need to read treatises
on estate management. Such knowledge was second nature to them.
Although, moreover, revenue from the demesne was bound to
fluctuate, its general trend was upwards until the 1260s whereafter it
was fairly stable.[2] The extent of the uncertainty was sometimes
mitigated by a second and more stable source of revenue from rents.
Inflation had not rendered these negligible or insignificant.

Coss has shown how the vigorous lordship of the *curialis* Geoffrey
de Langley 'revolutionized' the position of the tenantry at Stivichall
so that villein rents (in 1279) averaged out at 20s per virgate.[3]
Unfortunately, since there is virtually no evidence as to what rents
and services were in Oxfordshire knightly manors before 1279, there
is little certain proof of increased impositions. However in 1279 the
rents or the value of rents and services in nine manors belonging to
descendants of the 1220s knights exceeded or (in one case) equalled
the Stivichall figure. These manors were held by eight families, two
from group one, three from group two, two from group three and
one from group four.[4] In two manors rents, or rents and services,
were valued at between 15s and 20s per virgate,[5] and in eight more at
between 10s and 15s.[6] In three cases there is evidence of a shift from
works to rents. Probably, in the process, heavier burdens were imposed on the peasantry. At Rycote and Whitehill this took place on
the manors of single-manor families. In 1279 Rycote's nine and a half
virgates of villeinage gave 16s per virgate; but the tenants asserted
that 'anciently' they had given 5s per annum and various services.[7]
At Whitehill in 1279 the six villein half-virgaters each worked alter-
nate days between June and Michaelmas and gave aid and 22½d rent.
In 1304, on the death of the 1279 lord Walter of Whitehill (a former
coroner), the rents of the six villein half-virgaters averaged out at
10s annum for all services.[8] Finally, at Churchill in 1279 the
twenty-seven villein virgaters gave 1s 6d per annum rent and various
services – the total value of rent and services in each case was put at

1. *Fitz Nells Cartulary*, ed. Meekings, Shearman, p. xii; *CIPM*, vi. no. 123.
2. Postan, *The Medieval Economy and Society*, p. 234; once prices became more stable it was safer, of course, to lease property.
3. Coss, p. 15.
4. Group One: Shotteswell (fitz Guy); Stoke Goldington (Hastings), *RH*, p. 347. Group two: Sarsden (Golafre), pp. 729-30; Wheatfield, pp. 788, 817-18; Standlake (Mauduit), p. 702. Group three: Checkendon, Stoke (Marmion), p. 779; Shotteswell (Waundard). Group four: Haddon, p. 691. For Shotteswell, P.R.O. E 164/15, fos. 121ᵛ, 122.
5. Black Bourton (Mauduit), *RH*, p. 695; Rycote, p. 757.
6. Mursley, Salden (fitz Nigel), *RH*, pp. 335-6; Yelford (Hastings), p. 698; Asterley, Salford (Williamscot), pp. 734, 728 9; Newton Purcel, pp. 834-5; Tiddington (fitz Ellis), p. 714; Chastleton, p. 729.
7. *RH*, p. 757.
8. *RH*, pp. 857-8; P.R.O. C 133/111/16.

7s 1d. In 1298, on the death of Roger de Noers II, the twenty-five villein virgaters each gave 15s per annum for all services. The Noers were apparently as successful in increasing the burdens of their peasants as they were in expanding the area of their demesnes. Roger de Noers I (ob. 1292) left over £100 deposited for safe keeping in Osney abbey.[1]

With their many manors and large demesnes great barons and ecclesiastical institutions were perhaps the best placed to take advantage of the demesne farming of the thirteenth century. In this respect they had potential (which may or may not have been realized) to become more powerful relative to the knightly class. Perhaps the balance was reversed in the later Middle Ages when conditions favoured the gentry as against the larger landowners.[2] But this does not mean the gentry fared badly in the earlier period, and became easy prey. Whether within most knightly manors a major shift took place from rents to demesne farming between the twelfth and thirteenth centuries is difficult to say. Perhaps the demesne had always produced a significant slice of income, and the transition was one of degree rather than of kind.[3] If a major shift was necessary the period *circa* 1180–1220 probably required some care and enterprise from the gentry, especially as it coincided with a time of heavy financial pressure from the government. But many families made the transition with success. In the reign of Henry III, living off fixed and outdated rents may explain the difficulties of some individuals, but it hardly seems a reason 'why such a cross-section of the knightly class was affected' (by a crisis). On the contrary, the ability to maintain or develop demesnes of two hides supports the idea that the material position of many knightly families was potentially sound.

This view is reinforced by consideration of those families which did encounter serious material difficulties. Some, as has been mentioned, had small or non-existent demesne farms; but this was far from universally the case. The difficulties of several families seem to have had little to do with the crisis which Coss diagnoses. The Fritwells, Parles and Hamptons all had manors with two or more hides in demesne. The le Poures had six hides of demesne.[4] The immediate causes of distress were sometimes factors which were scarcely singular to the thirteenth century. Of particular importance was the high cost of litigation, and its consequences when unsuccessful. The 'great need' of Emma fitz Ellis was specifically the 'seeking of her inheritance'. The Fritwells and Rokeles were also engaged in

---

1. *RH*, p. 745; P.R.O. C13/85/1; *COA*, iii. 90.

2. Postan, *Cambridge Economic History of Europe*, i. 595–600.

3. For the contrast between the centuries see E. Miller, 'England in the Twelfth and Thirteenth Centuries: An Economic Contrast?', *Econ. Hist. Rev.*, 2nd ser., xxiv (1971), 1–14.

4. *RH*, pp. 693, 728, 835, 858–9; P.R.O. C 132/12/4. In 1279 some of these manors were leased; see above p. 362, n. 1, p. 369, n. 3.

extensive litigation.[1] In part this was aggressive – the pursuit of alluring if elusive claims to property – and was perhaps encouraged by the inflation. But it was also defensive – the product of uncertain right to land, and divisive family suits and settlements.[2] Hardest to identify and to estimate is the personal factor. 'The waste of a decent patrimony by an improvident [lord]' (like a long law suit) could prove fatal sooner or later in any age.[3] When Walter of Henley dolefully reflected on how men fell little by little into poverty and misery, it was largely on personal failings that he dwelt. 'Yowe see a sorte of men which have landes and tenementes and yet they be not able to lyve and whye? I wille telle youe, bycause that they lyve without setting downe any order at alle, and without making any provision before hande and doe dispend and waste more than theire landes be woorthe yearely . . . It is sayed to theire reproofe in Inglishe: He that wylle him further stretche than his blanket wille retche he into the chaffe must his feet stretche'.[4] Several Oxfordshire families may have fallen victim to such courses of incompetence and extravagance. Of course personal weaknesses are inseparable from the social and economic climate to which they are allied, and by which they may be aggravated; but once the degree of aggravation in the thirteenth century is considered, the view of Walter of Henley seems to some extent appropriate to the knightly class. The material position of the 'sorte of men' he characterized was potentially secure – they had lands and tenements. Failure to capitalize on them was a matter of ridicule and reproof.

The stress that has been laid on the round of manorial exploitation and improvement should not obscure the fact that, in the pursuit of prosperity, knightly families were not confined to such unspectacular activities. In addition they could accept employment, they could acquire new manors. The marriage, early in the century, which established Robert Mauduit and his descendants as leading Oxfordshire knights, was Robert's reward for his faithful service to King John's great minister, William Brewer.[5] Later in the century Fulk of Rycote, and two generations of Damories, entered the service of the earls of Cornwall. Robert Damory (1281–5) was granted a substantial property by the earl.[6] The most lucrative place of patronage was, of course, the king's court. It was not till the early fourteenth century

---

1. *Pipe Roll 1 John*, pp. 118–19; for the Fritwells see above p. 362, n. 1; for the Rokeles see *CRR*, vi. pp. xiii–xvi; *Feet of Fines Essex*, i, ed. R. E. G. Kirk (Essex Archaeological Soc., 1899), 35, 45, 95, 102.

2. For family settlements see, King, *ubi supra*, pp. 46–47.

3. E. Gibbon, *Autobiography* (Everyman edn., 1911), p. 125; see also pp. 88, 138. In Oxfordshire the properties husbanded and extended by the Quatremains for over three hundred years were finally dissipated in the early sixteenth century by the 'very onfrith' Sir Richard Fowler; W. F. Carter, *The Quatremains of Oxfordshire* (Oxford, 1936), p. 55.

4. *Walter of Henley*, ed. Oschinsky, pp. 309–11.

5. *Pipe Roll 1 John*, p. 282; *RLC*, i. 282; see above p. 361, n. 9.

6. *SC*, no. 27; *CPR 1247–58*, p. 589; *CIPM*, iii. 485–6.

that a family from the group – Damory – arrived there. But as many as thirty-two families had representatives employed in local government at some time in the thirteenth or early fourteenth centuries; twenty-four as sheriffs, coroners or forest officials,[1] the rest on *ad hoc* commissions.[2] The value of such employment is impossible to calculate. Some people positively sought exemption from it. Occasionally it could have highly unpleasant consequences. Yet it is unlikely that generations of Whitehills, Foliots, Rycotes, Pains, Fifields, Coombes, Sarsdens and le Moynes (all one-manor families) would have acted as coroners or forest officials had it been unprofitable.

During the course of the thirteenth century over twenty-five manors were acquired by thirteen families. Most of these went to families in groups one and two. Virtually all the manors came from other members of the knightly class, eleven of them by marriage; several were inherited through the extinction of other branches of the same family, or were secured from other branches by litigation. These acquisitions do not, therefore, suggest any overall increase in the land held by the gentry. But the provenance of the gains hardly affects the material success of the families which made them. It may indicate that gentry property was passing into fewer hands, although this process was limited by family settlements.[5] None of the families bought a manor outright, but considerable sums – sometimes well over 100 marks – were spent buying or securing claims to land, and purchasing wardships.[4] It is true that these sums are small compared with those expended by ambitious *curiales*. Between 1237 and 1261 the king's attorney, Laurence de Broke, spent over 650 marks on

1. Sheriffs: fitz Guy (Guy fitz Robert); Damory; Rycote; Williamscot; Cruce (Surrey); Mauduit (Wilts); Purcel; *PRO Lists and Indexes*, ix. 107–8, 135, 152; Coroners: Noers; Marmion; Whitehill; Quatremain; Coombe; Foliot; Waundard; Haddon; Salceto; fitz Guy; Rycote; P.R.O. Just 1/695, m. 20; Just 1/700, m. 1; Just 1/701, m. 19; Just 1/703, m. 1; Just 1/710, m. 32; *CR 1227–31*, p. 488; *CR 1234–37*, p. 128; *CCR 1296–1302*, p. 235. Forest officials: Hastings; Wheatfield; Golafre; Forester; le Moyne; Fifield; Pain; Sarsden; Coombe; *Pipe Roll 10 John*, pp. 138–9; *14 Henry III*, p. 247; *CR 1231–4*, p. 96; *56–59*, p. 20; *CAE*, ii. 209, 211–12; P.R.O. E 32/137, ms. 3d, 7, 8; E 32/251, ms. 4, 5.

2. Fitz Oger; le Poure; Finmere; Sandford; Bigstrup; Lisle; Chastleton; Wace; *PR 1225–32*, pp. 221, 518; *PW*, I, i. 708; *CAE*, ii. 169; P.R.O. C 66/14, m. 4d.

3. For acquisitions and family settlements see above p. 361, n. 9, p. 362, n. 1, p. 364, n. 3. For marriage see K. B. McFarlane, *The Nobility of Later Medieval England*, p. 59.

4. Group two: Williamscot: 180 marks, 150 marks (1281, 1293); Noers: 144 marks (1267, 1278, 1286) – with over 150 marks deposited at Osney abbey; fitz Ellis: 94 marks (1194–1230); le Poure: 40 marks, 60 marks (1253, 1280); Rokele: 102 marks (1205, 1210, 1228, 1232); Golafre: 20 marks (1285). Group three: Marmion: 130 marks (1246); Barton: 80 marks (1229); Rycote: 50 marks (1200); Gernon: 22 marks (1234–55), 15 marks (1299); Waundard: 34 marks (1272). *CCR 1279–88*, p. 178; P.R.O. CP 25(1)/188(12)/1; Bedfordshire County Record Office, County Hall Bedford, GA 95, no. lxiv; *FFO*, pp. 209, 224, 166, 216, 132, 85, 12, 92, 94, 171, 201; *COA*, iii. 90; v. 419–20; *BC*, pp. 16, 23; *Fines Wilts*, p. 45. For the fitz Ellises and Rokeles see above p. 361, n. 9, p. 362, n. 1. Some of the expenditure listed in this note was incurred in the course of family settlements.

property in Oxfordshire.[1] Equally, the individual acquisitions of knightly families cannot compare with the 'fifteen manors and lands and fifteen and a half advowsons' obtained by Walter de Merton between 1240 and 1277.[2] Yet the fact that others did better does not mean that the gentry did badly. A significant group of knightly families was strengthened by the acquisition of new manors. A larger number at some time enjoyed the advantages of office. In these ways the basic security derived from at least one manor of reasonable size could be consolidated.

IV

This paper has been based on the study of a solitary group of knights and their families, and it is natural to wonder how representative that group is. One problem obviously concerns the fourteen knights whose properties cannot be traced. Some perhaps were younger sons with life interests in their lands; some may have held small amounts of land, and been in an equivalent position to the knights in group four above. Families may also have disappeared through failure of heirs. It seems unlikely that many of the fourteen can have been lords of manors of any size who were forced to 'sell up' through financial difficulty. If they had been, especially if they had 'sold up' to religious houses, some record would probably have been left of the transactions.

The group may have a bias in favour of the more active 1220s knights, who were most likely to be chosen for assizes. But neither the significance nor the size of this bias should be exaggerated. Prominence in local affairs and government depended, in part at least, on inclination and ability, and thus tended to even itself out among the knightly class of a county in the course of a century. Even the families which produced generations of local officials went through long periods when they did not hold office. Moreover, although some of the 1220s knights were extremely busy in local affairs this was far from being universally the case. Over half, as far as is known, were not employed in local government. On the other hand, some prominent 1220s knights escape inclusion in the groups examined above altogether, because for one reason or another they do not appear on assizes.

There is clearly a distinction to be made in the thirteenth century between areas of England where lordship was strong and aggressive, and where it was not.[3] If Oxfordshire had been a county with large rather than medium-sized religious houses, perhaps more families

1. *FFO*, pp. 102, 112, 121, 123-4, 127, 151, 157-8, 188; BM Harl. Ch. 84, D. 55. See *VCH*, vi. 118; *CPR 1232-47*, p. 507.
2. *The Early Rolls of Merton College Oxford*, ed. J. R. L. Highfield (Oxford Hist. Soc., new ser., xviii, 1964), p. 41.
3. King, *ubi supra*, p. 49.

would have come under pressure and lost their lands. But the county was hardly unique in lacking a great house. Neighbouring Warwickshire was in a similar position.[1] Moreover, the number of families which a great house would put under pressure was not very large. It has been calculated that in the two centuries after 1086 Peterborough abbey recovered only 10 per cent of the land alienated after the Norman Conquest to its 'knights' – in all, just under five fees.[2] Dr King, who has studied the Peterborough evidence, concludes that while the great landowners were an important element in the thirteenth-century land market, 'certainly it is doubtful whether this shows the decline of a [knightly] "class" '.[3] How active was the trade in knightly properties? Coss himself makes the significant observation that entire manors can have come onto the market 'only sporadically'.[4]

The arguments advanced above have been largely based on families which held manors containing upwards of three hides of land. Indeed, the great majority of those in groups one to three held considerably more land than that.[5] However, in thirteenth-century England (given a virgate of twenty-five or thirty acres) there were numerous manors which contained little more than two hides of land. Kosminsky calculates that 65 per cent of all the manors in the hundred rolls contained under 500 acres. The average size of these manors was only 224 acres. There were fewer small manors in Oxfordshire, where the average sized lay manor was 575 acres, than there were in Cambridgeshire, where the average was only 368 acres.[6] Whether the position of families which held single small manors was unsound is unclear. Account should be taken of Kosminsky's finding that the smaller the manor, the greater was the size of the demesne. Kosminsky argues that it was precisely lords of small manors who were most concerned with 'the extraction of the greatest possible amount of revenue by producing for the market'.[7] Moreover, many lords of small manors may have been descendants of the professional fighting knights of the eleventh and twelfth centuries. Dr Harvey has shown that at the time of Domesday Book these knights usually held between one and two hides of land. They, and perhaps their descendants, even if they became lords of manors, may have made no claims to exalted social status.[8]

1. Coss, p. 19.
2. King, *ubi supra*, p. 48.
3. *Ibid.*, p. 50.
4. Coss, p. 20.
5. Of the twenty-five one manor families fourteen (largely on the basis of 1279 evidence) had manors of four or more hides. Three more held additional property of at least a hide.
6. Kosminsky, pp. 96–98.
7. *Ibid.*, p. 277.
8. S. Harvey, *ubi supra*, pp. 3–43. Lords of small manors and the many free tenants with one or two hides of land should probably be discussed together.

The chosen group of families is unrepresentative of the knightly class as a whole in one final respect. The group cannot provide an opportunity to study the new families which ascended into the ranks of the gentry, and were sometimes among its most prominent and prosperous representatives. As a result, this article may have underestimated the material well-being of the knightly class. In Oxfordshire the Louches and Adderburies rose from the ranks of the free tenants. Sometimes new families came from more unlikely quarters. The descendants of such hated foreign *curiales* as Falkes de Bréauté, Matthias Becille and Imbert Pugeis were all county knights, and accepted members of local society. The effect of Imbert's career was to bring land from the king's demesne into the hands of the gentry.[1]

How far examination of knightly families in other counties will reveal patterns similar to those found in Oxfordshire remains to be seen. Certainly the surviving non-Oxfordshire hundred rolls show many gentry manors with more than one hide in demesne.[2] Interest also attaches to Dr J. E. Newman's recent study of the traffic in thirteenth-century Yorkshire in advowsons which belonged to knightly families. In terms of their possession of advowsons, Newman's sixteen families of the 'highest level' roughly maintained their positions. Most had descendants summoned as peers to parliament in the fourteenth century. Of the eighty-two families below the highest level, thirty-one kept their advowsons. They went on to become members of the Yorkshire gentry of the fourteenth century. Fifty-one families disposed of advowsons. But in some cases these were the alienations of stable or prospering families.[3] Newman concludes that 'the number of distressed sellers is not large'.[4]

In any county in the thirteenth century there were obviously knightly families which suffered financial strangulation and material collapse. What is difficult to reconcile with a crisis which affected the whole knightly class and was 'severe' or 'prolonged and extensive' is the fact that there were also families (probably a much larger number) which either increased their properties in the thirteenth century, or at least retained their existing manors in reasonable condition. In Oxfordshire the underlying material position of many middling and upper knightly families seems secure. This view is confirmed by study of how such families responded to the social and economic conditions of the period, particularly the exigencies of demesne farming. There seems no reason why these conditions need

1. *VCH*, vi. 197; *CR 1261–64*, pp. 343, 381; P.R.O. Just 1/701, m. 9; *VCH*, vii. 9; 689, 750; *Cal. Charter Rolls*, i. 235; *PW*, I, i. 788; *RH*, pp. 699, 700; *CAE*, i. 328. For the Adderburies see above p. 352. For the Louches see *VCH*, v. 49, 51, 110; vii. 7, 11, 143 (references which could be greatly amplified).

2. *RH*, pp. 321–33 (Beds); 334–55 (Bucks); 356–590 (Camb); 591–687 (Hunts); P.R.O. E 164/15 (Warw).

3. J. E. Newman, 'Greater and Lesser Landowners and Parochial Patronage: Yorkshire in the Thirteenth Century', *EHR*, xcii. 305–7.

4. *Ibid.*, p. 301.

have forced a whole class into crisis. Were it possible, moreover, to diagnose the material health of the gentry at any one time in the century – rather than looking at it over the period as a whole – one would probably always find a crisis less of a class than of some individuals within it. Here a relevant fragment of evidence comes from the 1256 county by county returns of those eligible for knighthood through having a knight's fee or £15 per annum. The sheriff of an unidentifiable county noted that one man had a knight's fee 'sed est pauper', and another £15 per annum 'sed est pauper in magno debito'. These two were out of a total of twenty-four listed in the county as qualified for the honour.[1] Presumably the sheriff considered that the financial situation of the great majority of the potential knights was reasonably solvent. Yet this was at a time when, so it is suggested, the crisis of the knightly class was approaching its height. In overall terms the gentry almost certainly lost property to religious institutions in the thirteenth century, but this loss was scarcely heavy enough to threaten the position of more than a minority of the class. The gentry could obtain land from free tenants, from the baronage and from the king.

The thirteenth century is frequently portrayed as a period in which the peasantry suffered from increasingly harsh economic conditions. As the population grew, so did the number of small holders whose land was less than that needed for subsistence.[2] If knightly families, along with religious houses and great magnates, had the power to increase villein services this gloomy picture is compounded. Equally, manorial lords, intent on increasing their demesnes, may have bullied small free tenants to sell property. It may well have been the weakest sections of society, the villeins and small free tenants. who bore the brunt of rising prices in the thirteenth century.[3]

The financial difficulties of individual knightly families might certainly have important political consequences. Although the proportion of embittered debtors among Simon de Montfort's followers is unknown, there is no doubt that a significant number owed money to the Jews.[4] But how large a party did Simon have within the gentry? Coss believes that the 'reformist earls' received 'widespread support' from the knightly class.[5] But was this true of the whole period 1258–65? The gentry resented the way Henry III ran local government. Probably the early stages of the reform movement in 1258–9

1. P.R.O. C 47/1(1), m. 29.
2. J. Z. Titow, *English Rural Society*, ch. III.
3. On the other hand some villeins, and small free tenants acquired property; E. King, *Peterborough Abbey 1086–1310* (Cambridge, 1973), ch. VI; W. G. Hoskins, H. P. R. Finberg, *Devonshire Studies* (London, 1952), pp. 127–8.
4. Coss, pp. 31–4. In Oxfordshire the affairs of Robert fitz Nigel who was on the baronial side at Evesham seem in a prosperous condition; *Fines Bucks*, p. 104; P.R.O. C 47/1(1), m. 1; see also *Fitz Nells Cartulary*, ed. Meeking, Shearman, pp. lxxiii, xci–ii; *Early Rolls of Merton College*, ed. Highfield, pp. 28, 81, 104, 108, 114.
5. Coss, p. 34.

were generally welcomed. But the mood may have changed once involvement with the baronial cause meant rebellion. A detailed study of the knights in this period has been made by Dr C. H. Knowles. Knowles questions whether de Montfort retained the allegiance of the knightly class in 1264–5. Of the 150 knights appointed (in panels of four per county) to investigate grievances in 1258 the 'overwhelming bulk' seem to have disappeared thereafter from public life. The great majority of them refused to translate any sympathy for Simon into succour for his cause – or at least succour blatant enough to incur the displeasure of the king's party. The degree of sympathy itself is open to question since two thirds of the twenty-five knights whose stand in 1265 is known sided with the king.[1] If the knightly class was convulsed at this time by economic crisis, and inflamed by the 'horrors of debt' this apathy or caution seems strange. But it sits well with the picture of the class presented in this article. Many gentry lords had satisfactory material prospects. They would not risk them by rebellion. They were not desperate men. In this economic environment the cause of Simon de Montfort could only have a limited appeal.

The general recognition of the importance of the knightly class in the thirteenth century is explained by its power. That was the basic reason why it was courted by reformist earls and Edward I. The power derived from the large amount of land held by the class, whether or not that amount was diminishing. There is a good case for saying that it also stemmed from an economic climate which enabled many better endowed knightly families to preserve or amplify their material strength.

---

1. C. H. Knowles, ' "The Disinherited" 1265–80' (Univ. Wales Ph.D. thesis, 1959), part ii, pp. 81–2; see also part i, pp. 6–16. Of the twenty-nine knights associated with grand assize juries on the Hilary 1261 Oxfordshire eyre only five or six seem to have been associated with the rebels in 1264–5. (Materials which would reveal active support for de Montfort are fairly abundant); P.R.O. Just 1/701, ms. 3, 9. E. F. Jacob, *Studies in the Period of Baronial Reform and Rebellion* (Oxford, 1925), p. 298 observes that in Suffolk the proportion of manors of rebels to estates of loyal subjects 'will not be recognised as large'.

19

The Beginnings of Parliament

In November 1295 King Edward I assembled a parliament at Westminster. Looking back from the nineteenth century, in the pages of his great *Constitutional History of England*, William Stubbs[1] considered this to have been 'a model assembly . . . serving as a pattern for all future assemblies of the nation'. It was so because it 'fixed finally' the right of shire and borough representatives to attend parliament and thus ensured the future of the House of Commons. Thereafter, Stubbs affirmed, no assembly which did not conform to the model of 1295, was entitled to the name and authority of parliament.[2] Stubbs's 'Model Parliament' (it is so named in one of those marginal headings which ease one's passage through *The Constitutional History*) captured the imagination of the Victorian public.[3] Its subsequent history has mirrored the decline and fall of the self-confident age which gave it birth: first respectful qualification;[4] then contemptuous contradiction;[5] finally, as a serious academic argument, virtual extinction.[6] Whatever the rights and wrongs of Stubbs's model, and to these we will return, he was unquestionably right to see parliament in general and the commons in particular as creatures of the thirteenth century. It is with the development of parliament in the thirteenth century that the following pages are concerned.[7]

---

[1] *The Constitutional History of England in its Origin and Development*, to give the work its full title, was first published by Oxford University Press in three volumes between 1874 and 1878, and ran through many subsequent editions. The individual volumes went into new editions at different times and three-volume sets were often made up from different editions. In my own set, which appears to have been together throughout its life, volume I is from the fifth edition of 1891, volume II from the fourth edition, reprinted, of 1906, and volume three from the fifth edition of 1903. For a different combination see H.G. Richardson and G.O. Sayles, *The Governance of Mediaeval England* (Edinburgh, 1963), p. 491. In this chapter all references are to volume II of the fourth edition, reprinted, of 1906.

[2] Stubbs, *Constitutional History*, pp. 134, 235–6. Other relevant passages are on pp. 248, 266, 305.

[3] Ibid., pp. 133, 236.

[4] C.H. Jenkinson, 'The First Parliament of Edward I', *Eng. Hist. Rev.*, 25 (1910), 282–3. For F.W. Maitland, see below pp. 387,406.

[5] This reaches a climax in H.G. Richardson and G.O. Sayles, 'Parliaments and Great Councils in Medieval England', *Law Quarterly Review*, 77 (1961), reprinted as chapter 26 of their *English Parliament in the Middle Ages* (London, 1981).

[6] For example, M. Prestwich, *Edward I* (London, 1988), p. 441.

[7] The secondary literature on the subject is gigantic and I have made no comprehensive at-

In November 1236 King Henry III adjourned a law case to the 'parliament' which was to meet at Westminster in the following January.[8] This is the first 'official' use of the term parliament, 'official' because it appears in a government record, in fact in the rolls of the court of king's bench. A good deal is known about the ensuing assembly. It passed legislation, confirmed Magna Carta, voted taxation and, as we have seen, heard law cases. It was attended by the king, his councillors and large numbers of lay and ecclesiastical magnates.[9] But, as far as is known, there were no representatives from the shires and boroughs.[10] There was, in short, no embryonic House of Commons.

After 1237 both government records and monastic chronicles bestow the term 'parliament' with increasing frequency on assemblies of this kind, a usage both sanctioned and reinforced by the Provisions of Oxford in 1258, which called for regular meetings of parliament 'to review the state of the realm and to deal with the common business of the realm and of the king together'.[11]

In origin the word 'parliament', in French *parlement*, in Latin *parliamentum*, simply meant 'discussion', a usage which easily expanded to describe the assembly in which the discussion took place.[12] When the word first appears in England in the 1230s and 1240s, it was, up to a point, simply a new word for an old institution. From the earliest times the kings of England had always as-

---

continued

tempt to cite it. Particularly valuable are E. Miller, *The Origins of Parliament* (Historical Association pamphlet, London 1960); P. Spufford, *Origins of the English Parliament* (London, 1967), with translated sources; G.O. Sayles, *The King's Parliament of England* (London, 1975); H.G. Richardson and G.O. Sayles, *The English Parliament in the Middle Ages* (London, 1981) (their collected essays); M. Prestwich, *English Politics in the Thirteenth Century* (London, 1990), ch. 8 'Parliament and Community'; and the essays by various scholars in E.B. Fryde and E. Miller, ed., *Historical Studies of the English Parliament: Origins to 1399* (Cambridge, 1970), and R.G. Davies and J.H. Denton, ed., *The English Parliament in the Middle Ages: A Tribute to J.S. Roskell* (Manchester, 1981). G.O. Sayles, *The Functions of the Medieval Parliament of England* (London, 1988), brings together a large amount of source material in translation for the years 1258 to 1348. E.B. Fryde, D.E. Greenway, S. Porter and I. Roy, ed., *Handbook of British Chronology* (Royal Historical Soc., London, 1986), p. 533 onwards has a detailed list of parliaments and related assemblies from 1216.

[8] *Curia Regis Rolls* (London, 17 vols., 1922–91), xv, no. 2047. See H.G. Richardson and G.O. Sayles, 'The Earliest Known Official Use of the Term "Parliament"', *Eng. Hist. Rev.*, 82, (1967), 747–50.

[9] *Curia Regis Rolls*. xv, p. lvi note 5, p. lvii note 1; H.R. Luard, ed., *Matthaei Parisiensis . . . Chronica Majora* (Rolls Ser, London, 7 vols., 1884–9), iii, 380–4.

[10] I have used 'borough' by itself throughout this essay, although the town representatives were summoned both from boroughs' and from 'cities' (like London).

[11] Some of the chronicle references are usefully brought together in W. Stubbs, ed., *Select Charters*, ninth edn. revised throughout by H.W.C. Davis (Oxford, 1913), pp. 328–30 (all subsequent references to *Select Charters* are to this edition). For references to parliament in royal letters, see for example *Close Rolls, 1237–1242*, p. 447; *Close Rolls, 1247–1251*, pp. 104, 107, 109; *Close Rolls, 1253–4*, p. 43. For the Provisions of Oxford: R.F. Treharne and I.J. Sanders, ed., *Documents of the Baronial Movement of Reform and Rebellion* (Oxford, 1973), pp. 110–11 no. 21.

[12] H.G. Richardson, 'The Origins of Parliament', *Trans. Roy. Hist. Soc.*, 4th ser., 11 (1928), 137–49, reprinted in revised form as chapter 1 in Richardson and Sayles, *The English Parliament in the Middle Ages*.

sembled their great men to discuss the affairs of the realm. Under the Norman and Angevin kings such gatherings had been called 'councils' or 'great councils' and under the Anglo-Saxon kings they had been called 'witans'.[13] In this perspective, it was the Venerable Bede who described the earliest parliamentary debate: that in the royal hall in Northumbria between King Edwin and his priests and thegns over whether to embrace Christianity.[14]

This, however, is only part of the story. The word parliament was also used in the thirteenth century to describe an assembly which was changing fast and fundamentally both in terms of form and function. It was not merely, therefore, the name which was new. In many ways it was the institution itself. In discussing these changes we will look first at function and then at form.

Stubbs took it for granted that the essential purpose of parliament was to discuss the great affairs of the realm. A totally different view was advanced by two of the most learned, irascible and heterodox historians of the last generation, H.G. Richardson and G.O. Sayles: 'We would, however, assert that parliaments are of one kind only and that, when we have stripped every non-essential away, the essence of them is the dispensing of justice by the king or by someone who in a very special sense represents the king'.[15] Richardson and Sayles, in their extremist way, were wrong to stress the judicial role of parliament to the disadvantage of everything else ('the non-essentials'),[16] but they were right to grasp that the dispensation of justice, largely in the form of the hearing of petitions from the king's subjects, had played a vital part in parliament's development. By the end of the thirteenth century it was central to its activities. Take the parliament which Edward I held at Westminster between February and April 1305. Before it met, Edward called for petitions to be presented at the parliament and set up special committees to hear them. The result was that individuals and institutions presented 133 petitions which took up four-fifths of the parliament roll, the official record of the parliament's busi-

[13] H.R. Loyn, *The Governance of Anglo-Saxon England, 500–1087* (London, 1984), pp. 100–6.

[14] B. Colgrave and R.A.B. Mynors, ed., *Bede's Ecclesiastical History of the English People* (Oxford, 1969), pp. 182–7.

[15] H.G. Richardson and G.O. Sayles, 'The Parliaments of Edward I' *Bull. Inst. Hist. Res.,* 5 (1927–8), 133, reprinted with the same pagination as chapter 5 of their *English Parliament in the Middle Ages.* The statement was reiterated in their 'Parliaments and Great Councils in Medieval England', *English Parliament in the Middle Ages,* chapter 26, p. 6.

[16] To be fair, they completely accepted that legislation, taxation and the discussion of great affairs could take place in parliament, but argued that, unlike the dispensation of justice, these could equally take place in other assemblies, notably 'great councils'. Hence the dispensation of justice was parliament's 'essence' in the sense of 'distinctive quality'. See their 'Parliaments and Great Councils in Medieval England', *English Parliament in the Middle Ages,* chapter 26, p. 6 onwards. It is far from clear, however, that the dispensation of justice was parliament's 'essence' in the years when the name was becoming established; see below p. 384. For criticisms of Richardson and Sayles, see particularly J.G. Edwards, '"Justice" in Early English Parliaments', *Bull. Inst. Hist. Res.,* 27 (1954) reprinted in Fryde and Miller, ed., *Historical Studies of the English Parliament,* pp. 279–97, to which all subsequent references refer.

ness.[17] The tract the *Modus Tenendi Parliamentum* ('How to Hold a Parliament'), written in the early fourteenth century, even claimed that the assembly could not be dissolved so long as any petition remained unanswered; otherwise the king would be in breach of his coronation oath to dispense justice to everyone.[18] Likewise, one reason why the reforming Ordinances of 1311 called for regular parliaments was so that petitions could be determined along with a range of other judicial business.[19] This judicial aspect of parliament was well summarised by *Fleta*, a legal treatise written about 1300: 'there [in parliament] doubts are determined regarding judgements, new remedies are devised for wrongs newly brought to light, and there also is justice dispensed to everyone according to his deserts'.[20]

By 1300, therefore, the dispensation of justice was a primary feature of parliament's activities. This was due to developments which had taken place during the course of the century. Of course, great assemblies had always determined difficult and important law suits. What was new in the thirteenth century was the use of parliament to hear petitions from the king's subjects on a regular basis. There is no indication that the first assemblies called parliaments in the 1230s, 1240s and 1250s were used in this way. Nor indeed did the reformers in 1258 envisage such a role for the parliaments they wished to meet thrice annually. Rather, they set up a single official, the justiciar, who was to tour the country and 'do right to all persons'.[21] All this changed, as J.R. Maddicott has shown, early in the reign of Edward I. From the late 1270s Edward positively encouraged his subjects to present petitions to parliament. Sixty-one were presented to the parliament of 1278, their diverse form being testimony to the novelty of the procedure.[22] Two years later the pressure of hearing petitions at parliament was already prompting steps to reduce or share the burden. Edward I ordered the chancery, exchequer and justices to dispose of all they could directly; only those which 'be so great or are matters of grace' were to come before the king and his council in parliament.[23]

In opening up parliament to petitions, Edward was meeting a very real so-

---

[17] *Cal. Chancery Warrants, 1244–1326* (London, 1927), p. 246; F.W. Maitland, ed., *Memoranda de Parliamento Records of the Parliament Holden at Westminster . . . 1305* (Rolls Ser., London, 1893), pp. 3–320.

[18] N. Pronay and J. Taylor, ed., *Parliamentary Texts of the Later Middle Ages* (Oxford, 1980), pp. 90, 114 (cap. 24). For a useful discussion the debate surrounding the date and background of the *Modus*, see M. Prestwich, 'The *Modus Tenendi Parliamentum*', *Parliamentary History: A Yearbook*, 1 (1982), 221–5. In places the tract is more a work of opinion than of fact.

[19] H. Rothwell, ed., *English Historical Documents, 1189–1327*, (London, 1973), p. 536 (cap. 29).

[20] H.G. Richardson and G.O. Sayles, ed., *Fleta*, ii (Selden Soc., 72, 1953), p. 109.

[21] Treharne and Sanders, ed., *Documents of the Baronial Movement*, pp. 202–3, cap. 6; pp. 106–7, cap. 16.

[22] J.R. Maddicott, 'Parliament and the Constituencies, 1272–1377', in Davies and Denton, ed., *The English Parliament in the Middle Ages*, p. 62. See also Sayles, *The King's Parliament of England*, pp. 76–9.

[23] Edwards, '"Justice" in Early English Parliaments', p. 284 (*Cal Close Rolls, 1272–9*, pp. 56–7). For similar filtering measures in 1305, see *Cal. Chancery Warrants, 1244–1326*, p. 246.

cial need. During the long reign of King Henry III there had been a rising tide of complaint against the oppressions of both royal and seignorial officials in the localities. At the same time, litigation had become both far more popular and far more complex. Both developments had created grievances and difficulties which only the centre could redress. Yet central government, during the same period, had become more faceless and bureaucratic. How could a person outside the charmed circle of the court open its doors? The answer became by presenting a petition to parliament. At first sight the answers given to such petitions seem disappointing, for a few embodied final decisions. The majority were posted off to the appropriate government department: the exchequer was ordered to investigate a grievance; the chancery to issue a writ to enable litigation to begin.[24] Essentially what parliament was doing was oiling the clogged, slow-turning government machine. For the majority of the king's subjects this was its most important function.

Whether Edward I took the same view is another matter. He had solicited petitions, thereby fulfilling his coronation oath to dispense justice and strengthening his kingship after a disastrous civil war. But he did not want petitions to swamp other parliamentary business, as his filtering measures of 1280 showed. He wanted, as he said on that occasion, to be free with his council 'to attend to the great affairs of his realm and of his foreign lands'.[25] Discussion of great affairs had always been one of the chief functions of national assemblies. Now, from the middle years of the thirteenth century, it gained an altogether new importance; one which gave parliament a power and a place in the political constitution which it had never enjoyed before. This was brought about by a fact, new to the thirteenth century and cental to the rest of parliamentary history, namely the king's need for taxation which only parliament could grant.

The kings of the twelfth century had been able to fight wars without any need for general taxation. The kings of the thirteenth century could not. True, the revenue of Henry III (1216–72), as indicated by the pipe roll of 1230, was some £24,000, much the same as the revenue of Henry I, as revealed by the pipe roll of 1130, had been a hundred years before.[26] Henry III, however, unlike Henry I, had no revenue from Normandy for the Duchy had been lost to the king of France in 1204. Even worse, the real value of Henry's income had

[24] This is very much the impression gained from reading through the answers to the petitions in Maitland, ed., *Memoranda de Parliamento*, pp. 5–254.

[25] Edwards, '"Justice" in Early English Parliaments', p. 284 (*Cal Close Rolls, 1272–9*, pp. 56–7). For similar filtering measures in 1305, see *Cal. Chancery Warrants, 1244–1326*, p. 246.

[26] For the 1130 revenue, see J. Green, *The Government of England under Henry I* (Cambridge, 1986), pp. 220–5. For the inflation see P.D.A. Harvey, 'The English Inflation of 1180–1220', *Past and Present*, 61 (1973), pp. 3–30, but see the reservations in J.C. Holt, 'Magna Carta, 1215–1217: The Legal and Social Context', in *Law in Mediaeval Life and Thought*, ed. E.B. King and S.J. Ridyard (Sewanee, Tn., 1990), pp. 17–18 and J.L. Bolton, 'Inflation, Economics and Politics in Thirteenth-Century England', in *Thirteenth-Century England IV: Proceedings of the Newcastle upon Tyne Conference 1991*, ed. P.R. Coss and S.D. Lloyd (Woodbridge, 1992), p. 5. The comments about the revenues under King John and in 1230, I owe to forthcoming publications by Nicholas Barratt.

been eroded by a period of slow but steady inflation since 1180. As a result his revenue in 1230 was actually worth between two and three times less than that of Henry I. The sources of revenue had also changed in a significant way. The proportion of easy, politically inoffensive income from crown lands had diminished as those lands were given away to provide patronage. More and more money had to come from politically sensitive exactions from individuals. It was, therefore, very difficult to increase income without giving political offence. This was John's situation. For a few years after 1209 he hiked his real income substantially above the level achieved by Henry I. The result was Magna Carta, for the Great Charter was above everything else an attempt to limit the money-getting activities of royal government. Mindful of the political consequences, Henry III never resorted to the methods of his father, and never achieved his levels of revenue. Edward I (1272–1307) did rather better: he was the first king to exploit the customs and make use of Italian bankers; but even Edward found that his ordinary revenues were totally inadequate to meet the cost of war on four fronts – Scotland, Wales, Flanders and Gascony – in the 1290s. The conclusion was inescapable. To fight vigorously in war and even to live amply in peace there was no substitute for general taxation.

Such taxation could take several forms but far the most lucrative was a percentage tax on movable property: essentially a tax on each individual's animals and corn. Thus the seventh of 1207 had produced £60,000; the fifteenth of 1225 £40,000; the fortieth of 1232 £16,500; and the thirtieth of 1237 £22,500.[27] The bulk of these sums had come in within a year. Extraordinary taxation, therefore, had the power, depending on its rate, of doubling, tripling or even quadrupling the king's ordinary annual revenue. The only trouble was that it could only be levied by 'common counsel' of the realm. That principle had been asserted in chapters 12 and 14 of Magna Carta in 1215. The chapters were omitted from subsequent versions of the Charter but the principle was reaffirmed by Edward I in 1297. In any case, whatever the state of the law on the subject, the practical reality was the same. No extraordinary tax could be levied without common consent. The difficulties in collecting the taxes of 1220 and 1297, which were imposed, or so it was alleged, without such consent, sufficiently proved that.[28]

For practical purposes common consent could only be given by an assembly representative in some way of the realm. But such an assembly could refuse to

---

[27] T. Duffus Hardy, ed, *Rotuli de Oblatis et Finium . . .* (Record Commission, 1837), p. 459; H. Hall, ed., *The Red Book of the Exchequer* (Rolls Ser, London, 3 vols., 1896), iii, 1064. See S.K. Mitchell, *Studies in Taxation under John and Henry III* (New Haven, 1914), pp. 91, 205, 218 (fundamental for taxation in this period) and for 1225 F.A. Cazel, 'The Fifteenth of 1225', *Bull. Inst. Hist. Res.*, 34 (1964), 67–81.

[28] See D.A. Carpenter, *The Minority of Henry III* (London, 1990), pp. 210–11; Prestwich, *Edward I*, pp. 422–5. For the importance of securing common consent in 1268 see J.R. Maddicott, 'The Crusade Taxation of 1268 and the Development of Parliament', in P.R. Coss and S.D. Lloyd, ed., *Thirteenth Century England II: Proceedings of the Newcastle upon Tyne Conference 1987* (Woodbridge, 1988), pp. 97–8.

give its consent or to give it only upon conditions. The great lever with which parliament ultimately prised power from the king had arrived. There was no steady progression in the force with which it was used. The first king who went regularly to parliament to ask for taxation was King Henry III and he was answered at once by demands every bit as revolutionary as those made in the seventeenth century. The debates between Henry and his magnates in the parliaments between 1237 and 1258 were long and acrimonious. They covered the whole theory and practice of his kingship. In 1242 a detailed record was drawn up of the reasons why taxation was refused.[29] Parliament demanded the right to chose the king's chief ministers. Henry refused to accept such damaging inroads into the customary authority of the crown. In these confrontations the very nature of parliamentary assemblies was being transformed. The king needed their co-operation in a way he had never done before; the assemblies in their turn had a power they had never before possessed. They were now at the very centre of national political life. It was a position they were never to lose.

Alongside these changes in function, there were related chages in parliament's form. The king's council emerged as its inner core. Around that core parliament developed as an assembly of the estates of the realm with representatives of the lower clergy and, more importantly of the countries and boroughs, being summoned to attend for the first time. The great magnates, of course, had always attended but the basis on which they did so was quietly redefined.

'It seemed necessary to remind readers, who are conversant with the parliaments of later days, that about the parliaments of Edward I's time there is still much to be discovered, and that should they come to the opinion that a session of the king's council is the core and essence of every *parliamentum*... they will not be departing very far from the path marked out by books that are already classical'.[30] Thus F.W. Maitland in one of those long, leisurely sentences so characteristic of his style and so permissable in the spacious age in which he lived.

Maitland's view was based on his study of the parliament of 1305 whose roll he edited. He observed that some of the king's councillors received a special summons to parliament; that many of the petitions were addressed to the king and his council;[31] and that, on 21 March, after the parliament had been in session for some three weeks, the lay and ecclesiastical magnates together with the representatives from the counties and the boroughs were allowed to go home while the 'bishops, earls, barons, justices and others who are of the coun-

---

[29] Luard, ed., *Chronica Majora*, iv, 185–7; and see Stubbs, ed., *Select Charters*, pp. 325–30.

[30] Maitland, ed., *Memoranda de Parliamento*, p. lxxxviii. (Maitland's introduction to the *Memoranda de Parliamento* is partly reprinted in Fryde and Miller, ed., *Historical Studies of the English Parliament*, pp. 91–135).

[31] Edward had specifically called for petitions 'to be presented to the king and his council at the next parliament': *Cal. Chancery Warrants, 1244–1326*, p. 246.

cil' remained. Parliament thus constituted, constituted simply as the king's council, continued in session until 7 April.[32]

Up to a point there was nothing new about this. At great assemblies since Anglo-Saxon times the king had always been surrounded by an inner core of councillors and ministers. What had changed in the thirteenth century was that the core had become both larger and more formal. In the 1190s a bench of justices had emerged at Westminster separate from the exchequer. After 1234 there were professional judges staffing the court with the king, the court of king's bench. Two years later the council appears for the first time as a formal body with a defined and limited membership bound together by oath.[33] Much remains obscure about the history of the council, notably its composition and the formality and regularity of its sessions. The sworn council of 1236 had only twelve members. The revolutionary council of 1258 had fifteen, nearly all of them important lay and ecclesiastical magnates. The council under Edward I seems to have been considerably larger than this, for it contained, alongside great magnates, a large official element: the chancellor; the keeper of the wardrobe; the barons of the exchequer; the justices of the bench; and the justices of the court *coram rege*.[34] From this point of view the purpose of parliament was to assemble less 'the estates' of the realm than the diverse magnates and ministers who made up the king's council. It was that council which was at the heart of parliament's work.[35]

Chapter 14 of Magna Carta in 1215, in defining how the king should seek the common counsel of the realm, laid down that he should summon all the greater barons individually and other tenants-in-chief by a general summons through the sheriffs. Parliament, as thus conceived, was an assembly of the tenants-in-chief of the crown, dominated by the greatest of those tenants, the barons. By the end of the century the king still issued individual summonses to great men to come to parliament, but those men were no longer simply the baronial tenants-in-chief. Of the fifty-three magnates who received a personal summons to the parliament of 1295, twenty-two were outside that category.[36] For a while, after 1295, there was a great variation in the numbers of magnates summoned to parliament; but in the fourteenth century the right to a summons became the hereditary title of about seventy families.[37] A new grade had been created within the nobility: the parliamentary peerage.

---

[32] Maitland, ed., *Memoranda de Parliamento*, pp. xxxv-xlvii, cvi-cix.

[33] H.R. Luard, ed, *Annales Monastici* (Rolls Ser., London, 5 vols., 1864-9), iii, 145-6 (where misdated).

[34] B. Wilkinson, *Studies in the Constitutional History of the Thirteenth and Fourteenth Centuries* (Manchester, 1937), pp. 146-50.

[35] For this theme see particularly J.E.A. Jolliffe, 'Some Factors in the Beginning of Parliament', *Trans. Roy. His. Soc.* 4th ser., 12 (1940), reprinted in Fryde and Miller, ed., *Historical Studies in the English Parliament*, pp. 31-69.

[36] J.E. Powell and K. Wallis, *The House of Lords in the Middle Ages* (London, 1968), p. 226.

[37] Ibid., ch. 18, but see the reservations in C. Given-Wilson, *The English Nobility in the Later Middle Ages* (London, 1987), pp. 58-66.

This transition was painless and unnoticed, not surprisingly. Essentially in the thirteenth century, as in the twelfth, the king summoned his great magnates to national assemblies. In the twelfth century those magnates were nearly all baronial tenants-in-chief. In the thirteenth century they were not. What had changed was not the nature of the summons but the definition of the aristocracy. In 1215 it was still possible to regard the aristocracy, with Magna Carta, as coterminous with the baronial tenants-in-chief. A hundred years later it was not, as the *Modus Tenendi Parliamentum* recognised when it said that earls and barons were to receive personal summonses to parliament *and also* everyone with equivalent incomes.[38] The fact was that the termination and division of baronies and the rise of non-baronial families had made the equation of the baronage with the aristocracy increasingly meaningless.

A similar process took place in respect of the ecclesiastical tenants-in-chief, a group which embraced all the bishops and significant numbers of abbots and priors.[39] These ecclesaistical barons had been entitled to a personal summons under the terms of Magna Carta. Indeed as early as 1164 the Constitutions of Clarendon had laid down that ecclesiastics who held baronies in chief must attend judgements in the king's court along with other barons.[40] Once, however, lists of ecclesiastics receiving personal summonses survive, in the second half of the thirteenth century, it is clear that these summonses no longer corresponded to any precise tenurial criteria. Some of the abbots and priors summoned were not tenants-in-chief; some abbots and priors who were tenants-in-chief were not summoned. Eventually 'a class of ecclesiastical barons "by writ" ... emerged' to mirror the parliamentary peerage.[41]

The bishops and greater abbots, whether as tenants-in-chief or not, were summoned personally to parliament. But what of the lower clergy: the deans and priors of the cathedral churches, the archdeacons and above all the parish clergy?[42] Their representatives attended parliament in 1254 and again, in all probability, in 1268 and 1269. They were certainly summoned to the parliament of 1295, as they were with increasing frequency to parliaments thereafter.[43] In terms of appearance this was an important change in the structure of

---

[38] Pronay and Taylor, ed., *Parliamentary Texts of the Later Middle Ages*, pp. 81, 104 (cap. 3).

[39] J.H. Denton, 'The Clergy and Parliament in the Thirteenth and Fourteenth Centuries', in Davies and Denton, ed., *The English Parliament in the Middle Ages*, pp. 88–108, is essential reading for this paragraph and the next section.

[40] W. Stubbs, ed., *The Historical Works of Gervase of Canterbury* (Rolls Ser., London, 2 vols., 1879–80), II, 180, cap. 11: D.C. Douglas and G.W. Greenaway, ed., *English Historical Documents, 1042–1189*, 2nd edn. (London, 1981), p. 769, cap. 11.

[41] Denton, 'The Clergy and Parliament in the Thirteenth and Fourteenth Centuries', p. 91.

[42] The whole question of clerical representation has been fully examined in J.H. Denton and J.P. Dooley, *Representatives of the Lower Clergy in Parliament, 1295–1340* (Royal Historical Society, Studies in History, 50, 1987).

[43] *Close Rolls, 1253–4*, pp. 115–16; W.E. Lunt, 'The Consent of the Lower Clergy to Taxation during the Reign of Henry III', in *Persecution and Liberty: Essays in Honour of George Lincoln Burr* (New York, 1931), pp. 142–4; Maddicott, 'The Crusade Taxation of 1268–1270', p. 117; Stubbs, ed., *Select Charters*, pp. 480–1.

parliament. It meant the attendance of twenty-three cathedral priors or deans, sixty archdeacons, twenty-three proctors chosen by the cathedral clergy and forty-two (two from each diocese) chosen by the parish clergy. By the early fourteenth century parliament was formally representative of the whole body of the English church in a way it had never been before.[44]

In the long run, by far the most important change in the structure of parliament was the attendance of representatives from the counties and the boroughs. By the end of the thirteenth century this was becoming a normal though not a universal occurrence. By then, the form of summons was fairly standard.[45] Each sheriff was to send to parliament two knights from his county and two burgesses from each of his boroughs. Since there were thirty-two counties, this meant seventy-four knights attending parliament and, on average, about eighty-six burgesses.[46] The knights were almost certainly elected in the county courts. They were to have 'full power' from the 'communities' of their counties to 'do what is ordained by common counsel' about the affairs of the kingdom.[47] There was to be no doubt, therefore, about their representative nature.

In explaining the development of parliamentary representation, we will concentrate on the knights and begin by tracing chronologically the stages through which we reach in the fourteenth century the standard form of attendance, a form in which knights were summoned (a) to parliamentary assemblies, (b) on a regular basis, (c) as representatives of their counties, and, (d) although the importance of this was not that great, with a general brief rather than one requiring their participation for just some particular purpose.[48]

In August 1212 King John ordered the sheriffs to come before him 'with six law worthy and discrete knights' from their counties 'to do what we tell them'. Next year, knights from each county (we do not know how many) were again summoned before the king, this time with four men from each county, who were 'to speak with us on the affairs of our kingdom'.[49] There is no suggestion that either the knights or the men here were to be in any way representatives of their counties. The nature of the assemblies which they attended, if they took place, is obscure.[50] None the less, these are the first known examples of

---

[44] Denton, 'The Clergy and Parliament in the Thirteenth and Fourteenth Centuries', pp. 106–8.

[45] Stubbs, ed., *Select Charters*, pp. 481–2.

[46] M. McKisack, *The Parliamentary Representation of the English Boroughs during the Middle Ages* (London, 1932), p. 11. The number of town representatives attending fluctuated.

[47] See below p. 394. There is very little evidence as to how town representatives were elected in the reign of Edward I: Mckisack, *Parliamentary Representation of the English Boroughs*, pp. 11–16. They were likewise ordered to come with full power 'for themselves and for the community of the cities and boroughs'.

[48] For what follows see particularly, J.C. Holt, 'The Prehistory of Parliament', in Davies and Denton, ed., *The English Parliament in the Middle Ages*, pp. 1–28.

[49] T. Duffus Hardy, ed., *Rotuli Litterarum Clausarum* . . . (Record Commission, 2 vols., 1833–4), I, 132; Stubbs, ed., *Select Charters*, p. 282.

[50] In 1212 it is not known whether anyone was summoned to the king apart from the knights. In 1213 we do not have the original writ of summons. What survives is a supplementary writ in which the king ordered the sheriffs to cause 'all the knights' of their counties, who had been sum-

the king summoning small numbers of knights (or in 1213 of men) from each of the counties of England to come before him at the same time. Moreover, the brief to the men in 1213 'to speak with us on the affairs of our kingdom' was very much a general one. Indeed, it almost implied, however misleadingly, that they were to participate in some kind of parliamentary debate.[51]

In 1227, by a proclamation read out in the county court, the 'knights and honest men' of each county, were to elect, in the county court, four knights to come before the king to explain 'on behalf of all the county' (*pro toto comitatu*) grievances against the sheriffs over the implementation of Magna Carta.[52] Here, for the first time, the knights were clearly representatives of their counties, chosen by the county courts. On the other hand, their brief was particular one, to give information about the Charter, and if they did appear at Westminster in October 1227, as bidden, they did not attend an assembly exactly like a later parliament, for while at least eight bishops were present, the great lay magnates were conspicuously absent.[53]

In February 1254 the sheriffs were instructed to send before the king's council after Easter two knights from each county, chosen by the county court 'in place of all and each of the county' (*vice omnium et singulorum comitatus*). The knights were to say what tax they were prepared to grant 'on behalf of everyone in the county'.[54] Representatives of the lower clergy were summoned at the same time and an official record survives of the debate 'in the parliament at Westminster' where they conceded a tax only on the most stringent conditions.[55] If the knights from the counties also attended, and there is evidence that the elections did indeed take place,[56] then this was the first time they had appeared at an assembly specifically called a parliament,[57] although it was a parliament held by the king's regents, the king himself being absent in Gascony. Apart from that, the only difference between these knights and later representatives was that they were summoned, like the knights in 1227, for a stated

continued
moned, to now come armed. The barons, however, were to come unarmed. The sheriff was also to produce the four men. See Holt, 'The Prehistory of Parliament', pp. 6–9.

[51] Why the summons to *discretos homines* (not even free men) in 1214 rather than knights? Was John attempting to reach down to sections of society below the knights? Had he some particular task in mind unsuitable for those of knightly or even of free status? Or was the writ simply loosely drafted?

[52] *Rot. Litt. Claus.*, ii, 212b-213. The gathering of 1227 followed the cancellation of a similar summons to just nine counties the year before: ibid., p. 154 (Stubbs, ed., *Select Charters*, p. 353).

[53] This is shown by the witness lists to royal charters issued in October 1227: Public Record Office, C 53/ 19, mm. 2, 1.

[54] *Close Rolls, 1253–4*, pp. 114–15 (Stubbs, ed., *Select Charters*, pp. 365–6).

[55] *Close Rolls, 1253–4*, pp. 115–16; Lunt, 'The Consent of the Lower Clergy to Taxation during the Reign of Henry III', pp. 142–3.

[56] For the knights representing Essex: *Close Rolls, 1253–4*, p. 42. For the writ to the sheriff of Hertfordshire (and Essex) Luard, ed., *Chronica Majora*, vi, 286–7.

[57] Lunt, 'The Consent of the Lower Clergy to Taxation during the Reign of Henry III', pp. 142–3. For the assembly being called a parliament in a royal letter and memorandum, see *Close Rolls, 1253–4*, p. 43; *Cal. Patent Rolls, 1247–58*, p. 370.

specific purpose (in 1227 to provide information about local grievances; in 1254 to grant a tax), whereas the later representatives were summoned more generally 'to treat' or 'to do what is ordained by common counsel' about the affairs of the realm and thus were, by implication, to take a fuller part in the affairs of the parliament. This, however, may be a distinction without a difference since, on many later occasions, the business of taxation was almost certainly the main reason for the attendance of representatives, while the knights of 1254, if, like the clerical representatives they resisted the tax (and none certainly was ever granted) were already treating of the affairs of the realm at a level far above the heads of many of their successors.[58]

In August 1258 four knights from each county were ordered to bring the king's council in October (a time when parliament was in session) the inquiries which they had carried out into local abuses. Some of these knights later received expenses for the time they spent 'before the king's council at Westminster in parliament'.[59] Again, as in 1254 and 1227, the knights were attending parliament for a specific purpose. Indeed, the parallel with 1227 is close since in both cases the knights were bringing local grievances to the centre. Again that purpose may well have taken them into discussions about the great affairs of the realm. The attendance of the knights in 1258, as in 1254 and 1227, however, was still a particular expedient. It created no feeling that representatives were a necessary or normal part of parliament. This is sufficiently proved by the way parliament was conceived in the revolutionary Provisions of Oxford in 1258. The only representative element was provided not by knights elected by the counties but by twelve *prodeshomes* chosen by the magnates, the purpose being to spare the latter the cost of coming to the three annual parliaments for which the Provisions called.[60] None the less the frequency of knightly summonses to parliaments or kindred assemblies was quickening. There had been one in the 1220s; none in the 1230s and 1240s; two in the 1250s. In the 1260s there were between three and six.[61]

In September 1261 Simon de Montfort earl of Leicester, Richard de Clare earl of Gloucester, the bishop of Worcester and other opposition nobles summoned three knghts from each county to St Albans 'to treat with them about the common affairs of the kingdom'. The king *e contra* ordered the three knights to come instead to see him at Windsor.[62] The summonses of 1261 were the first

[58] A reason why neither a lay nor clerical tax was granted was also because the emergency in Gascony for which it had been demanded was seen quickly to evaporate.

[59] Treharne and Sanders, ed., *Documents of the Baronial Movement*, pp. 112–15 (*Cal. Patent Rolls, 1247–58*, pp. 645–9); *Close Rolls, 1256–9*, pp. 332–3. See H.M. Cam, 'The Parliamentary Writ "De Expensis" of 1258', *Eng. Hist. Rev*, 46 (1931), 630–2.

[60] Treharne and Sanders, ed., *Documents of the Baronial Movement*, pp. 104–5, no. 10, pp. 110–11, nos. 5, 21, 22.

[61] The uncertainty arises in the period 1268 to 1270 for which see below.

[62] *Close Rolls, 1261–4*, p. 490 (Treharne and Sanders, ed., *Documents of the Baronial Movement*, pp. 246–9). For the king's assembly being called a parliament, see Public Record Office, SC1/7, no. 33, translated in Sayles, *The King's Parliament of England*, p. 62.

occasions since 1213 that men had been summoned from the shires with the general brief of discussing the affairs of the kingdom, though we do not know how far the knights were in any sense representatives or indeed how many actually turned up either at Windsor or St Albans.

In May 1264 Simon de Montfort defeated King Henry III at the battle of Lewes and assumed control of the government. In effect, therefore, it was Simon, in June 1264, who summoned four knights from each county 'chosen by the assent of the county court' to come on behalf of all the county (*pro toto comitatu*) to a parliament at London 'to discuss the affairs of the king and kingdom'.[63] This parliament was a landmark. It was the first occasion in which all the characteristics of the later parliamentary summons appears: the knights were representatives of their counties; they were coming to a parliament; and their brief was general not specific. Later, in December, Simon went even further. He summoned the knights again, this time two from each county, and now, in addition, he summoned burgesses: each town was to send two. The ensuing parliament, which lasted from January to March 1265, was thus the first attended by representatives from both the counties and boroughs: the House of Commons in embryo.[64]

The precedent set by the parliament of 1265 was repeated with increasing frequency, although for many years it remained the exception rather than the rule. Knights alone were probably summoned to at least two parliaments between 1268 and 1270, and knights and burgesses together to at least one.[65] Both were summoned to the first parliament of Edward I in 1275.[66] All told, in Edward's reign, between 1272 and 1307, knights and burgesses were summoned to thirteen of the fifty to sixty parliaments and knights alone to another four.[67] The pace quickened markedly after 1294. Knights alone, or knights and burgesses together, were summoned to four of the eight parliaments held between 1294 and 1297. Of the nine parliaments held between 1300 and 1307 knights and burgesses were present at seven.[68] Their attendance was becoming the rule: the *Modus Tenendi Parliamentum* took it for granted, along with that of the lower clergy. Indeed, the *Modus* asserted that in all things 'which

[63] Treharne and Sanders, ed., *Documents of the Baronial Movement*, pp. 290–3 (*Cal. Patent Rolls, 1258–66*, p. 360).

[64] *Close Rolls, 1264–8*, pp. 84–7, 89, 96, 98–9 (Treharne and Sanders, ed., *Documents of the Baronial Movement*, pp. 300–9).

[65] Maddicott, 'The Crusade Taxation of 1268–70', p. 117. No writs of summons survive from these parliaments and their composition has to be judged from statements in chronicles and the occasional royal letter.

[66] Jenkinson, 'The First Parliament of Edward I', pp. 231–42. In January 1273, there was a general assembly at Westminster, attended by four knights from each county and four representatives from each city, in order to swear allegiance to the absent Edward I: Luard, ed., *Annales Monastici*, i, 113.

[67] For these figures see Fryde, Greenway, Porter and Roy, ed., *Handbook of British Chronology*, pp. 545–50. I have included the gathering of January 1273 (see next note above) and the Northampton/York and Shrewsbury assemblies of 1282/1283.

[68] Fryde, Greenway, Porter and Roy, ed., *Handbook of British Chronology*, pp. 550–2.

ought to be granted, refused or done by parliament' the knights from the shires carried more weight than the greatest earl.[69] The last parliament without representatives was that of 1325.

The form in which the representatives were summoned in the thirteenth century derived from administrative structures and practices of long standing. Both the county and its court dated back to Anglo-Saxon times. It had been the practice since at least the reign of Henry II for the county court to send groups of four knights to the king's court with the record of its proceedings.[70] Such knights were elected in the county court, just as were the later MPs. Indeed, by the early thirteenth century knights were elected in the county court to perform a whole series of local tasks. In 1215 Magna Carta stipulated such election, both for the four knights in each county who were to sit with the king's judges to hear petty assizes and for the twelve knights in each county who were to investigate the malpractices of local officials.[71] Equally established was the idea that knights so chosen represented the county court. Thus the knights bearing the record of the county court to the king were to come 'on behalf of all the county court' (*ex parte tocius comitatus*) or 'for the county court' (*pro comitatu*).[72] It was but a small extension for knights to come on behalf of the county as a whole, as they did in 1227 when they were summoned to explain grievances over Magna Carta 'for all the county' (*pro toto comitatu*). Thereafter various attempts were made to express the idea that the knights were indeed representative of everyone in the county. In 1254 they came specifically 'in place of all and each of their counties' (*vice omnium et singulorum comitatuum*) but ultimately the government preferred to stress the community rather than the individual. In the final form of the writ of summons in 1295, the knights were to have power 'for themselves and the communities of their counties' (*pro se et communitate comitatus*).[73]

The Edwardian writs of summons rarely state specifically why representatives were being called to parliament: from 1295 they were simply 'to do what is ordained by common counsel'. Under Henry III, by contrast, both the writs and the circumstances in which they were issued are more informative. Together they suggest three broad and interrelated reasons for the summoning of representatives. First the need for political support, support which could be obtained by explaining to representatives the government's case and actions; secondly the desire for information about grievances and conditions in the localities, information which representatives could bring; and thirdly the need for taxation which the representatives alone could grant. Fundamentally, these

---

[69] Pronay and Taylor, ed., *Parliamentary Texts of the Later Middle Ages*, pp. 77–9, 89–91 (caps. 23, 26).

[70] G.D.G. Hall, ed., *Glanvill* (London, 1965), p. 99.

[71] Stubbs, ed., *Select Charters*, pp. 295, 298, caps. 18, 48.

[72] Hall, ed., *Glanvill*, p. 9. There are numerous examples in the plea rolls of knights coming *pro comitatu*: see *Curia Regis Rolls*, v, 16, 45, 150, 160.

[73] *Rot Litt Claus*, ii, 154, 212b-213; *Close Rolls, 1253–4*, pp. 114–5; Stubbs, ed., *Select Charters*, pp. 481–2.

reasons continued to operate under Edward I and under Edward II, ultimately transforming the summons of representatives from an occasional event into a general practice.

When the king and the rebellious magnates summoned knights to rival assemblies in 1261, when Montfort summoned knights in 1264, and knights and burgesses in 1265, the aim in all cases was the same: to gain political support. The same was true, in all probability, of John's summoning of knights and men in 1212 and 1213. All these summonses took place at moments of political uncertainty, even of crisis.[74] The aim of the regime was to explain and justify its proceedings. As Henry III put it in 1261, the knights were to come 'in order that they might see and understand that we propose to attempt nothing save what we know will conform to the honour and common utility of our kingdom'.[75] Having thus seen and understood, the knights were to return to their counties as the regime's apostles and recruiters. Even in more tranquil times, kings coveted popularity and support. They wished to broadcast triumphs just as much as they needed to refute slander. If, as seems likely, knights and burgesses attended Henry III's parliament of October 1269, it was to witness the greatest triumph of his reign: the translation of Edward the Confessor's body to its shrine in the new church at Westminster.[76] Likewise in 1283 it was to witness the completion of Edward I's greatest triumph, the conquest of Wales, with the trial and execution of the Welsh prince David, that knights and burgesses were summoned to the parliament at Shrewsbury.[77] Indeed, the representatives from London took David's head back with them so that it could be set up on the Tower.[78]

Parliamentary representatives could thus take back information from the court to the counties and the boroughs. They could also bring information from the counties and boroughs to the court. Indeed, both in 1227 and 1258, as we have seen, knights were specifically summoned to councils or parliaments in order to ventilate local grievances. Later representatives were not specifically charged in this way. Few, moreover, seem to have presented individual petitions, and it was not till the fourteenth century that petitions from the commons as a whole formed the basis for legislation. None the less, the informal information which representatives could bring must have been extraordinarily valuable to the government. They could report on the political situation in their counties and on the competence and honesty of the king's local officials. They could be a vital link between the centre and the localities.

In 1254, as we have seen, two knights from each county were summoned to

[74] For 1212 and 1213, see Holt, 'The Prehistory of Parliament', pp. 5–9; for 1261 and 1264–5, see J.R. Maddicott, *Simon de Montfort* (Cambridge, 1994), pp. 213, 285, 316–17.

[75] *Close Rolls, 1259–61*, p. 490 (Treharne and Sanders, ed., *Documents of the Baronial Movement*, pp. 246–9).

[76] Maddicott, 'The Crusade Taxation of 1268–1270', pp. 105, 117.

[77] Stubbs, ed., *Select Charters*, pp. 460–1.

[78] W. Stubbs, ed., *Chronicles of the Reigns of Edward I and Edward II* (Rolls Ser., London, 2 vols., 1882, 1883), i, 92; Luard, ed., *Annales Monastici*, iv, 294.

parliament quite specifically to say what tax everyone in the county was prepared to grant the king. Likewise, in October 1269, knights and burgesses came not merely to witness the translation of Edward the Confessor but to give consent to taxation.[79] There can be no doubt that the need to get consent to taxation was a major factor in establishing the place of the Commons in parliament. The cardinal fact was this: from the 1260s no general tax was levied in England without the consent of representatives. The result was that representatives *were* *always* summoned to parliament if taxation was in question. If the king wanted regular taxation, then representatives would have to be summoned regularly. More than anything else, this linkage established parliamentary representation during the reign of Edward I. Between 1275 and 1290 parliaments made four grants of general taxation to Edward I. Knights, or knights and burgesses, attended all of these parliaments; and, with one exception, these were the only parliaments which they did attend, the exception being the Shrewsbury meeting of 1283 where the business was the condemnation of David.[80] From 1294, as Edward's need for taxation multiplied with the wars in France and Scotland, so did the frequency with which representatives were summoned. Between 1294 and 1297 they came to four out of the eight parliaments, precisely those at which taxation was granted.[81]

In these watershed years the very formula in the writ which summoned representatives to parliament was developed so as to leave no doubt about their authority to grant taxation.[82] In the final version, in 1295, two knights were to be sent from each county 'with full and sufficient power for themselves and for the community of the county to do what is ordained by common council . . . so that for lack of that power the business will not remain unfinished in any way'.[83] The purpose of thus requiring full power was to ensure that the consent of the representatives to taxation was completely binding on the local communities. Thus the only occasion, between November 1282 and October 1297, on which it was not demanded was likewise the only occasion on which there was no taxation, the business being instead the condemnation of David.[84] Consent to taxation was not the only reason for the summons of representatives, as we have seen. Indeed, with the form of the writ now standardised, they appeared at parliaments after 1297 equipped with full power although no taxation was

---

[79] Maddicott, 'The Crusade Taxation of 1268–1270', pp. 105, 117.

[80] I am including as taxation the grant of the customs to Edward in 1275. For the role of the commons in making this grant ('the communities of the kingdom'), see Stubbs, ed., *Select Charters*, p. 443. I am also including as one parliament the northern and southern assemblies of 1283 and the Shrewsbury assembly of the same year. None of these meetings were actually described as parliaments in surviving records. See Fryde, Greenway, Porter and Roy, ed., *Handbook of British Chronology*, pp. 545–8.

[81] This is including all the assemblies of this period as parliaments.

[82] For what follows, see J.G. Edwards, 'The *Plena Potestas* of English Parliamentary Representatives', in Fryde and Miller, ed., *Historical Studies in the English Parliament*, pp. 136–49.

[83] Stubbs, ed., *Select Charters*, pp. 481–2. Full power was also demanded of the burgesses.

[84] Edwards, '*Plena Potestas*', p. 141. I have slightly modified the dates.

granted.[85] But the need for consent had played a central role, first in ensuring occasional attendance between 1275 and 1290 and then, between 1294 and 1297, in placing representatives in parliament on a more regular footing.

This conclusion is confirmed by two final considerations. First, the failure to summon representatives from the Welsh Marches to parliament before the sixteenth century seems closely linked to the fact that no taxation was levied there.[86] Secondly, the summoning of representatives of the lower clergy to parliaments and other assemblies was closely related to the desire to secure their consent to taxation.[87] Indeed, as we have seen, the first known summons of such representatives to parliament in 1254 was specifically stated to have that purpose.[88]

Knights and burgesses, therefore, were summoned to parliament for reasons of politics, administration and finance. They provided a channel of communication between the centre and the localities; they granted taxation. But if these were the immediate reasons for their summoning, why did those reasons operate in the second half of the thirteenth century but not in the first? The problem can be posed most starkly in terms of taxation. In 1207, 1225, 1232 and 1237 assemblies without any formal representative element granted taxes to the king. Then things began to change: in 1254, as we have seen, knights were summoned to say what aid the counties would grant;[89] in 1268–9 they were present at several parliaments where taxation was discussed; in May 1270 they attended the parliament which finally granted it.[90] Thereafter the knights attended every subsequent parliament at which taxation was granted. What had altered? To answer that question, we need to look at theories of consent, changes in society and developments in politics.

First, theory. In 1215 Magna Carta had laid down that general taxation could only be levied by 'the common counsel' of the realm. It had then, as we have seen, defined how 'common counsel' was to be obtained. The greater barons were to receive individual writs of summons. The other tenants-in-chief were to be summoned generally through the sheriffs. An assembly of tenants-in-chief, dominated by the greater barons, therefore, apparently could answer for the realm in the granting of taxation. The theory behind this has been suggested by J.C. Holt: 'The magnates could give consent on behalf of the whole community, and they could do so because they spoke for the tenants-in-chief,

---

[85] This point is made in Prestwich, *Edward I*, pp. 456–7.

[86] R.R. Davies, *Domination and Conquest: The Experience of Ireland, Scotland and Wales, 1100–1300* (Cambridge, 1990), p. 74.

[87] Denton, 'The Clergy and Parliament', pp. 102–3. The revenues of the parish churches (from tithes, oblations and glebe lands) were nearly double the temporal revenues of the bishops, abbots and priors and other clergy which were tapped by ordinary secular taxation.

[88] *Close Rolls, 1253–4*, pp. 115–16; see Lunt, 'The Consent of the Lower Clergy to Taxation during the Reign of Henry III', pp. 142–3.

[89] See, however, below note 120.

[90] For the years 1268–70, this is to accept the arguments advanced in Maddicott, 'The Crusade Taxation of 1268–70', pp. 93–117.

whose consent embodied that of their tenants and therefore that of the whole realm'.[91] A hundred years later this confidence that the magnates could speak for the realm had entirely gone. The *Modus Tenendi Parliamentum* asserted that 'each [of the magnates] is at parliament for his own individual person, and for no one else'.[92]

Even in the early thirteenth century there had been doubts over the theory that baronial consent could bind everyone to pay taxation, particularly taxation levied on everyone's movable property. Rather, it was believed that the only taxes the baronage could answer for were taxes, in the first instance, paid only by themselves; taxes, that is, which took the form of scutages levied on the number of knights' fees which they held in chief. To put it another way, a feudal assembly could only impose a feudal tax. If, on the other hand, the tax was one paid by everyone, then everyone in theory needed to consent to it, or at least everyone who was free.

These doubts over the authority of baronial consent were not universal. Occasionally, especially when writing to an individual baron, the king could imply that the great magnates alone had bound everyone to pay taxation on movables.[93] But usually, especially when announcing such taxes to the nation at large, the king shied away from any such suggestion.[94] Indeed, on occasion, he positively indicated that a tax paid by everyone had received everyone's consent. Thus in 1225 Magna Carta itself stated that the fifteenth on movables had been granted by archbishops, bishops, earls, barons, knights, free tenants and everyone in the kingdom.[95] The fortieth of 1232 was likewise conceded, so the writ said, by lay and ecclesiastical magnates, knights, free tenants 'and villeins', the addition of 'villeins' indicating that the tax had received consent even from the unfree.[96] In 1237 the writ for the levy of the thirtieth did not go so far, stating that earls, barons, and also knights and freemen, had answered for their villeins; but that only made more pointed the absence of any claim that it was the earls and barons alone who had answered for everyone else. The writ of 1237, indeed, suggests that the clerk had quite deliberately widened the circle of consent beyond the purely baronial. The sheriffs were informed that the archbishops, bishops, abbots, priors, earls and barons 'of all our kingdom' had

---

[91] Holt, 'The Prehistory of Parliament', p. 26.

[92] Pronay and Taylor, ed., *Parliamentary Texts of the Later Middle Ages*, pp. 77, 89–90 (cap. 23).

[93] For example: *Rot. Litt. Claus.*, ii, p. 75; *Close Rolls, 1231–34*, p. 311. See S.K. Mitchell, *Studies in Taxation under John and Henry III* (New Haven, 1914), pp. 200–1, note 109. Likewise, according to the writ which announced it, the poll tax of 1222 for the help of the Holy Land was conceded simply 'in the presence' of lay and ecclesiastical barons and magnates. On the other hand the actual agreement to the tax was said to be 'by the common will of all'. The king stressed that no one was to be distrained to pay the tax which effectively made it voluntary though, later, arrangements for distraint were made. See *Rot. Litt. Claus.*, ii, 516b, 517, 518b, 566–566b; Mitchell, *Studies in Taxation*, pp. 141–2.

[94] For a different perspective on what follows see Holt, 'The Prehistory of Parliament', pp. 25–6.

[95] Stubbs, ed., *Select Charters*, pp. 350–1.

[96] *Close Rolls, 1231–34*, pp. 155–6 (Stubbs, ed., *Select Charters*, p. 356).

assembled at Westminster. But in the next sentence, when it comes to the tax, this exclusively baronial assembly suddenly expands. The tax has been conceded by 'archbishops, bishops, abbots, priors *and clerks having lands which do not belong to their churches*, earls, barons, *knights and free men for themselves and their villeins*'.[97]

It is only the writs dealing with taxation in the form of a scutage that make no claims to wide consent. The scutage of 1235, for example, was granted by 'archbishops, bishops, abbots, priors, earls, barons and all others of our kingdom *who hold from us in chief*';[98] that of 1245 was 'by the common counsel of the magnates of England';[99] that of 1253 by 'archbishops, bishops, earls, barons, abbots, priors and other magnates of our kingdom'.[100] It is easy to see the basis for this distinction. A scutage was a tax paid by the tenants-in-chief and levied on the number of fees they held by knight service. They then recouped the tax from their undertenants, who were bound to pay because they were simply fulfilling a basic obligation of their tenure.[101] The whole way in which the scutages were actually collected reflected and supported this theory. In 1235, the lay tenants-in-chief, through their bailiffs, collected the tax from their own tenants and then handed it to the knights appointed as receivers in each shire. Ecclesiastical tenants-in-chief were to pay the tax not to the knights at all but directly to the king.[102] This then was a tax which the barons collected themselves from their own tenants. No wonder they felt able to consent to it. Taxation on movables was very different. It was paid not simply by barons and their tenants but, as John put it in 1207, 'by every layman of the whole of England'.[103] It was usually collected not by baronial officials within each barony but by royal officials working within the shire. Only for the tax of 1232 was an exception made to this rule: then, after the tax had been assessed on each individual by the men of each village, the particulars were to be handed over to the steward of the baron in whose fee the village was, who could then collect

---

[97] *Close Rolls, 1234–37*, p. 545 (Stubbs, ed., *Select Charters*, p. 358).

[98] *Close Rolls, 1234–37*, p. 186. Another writ, (ibid., p. 189, printed in Stubbs, ed., *Select Charters*, pp. 357–8) states that the tax was granted by 'earls, barons and all others of all our kingdom'. I suspect that the additional phrase 'who hold from us in chief' has been accidentally omitted.

[99] T. Madox, *The History and Antiquities of the Exchequer*, (2nd edn., London, 2 vols, 1769), i, 593 note f.

[100] Luard, ed., *Chronica Majora*, vi, 250; *Close Rolls, 1251–3*, p. 353.

[101] According to the writ of 1235, after the tenants-in-chief had granted an aid to the king, it was likewise 'provided by their counsel' that they could levy a scutage of two marks from each of their fees to pay it (*Close Rolls, 1234–37*, pp. 186, 189). In 1253, the barons having conceded an aid to the king of forty shillings from each of their fees, the king conceded that they might raise an equivalent amount from their tenants by knight service (Luard, ed., *Chronica Majora*, vi, 250–1). No consent, therefore, was needed from the undertenants themselves. They could be obliged to pay the tax by the consent of their lords and the will of the king.

[102] *Close Rolls, 1234–37*, pp. 186–91.

[103] T. Duffus Hardy, ed., *Rotuli Litterarum Patentium* (Record Commission, 1835), p. 72 (Stubbs, ed., *Select Charters*, pp. 278–9). Alternatively the particulars were to be handed to the steward of the lord of the liberty in which the vill was situated.

it.[104] For all the other taxes of the early thirteenth century collection was entirely in the hands of the sheriff and knights appointed by the king, who collected the tax from each village irrespective of the barony to which it belonged.[105] As John put it in 1207, the tax was to be paid 'by every layman of the whole of England *of whosoever's fee he may be*'.[106]

In the early thirteenth century, therefore, there was a growing feeling that an assembly of tenants-in-chief could consent to a scutage paid and collected by themselves but not to a tax on movables paid by everyone else and collected by the king. The fundamental principle underlying the distinction was that no one, or at least no one who was free, need pay taxes to which they had not consented, unless they were bound to it, as in the case of scutage, by the conditions of their tenure. This principle of individual consent to taxation was strenuously asserted by several great magnates in the reign of Henry III.[107] It also applied lower down the social scale; even, so the writs of 1232 implied, to the villeins. It was a principle which derived both from Roman and from canon law. The Roman law tag, 'what touches all shall be approved by all' (*quod omnes tangit ab omnibus approbetur*), was familiar in England long before Edward I cited it famously in his writ of summons to the parliament of 1295.[108] A canon of the Fourth Lateran council in 1215 reflected the same basic principle when it stipulated that taxation of the church for secular purposes required the consent of the bishop and his clergy as well as the permission of the pope.[109] The necessity for the consent of the lower clergy, who held the bulk of the church's spiritual property, was widely accepted in thirteenth-century England. In 1226 Henry III suggested that the bishops should convoke the deans and chapters, men of religion and all the clergy of their dioceses 'whom this affair touches' (*quos dictum tangit negotium*) in order to induce them to grant a tax.[110] In 1240, according to Matthew Paris, the bishops delayed an attempt, this time by the pope, to tax the lower clergy with the declaration that 'this affair touches all; all therefore ought to be convoked; without them it is neither fitting nor expedient to reply'.[111] In 1256 Lincolnshire clergy complained that, without any consultation, they had been taxed by the king; 'something all the more grievous since when it is a question of anyone being taxed, his express consent is neces-

---

[104] *Close Rolls, 1231–34*, pp. 155–6 (Stubbs, ed., *Select Charters*, p. 356).

[105] The varying methods of assessment and collection can be followed in Mitchell, *Studies in Taxation under John and Henry III*, which surveys each tax in turn in splendid detail.

[106] *Rot. Litt. Pat.*, p. 72 (Stubbs, ed., *Select Charters*, pp. 278–9).

[107] Mitchell, *Studies in Taxation*, pp. 386–8.

[108] Stubbs, ed., *Select Charters*, p. 480. Matthew Paris seems to refer to it in describing episcopal resistance to papal taxation in 1240 mentioned below; Lunt, 'The Consent of the English Lower Clergy to Taxation', p. 129; see also *Chronica Majora*, iii, 109.

[109] Rothwell, ed., *English Historical Documents, 1189–1326*, p. 663, cap. 46.

[110] *Rot. Litt. Claus.*, ii, 152. This writ is more informative than the one printed in F.M. Powicke and C.R. Cheney, ed., *Councils and Synods with Other Documents relating to the English Church, 1205–1265* (Oxford, 1964), pp. 160–1. See ibid., pp. 158–65, for the whole episode.

[111] Luard, ed., *Chronica Majora*, iv, 37; Lunt, 'The Consent of the English Lower Clergy to Taxation', p. 129.

sary'.[112] Ecclesiastical and secular ideas were closely intermingled in thirteenth-century England. The widely expressed principle that the lower clergy needed to consent to taxation may well have encouraged the belief that the same was true of knights and freemen.[113] Indeed, the principle was applied on both ecclesiastical and secular fronts in the writ which levied the thirtieth of 1237. The clerk, as we have seen, did not merely affirm that knights and freemen had given their consent; he also said the same of 'clerks having lands which do not belong to their churches'.[114]

In 1237, of course, as in 1225 and 1232, the claim that knights and freemen had consented to taxation was fraudulent, or at least bore limited relation to reality. Knights and freemen may well have attended the assemblies but there is no evidence that there was any formal representation of the counties or the boroughs. Whatever the theory expressed in the writs, in practice the great magnates alone were granting taxation on behalf of the whole realm. What happened in the second half of the century was simply that practice came into line with theory. It was impossible, of course, for all knights and freemen personally to consent to the taxes they paid. The election of knights with full power to bind the whole community of the shire solved the problem.

In asking why theory and practice came to coincide, we should not underestimate the influence of the theory itself. We should also acknowledge the force of ecclesiastical example. In 1254, as we have seen, the government ordered each sheriff to explain the king's needs to 'the knights and others of their county', after which two knightly representatives were to come before the council after Easter to say what aid 'everyone' in the county would grant. Each bishop was likewise to explain the king's needs to the assembled clergy of his diocese after which 'discrete men' were to come before the council on the same day as the knights to say what aid the lower clergy would grant.[115] Here both ecclesiastical and secular representation at parliament moved in parallel; but the letter in which the regency government explained these events to the king suggests that it was from the church that both the principle and the practice derived. It was the bishops, so the king was informed, who protested that 'they were able to do nothing about giving an aid from their clergy, without the assent of the clergy'. However, they promised to discuss the matter with them and try to in-

[112] Powicke and Cheney, *Councils and Synods*, p. 506: 'maxime cum agitur de aliquo obligando, necessarius est eius expressus consensus'.

[113] The importance of looking at the representation of the lower clergy and that of the counties and towns together, and not isolating one from the other, is particularly stressed in Denton and Dooley, *Representatives of the Lower Clergy in Parliament, 1295-1340*, for example on pp. 1-3, 76-7.

[114] *Close Rolls, 1234-37*, p. 545. Land not belonging to churches referred to secular as opposed to spiritual property in the hands of parish clergy. For a different way of looking at the question of consent, one which stresses the importance of the Roman law doctrine of necessity, see G.L. Harriss, *King, Parliament and Public Finance in Medieval England to 1369* (Oxford, 1975), especially chapters 1 and 2, and the criticisms in Prestwich, *English Politics in the Thirteenth Century*, pp. 109, 115-16.

[115] *Close Rolls, 1253-54*, pp. 114-16.

duce them to make a grant. On the secular side there was no statement of principle and no mention of discussion.[116] It is hard not to think that the procedure in 1254 – the sheriffs explaining the king's needs locally (clearly in the county courts), and the knights coming to the council to say what aid everyone in the counties would grant – was modelled, at least in part, on the ecclesiastical procedure where the bishops explained the king's needs to their assembled clergy, and representatives ('the discrete men') came to parliament to report the results.

Neither the power of principle nor the force of ecclesiastical example, however, are sufficient to explain the transition from theory into practice, and fundamentally the explanation lies in the realm of practice rather than of theory. The essential problem with all taxation is its actual collection. Down to 1237 the perception was that the counties could be carried and the tax collected by assent given professedly by everybody but in practice by an assembly dominated by great magnates and without any formal representation from the shires and boroughts. The perception was essentially correct, for the taxes on the whole seem to have been efficiently collected.[117] Indeed, the counties may have been less worried about the theory of universal consent that the government. In Yorkshire in 1220 the complaint in the county court was of the king's failure to consult the magnates, not the knights.[118] In the second half of the century, by contrast, the confidence that magnate assent alone could carry taxation evaporated. Reality and rhetoric had to come into line. Unless the counties had actually agreed the tax, the perception grew that it would not be possible to collect it. This was the crux which the regents recognised in 1254. As they told the king 'from the other laymen [in the counties] we do not believe that we can obtain any aid for your use'.[119] The necessity of consent, in some form, was here taken for granted. Indeed, it was already essential, as the regents went on to explain, to make political concessions to obtain it.[120] The situation was much the same between 1268 and 1270, the next occasion on which taxation was sought. Again the need to consult the knights was taken for granted, and this time concessions were actually made to secure their consent.[121]

---

[116] W.W. Shirley, ed., *Royal and Other Historical Letters Illustrative of the Reign of Henry III* (Rolls Ser., London, 2 vols., 1862, 1866), ii, 103–4.

[117] F.A. Cazel and A.P. Cazel, ed., *Rolls of the Fifteenth* . . . (Pipe Roll Soc., new ser., 45, 1976–77), pp. ix-x.

[118] Shirley, ed, *Royal Letters*, i, 151–2. The tax in 1220 was a carucage not a levy on movables.

[119] Ibid., ii, 103–4.

[120] It should be recognised, however, as J.C. Holt has pointed out, that the tax envisaged in 1254 was not a general levy on the kingdom. The earls, barons and other tenants-in-chief, who were to cross personally to help the king in Gascony, were to be exempt. The tax payers were to be 'the other laymen who are not to cross'. This division encouraged the perception that the earls and barons could or should not answer for the tax. But the perception was also strongly reinforced by the discontent in the counties to which the regents referred in their letter to the king. See Shirley, ed., *Royal Letters*, ii, 101–2; Holt, 'The Prehistory of Parliament', pp. 26–7.

[121] This is to follow the reconstruction in Maddicott, 'The Crusade Taxation of 1268–1270', pp. 97–8, but see the reservations in Prestwich, *English Politics in the Thirteenth Century*, p. 141.

That the political perceptions of 1254 and 1268 were correct, that taxes could no longer be levied without the consent of the commons, was finally proved by the events of 1297. In July of that year Edward I attempted to levy an eighth on movable property. It had been agreed by a parliament but one to which the magnates, it seems, had been improperly summoned, and no representatives of the counties and boroughs had been summoned at all.[122] Edward, however, attempted to cover this up just as his father had done earlier in the century. The writ ordering the collection of the tax claimed that it had been granted 'by earls, barons, knights and laymen of all our kingdom'.[123] This time the bluff was called. The earls of Hereford and Norfolk marched into the exchequer and declared that the writ lied; the tax had not been granted by the magnates or by 'the community of the realm'.[124] A little later the opposition manifesto, the *De Tallagio Non Concedendo*, demanded that no tax be imposed without the consent of lay and ecclesiastical magnates, and the knights, burgesses and other freemen of the kingdom.[125] In 1220 the complaint was the failure to consult the magnates. In 1297 the failure to consult the knights and burgesses seemed equally important. In 1215 Magna Carta had envisaged consent to taxation being given by a purely baronial assembly. In 1297 when Edward I accepted that taxes needed 'the common assent of all the realm', he envisaged an assembly including knights and burgesses.[126] It was they, as the *Modus Tenendi Parliamentum* later stated, who, together with the proctors of the lower clergy, represented the community of the realm.[127]

Underlying these shifting perceptions were long-term changes in the nature of baronial power. In the twelfth century, when the structure of baronies was more intact, great barons might have felt confident about collecting a tax on movables for the king and by extension of agreeing to it on behalf of everyone else. But in the thirteenth century this structure was in decay. The arrangements of 1232 were a lone attempt to put the clock back; to restore a world which had gone, or at least was going. Tenants holding from several baronies; tenants living far from the chief residence of their lord; the division of baronies between co-heiresses; their passage to new families through the process of forfeiture, marriage and escheat; all these factors over time, and at different speeds, tended to weaken the structure of baronies. This did not necessarily create a crisis for lords. If feudal ties weakened, they could be replaced by bastard feudal ones. But the barons recognised that they no longer had the administrative structures to collect a tax on movables. Indeed they often lacked

---

[122] Prestwich, *Edward I*, p. 422.

[123] M. Prestwich, ed., *Documents Illustrating the Crisis of 1297–98 in England* (Camden Soc., fourth ser., 24, 1980), p. 110.

[124] Ibid., pp. 137–8 (translated in Rothwell, ed., *English Historical Documents, 1189–1327*, p. 482).

[125] Prestwich, ed., *Documents Illustrating the Crisis of 1297–98*, p. 151, cap.1 (translated in Rothwell, ed., *English Historical Documents, 1189–1327*, p. 486, cap. 1).

[126] Prestwich, ed., *Documents Illustrating the Crisis of 1297–8*, p. 27 and note 157; and p. 159 (cap. 6).

[127] Pronoy and Taylor, ed., *Parliamentary Texts of the Later Middle Ages*, pp. 77, 90 (cap. 23).

the power even to collect scutages, having to rely on the sheriffs to distrain their tenants to pay up.[128] The fact was that taxation, especially taxation on movables, was far more efficiently collected through the county administration of the king.[129]

The nature of that county administration was also changing in a significant way. The running of local government was passing into the hands of the knights and gentry. In the thirteenth century they came to dominate the most important local offices, those of sheriff, coroner, escheator, justice of assize and, above all, collector of taxation. This was the king's system of local government which he had commissioned the knights to run. No baron could anser for it, at least not in any formal way, however much he might retain and control some of its agents. Indeed, the very taxes themselves could not be collected without the cooperation of the knights. Why not make sure of the cooperation by summoning them to parliament to consent to it? Significantly there was a close connection between the knights who came as representatives to parliament and the knights who actually collected the taxes. In 1295, in twenty-one of the thirty-five counties, tax collectors were also representatives.[130]

In the first half of the century the castle of baronial consent still stood, although undermined. It was the politics of the mid-century which fired the last props holding up the tunnels, and brought it tumbling down. In the course of the thirteenth century the counties of England were radicalised politically. Already in John's reign the counties had a political programme: they wished local government to be run by local men; an aspiration to which several clauses in Magna Carta bore witness. In the minority of Henry III, and during his personal rule, the counties struggled both to implement clauses in the Great Charter on the local courts and to secure the deforestation promised by the companion Charter of the Forest. After 1234 the abolition of the justiciarship rendered central government more remote while the financial needs of the crown made both the sheriffs and the justices in eyre more oppressive. In 1254, when the regents advised the king that no tax could be obtained from the counties, it was precisely because of the widespread local discontent: above all, so it was claimed, Magna Carta was not kept by the sheriffs and other royal bailiffs. If the king was to secure a tax, he was advised to publicly proclaim the Charters through the counties and order the sheriffs to keep them.[131] The king took this advice but too late to influence the results of the ensuing parliament, and

---

[128] Such distraint was arranged in the writs ordering the collection of scutages (*Close Rolls, 1234–37*, pp. 186, 189; Luard, ed., *Chronica Majora*, vi, 250–1) and there is much evidence in the memoranda rolls of the exchequer for it actually taking place.

[129] This point is made by Holt, 'The Prehistory of Parliament', pp. 26–9.

[130] D. Pasquet, *An Essay on the Origins of the House of Commons* (Cambridge, 1925), pp. 186–7 (cited by Prestwich, *Edward I*, p. 458 note 102). However Pasquet (p. 187) goes on to show that in some other parliaments the proportion of deputies amongst the collectors was much smaller.

[131] Shirley, ed., *Royal Letters*, pp. 101–2. For local grievances in the reign of Henry III see J.R. Maddicott, 'Magna Carta and the Local Community', *Past and Present*, 102 (1984), 25–65.

no tax was forthcoming.[132] Local grievances, moreover, were not merely against the officials of the king; the officials of great magnates were equally unpopular. Indeed, the demand that the magnates should observe Magna Carta towards their own tenants and neighbours was one of the king's most constant refrains.

By 1254, therefore, it was already clear that neither the king nor the barons could take the counties for granted. Yet the pattern was not quite set. As we have seen, there was no suggestion that the three annual parliaments envisaged in 1258 should have representatives from the counties; and, despite the precedent of 1254, it was still possible to think that a purely magnate assembly might grant a tax to the king: at any rate the Oxford parliament of 1258, at which no representatives were present, appointed a body of twenty-four magnates 'to negotiate about an aid for the king'.[133] It was the revolutionary events of the next decade which tipped the balance firmly in favour of the counties. In 1258 itself the whole structure of local government was overhauled to meet the grievances of the knights and those below them in local society. In 1259 the protest at the Westminster parliament of 'the community of the bachelory of England', a body broadly representing the knightly class, forced through legislation very much against baronial interests. In 1261 there was widespread resistance in the counties to the visitations of the king's justices and to the new sheriffs appointed in the royal bid to recover power. Both sides vied for the support of the knights, summoning them to rival assemblies at Windsor and St Albans. Then Montfort, drawing logical conclusions from these events, summoned the knights to his famous parliaments of 1264 and 1265. The middle years of the century had brought the counties into the political limelight. Thereafter the king never obtained taxation without their consent.

During the course of the thirteenth century, therefore, assemblies of the realm had changed fundamentally both in terms of form and function and had been given a new name: parliament. The king's council had emerged to become the heart of the institution. Lay and ecclesiastical magnates were summoned not as barons but as their importance warranted. Increasingly representatives of the counties, boroughs and lower clergy were joining the assembly. One new function was the dispensing of justice through the hearing of petitions; another was the granting of taxation. It was the granting of taxation, or rather the constant refusal to grant it, which put parliament on the political map between 1237 and 1258. The name parliament became established in precisely that period. This was no accident. The institution had achieved an altogether new political prominence. A new word seemed appropriate to describe it.

The structure of parliament by the early fourteenth century was, of course,

---

[132] *Cal Patent Rolls, 1247–58*, p. 281. However, as noted above, the emergency for which the tax was required (a threatened invasion of Gascony by the king of Castile) did not materialise.

[133] Treharne and Sanders, ed., *Documents of the Baronial Movement*, pp. 104–7 (cap. 11). It should also be noted that Henry III demanded a tax from the April 1258 Westminster parliament at which no representatives were present.

far from settled. In the next half century a fixed list of parliamentary peers evolved to end the fluctuating numbers summoned around 1300. It was not till after 1325 that the summoning of representatives from the counties and boroughs became the absolute rule. Representatives of the lower clergy continued to attend parliament throughout the fourteenth century but also formed a quite separate clerical assembly: convocation. Since it was in convocation that the clergy granted taxation to the crown, this became the focus of their activities. They were present at parliament but had little role. In this sense the parliaments of the later fourteenth century were less representative than those of a hundred years earlier, which had witnessed an important but abortive 'attempt by the crown to bring the clergy and the laity of the realm into one assembly'.[134]

The functions of parliament also developed in the fourteenth century. The hearing of private petitions as an important part of business dried up, while the petitions presented by the representatives of the shires and boroughs became a major source of legislation.[135] As the king's demand for taxation, faced with the costs of the 100 Years War, became more and more insistent, the knights conceived a whole series of demands in return for granting it. We have stressed that as early as 1254 the knights may well have demanded concessions before granting taxation. But a hundred years later this was taking place with an altogether new regularity: the House of Commons had arrived.

Where then does all this leave Stubbs's parliament of 1295, that 'model assembly . . . serving as a pattern for all future assemblies of the nation', that assembly which 'established' or 'finally fixed' the right of shire and town representation and, after which, 'it may be fairly questioned whether any assembly afterwards held is entitled to the name and authority of parliament which does not in the minutest particulars of summons, constitution, and formal dispatch of business, answer to the model then established'?[136]

It is easy, in the light of what we have said above, to dismiss these claims. In the first place Stubbs concentrated almost exclusively on parliament's development as an assembly of estates, with the key feature being the emergence of the representatives from the shires and boroughs. He had thus sidelined the role of the king's council in parliamentary development and the central part it had played in the dispensation of justice through the hearing of petitions. When Maitland told his readers that they would not be departing very far from the path marked out by works which were already classical, if they concluded that a session of the king's council was the core and essence of every *parliamentum*, he was distancing himself from Stubbs while diplomatically pretending not to do so. For the whole thrust of Stubbs's discussion had been to see the king's

---

[134] Denton, 'The Clergy and Parliament', p. 106.

[135] Sayles, *The King's Parliament of England*, pp. 110–11, 115. Ultimately such petitions were heard in the court of chancery.

[136] Stubbs, *Constitutional History*, pp. 133, 134, 235–6.

council as something growing up alongside parliament rather than as part of it.[137]

Even on his own terms Stubbs's claims for the 1295 parliament were overstated, as he himself came close to recognising. That parliament can hardly be said to have established or fixed the right of town and country representation when many subsequent assemblies down to 1325, which contemporaries called parliaments, met without any such representation at all. Stubbs was perfectly aware of this and skated round the difficulty by admitting that, though the parliament of 1295 established the rule and pattern, the rule 'was not at once recognised'. Thus 'for many years' assemblies of councillors and magnates without any representatives 'share with the constitutional assembly of estates the name of parliament'.[138] That this admission virtually destroyed his whole hypothesis Stubbs did not appreciate, or at least hoped his readers would not appreciate. For how can the parliament of 1295 be a model if it was a model unrecognised by contemporaries? Stubbs talked of anomalies, exceptional practices, irregularities and confusion amidst the 'tender growth of the new system',[139] but of course the irregularities and confusion were entirely of his own making; the product of setting up a standard which at the time simply did not exist.

Why did Stubbs seize on the 1295 parliament? There were various reasons but one particularly stands out, namely the principle enunciated in the writ of summons to the bishops: 'that which touches all shall be approved by all'.[140] It was this which made Stubbs sit up. The 1295 parliament was, he wrote, a 'precedent for all time to come, worthy of the principle which the king had enunciated in the writ of summons'. 'This was to be a model assembly, bearing in its constitution evidence of the principle by which the summons was dictated, and serving as a pattern for all future assemblies of the nation'.[141] Perhaps, however, there was also another, more artistic reason for Stubbs's elevation of the parliament of 1295. His account of the origins of parliament is not easy going. Reading Maitland is like galloping a fine horse across open country; reading

---

[137] Ibid., pp. 268, 274–5.

[138] Ibid., p. 236.

[139] Ibid, pp. 235–6, 274.

[140] *Select Charters*, ed., Stubbs, p. 480.

[141] Ibid, pp. 236, 133–4. Stubbs also believed that the 1295 parliament was the first to which both town and county representatives were summoned through writs addressed to the sheriffs, previously the towns having been summoned individually. The result, Stubbs argued, was that the final process of the election took place in the county court and that 'the parliament that results contains a concentration of the persons and the powers of the shiremoot'. Thus 'the parliament of 1295 differed, so far as we know, from all that had preceded it, and was a precedent for all time to come'. Stubbs was right to inject a note of caution with his 'so far as we know' for in fact the representatives had been summoned though a single writ to the sheriffs as early as 1275 (Jenkinson, 'The First Parliament of Edward I', pp. 232–3; these pages have a useful summary of the elements supposedly combined for the first time in the parliament of 1295). The parliament of 1295 probably was the first at which representatives of the lower clergy were summoned through writs addressed to the bishops, which was to become the standard form. See Stubbs, *Constitutional History*, pp. 204, 209–10.

Stubbs is like following the plough through heavy soil. Stubbs desperately needed some landmark on which his readers could sit and view the surrounding fields. He found it in the Model Parliament. Having found it he was too good a historian not to recognise its difficulties; but he was not good enough to abandon the hypothesis altogether. So he compromised, establishing the Model Parliament and then immediately surrounding it with qualifications and explanations which, to the careful reader, destroyed much of its value. Fortunately for Stubbs, the great Victorian and Edwardian public were not careful readers. They bought the book for show not for use; hence the many uncut copies, in their fading maroon covers, which gather dust in second-hand book shops.

We should not, however, abandon Stubbs and his model altogether. In concentrating on parliament as an assembly of estates he was looking at only one aspect of its development in the thirteenth century. Yet, for the future, he was looking at by far its most important aspect. There was also something important going on around 1295. In the first half of Edward I's reign, representatives had attended parliament on an occasional basis. After 1294 their attendance became much more regular. Between 1294 and 1297, knights alone, or knights and burgesses together, attended four of the eight parliaments. Between 1300 and 1307, as we have seen, they attended seven out of nine. If Stubbs's 'Model Parliament' plants in the public mind the idea that parliament was a construct of the thirteenth century and that the years around 1295 were decisive in its development, then it has not been without its value.

20

King Henry III and the Cosmati Work
at Westminster Abbey

The Cosmati work at Westminster abbey has long attracted the attention of historians, not surprisingly since it lies at the heart of the abbey built by King Henry III.[1] The base of the new shrine of Edward the Confessor, its altar, the pavement in the Confessor's chapel, the great sanctuary pavement before the high altar, and the tomb of King Henry III were all produced by Cosmati marblers. There is a degree of consensus about the chronology of this work. The pavement in the sanctuary was largely completed by 1269. The tomb of Henry III, on the other hand, was almost certainly later, being under way in 1279 and complete by 1290. Over the date of Edward the Confessor's shrine, however, a debate has recently been kindled. Like many shrines, Edward's was made up of two parts. There was first the reliquary, the wooden casket covered with gold and jewels in which the saint's body lay. This is totally lost. And there was secondly the Cosmati base on which the reliquary reposed, a base which survives in the battered reconstruction made during the Marian restoration of the abbey between 1553 and 1558.[2] In the thirteenth century, contemporaries could apply the term 'feretory' indifferently both to the whole shrine or to either of its parts. Since the Confessor's body was ceremonially translated to a new shrine on 13 October 1269, scholars have generally assumed that, for practical purposes, both parts were finished by that date. It is this conviction that Paul Binski has challenged in an article which examines the chronology of the Cosmati work at Westminster and considers what the 'whole hearted Romanizing' at the abbey tells us about the ethos and self-image of the English court. Briefly, Binski has argued that the base of the Confessor's shrine was commissioned not by Henry III but by Edward I. Work probably started some time after the king's return to England in 1274 and was completed in 1279, leaving the craftsmen free to concentrate on the tomb of Henry III.[3] Binski's thesis is power-

[1] P.C. Claussen, *Magistri Doctissimi Romani: Die Römischen Marmorkünstler des Mittelalters (Corpus Cosmatorum I)* (Stuttgart, 1987), 176 n. 988 has an extensive bibliography.

[2] J.G. O'Neilly and L.E. Tanner, 'The shrine of St Edward the Confessor', *Archaeologia*, c (1966), 129–54. For shrine bases see particularly N. Coldstream, 'English Decorated Shrine Bases', *Journal of the British Archaeological Association*, 3rd ser. xxxix (1976), 15–34.

[3] P. Binski, 'The Cosmati at Westminster and the English Court Style', *Art Bulletin*, no. 1 (1990), 6–34 and, for the dating, especially 13–19 and 21–2. For another recent discussion, which suggests that the shrine base had not been finished by 1272, see J. Gardner, 'The Cosmati at Westminster: some Anglo-Italian Reflections', in *Skulptur und Grabmal des Spätmittelalters in Rom und Italien: Akten*

fully presented. Features of it may be right. Yet, as this essay will show, there remain strong grounds for accepting the traditional view that the Cosmati base was begun by Henry III and was substantially in place for the translation of 1269.

The case for the traditional chronology begins with what appear to be documentary references to the new base of the shrine and its surrounding Cosmati pavement in the 1260s. These are in the accounts of the keepers of the works at Westminster enrolled on the pipe rolls. The first surviving account, for the period January 1264 to December 1266, mentions neither base nor pavement. The next two accounts, however, covering the periods from December 1266 to September 1267 and from September 1267 to December 1269, both record the payment of wages to, among others, 'paviors before the feretory of St Edward' (*in stipendiis . . . pavatorum ante pheretrum Sancti Edwardi*). Thereafter the references to the feretory and the paviors disappear.[4] There could at this time have been three objects able to be described as the 'feretory' of St Edward.[5] The first, the new reliquary being worked on, primarily by goldsmiths, somewhere in the abbey precincts, can hardly be that in question since a new pavement would scarcely have been installed around it. The second, the old feretory in which the saint's body resided prior to translation, seems at first sight a more plausible candidate. For several years before 1269 it had stood somewhere *ante* or *coram* the high altar of the abbey. Consequently the paviors working before it could have been working on none other than the great sanctuary pavement itself.[6] In fact, however, it is unlikely that this is the feretory referred to. The sanctuary was dominated by the high altar, not the temporary feretory, and the new pavement installed there was called, as early as May 1269, the pavement 'in the presence of the great altar' (*coram magno altari*). Paviors working in the area would almost certainly have been described in the same way.[7]We

continued

des Kongresses 'Scultura e Monumento Sepolcrale del Tardo Medioevo a Roma e in Italia' (1985), ed. J. Garms and A.M. Romanini (Österreichische Akademie der Wissenschaften, Wien, 1990), 201–15, especially 210.

[4] *Building Accounts of King Henry III*, ed. H.M. Colvin (Oxford, 1973), 416–19, 422–3, 426–7, 428–35. The accounts closed on 20 November 1272.

[5] Binski's postulation of a fourth possibility is discussed below.

[6] The chronicler Thomas Wykes says that Henry III was buried in the place where Edward the Confessor's body had rested 'for several years' before his translation: *Annales Monastici*, ed. H.R. Luard (5 vols. Rolls Ser., 1864–9), iv.252. A large number of other sources say that Henry was buried *ante* or *coram* the high altar, for example: *Foedera, Conventiones, Litterae*, ed. T. Rymer, new edn. ed. A. Clarke and F. Holbrooke, 3 vols. in 6 (Record Comm., 1816–30), I, ii, 497; *Flores Historiarum*, ed. H.R. Luard, 3 vols. (Rolls Ser., 1890), iii, 28; *Liber Memorandorum Ecclesie de Bernewelle*, ed. J.W. Clark (Cambridge, 1907), 153; *Annales Monastici*, ii.112, 378; iv.461; *De Antiquis Legibus Liber: Cronica Maiorum at Vicecomitum Londoniarum*, ed. T. Stapleton (Camden Soc., 1846), 153. For the view (though for reasons unexplained) that the sanctuary pavement was that referred to in the accounts, see W.R. Lethaby, *Westminster Abbey and the King's Craftsmen* (London, 1906), 328n, and his *Westminster Abbey Re-Examined* (London, 1925), 224–5.

[7] Public Record Office [henceforth PRO] C 66/87, m. 17 (pencil) (*Cal. Patent Rolls 1266–1272*, 338). It is noticeable that whereas Wykes says that Henry was buried in the place where Edward

are left, therefore, with the third and by far the most likely candidate for the feretory mentioned in the accounts, namely the new Cosmati base in the Confessor's chapel. If this identification is correct, the accounts would seem to prove both that this base was in existence between December 1266 and December 1269 and that the paviors were installing the new Cosmati pavement around it.[8]

Binski accepts that the paviors were indeed working in the area intended for the new feretory, but questions whether it had actually been built. Instead he suggests, as one possibility, that the feretory referred to was a much earlier base constructed in the 1240s at the time when Henry III began work on the Confessor's new reliquary.[9] It is true that in October 1241 Henry assigned £6 10s for the marble of the new feretory. Perhaps this was indeed for the base. Next year, in May 1242, just before leaving for Poitou, he ordered the exchequer to provide whatever was necessary for the feretory's gold and marble. When, however, on his return, he issued a writ covering this expenditure, it was simply for gold and the wages of goldsmiths, which would seem to cover work on the reliquary rather than the base.[10] Since these are the only references which could relate to an earlier base, we cannot know how far it had progressed either before 1245 or after it, when Henry was rebuilding the whole abbey church. In April 1251 the pope both granted indulgences to those who attended the Confessor's translation and acknowledged Henry's intention of knighting his son on the same day. Both nothing came of this scheme and Edward was knighted in November 1254 at Las Huelgas in Castile. In the same month, Henry, in Gascony, hoped to consecrate the new church on 13 October 1255 and presumably, though this is not said, to translate the Confessor at the same time. This scheme too was abandoned. Since, in the event, it was not till 1269 that either church or reliquary was deemed ready for the great ceremony, there is no reason to think that the base was ready either. Indeed, whatever was pro-

---

continued

the Confessor had rested, all the other sources say he was buried *ante* or *coram* the high altar: see above n. 6. I am grateful to Nicola Coldstream for discussing this point with me. She suggests that the Confessor's body may have been placed on the north side of the sanctuary in the space now occupied by Crouchback's tomb. If so, it is even more unlikely that the sanctuary pavement would have been identified by reference to it.

[8] The work of the paviors was evidently expensive and time-consuming and it seems unlikely, therefore, that it was merely on some temporary floor later replaced by the Cosmati one. It is also unlikely that 'before the feretory' was being used very vaguely and referred to work in, say, the ambulatory. Only the skilled men installing highly decorated pavements in chapels were singled out in the accounts. (The one other reference to paviors is to those, between February and November 1272, working in front of 'diverse altars': *Building Accounts of Henry III*, 434–5). For the view (unsupported by evidence) that the pavement in the Confessor's chapel belongs to the reign of Edward I, see W. Burges, 'The Mosaic Pavements', in G.G. Scott, *Gleanings from Westminster Abbey* (Oxford, 1863), 102 and Lethaby, *Westminster Abbey and the King's Craftsmen*, 327–8. Lethaby later changed his mind: *Westminster Abbey Re-Examined*, 225.

[9] Binski, 'The Cosmati at Westminster', 14, 17.

[10] *Cal. Liberate Rolls 1240–5*, 83–4, 134, 248; *Cal. Patent Rolls 1232–47*, 285; *Receipt and Issue Rolls 26 Henry III*, ed. R.C. Stacey (Pipe Roll Soc., new ser., xlix, 1987–8), 84.

duced in the 1240s and 1250s must have been deemed inadequate, otherwise it would not have been replaced by the Cosmati structure. Most probably, once the east end and transepts of the new church were finished in 1259 and Henry could view the new site in all its splendour, he decided to make an entirely fresh start on the base, a suggestion to which we will return.[11]

Aside from raising the question of an earlier feretory, Binski also suggests another possibility, namely that 'feretory' in the accounts does not refer to an actual structure at all. It simply indicates 'the place where it was intended that the metal shrine with its base should eventually be installed'. The implication, apparently, is that at the time of the 1269 translation the shrine base was actually 'non-existent' and that the reliquary was placed on some purely 'provisional' structure.[12]

If either of Binski's hypotheses is right, the translation on 13 October 1269 was a bizarre affair. All the nobles of the kingdom were summoned to Westminster. The Confessor's body was removed from its old feretory by the high altar and carried round the new church on the shoulders of King Henry, King Richard of Germany, the princes Edward and Edmund, the Earl of Surrey, and Philip Basset.[13] When this imposing party reached the Confessor's chapel, it must have looked down on the shimmering marble of the Cosmati pavement, gazed up at the gleaming gold of the reliquary, and then shuddered as it saw the totally unworthy 'provisional or earlier' base.[14] Those present must have been painfully aware that the Confessor would soon have to resume his travels to allow the construction of a more worthy feretory. If they imagined that he could simply take a return ticket back to his old station before the high altar, they were to be disappointed since, in 1272, that space was used for the body of Henry III himself.[15]

Just why King Henry put his patron saint through such humiliation is far from clear. The climax of all the work at the abbey was to be the translation of the Confessor to his new shrine. As the essential parts of the new church neared completion, as Henry himself entered old age, as the Lord Edward's departure on crusade drew closer (he took the cross in June 1268),[16] so the translation became both increasingly possible and increasingly urgent. In 1266 Henry was hastening the completion of the reliquary. In March 1267 the pope gave the abbot and convent permission to effect the translation at a suitable opportunity 'having convened clergy and people with due solemnity'. In August 1269 Henry was taking explicit and emphatic measures to finish the reliquary in time

---

[11] Westminster Abbey Muniments [henceforth WAM] Book 11 ('Westminster Domesday'), f. 406v; *Building Accounts of Henry III*, 194–5; see also *Cal. Papal Registers*, i.271. I am grateful to Nicholas Vincent for drawing my attention to the indulgences in the 'Westminster Domesday'.

[12] Binski, 'The Cosmati at Westminster', 14, 15, 17.

[13] *Annales Monastici*, iv. 226 (from the chronicle of Thomas Wykes); *De Antiquis Legibus Liber*, 117.

[14] Binski, 'The Cosmati at Westminster', 17.

[15] See above, n. 6.

[16] S.D. Lloyd, *English Society and the Crusade 1216–1307* (Oxford, 1988), 114–15.

for the translation, now less than two months away.[17] And yet we are asked to believe that the base which was to hold the reliquary aloft for clergy and people to see, the base in whose niches the sick were to be cured by the saint's miraculous powers, this base remained so skeletal or outmoded that in a few years it had to be entirely swept away.

Binski suggests that the nature of the 1269 translation is in fact 'obscure. No contemporary reference gives us any idea as to [the feretory's] location'.[18] The implication is almost that the body might not have been placed in the Confessor's chapel at all. But the chronicle of Bury St Edmunds states specifically that the saint was translated to 'the new presbytery which [King Henry] had built with great splendour for him, and there he was interred in a new shrine (*in novo loculo*'.[19] That 'presbytery' here refers to the Confessor's chapel is confirmed by the chronicler Wykes's remarks about the body being translated to a 'supereminent place'.[20] In fact, no source indicates that this translation was to anything other than the Confessor's final resting-place. Admittedly, a London chronicler recorded Edward's removal to 'a gold feretory, fittingly decorated with precious stones and gems, although not yet finished completely'. This, however, seems to refer to the reliquary rather than the base.[21] That the former, despite Henry's efforts, needed further work after October 1269 is confirmed by the record evidence; nor is that surprising since it was a hugely elaborate structure. Quite probably the Cosmati base too needed some finishing, but that is totally different from its being non-existent.[22] The most circumstantial de-

---

[17] *Close Rolls 1264–8*, 262; WAM Book 11, f. 386. On 19 August 1269 Henry informed the Constable of the Tower that *quia volumus quod feretrum beati Edwardi citra festum eiusdem sancti quod in quindena sancti Michaelis proxima futura cum solempnitate apud Westmonasterium celebraturi sumus perficiatur*, he was to give 20 marks from the issues of the city of London to Walter the monk of Westminster and Richard Bonaventure, keepers of the feretory, *ad idem feretrum inde faciendum. Et hoc sicut nos et honorem nostrum et vestrum diligitis et sicut de vobis confidimus nullo modo omitattis.* If the 20 marks could not be raised from the issues, they were to be obtained on loan: PRO, SCI/2, no. 88. *Cal. Liberate Rolls 1267–72*, no. 88, and PRO, E 372/114, m. 20 show that the money was raised from the issues.

[18] Binski, 'The Cosmati at Westminster', 17.

[19] *The Chronicle of Bury St Edmunds 1212–1301*, ed. A. Gransden (London, 1964), 45.

[20] *Annales Monastici*, iv.226. I cannot agree that Wykes's remarks about the translation 'simply preserve a *topos* about the elevation of relics': Binski, 'The Cosmati at Westminster', 17 and n. 55. If Wykes re-employed phraseology, it was because it was appropriate. His statement, quoted above, about the body being carried on the shoulders of the two kings, the two princes, the Earl of Surrey, and Philip Basset, is found in no other source and suggests he had good informants. Indeed, he may well have been present.

[21] *Chronicles of the Reigns of Edward I and Edward II*, ed. W. Stubbs (2 vols., Rolls Ser., 1882–3), i.80.

[22] *Building Accounts of Henry III*, 428–9; Binski, 'The Cosmati at Westminster', 17 and n. 52. In January 1270/1 the Bishop of Meath issued indulgences to all who contributed to the *reperationi feretri sive capse in qua corpus ipsius sancti [Edwardi] requiescit*, phraseology which may or may not have been designed to refer to base as well as reliquary: WAM Book 11, fos. 394–394v. To a degree reliquaries like the Confessor's were never finished, since fresh gold and jewels could always be attached to them. In 1299 there is a reference to gold assigned to the Confessor's feretory but not

scription of the translation, that by the London alderman, Arnold fitz Thedmar, who was almost certainly present, registered no doubts about either base or reliquary. King Henry, he wrote, caused the saint's body to be transferred to 'another place where it now lies, and above the saint he caused a new *basilica* [a good description of the reliquary] to be made all covered and decorated with the purest gold and precious gems'. Fitz Thedmar's statement, later reiterated, that the Confessor's body was moved to the place 'where it now lies' is itself significant, given that his chronicle was completed after Edward I's return to England and coronation in August 1274. Clearly fitz Thedmar had no information about any plan to replace the 1269 base, and, if we may sense an air of finality about the 'where he now lies', no expectation that there would be one.[23]

There are therefore considerable arguments, both evidential and circumstantial, for accepting the traditional view that Edward's shrine was substantially complete by 1269. Binski's case for overturning them has several strands; one centres on an argument from silence; another on questions of style; and yet another on the date of the base's completion as recorded by the contemporary inscription placed upon it.

Any argument from silence in this matter might seem to be a two-edged weapon, given the total failure of the chroniclers to mention the pulling down of the 'provisional or earlier' shrine, the removal of the Confessor's body, the building of the Cosmati base and the restoration of the saint to his new home - striking events which would surely have claimed attention; at least two chroniclers, after all, mentioned the parallel, and in some ways less significant translation of Henry III to his new Cosmati tomb in 1290.[24] Binski's argument, however, is more specific than this, and concerns the chancery rolls, the rolls on which the king's letters, issued under the great seal, were recorded. In Henry III's reign these contain large numbers of orders concerning the king's building and artistic works. Their apparent failure to make any reference to the base of the shrine is therefore 'suspicious'. The chancery rolls are equally silent under Edward I; but this is now explicable since a 'change in administrative practice in the early 1270s' meant that the chancery thereafter was 'seldom used to record such business'.[25] Instead the king, because he was now frequently separated

---

continued
yet placed on it: WAM 9464**. On the other hand, in August 1269 Henry thought 20 marks would complete the reliquary (see n. 17 above), which hardly suggests that there was much more basic work to do. In 1253, by contrast, Henry had assigned 500 marks to the completion of the feretory, though this may have been for the base as well as the reliquary. See below, p. 420.

[23] *De Antiquis Legibus Liber*, 117, 173.

[24] *The Chronicle of Bury St Edmunds*, 94; *Chronicles of the Reigns of Edward I and Edward II*, 98. Binski points out ('The Cosmati at Westminster', 17) that shrines could be rebuilt without the necessity of any formal translation but in the case he mentions (that of the shrine of St Alban in the 1300s) the rebuilding was still considered a significant event worthy of comment: *Gesta Abbatum Monasterii Sancti Albani*, ed. H.T. Riley, 3 vols. (Rolls Ser., 1867–9), ii.107.

[25] Binski, 'The Cosmati at Westminster', 17–18.

from the chancery, used letters, sealed by the privy seal, of which we have only very partial records.

There are, however, serious problems with this hypothesis. The change in chancery practice, first commented on in relation to building works by Colvin,[26] did not originate in a sudden break in the 1270s. The use of the privy seal developed gradually over Edward I's reign, with the decisive change taking place after the death of Edward's trusted chancellor, Robert Burnell, in 1292.[27] As late as 1291 Edward used great seal letters when commissioning the effigy for his father's tomb.[28] The following table gives the numbers of surviving privy seal letters of the 1270s addressed to the chancery:

1274–5: 4
1275–6: none
1276–7: 23
1277–8: 6
1278–9: 6[29]

That these letters are not survivals of a much large number is suggested both by the exiguous references to authorizations via the privy seal on the chancery rolls, and by the logical rather than haphazard pattern of survival of the privy seal letters themselves. Thus the twenty-three letters of 1276–7 were issued while Edward was separated from the chancery during his Welsh campaign; several of those in 1278–9 were produced by a similar separation while Edward visited France. Of course, privy seal letters were not simply addressed to the chancery. They were used for all manner of other purposes. But if those sent to the chancery may be taken as any guide, then the privy seal was not being used on any great scale in the 1270s.[30] Consequently, during this period, one would expect orders concerning the king's building operations to appear on the chancery rolls, just as they do under Henry III. And in fact that is the case. The *liberate* rolls for the period November 1274 to November 1276 (the rolls recording letters dealing with royal expenditure) order payments for the works at Westminster, Charing, Windsor, and the Tower, as well for smaller items such as the fourteen pearls placed in the queen's crown at her coronation.[31]

If, therefore, the silence of the chancery rolls is an argument against the shrine base being in progress under Henry III, it is just as much an argument against its construction in the early years of his son. In fact the silence is conclusive against neither king. Not all chancery letters were enrolled and, in any

[26] *The History of the King's Works*, I, ed. H.M. Colvin (London, 1963), 162–3.

[27] T.F. Tout, *Chapters in Mediaeval Administrative History*, 6 vols., (Manchester, 1920–33), ii.78; M. Prestwich, *Edward I* (London, 1988), 136–7.

[28] *Cal. Close Rolls 1288–1296*, 171.

[29] PRO, C 81/1, nos. 2–32B. See *Cal. Chancery Warrants 1244–1326*, 1–6.

[30] There are equally very few specifically privy seal letters enrolled on the memoranda rolls of the exchequer in this period. For two examples: PRO E 368/50, m. 2d; E 368/51, m. 3d.

[31] PRO, C 62/51, mm. 12, 10, 9, 8, 3, 1; C 62/52, mm. 11, 8, 2.

case, the king could have funded the shrine base without resorting to royal letters at all.

If indeed we widen the discussion to consider the evidence on payment, then, if anything, the silence under Henry III is more explicable than the one under his son. There were various ways in which Edward I could have met the expense of the shrine base. The most conventional was via a writ of *liberate* ordering the necessary money to be disbursed by the exchequer. As we have seen, no such writ was ever enrolled on the *liberate* rolls. Edward could also have written to the exchequer by a privy seal letter. But, either way, the resulting payments should appear on the issue rolls of the exchequer. There is no sign of them. The only possibility is that expenditure on the shrine was contained within the general payments to the king's mason, Robert of Beverley, for works at Westminster, or at Westminster and the Tower, which were ordered by writs of *liberate* in 1274–5, the corresponding payments appearing on the issue rolls.[32] However, Robert of Beverley's detailed lists of expenditure, both in purchasing materials and paying wages, which survive for the period March 1274 to May 1277, ignore the shrine, although there are references to the tomb for Henry, King Edward's son. The lists also make plain that the works at Westminster were on the palace rather than the abbey.[33]

King Edward could also have paid for the shrine through his Italian bankers, who took over from the exchequer the financing of a wide variety of royal activity in the 1270s. In 1276 a writ of *liberate* ordering the exchequer to fund Robert of Beverley's works on the palace of Westminster and the mews at Charing was cancelled, with a note that he had been satisfied instead by Luke of Lucca, one of the chief Italian bankers.[34] Indeed, between 1276 and 1279 the scale of this Italian activity greatly reduced the numbers of writs of *liberate* ordering disbursements to be made by the exchequer.[35] Yet, had the Italians met the cost of the shrine, their instructions might well have survived, since large numbers of letters directing them to make payments were enrolled on the patent rolls, including, for example, the letter which led to the cancellation of Robert of Beverley's writ of *liberate* mentioned above.[36] In June 1278 the Italians were ordered to give Giles de Audenard £100 a week until the following November, to maintain the works on the Tower and Westminster, but the possibility that these works might have included construction of the shrine is removed by Giles's

[32] PRO, C 62/51, mm. 12, 8, 1 (£65, £154, £100); E 403/27, m. 2; E 403/30, m. 2; E 403/33, m. 2.

[33] PRO, E 101/467 6(2); E 101/467 7(2). The reference to Henry's tomb is on m. 1 of both rolls. The same items appears in Beverley's accounts enrolled on the pipe roll: E 372/125, m. 6d.

[34] PRO, C 62/52, m. 2. For these bankers see R.W. Kaeuper, *Bankers to the Crown: The Riccardi of Lucca and Edward I* (Princeton, 1973).

[35] This is especially the case in PRO, C 62/53, 54, 55.

[36] *Cal. Patent Rolls 1272–81*, 167; PRO, C 62/52, m. 2. Payments made by the bankers on the king's behalf are summarized in the index to the patent rolls: *Cal. Patent Rolls 1272–81*, 562–3.

accounts for the period Easter 1278 to Easter 1279, which show, once again, that the operations at Westminster were confined to the palace.[37]

Edward might equally have financed the shrine base directly out of the wardrobe. He was certainly not doing so, however, between January and November 1278, the period covered by the first surviving wardrobe book, since this contains no reference to such expenditure.[38] Outside 1278, wardrobe activity has largely to be followed in the accounts of the keepers of the wardrobe enrolled on the pipe rolls. While these are far less detailed than the wardrobe books, they do record building works as separate items. Thus Edward's castle expenditures (for example the £120 spent on Lampeter), entered in the Wardrobe book for 1278, appear again in the pipe roll wardrobe account covering the same period.[39] Earlier, between October 1274 and November 1275, the accounts itemized £113 spent on the park of Windsor Castle and £153 on the Tower of London. Under Henry III they had recorded the money spent on the tomb of the king's daughter, Katherine.[40] The failure of the enrolled accounts in the 1270s to make any reference to work on the shrine is therefore significant. Edward was apparently not financing that work through the wardrobe.

A final possibility is that Edward paid for the base by assigning to it some existing source of revenue. Such an arrangement would normally appear on the pipe rolls, but for the reign of Edward these are both voluminous and unprinted. There must, however, be a good chance of such an assignment being initially set up by letters enrolled on the chancery rolls, and of these there is certainly no trace.[41]

If, therefore, Edward I paid for the shrine base in the 1270s, the silence of the relevant material take some explaining. After all, references to the tombs of his sons, John and Henry, reverberate through the *liberate*, issue, pipe, and exchequer account rolls.[42] An explanation is somewhat easier to formulate for the silence under Henry III. If Henry had financed the base, as he did the reliquary, direct from the wardrobe, the exchequer, and assigned revenues, the evidence would probably have survived. If, on the other hand, he had financed it as part of the general works on the abbey, then it might well not have done so, and this for two reasons. First, it is only from January 1264 that the accounts of the keepers of the Westminster works were enrolled on the pipe rolls and thus survive. Had the shrine base been largely paid for before that date, there would be no record of it. Second, assuming that work on the shrine was still continuing later than 1263, it is possible that payments for it were in-

---

[37] *Cal. Patent Rolls 1272–81*, 273; PRO, E 372/123, m. 40.

[38] PRO, C 47/4/1. The book originally covered the period from November 1277 but the early pages are lost or damaged. On p. 24 there is a reference to Edward offering a brooch 'to the feretory of St Edward'.

[39] PRO, C 47/4/1, 35; E 372/123, m. 42d.

[40] PRO, E 372/119, m. 43d; E 361/1, m. 1.

[41] For a sign that the shrine was not completed by Henry's executors, see below, p. 420.

[42] John: PRO, E 101/467 8, m. 1; E 403/21A, m. 1; C 62/50, m. 4; E 403/25, m. 2. Henry: C 62/51, m. 12; E 101/467 6(2), m. 1; E 101/467 7(2), m. 1; E 372/125, m. 6d.

cluded within the general item of 'wages of certain masons, carpenters and labourers and in works put out to task to masons and carpenters', which always form by far the largest item in the accounts.[43]

We move, then, to the question of style. In Binski's view, the shrine base of the Confessor and the tomb of King Henry (which was probably under construction in 1279), came from the same workshop. Indeed, having finished the base around 1279, the artists then moved across to the tomb. Yet the contrasts between the two present problems for this hypothesis, at least as thus postulated. On the one hand we have the base, in Binski's words, 'an oddly unharmonious hybrid . . . a gimcrack compromise of Roman and Gothic'; on the other hand, the tomb, 'a magnificent if austerely experimental edition of the more richly handled Roman monuments of the last decades of the thirteenth century'.[44] 'The tomb is stylistically related to the shrine' as Binski points out, 'only with respect to its small trefoil-headed *fenestellae* and twisted colonettes'[45] and even the trefoils of the *fenestellae* (the two cavities set in the tomb in which relics were probably housed) are markedly less pointed than those of the niches on either side of the base. The real parallel, as Binski observes, is not between the tomb and the base, but the tomb and the shrine's altar, which is now in the south ambulatory.[46] It may well be that tomb and altar came from the same craftsmen and were constructed around the same time. But this tells us nothing about the date of the base. If anything, the uncertainty of the base's design and the assurance of the tomb's suggest that the former belonged to a different campaign and was considerably earlier in date.

And so finally to the contemporary inscription on the tomb. This is now virtually lost but in a fifteenth-century transcription it appears as follows:

> Anno milleno domini cum septuageno
> et bis centeno cum completo quasi deno,
> hoc opus est factum quod Petrus duxit in actum,
> Romanus civis, homo, causam noscere si vis,
> rex fuit Henricus, sancti presentis amicus.

Binski's translation runs thus: 'In AD one thousand, with seventy and two hundred, and ten nearly complete, this work was made which Peter the citizen of Rome brought into being: if you wish to know the cause, it was King Henry, the friend of this saint'[47]

Binski argues, perfectly reasonably, that in the crucial passage 'and ten nearly

---

[43] Paviors are the only specialist craftsmen singled out in the accounts. Between February and November 1272 there is a reference to 'paviors making pavements in front of various altars': *Building Accounts of Henry III*, 432–5.

[44] Binski, 'The Cosmati at Westminster', 13, 18, 24.

[45] Ibid. 21.

[46] Ibid. 22.

[47] *The History of Westminster Abbey by John Flete*, ed. J.A. Robinson (Cambridge, 1909), 114, Binski, 'The Cosmati at Westminster', 14.

complete' (*cum completo quasi deno*) the *cum* means plus or in addition to and thus indicates that nearly ten has to be added to 1270. Hence the inscription meant that the shrine was *factum* in 1279. Other scholars have accepted this reading of *cum* but have still reached a date of 1269 by supposing that, in the fifteenth-century copy, *septuageno*, seventy, was a mistake for *sexageno*, sixty. However, this possibility is rendered implausible both by the scansion of the verses and by Binski's careful examination of how the inscription was laid out. Binski also acknowledges, very fairly, the possibility of reaching 1269 by another route, namely by assuming that the *cum completo quasi deno*, 'with ten nearly complete', was meat to qualify the 'one thousand, with seventy and two hundred', indicating that the last ten of the 1270 years was nearly concluded, hence making the date 1269. But this reading requires the *cum* to be employed in an apparently unique fashion, one different from that found both in the first line of the inscription (*Anno milleno cum septuageno*) and in many other dating verses of this type, in all of which its effect is additive.[48]

The balance of the argument, therefore, weighs quite heavily in favour of 1279 as the date recorded in the inscription. Yet the inscription, taken as a whole, like so much other evidence, still points to the shrine as the work of the 1260s, for it states emphatically that King Henry was its 'cause', an odd claim if the structure was commissioned by Edward I. Had Edward wanted to pay tribute to his father's wishes or inspiration, would he not have linked their names together, thus making his filial salute explicit, enhancing his own credit, and binding the dynasty as a whole to its sainted predecessor? He had, after all, a clear precedent in the sanctuary floor at the Abbey, paid for by Abbot Ware, where lines joined together Ware's name and King Henry's.

The evidence thus diverges, yet there is a means of reconciling it, namely by accepting that the inscription recorded not the substantive construction of the base (which took place in the 1260s) but the date of its final completion. In any scenario the inscription is likely to have come last, after the conclusion of the rest of the work. In any scenario too, whether the date is 1269 or 1279, the *opus* is unlikely to have been *factum* in one calendar year: the meaning of *factum* must, in effect, be 'completed'. This is indeed precisely its meaning in the royal letter of August 1269 which ordered the finishing of the reliquary.[49] The careful phrasing of the verse thus hints at a distinction between completion and creation: 'in 1279 this work was completed which Peter, the Roman citizen, brought into being'. This does not mean that the base was under continuous construction from the 1260s through to 1279 for, as we shall see, there are reasons to think that the Cosmati had left Westminster by the early 1270s (see below, pp. 422–3). They returned at the end of the decade and they returned to make King Henry's tomb. How natural, therefore, to celebrate at the same time Henry's responsibility for the Confessor's shrine. How natural too to re-

---

[48] Binski, 'The Cosmati at Westminster', 14–15, 22 and 15 n. 41 and 42. I am most grateful to Carlotta Dionisotti and Anne Duggan for advising me about the inscription.

[49] See above, n. 17.

member Peter *civis Romanus*, who had made it. For it may well be that it was
Peter's workshop, perhaps even Peter himself, who had returned to the abbey.
The stylistic contrasts between the shrine base and Henry's tomb, stressed earlier, simply reflect the considerable interval between the two works. Binski may
be right in thinking that they come from the same workshop, but with at least
ten years in between.

The completion of the base probably involved elaboration and refinement
of the surface decoration as well as the addition of the inscription. But if the
base was in place for the translation in 1269, as we have argued it was, Henry
would surely have remedied any major defects, as a matter of urgency, in the
three years before his death in 1272 and before, of course, the departure of
the Cosmati. There is one small but telling piece of evidence here. In the will
he drew up in 1253, just before leaving for Gascony, Henry asked Edward to
finish the fabric of the abbey and his executors to finish the feretory. The executors were to find the necessary 500 marks by selling his jewels. If Henry
made another will after 1253 it does not survive; however, we do know what
happened to his jewels. The keeper of his wardrobe, Peter of Winchester, wished
to sell them, not to finance a new base for the shrine but to support poor members of the late king's household.[50] As far as Henry III was concerned the feretory of the Confessor was complete.

There remain, therefore, compelling reasons for accepting that the base of
the Confessor's shrine was ready for the translation in 1269.[51] The arguments
to the contrary derived from the silence of the sources, questions of style, and
the inscription around the base are ambiguous and are either compatible with
construction in the 1260s or actually in favour of it. The references in the accounts to the paviors working around the feretory, and the whole circumstances of the 1269 translation itself, tip the balance firmly in that direction. A
date for the base, which sees it constructed around the middle 1260s, is also
compatible with the state of Cosmati work in Italy. There the earliest datable
examples in the base's Italianate Gothic idiom, for example, the tomb of Clement IV at Viterbo, come from the end of the decade and are therefore later,
which precisely explains the uncertainty of the Westminster design, why it seems,

---

[50] *Foedera*, I, i, 496; PRO, E 352/74, r. 2, m. 2 (E 372/125, m. 6): John of London, accounting at
the exchequer, was allowed 200 marks he had given to Bartholomew de Castro [Castello], 200
marks which Bartholomew himself had given to Peter of Winchester *pro jocalibus Regis Henrici de-
functi que vendere volebant pro deliberaicone pauperis familie ipsius Regis.* Bartholomew, apparently associated in Peter's wish, was a former household clerk of King Henry's and keeper of the exchange.
See also *Cal. Patent Rolls 1272–1281*, 3.

[51] That Edward I ordered payment in 1291 for three marble columns placed *circa* the feretory
does not indicate that it was still incomplete at that date since the columns were probably not part
of the structure but free-standing around it: PRO, E 403/1256, m. 2 (*Liberate de thesauro nostro fratri
Reymondo de Wenlok' monacho Westmonasteriensis quadraginta sex solidos et octo denarios pro factura trium
columpnarum marmorum quas nuper per preceptum nostrum fieri fecit circa feretrum sancti Edwardi in eccle-
sia Westmonasteriensis. teste me ipso apud asserugg' xii die januarii anno regni nostri xix*); G.G. Scott,
Gleanings from Westminster Abbey, 136 n. See Binski, 'The Cosmati at Westminster', 18.

as Binski puts it, 'an improvisation', made up almost as it went along and influenced by some of the motifs in the abbey church rising around it.[52]

This dating is further confirmed if we relate the evidence about the base to the sequence of events which might have led to the commissioning of the Cosmati work. A central role in making contact with the Cosmati, as Claussen, Binski, Foster, and Gardner have pointed out, was almost certainly played by Abbot Ware.[53] Following his election to the abbacy of Westminster, Ware left England in December 1258 to seek confirmation from the pope. He had probably returned by the following August.[54] As Foster observes, in 1259 the papal court was resident at Anagni. It was there, in March 1259, that Ware was made a papal chaplain. And there in the cathedral he would have seen the superb Cosmati pavements which still survive in the crypt and the nave.[55] It seems unlikely, however, that on this first visit Ware brought back Cosmati stones and workers, although Flete, the Westminster monk, in his history of the Abbey written in the 1440s, states that he did so.[56] Apart from other difficulties with Flete's account, which will be mentioned later, such a major decision about the church would have needed the closest consultation with Henry III. What Ware did was rather give King Henry first-hand information about the Cosmati.

This information came at a critical time. In June 1259 Henry had ordered the demolition of a further section of the Confessor's church and the commencement of work on the new choir.[57] Clearly the east end and transepts of the abbey were at last complete. This was a natural moment to give practical thought to the shrine base and pavement in the Confessor's chapel. With his enthusiasm fired by Abbot Ware, Henry decided to commission both from Peter *civis Romanus*. Probably the contract was fixed up during the visits Ware made to the papal court 'on the affairs of the king and the church of Westminster' early in 1260 and again early in 1261, both of which have hitherto passed unnoticed by historians.[58] If this is right, then Peter *civis Romanus* arrived in England some time in the early to mid 1260s, began work on the shrine and then, with its structure in place, commenced the pavement, hence the paviors working before the feretory of the Confessor between December 1266 and December 1269. As we have seen, this suggestion is compatible both with the base's style and the surviving accounts. It also corresponds with what would be the natural sequence of such work, the base itself coming before the pavement.

King Henry evidently judged the Cosmati work a success and hence decided to place another and much greater Cosmati pavement before the high altar, a

[52] Binski, 'The Cosmati at Westminster', 18.

[53] Claussen, *Magistri Doctissimi Romani*, 178; Binski, 'The Cosmati at Westminster', 28; R. Foster, *Patterns of Thought The Hidden Meaning of the Great Pavement of Westminster Abbey* (London, 1991), 14–21; Gardner, 'The Cosmati at Westminster', 204–5.

[54] *Close Rolls 1256–9*, 351; *Cal. Patent Rolls 1258–66*, 7, 39, 59.

[55] *Cal. Papal Registers*, i.364; Foster, *Patterns of Thought*, 17.

[56] *The History of Westminster Abbey by John Flete*, 113.

[57] *Close Rolls 1256–9*, 390 (*Building Accounts of Henry III*, 196–7).

[58] *Cal. Patent Rolls 1258–1266*, 117, 135.

pavement he described, in a letter patent of 1269, as having been obtained 'for our use' (*ad opus nostrum*).[59] Flete, as we have seen, believed that Ware brought the new pavement and the workers to assemble it back from his first visit to Rome in 1259–60. But the inscription on the pavement itself, which states that it was finished in 1268, makes this unlikely. Would it really have taken eight years to complete? Equally, it was not till May 1269 that Henry, as far as the evidence goes, gave Ware any financial compensation for his mission.[60] Since, in addition, the sanctuary pavement is more sophisticated in its planning and grander in its materials than the pavement in the Confessor's chapel, it seems highly likely that it is the product of a different and slightly later campaign.[61] Quite probably, therefore, Ware obtained the pavement on a later visit to Rome, either that in 1266 or the one that started in September 1267.[62]

There is no indication that Henry III paid in anything like full measure for the sanctuary pavement. In May 1269 Abbot Ware, in return both for obtaining it and for other expenses, was merely pardoned a debt of £50, surely inadequate compensation. Contemporaries would have been highly amused by Foster's suggestion that the cost was borne by the pope. In fact, Fleet may well be right in asserting that the pavement was paid for by Ware himself.[63] The abbot was something of a financial expert, the abbey was a wealthy house, and its debt to King Henry was immense.[64]

By the time of Henry III's death in 1272 the first phase of the Cosmati work at Westminster was over.[65] Henry himself was buried, not in his later Cosmati tomb, but in the place where the Confessor had lain before the high altar prior

---

[59] PRO, C 66/87, m. 17 (pencil); *Cal. Patent Rolls 1266–1272*, 338. The normal meaning of *ad opus nostrum* is 'for our use' and it is naturally translated thus in this letter, but for the view that it should rather be translated 'for our work', see Binski 'The Cosmati at Westminster', 13 n. 26.

[60] See above, n. 59. These points have often been made by previous commentators. See Binski, 'The Cosmati at Westminster', 29, n. 107.

[61] Binski (*The Cosmati at Westminster*, 14) suggests, as one possibility, that this 'stylistic discrepancy ... could ... be evidence of the work of a different campaign'. The pavement before the high altar, according to its inscription, was the work of 'Odoricus'. Claussen has suggested that he was identical with the Peter *civis Romanus*, who constructed the Confessor's shrine, both thus being the work of the Petrus Oderisius whose career Claussen reconstructs. Alternatively, Claussen postulates, 'Odoricus' may have been Oderisius Stephani, the supposed father of Peter, who signed pavements in Rome: Claussen, *Magistri Doctissimi Romani*, 181–3. For contrary arguments see Binski, 'The Cosmati at Westminster', 18–19 and Gardner, 'The Cosmati at Westminster', 209–11.

[62] *Cal. Patent Rolls 1258–1266*, 681; *Close Rolls 1264–8*, 332. Its inscription states that the pavement was finished in 1268 but this, following papal and English royal practice, is probably the year March 1268-March 1269.

[63] See above, n. 59; Foster, *Patterns of Thought*, 21; *The History of Westminster Abbey by John Flete*, 113.

[64] B. Harvey, *Westminster Abbey and its Estates in the Middle Ages* (Oxford, 1977), 97. Miss Harvey shows that Ware and the monks must have lent Ralph de Limesi 'a substantial sum of money' in 1263 and in 1269 they agreed to buy his manor of Great Amwell for £566 13s 4d: ibid. 191, 194, 196.

[65] For the suggestion that the great pavement's inscription may not have been installed until after Henry III's death, see Binski, 'The Cosmati at Westminster', 10–11.

to his translation in 1269.[66] The tombs of the princes John and Henry, the sons of Edward I, under way respectively in 1272 and 1274, were almost certainly made of Purbeck marble since the craftsmen, under the king's mason, Robert of Beverley, were Ralph of Guildford, Ralph and William of Corfe, and Robert and Osbert the Polishers.[67] The first sign of activity around Henry's tomb comes in a statement from the chronicler Trevet to the effect that Edward returned from France in 1280 (in fact the visit was in 1279) and 'caused the paternal sepulchre to be repaired with stones of jasper which he brought with him'.[68] If this indicates that the Cosmati work was already in progress, then perhaps it had been commissioned by Abbot Ware when he visited Rome in 1276 and 1277.[69] It was not, however, until 1290 that Henry's body was actually moved to his new tomb.[70]

Unless work on the tomb progressed very slowly, this delay is puzzling. Is the explanation that King Edward, aware of the growing cult of the future St Louis, was hoping for a similar cult to develop around his father, leading likewise to his translation as a saint? Was the Cosmati tomb thus intended as a shrine?[71] Such hopes were not without substance. The Furness chronicler, under the year 1275, noted that 'in these days it was said that frequent miracles were done at the tomb of the blessed King Henry'. Westminster Abbey's own *Flores Historiarum* claimed that Henry's merits in life were demonstrated by miracles after his death.[72] The cult certainly had some official sanction and encouragement. In October 1274, when Henry, King Edward's son, was on his deathbed, two 'measures' (candles measuring his height) were sent to Westminster Abbey,

---

[66] See above, n. 6.

[67] John: E 101/467 8, m. 1; E 403/21A, m. 1; C 62/50, m. 4; E 403/25, m. 2. Henry: C 62/51, m. 12 (where the tomb is specifically stated to have been of marble); E 403/27, m. 2; E 101/467 6(2), m. 1; E 101/467 7(2), m. 1; E 372/125, m. 6d. William of Corfe worked on Henry's tomb, the others on John's.

[68] *Nicholai Triveti Annales*, ed. T. Hog (London, 1845), 301. A slightly more elaborate version, which changes *reparari* to *plurimum honorari*, is found in *Willelmi Rishanger Chronica et Annales*, ed. H.T. Riley (Rolls Ser., 1865), 96. This was probably written up from Trevet: see ibid., p. xxiv. For the date of Edward's visit see Binski, 'The Cosmati at Westminster', 19. The wardrobe accounts show that while abroad Edward spent £741 purchasing 'diverse jewels' which had belonged to his late mother-in-law, the Countess of Ponthieu: PRO, E 372/124, m. 47d. Did these include the 'stones of jasper' he used to decorate his father's tomb?

[69] PRO, C 62/52, m. 11; *Cal. Close Rolls 1272-9*, 349; *Cal. Pat. Rolls 1272-1281*, 171, 231. This suggestion is made by Binski, 'The Cosmati at Westminster', 22. He also wonders whether Ware arranged for the shrine base at the same time. For Claussen's view that Henry's tomb was the work of Arnolfo de Cambio and Binski's reservations, see Claussen, *Magistri Doctissimi Romani*, 183; Binski, 'The Cosmati at Westminster', 24-6. Since there is no sign that Edward paid for his father's tomb, perhaps Ware funded it, paying at the same time for the completion of the shrine base.

[70] *The Chronicle of Bury St Edmunds*, 94; *Chronicles of the Reigns of Edward I and Edward II*, 98.

[71] This suggestion is also made by Gardner, 'The Cosmati at Westminster', 213.

[72] *Chronicles of the Reigns of Stephen, Henry II and Richard I*, ed. R. Howlett, 4 vols. (Rolls Ser., 1884-79), ii.571; *Flores Historiarum*, ed. H.R. Luard, 3 vols. (Rolls Ser., 1890), iii.28; and see the references in Binski, 'The Cosmati at Westminster', 27 n. 95.

one to be placed by Saint Edward, the other by King Henry.[73] In May 1276 King Edward's chancellor, Robert Burnel, Bishop of Bath and Wells, issued indulgences to all from his diocese who visited Henry's tomb. He was followed on the same day by the Bishop of Verdun and later by the Bishops of Laon (1277/8), Kildare (1280/1), Ely, St Andrews, and Emly (all 1287).[74] In the end, however, the cult faltered and died. And thus in 1290, with a sense of disappointment, and without much ceremony – 'suddenly and unexpectedly' as the chronicle of Bury St Edmunds put it[75] – Edward moved his father to his Cosmati tomb, magnificent and soon to be made more so with an effigy, but still not the shrine he had once hoped it might be.

All this is speculation. What is less so is that King Henry played a central role in bringing the Cosmati to Westminster to construct the pavement in the Confessor's chapel, the sanctuary pavement before the high altar, and the shrine of the Confessor himself. Such work affirmed King Henry's special devotion to the papacy, symbolized (though this is more speculative) his view that royal authority had parallels with papal,[76] and above all, for a king who was more aesthete than intellectual, honoured in the most magnificent way possible the memory of Edward the Confessor. 'Since we recall that you have told us' ran a well-known letter from Henry to Edward of Westminster, 'that it would be rather more splendid to make two leopards which are to be either side of our throne at Westminster of bronze instead of cutting them out of marble, we command you to have them made of metal as you said'.[77] We may well imagine Henry speaking to Abbot Ware in similar terms about the employment of the Cosmati on the Confessor's shrine in preference to Purbeck marblers.

Henry III was a king much concerned with his name and fame. He ordered all the silk cloths which he gave to St Albans abbey to be inscribed 'indelibly' with the name, 'Henry III, King of the English'. At Westminster an inscription on the pavement of the new Chapter House declared: 'This Chapter House as superior to others as the rose is among flowers: it King Henry friend of the Holy Trinity: to Christ dedicated who him loved.' On the great Sanctuary pavement, likewise, an inscription told how in 1268 'King Henry the Third, the city [Rome], Odoricus, and the abbot joined together these porphry stones'.[78] And

[73] PRO, E 101/350/18, m. 3. Nicholas Vincent kindly drew this roll to my attention.
[74] WAM Book 11, ff. 404v, 405, 398–9. Henry III's tomb does not appear in indulgences after 1287.
[75] *The Chronicle of Bury St Edmunds*, 94. See also *Chronicles of the Reigns of Edward I and Edward II*, 98. However, Edward was not taken in by fraudulent miracles wrought at his father's tomb: see *Triveti . . . Annales*, 302–3. Binski, 'The Cosmati at Westminster', 27–8 discusses the possibility of Henry's translation from a different angle.
[76] *Robert Grosseteste Epistolae*, ed. H.R. Luard (Rolls Ser., 1861), 338–9; *Matthaei Parisiensis . . . Chronica Majora*, ed. H.R. Luard, 7 vols. (Roll Ser., 1872–83), v. 129–30. See above, p. 78.
[77] *Close Rolls 1242–7*, 293; *The History of the King's Works*, ed. Colvin, i.102.
[78] *Matthaei Parisiensis . . . Chronica Majora*, vi. 389; W.R. Lethaby, *Westminster Abbey Re-Examined*, 112; *Flete's History of Westminster Abbey*, 113.

at the spiritual heart of the whole church the inscription on the Confessor's shrine proclaimed:

> ... Man, if you wish to know the cause,
> it was King Henry, of the present saint a friend.[79]

To this proud boast Henry III had every right.[80]

[79] There are distinct parallels between the inscription on the Chapter House floor and that on the Confessor's shrine. Both are in Leonine verse and both describe Henry as a 'friend' (*amicus*), respectively of the Holy Trinity and the Confessor.

[80] I am most grateful to Paul Binski, Jinty Nelson, and Michael Prestwich for commenting on a draft of this article.

21

The Burial of King Henry III, the Regalia and Royal Ideology

On 28 November 1871 Dean Stanley led a party of ecclesiastics, antiquaries and workmen into the chapel of Edward the Confessor at Westminster Abbey.[1] Stanley's purpose was to open the tomb of King Henry III which stood, as it still stands, immediately to the north of the Confessor's shrine. The king's effigy was removed, the marble slabs beneath it were lifted, and the coffin was revealed, covered in cloth of gold. But then, as Stanley later recorded, 'a feeling was found to prevail that there did not seem, upon historical grounds, to be sufficient motive to warrant the opening of the coffin'.[2] Perhaps the assembled party recoiled from violating the king's body, so long undisturbed. Perhaps, or so the story ran at the abbey, Queen Victoria was unamused by the plans to tamper with the bones of her predecessor, and ordered Stanley to desist.[3] Whatever the reason, Henry III was left unexamined, thus avoiding the fate of his father and son, Kings John and Edward I, whose coffins were opened by eighteenth-century antiquaries, more inquisitive or less restricted than their nineteenth-century successors.[4] As far as Henry's burial robes and *insignia* are concerned, this gap in our knowledge can be filled, at least in part. Henry III is the first king of England for whose *funeralia* there is documentary evidence. This essay will set out that evidence and discuss the significance of what it reveals, namely that Henry III was buried in coronation *regalia*, quite possibly the *regalia* used at his own coronation in 1220.[5]

[1] I am most grateful to Jinty Nelson for commenting on a draft of this essay.

[2] A.P. Stanley, 'On an Examination of the Tombs of Richard II and Henry III in Westminster Abbey', *Archaeologia*, 45 (1880), p. 322 and pp. 317–22. Richard Mortimer, keeper of the muniments at the abbey, has kindly showed me a fragment of the cloth of gold which is now preserved in the library.

[3] I owe this story to the late Lawrence E. Tanner, keeper of the muniments and librarian at the abbey. For Stanley's examination of the royal vaults under Henry VII's chapel, see his *Historical Memorials of Westminster Abbey* (fifth edn., London, 1882 and subsequent editions), appendix. According to Lawrence Tanner, Stanley had one great advantage in examinations of this kind: he had no sense of smell.

[4] V. Green, *An Account of the Discovery of the Body of King John* (London and Worcester, 1797); J. Ayloffe, 'An Account of the Body of King Edward I, as it Appeared on the Opening of his Tomb in the Year 1774', *Archaeologia*, 3 (1786), 376–431. See M. Prestwich, *Edward I* (London, 1988), pp. 566–7.

[5] This was Henry's second coronation. The first was held in the turmoil of the civil war at Gloucester in October 1216.

Henry III died late in the day on 16 November 1272, in his palace at Westminster in the sixty-sixth year of his age.[6] He had left his body to the abbey, to
lie close to the shrine of Edward the Confessor, and had given his heart to Fontevrault to be with the tombs of his mother, grandmother, uncle and grandfather – Isabel of Angoulême, Eleanor of Aquitaine, Richard I and Henry II.
Henry's heart was probably extracted at once for eventual transport to the Touraine; his body was buried on 20 November in the place before the high altar
where the Confessor had rested prior to his translation in 1269.[7] It was not till
1290 that Henry himself was translated to the tomb made by Cosmati marblers
beside the Confessor's shrine.[8] Next year, the abbess of Fontevrault, risking death
by shipwreck (as the cartulary of the abbey put it) came to England and took
home 'that most excellent treasure, namely the heart of the illustrious English
king of famous record'.[9] This was not the end of the heart's journeys, however,
or at least not by repute: a heart, claimed as Henry's, escaped the destruction
at Fontevrault at the time of the Revolution, and is now possessed by a convent
of Ursuline nuns in Edinburgh.[10] When inspected by Michael Clanchy and myself around 1980 it was encased in a plain lead heart-shaped container and appeared (through a hole in the container's side) to be like a small lump of pumice
or desiccated wood. We have one clue to the size of the body which the heart
graced. Stanley did at least measure Henry's coffin and found it six feet one
inch long. Probably Henry was much the same height as his father John, whose
coffin was likewise six feet one inch, and whose body, when measured in 1797,
was found to be five feet six and a half inches tall. The chronicler, Trevet, was
therefore right in saying that Henry was a man of middle height. He was certainly considerably shorter than his son, Edward I, who was found in 1774 to
measure a princely six feet two inches.[11]

The evidence for the robes and *insignia* used for Henry's burial comes from
the accounts of the keeper of his wardrobe enrolled on the pipe rolls. From
1234 these were divided into two halves. There was firstly a section dealing with
the money received and spent by the keeper; and secondly an equivalent section dealing with precious objects under his control: 'concerning jewels, gold
and silver vessels, cloths of gold and arest' (*de jocalibus, vasis aureis et argenteis,*

---

    [6] *Close Rolls, 1268–72*, p. 588.
    [7] *Annales Monastici*, ed. H.R. Luard, 5 vols. (Rolls Ser., 1864–9), iv, 252.
    [8] *The Chronicle of Bury St Edmunds, 1212–1301*, ed. A. Gransden (London, 1964), pp. 94–5; *Chronicles
of the Reigns of Edward I and Edward II*, 2 vols. ed. W. Stubbs (Rolls Ser., 1882–3), i, 98.
    [9] Bibliothèque Nationale, Paris, MS Latin 5480, f. 4; Westminster Abbey Muniments no. 6318B;
Cal. Patent Rolls 1281–92, p. 463.
    [10] A. Pommier, *Observations sur une Relique Possédée autrefois par Le Musé d'Orléans sous le Nom de
Coeur de Henry II (Plantagenet)* (Orléans, 1917).
    [11] Stanley, 'On an Examination of the Tombs of Richard II and Henry III in Westminster Ab-
bey', p. 320; Green, *An Account of the Discovery of the Body of King John*, p. 6; Ayloffe, 'An Account of
the Body of King Edward I', p. 385. According to another, but less authoritative account, John's
body measured five foot five inches: A.L. Poole, *From Domesday Book to Magna Carta* (Oxford, 1951),
p. 486 n. 2.

pannis ad aurum et pannis de aresta) as it was put in 1268–9.[12] From one point of view, these jewel accounts, with their serried ranks of rings, cups, brooches and garlands all massed together without columns or paragraphs through membranes of the pipe rolls, can be tedious and difficult to work through;[13] from another, with a touch of imagination, they suggest, more than anything else, the immense glitter of medieval monarchy and remind us that the Plantagenets, like their Anglo-Saxon predecessors, were still very much the givers of rings. In the two years between February 1238 and February 1240 Henry dispensed 409 rings and 103 brooches 'in gifts to diverse people'.[14] When the jewel accounts came to the period between July 1258 and July 1261, a new section appeared within them, one dealing with objects which seem to have been on semi-permanent deposit in the wardrobe. Up to a point these were rather a mixed bag but the section began with 'a great crown of gold with precious stones' and then listed together, one after the other, a series of items of what, as we shall see, were *regalia*.[15] In the next account, that covering the period from July 1261 to Christmas 1264, these items of *regalia* were again listed together in virtually the same order, and this continued to be the case down to the end of the reign.[16]

In the last jewel account of the reign, however, instead of the customary statement, after the list of *regalia*, that everything remains, one comes, with a sudden shock, to a very different conclusion:

> from which [items] one royal rod, one dalmatic of red samite with orphreys and stones, one mantle of red samite most splendidly adorned with orphreys and precious stones, a gold brooch, one pair of stockings of red samite with orphreys, one pair of shoes of red samite are handed over for the burial of the king. And all the other things remain.

> De quibus una virga regalis, una dalmatica de rubeo samicto cum aurifragio et lapidibus, unum mantellum de rubeo samicto cum aurifragio et lapidibus preciosis peroptime hornatum, una brochea auri, unum par caligarum de samicto rubeo cum aurifragio, et unum par sotularium de rubeo samicto liberantur ad sepulturam Regis. Et omnia alia remanent.[17]

---

[12] Public Record Office London (from whence all future manuscript references come unless stated) E 372/113, m. 3d..

[13] They may have had a depressing effect on those who wrote them. On the dorse of a schedule attached to one of Edward I's jewel inventories is the bleak note: 'Ego dixi in dimidio dierum meorum vadam ad portas inferi' (E 101, 353/30).

[14] E 372/83, m. 13. Anglo-Saxon rings, however, were usually arm rings.

[15] E 361/1, m. 2. The great crown is followed immediately by a great brooch, great ring, sceptre and three rods but other items then intervene before the rest of the *regalia* is listed *en bloc*.

[16] E 372/113, mm. 3d, 4d; E 372/114, m. 41d; E 372/115, m. 2d; E 372/116, m. 1d. The main differences are first, that the items listed either side of the *regalia* change between 1258–1261 and 1261–1264, though thereafter they remain the same; and second that after the 1258–1261 account there is no further reference to the great crown, great brooch and great ring; see below p. 453.

[17] E 372/116, m. 1d.

As the accounts make clear, the *regalia* taken for Henry's burial did not return to the wardrobe. The rod, dalmatic and the rest, were not, therefore, required for mere temporary display, for example to clothe a wooden effigy of the king placed above his coffin at the funeral. They were used instead to adorn the king's body and were entombed with him. By the same token, since the articles in question had been in the wardrobe since at least 1258–61, they had not been acquired simply for the burial, as was to happen for example with royal burials in early fourteenth-century France.[18]

There can be little doubt that Henry was buried in coronation *regalia*.[19] There is no detailed description of the 1220 coronation, but we can see the place of Henry's burial robes and *insignia* in the coronation service through following Roger of Howden's account of the coronation of Richard I in 1189.[20] After Richard had taken the customary oaths, he was stripped to his shirt (*camisia*) and breeches, shod with sandals worked with gold (*sandalis auro contextis*) and then anointed with holy oil on his head, breast and arms. After the anointing, he was dressed in his 'royal vestments', 'first namely the tunic, then the dalmatic'. And then, having been girded with sword and spurs, 'he was vested with the mantle'. There followed the actual crowning, after which the archbishop put the royal sceptre, surmounted with a cross, in Richard's right hand and the royal rod (*virga*) surmounted with a dove, in his left.

Now, in 1272, the wardrobe did not supply Henry's body with all the *regalia* mentioned here. There was, and we will discuss the significance of some of these omissions later, no shirt, tunic, sword, spurs, crown or sceptre. The 'one pair of shoes (*sotularium*) of red samite' which were provided may, or may not, be the equivalent of the *sandali* of 1189.[21] In other areas, however, there is a clear correlation. Henry was buried with a dalmatic,[22] a mantle, and a *virga*

[18] E.A.R. Brown, 'The Ceremonial of Royal Succession in Capetian France: The Double Funeral of Louis X', *Traditio*, 34 (1978), 229–30, and idem., 'The Ceremonial of Royal Succession in Capetian France: The Double Funeral of Philip V', *Speculum*, 55 (1980), 279, 281, 290–3, both reprinted in idem., *The Monarchy of Capetian France and Royal Ceremonial* (Aldershot, 1991), as chapters 7 and 8. See also below p. 444 and note 100.

[19] For a valuable survey of coronation *regalia* between the Conquest and 1483, see W.H. St. John Hope, 'The King's Coronation Ornaments', *The Ancestor*, 1 (1902), 127–59.

[20] *Chronica Rogeri de Houedene*, ed. W. Stubbs, 4 vols. (Rolls Ser., 1868–71), iii, 9–12 reprinted in *English Coronation Records*, ed. L.G. Wickham Legg (Westminister, 1901), pp. 46–53. See K.J. Leyser, 'Frederick Barbarossa, Henry II and the Hand of St. James', in his *Medieval Germany and its Neighbours* (London, 1982), at p. 225 note 1. For the coronation *ordo* see J. Brückmann, "The Ordines of the Third Recension of the English Coronation", *Essays in Medieval History Presented to Bertie Wilkinson*, ed. T.A. Sandquist and M.R. Powicke (Toronto, 1979), pp. 99–115.

[21] In the *regalia* as listed in 1220 pairs of *sotularium* and *sandalium* are distinct but linked together: *unum par sandalium novorum et sotularium*: E 401/3B, r. 1, printed and translated in *English Coronation Records*, ed. Legg, pp. 54–6.

[22] A dalmatic is not mentioned specifically in the *regalia* between 1258 and 1272 but, since the accounts are specific that Henry's dalmatic came from that *regalia*, it must have been one of the two 'royal tunics of red samite with orphreys and precious stones'. There is some indication from John's reign that 'dalmatic' and 'royal tunic' could be used interchangeably. See *Rot. Litt. Pat.*, pp. 54b, 173a.

regalis, the last almost certainly being the dove-topped rod. The gold brooch, which was also supplied, was probably used to attach the mantle to the dalmatic like that listed in the coronation *regalia* in 1220.[23] It is just possible, moreover, that the tunic worn in the coronation beneath the dalmatic was also provided in 1272 from the *regalia*, coming unmentioned, since it was a far simpler garment, with the dalmatic. At any rate, in the description of the *regalia* in 1220, two 'tunics' are described as being 'with' highly decorated dalmatics.[24]

The appearance of Henry's dalmatic, mantle, brooch and rod may be suggested by the robes and *insignia* with which Edward I was found when his tomb was opened in 1774. He was clothed in 'a dalmatic . . . of red silk damask', over which was 'the royal mantle, or pall, of rich crimson sattin, fastened on the left [his right] shoulder with a magnificent *fibula* of metal gilt with gold', four inches long and decorated with twenty-two 'beads or mock pearls'. Down Edward's left side, held by his left hand, lay a rod, five foot and half an inch long and topped by a dove made of white enamel.[25] On Henry's own gilt bronze effigy, erected some twenty years after his death,[26] the *insignia* have been lost but the body is swathed in a great mantle, fastened by a brooch on its right shoulder. Beneath the mantle is what may be a dalmatic with loose sleeves, underneath which is a tight-sleeved inner tunic. Both the mantle and the dalmatic were once studded at the edges with jewels. The effigy of King John in Worcester cathedral, a work probably of the 1230s,[27] likewise has a loose-sleeved dalmatic, ornamented with fringes inset with jewels around the kneck and cuffs. One minor puzzle relates to the length of Henry's dalmatic. In John's effigy it is cut off well above the feet to reveal the tunic underneath. Most dalmatics took this short form. On the other hand, the much-perished robe found on John's body, apparently of crimson damask, reached from the neck nearly to the feet, as does the dalmatic on Henry's effigy.[28] It may be noted that in the

---

[23] See below p. 460.

[24] *English Coronation Records*, ed. Legg, pp. 54–6 and see above note 22. The one item with which Henry was buried not mentioned in the coronation service, were the stockings (*unum par caligarum de samicto rubeo cum aurifragiis*). The Emperor Otto IV ordered that he be buried with stockings of samite (*caligis de samito*): A. Erlande-Brandenburg, *Le Roi est Mort: Etude sur les Funérailles, les Sépultures et les Tombeaux des Rois de France jusqu' à la Fin du XIIIe siécle* (Bibliothèque de la Française D'Archéologie, 7, 1975), p. 19 note 9.

[25] Ayloffe, 'An Account of the Body of King Edward I', pp. 382–4. Ayloffe mentions no jewels on either Edward's dalmatic (which he also called a 'tunic') or mantle. Unlike his father, as far as the evidence goes, Edward had (in his right hand) a sceptre, which was surmounted with a cross made of copper gilt of 'most elegant workmanship', and a stole, decorated with 'philligree work', transparent glass and beads, which was wrapped round the body. For Edward's crown, see below p. 444. A contemporary sketch of the body is reproduced in *Age of Chivalry: Art in Plantagenet England, 1200–1400*, ed. J. Alexander and P. Binski (London, 1987), p. 369. For the significance of the stole see P.E. Schramm, *A History of the English Coronation*, translated by L.G. Wickham Legg (Oxford, 1937), p. 135.

[26] Henry's effigy was commissioned in 1291: *Cal. Close Rolls, 1288–96*, p. 171.

[27] John was placed *in novo sarcofago* in Worcester cathedral in 1232: *Annales Monastici*, i, 84.

[28] Green, *An Account of the Discovery of the Body of King John*, p. 6.

ritual as set out for the coronation of Richard II in the *Liber Regalis*, the garment beneath the mantle was a highly decorated tunic which likewise touched the feet.[29] As the lower part of Edward I's body was covered in a cloth of gold, we cannot know if his dalmatic was of this kind.[30]

Henry, therefore, was certainly buried with the kind of *regalia* used at coronations. Was it the actual *regalia* used at his coronation in 1220? This is quite possible but not quite provable. On 26 May 1220, six days after the coronation, a set of *regalia* (it is so called at the time) was delivered to the treasurer of the exchequer by the king's tutor, Peter des Roches, bishop of Winchester. That some of this had been used at the coronation is clear both from the objects themselves and from the fact that the gold spurs, when they were subsequently given to the new Lady Chapel at the abbey, were specifically described as 'having been made for us at our first coronation at Westminster'.[31] The Appendix at the end of the essay shows how most of the items used for Henry's burial in 1272 can be matched up with items in the 1220 *regalia*. Thus the *virga regalis* of 1272 could correspond to the *virga argentea et deaurata* of 1220;[32] the *dalmatica de rubeo samicto cum aurifragio et lapidibus* to the *tunica cum dalmatica de rubeo samit. cum uno monili et lapidibus in aurifragio*; the *mantellum de rubeo samicto cum aurifragio et lapidibus preciosis peroptime hornatum* to the *pallium de rubeo samit. cum lapidibus*; the *brochea auri* to one of the two *broche auree ad pallium et dalmaticam quarum in una est saphirus et in alia perla*; and the *unum par sotularium de rubeo samicto* to the *unum par sotularium de rubeo samit. cum aurifragio*. There are problems with such a match. One dalmatic of red samite sounds much like another; the number of *virgae* had multiplied from one to three between 1220 and 1258–61, so perhaps Henry was buried with a new one;[33] and already in 1220 there were more robes than seem to have been needed for the actual coronation ceremony: conceivably Henry's dalmatic, mantle and brooch dated back to 1220 but were second pairs not used for the ceremony. On the other hand, there was only *unum par sotularium* of red samite both in the 1220 *regalia* (apart from a pair surviving from King John) and in the wardrobe after 1258, so here it seems very likely that the 1220 *sotulares* were used. There was also nothing new, as we shall see, about a king being buried with his actual coronation *regalia*. My own feeling is that the articles taken from the wardrobe in 1272

---

[29] *English Coronation Records*, ed. Legg, pp. 94, 119. For Edward II's coronation robes see W.H. St. John Hope, 'On the Funeral Effigies of the Kings and Queens of England', *Archaeologia*, 60 (1906), 531 citing E 361/3, r. 8/16 (pencil).

[30] Ayloffe, 'An Account of the Body of King Edward I', p. 383; *Age of Chivalry*, ed. Alexander and Binski (London, 1987), p. 369.

[31] *English Coronation Records*, ed. Legg, pp. 55, 56.

[32] Henry's *virga* was one of three *virgae* in the wardrobe between 1258 and 1272. In the account for 1258–61 these are three *virgae auri*; from the account of 1265 onwards (E 371/114, m. 41) they become *virgae argenti*. Most probably they were all silver gilt, like the *virga* in the wardrobe in 1220. For an occasion when rods and sceptres in the *regalia*, thought to be gold, turned out to be silver gilt, see M. Holmes, 'New Light on St. Edward's Crown', *Archaeologia*, 97 (1959), 213–4.

[33] For further discussion see below note 151.

had been used for Henry's coronation in 1220, although the following discussion does not depend on that assumption.[34]

At least two kings of England before 1272 were buried in robes connected with their coronations, namely Henry, the young king, the eldest son of Henry II; and Richard I.[35] That did not mean, however, that the manner of Henry III's interment was entirely dictated by precedent. On the contrary, Henry, it may be suggested, had thought deeply about his death and the form and meaning of his burial. He was not alone in that for his kinsman, the Emperor Otto IV, in 1218, left detailed instructions about the robes and *insignia* with which he was to be buried.[36] Death surrounded a medieval king. Life expectancy was short and the king's circle of acquaintance large. Henry marked the deaths of favoured ministers and magnates by distributing alms for their souls and giving palls to cover their bodies.[37] He commissioned a marble tomb for his sister, Joan, and first a marble effigy and then one of silver for his beloved daughter Katherine.[38] When the courtier Hugh Giffard collapsed and died in May 1246, Henry immediately appointed a special chaplain to sing the *salus populi* daily at mass 'to preserve the king and his household from sudden death'.[39] In 1231, affected by the death of his brother-in-law, William Marshal earl of Pembroke,

---

[34] See also below note 138. Edward I, as we have seen, was certainly buried in *regalia* suitable for a coronation (Schramm, *The English Coronation*, p. 135 says he was buried in 'coronation robes') but, in the absence of any documentary evidence (in part because there were no wardrobe accounts for the end of the reign), it is impossible to know whether any of the items had actually been used at his coronation. It may be noted that Henry's burial dalmatic had orphreys and stones and there was only one dalmatic of that type in the *regalia* in 1220, the other being only of red samite. However, by 1258 both dalmatics ('royal tunics') were described as having orphreys and stones. Perhaps the second dalmatic had been re-worked by then. The same may have been true of the 1220 *pallia* which, if they are the same, had both become more elaborate between 1220 and 1258. Henry was aged thirteen years and six months at the time of his coronation and his robes may well have needed alteration to fit later in life, for example if they were worn at the queen's coronation in 1236.

[35] Schramm, *The English Coronation*, p. 135, refers briefly to the case of the young king. For a valuable survey of royal effigies and burials see St. John Hope, 'On the Funeral Effigies on the Kings and Queens of England', 517–70. For an examination of the French and some of the English and imperial evidence see Erlande-Brandenburg, *Le Roi est Mort*, especially pp. 12–22. No Capetian king is specifically said to have been buried with robes and *insignia* used at his coronation, and in the early fourteenth century the practice was to acquire *regalia* for the burial (see above note 18). The first king known to have been buried in state, with tunic, dalmatic, crown and sceptre, was Philip Augustus and Erlande-Brandenburg suggests (pp. 14–18) that the Capetians lagged behind the Angevins in this area.

[36] *Monumenta Germaniae Historica Legum Sectio IV, Constitutiones et Acta Publica*, ii (Hanover, 1896), ii, 51–3; Erlande-Brandenburg, *Le Roi est Mort*, p. 19 note 9. For the details, see below note 112. For the elaborate arrangements made by Philip V for his burial, see Brown, 'The Ceremonial of Royal Succession in France: the Funeral of Philip V', pp. 273–6.

[37] For example, *Cal. Liberate Rolls, 1226–40*, p. 474; *Close Rolls, 1237–42*, p. 339; *Cal. Liberate Rolls, 1245–51*, pp. 68, 69; *Cal. Liberate Rolls, 1251–60*, p. 346; *Close Rolls, 1256–9*, p. 345.

[38] *Cal. Liberate Rolls, 1226–40*, p. 316; *Cal. Liberate Rolls, 1251–60*, pp. 376, 385; E 361/1, m. 1.

[39] *Matthaei Parisiensis . . . Chronica Majora*, ed. H.R. Luard, 7 vols. (Rolls Ser., 1872–83), iv, 553; *Cal. Liberate Rolls, 1245–51*, p. 54.

he decided to lie with the Marshals in the Temple Church in London. Later, in 1246, he decided to be buried beside the Confessor in Westminster Abbey.[40] During his visit in 1254, he decided to leave his heart to Fontevrault.[41] Long and dangerous illnesses in 1252, when he was 'gripped by fear of terrible death', in 1262–3, when there were rumours that he had actually died, and in 1271 when the doctors despaired of his life, gave Henry plenty of time to refine the details of the funeral ceremony.[42] He had time again during the weeks of his last illness.[43] Quite probably, therefore, Henry, like Otto IV, decided upon his grave robes and *insignia*. In so doing he was above all concerned with his passage to the life hereafter, a point to which we will ultimately return. But he was also making a final statement about his kingship, something all the more important given the fragility of peace after the civil war and the absence of Edward, the new king, on crusade.[44] Henry's funeral, as described by the chronicler Thomas Wykes, who perhaps was present, was a great public ceremony attended by the magnates of the kingdom. The king's body 'adorned as was fitting in the most precious garments and a royal diadem' was borne to the grave by chosen nobles *in locello portatili*, some kind of portable reliquary which clearly enabled the king's body to be seen.[45] Henry's funeral was thus 'his final blazon'.[46]

There were, in all probability, two quite distinct traditions regarding royal interments and the coronation *regalia*, one represented by the rites of the young king, one by those of Richard I. In 1183 the body of the young king was buried, according to the chronicle of Ralph de Diceto, 'wrapped most carefully in the linen clothes, anointed with the chrism, which he had at his consecration' (*corpus regis, quas habuit in sua consecratione lineis vestibus crismate delibutis diligentius*

[40] *Chronica Majora*, iii, 201; *Cal. Charter Rolls, 1226–57*, p. 135; Westminster Abbey Muniments, no. 6318A (*Cal. Charter Rolls, 1226–57*, p. 306).

[41] Westminster Abbey Muniments, no. 6318B. For the problems arising from the division of the body, see E.A.R. Brown, 'Death and the Human Body in the Later Middle Ages: The Legislation of Boniface VIII on the Division of the Corpse', *Viator*, 12 (1981), 221–70, reprinted as ch. 6 of *The Monarchy of Capetian France and Royal Ceremonial*.

[42] *Chronica Majora*, v, 304; *Close Rolls, 1251–3*, p. 433; *Close Rolls, 1268–72*, pp. 397–8.

[43] Henry died on 16 November and was already in bed seriously ill on 28 October: *Cronica Maiorum et Vicecomitum Londoniarum*, ed. T. Stapleton (Camden Soc., 1846), pp. 149–50. However, there were hopes of recovery early in November: *Close Rolls, 1268–72*, pp. 585–6.

[44] During his illness in 1271 Henry had urged Edward to return from his crusade: *Close Rolls, 1268–72*, pp. 397–8. On the day of Henry's death, as he laboured *in extremis*, the potentially disruptive earl of Gloucester came before him and swore to maintain the peace of the realm: *Cronica Maiorum et Vicecomitum*, p. 155.

[45] *Annales Monastici*, iv, 252; see also *Cronica Maiorum et Vicecomitum*, pp. 153–4, and *Foedera, Conventiones, Litterae . . .*, ed. T. Rymer, revised by A. Clarke and F. Holbrooke, vols. I, i and ii and II, i (London, 1816–18) I, ii, 497. Erlande-Brandenburg (*Le Roi est Mort*, pp. 18–22) discusses the circumstances in which the bodies of the Capetian kings, from Philip Augustus onwards, were exposed before burial.

[46] For the way increasingly elaborate burials were used to demonstrate the power and authority of kingship, see E.M. Hallam, 'Royal Burial and the Cult of Kingship in France and England, 1060–1330', *Journal of Medieval History*, 8 (1982), 359–80.

involutum . . .).[47] The young king, therefore, was buried in the shirt in which he had been anointed at his coronation in 1170. He was not the last king to be interred after this fashion. In 1327 there were sent to Gloucester from the great wardrobe two sets of vestments for the funeral of Edward II. On the one hand, there was the mantel, tunic, dalmatic, gloves, belt, hose, shoes and spurs 'which the king used on the day of his coronation'; on the other a tunic, shirt (*camisia*), cap and coif (*pillium* and *tena*) 'in which the king was anointed on the day of his coronation'. Nearly all the first set of robes eventually returned to the great wardrobe, as did the cap. Only the gloves, and the vestments of unction, the tunic, shirt and coif, were used for the burial.[48]

Was the practice of visibly burying kings in articles associated with the unction in any way kept alive between 1183 and 1327? It is just possible that it was, which brings us to the most extraordinary feature of the burial of King John, namely that he did not wear a crown. Instead, on his skull the antiquaries in 1797 found what they took to be 'the celebrated monk's cowl, in which he is recorded to be buried, as a passport through the regions of purgatory'. 'This sacred envelope', the report continued, 'appeared to have fitted the head very closely, and had been tied or buckled under the chin by straps, parts of which remained'.[49] But were the antiquaries right in this identification? There appears to be no contemporary warrant for the assertion that John was buried in a monk's cowl. Much more likely is that, just like Edward II, and quite probably his own elder brother, the young king, he wore head-gear used during the ceremony of unction at his coronation. At the 1189 coronation the coif was carried into the Abbey by Geoffrey de Lucy and was placed on the king's head (above a linen cloth) immediately after the consecration. According to the fourteenth-century ritual in the *Liber Regalis*, perhaps here reflecting earlier practice, the coif (*amictus*), placed on the king's head 'on account of the anointing', was worn continuously for seven days. On the eighth day the archbishop celebrated mass, removed the coif, washed and arranged the king's hair, and then put a golden circlet on the king's head which was worn all that day bareheaded 'in reverence of his cleansing'.[50] It is clear, therefore, that the coif was a highly significant garment. It was ceremonially carried into the abbey and had to remain in place over a linen cloth and under various crowns, hence no doubt the need for straps. It protected the sacred oil on the king's head, and thus symbolically the spiritual benefits which the oil conferred, from any taint throughout the rest of the ceremony and in the days thereafter. Since John, as we have seen, wore on his body a robe of crimson damask, he was not buried in

---

[47] *Radulfi de Diceto . . . Opera Historica*, ed. W. Stubbs, 2 vols. (Rolls Ser., 1876), ii, 20.

[48] St. John Hope, 'On the Funeral Effigies on the Kings and Queens of England', 531, citing E 361/3, r 8/16 (pencil).

[49] Green, *An Account of the Burial of the Body of King John*, pp. 4–5. The engraving of the body gives little help as to the appearance of the head-gear.

[50] *Chronica Rogeri de Houedene*, iii, 9–10; *English Coronation Records*, ed. Legg, pp. 48–9, 51–2, 94, 119.

his unction shirt. But it may well have been the coif of unction, rather than the monk's cowl, which he took 'as a passport through the regions of purgatory'.

Some kings, therefore, were overtly buried in the vestments of unction. Others, however, either did not wear them at all, or concealed them beneath the splendid 'top' robes and *insignia* of the coronation. According to the annals of Winchester, Richard I was buried 'in the same crown and other royal *insignia* in which he had been crowned five years before at Winchester'. The annalist was here referring to Richard's crown-wearing in 1194, after his return from captivity in Germany, an event which most chroniclers referred to simply as a coronation and which certainly employed coronation *regalia*, indeed that was the whole point.[51] Richard is the first king specifically stated to have been buried with coronation *insignia* but he may possibly have been following the example of his father. At any rate, according to Howden, Henry lay in state before his burial 'dressed in royal apparel, having gloves on his hands, a gold ring on his finger, a sceptre in his hand, shoes covered with gold and spurs on his feet, girded with a sword'.[52] Both Richard and Henry, in their effigies at Fontevrault, are shown crowned, sceptred and splendidly attired.[53] So was John in his effigy at Worcester and Louis VII in his at St-Denis. All these effigies Henry had almost certainly seen.[54] Yet he may well have been aware of the rival custom of burial in the vestments of the anointing. Indeed, it is possible that he had actually seen his father's crownless head, covered with the coif of unction, when he attended John's reburial at Worcester in 1232, just as his own face 'with a long beard' (*cum barba prolixa*) was revealed at his translation in 1290.[55] In the end, of course, Henry was buried very much in the second tradition, with the *insignia* and 'top' robes of the coronation.[56] It is worth canvassing some reasons as to why burial in the visible vestments of unction did not appeal to him.

The anointing was, in some ways, the supreme spiritual moment of the coronation. Derived from the way the prophet Samuel had anointed David, it pro-

---

[51] *Annales Monastici*, ii, 71. After the ceremony Richard took off the heavy vestments and crown and put on lighter ones. There are detailed descriptions of the ceremony in *Chronica Rogeri de Houedene*, iii, 247–9, and *The Historical Works of Gervase of Canterbury*, ed. W. Stubbs, 2 vols. (Rolls Ser., 1879, 1880), i, 524–7. See also *Radulphi Coggeshall Chronicon Anglicanum*, ed. J. Stevenson (Rolls Ser. 1875), p. 64; *Chronicles and Memorials of the Reign of Richard I*, 2 vols., ed W. Stubbs (Rolls Ser., 1864, 1865), i, 446; *Radufli de Diceto Opera*, ii, 114, and see J. Gillingham, *Richard the Lionheart* (London, 1978), p. 242.

[52] *Chronica Rogeri de Houedene*, ii, 71.

[53] W. Sauerländer, *Gothic Sculpture in France 1140–1270* (London, 1972), p. 448 and plate 142. St. John Hope goes so far as to say that 'the robes in which [Henry II] is shown arrayed are those that were put upon him at his coronation'. He likewise thought Richard's effigy showed him with his coronation ornaments: 'On the Funeral Effigies of the Kings and Queens of England', pp. 523–4.

[54] See below p. 443. For the robe in which John was buried, see above p. 431.

[55] *Annales Monastici*, i, 84 (the correct date is 19 May); *Chronicles of the Reigns of Edward I and Edward II*, i, 98.

[56] For Henry's crown, see below p. 444.

claimed that the king had been chosen by God and had received from him the gifts of the Holy Spirit. From thenceforth he did indeed rule 'by the grace of God'.[57] No wonder, therefore, that kings were sometimes buried in the garments hallowed by this part of the ceremony. None could be more holy.

Henry himself had pondered the importance of unction and had asked Robert Grosseteste what it added to the royal dignity. Grosseteste, in reply, expanded on the seven-fold gifts of the Holy Spirit, although in such a way as to emphasise the duties which they imposed, and then warned that unction in no way placed the royal power on a level with the sacerdotal or gave the king any kind of priestly authority.[58] Henry seems to have accepted this. According to Matthew Paris, he refused to hold a candle during an excommunication ceremony in 1253 on the grounds that he was not a priest.[59] Had the exchange with Grosseteste, therefore, diminished Henry's sense of the importance of unction? Certainly, the picture of the coronation of St Edward (a work of the 1260s) placed behind Henry's bed in his chamber at Westminster, instead of depicting both crowning and unction like other portrayals of the scene, depicted crowning alone.[60]

All this is highly speculative. Henry also, according to Matthew Paris, swore in 1253 to observe Magna Carta, 'as I am crowned and anointed king'.[61] His preference for the full coronation *regalia* at his funeral is better perhaps approached from other angles. One of the attractions of the robes of unction was their very austerity. On his death bed the young king was urged by a *vir religiosus* to remove even the ring from his finger: 'naked you left the womb of your mother and naked you should return'.[62] But there was nothing austere or indeed intellectual about Henry's piety. He wore no Montfortian hair-shirt and preferred, as he told Louis IX, to see God in the mass rather than to hear about him in sermons.[63] Henry's piety was warm-hearted, opulent and theatrical. On special occasions he would feed one thousand, fifteen thousand, even a hundred thousand paupers.[64] He delighted in ecclesiastical ritual, lavished money

[57] For unction in the coronation *ordo*, see *English Coronation Records*, ed. Legg, pp. 31–3, 39–40. For a discussion of the origins and development of unction, see J.L. Nelson, *Politics and Ritual in early Medieval Europe* (London, 1986), especially pp. 247–57, 274–81, 288–96, and chapter 13.

[58] *Roberti Grosseteste Epistolae*, ed. H.R. Luard (Rolls Ser., 1861), pp. 348–51, also printed and translated in *English Coronation Records*, ed. Legg, pp. 66–8.

[59] *Chronica Majora*, v, 377.

[60] P. Binski, *The Painted Chamber at Westminster* (The Society of Antiquaries, Occasional Paper, new ser., 9, 1986), pp. 38–40, and colour plate 1 and plates 2, 36, 37.

[61] *Chronica Majora*, v, 377.

[62] *Radulphi de Coggeshall Chronicon Anglicanum*, ed. J. Stevenson (Rolls Ser., 1875), p. 265. The long tract printed here (pp. 265–73) on the death and burial of the young king does not mention his burial in the robes of unction but is perfectly compatible with it.

[63] *Nicholai Triveti Annales*, ed. T. Hog (London, 1845), p. 280. For an illuminating discussion of the piety of Simon de Montfort, Louis IX and Henry III see J.R. Maddicott, *Simon De Montfort* (Cambridge, 1994), pp. 90–3.

[64] *Cal. Liberate Rolls 1240–5*, pp. 124, 220, 281, 306; *Annales Monastici*, iv, 77. See H. Johnstone, 'Poor Relief in Royal Households of Thirteenth-Century England', *Speculum*, 4 (1929).

on candles and vestments, and so the stories went, heard as many as four masses a day.[65] Westminster Abbey breathes Henry's expansive spirit. Like the great French cathedrals on which it was partly based, it reached high, higher than any other church in England; yet, unlike the French cathedrals, instead of the blank wall behind the triforium arcades, it boasted a great windowed gallery. Unlike the French churches, it was also extravagantly decorated with all the internal surfaces covered with marble, figure sculpture, painting and diaper. As the church progressed, so the decoration multiplied. In the choir, begun in 1259, the pillars of the main arcade, were given eight shafts instead of four; the single octafoil windows of the galleried triforium were replaced by three cinquefoils and more shafting was added in the vault. It would, therefore, have been utterly foreign for Henry to have been buried in robes and *insignia* which did not proclaim his majesty in all its jewelled and coloured splendour. Such *regalia*, moreover, even though they hid the robes of unction, still testified to the monarchy's unique authority. No other English layman wore a crown and, if Henry claimed no priestly power, his dalmatic with its jewels and orphreys was still very much an ecclesiastical garment worn by bishops and deacons on festal occasions, most notably when celebrating mass.[66]

Moving now to the *insignia* with which Henry was entombed, we may note several innovations. To start with, as far as the evidence goes, Henry was buried without a sword. At the time of his death, no fewer than seven swords lay amongst the *regalia* of which five had also been there in 1220. Yet none of these was taken out to adorn Henry's body.[67] The possibility that some other sword was used is reduced both by Henry's swordless effigy and by the fact that no sword was found in the tomb of Edward I. All this was a clear breach with the Angevin past. When John's tomb was opened in 1797 his left arm was found lying on his breast and in its hand there was a sword in a leather scabbard pointing downwards along the body.[68] The effigy on John's tomb likewise depicts the king gripping a downward pointing sword in his left hand.[69] The body of

---

[65] *Annales Monastici*, iv, 254; *Nicholai Triveti Annales*, p. 280, and see the index under 'Ecclesiastical matters: *church ornaments*' in any volume of the *Cal. Liberate Rolls*. The two surviving rolls recording Henry III's oblations at mass (and elsewhere) show that he usually heard one mass a day. However, he sometimes heard two and on special occasions (like Christmas Day 1238) he heard three. There is no recorded occasion when he heard four. C 47/3/44; E 101/349/30.

[66] J. Mayo, *A History of Ecclesiastical Dress* (London, 1984), pp. 31–2, 56, 147–51. See the discussion in Schramm, *The English Coronation*, pp. 134–6. I am grateful to Kay Staniland for much help over ecclesiastical dress. For aristocratic coronets, see D. Crouch, *The Image of Aristocracy in Britain, 1100–1300* (London, 1992), pp. 198–211.

[67] The three swords born before the king in the coronation procession would not have been used for this. The appropriate sword would have been the one with which he was ceremonially girded.

[68] Green, *An Account of the Discovery of the Body of King John*, p. 5.

[69] J. Martindale, 'The Sword on the Stone: Some Resonances of a Medieval Symbol of Power (the Tomb of King John in Worcester Cathedral', *Anglo-Norman Studies*, 15, ed. M. Chibnall (Woodbridge, 1992), pp. 199–241. This wide-ranging article brings together a great deal of valuable material about the use of swords in effigies and burials.

John's father, Henry II, was girded with a sword, as we have seen, and both his effigy and that of Richard I were shown with swords by their sides. The likelihood that Richard I was buried with a sword, indeed the sword with which he had been girded at his coronation, is strengthened by the fact that John had to have a new sword made for his own coronation.[70]

The role of the sword in the coronation ceremony was, of course, wholly positive. Three were borne before the king as he progressed into the abbey and another was girded around him, after he had donned tunic and dalmatic. 'Receive the sword', intoned the archbishop, to 'exercise justice, powerfully destroy the forces of iniquity and protect the church'.[71] And yet it was impossible not to be aware of very different resonances. As Jane Martindale has remarked, 'the sword was primarily a weapon whose associations were with violence and bloodshed'.[72] For a king like Richard that was completely appropriate. The sword beside his effigy told of great deeds and mighty victories. The sword in King John's sepulchral hand, by contrast, simply risked the jibe 'swoft-sword', *mollegladium*.[73] It was a jibe to which Henry was equally vulnerable. His campaigns in France in 1230 and 1242 were dreary failures. In the 1250s he projected first a crusade to the Holy Land and then a campaign in Sicily and achieved neither. In 1264, at the battle of Lewes, he had two horses killed under him and was 'much beaten with swords and maces'. Next year, at the battle of Evesham, he was wounded and lost the two sword-belts with which he was girded before the battle.[74] The last thing Henry wanted to remember at the end of his life was a sword. Indeed, long before that he had begun to abandon it as a symbol of royal authority. On his seal, made in 1218, Henry was depicted like all his Norman and Angevin predecessors enthroned and holding sword and orb. But when Henry showed himself again enthroned on his gold penny in 1257, on his first and second substitute great seals, one made before 1259 and one after, and on the new great seal of 1259 itself, about whose form he gave personal directions, the sword had vanished.[75]

Henry's abandonment of the sword was not entirely negative, for he had

---

[70] *Rott. Litt. Pat.*, pp. 54b-55. The emperors Otto IV and Frederick II were both buried with swords, Otto's by his right side, Frederick's girded about the body: Erlande-Brandenburg, *le Roi est Mort*, p. 19 note 9; Martindale, 'The Sword on the Stone', p. 222.

[71] *English Coronation Records*, ed. Legg, p. 98. For the origins of the sword in the coronation ceremony, see Nelson, *Politics and Ritual in Early Medieval Europe*, pp. 313–4, 378–9, 395 note 104.

[72] Martindale, 'The Sword on the Stone', pp. 234–5. For other symbolic connotations of the sword, see Crouch, *The Image of Aristocracy*, pp. 190–8; and E. Mason, 'The Hero's Invincible Weapon: An Aspect of Angevin Propaganda', *The Ideals and Practices of Medieval Knighthood*, 3, ed. C. Harper-Bill and R. Harvey (Woodbridge, 1990), pp. 121–37.

[73] Martindale, 'The Sword on the Stone', p. 237.

[74] British Library, MS Tiberius AX, f. 170; E 372/114, m. 40d.

[75] A.B. and A. Wyon, *The Great Seals of England* (London, 1887), pp. 21–6; plates 6–7 nos. 41–6; D.A. Carpenter, 'Gold and Gold Coins in England in the mid-thirteenth century', *Numismatic Chronicle*, 147 (1987), plate 19 no. 5; P. Chaplais, 'The Making of the Treaty of Paris (1259) and the Royal Style' in *Essays in Medieval Diplomacy and Administration*, (London, 1981), ch. 1, p. 249 n. 2 (*Cal. Liberate Rolls 1251–60*, p. 472); idem, *Piers Gaveston: Edward II's Adoptive Brother* (Oxford, 1994), pp.

something to put in its place.[76] In the coronation of 1189, immediately after the crowning, Richard received a sceptre in his right hand, and a gold *virga* 'having at its summit a gold dove' in his left. When the body of Edward I was examined he was likewise found holding a rod topped by a dove in his left hand. We can be fairly confident, therefore, that the *virga regalis* with which Henry was buried, perhaps identical to the *virga argentea et deaurata* in the treasury in 1220, was likewise a rod, surmounted by a dove.[77]

In being entombed with the dove-topped rod, Henry III was breaking with past practice. John, as we have seen, held only a sword. Henry II's body, according to Howden, lay with a sceptre; and it was with a sceptre likewise that the effigies of Henry and Richard at Fontevrault were most probably adorned.[78] Henry's preference for the doved rod over both sword and sceptre had already been signalled in the 1250s. In his new gold penny, minted in 1257, the sword gave way to the sceptre; but in all the new seals mentioned above it surrendered to a dove.

There was one reason above all for Henry's adoption of the dove, namely its association with Edward the Confessor.[79] The penny of the Confessor had already provided the model for the gold penny of Henry III. Edward's penny showed him enthroned and holding orb and sceptre. Henry's gold penny followed suit, thus becoming the first coin since the Conquest to show the king enthroned.[80] The sceptre was certainly a symbol of the Confessor's. Indeed, in 1242 Henry gave orders for 'the sceptre of Saint Edward' to be gilded and repaired.[81] Yet when he came to study the question of commissioning new great seals to supplement or replace his great seal of 1218, Henry came to realise that it was the doved rod which was most intimately associated with the Confessor, and which was the most fitting symbol for both his own and the Confessor's rule. Henry's new seals were inspired by the seal of the Confessor which showed him enthroned and holding in his left hand a sword and in his right

---

continued

37–9 where the whole question of Henry III's substitute seals is clarified. They are illustrated as plates 2 and 3.

[76] The arrangement of Henry's hands in his tomb, if they were placed as we suggest below, would have left no room for a sword; however he could still have been girded with a sword or one could have been put by his side, as with the emperors Otto IV and Frederick II; see above note 70. The abandonment of the sword in his tomb was thus a more positive act of discrimination than on his new seal where there really was no room for a sword.

[77] For the question of in which hand Henry held the rod, see below note 96.

[78] The current sceptres are modern restorations. Both hands are placed to hold the *insignia* but the right is the 'gripping' hand. See the engravings in C. Stothard, *The Monumental Effigies of Great Britain* (London, 1817) and below p. 443.

[79] For Henry and the Confessor, see now P. Binski, *Westminster Abbey and the Plantagenets: Kingship and the Representation of Power, 1200–1400* (New Haven, 1995), chapter two. Binski's book appeared as I was completing this essay and I have not made changes in the light of it. It contains a bravura discussion of many of the points I touch on.

[80] Carpenter, 'Gold and Gold Coins', pp. 110–11.

[81] *Cal. Liberate Rolls, 1240–5*, p. 120.

hand a rod ending in a large and very striking dove. Even the Confessor's example could not persuade Henry to retain the sword, but the doved rod caught his imagination. It seemed uniquely an emblem of the Confessor, for subsequent kings had omitted it from their seals: like Henry III in his first great seal of 1218, they sat with sword and orb.[82] Henry was, therefore, acting very much in the Confessor's image, when he replaced the sword with the doved rod on the substitute great seal of before 1259, on the new great seal of 1259, and on the substitute great seal of the 1260s.[83] The dove appeared too atop Edward's rod, gaily presiding over the whole ceremony, in the coronation of the Confessor painted in the king's Westminster chamber in the 1260s, this in contrast to the painting of the same scene in *La Estoire de Seint Aedward le Rei* of perhaps ten years before where Edward held a sceptre.[84] The association thus forged by the dove between himself and the Confessor, Henry made all the more personal and powerful by denying it to anyone else. In the golden *bulla* he made for his son Edmund, as king of Sicily in 1255–6, Edmund held an orb and sceptre.[85] Even more striking, while Henry adopted the doved rod on his own seal, he removed it from the seal of his wife. In her pre-1259 seal Eleanor of Provence held both sceptre and dove-topped rod. In her post 1259 seal she held only a sceptre while her free hand was left fingering the strings of her cloak.[86]

Henry's use of the doved rod testified to his very personal devotion to the Confessor and also to his wider conception of kingship with which the Confessor was bound up. In the great proclamations of the 1260s Henry stressed one thing above all about his rule: it had brought peace.[87] He was quite right about that, for there had indeed been almost unbroken political peace since the end of the civil war in 1217. With peace as his aim, the dove by itself was an appropriate symbol. As one prayer during the coronation put it, God, having chastised the world with the flood, had then sent a dove bearing an olive branch to reveal 'the return of peace to the earth'.[88] The dove's association with the Con-

---

[82] Wyon, *Great Seals of England*, pp. 3–4, plate 1, no. 6. See plates 3–5, nos. 19, 21, 23, 25, 27, 30, 32 which show a dove appearing on top of the orb in the seals of Henry I, Stephen and Henry II.

[83] There appears to be no documentary evidence bearing on the date of the pre-1259 substitute great seal and it is hard to place on stylistic grounds. It lacks the elaborate throne of the 1259 great seal, but that was also true of Edmund's gold *bulla* of 1255–6. Its form was also followed very closely by the post 1259 substitute great seal, apart from the altered legend. See Chaplais, *Piers Gaveston*, pp. 38–9 and plates 2 and 3; Carpenter, 'Gold and Gold Coins', plate 19 no. 4.

[84] Binski, *The Painted Chamber at Westminster*, pp. 38–40, and colour plate 1 and plates 1, 37b, and see plate 4b, 5b.

[85] Carpenter, 'Gold and Gold Coins', plate 19 no. 4.

[86] F. Sandford, *A Genealogical History of the Kings and Queens of England and Monarchs of Great Britain from 1066 to the Year 1707* (London, 1701), p. 57. I owe this information to the kindness of Margaret Howell. I suspect that when Eleanor's first seal was made, presumably in 1236, Henry had not appreciated just how intimately the rod was associated with the Confessor's kingship.

[87] *Foedera*, I, i, 408–9; *Close Rolls, 1268–72*, pp. 242–3. See above pp. 96–8.

[88] *English Coronation Records*, ed. Legg, p. 91. It is not clear whether this prayer was said at Henry's coronation, though he was doubtless well aware of the episode to which it referred (Genesis, chapter 8, verse 11). The prayer appears in the first and second English Ordo and in that of 1308

fessor reinforced this message for the Confessor, like Henry, had been a *rex pacificus*, a king of the dove not the sword. Matthew Paris, indeed, in the prologue to *La Estoire de Seint Aedward le Rei* made the contrast explicit. Some kings, he wrote, 'were mighty and very bold', famous for 'strength and courage'. Others, like the Confessor, 'were more wise, peaceable and temperate'.[89] By adopting the doved rod, therefore, Henry associated his own governance with the wise, peaceable and harmonious rule of the Confessor.[90] He also reached back into the Anglo-Saxon past and stressed the descent of his dynasty from pre-Conquest kings, a theme likewise developed by Matthew Paris in *La Estoire de Seint Aedward le Rei*. In allegorical fashion Paris explained how Henry I, by his marriage to 'the daughter of King Edward's neice', had grafted the dynasty on to its old Anglo-Saxon root, a union of which the ultimate fruit was King Henry III himself.[91]

Dynastic continuity was also, it may be suggested, stressed in another way by Henry's burial, though this time the continuity was with Henry's more immediate Angevin predecessors. This brings us to another puzzle. Henry, as far as the evidence goes, was buried with a rod but not with a sceptre, unlike his son Edward I who lay with both.[92] What then was done with Henry's free hand? Henry had seen at least three models of how kings might be laid out in death.[93]

---

continued

but not in the third Ordo in between: Schramm, *The English Coronation*, p. 107; Nelson, *Politics and Ritual in Early Medieval Europe*, p. 378.

[89] *Lives of Edward the Confessor*, ed. H.R. Luard (Rolls Ser., 1858), pp. 25–6, 179–80.

[90] Another influence on Henry could have been the very civilian image of the Capetian kings of France, for which see Martindale, 'The Sword on the Stone', pp. 212–13. On his seal Louis IX sat enthroned without a sword and there was no sword on the effigy of Louis VII at St-Denis which Henry might have seen in 1254. Philip Augustus was buried without a sword: Erlande-Brandenburg, *Le Roi est Mort*, p. 18.

[91] *Lives of Edward the Confessor*, ed. Luard, p. 287.

[92] For Edward's sceptre, see above note 25. Burial of the king with crown, rod and sceptre is stipulated in Westminster Abbey's Litlington Missal (1383–4) where other features too correspond to the way Edward I was buried: *Missale ad Usum Ecclesie Westmonasteriensis*, ed. J. Wickham Legg, 3 vols. (Henry Bradshaw Soc., i, v, xii, 1891, 1893, 1896), ii, 734–5, a passage also found in British Library, Cotton MS Nero DVI, f. 75, a reference I owe to the kindness of Philip Morgan. Henry's effigy once held both rod and sceptre. Effigies are, however, far from infallible guides as to how kings were actually buried. John's effigy had both crown and sceptre yet neither were found in his tomb. For further reflections on why Henry was not buried with a sceptre, see below note 151.

[93] It is conceivable, as we have suggested, that he also saw his father's head. Indeed, perhaps he saw the body as well. Henry may also have seen the Confessor's body in 1269 but it was probably by then without *regalia*. See *The Life of King Edward who Rests at Westminster*, ed. F. Barlow (2nd edn., Oxford, 1992), p. 153 and the same author's *Edward the Confessor* (London, 1970), pp. 269, 277. Contrast, Holmes, 'New Light on St. Edward's Crown', p. 214. Osbert de Clare's description of the crown, ring and sceptre found with the Confessor when his tomb was opened in 1102 was omitted from the subsequent lives by Ailred and Matthew Paris: M. Bloch, 'La Vie de S. Édouard le Confesseur par Osbert de Clare', *Analecta Bollandiana*, 41, fasc. I et II (1923), 121–2; *Historiae Anglicanae Scriptores X*, ed. R. Twysden (London, 1652), p. 407b; *Lives of Edward the Confessor*, ed., Luard, pp. 156, 310.

One, which came from the effigy of his own father in Worcester Cathedral, he decisively rejected. As we have seen, he would lie with neither sword nor sceptre. The second came from the tombs of the Capetians at Saint-Denis just outside Paris. Henry last visited Paris in 1262, just too soon to see the series of royal effigies commissioned by Louis IX. He could, however, have seen the existing effigy of Louis VII, which depicted the king holding a sceptre in his right hand, with its top resting on his shoulder, and with his left hand lying upon his heart.[94] Again, Henry rejected the sceptre, but it is just possible that the rod was placed on his shoulder and his free hand upon his heart. Much more likely, however, is that Henry lay in death after the fashion of the effigies at Fontevrault which he saw during his emotive visit in 1254. Henry II and Richard I both rested in the same way with the sceptre, placed vertically along the centre of the body, gripped by the right hand. The left hand was placed across the centre of the body, just beneath the right hand in Henry's effigy, and a little above it in Richard's, with the sceptre either running through or over the fingers.[95] Henry's heart lay with Henry and Richard at Fontevrault and his body rested with the Confessor at Westminster. Was it likewise, in the manner of Henry and Richard, that Henry clasped the doved rod, the emblem of the Confessor, to his breast?[96] The union of the Angevin and Anglo-Saxon dynasties could not have been more perfectly expressed.

King Henry's burial thus reached back to the dynastic past; yet it also tried to shape the dynastic future, though more through what was left out of the tomb than what was put in it. This brings us to the question of the crown. The placing of the crown on the king's head was the climax of the coronation. 'O God, bless and sanctify the crown', the archbishop prayed, 'that your servant may be filled with virtue'. 'God crown you with the crown of glory, justice, honour and fortitude that by his blessing, through the fruits of many good works,

[94] Erlande-Brandenburg, *Le Roi est Mort*, pp. 81–2, 111, 161–2 and plate 10 no. 38.

[95] The hands of the effigies have been partly restored but the form is fairly clear from early engravings in Stothard, *The Monumental Effigies of Great Britain* and see Sauerländer, *Gothic Sculpture in France*, pp. 448–9 and plate 142.

[96] The length of the rod may have necessitated it lying slightly off centre, however, unless the dove lay over the king's face. Arranging both Henry's hands to hold the rod solved another problem. In Henry's first great seal the sword was in the right hand and the orb in the left. If, therefore, the rod directly replaced the sword, it would end up, as far as the coronation ritual was concerned, in the wrong hand. This problem was avoided by completely recasting the seal. Both sword and orb were dropped and, in conformity with the coronation ritual, a sceptre was placed in the right hand and a rod in the left. The only trouble with this was that, in the Confessor's own seal, the rod was in the right hand. In Henry's second great seal the Confessor's example triumphed over coronation ritual and the rod was placed in the right hand and an orb returned to the left. By associating both hands with the funeral rod, the problem of deciding in which hand to place it was reduced. However, we may be reading too much into all this. That fact that the second substitute great seal of the 1260s retained the pattern of the first suggests Henry did not feel very strongly about which hand he held the rod in. In any case the issue was somewhat fudged by the rod on all the seals being more of sceptre like length.

you may arrive at the crown of the heavenly kingdom'.[97] The crown was the supreme symbol of regality and far and away the most important part of the *regalia*. Its use at the 1220 coronation had a particular significance because in 1216, during the turmoil of the war, Henry had been crowned with a *circulum aureum* or *sertum quoddam loco diadematis*.[98] Yet, as we have seen, the wardrobe accounts make no mention of a crown being used for Henry's burial. Wykes's statement that Henry's body was fittingly adorned with 'a royal diadem' makes it fairly certain, however, that he wore one and was not buried like his father in his coif of unction.[99] Edward I was found in a crown 'of tin, or latton . . . of inferior workmanship' and perhaps Henry's too was a cheap one made especially for his burial.[100] On the other hand, Henry may have been buried in one of the magnificent crowns he acquired in the course of the reign.[101] Whatever the truth here, Henry was not buried with the crown he had worn at his coronation, the 'gold crown decorated with diverse stones' handed over to the treasurer in 1220. This coronation crown was probably the 'one great crown of gold with precious stones' referred to in 1258–61 but it then vanishes until the final jewel account of the reign. Then, at the end of that account, comes the following statement: 'the same [keeper of the wardrobe] has handed over the great royal crown with most precious rubies and other precious stones (*magnam coronam regalem cum rubeis preciossimis et aliis lapidibus preciosis*) with all the other aforesaid remaining jewels, and the other things annotated above to John of London, clerk of the lord King Edward'.[102] Presumably this then was the crown used for the eventual coronation of Edward in August 1274, after he had returned from his crusade, the 'great crown of gold which the king used on the day of his coronation with precious jewellery of great stones, rubies and emeralds' (*magna corona auri qua Rex usus fuit die coronacionis sue cum preciosa pretraria magnorum balesiorum rubettorum et ameraldarum*), as it was described in 1303.[103]

Trying to trace the history of any particular coronation crown is a hazardous business. Crowns could be altered and, in any case, most kings had several of various shapes and sizes. Nearly all the Norman and Angevin kings, moreover,

[97] *English Coronation Records*, ed. Legg, pp. 34–5.

[98] *Chronica Majora*, iii, 1; *Annales Monastici*, iv, 60.

[99] *Annales Monastici*, iv, 252.

[100] Ayloffe, 'An Account of the Body of King Edward I', p. 384. Philip V's crown was likewise comparatively cheap (Brown, 'The Funeral of Philip V', p. 291 no. 36). Burial in cheap, specially made crowns was an ancient practice in Germany and elsewhere. On the other hand, from the late twelfth century it was also the practice to be buried in crowns (and other *regalia*) worn in life. See P.E. Schramm, *Herrschaftszeichen und Staatssymbolik*, 4 vols. (Schriften der Monumenta Germaniae historica, 13, Stuttgart, 1954–76), iii, 911–2.

[101] For Henry buying a crown for 500 marks in 1253, and later having one repaired, see *Cal. Liberate Rolls, 1251–60*, p. 105; E 403/9; *Cal. Liberate Rolls, 1267–72*, no. 899.

[102] E 372/116, m. 1d. Henry seems to have left two large crowns to his son, one smaller than the other (*Cal. Patent Rolls, 1272–81*, p. 212).

[103] *Documents Illustrative of English History in the Thirteenth and Fourteenth Centuries*, ed. H. Cole (London 1844), p. 277. Three other crowns are also listed here.

enjoyed more than one coronation (or what chroniclers called coronations), quite apart, under the Normans, from more regular festal crown-wearings. On the day of the coronation itself, more than one crown was used with a lighter one being put on immediately after the ceremony. None the less, if we are right in thinking that Henry III passed on his coronation crown, he was not, it may be suggested, following any firmly established custom. William I, on his death bed, left one crown and set of *regalia*, to St-Etienne at Caen and another to his successor, William Rufus.[104] In 1141 the Empress Matilda found the *corona regni*, which may or may not have been that left to Rufus, in the treasury at Winchester.[105] It was from Winchester too in 1158 that Henry II ordered 'the crowns of the king' to be despatched for the crown wearing or coronation of himself and his queen at Worcester. These 1158 crowns, however, then went into retirement at Worcester for, so Howden records, 'when they came to the oblation [Henry and Eleanor] took off their crowns, and offered them on the altar, vowing to God that they would never in their life be crowned again'.[106] Henry's 1158 crown, in any case, was not apparently that used for his first coronation since a good source states that he was crowned with the great imperial crown which his mother, the Empress Matilda, had brought back from Germany. This crown too entered a religious house, for the empress gave it to the abbey of Bec where it probably remained after her death in 1167.[107] Of course crowns could leave religious houses as well as enter them, and it has been suggested that the imperial crown was used for Richard's coronation in 1189,[108] in which case it may have ended life not at Bec but at Fontevrault. As we have seen, the Winchester annals state that Richard was buried in the crown he had worn at his 1194 coronation, and there are several indications that this was the coronation crown which he had used in 1189. Richard certainly had the *regalia* with him in 1194 for, as soon as he was released, he ordered their despatch out to

[104] F. Barlow, *William Rufus* (London, 1983), p. 50 note 200; *English Historical Documents 1042–1189*, ed. D.C. Douglas and G.W. Greenaway, 2nd edn. (London, 1981), p. 303. For the Conqueror's crowns see also below p. 449 and *The Carmen de Hastingae Proelio*, ed. C. Morton and H. Muntz (Oxford, 1972), pp. 48–51; *The Life of King Edward*, ed. Barlow, p. 153 note 19, and Schramm, *Herrschaftszeichen und Staatssymbolik*, ii, 393–4.

[105] *Gesta Stephani*, ed. K.R. Potter (London, 1955), p. 79.

[106] *Pipe Rolls of 2-3-4 Henry II* (reproduced in facsimile from the edition of 1844, London, 1930), p. 175 (I am grateful to John Maddicott for pointing me in the direction of this reference); *Chronica Rogeri de Houedene*, i, 216; *Radulfi de Diceto Opera*, i, 302.

[107] *Chronicles of the Reigns of Stephen, Henry II and Richard I*, ed. R. Howlett, 4 vols. (Rolls Ser., 1884–9), ii, 758 (a contemporary inventory of the empress's gifts to Bec). See M. Chibnall, *The Empress Matilda, Queen Consort, Queen Mother and Lady of the English* (London, 1991), pp. 189–90. For the empress's crown, see Schramm, *Herrschaftszeichen und Staatssymbolik*, iii, pp. 759–62. The empress also gave to Bec a small gold crown which the emperor had used *in majoribus sollemnitatibus*.

[108] Schramm, *Herrschaftszeichen und Staatssymbolik*, iii, 762–3 (though Schramm stressed this was only one possibility); see also Leyser, 'Frederick Barbarossa, Henry II and the Hand of St. James', *Medieval Germany and its Neighbours*, pp. 224–5. For Rufus and Henry I recovering the crown which their father had given to St-Etienne at Caen: Barlow, *William Rufus*, p. 50 note 200.

Germany. Diceto remarks of the 1194 coronation that Richard was crowned with 'the diadem of the kingdom', and Howden states that, after the ceremony, Richard took off the crown and put on a lighter one, in other words it was indeed a great coronation crown.[109] That no coronation crown, accordingly, was left to John is suggested by the pipe roll entry which recorded the working of £65 worth of gold 'for crowns and other ornaments made for the king's coronation'.[110] Likewise, in the first list of John's *regalia* his 'gold crown' was said to have been 'made in London'; in other words it was new.[111]

While the evidence is therefore fragmentary, the conclusion is clear. Under the Norman and Angevin kings there was no single coronation crown which was passed on from one reign to the next. New crowns could be introduced while old ones could be given to religious institutions or used to adorn kings in tombs.[112] If there was a feeling that the *regalia* should be passed on, it was not strong enough to restrict the will of individual kings. Henry III, therefore, in handing on his coronation crown, was bound by no immutable tradition.[113] His decision was governed by considerations which were old but which, in the course of his reign, filled with new and more powerful meaning. To start with there was a growing sense of the apartness and inviolability of the *regalia*, with the crown in particular coming to symbolise inalienable royal rights.

Under John the *regalia* were already kept intact and apart from the king's everyday clothes and *insignia*, and this continued to be the case under Henry.[114] As we have seen, the *regalia* of 1220 were still there in 1258–61 and thereafter

---

[109] *Annales Monastici*, ii, 71; *Chronica Rogeri de Houedene*, iii, 248; *Radulfi de Diceto Opera*, ii, 114; *Pipe Roll 6 Richard I*, p. 176. For 'diadem' as a kind of 'double crown' in which 'another *circulus* with gems' is added to the 'simple crown of a gold *circulus*', see Schramm, *Herrschaftszeichen und Staatssymbolik*, iii, 760 note 5 but see also pp. 912–13.

[110] *Pipe Roll 9 John*, p. 50. These crowns could, however, have been made for John's second coronation and his wife's first in 1200. For John's 'small' crown, see *Pipe Roll 3 John*, p. 258, and for other crowns, *Pipe Roll 14 John*, pp. 16, 43, 49, 50 and next note.

[111] *Rot. Litt. Pat.*, pp. 54b-55. It should be noted, however, that the crown is not stated specifically to have been made for the coronation whereas that is said of the sword. John still had the *magnum regale* of the empress which he called in in May 1215, and probably sold. Certainly it is never heard of again. This may be the same *regalia* as that listed in 1207 headed by a 'great crown which came from Germany', in which case the empress's crown had avoided Bec and Fontevrault after all. Alternatively, it could have been another of the empress's crowns (that for example which Henry I took and stored in his treasury), or again, as Schramm suggests, the 'great crown of gold' sent to Richard I by the emperor Henry VI in 1195. See *Rot. Litt. Pat.*, pp. 77b, 142a; *Chronica Rogeri de Houedene*, i, 181; iii, 300; Schramm, *Herrschaftszeichen und Staatssymbolik*, iii, 763.

[112] Schramm came to a similar conclusion (*Herrschaftszeichen und Staatssymbolik*, iii, 762–4) and contrasted Angevin practice with that in the empire. The emperor Otto IV in his will in 1218 specifically left the imperial cross, lance, crown and other unspecified *insignia* to his successor: *Monumenta Germaniae Historica Legum Sectio IV, Constitutiones et Acta Publica*, ii, 51–3; Erlande-Brandenburg, *Le Roi est Mort*, p. 19 note 9. He was probably following long-established practice: see Leyser, 'Henry II and the Hand on St. James', *Medieval Germany and its Neighbours*, p. 224.

[113] Whether Henry inherited a crown and other *regalia* from his father is discussed below.

[114] *Rot. Litt. Pat.*, pp. 54b-55, 173a. It may also be noted that John still possessed the *regalia* of the Empress Matilda: *Rot. Litt. Pat.*, pp. 77a-b, 142a.

can be followed from account to account down to the end of the reign in 1272. Although one cannot be certain about this, it seems highly likely that the coronation *regalia* were employed once at the ceremony and were then largely treasured up unused. Henry had separate robes made for the great feasts of Christmas, Easter and Pentecost and ordered a new set of *insignia* and robes – crown, rod, sceptre, royal tunic, shoes and gloves – for his French expedition of 1230.[115] In particular, by the end of the reign, Henry may have regarded the coronation crown as having a unique and singular function. In 1158 Henry II, as we have seen, had vowed not to be crowned again, a decision which he emphasised by giving his crown to Worcester. In thus signalling the end of the great Anglo-Norman crown wearings, Henry emphasised the uniqueness of both the 1158 ceremony in particular (at which Eleanor was crowned) and the coronation in general.[116] Henry III found that what his grandfather had begun was hardening into custom. In 1269, on the triumphal day when he planned to translate the body of the Confessor to its new shrine in Westminster Abbey, Henry had intended to wear his crown. At the last minute he changed his mind. A proclamation was read in Westminster Hall: the king 'was not advised that he should then wear his crown for it ought to be sufficient for him to wear his crown once'.[117] 'Wear his crown' here may, of course, be describing a ceremony rather than a specific object, yet the implication that the coronation crown itself should only be worn once may not be incorrect. The way possession of the crown was recorded in 1220, 1258–61 and 1272 shows, at the very least, that it had a very special status. Henry may well have come to see it as 'coronation dedicated'. If so, he had no right to take it to his grave.

This belief was reinforced by a growing feeling that the *regalia* were inalienable, that the physical crown must remain attached to the intangible crown, the crown that is in the sense of the enduring rights and possessions of kingship. Henry, as we have seen, was buried with robes and rod taken from the *regalia* but he was uneasy about putting them to other uses. In 1267, he excepted the *regalia* from the great sale of his jewels and indeed reserved, 'by word of mouth', a brooch, gold ring and belt 'which belonged to the crown'.[118] Henry's declaration here reflected the theory that certain lands, possessions and rights were indeed inseparable from the crown, the crown, that is, in the intangible sense defined above.[119] Already in 1154 Henry II had set about recovering lands alienated from 'the demesne' of his predecessors,[120] but down

---

[115] *Close Rolls, 1227–31*, p. 323. The wardrobe accounts enrolled on the pipe roll have a great deal of material about the king's robes.

[116] See also Schramm, *The English Coronation*, p. 58.

[117] *Cronica Maiorum et Vicecomitum*, pp. 116–17.

[118] *Cal. Patent Roll, 1266–72*, pp. 50, 52, 69.

[119] See J.R. Studd, 'The Lord Edward and King Henry III', *Bull. Inst. Hist. Res.*, 41 (1977), 7; H.W. Ridgeway, 'Foreign Favourites and Henry III's Problems of Patronage, 1247–1258', *Eng. Hist. Rev.*, 109 (1989), 598–9; D.A. Carpenter, *The Minority of Henry III* (London, 1990), pp. 285–6, and the other authorities cited there.

[120] W.L. Warren, *Henry II* (London, 1973), pp. 61–2, 263–4.

to 1234 kings still granted royal demesne away in hereditary right. The political revolution of 1234 brought such grants to an end. In 1257 Henry III's councillors swore never to consent to the alienation of those things 'which belong to the ancient demesne of the crown'.[121] How natural, therefore, to think that the crown itself, as a physical entity, should have a continuous life and be passed down from one coronation to the next, as a permanent visual symbol of inalienable royal rights. That symbolism was grasped by Edward I for after his coronation, according to the Hagnaby chronicle, he took off his crown and vowed not to wear it again until he had recovered lands alienated from the crown. Later Edward swore by Edward the Confessor to preserve 'the right of his kingdom and of the crown of Saint Edward'.[122]

Mention of Saint Edward's crown brings us to the second reason why Henry III might wish to leave his coronation crown to his successors: the association of that crown with Edward the Confessor. According to the Barnwell annalist, a good contemporary source, Henry III was crowned in 1220 with the 'diadem of the most saintly King Edward'.[123] This association of the coronation crown with the Confessor dated back, at the very least, to the 1120s and 1130s and to the campaign by the then prior of Westminster, Osbert de Clare, to secure the Confessor's canonisation and protect and expand, sometimes through forgery, the abbey's rights and properties. Thus in a spurious charter William the Conqueror declared that the Confessor had left the *coronam et alia regalia regni prima* to the abbey, while Pope Innocent II, in an equally spurious bull (of 1139) ordered this *regalia* to be preserved intact at the abbey and forbade its removal or sale without the consent of the convent.[124] When first inventoried in 1359 the abbey certainly had a large set of *regalia* claimed as the Confessor's, some of which was used at the coronation of 1377 and probably that of 1327 as well.[125] The Westminster monk, William of Sudbury, who researched the matter under Richard II, went further and averred that this *regalia* had been used at all the coronations since 1066. Yet there appears to be no independent evidence to support this claim, itself scarcely enhanced by Sudbury's further opinion that the abbey's *regalia* originated not with the Confessor but with Alfred, having been brought back from Rome after his coronation by Pope Leo.[126] Even if

[121] *Annales Monastici*, i, 396.

[122] British Library, Cotton MS Vespasian B.XI, f. 26/7; *The Chronicle of Walter of Guisborough*, ed. H. Rothwell (Camden Soc., 89, 1957), p. 235; Prestwich, *Edward I*, pp. 90–1.

[123] *Memoriale Fratris Walteri de Coventria*, ed. W. Stubbs, 2 vols. (Rolls Ser., 1872, 1873) ii, 244.

[124] *Westminster Abbey Charters 1066–1214*, ed. E. Mason (London Rec. Soc., 25, 1988), nos. 1, 161, 153, 154 and pp. 8–11; *Cal. Charter Rolls 1327–41*, p. 330; *The History of Westminster Abbey by John Flete*, ed. J.A. Robinson (Cambridge, 1909), pp. 47–9, 91. For Osbert's forgeries see also P. Chaplais, 'The Original Charters of Hervey and Gervase, Abbots of Westminster (1121–1157)', ch. 18 of his *Essays in Medieval Diplomacy and Administration* (London, 1981); and B. Harvey, 'Abbot Gervase de Blois and the Fee Farms of Westminster Abbey', *Bull. Inst. Hist. Res.* 40 (1967), 127–41.

[125] *History of Westminster Abbey by John Flete*, pp. 18–20.

[126] *Ricardi de Cirencestria Speculum Historiale*, ed. J.E.B. Mayor, 2 vols. (Rolls Ser., 1863, 1869), ii, 26–39. For Sudbury, see *The Westminster Chronicle, 1381–94*, ed. L.C. Hector and B.F. Harvey (Ox-

the Confessor did give his *regalia* to the abbey, it seems unlikely, as Frank Barlow has observed, that the Conqueror would have left it there to be used by the next claimant who came along.[127] In 1069 it was from Winchester that William ordered 'his crowns, royal *insignia* and plate' to be sent to York for a crown-wearing;[128] and we have already seen that crowns were likewise kept at Winchester in the twelfth century. In France the abbey of St-Denis was busy, at much the same time as Osbert de Clare, in forging charters to support (amongst other things) its claims to hold the Capetian *regalia*. It met with considerable success.[129] But here the relationship between dynasty, monastery and saint was genuinely close. The Norman and Angevin kings had no particular devotion to the abbey or the Confessor.[130]

Was Henry III, then, the first king to be crowned with the crown of the Confessor preserved at the abbey? This is an attractive hypothesis. Certainly Henry is the first king to be described by any contemporary source as being crowned with the Confessor's crown. Whatever their origins, a crown and other items claimed as the Confessor's coronation *regalia* were clearly possessed by the abbey in the time of Osbert de Clare. Perhaps, as Barlow has suggested, the collection had begun with the removal of the crown, sceptre, and *pallium* found in the Confessor's tomb, according to Osbert, when it was opened in 1102.[131] Accordingly, in 1220 Henry wore the crown of the Confessor; in 1242 he took steps to gild and repair St Edward's sceptre, and in the 1260s the abbey itself possessed the '*indumen* [*pallium?*] *coronacionis beati regis Edwardi*'.[132] If the abbey had all these items in 1220, it was well placed to get them used at the coro-

---

continued

ford, 1982), pp. xxxvi-viii. For Alfred's 'coronation', see J.L. Nelson, 'The Problem of King Alfred's Royal Anointing', ch. 15 of her *Politics and Ritual in Early Medieval Europe*.

[127] *The Life of King Edward*, ed. Barlow, p. 153 and pp. 152-4, where there is an excellent discussion of the Abbey's claims to hold the Confessor's *regalia*. See also the discussion in Schramm, *Herrschaftszeichen und Staatssymbolik*, iii, 757-9.

[128] *The Ecclesiastical History of Orderic Vitalis*, ed. M. Chibnall, 6 vols. (Oxford, 1969-80), ii, 232.

[129] G.M. Spiegel, 'The Cult of Saint Denis and Capetian kingship', *Journal of Medieval History*, I (1975), 59-60 and note 30, and idem, *The Chronicle Tradition of Saint-Denis: A Survey* (Medieval Classics: Texts and Studies, Brookline, Mass., and Leyden, 1978) pp. 31-3.

[130] A point made by Emma Mason: *Westminster Abbey Charters*, ed. Mason, pp. 3, 9, 12. I am most grateful to Emma Mason for a highly instructive letter about the Abbey's claims to hold the *regalia*.

[131] Bloch, 'La Vie de S. Édouard le Confesseur par Osbert de Clare', pp. 121-2. A late fourteenth-century account of the reopening of the tomb in 1163 mentions no *insignia* apart from the Confessor's ring, which was removed by the abbot. The abbot also made three copes out of the cloths in which the saint was wrapped. *Ricardi de Cirencestria Speculum Historiale*, ii, 324-5; *History of Westminster Abbey by John Flete*, p. 71; *Lives of Edward the Confessor*, ed., Luard, pp. 156, 310. See *The Life of King Edward*, ed. Barlow, pp. 152-3, and his *Edward the Confessor*, pp. 269, 277; contrast Holmes, 'New Light on St. Edward's Crown', p. 214. For further discussion of the Confessor's *regalia*, see Schramm, *Herrschaftszeichen und Staatssymbolik*, iii, 757-8, 911.

[132] *Cal. Liberate Rolls, 1240-5*, p. 120; *Customary of the Benedictine Monasteries of Saint Augustine, Canterbury and Saint Peter Westminster*, ed. Sir E.M. Thompson, 2 vols. (Henry Bradshaw Soc., 23, 28, 1903, 1904), ii, 62.

nation.[133] The ceremony was designed, at least in part, to confirm Westminster's coronation rights, so grievously breached by Henry's first coronation in October 1216, which had taken place, thanks to the civil war, at Gloucester. If, moreover, John's coronation crown and other *regalia* had been lost in the war (as is often suggested) then the Westminster set had a clear field. Certainly Henry's *regalia* were not made specifically for the 1220 coronation for only 31s. 8d. were spent on 'the repair of our crown and our *regalia* for our coronation at Westminster', a sum far too small for their actual fabrication.[134]

There are, however, problems with this hypothesis. After the coronation of 1220, the *regalia*, including the crown, instead of returning to the abbey, were handed over to the treasurer of the exchequer. Only the king's spurs were given to the abbey and they were simply a donation towards the building of the new Lady Chapel. In 1258 the crown of gold, ring and brooch (*firmaculum*) of the *regalia* were in the abbey treasury at Westminster, and Henry promised not to remove them from the custody of the abbot and convent; but this was only until a loan was repaid, which next year it was.[135] What was probably Henry's coronation crown was in the custody of the keeper of the wardrobe between 1258 and 1261, and again at the end of the reign. Crown and *regalia* continued to be kept by the wardrobe into the fourteenth century.[136] If, therefore, the abbey succeeded in pressing the Confessor's crown into service at the 1220 coronation, it failed apparently to retain it afterwards. Its rights as custodian of the *regalia* were both vindicated and violated at the same time. This paradox is not inexplicable. If fresh items could be added to the Confessorial collection at each coronation, as Barlow has suggested, they could also be taken away.[137] Perhaps Henry's government, having obtained the crown from the monks, was loth to return it, and later quietened protests by sometimes storing the *regalia* within the abbey's precincts.[138]

These explanations may or may not convince, and there are other difficulties. There is no proof that the Confessor's crown and *regalia* had a continuous life at the abbey from the time of Osbert de Clare through to 1359 when they

---

[133] See the letter of Guala the papal legate: Westminster Abbey Muniments, no. 51111.

[134] *Rot. Litt. Claus.*, i, 431. Ten marks were also spent purchasing the king's spurs (p. 422).

[135] PRO, C 66/72, m. 7 (*Cal. Patent Rolls, 1247–58*, p. 634); *Cal. Liberate Rolls, 1251–60*, p. 459.

[136] See below note 162. Interestingly, in 1223 Louis VIII appears to have recovered the *regalia* from St-Denis; storing it instead in the Royal Treasury: Spiegel, *The Chronicle Tradition of Saint-Denis*, p. 32.

[137] *The Life of King Edward*, ed. Barlow, p. 153.

[138] The problem would also be solved could we assume that *regalia* handed over to the treasurer in 1220 and later controlled by the wardrobe were simply those used after the coronation ceremony. This cannot apply to the sceptre and rod, however, since a single set was used throughout the day (see the practice mentioned in the *Liber Regalis*, below p. 456) and, in any case, Howden's description of the 1189 coronation does not suggest any particular status attached to the secondary crown and vestments: 'rex deposuit coronam regalem et vestes regales; et leviores coronam et vestes cepit': *Chronica Rogeri de Houedene*, iii, 11. However, Edward I in the late 1290s, did assign a special crown (surprisingly a 'great' one) to be worn after the ceremony and it is just possible that the situation changed in the fourteenth century. See below notes 159, 162.

were first inventoried by the monks. Osbert himself, in making the pope forbid the *regalia's* removal or sale without consent of the convent, seems to have feared for their survival at the abbey, and they may have been lost before the coronation of 1220. In the thirteenth century, the only object of the Confessor's *regalia* quite certainly possessed by the abbey was the '*indumen coronacionis beati regis Edwardi*', mentioned above, which Abbot Ware's customary (of the 1260s) ordered to be displayed on the saint's festivals.[139] For all we know, the abbey's claims before and after 1220 were more to recover *regalia* which they alleged they had lost, than to press into service a set which they had preserved. If, moreover, the crown and other *regalia* were not made for Henry's coronation, they may well have been inherited, at least from King John. It is often said that little of John's *regalia* descended to his son, having been lost in the disaster in the Wash or sold to raise money in the civil war.[140] It is certainly true that the *regalia* which survived from the Empress Matilda seems to have disappeared at this time.[141] Yet, the crown, sword, sceptre, royal tunic of red samite with orphreys containing stones, white tunic *de diaspre*, two brooches to attach a *pallium*, shoes and two pairs of gloves belonging to John's own *regalia* in 1216 could all match up with items on the 1220 list.[142] An official account of the queen's 1236 coronation described the stone chalice as 'from the *regalia* of kings of old' (*de regalibus Regis a veteri*).[143] Likewise the three swords borne before the king in 1236 may well have existed before 1189. At any rate, in Howden's account of the 1189 coronation, the three swords were brought from the treasury, in other words they already existed. They may still have existed in 1220 for the three swords used at the coronation had been brought up from Corfe where John had stored a large part of his treasure.[144]

If, then, Henry's crown came not from the abbey, but from his father, this does not make its association with the Confessor inexplicable. Although the abbey had failed to get its *regalia* (such as it was) accepted, it had succeeded in

[139] *Customary of the Benedictine Monasteries of Saint Augustine, Canterbury and Saint Peter Westminster*, ii, 62. The sceptre of 1242 seems in the king's possession: *Cal. Liberate Rolls, 1240-5*, p. 120. There was a larger collection by 1327, however; see below p. 456.

[140] A.V. Jenkinson, 'The Jewels Lost in the Wash', *History*, 8 (1924), 167–8; J.C. Holt, 'King John's Disaster in the Wash', in *Magna Carta and Medieval Government* (London, 1985), p. 121.

[141] See above note 111.

[142] *Rot. Litt. Pat.*, p. 173; *English Coronation Records*, ed. Legg, pp. 54–6. John's crown was not used for Henry's 1216 coronation, but it may simply have been unavailable in some castle treasury, for example at Corfe. Before the coronation of 1220 Peter de Maulay was ordered to bring up all the king's *regalia* which he had with him at Corfe. In the subsequent list of the *regalia* only the three swords were said to have come from there. But this does not necessarily mean all the rest of the *regalia* had been freshly made; they may have been kept elsewhere. The only item in 1220 specifically identified as having been King John's was a pair of shoes; but, on the other hand, only one pair of sandals are specifically identified as being 'new': *English Coronation Records*, ed. Legg, pp. 55–6; *Rott. Litt. Claus.*, i, 417b; and see the Appendix below.

[143] *The Red Book of the Exchequer*, ed. H. Hall, 3 vols. (Rolls Ser., 1896), iii, 755.

[144] *Chronica Rogeri de Houedene*, iii, 9; *English Coronation Records*, ed. Legg. pp. 49, 51, 55–6; *Rot. Litt. Claus.*, i, 417b.

spreading the idea that the coronation crown, whatever its provenance, was connected with the Confessor.[145] This was a belief that Henry himself could easily have come to share and celebrate. He was both inquisitive and credulous about the Confessor. He came to believe that the Confessor had given his ring to Saint John at Clavering in Essex, although the place was mentioned in none of the principal lives of the king.[146] Henry is unlikely to have subjected the antiquity of his crown to any precise historical examination; that it was inherited was probably enough to vouch for its antiquity and descent from the Confessor. The Westminster monks had no interest in challenging that belief, either by pointing out that the crown only dated from John's reign or by alleging that Henry had been crowned with the wrong one. On the contrary, the more they could associate the 1220 crown with the Confessor, the more they were likely to secure its custody.

Whether, therefore, Henry got his coronation crown from the monks or from his father, he could still see it as the Confessor's. Edward I's reference to 'the crown of the Confessor' suggests that he did the same. Indeed, the general association between the Confessor and the *regalia* probably grew apace during Henry's reign. Thus Matthew Paris observed that the sword 'Curtana', one of the three swords, carried before the king at the queen's coronation in 1236, was 'the sword of Saint Edward',[147] while Henry himself, as we have seen, was gilding and repairing 'the sceptre of Saint Edward' in 1242. Henry may also have gone some way towards acknowledging the abbey's claims to keep the crown and *regalia*.[148] If, as we have said, in 1258 the crown, ring and *firmaculum* were 'in deposit in the treasury of the church of Westminster' only as security for a loan, it is not clear that this was likewise the reason why the *regalia* were again in the keeping of the abbey at the time of the great sale of jewels in 1267.[149] The crown, ring and *firmaculum*, moreover, appear in the list of the *regalia* con-

---

[145] There are, of course, many intermediate positions (all equally unprovable) between the hypothesis that a full set of *regalia* from the abbey was used and that nothing at all was used. Perhaps, for example, just the Confessor's *indumen* was put in service.

[146] V.H. Galbraith, 'Edward the Confessor and the Church of Clavering', *Essex Arch. Soc. Trans.*, new ser., 16 (1923), 187–9. Schramm, in discussing the Confessor's crown, cites the example of relics and notes how easily labels of ownership could attach to particular objects: *Herrschaftszeichen und Staatssymbolik*, iii, 758.

[147] *Chronica Majora*, iii, 337. Paris's remark reflects the general connection between the *regalia* and the Confessor rather than any particular knowledge about the sword since, in actual fact, the three coronation swords were never claimed by the abbey as part of the Confessor's *regalia*. For the possible association of *Curtana* with a sword of Tristram, see Mason, 'The Hero's Invincible Weapon', pp. 133–4.

[148] A brief allusion to the claim appears in *Lives of Edward the Confessor*, ed. Luard, pp. 156–7.

[149] C 66/72, m. 7; C 66/85, m. 22 (*Cal. Patent Rolls, 1247-58*, p. 636; *Cal. Patent Rolls, 1266–72*, pp. 50, 52). This may have been the start of storing the wardrobe treasure in the crypt of the Westminster Abbey chapter house: see T.F. Tout, *Chapters in The Administrative History of Mediaeval England*, 6 vols. (Manchester, 1920–33), ii, 53–4. In 1261 Louis IX confirmed St-Denis' right to hold the *regalia* (Spiegel, *The Chronicle Tradition of Saint-Denis*, p. 32, and above note 137.) Henry III was with Louis in Paris both in 1259–60 and 1262.

trolled by the wardrobe between 1258 and 1261; but they then disappear from subsequent lists until the crown, as we have seen, reappears after Henry's death. Was this disappearance because they had been officially placed in the abbey's custody?[150]

To return at last to the point. By leaving 'the diadem of the most saintly King Edward' to his successors for use at their coronations, Henry was making a gift of numinous significance. He himself thought constantly about the Confessor's own coronation and wished others to do so too. The subject was thus depicted in the magnificent painting placed above his bed in his great chamber at Westminster, the most public and private room in the whole kingdom and the one in which Henry lived far more than any other. Above the crown on the Confessor's head ran the legend CEST LE CORONEMENT SEINT EDEWARD in large gold letters, just in case anyone was unsure. It was natural for Henry to celebrate this zenith of the Confessor's regality and spirituality; but how much more resonant became the whole scene if the crown it depicted had been used at Henry's own coronation. By now passing it on to his successors for use at their coronations Henry was placing the dynasty, at the transcendent point at the start of each reign, under the saint's over-arching care.[151] From that care, in life, Henry had already obtained much. In the months between 1 January and 25 June 1265, when a virtual captive of de Montfort, he had heard no less than nineteen special masses of the Confessor in his chapel.[152] No doubt he saw Evesham as the reward for such devotions. Much earlier, in 1244, he had personally helped transmit the saint's miraculous powers. When, in that year, the queen's uncle, Thomas of Savoy, lay grievously ill, Henry assured him of recovery if he placed his trust in the Confessor. 'I pray God that the fever should pass to me if my words lack truth'. Recover Thomas did, whereupon he gave thanks 'to God, to Saint Edward and to the king'. Henry ordered Matthew Paris 'secretly' to record the miracle 'lest the memory of such a great benefit, which

---

[150] At first sight there appears a different explanation for the disappearance of the crown, *firmaculum* and ring. On 14 June 1261 a great crown, *firmaculum* and ring, together with other jewels were pawned at the Paris Temple. They were recovered in February 1272. However these were not apparently the same as the crown, *firmaculum* and ring in the wardrobe between 1258 and 1261 which were still said to 'remain' when the keepers closed their account on 25 July 1261. The jewels pawned in Paris were not described as *regalia* and may have all belonged to what the king called, on their recovery in 1272, his 'new treasure': *Foedera*, I, i, *410, 492* (*Cal. Patent Rolls, 1258–66*, p. 190; *Cal. Patent Rolls, 1266–72*, p. 627); E 361/1, m. 1.

[151] Henry may also have believed that the doved rod used at his coronation had been the Confessor's. That gave him a reason for leaving it to his successors but also for taking it with him to his grave. One can play it either way. Henry had some leeway here since the number of rods had multiplied from one to three between 1220 and 1258 (see above p. 432). It was perfectly possible for him to believe that all three were associated in some way with the Confessor. In 1359 the Westminster monks listed three rods as part of the saint's *regalia*: *History of Westminster Abbey by John Flete*, p. 19. By contrast there was only one sceptre in the *regalia* both in 1220 and between 1258 and 1272, so Henry may have felt less free to be buried with it, especially if it was the same as the sceptre of the Confessor mentioned in 1242.

[152] E 101/349/30.

God thought fit to bestow through Saint Edward, should through the carelessness and ingratitude of men pass into oblivion'.[153] By leaving the Confessor's
crown to his successors, Henry ensured that they would never be oblivious of
the multitudinous benefits which the saint could bestow.

King Henry's *regalia* in death thus projected his view of royal authority in
life. The vestments of unction were unused, or at least unseen, but the dalmatic, mantle and *insignia* still proclaimed the magnificent uniqueness conferred on monarchy by the coronation. The abandonment of the sword and
the embracing of the doved staff reflected Henry' pacific rule and linked him
with both the Angevin kings at Fontevrault and the Sainted Edward. Saint Edward's crown, passed on for future coronations, reminded kings of both the
protection which the saint conferred and the inalienable rights which they had
inherited. Edward I, indeed, linked both these point when he swore by the
Confessor to preserve 'the right of his kingdom and the crown of Saint Edward'.[154]

Not everyone, however, indeed not even Edward himself, accepted unqualified Henry's visual rhetoric. Henry faced a commonsensical audience, very able
to distinguish between symbol and substance. On his new gold penny he sat
elegantly enthroned but the citizens of London told him to his face that the
coinage was useless. The replacement of the sword with the doved rod on the
new seal merely reflected, in the view of chroniclers, the shameful loss of the
continental possessions.[155] The more elaborate throne on the new seal merely
elicited an insulting question from the pope: why was the new seal more magnificent than the old one made when the king had been duke of Normandy?[156] The splendid robes of Henry's funeral themselves provoked ironic
comment. The chronicler Thomas Wykes noted that the king's body 'was adorned
with the most precious garments and a royal diadem as was fitting' but then
continued 'so that he shone forth with greater splendour dead than before
when he was alive'.[157] Even Edward I joined in the criticism. When, as we have
seen, he swore at his coronation not to wear the crown again until he had recovered alienated lands, the lands in question were those 'which his father had
alienated by giving them to the earls and barons of England and to aliens'.[158]

Yet Henry's association of English monarchy with the Confessor has its effect. Henry's crown, Saint Edward's crown, may well have gone on to become

---

[153] *Chronica Majora*, vi, 92–4.

[154] *Chronicle of Walter of Guisborough*, p. 235.

[155] *Cronica Maiorum et Vicecomitum*, pp. 29–30, 43; *Annales Monastici*, i, 486–7; *The Chronicle of Bury St Edmunds*, p. 25. 'Such is the fate of rulers: this episode stands as the most trenchant con-temporary illustration of the failure of royal image-making at its most sensitive': Binski, *Westminster Abbey and the Plantagenets*, p. 86.

[156] *Diplomatic Documents, 1101–1272*, ed. P. Chaplais (London, 1964), no. 367: *sigillum majoris magnitudinis.*

[157] *Annales Monastici*, iv, 253.

[158] British Library, Cotton MS Vespasian BXI, f. 26/27 (the Hagnaby chronicle); Prestwich, *Edward I*, p. 91.

the coronation crown of the kingdom. At any rate, Edward I still had his coronation crown, presumably that left him by Henry, in 1303 and was not buried with it.[159] If, moreover, the Confessor achieved no general popularity, he gained a central role in the coronation ceremony. At the coronation of 1308, the chalice which Matthew Paris had described in 1236 as coming 'from the *regalia* of kings of old' was officially described as the chalice of the Confessor.[160] A memorandum copied by the chancery in connection with the coronation of Edward III in 1327, assigned no provenance to the crown, and declared that the three processional swords (including *Curtana*), the sword with which the king was girded, and the two processional sceptres (probably the same as the sceptre and rod used later in the ceremony) were to come from the treasury of the king, while the king's ministers were to provide the spurs. However, besides Saint Edward's chalice, the memorandum also referred to 'Saint Edward's ring', as well as the saint's '*Tunycle* which is of the church of Westminster' and his '*cote* which lives at Westminster', both of which the king was to put on after the anointing. After the ceremony, the memorandum stressed that the king should take off the 'royal ornaments of Saint Edward' and return them to the abbey 'as of right'.[161] In 1339 Edward III confirmed the Conqueror's spurious charter, mentioning the Confessor's gift of his crown and *regalia* to the Abbey (the first king to do so); and in 1359, when the monks drew a detailed inventory, this *regalia* included a crown, tunic, supertunic, *pallium*, sceptre and three rods, as well as gloves, stockings, shoes and chalice. There seems no doubt that the abbey *regalia* were used for the coronation of Richard II in 1377 and, apart from a lost shoe, were recovered afterwards.[162] To avoid further accidents, the

[159] Edward decided that a great crown he had acquired from Blanche of Navarre should be worn 'by kings of England' on leaving the church and at the coronation feast. He did not replace the coronation crown itself. See *Liber Quotidianus Contrarotulatoris Garderobae Anno Regni Regis Edwardi Primi Vicesimo Octavo*, ed. J. Nichols (London, 1787), p. 353; E 101/357/13, m. 1d (a roll which Wendy Childs and Robert Stacey kindly looked at with me).

[160] *Foedera*, II, i, 36.

[161] *Three Coronation Orders*, ed. Legg, pp. 120–4. This is now C 49/Roll 11, a reference I found thanks to a suggestion of Mark Ormrod. The mantle was described as 'of the treasury of Westminster' (p. 123).

[162] *Cal. Charter Rolls, 1327–41*, p. 330; *The History of Westminster Abbey by John Flete*, pp. 18–20, 71; *The Westminster Chronicle*, ed. Hector and Harvey, pp. 90–1, 156–7, 414–17. There are still problems, however, because in 1356 the treasury in the Tower of London contained not merely the three coronation swords (one again *Curtana*), the coronation spurs, rods and sceptres, but also 'the vestments of red samite for the coronation of the king', including two tunicles and a mantle: *English Coronation Records*, ed. Legg, pp. 79–80. At the same time, four royal crowns, including a 'great' one, once pledged in Flanders, were stored in the treasury in the abbey cloisters. Earlier, in 1299, the ring with which Edward I had been consecrated was in the treasury of the wardrobe in the crypt of the abbey chapter house: E 101/357/13. Edward I's coronation crown was likewise there in 1303 but after the famous robbery it was moved to the Tower of London: *Documents Illustrative of English History*, ed. Cole, p. 277; Tout, *Chapters in Administrative History*, ii, 53–8. In 1327 Edward II's coronation vestments were controlled by the great wardrobe: St. John Hope, 'On the Funeral Effigies on the Kings and Queens of England', 531 citing E 361/3, r. 8/16 (pencil). Conceivably some of the apparent conflict between this *regalia* and that kept by the abbey can be re-

Liber Regalis, the magnificent coronation service book prepared for Richard II at Westminster in the 1380s, stipulated, in a series of new rubrics, that after the ceremony the king was to enter the chapel of the Confessor and lay the crown and other *regalia* on its altar. At the same time the king was to resign his shoes and sandals to the abbot, while the rod and sceptre were to be returned after the coronation feast. The abbey was to be 'the repository of the royal *insignia* for ever'.[163]

As so often with Henry's own triumphs, the Confessor's was not unalloyed. At this very time in the reign of Richard II, the Westminster monk William of Sudbury was ungratefully suggesting that the *regalia* dated back to Alfred, and this idea persisted in later centuries.[164] Still the Confessor too held his ground. Henry IV, according to Froissart, was crowned with Saint Edward's crown, and another Westminster monk, John Flete, writing in the mid fifteenth century, had no doubt that the coronation *regalia* were Edward's and that he had ordered their preservation at the abbey.[165] The end of the Angevin empire, which helped Westminster develop as an administrative capital, and meant that *regalia* had no longer to be transported across France, were factors in the success of the abbey and its saint. But the most immediate reason was Henry III's own overwhelming devotion to the Confessor. It was that which had put the Confessor on the map. There was one other reason. The political status of the Confessor, as Paul Binski has pointed out, had always been ambivalent. He was both royal icon and rallying point for opposition. The Laws of the Confessor were brandished in the face of tyrannical kings, and it was not perhaps through royal initiative that Edward II swore to observe them in the coronation oath of 1308.[166]

continued

solved by assuming that parts of the former were items put on after the ceremony (or indeed before it). Note the combination of red and purple robes at the coronation of 1483: St. John Hope, 'The King's Coronation Ornaments', pp. 157–9. The Confessor's vestments in 1359 were described as being of purple or black samite, whereas those in the Tower were of red samite. Interestingly, the *pallium* worn by the Confessor in the coronation painting in Henry III's chamber at Westminster was of a dark colour. However, the tunic or dalmatic beneath it was green (Binski, *The Painted Chamber*, colour plate I). I am grateful to Nigel Saul and Mark Ormrod for discussing the problems of the fourteenth-century evidence. There is other relevant material in *Antient Kalendars and Inventories.* . . . ed. Sir F. Palgrave, 3 vols. (Ricard Com., 1836), for example i, 156–7, 160, 162.

[163] *English Coronation Records*, ed. Legg, pp. 84–5, 99, 106–7, 115, 121, 127–8. The memorandum of 1327 had given the king the option of removing the ornaments of Saint Edward either in the abbey or (as happened in 1377) in the palace: *Three Coronation Orders*, ed. Legg, pp. 123–4. For Walsingham's account of Richard II's coronation, which mentions the Confessor's tunic and dalmatic see *Thomae Walsingham* . . . *Historia Anglicana*, ed. H.T. Riley, 2 vols. (Rolls Ser., 1863–4), i, 334.

[164] *Ricardi de Cirencestria Speculum Historiale*, ii, 26–39; Holmes, 'New light on St. Edward's Crown', pp. 214, 216–17. The idea was developing in the late thirteenth century when Robert of Gloucester noted that the pope had crowned Alfred with 'the crown of this land that in this land yet is': *The Metrical Chronicle of Robert of Gloucester*, ed. W.A. Wright, 2 vols. (Rolls Ser., 1887), i, 388.

[165] *Froissart Chronicles*, ed. G. Brereton (Penguin classics, Harmondsworth, 1968), p. 465; *History of Westminster Abbey by John Flete*, p. 71.

[166] P. Binski, 'Reflections on *La Estoire de Seint Aedward le Rei*: Hagiography and Kingship in

Henry, however, saw no conflict. The great strength of his rule was its ideological integrity. He wished to be exalted and protected by his sainted predecessor but also to imitate the fabled peace and justice of his rule. Put another way, Henry accepted the duality which ran through the whole ceremony of the coronation. The coronation, on the one hand, set the king apart, and, on the other hand, bound him to rule for the welfare of his subjects. The latter Henry certainly wished to do, yet there was an all too obvious gulf between aspiration and achievement. Henry achieved long periods of peace, but often, so contemporaries thought, at the cost of ignoring or condoning acts of injustice. Hence, in part, the political troubles which ultimately engulfed him. To steer through those troubles the support of the Confessor seemed vitally important. It was even more important in securing the king's passage to the life hereafter.

We come at last to what Henry would undoubtedly have put first about his burial. His father's torments after death were common knowledge. One of John's former priests had attempted to pray for him, only to be told in a vision to read the fifty-first psalm 'and he, finding no hope (*nichil boni*) in that psalm, gave up his prayer'.[167] Henry did not want to be left thus alone and hopeless after death. By vesting himself in his coronation *regalia* he went some way to ensuring that he would not be. He thus returned at death to the supreme moment in his life, the moment when he was filled with the gifts of the Holy Spirit and was promised 'the crown of the heavenly kingdom'. But for Henry there was even more to his burial than that. By rebuilding the abbey in honour of the Confessor, by translating him to his new shrine, by being buried first in the old shrine and then beside the new one, and by clutching the doved rod, the emblem of the Confessor to his breast, he secured a powerful advocate with the Father. As Henry himself put it, in conversation with Thomas of Savoy: the Confessor 'ought not to be loved because I love him but because God [loves him]. Nor do I love him, save on account of God'.[168]

Henry had every reason to feel confident about the Confessor's heavenly connections. The Confessor's special patron, as the life written by Ailred of Rievaulx (the basis for all subsequent hagiographies) repeatedly stressed, was Saint Peter, the primate of the whole church and keeper of the keys of Heaven.[169] His second protector was Saint John the Evangelist, the disciple whom Jesus loved, so often (as Ailred noted) present with Peter at the key moments of Christ's life. Together, therefore, Peter and John were a complementary and uniquely powerful combination. Saint John loved Edward for his chastity, so like his own, and once visited him disguised as a pauper begging for alms. Edward, for he

Thirteenth-Century England', *Journal of Medieval History*, 16 (1990), 347–8; J.C. Holt, *Magna Carta*, 2nd edn. (Cambridge, 1994), pp. 93–5, 113–15; Nelson, *Politics and Ritual*, pp. 73–4; H.G. Richardson, 'The English Coronation Oath', *Speculum*, 24 (1949), 59–64, 75 (though some of Richardson's arguments are open to question).

[167] *The Chronicle of Walter of Guisborough*, p. 156; see *Chronica Majora*, iii, 112.

[168] *Chronica Majora*, vi, 93.

[169] *Historiae Anglicanae Scriptores X*, ed. Twysden, pp. 373–5, 381–4, 397–8.

could find nothing else, gave him a ring from his finger, the last and most famous of all the Anglo-Saxon ring-givings. A little later John reappeared before two English pilgrims in the Holy Land and told them to take the ring back to Edward with the assurance that he would die within six months and that he, John, would conduct him to heaven.[170] John kept his promise and *La Estoire de Seint Aedward le Rei* has a moving picture of the Confessor's entry into heaven, with Saint John pointing him forward with a reassuring hand on the shoulder, Saint Peter standing by with his keys, and Christ placing a crown upon his head, 'the crown of the heavenly kingdom'.

> And Saint Peter, his dear friend
> Opens the gate of Paradise,
> And Saint John, his own dear one,
> Conducts him before his Majesty,
> And God gives him his kingdom,
> Who puts the crown on his head[171]

No wonder, therefore, that the dramatic scene of Edward giving the ring to Saint John seemed to Henry more important than any other episode in the Confessor's life. He had it depicted at Everswell, Guildford, the Tower of London and Winchester.[172] In the great chamber at Westminster it was painted in the splays of the window opposite the king's bed, so that it was the first thing Henry saw when he woke up in the morning.[173] And likewise, as the crowds entered the Abbey through the ceremonial north door, their eyes were immediately swept upward to the great painted statues of the Confessor and Saint John centrally placed beneath the rose window of the south transept.[174] Everyone thus learnt about how John had prophesied Edward's death and promised that he would ascend to heaven.

Edward was, therefore, a saint of 'mighty power' and had frequently demonstrated as much.[175] Through his miraculous help, the crippled walked, the blind saw and the scrofulous became whole.[176] A prayer for aid when destitute in exile brought, through Saint Peter's intervention, his accession to the throne; a prayer during mass for the peace of his people was answered at once by the drowning of the king of Denmark; the treacherous Earl Godwin choked to death

[170] Ibid., pp. 397–8, 402. This supposedly was the ring taken from Edward's coffin in 1163: *History of Westminster Abbey by John Flete*, pp. 71–2.

[171] M.R. James, *La Estoire de Seint Aedward le Rei* (Roxburgh Club, 1920), plate 53; *Lives of Edward the Confessor*, ed. Luard, pp. 18–19, 174, 136, 290.

[172] *Cal. Liberate Rolls, 1245–51*, pp. 177, 186; *Cal. Liberate Rolls, 1260–7*, p. 21; *Cal. Liberate Rolls, 1240–5*, p. 14; *Cal. Liberate Rolls, 1251–60*, p. 308; see T. Borenius, 'The Cycle of Images in the Palaces and Castles of Henry III', *Journal of the Warburg and Courtauld Institute*, 4 (1943), 488–9.

[173] Binski, *The Painted Chamber*, plates 4, 5 and pp. 37–40.

[174] At the abbey the scene also appeared in figures either side of the north door and in the tiles of the chapter house.

[175] *Lives of Edward the Confessor*, ed. Luard, line 4516.

[176] *Historicae Anglicanae Scriptores X*, ed. Twysden, pp. 383–4, 390, 390–4.

when Edward blessed his bread; King Harold won his only victory when afforded the saint's protection.[177] The Confessor had also the gift of prophesy and had foreseen both the disaster of the Norman Conquest and the restoration of the tree of monarchy to its true root with Henry I's marriage to the daughter of Margaret of Scotland, a tree, which as Matthew Paris said, had now born fruit with Henry III.[178] The Confessor had helped Henry in this life, as we have seen; now he would place his hand on his shoulder and guide him to the life to come. As *La Estoire de Seint Aedward le Rei* put it:

> By his virtues and his prayers
> He governs you and comforts you
> He will cause to be opened for you the gate of Heaven.[179]

---

[177] Ibid., pp. 374–5, 378–9, 394–5, 403–4. The deaths of the king of Denmark and Earl Godwin were depicted on Abbot Berking's tapestry in Westminster Abbey: P. Binski, 'Abbot Berking's Tapestries and Matthew Paris's Life of St Edward the Confessor', *Archaeologia*, 109 (1991), 95–6.

[178] *Historiae Anglicanae Scriptores X*, ed. Twysden, p. 398; *Lives of Edward the Confessor*, pp. 133, 287.

[179] *Lives of Edward the Confessor*, ed. Luard, pp. 27, 181.

Appendix

Used for Henry III's Burial 1272[1]	Taken from Following Items in the Wardrobe, 1258–1272[2]	*Regalia* in 1220[5]
una virga regalis	tribus virgis auri Regalibus et longis[3]	Virga argentea et deaurata
una dalmatica de rubeo samicto cum aurifragio et lapidibus	duabus tunicis regalibus de rubeo samito cum aurifrigio [et] lapidibus diversis	Tunica cum dalmatica de rubeo samit. cum uno monili et lapidibus in aurifragio Tunica de Diaspro blanco cum dalmatica de rubeo samit.
unum mantellum de rubeo samicto cum aurifragio et lapidibus preciosis peroptime hornatum	duobus mantellis regalibus de rubeo samito cum aurifrigio et lapidibus preciosis	Pallium de rubeo samit. cum lapidibus vetus pallium de rubeo samit.
una brochea auri	et duobus brocheis auri	Due broche auree ad pallium et dalmaticam quarum in una est Saphirus et in alia Perla
unum par caligarum de samicto rubeo cum aurifragio	uno pari caligarum de samito rubeo cum aurifrigio	
unum par sotularium de rubeo samicto	uno pari sotularium brudatarum de samito rubeo cum lapidibus	Unum par Sandalium novorum et Sotularium de Rubeo Samit. cum aurifragio Duo Freselli de aurifragio ad Fratandam sandalia Regis Item unum par veterum sandalium de Rubeo Samit. cum aurifragio cum uno pari veterum sotularium Brodlatorum auro que fuerunt Regis Johnannis

[1] E 372/116, m.1d.
[2] Taken from the account of 1258–1261: E 361/1, m.2. Order changed. Cases as in original.
[3] From the 1265 account onwards these become *argenti* rather than *auri*: E 372/114, m.41.
[5] E 401/3B, r.1. Order changed. Capitalisation as in original. Printed in *English Coronation Records*, ed. Legg, pp. 54–6.

Items in the Wardrobe, 1258–1272, Untouched for the Entombment	*Regalia* in 1220 continued
[una magna corona auri cum lapidibus preciosis	Corona aurea integra diversis lapidibus ornata
uno magno firmaculo cum pulcherimis rubicis	
uno anulo magno cum magno rubico pulcherimo][4]	Anulus aureus cum rubeyo
uno ceptro auri et regali	Ceptrum aureum
duabus tunicis regalibus de rubeo samito cum aurifrigio sine lapidibus	
una tunica de serico linata cendallo viridi	
quatuor ensibus cum scaubergiis de rubeo samicto et zonis de aurifrigio quarum una est sine bucula et pendente	Duo gladii cooperti de rubeo samit. frettati aurifragio
tribus ensibus cum scabergiis de corio nigro quorum due sunt sine zonis	Tres gladii qui fuerunt apud Corf' cooperti coreo
uno pari caligarum brudatarum de samito rubeo	
uno pari sotularium brudatarum cum samito nigro	
uno pari calcarium deauratorum cum lapidibus	[calcarea aurea][6]
duobus paribus cyrotecarum cum lapidibus	Duo paria cirotecarum
uno pari cyrotecarum sine lapidibus	
una zona de samito rubeo cum chamautis et aliis lapidibus	
uno aurifragio delicato	
	Baltheus cum apparatu aureo cum lapidibus

[4]These first three items disappear after the 1258–61 account: see above pp. 452–3.
[6]Erased with note *que in exitu per Breve*. A writ ordering the delivery of the spurs, made for the king's coronation at Westminister, to the prior of Westminister *ad opus* the work on the new Lady Chapel is enrolled. This is the same as *Rot. Litt. Claus.*, I, 440b.

Index

absolutism 37–43, 75–80, 85
Abthorpe, manor of, Northants. 169
accounts 116
—. of gold treasure 112, 114, 115, 127, 128, 131–6
—. jewel 429, 444
—. Wardrobe 108–9, 112, 121, 131–6, 417
Adderbury family 378
Adderbury, Thomas of 352
Aigueblanche, Peter de, bishop of Hereford 271
Akeny, Sir Baldwin de 315, 320
Alexander III, king of Scotland 177
Alexander IV, pope 184, 185
Alfred, king 449, 456
aliens, see foreigners
Almain, Henry of (son of Richard of Cornwall) 94, 195, 266, 270, 275
—. hostage for Mise of Lewes 281, 288, 289, 290
Almohade dynasty 109
Alton, Yorks. 87
amercements 85–6, 89, 143, 144, 147
—. forest 89, 91, 92, 93
—. and *Walter of Henley* 345
Anagni Cathedral 421
annals, see chronicles
anointing 435–7
Ardern, Thomas of 229
Argentan, Giles de 24, 301, 304
Argentan, Richard de 24, 57, 315
aristocracy, definition of 389
Aristotle 236
Arlot, Master (papal envoy) 185, 195
armies 155, 317, 318–19, 319, 322
—. mercenaries 270, 272, 273, 275, 277
—. of Queen Eleanor 275, 277, 284, 318, 338
Articles of the Barons 1215 1–2, 7, 12, 13, 16
—. omissions in Magna Carta 6
Arundal, countess of 141

Ascot, manor of, Oxon. 363
Ashridge, Peter of 330
Ashton, Stephen de 176
Aspley Guise, manor of, Beds. 42
Assize of Arms 319, 343
Assize of Northampton 343
Astley, Thomas of 228
Aston Cantlow, War. 227, 298
Audenard, Giles de 416–17
Audley, Henry of 162, 164
Audley, James de 288
Aylesbury, Bucks. 314

Babraham, Camb., Hundred Rolls 317
Balliol, John de 321
Bamborough castle, Northumb. 177
Bampton, manor of, Oxon. 196, 329, 330, 332, 348
Banbury, Henry of 255
Bank of England 109
Barbling, Robert de 331
Bardolf, William 92, 96
Barentin, Drogo de 323
Barliwey, Simon 316
Barlow, Frank 449, 450
Barnstaple, Devon 29
Barnwell priory 16, 322, 448
baronial wars 181, 183
Barrow, G.W.S. 75
Barton family 364
Basset family of Shutford 370
Basset, Fulk, bishop of London 84, 94, 100
Basset, Gilbert 49, 58, 59
—, and litigation 23, 38, 39, 40, 41
Basset, Philip 84, 287, 412
Basset, Ralph, of Sapcote 228
Basset, Thomas, of Headington 158, 180
Bath, Henry of 25, 83, 84, 87, 177
Bath and Wells, bishop of 100
Battle abbey 100, 322
—, chronicles 284, 285, 288, 322, 348
Bayford, manor of, Herts. 196

Beaudesert, War. 227, 298
Beaulieu abbey 122, 126
Bec, abbey of 445–6
Bede, the Venerable, St 383
Bedford castle 257, 320
Bekeford, William de 189
Bémont, Charles 241, 242
Bendford, Nicholas de 370
Bere, Richard de 192
Berkshire 166, 170
Berksted, Stephen de, bishop of
    Chichester 230, 294, 295, 296
—, and *Song of Lewes* 231, 277
Bermondsey, prior of 331
Berwick, Sussex 342
Beverley, Robert of 416, 423
Bezill, Matthias 57, 264, 269, 271–2
Bibliothèque Nationale, Paris 241
Biddlesden abbey 364
Bigod, Hugh 34, 92, 94, 194, 196
—, and battle of Lewes 285
—, eyres of 43, 99, 269, 326, 329–32, 333
Bigod, Roger, 6th earl of Norfolk 37, 72,
    221
—, and alliance of the barons 194
—, ally of de Montfort 247
—, on council of fifteen 247
—, and debts to king 89–90, 91, 96
—, disputes with Aymer Lusignan 191, 192
—, disputes with king 97, 141
—, and disseisin 83, 96
—, and litigation 30–2
—, and march to king's hall 32, 35, 188–9,
    195, 263
—, receives gifts from king 95
Bigod, Roger, 7th earl of Norfolk 403
Bingley, manor of, Yorks.
Binski, Paul x, 413, 418, 421
—, on chronology of Cosmati work 409–10,
    412, 414
—, on political status of Confessor 457
Birling, Kent 331
Birmingham, William of 229
Black Death 348
Blancpain, Roger, of Madingley 322
Blockley, William of 53, 54
Bodmin priory 4
Bohun, Henry de, earl of Hereford 27, 48
Bohun, Humphrey de, 6th earl of
    Hereford 72, 89, 91, 191, 247
—, and alliance of barons 195
—, conflict with Valence 191
—, and debts to king 96

—, and gallows 101
—, and Gascon campaign 96
—, receives gifts from king 95
Bohun, Humphrey de, 7th earl of
    Hereford 403
Bois, Arnold de 227
Bonet, John 162
Boreham, Hervey of 102
Borre, Richard 314
Boston fair, Lincs. 301, 304
Bovill, John de 101
Boxley, abbot of 100
Bracton 30, 40–2, 77, 78, 344, 345, 346
Bracton, Henry de 40, 77, 82, 105
Bradenham, manor of, Bucks. 34
Brand, Paul x, 21, 335
Braose, John de 29
Braose, Reginald de 28, 29
Braose, William de 29
Bray, Ralph de 47, 58
Braybrook, Robert of 159
Bréauté, Falkes de 46, 58, 59, 70
—, death (1226) 47
—, debts 161
—, disputes with earl of Pembroke 48
—, disputes with Hubert de Burgh 46, 164
—, as sheriff 60, 161, 180
Breton, Ranulf the 51
Brewer, William *see* Briwerre, William
Brid, William le 330–1
Bridecote, William de 315
Bridgnorth castle, Shrops. 162
Brill, manor of, Bucks. 331, 339
Bristol castle 243, 249
Brittany campaigns 162, 174
Briwerre, William 151, 158, 159, 160, 180,
    374
Broke, Laurence de 353, 375–6
Bromholm priory 50, 51, 52, 53, 54
Bucknell, manor of, Oxon. 364
Burdeleys, John de 322
Burgeis, Walter de 174
Burgh, Hubert de 62, 151, 165
—, capture at Chinon 59
—, correspondence 70
—, enemies 46, 47, 48, 49, 56, 164
—, —, Roches, Peter des 45, 46, 47, 50, 56
—, fall of 38, 45–60, 165
—, imprisonment at Devizes 45, 49, 58
—, justiciar 27, 36, 38, 68, 71
—, life-grants 63, 64, 65
—, and litigation 25, 28, 29, 30, 40, 42
—, and petitions 70

—, wives of 52, 56, 66n.
Burgh, John de 53
Burgh, Margaret de 56
Burgh, Norfolk 52, 53, 54, 58, 64
Burgh, Theobold de 157
Burgh, Walter de 169
Burgundy, duke of 281, 290
Burham, Surrey 331
Burhurst, William of 331
Burnel, Robert, bishop of Bath and
    Wells 371, 415, 424
Burton abbey annals 195, 263, 264, 271
Bury St Edmunds, abbey of 56, 79, 278
—, chronicles 413, 424
Bussey, William de 102, 327–8
Butler, Nicholas 100
Buttevilt, Thomas de 298

Cahorsin money-lenders 263, 272
Cam, Helen 2
Cambridgeshire 55, 57, 315, 316, 327–8
Camoys, John de 316
Camoys, Ralph de 316
Campden, Gloucs. 81
Canisio, Ralph de Monte 104
Canisio, Warin de Monte 95, 100, 101, 104
Canterbury Peace 275, 276, 277
Cantilupe family seat 298
Cantilupe, master Robert de 101
Cantilupe, Thomas de 293, 294, 295, 299,
    303, 306
—, arms 293
—, elected bishop of Hereford 305
—, friends 298, 299
—, as keeper of the king's seal 299–300,
    302, 304
—, —, career after Evesham 304–5
—, —, salary 300–1
—, and Provisions of Oxford 294, 295
—, tomb 293
Cantilupe, Thomas, St *see* Cantilupe, Thomas
    de
Cantilupe, Walter de, bishop of
    Worcester 100, 296–7, 298, 299, 305
—, elected bishop of Worcester 297
—, and *forma pacis* 266, 267
—, negotiation with Gilbert de Clare 304
—, one of council of fifteen 297–8
—, opposes Sicilian venture 297
—, and plan of reform 94
—, reconciled with king 297
—, supports Simon de Montfort 227, 230,
    296, 297, 298

Cantilupe, William de (nephew of
    Thomas) 300
Cantilupe, William (I) de 151, 293
Cantilupe, William (II) de 72, 293, 297
Cantilupe, William (III) de 297, 298
Capella, Henry de 57
Chaceporc, Peter 108, 110, 119
—, treasure accounts 112, 114, 115, 127,
    128, 131–6
Chalgrove, Oxon. 39
chalice, St Edward's 455
Champagne, count of 95–6
chancery practice 4–5, 61–73 *passim*, 211–8
    passim, 299–304 *passim*, 414–6
chancery rolls 201, 414, 415, 417
Channel Islands 92
chapel of Edward the Confessor 409, 410,
    412, 421, 424
Charles of Anjou 281, 290
Charles the Simple 238
Charter of the Forest 16, 404
charter rolls 53, 65, 66–70
charters (1232) 64, 65, 67
charters, royal 52, 54, 56, 58, 200–1, 302
—, and amercements 85
—, dating formula 4–5, 65, 302
—, and Paper Constitution 63
—, and witnesses 174, 366
Chartley castle and manor, Staffs. 32, 33
Chaworth, Payne de 24
Cheddar wood, Som. 42
Chelmsford, Essex 99
Chenduit, Sir Ralph de 371
Chenduit, Stephen de 371
Cheney, C.R. 2, 6, 8, 9, 12
Chester castle 235
Chester, Ranulf, earl of 28, 30, 46, 47, 48,
    57, 227
—, last earl of (d. 1237) 227
Cheveley, manor of, Cam. 315
Chevreuse, duke de 241
Childwick, Geoffrey of 78, 79, 84, 336
Chingford, Essex 332
Chinon 59
Chippenham, Cam. 53
Chishill, John of 295, 300
chronicles:
—, Barnwell priory 16, 448
—, Battle abbey 284, 285, 288, 322, 348
—, Burton abbey 195, 263, 264, 271
—, Bury St Edmunds abbey 413, 424
—, Canterbury/Dover 270, 272

—, Dunstable priory   50, 56, 111, 185, 273, 277
—, Furness abbey   97, 259, 281, 282, 284, 285, 288, 318
—, Hagnaby abbey   448
—, Hailes abbey   259
—, London   413
—, Melrose abbey   220, 274
—, Merton priory   285, 287, 288, 289, 290, 291
—, Osney abbey   256, 262
—, Rishanger   222, 230
—, Robert of Gloucester   284, 285
—, St Alban's abbey   266, 272, 273
—, St Benet at Hulme abbey   284
—, Waverley abbey   45, 101
—, Westminster abbey   259
—, Winchester cathedral priory   436
—, Worcester cathedral priory   284
—, *see also under* fitz Thedmar, Arnold; Paris, Matthew; Tewkesbury abbey; Wendover, Roger; Wykes, Thomas
Churchill, manor of, Oxon.   371, 372
Cigogné, Engelard de   57, 162–3, 164, 166, 170
—, dismissed from office   59, 167, 174
—, opposes Hubert de Burgh   47, 164
—, as sheriff   60, 159, 166
Cinque Ports   224, 225
Cistercians   80
civil war (1215–17)   60, 70, 98
civil war (1263)   278
—, beginnings of   181, 224
—, causes of   183, 278, 294, 311
—, military decisions   224–5
—, *see also* Evesham, battle of; Lewes, battle of; Wales
Clairambault, Pierre   241, 242
Clanchy, Michael T.   x, 75, 77, 78, 428
Clare, Gilbert de, 4th earl of Gloucester   48
Clare, Gilbert de, 6th earl of Gloucester   214, 256, 278, 294, 304
—, birth of daughter   255
—, and Evesham, battle of   225–6
—, and Lewes, battle of   285, 288, 289
—, marriage   95
Clare, Osbert de, prior of Westminster abbey   448, 449, 451
Clare, Richard de, earl of Hertford   9
Clare, Richard de, earl of Gloucester   89, 92, 94, 99, 100, 243, 244
—, and accord with Edward   248, 249
—, and alliance of the barons   194

—, conflict with Valence   191, 193
—, on council of fifteen (1258)   247
—, death (1262)   255, 256
—, financial resources   226
—, illness   197
—, king protects liberties   104
—, king protects from writs   82
—, and quarrel with de Montfort   221, 222, 230, 236, 247, 248
—, and quarrel with King Henry   141
Clare, William de, death of (1258)   197
Clarendon house, Wilts.   202
Claussen, P.C.   421
Clavering church, Essex   452
Clement IV, pope   420
clergy, lower   389, 397, 400–1, 406
Clifford, Roger of   270, 275
—, and letter to king on Provisions of Oxford   265, 266, 271, 272
Clinton, Thomas de   232
coats of arms   96, 293
Cobham, Reginald of   175
Cockfield, Robert of   51, 53
coif, coronation   435–6, 444
coinage   110, 121, 148
—, *see also* currency; gold; new money; treasure
Colchester castle, Essex   177
Coleby, Lincs.   331
Colvin, H.M.   415
Comberton, Cam.   315
commissioners of array   154
common law   18–19, 20, 43
—, *see also* writs
constables   154, 155, 178
Constitutions of Clarendon   389
Corbet, William   315
Corfe castle, Dorset   47, 175, 177, 452
Corfe, William of   423
Cornard, John of   158
Cornwall, Richard earl of   72, 80, 83, 84, 94, 99, 412
—, as a diplomat   223–4
—, dispute with Waleran the German   59
—, and escheats from king   196
—, and fall of de Burgh   48, 57
—, financial resources   226
—, in Holy Land (1241)   117
—, honours granted   353
—, and Lewes, battle of   285, 287
—, loans to king   116, 117, 123, 124, 129
—, —, for Gascony expedition   109, 118
—, —, for new money   125

—, and secret wedding of Montfort and Eleanor 203
—, and sheriffs 100, 101
—, son 94, 195, 281
coronation 427–61 *passim*
coroners, introduction of 152, 154
Cosmati 409, 419, 420, 421, 422, 424
Coss, Peter R. ix, x, 349–79 *passim*
Cottingham, manor of, Yorks. 23, 37, 39, 42
council of fifteen 1258 102, 228, 247, 264, 294, 297–8
council of nine 1264 294, 295, 298, 301, 303
county farms 169, 170, 173, 174, 177, 179
—, in Magna Carta 160
—, revenue above the 155, 156–60, 163, 170, 172, 180
—, —, defined 153
—, —, and sheriffs 157, 171, 176
courts, manorial 99–100
Cowick ordinance 147–8
Cranbourn, prior of 255
Creepping, Robert of 175
Crevequor, Hamo de 331
Criel, Bertram de 175, 177
Cripa, Geoffrey 315–16
Crowcombe, Godfrey of 52, 53, 68, 164, 170
—, granted castle of Oxford 163
—, removed from office 57, 164, 167
—, returned to office 165, 166
—, satisfaction of magnates with 170
crown jewels 50
crowns 444–54
Croyden, Thomas (the Reaper) of 315
Croydon, Philip of 315
crusades 49, 96, 107, 115, 116, 118
—, and treasure 116, 120
Cumberland 27
curial magnates 94–5
currency 107, 109, 116
—, *see also* coinage; gold; new money; treasure
Curzon, Henry de 229
Cuxham, Oxon. 371

Dale, John de la 317, 320
Damory family 369
Damory, Robert 374
Damory, Roger 364
Darlington, John of 267
David (prince of Wales), executed (1283) 395

Denholm-Young, N. 63, 281
Despencer, Hugh de 228, 301, 304, 326, 342
—, death (1265) 222
—, and debts to king 92
Devizes castle, Wilts. 45, 49, 58, 117
Devon 180
Diceto, Ralph de 435, 446
Dictum of Kenilworth 312, 323
'Disinherited' 278, 312, 315, 347
disseisins 19, 34, 58, 77
—, of Henry III 38–9, 41, 42, 43
—, John, king 25–6, 27, 42, 43
Dorton, Bucks. 314
dove, symbolic 440, 441, 442, 454
Dover priory annals 270, 272, 318
—, and battle of Lewes 285, 286–7, 289
Dover castle 45, 59, 175, 256
Dublin castle 96
Dunstable annals 50, 56, 111, 185, 273, 277
Durham 48
Dwelly, Surrey 331

Earsham hundred, Norfolk 32
East Anglia 64, 66
ecclesiastics 72, 85, 389, 401–2
—, fines 111, 114, 115
—, challenge to liberties 85–6
Edenham, manor of, Lincs. 26, 27, 37
Edmund, prince 120, 412, 441
—, and throne of Sicily 120, 184
Edward the Confessor, St 96, 117, 259, 455, 458
—, biographies of 97, 98
—, chapel 409, 410, 412, 421, 424
—, coinage 440
—, crown 448, 449, 450–1, 454
—, feast days of 206, 208
—, Henry III's devotion to 97, 208, 441, 442, 456–7
—, miracles of 459
—, as patron 457–8, 458
—, political status 457
—, regalia 448–9, 451
—, shrine 409, 416, 417
—, —, base 410, 412, 413, 416
—, —, date of 414, 420, 421
—, —, inscription 418, 419, 420
—, —, pavement 410, 411
—, —, style 418–20, 421
—, tomb 425, 449
—, translation 395, 396, 409, 412, 413

Edward I, king of England   33, 73, 105, 147,
    151, 454
—, burial regalia   431, 442
—, coffin opened   427
—, crowns   444–5, 448, 454–5
—, on crusade (1270–4)   181
—, and debt collection   91
—, first parliament of (1275)   393
—, height of   428
—, itinerary   215
—, and petitions   384–5
—, and professional administrators   151
—, and taxation   148, 403
—, and Tower of London   199, 203, 209
—, Westminster parliament (November
    1295)   381
Edward I, king of England (as Lord Edward)
    195, 206, 254, 270, 412
—, crisis of 1263   270–2
—, crusades   181, 412
—, and Evesham, battle of   225–6
—, and foreign troops   271, 337
—, knighted   411
—, and Lewes, battle of   284–91, 305
—, —, as hostage   281, 288, 289, 290, 294
—, oath to aid Simon de Montfort   241–52
—, preparations against Llywelyn   195, 271
—, revenges insult to mother   206
—, writ of 21 August (1259)   241
Edward II, king of England   210, 218, 278,
    435, 457
Edward III, king of England   105, 128, 210,
    218, 455
Edwin, king of Northumbria   383
Eleanor of Aquitaine   428
Eleanor, countess of Leicester see Montfort,
    Eleanor
Eleanor of Provence   31, 33, 194, 270, 441
—, her armies   276, 277, 284, 338
—, crisis of 1263   270–2
—, hostility towards   206, 214, 268
—, see also Savoy, Savoyards
Ely, bishop of   424
Ely, prior of   316–7
Erdington, Thomas of   159, 162
'esquire' defined   366
Essendon, manor of, Herts.   196
Eu, countess of   27
'European Gold Famine'   107, 129
Eustace the monk   46
Evesham, battle of   225–6, 311–12, 439
—, casualties   228, 229, 290, 298, 313, 314
—, —, Montfort, Simon de   220, 298, 305

exchequer   127, 175, 176, 179, 190, 403
—, Henry III's speech at (1250)   80, 86, 142
—, Henry III's speech at (1256)   137–50,
    344
—, —, official version   139, 140, 142
—, —, Paris's version   138, 139–41, 142
Exeter, bishop of   267
Eye, Philip of   53, 54
eyres   81, 87, 105, 152, 190
—, of Gloucestershire   81
—, of Hampshire   192
—, of Norfolk   87, 101
—, of Suffolk   92
—, see also Bigod, Hugh

fairs   113, 301, 304
famine   340
Farnham castle, Surrey   191, 192
Ferrers, Alice de   33
Ferrers, Robert de (later earl of Derby)   33,
    95
Ferrers, Thomas de   32, 33, 35
Ferrers, William de, earl of Derby   32–3, 48,
    104
Fifield, John of   370
Fifield, manor of, Oxon.   370
financial reserves see gold; treasure
fine rolls   108–121 passim, 124, 128
fines   108, 112, 114, 115, 123, 129
—, of Bloxham, Oxon.   336
—, ecclesiastical   111, 114, 115
—, and knighthood   124
—, murdrum fines   334, 335, 341, 342
Finmere family   364, 371
fitz Alan, John   100
fitz Count, Henry   29
fitz Ellis, Emma   364, 373
fitz Ellis, Robert (descendant of Emma)   365
fitz Fulk, Ralph   315
fitz Geoffrey, John   72, 93, 105, 192, 193
—, and alliance of the barons   194, 195
—, dispute over Shere, Surrey   36, 82,
    192–3, 195
—, king's offence to, causes parliamentary
    fury (1258) 193, 195
—, and plan of reform (1258)   94, 221
fitz Gregory, Gilbert   364–5
fitz Gregory, William   364
fitz Guy, John (and family)   365, 369, 371
fitz Hugh, Richard   57
fitz John, John   313, 323
fitz John, Walter   34
fitz Nicholas, Henry   166, 167

fitz Nicholas, Ralph 52, 58, 161, 166, 170
—, at court (royal) 167, 174
—, death (1257) 174
—, as sheriff 162, 180
fitz Nigel, Robert 313, 314, 369, 370
fitz Nigel, Robert, jr 314, 371
fitz Peter, Geoffrey 193
fitz Ranulf, Peter 316, 320
fitz Reinfrey, Gilbert 159
fitz Richard Herbert, Richard 330
fitz Robert, Walter 100–1
fitz Roger, Robert 158
fitz Stephen, William 207, 208
fitz Thedmar, Arnold (chronicler) 265,
    281–91, 318, 330, 340, 414
fitz Thomas, Eustace 313
fitz Walter, Robert 33, 34, 35
Flete, John 421, 422, 456
Fontevrault 428, 434, 436, 440
foreigners 58, 82, 231, 262–80 *passim*,
    337–8
—, mercenaries/soldiers 11–12, 270, 272,
    273, 275, 277
forests, royal 15–16, 47, 51, 55, 60
forma pacis 1263 266–7, 267, 272, 273, 279
Fors, Isabella de 235
Forz, William de, count of Aumale 26–7,
    48, 104
Foster, R. 421, 422
Fotheringhay castle, Northants. 9, 321
Fourth Lateran council (1215) 400
Franc, John le 314
Francis, John le 81
Frederick II, emperor 76, 107, 109, 126,
    203
Fressingfield, Suffolk 99
Fritwell family 362, 373–4
Froissart 456
Furness abbey chronicles 97, 259, 423
—, and Battle of Lewes 284, 285, 318
—, and Mise of Lewes 281, 282, 288

Galbraith, V.H. 2–13 *passim*, 137
Gant, Gilbert de 10, 26, 37
Gant, Maurice de 28
Gardner, J. 421
Gascony 109, 117, 223, 233
—, (1243) 108, 110, 117
—, (1253) finance 116, 118, 119, 174, 177
Geddington, manor of, Northants. 169
gentry class defined 350–1
Geoffrey *prepositus* of Salden 314
Gernon family 371

Gervaise, John, bishop of Winchester 230,
    296
Giffard, Hugh 433
Gloucester castle 177
Gloucester, great council of 40, 165, 168
Gloucester, Robert of, chronicles 284, 285
Gloucester, William of 121, 123, 125
Godstow, abbess of 100
Golafre, Thomas (and family) 366, 371
gold 109, 110, 114, 121, 128
—, coinage 107, 129, 130, 148, 454
—, —, design 126, 129, 439, 440
—, —, of Louis IX 130
—, gold leaf 125, 126
—, treasure of Henry I 129
—, treasure of Henry III 107–30, 131–6,
    142, 148
—, —, the first (1243–53) 108–20, 123
—, —, the second (1254) 120–9
—, *see also* coinage; currency; new money;
    treasure
government, local 151–82 *passim*, 178,
    230–1, 232, 375, 404
—, Magnate control of 98–106
Granson, Otto de 151
Grant, Richard, archbishop of
    Canterbury 48, 56
Gravesend, Richard, bishop of Lincoln 230,
    238, 266, 267, 296
Green, William de la 332
Grelle, Robert 9
Grelle, Thomas de 84
Gretton 322
Grey, John de 4, 92, 97, 100–1, 177, 313
Grey, Richard de 92, 94, 167, 228
Grey, Walter de, archbishop of York 5, 332,
    353
Grey, William de 95
Grosset, Richard 313, 314
Grosseteste, Robert, bishop of Lincoln 229,
    230, 231, 236, 437
—, and Simon de Montfort 230, 275, 296
Guildford, Ralph of 423
Guisborough, Walter of 256, 259, 264,
    285–7, 290

Hagnaby chronicle 448
Hailes abbey chronicle 259
Hale Bridge, Kent 331
Hampton family 373
Harcourt, Saer de 227
Hardwick, manor of, Oxon. 332, 348
Harestan castle, Derbs. 178

Hartshill, Robert of   229
Harvey, S.   377
Hastings, Henry de   191, 315
Hastings, Miles de   364
Haverhill, William of   180
Havering, Richard of   228
Hay, Robert de   164
Hemington, Northants.   338
Hengrave, Thomas of   166, 167, 174
Henley, Walter of   343, 345, 368–9, 374
Henlow, Beds.   25
Henry I, treasure of   107, 117, 129
Henry II   6, 15, 95, 119, 152
—, burial regalia   440
—, crowns   445, 447
—, effigy   439
—, tomb of   428
Henry III, king of England   34, 45, 46, 105,
    265
—, abilities   33, 37, 39, 43, 58, 98–9, 119,
    128–30, 141–8, 456–7
—, and absolutism   75–9
—, birth   262
—, body bequeathed to Westminster
    abbey   428
—, burial   422, 427
—, —, funeral robes   454
—, —, insignia   438
—, —, regalia   430, 431, 432, 432–3, 460–1
—, —, robes   427, 438
—, children   80, 210, 417, 433
—, —, see also Edward I
—, coronation   64, 448, 450
—, —, crown   444, 450, 452, 453
—, and crusades   115, 116, 118
—, death   206, 253, 428, 436
—, —, preparations for death   434, 442–3,
    457
—, —, rumours of   253–4, 434
—, disseisins   38–9, 41, 42, 43, 79
—, ecclesiastical quarrels   297
—, and Edward the Confessor   97, 208, 412,
    441, 442, 456–7
—, effigy   431, 432, 436, 440
—, financial position   129, 143, 145, 153,
    385
—, —, poverty   50, 51, 88, 122–3, 176, 206
—, and foreign relatives   93–6, 190–4, 295
—, heart bequeathed to Fontevrault   428,
    434
—, height of   428
—, illness (1262)   253–4, 256
—, itinerary   200, 207, 209, 211–13

—, jewels of   420
—, justice, denial of   30–36, 79–85, 191–3
—, kingship   60, 98–9, 141–8
—, law, subject to   39–43, 76–9
—, and Lewes, battle of   284–91
—, and Magna Carta   9, 36–42, 76–85,
    191–3, 404
—, magnates debts to   88–93
—, marriage (1236)   59, 166, 202, 262
—, marriage alliances   80, 95
—, and Mise of Lewes   281
—, and Montfort/Marshall litigation   35
—, obituary of (1263)   253–60
—, piety   50, 255, 438
—, peace, desire for   96–8, 257, 259,
    439–42
—, prisoner of Montfort   294
—, and Redenhall litigation   31–2
—, residences of   202, 207, 208
—, riots (1232)   55
—, seal   62
—, speech at the Exchequer (1250)   80, 86,
    142
—, speech at the Exchequer (1256)   137–50,
    344
—, —, official version   139, 140, 142
—, —, Paris's version   138, 139–41, 142
—, and taxation   387
—, tomb   409, 427
—, —, of Cosmati in (1290)   414, 423, 428
—, —, Edward refurbishes (c.1279)   423
—, —, first   422
—, —, position of body in   443
—, will   115, 117, 420
Henry IV, king of England   456
Henry, young king (son of Henry II)   433,
    435
Henry, prince, (son of Edward I)   416, 417,
    423
Hereford cathedral   293
Heron, William   175
Hertford castle   177, 190, 196
Hilton, R.H.   310, 349
Historic Royal Palaces Agency   214
Hohenstaufen rulers of Sicily   120, 184
Holt, J.C.   17, 36–7, 349, 397
—, on Magna Carta   1–16 passim, 137
Holy Land   116, 117, 119, 129, 439
Hoppere, Richard le   317
Horton, William of   83, 84
House of Commons   43, 406
Howden, Roger of (chronicler)   430, 436,
    440, 445, 446, 451

Hubert of Stapelford   327
Hugh of Pattishall   180
Hundred Rolls   313, 316, 335
Hungerford, Berks.   321
Huntercombe, William of   39
Huntingdon, David, earl of   9
Huntington Library, California   2, 3, 7
Hyldeborw, Walter de   339
Hyldeston, Kent   331

Innocent II, pope   448
Innocent III, pope
Ireland   49, 118
Irish register of writs   22
Isabel of Angoulême   428
Isle of Ely   338
Italian banking operations   116
Italian clerks riots against   55, 56, 59
itinerary of Edward I   215
itinerary of Henry III   200, 207, 209, 211–13
itinerary of John   209

Jesmond, Adam of   100
jewel accounts   444
Jews   111, 114, 118, 124
—, money owed to   351, 364, 379
Joan (sister of Henry III), tomb of   433
John, king of England
—, and aliens   262
—, biographers   2
—, burial at Worcester (1232)   435, 436,
        440, 444
—, crown of   446, 450
—, debts owed to   90
—, disseisins   25–6, 27, 42, 43
—, effigy   431, 436, 443
—, grants made by   59–60
—, height   428
—, and income   145–6, 386
—, itinerary   209
—, and litigation   19–20, 21, 22, 28, 29
—, and Magna Carta   1–16 *passim*
—, and parliament   390
—, regalia lost in Wash   451
—, and sheriffs   146, 151, 159, 160
—, and taxation   399, 400
—, tomb opened   427, 438–9
—, treasure of   117, 120
John, prince (son of Edward I)   417, 423
judges   41, 84, 168
justice   79–85, 191–3
—, judicial role of parliament   383, 384, 405
—, under King John and Henry III   17–43

justices in eyre   73, 152
justices of the peace   105, 154
justiciars, chief   73, 165, 329, 404

Katherine (daughter of Henry III)   417, 433
Kautona, R. de   250
keepers of the peace   154
Kempton, Surrey   213
Kenilworth castle, War.   15, 225, 226, 298
Kent   34, 91, 175, 177
Kent, countess of (wife of Hubert de
        Burgh)   52, 66n., 104
Kent, earldom of   56
Kenteis, Adam de   319–20
Kildare, bishop of   424
Kimberle, Richard de   298
King, Edmund   377
Kingsthorpe manor, Northants.   169
Kingston, treaty of   60
Kirkebi, Alan de   323
Kirketot, William de   322
Knaresborough, Yorks.   57
knightly class
—, defined   350–1
—, rising costs of knighthood   351, 367–8
—, supposed crisis of   ix, 349–80
Knowles, C.H.   219, 380
Kosminsky, E.A.   377

Lambeth palace attacked   191, 193
Lancaster, Thomas of   226
Langley, Geoffrey de   352, 372
Langton, Stephen, archbishop of
        Canterbury   15, 38, 46, 47, 60
Langton, Walter de   353
Laon, bishop of   424
Larkfield, Kent   331
Latimer, Edward   151
law *see* justice
—, king subject to   39–43,
        76–9
Lawrence, C.H.   286
Laxton, John of   177, 180
Lechlade, manor of, Gloucs.   43
Leeds, manor of, Yorks.   28
Leicester abbey   342
Leigham, Surrey   331
Lenham, Nicholas of   30–1, 32, 35
Leo, pope   449
Lestrange, Hamon   270, 275
Lewes, battle of   225, 275, 281, 284–91,
        294, 311
—, casualties   317–18

—, king loses two horses 439
Lewes priory 285, 287, 289
Lewknor, Nicholas of 100
Leybourne, Roger of 34, 192, 275, 288
liberties 85–8, 112, 113, 114, 120, 124
—, 'non-usage' 104
—, usurpation of 87, 99–101
Lichfield, bishop of 266, 267
Lilley, manor of, Herts. 24
Limminge, Richard of 103
Lincoln, earl of 95
Lincolnshire proffers 144
Lisle, Brian de 47, 57, 59, 60, 164
Little, William 317
Little Billing, Northants. 339
Llywelyn ab Iorwerth 49, 50, 162
Llywelyn ap Gruffydd 123, 190, 193, 271
London 15, 125, 127, 225
London chronicles 413
—, and Battle of Lewes 284
—, and Mise of Lewes 281, 282, 283, 288, 291
—, *and see* Tower
London, John of 444
Longespee, Stephen de 104
Longespee, William de, earl of
        Salisbury 27–8, 48, 84
Lopez, R.S. 127
Lossenham, Kent 331
Louches family 378
Louis IX, king of France 36, 73, 173, 235
—, as arbiter in baronial conflict 284, 294, 311
—, and civil war 45
—, and coinage 130
—, condemns Provisions of Oxford 224
—, and crusades 116, 117
—, gift of elephant to Henry 203
—, and Mise of Amiens 268
—, and peace treaty with Henry 245
Louis VII, king of France 436, 443
Lovel, Philip 119
Luard, H.R. 137, 150, 253
Lucy, Geoffrey de 191, 435
Luke of Lucca 416
Lusignan, Aymer de, bishop-elect of
        Winchester 82, 90, 190, 192, 262
—, dispute over advowson of Shere 192–3
—, and robbery at Lambeth Palace 191
Lusignan, Geoffrey de 190, 191, 262, 332
Lusignan, Guy de 118, 190, 191, 262, 285
Lusignans 75, 76, 77, 82, 197, 262, 268
—, and conflict with Simon de Montfort 94

—, dislike of 98, 99, 183, 190, 231, 326, 337, 338
—, —, expelled from England 197, 263, 265, 327
—, —, king's protection of 82, 93, 192, 193, 269
—, —, oppression by 193, 326
—, —, and papal letter re reforms of (1258) 347
—, —, and Tewkesbury annals 257
—, marriage alliances 95, 190
—, and Savoyard conflicts 190, 268–9

McKechnie, W.S. 1, 2, 7
Maddicott, J.R. ix, 135, 281–3, 384
Madingley, Cam. 322
Madox, T. 149
Magna Carta
—, Henry III's breaches and
        observance 37–42, 76–85, 191–3, 404
Magna Carta (1215) 19, 20, 61, 102
—, cap. 14 (taxation) 388, 398, 403
—, cap. 18 (local judges) 394
—, cap. 20 (amercements) 341
—, cap. 25 (increments) 160
—, cap. 36 (writ of life and limb) 22
—, cap. 39 (lawful judgement) 37, 38, 39, 42, 43, 77, 78, 79, 80
—, cap. 40 (denial of justice) 20, 36, 37, 42, 79, 80, 192
—, cap. 50 (dismissal of alien officers) 59
—, cap. 51 (dismissal of mercenaries) 11
—, cap. 52 (disseisin) 37
—, cap. 61 (the twenty-five) 10
—, oath to observe 13
—, witnesses 9–10
—, dating and making 1–16
—, St Albans' version 15, 59, 137
Magna Carta (1216) 9, 60
Magna Carta (1217) 60
Magna Carta (1225) 60
Magna Carta (1237) 79
Magna Carta (1253) 79
magnates 94–5, 99, 105–6, 170, 186
—, and absolutism 85
—, and appeasement policies 79, 85, 93, 98
—, confrontations with king 195, 204
—, control of local government 99–106
—, debts to king 75, 76, 88–93, 94
—, grievances against 405
—, and judges 84

—, and king's breach of Magna Carta 40, 80, 81
—, liberties of 76, 86–8
—, oppression by 101–2
—, and professional officials 102, 105
—, and reforms 183
Maitland, F.W. 387, 406, 407
manorial courts 99–100
Mansel, John 83, 84, 206, 235
Mansel, William 232
Mara, Henry de 83, 84
Marcher lords, liberties of 88 n.62
Mares, Robert de 325, 348
Mares, Sibyl de 325–6, 348
Mark, Philip 159
markets, grants of 113
Marlborough, Wilts. 202, 320–1
Marmion family 363, 364
Marmion, John 363, 370
Marmion, William 326, 342
Marsh, Adam 229, 236, 237, 238, 297, 346–7
Marsh, Richard 5
Marshal, Richard, earl of Pembroke 39, 40, 49, 58, 89
—, and alliance with Bassets 59
—, and fall of de Burgh 48–9, 57
—, Irish lands 63
—, and rebellion against des Roches 39, 77, 257
Marshal, William (custodian of Northamptonshire) 100, 326
Marshal, William, 4th earl of Pembroke and regent 46, 158
Marshal, William, 5th earl of Pembroke 35, 48, 246–7, 434
Martindale, Jane 439
Matilda, empress (Maud) 445, 451
Mauclerc, Walter, bishop of Carlisle 52, 57, 58, 161, 162
—, charters granted to 64, 65
Mauduit family 363, 364, 371
Mauduit, Robert 374
Mauduit, William 227n.
Maulay, Peter de 23, 38, 39, 47, 57
—, absence from court 49
—, and claim to Upavon manor 58, 59
—, dismissed from office 167
—, king's measures against 80
—, as opponent of de Burgh 164
Maxwell-Lyte, H.C. 218
Maytham, Kent 331
Mears Ashby *see* North Ashby

Meldreth, Hebbe of 315
Melrose chronicles 220, 274
mercenaries/soldiers *see* armies
Merton priory 100, 148, 211, 283
—, chronicles 285, 287, 288, 289, 290, 291
Merton College charters 371
Merton family 370
Merton, Walter de 266, 298, 353, 371, 376
Meulant, Roger de, bishop of Coventry 266, 267, 353
Meulles (Molis), Nicholas de 166, 167, 174
Mills, Mabel 152, 166, 173, 180
Milstead, Kent 331
Milton, manor of, Kent 175
miracles 306, 339, 423, 454, 459
Mise of Amiens 261, 268, 273, 294, 311
Mise of Lewes 281–91
'Model Parliament' (Stubbs) 381, 406, 407, 408
Montacute, William de 83, 84, 105
Montbegon, Roger de 9
Montfort, Eleanor de (wife of Simon) 89–90, 202–3, 233, 234, 235
—, and litigation 35, 246–7
Montfort, Peter de 94, 104, 194, 297, 298, 304
—, council membership 228, 297–8, 301, 304
—, and debts to king 92
—, as sheriff 177
—, and Simon de Montfort 194, 227, 228
Montfort, Simon de, earl of Leicester ix, 34, 84, 100, 104, 233, 298
—, army 318
—, background 220, 273, 274
—, barons recall to England 206, 265, 271, 294
—, Canterbury Peace 275
—, and Thomas de Cantilupe 293, 297
—, conflict with Valence 94, 191, 193, 197
—, Constitution of June 1264 275, 282
—, death at Evesham 220, 298, 305
—, and debts to king 89, 91
—, departs to France 222
—, disputes with king 80, 97, 141, 233, 238
—, and ecclesiastics 296
—, and Evesham, battle of 225–6
—, followers/supporters 226–9, 230, 296, 338
—, and foreigners 190, 274, 277
—, and Gascony 117, 234, 297
—, and Grosseteste 275, 296

—, Henry sends to the Tower   210
—, Henry surrenders to   206
—, and Kenilworth castle   226, 298
—, and Lewes, battle of   275, 393
—, and litigation   35
—, Lord Edward's oath to   241–52
—, marriage to Eleanor (king's
    sister)   202–3, 220, 233
—, militarism of   222–3, 224, 226, 248–9
—, and Mise of Lewes   281–91
—, and Mortimer   43, 247
—, as one of '3 electors'   294
—, one of council of fifteen   297–8
—, parliaments/counsels summoned   392,
    393, 405
—, and plan of reform (1258)   94
—, as political leader   219–40
—, and Provisions of Oxford   220, 232, 265,
    311
—, religiosity of   229–30, 232, 296
—, resources   226, 233
—, and self-interest   233–8, 248
—, son born at Kenilworth   274
—, will of   347
Montfort, William de (son of Peter de
    Montfort) 298
Mora, Simon de   316
Mortimer, Isabella   43
Mortimer, Roger   43, 92, 247, 288, 290
Mowbray, William de   9
Moyne, John le   176
murdrum fines   334, 335, 340, 341, 342
Musson, John de   321
Mustac, William de   20, 23, 24

Nashenden, manor of, nr Rochester, Kent   34
Nerbonne family   368
Netley, abbot of   100
Neville, Hugh de   100, 151
Neville, Nicholas de   65n
Neville, Peter de   309, 323, 336
Neville, Ralph de, bishop of Chichester   5,
    49, 52, 54
—, appointment as keeper of the seal   62
—, career, 62–73
—, death   62
—, deprived of seal   65, 302
—, and petitions   70
—, regains seal   69
new money   125–7, 128, 129, 130
—, *see also* coinage; currency; gold; treasure
New Temple, treasury at   119
Newcastle-under-Lyme, Staffs.   235

Newington, Kent   331
Newman, J.E.   378
Newmarket, Adam of   301
Newton Longville priory   314
Noers, Roger de, family   370, 371, 373
Norbiton, Surrey   331
Norfolk eyre   101
Norgate, Kate   4
Normandy   262, 385
North Ashby, Northants.   325, 326, 336, 339,
    348
North Weston, manor of, Oxon.   363
Northampton castle   15, 47, 177, 224, 296
Northumberland   22, 144, 158, 175
Nottingham castle   15, 174, 178
Nottinghamshire   161
novel disseisin   26, 31, 34

obituary of King Henry III (1263)   253–60
oblations, king's   117, 211, 212
Odiham castle   47, 55, 64
Oilly, Roger de   329–30, 332, 348
Ordinance of the Magnates 1259   221, 222,
    230, 244, 328
Ordinance of the Sheriffs 1258   328
Orrebi, R. de   250
Orwell Hundred Rolls, Cam.   316
Osbert and Robert (polishers)   423
Osney abbey   353
Osney abbey chronicles   256, 262
Otto IV, emperor   433
Oxfoot, Richard,   321–2
Oxford   54
Oxford castle   163, 177
Oxford parliament 1258   183–4, 195, 196,
    325, 405
—, descriptive newsletter   263
—, *see also* Provisions of Oxford
Oxford University   295, 296
Oxfordshire   54, 349–80 *passim*
Oxfordshire Hundred Rolls   354

Painscastle nr Builth   49, 50, 51
Painter, Sidney   160
paintings at Westminster   98, 437, 441, 453,
    458
Pandulf, papal legate   27
Paper Constitution (1244)   61, 62–3, 65, 69,
    71–2, 237
Paris, Matthew   45, 49, 137–8, 140, 141
—, and absolutism   79
—, and biography of Edward the
    Confessor   97

—, on coronation swords 452
—, on excommunication 437
—, on exactions 114
—, on famine 340
—, on foreigners 193–4, 268
—, on Gascony campaign 223
—, on gifts to king 110–11
—, on Griffin's escape from Tower 199
—, and Henry's court 95, 96
—, on justice 329
—, on King Henry III 76, 78, 96, 97, 118
—, on king's residence in Tower 202
—, on kingship 442
—, on Lusignans 193–4
—, on magnate privileges 99
—, and cure of Thomas of Savoy 454
—, on money 115, 116
—, on Neville 62, 63, 69, 70
—, on parliaments 70, 187, 195–6, 196
—, on preaching of crusade 117–18
—, prejudice of 137, 141
—, on Robert Grosseteste 230
—, on royal grants 112–13
—, and sheriffs 170, 179
—, on Simon de Montfort 221, 231, 232, 235, 244, 274
—, on speech to Exchequer (1256) 138, 139–41, 142
—, on taxes 400
—, on Trumpington outrage 327–8
—, on Westminster Parliament 1258 194–5
—, on writs 82
Paris, money of 116
Parles, William de, and family 362, 373
parliaments 381, 387–97, 405–6, 406
—, of (1236) 202
—, of (1258) 183–4, 187, 192, 195, 196, 204
—, of (1259) 243
—, of (1262) 235
—, of (1264) 281, 282, 294, 393
—, of (1265) 284
—, of (1295) 381
—, general development 381–408
Passelewe, John 313
Passelewe, Robert 25, 47, 57, 164, 177
Pattishall, Martin of, judge 70
peace in England 97, 98, 245, 248
Peak castle, Derbs. 235
peasants 312
—, and allegiance 343
—, in armies 317, 318, 319
—, arms and weaponry of 319–20

—, classification of 310–11, 314, 316
—, exploitation by barons 326, 341
—, in litigation 325–6, 329–31, 334, 344–5
—, and local administration 324–5
—, loyalties of 313, 315
—, and oath of reform 328
—, in raiding parties 316, 320, 336
—, revolts 348
Peatling Magna, Leics. 309–10, 320–1, 323, 336, 339, 347–8
Pecche, Bartholomew 331
Pecche, Herbert 331
Peche, Gilbert de 322
peerage, parliamentary 388
Percy, Richard de 27
Percy, William de 27
Perot, Ralph 315, 317
Peter the Roman citizen 418, 419–20, 421
Peterborough abbey 377
Petition of the Barons 1258 85, 172–3, 263, 266–7, 268, 272, 279, 340–1
petitions 383–5, 405, 406
Pevensey castle, Sussex 225
Peyvre, Paulinus 24
Pickering castle, Yorks. 177
Pipard family 370
pipe rolls 91, 153, 385
—, on crowns 446
—, of Edward I 417
—, on Henry's burial 428, 430
—, and Henry's treasure 108, 418
—, jewel accounts 428, 429, 430
Plescy, John de, earl of Warwick *see* Plessis, John du
Plessis, Hugh de (son of John) 34
Plessis, John du, earl of Warwick 34, 39, 57, 94, 227, 264
Poitevin campaign (1242–3) 49, 89, 177, 223
Popping, William 313–14, 320
population 311, 348
Portchester castle, Hants. 178
Porter, Peter le 227
Postan, M.M. 349
Poure, le, family 362, 373
Poure, Richard le, bishop of Salisbury and Durham 48
Powicke, Sir Maurice 45, 152, 172
—, on baronial quarrels 204
—, on Henry III 58, 59, 119
—, on Neville 62
—, on reforms of (1258) 183, 184, 185, 192, 195

—, on des Roches and de Burgh 50, 52, 53, 54, 55
—, on sheriffs 172, 173
—, on Thomas Cantilupe 304
Preston, Gilbert of 84, 326
Preston, Kent 192
Prestwich, J.O. x, 8 n.49, 273 n.1
Prestwich, M.C. x
Pricke, Geoffrey 317
privy seal 415
proffers at exchequer 142, 143, 144–5
—, and Cowick ordinance 147–8
—, from Bedfordshire-Buckinghamshire 144
—, from Lincolnshire 144
—, from Northumberland 144
—, sheriffs attendance at 146–7
Provisions of Oxford 42, 61, 99, 141, 142, 170
—, and chancellor 303
—, and conciliar control of the king 250
—, and countess of Leicester 246
—, and de Montfort 220, 232
—, defined 294, 300
—, effectiveness 204
—, on exactions 173
—, and foreigners 263, 265
—, Henry rejects (1261) 205, 222, 256, 265
—, king reaffirms the 224, 294
—, Louis IX condemns 261, 275
—, and Mise of Lewes 281, 283, 290
—, and papal letters 222
—, on parliament 221, 382
—, queen opposes 269, 337
—, rebels demand restoration 206
—, re-establishes office of justiciar 193
—, restoration of (1263) 275
—, and sheriffs 171, 173–4, 179
Provisions of Westminster 102, 221, 235, 348
—, finalised 244
—, and *murdrum* fines 334
—, and parliament of (1259) 243
—, and peasantry 333
Public Records Office 66, 354
Pugeys, Imbert 177, 180, 264, 378
Purcel family 371

Quatremain family 363, 364
Quincy, Roger de, earl of Winchester 104, 227, 247
quo warranto cases 75, 88, 105

Rabayne, Elias de 174, 176, 263, 270

Ralegh, William 39, 40, 41, 77, 346
Ramsay, James H. 223–4
Reading, abbot of 100
receipt rolls 142, 145
Redenhall manor, Norfolk 30, 31, 32
religious houses 85–6, 352, 356, 379
revolution of (1258) 35–6, 99, 147, 197
—, from within the court 99, 191
—, and Savoyards 264
—, *see also* civil war
Rich, Edmund, archbishop of Canterbury 58, 100
Richard I, king of England 6
—, burial 433, 435, 436
—, coronation of 430
—, crown of 445–6
—, effigies 436, 439, 440
—, tomb of 428
Richard II, king of England 105, 432, 455–6
Richard, king of Almain *see* Cornwall, earl of
Richard, king of Germany *see* Cornwall, earl of
Richardson, H.G. 383
Richmond, Yorks. 28, 31
Ridgeway, Huw ix, 262, 268
Rievaulx, Ailred of 97, 98, 259, 457, 458
ring, St Edward's 455
rings 429, 458
Rishanger (chronicler) 222, 230
Rivaux, Peter des 58, 60, 163, 164
—, charters granted to 63, 64, 65, 66, 68, 69
—, fall of 165
—, and fall of de Burgh 56
—, granted forest of England for life 55
—, removed from office 46–7
—, as treasurer 51, 52–3, 57
Robert and Osbert (polishers) 423
robes, royal 427, 431, 438, 447, 454
Roches, Peter des, bishop of Winchester 5, 37, 40, 45, 46
—, and absolutism 38–9, 77
—, and Aumale litigation 26–7
—, and coronation regalia 432
—, and crusades 49
—, and fall of de Burgh 47, 49–50, 52, 56, 57, 165
—, in favour at court 51
—, and King John 46, 59, 60
—, misguides king 98
—, not present at oath of Burgh 53
—, removed from office 39, 58
—, replaces de Burgh 38

—, and revenue 163, 164
—, and Roger fitz John 70
—, sheriffdoms 46, 164, 165
—, split with Richard Marshal 49
Rochester castle 209, 225
Rochford, Guy de 263, 270
Roffa, Peter de 114
Rokele family 373–4
rolls
—, Babraham hundred rolls 317
—, chancery rolls 201, 414, 415, 417
—, charter 53, 65, 66–70
—, close rolls and royal letters 303
—, fine rolls 108–121 *passim*, 124, 128
—, and gold treasure of Henry III 108
—, household rolls 201, 216, 217
—, hundred rolls 313, 316, 335
—, issue rolls 122
—, legal and financial 353–4
—, memoranda 142, 143, 145
—, originalia 111, 112
—, Orwell hundred 316
—, Oxfordshire hundred 354
—, patent 113, 277
—, pipe 91, 153, 385
—, —, on crowns 446
—, —, of Edward I 417
—, —, on Henry's burial 428, 430
—, —, on Henry's treasure 108, 418
—, —, on jewel accounts 428, 429, 430
—, plea 30
—, receipts 142, 145
—, Thriplow hundred 327
rolls of eyre (1267–72) for Dictum of
    Kenilworth (Oct 1266) 312–13
Romillies family 352
Ros, Robert de 80
Ros, William de 100
Runnymede 1–16 *passim*, 45, 59
Rycote, Fulk of 371–2, 374
Rycote, manor of, Oxon. 372

Safford, E.W. 215–16
St Albans abbey 78, 79, 191, 424
—, annals 266, 272, 273, 329, 337–8
—, —, and Lewes, battle of 284
—, —, *see also* Paris, Matthew and
    Wendover, Roger
St Amand, Amaury de 166
St Andrew's, bishop of 424
St Benet at Hulme abbey chronicles 284
St Briavels 195
St Denis, abbey of 443, 449

St Etienne at Caen 445
St Evroul abbey 321
St John, Richard de 51, 57
St John, Roger de 304
St Pancreas priory *see* Lewes priory
St Paul, palace of 206
St Romain, Artald de 120, 127–8
St Valery 353
Saintes, debacle at (1242) 238
Salden, Thomas of 314, 320
Salisbury, countess of 27
Saluzzo, marquis of 95
Sanchia (wife of earl of Cornwall) 101
Sancta Ermina, William de 263, 268, 270
Sandwich, Henry of, bishop of London 230,
    266, 267, 295, 296
Sandwich, Ralph of 304, 305
Sandwich, sea battle off 46
Savoy, Beatrice of 95
Savoy, Boniface of, archbishop of
    Canterbury 190, 191, 192, 262, 264
—, robbed by Poitevins 191
Savoy marriage alliances 95
Savoy, Peter of 30, 32, 33, 93, 99, 100, 103,
    342
—, and alliance of the barons, 194
—, and Boston fair tolls 301
—, elected to council of fifteen 264, 297–8
—, honour of Richmond 190, 262
—, and Lusignans 190–1
Savoy, Thomas of 65, 95, 268, 454
Savoy, William of 166, 167, 168, 170
Savoyards 94, 190, 191, 262–3, 268
—, kinsmen of Queen Eleanor of
    Provence 75, 93, 262
Sayles, G.O. 383
Scaccario, Roger de 102
Scalariis, John de 100, 315
Scarborough castle, Yorks. 15, 114, 177
sceptre 440, 442, 452
Scotland 177
Seagrave, Gilbert of 228
Seagrave, Nicholas of 228
Seagrave, Stephen of 39, 49, 54, 57, 58, 162
seals 201, 439–40, 441, 454
Seward, Richard 49
Shardlow, Robert of 55
Shere, Surrey 192, 193
sheriffs 76, 80, 86, 146, 151–82 *passim*, 230
—, amercement of (1237) 140, 143, 147
—, appointment of 105, 168
—, change in type of person selected
    as 102–3

—, control over 148
—, corruption of 295
—, curial 100, 103, 151–82
—, and knighthood fines 124
—, loss of power to check magnates 89, 99,
        102–3, 105, 181
—, oppression by 73, 190
—, and proffers 142, 143, 144–5, 145, 146
—, reform of, 1258 172–3, 178–9
—, sheriff's tourn 86
—, and speech at the exchequer (1250) 80,
        86
Shrewsbury castle 50, 162, 395
Sicily 183, 184, 185, 186, 190
—, expedition to 126
—, and finance 123, 129, 195
—, pope offers throne to Edmund 120, 184
—, Sicilian venture 96, 99, 107, 187, 296,
        439
—, —, opposed by Walter de Cantilupe 297
silver 107, 110
Simon (chaplain to de Burgh) 55
Simon the Norman, Master 65, 66, 71
Somerset assizes 82, 83
Somery, Roger de 81
Song of Lewes 231, 232–3, 235, 236, 237,
        277
Southwark, Surrey 237
speech at Exchequer (1250) 142
speech at Exchequer (1256) 138, 139,
        139–41, 140, 142
Spoleto, papal letters from 55
Stacey, Robert ix, 72
Staine, Cam. 316
Stamford, Robert de 101
Stanley, A.P. 427
Stanton, Philip of 315, 320
Stanwick 348
statute against aliens 261–80
Statute of Marlborough (1267) 335
Stephen, king, treasure of 107
Stivichall, manor of, War. 372
Stokes, Peter de 158
Stratford-at-Bow 203
Stubbs, Bishop William 4, 219
—, on parliament 381, 383, 406, 407, 408
—, *Select Charters* 6
Stuteville, Eustace de 23, 37, 42
Stuteville, Robert de 87, 105
Sudbury, William of 448–9, 456
Sutton, king at 211
Swaffham Bulbeck, Cam. 316
Swaffham Prior, Cam. 316, 335

Swinfield, Richard de 293, 300
sword belt 95–6
swords 438, 439, 440, 451, 454, 455
—, role of in coronation 439

Talbot, William 166
taxation 120, 121, 386, 397–403
—, collection of 402, 403–4
—, granting 405
—, and king 107, 204, 385, 386–7, 396–7
—, moveable property 343, 386, 398, 400
—, scutage 399, 400
—, tax collectors 168
Templars 100, 116
Temple Church, London 434
tenants-in-chief 18–19, 20, 25
Tewkesbury abbey annals 253, 254–5,
        257–8, 259, 263–4
—, burial of Richard de Clare, earl of
        Gloucester 255
—, on invasion threats 319
—, on king's desire for peace 97
—, on march to the king's hall 204
—, obituary of Henry III 260
—, on papal interdict on England 185
—, on removal of aliens 263–4
—, on Westminster parliament (1258) 187–9
Thetford Leper hospital 69
Thirkleby, Roger de 83
Thomas, Master (king's cook) 322
Thomley family 370
Thorne, S.E. 41
Thornham, Robert of 158
Three Castles 28–9, 38
Thriplow Hundred, Cam. 327
Thriplow, manor of, Cam. 315
Tickhill, Yorks. 27
Tiffenden 331
Tiptoft, Robert 151
Todding, Hervey 317
Tonney, Nicholas 323
Totehale, Robert de 101
Totnes, Devon 29
Tours, money of 116
Tout, T.F. 304
Tower of London 55, 64, 199, 200, 205,
        256
—, and Edward I 199, 203, 214–18, 215
—, expenditure on 417
—, Henry III resident at 199, 201–2, 202,
        203, 206, 207
—, Henry III's work on 199–200, 203, 204,
        207

—, and King John 207
—, menagerie 203, 204
Tracy, Henry de 29
treasure 118, 129
—, first gold 109, 110–14, 123, 124
—, second gold 121–3
—, *see also* coinage; currency; gold; new
    money
Treaty of Paris 235
Treharne, R.F. 75, 264
—, on de Montfort 219
—, and itinerary 213
—, on knights and gentry 312, 349, 365
—, on reforms of (1258) 183, 184–5, 192
Trevet, Nicholas 256, 291, 423, 428
troops *see* armies
Trowbridge, Wilts. 27, 43
Trumpington, Roger of 322
Trussel, Richard 229
Trussel, William 84, 229
Tugge, William 317
Turner, R.V. 2, 3
Twain, Mark 253
Tweng, Robert 55

Umfraville, Gilbert de 233
under-sheriffs 145, 168, 174
Upavon, manor of, Wilts. 23, 38, 39, 43, 49,
    59

Vache, Richard le 313
Valence, William de 35, 99, 103, 180, 202,
    270
—, and act of resumption 196
—, conflict with Archbishop Boniface 191
—, conflict with earl of Gloucester 191, 195
—, conflict with earl of Hereford 191
—, conflict with earl of Leicester 191, 195,
    232, 236
—, conflict with Humphrey de Bohun 191
—, grants from king 79
—, and Lewes, battle of 285
—, and Llywelyn 195
—, marriage 95, 190, 262
—, and Pembroke 193
—, and sheriffs 100, 101
Vaughan, R. 137
Vaux, John de 270, 275, 301
Verdun, bishop of 424
Vesci, Eustace de 9
Vesci, John de 95
Vescy, John de 151
vestments of unction 454

Victoria, queen of England 427
Vieuxpont, Robert de 27, 36
Vincent, N. 38 n.112, 60 n.99
Vivonne, Hugh de 175, 176

Wace family 366
Wake, Andrew 83
Wake, Hugh 20, 23, 24
Waldis, William de 348
Waleran the German 59
Walerand, Robert 174, 191, 192, 249
Wales 48, 59, 124, 177, 257
—, conflict costs 123, 126
Wales, John of 346
Wallingford, Oxon. 353
Walter, Hubert 4, 154, 155
Walthamstow, Essex 331
Walton, Bucks. 314
Walworth, Surrey 331
Wapurnet, John 323–4
war 162, 386, 406
—, baronial wars 181, 183
—, Brittany campaigns 162, 174
—, *see also* civil war; revolution; Wales
Wardrobe Accounts 108–9, 112, 121, 131–6,
    417
Ware, Richard of abbot, of Westminster 419,
    421, 422, 423
Ware, prior of 100
Warenne, John de, earl of Surrey 94, 104,
    195, 270, 412
—, and Lewes, battle of 285
—, marriage 95
—, reconciled with Edward 275
Warren, W.L. 2
Watson, A.M. 115
Waugh, Scott ix
Waundard family 371
Waverley abbey annals 45, 101, 284, 285,
    288
Wellow, Notts. 336
Wells, Jocelin of, bishop of Bath 42, 48
Wells, Simon, archdeacon of 4
Wendover, Bucks. 314
Wendover, Roger of 15, 49, 50, 51, 58, 137
—, on de Burgh's dismissal 45, 54, 56
—, on royal charters 63
Westminster abbey 96, 118–19, 208, 209,
    438
—, annals 97, 259, 271
—, choir 96
—, Confessor's chapel 409, 410, 412, 421,
    424

—, Cosmati work at 409–26
—, Lady Chapel 450
—, sanctuary floor 409, 410, 419, 421–2
—, shrine of Edward the Confessor 409, 410, 424
—, statues of Confessor and Saint John 458
—, tomb of Henry III 409
Westminster, abbot of 100, 197, *see also* Ware
Westminster, Edward of 119
Westminster palace 206, 208, 209, 210, 416
—, painting 453
—, as residence of Edward I 216, 217
—, as residence of Henry III 202, 208
Westminster parliaments 195, 243, 382
Westminster treasury 108
Wheatfield, Oxon. 362
Whitehill, manor of, Oxon. 372
Whitehill, Walter of 372
Wiggenholt, John of 159
William I, king of England 445, 448, 449
William II (Rufus), king of England 208, 445
William the Lion, King of Scotland 56
William, master (parson) 331
Williamscot family 363, 364
Willian, manor of, Herts. 24
Wilton, William of 267
Wiltshire 269
Winchester 202, 263, 445

—, annals 289, 318, 436
Winchester, Peter of 420
Winchester parliament 263
Winchester, treasury of 445
Windsor castle 2–3, 47, 55, 64, 166, 323
—, expenditure on 417
—, as residence of Henry III 202
Wissett, manor of, Suffolk 31
Woodstock 50, 54, 202
Woodstock, manor of 163
Worcester cathedral priory chronicles 284
writs 19, 70, 71, 73, 82
—, *de cursu* 19, 20, 22, 24, 36, 40, 79
—, difficulty in obtaining 24–5, 36, 82, 101
—, irregular 301
—, of Lord Edward 21 August (1259), latin text of 251–2
—, *mort d'ancestor* 19, 20, 23
—, *novel disseisin* 19, 34, 82, 93, 96
—, *praecipe in capite* 19, 20, 21, 21–4, 28
—, *quo warranto* 23, 24, 75, 88, 105
Wykes, Thomas (chronicler) 238, 296–7
—, on funeral of Henry III 434, 444, 454
—, and Lewes, battle of 285
Wymington, manor of, Beds. 370

York 142, 143, 144
Yorkshire 159, 164
—, Henry of Bath as custodian 177

CPSIA information can be obtained at www.ICGtesting.com
Printed in the USA
LVOW071506131212

311545LV00008B/187/P